Rick Steves®

LONDON

Rick Steves & Gene Openshaw

2015

CONTENTS

CITY OF LONDON

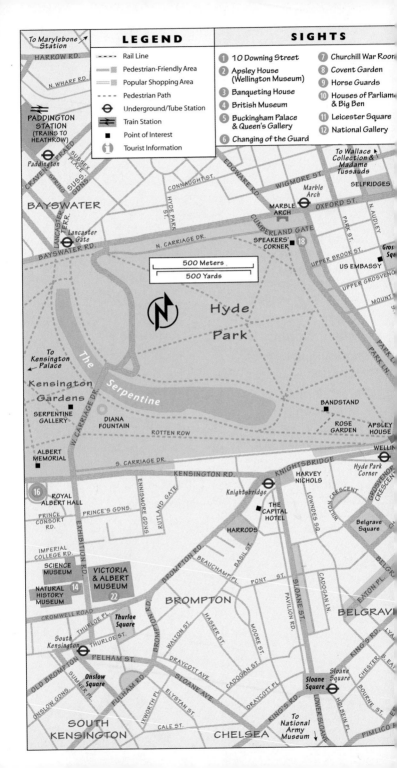

LEGEND

- ----- Rail Line
- ▦ Pedestrian-Friendly Area
- ▦ Popular Shopping Area
- ----- Pedestrian Path
- ⊖ Underground/Tube Station
- ⇄ Train Station
- ■ Point of Interest
- ⚐ Tourist Information

SIGHTS

1. 10 Downing Street
2. Apsley House (Wellington Museum)
3. Banqueting House
4. British Museum
5. Buckingham Palace & Queen's Gallery
6. Changing of the Guard
7. Churchill War Room
8. Covent Garden
9. Horse Guards
10. Houses of Parliament & Big Ben
11. Leicester Square
12. National Gallery

To Marylebone Station

HARROW RD.

N. WHARF RD.

PADDINGTON STATION (TRAINS TO HEATHROW)

Paddington

CRAVEN RD.

SPRING ST.

SUSSEX PL.

SUSSEX GDNS.

PRAED ST.

CONNAUGHT ST.

EDGWARE RD.

WIGMORE ST.

Marble Arch

SELFRIDGES

BAYSWATER

MARBLE ARCH

OXFORD ST.

N. AUDLEY

To Wallace Collection & Madame Tussauds

LANCASTER TERR.

Lancaster Gate

BAYSWATER RD.

HYDE PARK ST.

CUMBERLAND GATE

SPEAKERS' CORNER ■ 18

N. CARRIAGE DR.

PARK ST.

UPPER BROOK ST.

Gros Squ

US EMBASSY

UPPER GROSVENO

MOUNT

500 Meters

500 Yards

Ⓝ

Hyde Park

PARK LN.

To Kensington Palace

Kensington Gardens

The Serpentine

W. CARRIAGE DR.

SERPENTINE GALLERY

DIANA FOUNTAIN

ROTTEN ROW

BANDSTAND ■

ROSE GARDEN

APSLEY HOUSE

ALBERT MEMORIAL ■

S. CARRIAGE DR.

KENSINGTON RD.

KNIGHTSBRIDGE

HARVEY NICHOLS

WELLIN

Hyde Park Corner

16

ROYAL ALBERT HALL

PRINCE CONSORT RD.

PRINCE'S GDNS.

RUTLAND GATE

ENNISMORE GDNS.

Knightsbridge

THE CAPITAL HOTEL

HARRODS

LOWNDES SQ.

NILTON

CRESCENT

GROSVENOR CRESCENT

Belgrave Square

BELGRA

IMPERIAL COLLEGE RD.

EXHIBITION RD.

SCIENCE MUSEUM

NATURAL HISTORY MUSEUM

14

VICTORIA & ALBERT MUSEUM

22

BROMPTON

BROMPTON RD.

BEAUCHAMP PL.

BASIL ST.

PONT ST.

SLOANE ST.

CADOGAN LN.

PAVILION RD.

EATON PL.

BELGRAVI

CROMWELL ROAD

THURLOE PL.

Thurloe Square

WALTON ST.

HASKER ST.

MOORE ST.

DRAYCOTT ST.

KING'S RD.

CHESTER S. EA

BOURNE ST.

South Kensington

THURLOE ST.

PELHAM ST.

CADOGAN PL.

SLOANE SQUARE

KING'S RD.

LYON

OLD BROMPTON RD.

SUMNER PL.

Onslow Square

FULHAM RD.

DRAYCOTT AVE.

SLOANE AVE.

CADOGAN ST.

Sloane Square

LOWER SLOANE

HOLBEIN PL.

PIMLICO T

ONSLOW GDNS.

SOUTH KENSINGTON

LYWORTH PL.

CALE ST.

ELYSTAN ST.

CHELSEA

To National Army Museum ↓

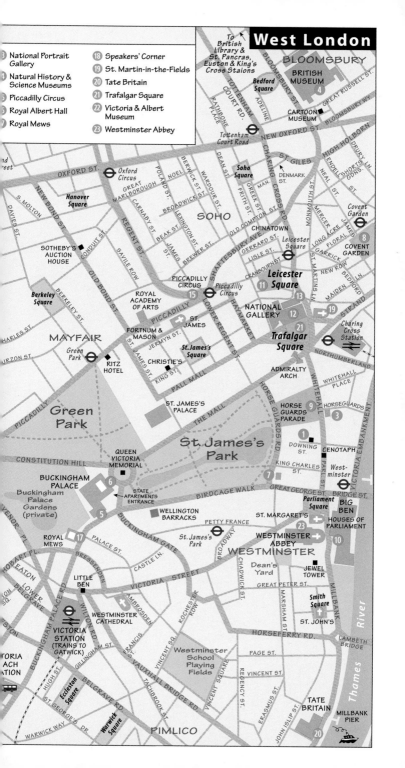

West London

Legend

3 National Portrait Gallery
4 Natural History & Science Museums
5 Piccadilly Circus
6 Royal Albert Hall
7 Royal Mews

18 Speakers' Corner
19 St. Martin-in-the-Fields
20 Tate Britain
21 Trafalgar Square
22 Victoria & Albert Museum
23 Westminster Abbey

To British Library & St. Pancras, Euston & King's Cross Staions

BLOOMSBURY

BRITISH MUSEUM

Bedford Square

CARTOON MUSEUM

NEW OXFORD ST.

HIGH HOLBORN

Tottenham Court Road

ST. GILES

DENMARK ST.

OXFORD ST.

Oxford Circus

Covent Garden

Hanover Square

SOHO

Soho Square

CHINATOWN

Leicester Square

COVENT GARDEN

SOTHEBY'S AUCTION HOUSE

Berkeley Square

PICCADILLY CIRCUS

Piccadilly Circus

Leicester Square

NATIONAL GALLERY

STRAND

Charing Cross Station

MAYFAIR

ROYAL ACADEMY OF ARTS

ST. JAMES

Trafalgar Square

Green Park

FORTNUM & MASON

St. James's Square

CHRISTIE'S

ADMIRALTY ARCH

WHITEHALL PLACE

RITZ HOTEL

PALL MALL

ST. JAMES'S PALACE

THE MALL

HORSE GUARDS PARADE

HORSEGUARDS

Green Park

St. James's Park

DOWNING ST.

CENOTAPH

CONSTITUTION HILL

QUEEN VICTORIA MEMORIAL

KING CHARLES ST.

Westminster

BUCKINGHAM PALACE

Buckingham Palace Gardens (private)

STATE APARTMENTS ENTRANCE

BIRDCAGE WALK

GREAT GEORGE ST.

Parliament Square

BIG BEN

WELLINGTON BARRACKS

ST. MARGARET'S

HOUSES OF PARLIAMENT

ROYAL MEWS

St. James's Park

PETTY FRANCE

WESTMINSTER ABBEY

PALACE ST.

BROADWAY

WESTMINSTER

LITTLE BEN

CASTLE LN.

VICTORIA STREET

Dean's Yard

JEWEL TOWER

GREAT PETER ST.

Smith Square

WESTMINSTER CATHEDRAL

ST. JOHN'S

VICTORIA STATION (TRAINS TO GATWICK)

HORSEFERRY RD.

LAMBETH BRIDGE

Eccleston Square

Westminster School Playing Fields

PAGE ST.

Warwick Square

VAUXHALL BRIDGE RD.

PIMLICO

TATE BRITAIN

MILLBANK PIER

River Thames

WARWICK WAY

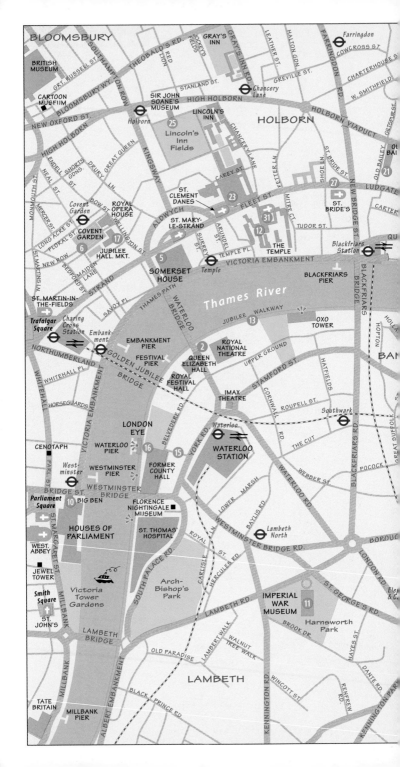

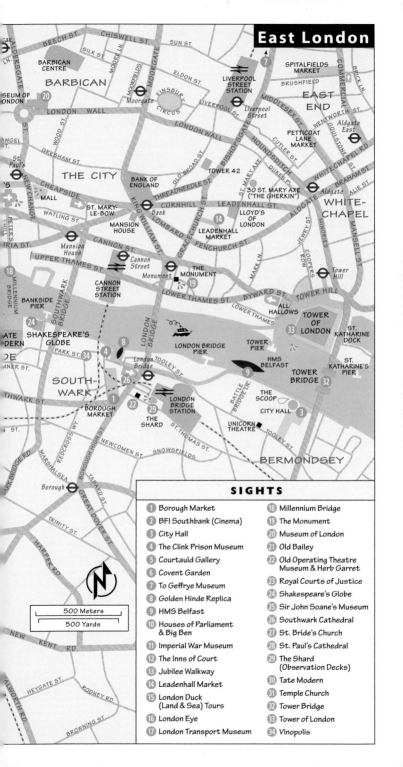

East London

SIGHTS

1. Borough Market
2. BFI Southbank (Cinema)
3. City Hall
4. The Clink Prison Museum
5. Courtauld Gallery
6. Covent Garden
7. To Geffrye Museum
8. Golden Hinde Replica
9. HMS Belfast
10. Houses of Parliament & Big Ben
11. Imperial War Museum
12. The Inns of Court
13. Jubilee Walkway
14. Leadenhall Market
15. London Duck (Land & Sea) Tours
16. London Eye
17. London Transport Museum
18. Millennium Bridge
19. The Monument
20. Museum of London
21. Old Bailey
22. Old Operating Theatre Museum & Herb Garret
23. Royal Courts of Justice
24. Shakespeare's Globe
25. Sir John Soane's Museum
26. Southwark Cathedral
27. St. Bride's Church
28. St. Paul's Cathedral
29. The Shard (Observation Decks)
30. Tate Modern
31. Temple Church
32. Tower Bridge
33. Tower of London
34. Vinopolis

500 Meters
500 Yards

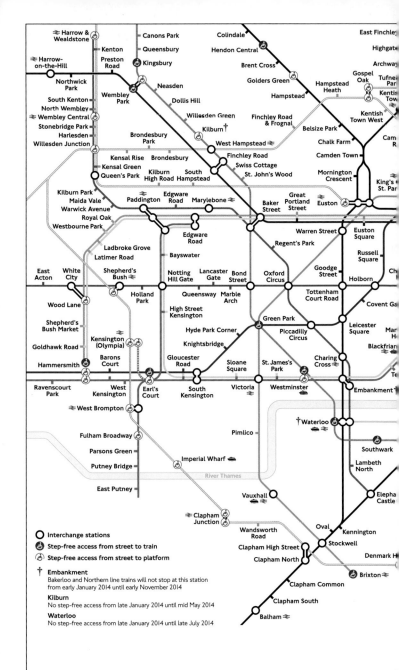

MAYOR OF LONDON

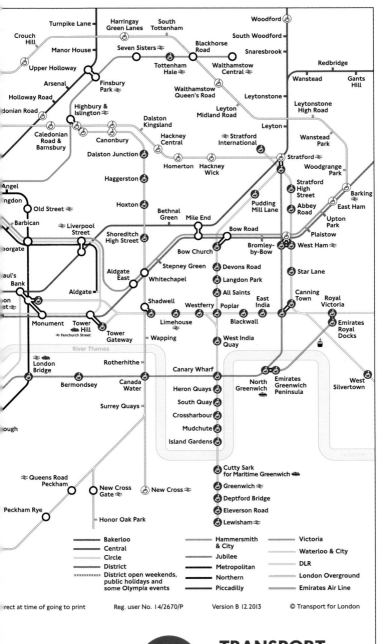

Crouch Hill
Turnpike Lane
Harringay Green Lanes
South Tottenham
Woodford
South Woodford
Snaresbrook
Redbridge
Manor House
Seven Sisters
Blackhorse Road
Wanstead
Gants Hill
Upper Holloway
Tottenham Hale
Walthamstow Central
Arsenal
Finsbury Park
Walthamstow Queen's Road
Leytonstone
Leytonstone High Road
Holloway Road
Highbury & Islington
Leyton Midland Road
donian Road
Caledonian Road & Barnsbury
Dalston Kingsland
Leyton
Wanstead Park
Canonbury
Hackney Central
Stratford International
Dalston Junction
Homerton
Hackney Wick
Stratford
Woodgrange Park
Angel
Haggerston
Stratford High Street
Barking
ngdon
Hoxton
Pudding Mill Lane
Abbey Road
East Ham
Old Street
Bethnal Green
Mile End
Upton Park
Barbican
Liverpool Street
Bow Road
Plaistow
Shoreditch High Street
Bromley-by-Bow
West Ham
oorgate
Aldgate East
Bow Church
Devons Road
Star Lane
aul's
Stepney Green
Langdon Park
Bank
Aldgate
Whitechapel
All Saints
Canning Town
Royal Victoria
on et
Shadwell
Westferry
Poplar
East India
Monument
Limehouse
Blackwall
Emirates Royal Docks
Tower Hill
Fenchurch Street
Tower Gateway
Wapping
West India Quay
River Thames
London Bridge
Rotherhithe
Canary Wharf
Bermondsey
Canada Water
Heron Quays
North Greenwich
Emirates Greenwich Peninsula
West Silvertown
Surrey Quays
South Quay
Crossharbour
Mudchute
Island Gardens
ough
Queens Road Peckham
New Cross Gate
New Cross
Cutty Sark for Maritime Greenwich
Greenwich
Peckham Rye
Honor Oak Park
Deptford Bridge
Eleverson Road
Lewisham

━━━ Bakerloo	━━━ Hammersmith & City	━━━ Victoria
━━━ Central	━━━ Jubilee	━━━ Waterloo & City
━━━ Circle	━━━ Metropolitan	━━━ DLR
━━━ District	━━━ Northern	━━━ London Overground
┄┄┄ District open weekends, public holidays and some Olympia events	━━━ Piccadilly	━━━ Emirates Air Line

rect at time of going to print   Reg. user No. 14/2670/P   Version B 12.2013   © Transport for London

TRANSPORT FOR LONDON

UNDERGROUND

EVERY JOURNEY MATTERS

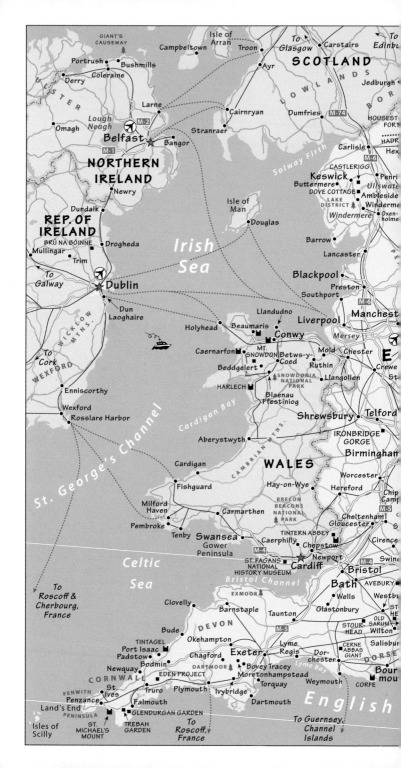

Berwick-upon-Tweed
Holy Island
BAMBURGH CASTLE
Alnwick
Newcastle-upon-Tyne
MISH EUM
Durham
A-1
Middlesbrough
RK IRES LES
Staithes
Grosmont
VAULX BBEY
NORTH YORK MOORS
Whitby
Robin Hood's Bay
Thirsk
Goathland
Hutton-le-Hole
Pick.
Scarborough
CASTLE HOWARD
EDEN CAMP
York
Bridlington
Doncaster
ds
Kingston-upon-Hull
Sheffield
Grimsby
M-1
North Sea
LAND
DLANDS
Lincoln
Newark
Skegness
rby
Boston
Nottingham
The Wash
M-1
Cromer
cester
Stamford
King's Lynn
oventry
Peterborough
Norwich
Warwick
Ely
Great Yarmouth
atford
Northampton
EAST
eton
Cambridge
ANGLIA
BLENHEIM PALACE
M-1
Ipswich
Luton
Oxford
Hertford
Stansted
Harwich
M-40
Leavesden
M-11
Colchester
cot
Thames
London
Reading
City
Windsor
Heathrow
Greenwich
Southend
Southend-on-Sea
M-3
Whitstable
Gatwick
Ramsgate
M-23
M-20 M-2
Canterbury
nchester
KENT
WHITE CLIFFS OF DOVER
Ostende
Bruges
uthampton
ARUNDEL
SISSINGHURST GARDENS
Ashford
Dover
Portsmouth
Battle
Folke-stone
Dunkerque
E-40
FISHBOURNE ROMAN PALACE
PEVENSEY
Rye
Calais
BELGIUM
port
Brighton
Hastings
Channel Tunnel
e of
Newhaven
Alfriston
ght
Eastbourne
FRANCE
BEACHY HEAD
Lille
E-17
Channel
A-16
A-26
E-42
To Cherbourg, France
To Ouistreham, France
To Dieppe, France
To Paris
To Paris
To Brussels

To Esbjerg, Denmark

To Amsterdam, Netherlands

To Hoek van Holland, Netherlands

Zeebrugge

Rick Steves

LONDON

2015

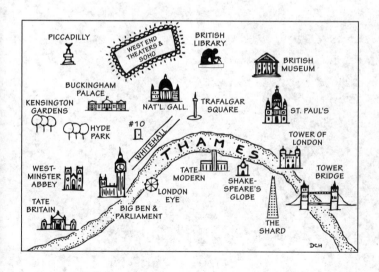

PICCADILLY

WEST END THEATERS & SOHO

BRITISH LIBRARY

BRITISH MUSEUM

BUCKINGHAM PALACE

KENSINGTON GARDENS

NAT'L. GALL.

TRAFALGAR SQUARE

ST. PAUL'S

HYDE PARK

#10

WHITEHALL

THAMES

TOWER OF LONDON

WEST-MINSTER ABBEY

TATE MODERN

SHAKE-SPEARE'S GLOBE

TOWER BRIDGE

TATE BRITAIN

LONDON EYE

BIG BEN & PARLIAMENT

THE SHARD

DCH

INTRODUCTION

Blow through the city on a double-decker bus, and take a pinch-me-I'm-in-London walk through the West End. Ogle the crown jewels at the Tower of London, hear the chimes of Big Ben, and see the Houses of Parliament in action. Cruise the Thames River, and take a spin on the London Eye. Hobnob with the tombstones in Westminster Abbey, visit with Leonardo, Botticelli, and Rembrandt in the National Gallery, and explore Harry Potter's magical realm at the film studio in Leavesden. Enjoy Shakespeare in a replica of the Globe Theatre and marvel at a glitzy, fun musical at a modern-day theater. Whisper across the dome of St. Paul's Cathedral, then rummage through our civilization's attic at the British Museum. And sip your tea with pinky raised and clotted cream dribbling down your scone.

You can enjoy some of Europe's best people-watching at Covent Garden, and snap to at Buckingham Palace's Changing of the Guard. Just sit in Victoria Station, Piccadilly Circus, or a major Tube station and observe. Tip a pint in a pub with a chatty local, and beach-comb the Thames. Spend one evening at a theater and the other nights catching your breath.

London is more than its museums and landmarks. It's the L.A., D.C., and N.Y.C. of Britain—a living, breathing, thriving organism...a coral reef of humanity. The city has changed dramatically in recent years, and many visitors are surprised to find how "un-English" it is. ESL (English as a second language) seems like the city's first language, as white people are now a minority in major parts of the city that once symbolized white imperialism. Arabs have nearly bought out the area north of Hyde Park. Chinese takeouts outnumber fish-and-chips shops. Eastern Europeans pull pints in British pubs. Many hotels are run by people with foreign accents (who hire English chambermaids), while outlying suburbs

Map Legend

½	Viewpoint	✈	Airport	▮ ▮	Tunnel
↟	Entrance	Ⓣ	Taxi Stand		Pedestrian Zone
✚	Tourist Info	▮	Tram Stop		Railway
WC	Restroom	Ⓑ	Bus Stop		Ferry/Boat Route
▮	Castle	Ⓟ	Parking	├─┼─┤	Tram
⬚	Church	⊖	Tube		Stairs
▪	Statue/Point of Interest	)(	Mtn. Pass		Walk/Tour Route
▼	Pub		Park		Trail

Use this legend to help you navigate the maps in this book.

are home to huge communities of Indians and Pakistanis. London is a city of eight million separate dreams, inhabiting a place that tolerates and encourages them. With the English Channel Tunnel and discount airlines making travel between Britain and the Continent easier than ever, London is learning—sometimes fitfully—to live as a microcosm of its formerly vast empire.

The city, which has long attracted tourists, seems perpetually at your service, with an impressive slate of sights, entertainment, and eateries, all linked by a great transit system. You'll still see the effects of a banner year for London—2012—when the city hosted both the Olympics and the Queen's "Diamond Jubilee" celebration for her 60th year on the throne. Consequently, this already spiffed-up city shines brighter than ever.

ABOUT THIS BOOK

Rick Steves London 2015 is a personal tour guide in your pocket. Better yet, it's actually two tour guides in your pocket: The co-author of this book is Gene Openshaw. Since our first "Europe through the gutter" trip together as high school buddies in the 1970s, Gene and I have been exploring the wonders of the Old World. An inquisitive historian and lover of European culture, Gene wrote most of this book's self-guided museum tours and neighborhood walks. Together, Gene and I keep this book current and accurate (though, for simplicity, from this point "we" will shed our respective egos and become "I").

In this book, you'll find the following chapters:

Orientation to London includes specifics on public transportation, helpful hints, local tour options, easy-to-read maps, and tourist information. The "Planning Your Time" section suggests a schedule for how to best use your limited time.

Sights in London describes the top attractions and includes their cost and hours.

Key to This Book

Updates

This book is updated every year. For the latest, visit www. ricksteves.com/update.

Abbreviations and Times

I use the following symbols and abbreviations in this book:
Sights are rated:

▲▲▲   Don't miss

▲▲   Try hard to see

▲   Worthwhile if you can make it

No rating   Worth knowing about

Tourist information offices are abbreviated as **TI,** and bathrooms are **WCs.** To categorize accommodations, I use a **Sleep Code** (described on page 377).

Like Europe, this book uses the **24-hour clock.** It's the same through 12:00 noon, then keeps going: 13:00, 14:00, and so on. For anything over 12, subtract 12 and add p.m. (14:00 is 2:00 p.m.).

When giving **opening times,** I include both peak season and off-season hours if they differ. So, if a museum is listed as "May-Oct daily 9:00-16:00," it should be open from 9:00 a.m. until 4:00 p.m. from the first day of May until the last day of October (but expect exceptions).

If you see a ✪ symbol near a sight listing, it means that sight is described in far greater detail elsewhere—either with its own self-guided tour, or as part of a self-guided walk.

For **transit** or **tour departures,** I first list the frequency, then the duration. So, a train connection listed as "2/hour, 1.5 hours" departs twice each hour, and the journey lasts an hour and a half.

The **Self-Guided Walks** cover Westminster (from Big Ben to Trafalgar Square); the West End (it's the thee-ah-ter district, dahling, with restaurants and shops galore, from Leicester Square and Covent Garden to Soho, Regent Street, and Piccadilly Circus); The City (the financial district—banks, churches, and courts busy with barristers and baristas); Bankside (on the South Bank, through Shakespeare's world to the Tate Modern); and the Docklands (London's new and creatively planned urban district).

The **Self-Guided Tours** lead you through London's most fascinating museums and sights: Westminster Abbey, the Houses of Parliament, the National Gallery, the National Portrait Gallery, the Courtauld Gallery, the British Museum, the British Library, St. Paul's Cathedral, the Tower of London, the Tate Modern, the

Victoria and Albert Museum, and the Tate Britain. The Greenwich Tour ties together the major sights of that London borough.

Sleeping in London describes my favorite hotels, from good-value deals to cushy splurges.

Eating in London serves up a range of options, from inexpensive pubs to fancy restaurants.

London with Children includes my top recommendations for keeping your kids (and you) happy in London.

Shopping in London gives you tips for shopping painlessly and enjoyably, without letting it overwhelm your vacation or ruin your budget.

Entertainment in London is your guide to fun, including theater, music, walks, and wintertime activities.

London Connections lays the groundwork for your smooth arrival and departure, covering transportation by train (including the Eurostar to Paris and Brussels) and by plane (with detailed information on London's major airports), plus connections to the cruise-ship ports of Southampton and Dover.

Practicalities is a traveler's tool kit, with our best travel tips and advice about money, sightseeing, and staying connected. There's also a list of recommended books and films.

Day Trips from London includes Windsor, Cambridge, and Stonehenge.

Great Britain: Past and Present gives the background of this country, including a timeline of London history, information about British architecture, and a rundown of contemporary events and current challenges.

The **appendix** has nuts-and-bolts information, including useful phone numbers and websites, a festival list, a climate chart, a handy packing checklist, and a fun British-Yankee dictionary.

Browse through this book and select your favorite sights. Then have a brilliant trip! Traveling like a temporary local, you'll get the absolute most out of every mile, minute, and dollar. As you visit places I know and love, I'm happy you'll be meeting my favorite Londoners.

Planning

This section will help you get started planning your trip—with advice on trip costs, when to go, and things to know before you take off.

TRAVEL SMART

Your trip to London is like a complex play—it's easier to follow and really appreciate on a second viewing. While no one does the same trip twice to gain that advantage, reading this book in its entirety before your trip accomplishes much the same thing.

Design an itinerary that enables you to visit sights at the best possible times. Note festivals, holidays, specifics on sights, and days when sights are closed. Visit The City (London's old center) during the day on weekdays, when it's lively, not at night or on weekends, when it's completely dead. The two-hour orientation bus tour is best on Sunday morning (when some sights are closed anyway, and traffic doesn't slow down the bus) or evenings (when it's cheaper). There are almost no plays on Sundays, except for Shakespeare's Globe and family fare (like *The Lion King*). Treat Saturday as a weekday, except for transportation connections outside of London (which can be less frequent than on Mon-Fri, and downright meager on Sun). A smart trip is a puzzle—a fun, doable, and worthwhile challenge.

When you're plotting your itinerary, strive for a mix of intense and relaxed stretches. Every trip—and every traveler—needs slack time (laundry, picnics, people-watching, and so on). Pace yourself. Assume you will return.

Update your plans as you travel. You can carry a small mobile device (phone, tablet, or laptop) to find out tourist information, learn the latest on sights (special events, tour schedules, etc.), book tickets and tours, make reservations, reconfirm hotels, research transportation connections, and keep in touch with your loved ones. If you don't want to bring a pricey device, you can use guest computers at hotels and make phone calls from landlines.

Enjoy the friendliness of the British people. Connect with the culture. Set up your own quest for the best pub, silly sign, or chocolate bar. Slow down and be open to unexpected experiences. You speak the language—use it! Ask questions—most locals are eager to point you in their idea of the right direction. Keep a notepad in your pocket for confirming prices, noting directions, and organizing your thoughts. Wear your money belt, learn the currency, and figure out how to estimate prices in dollars. Those who expect to travel smart, do.

TRIP COSTS

Five components make up your trip costs: airfare, surface transportation, room and board, sightseeing and entertainment, and shopping and miscellany.

Airfare: A basic round-trip flight from the US to London can cost on average, about $1,000-2,000 total, depending on where you fly from and when (cheaper in winter). If London is part of a longer trip, consider saving time and money in Europe by flying into one city and out of another; for instance, into London and out of Paris.

Overall, Kayak.com is the best place to start searching for flights on a combination of mainstream and budget carriers.

Surface Transportation: For a typical one-week visit, allow about $52 for the Tube and buses (for a Seven-Day Travelcard transportation pass). The cost of round-trip train rides to day-trip destinations is about $28 for Windsor, $15 for Greenwich (two rides on a 1-2-zone pay-as-you-go Oyster card—see page 24), and $38 for Cambridge. You can save money by taking buses instead of trains. Add $90 if you plan to take a taxi ride between London's Heathrow Airport and your hotel (or save money by taking the Tube, train, bus, or airport shuttle).

Room and Board: London is one of Europe's most expensive major capitals. But if you're careful, you can manage comfortably in London in 2015 on $135 a day per person for room and board. A $130-a-day budget allows $15 for lunch, $30 for dinner, and $90 for lodging (based on two people splitting the cost of a basic $180 double room that includes breakfast). Students and tightwads can do it for as little as $70 a day ($45 for hostel bed, $25 for groceries).

Sightseeing and Entertainment: You'll pay more in London for sights that charge admission than you will anywhere else in Europe. Fortunately, most of London's best sights are free (although many request a donation), including the British Museum, National Gallery, National Portrait Gallery, Tate Britain, Tate Modern, British Library, and the Victoria and Albert Museum. (For a full list of free museums—and advice on saving money on sightseeing—see "Affording London's Sights," page 70.)

Figure on paying roughly $25-35 each for the major sights that charge admission (e.g., Westminster Abbey-$30, Tower of London-$36), $12-20 for guided walks, and $50 for bus tours and splurge experiences (plays range $25-100).

An overall average of $50-60 a day works for most people. Don't skimp here. After all, this category is the driving force behind your trip—you came to sightsee, enjoy, and experience London.

Shopping and Miscellany: Figure roughly $2 per postcard, $3 for tea or an ice cream cone, and $6 per pint of beer. Shopping can vary in cost from nearly nothing to a small fortune. Good budget travelers find that this category has little to do with assembling a trip full of lifelong and wonderful memories.

WHEN TO GO

July and August are peak season—my favorite time—with long days, the best weather, and the busiest schedule of tourist fun. Prices and crowds don't go up in summer as dramatically in Britain as they do in much of Europe, except for holidays and festivals (see page 584). Still, travelers during "shoulder season" (May, early

London Almanac

Population: Approximately 8.2 million people

Currency: British pound (GBP)

City Layout: London is divided into the City of London (the main financial district) and 32 administrative boroughs—12 in inner London.

Tallest Building: The Shard stands at 1,020 feet, making it the tallest building in Western Europe—for now.

Tourist Tracks: Each year London hosts 26 million tourists, most of whom stop to take a photo at Trafalgar Square. London's most popular attraction, the British Museum, sees 5.9 million visitors annually.

Popular Misconception: "Big Ben" refers not to the clock, but instead to its 13-ton bell.

Culture Count: While the Queen's English is still the language of the land, fewer than half the residents of inner London speak English as their first language. Nearly 300 different languages are spoken in London's schools. About 60 percent of Londoners are white (many of them Continental Europeans rather than Brits), 18 percent are Asian, 13 percent are black, 5 percent are mixed race, and 4 percent are "other." Six in 10 Brits call themselves Christian (half of those are Anglican), but in any given week, more Londoners visit a mosque than an Anglican church.

Fun Food Facts: Traditionally, London's most popular take-away foods have been fish-and-chips and minced-meat pie (the pies were originally filled with eels...so minced-meat is an improvement). But it's not all about meat; PETA recently named London the world's most vegan-friendly city. These days you'll find more gourmet sandwich and prepackaged-meals shops than "chippies."

Need a Restroom? Ask for the toilet, loo, lavatory, or bog.

Oldest Pub: The Lamb and Flag in Covent Garden. First licensed in 1623, it was once known as the Bucket of Blood, thanks to rowdy, bare-knuckle fights held there.

Average Londoner: The average Londoner is about 40 years old, has 1.7 children, and will live until the age of 80. He/she will drink 75,000 cups of tea in a lifetime and consumes less alcohol per week than the average Brit. Over the course of a year, he/she spends 276 hours riding the Tube.

INTRODUCTION

Rick Steves Audio Europe

If you're bringing a mobile device, be sure to check out **Rick Steves Audio Europe,** where you can download free audio tours and hours of travel interviews (via the Rick Steves Audio Europe smartphone app, www.ricksteves.com/audioeurope, Google Play, or iTunes).

My self-guided **audio tours** are user-friendly, easy-to-follow, fun, and informative, covering the major sights and neighborhoods in London: the British Museum, British Library, St. Paul's Cathedral, and the Westminster and City of London walks. Compared to live tours, my audio tours are hard to beat: Nobody will stand you up, the quality is reliable, you can take the tour exactly when you like, and they're free.

Rick Steves Audio Europe also offers a far-reaching library of intriguing **travel interviews** with experts from around the globe. The interviews are organized by destination, including many of the places in this book.

June, Sept, and early Oct) enjoy lower prices, smaller crowds, decent weather, and the full range of sights and tourist fun spots.

Winter travelers find fewer crowds and soft room prices, but shorter sightseeing hours. The weather can be cold and dreary, and nightfall draws the shades on sightseeing well before dinnertime. While England's rural charm falls with the leaves, London sightseeing is fine in the winter, and is especially popular during the Christmas season. For more on planning a winter holiday visit, read "Winter Diversions" (at the end of the Entertainment in London chapter).

Plan for rain no matter when you go. Just keep traveling and take full advantage of "bright spells." The weather can change several times a day, but rarely is it extreme. As the locals say, "There's no bad weather, only inappropriate clothing." Bring a jacket, and dress in layers. Temperatures below 32°F cause headlines, and days that break 80°F—while more common in recent years—are still infrequent in London. (For more information, see the climate chart in the appendix.) Weather-wise, July and August are not much better than shoulder months. May and June can be lovely. While sunshine may be rare, summer days are very long. The midsummer sun is up from 6:30 to 22:30. It's not uncommon to have a gray day, eat dinner, and enjoy hours of sunshine afterward.

KNOW BEFORE YOU GO
Your trip is more likely to go smoothly if you plan ahead. Check this list of things to arrange while you're still at home.

You need a **passport**—but no visa or shots—to travel in Great

Britain. You may be denied entry into certain European countries if your passport is due to expire within three months of your ticketed date of return. Get it renewed if you'll be cutting it close. It can take up to six weeks to get or renew a passport. (For more on passports, see www.travel.state.gov.) Pack a photocopy of your passport in your luggage in case the original is lost or stolen.

Book rooms well in advance if you'll be traveling during peak season or any major holidays or festivals (see page 584).

To book a **London play,** you can call from the US as easily as from London, using your credit-card number to pay for your tickets. For the current schedule and phone numbers, visit www.officiallondontheatre.co.uk. For simplicity, I book plays while in London (but if you have your heart set on a hot show, prebooking is safer). For more information, see the Entertainment in London chapter.

To visit **Stonehenge,** it's best to reserve your ticket at least 24 hours in advance (see page 521); if you want to go inside the stone circle, book your visit as soon as you know the date you'll be there.

Call your **debit- and credit-card companies** to let them know the countries you'll be visiting, to ask about fees, request your PIN code (it will be mailed to you), and more. See page 559 for details.

Do your homework if you want to buy **travel insurance.** Compare the cost of the insurance to the likelihood of your using it and your potential loss if something goes wrong. Also, check whether your existing insurance (health, homeowners, or renters) covers you and your possessions overseas. For more information, see www.ricksteves.com/insurance.

If you plan to hire a **local guide,** reserve ahead by email. Popular guides can get booked up.

If you're bringing a **mobile device,** download any apps you might want to use on the road, such as maps and transit schedules. Check out **Rick Steves Audio Europe,** featuring audio tours of London's major sights, hours of travel interviews on Great Britain, and more (for details, see the sidebar).

Check the **Rick Steves guidebook updates** page for any recent changes to this book (www.ricksteves.com/update).

You won't want to drive in London because of the traffic and congestion charge (covered on page 33), but if you'll be **renting a car** for touring Britain, you'll need your driver's license.

If you'll be taking the **Eurostar train,** consider buying your ticket in advance; for details, see page 481.

Check the **Rick Steves guidebook updates** page for any recent changes to this book (www.ricksteves.com/update).

Because **airline carry-on restrictions** are always changing, visit the Transportation Security Administration's website (www.tsa.gov) for a list of what you can bring on the plane and for the

INTRODUCTION

How Was Your Trip?

Were your travels fun, smooth, and meaningful? If you'd like to share your tips, concerns, and discoveries, please fill out the survey at www.ricksteves.com/feedback. I value your feedback. Thanks in advance—it helps a lot.

latest security measures (including screening of electronic devices, which you may be asked to power up).

Traveling as a Temporary Local

We travel all the way to Europe to enjoy differences—to become temporary locals. You'll experience frustrations. Certain truths that we find "God-given" or "self-evident," such as cold beer, ice in drinks, bottomless cups of coffee, hot showers, and bigger being better, are suddenly not so true. One of the benefits of travel is the eye-opening realization that there are logical, civil, and even better alternatives. A willingness to go local ensures that you'll enjoy a full dose of British hospitality.

Europeans generally like Americans. But if there is a negative aspect to the image the British have of Americans, it's that we are loud, wasteful, ethnocentric, too informal (which can seem disrespectful), and a bit naive.

The British (and Europeans in general) place a high value on speaking quietly in restaurants and on trains. Listen while on the bus or in a restaurant—the place can be packed, but the decibel level is low. Try to adjust your volume accordingly to show respect for the culture.

Although the British look bemusedly at some of our Yankee excesses—and worriedly at others—they nearly always afford us individual travelers all the warmth we deserve.

Judging from all the happy feedback I receive from travelers who have used this book, it's safe to assume you'll enjoy a great, affordable vacation—with the finesse of an independent, experienced traveler.

Thanks, and have a brilliant holiday!

Rick Steves

Back Door Travel Philosophy

From Rick Steves Europe Through the Back Door

Travel is intensified living—maximum thrills per minute and one of the last great sources of legal adventure. Travel is freedom. It's recess, and we need it.

Experiencing the real Europe requires catching it by surprise, going casual..."through the Back Door."

Affording travel is a matter of priorities. (Make do with the old car.) You can eat and sleep—simply, safely, and enjoyably—anywhere in Europe for $125 a day plus transportation costs. In many ways, spending more money only builds a thicker wall between you and what you traveled so far to see. Europe is a cultural carnival, and time after time, you'll find that its best acts are free and the best seats are the cheap ones.

A tight budget forces you to travel close to the ground, meeting and communicating with the people. Never sacrifice sleep, nutrition, safety, or cleanliness to save money. Simply enjoy the local-style alternatives to expensive hotels and restaurants.

Connecting with people carbonates your experience. Extroverts have more fun. If your trip is low on magic moments, kick yourself and make things happen. If you don't enjoy a place, maybe you don't know enough about it. Seek the truth. Recognize tourist traps. Give a culture the benefit of your open mind. See things as different, but not better or worse. Any culture has plenty to share.

Of course, travel, like the world, is a series of hills and valleys. Be fanatically positive and militantly optimistic. If something's not to your liking, change your liking.

Travel can make you a happier American, as well as a citizen of the world. Our Earth is home to seven billion equally precious people. It's humbling to travel and find that other people don't have the "American Dream"—they have their own dreams. Europeans like us, but with all due respect, they wouldn't trade passports.

Thoughtful travel engages us with the world. In tough economic times, it reminds us what is truly important. By broadening perspectives, travel teaches new ways to measure quality of life.

Globetrotting destroys ethnocentricity, helping us understand and appreciate other cultures. Rather than fear the diversity on this planet, celebrate it. Among your most prized souvenirs will be the strands of different cultures you choose to knit into your own character. The world is a cultural yarn shop, and Back Door travelers are weaving the ultimate tapestry. Join in!

ORIENTATION TO LONDON

London is more than 600 square miles of urban jungle—a world in itself and a barrage on all the senses. On my first visit, I felt extremely small. To grasp London more comfortably, see it as the old town in the city center without the modern, congested sprawl. (Even from that perspective, it's still huge.)

The Thames River (pronounced "tems") runs roughly west to east through the city, with most of the visitor's sights on the North Bank. Mentally, maybe even physically, trim down your map to include only the area between the Tower of London (to the east), Hyde Park (west), Regent's Park (north), and the South Bank (south). This is roughly the area bordered by the Tube's Circle Line. This four-mile stretch between the Tower and Hyde Park (about a 1.5-hour walk) looks like a milk bottle on its side (see map on next page), and holds 80 percent of the sights mentioned in this book.

With a core focus and a good orientation, you'll get a sampling of London's top sights, history, and cultural entertainment, and a good look at its ever-changing human face.

The sprawling city becomes much more manageable if you think of it as a collection of neighborhoods.

Central London: This area contains Westminster and what Londoners call the West End. The Westminster district includes Big Ben, Parliament, Westminster Abbey, and Buckingham Palace—the grand government buildings from which Britain is ruled. Trafalgar Square, London's gathering place, has many major museums. The West End is the center of London's cultural life, with bustling squares: Piccadilly Circus and Leicester Square host cinemas, tourist traps, and nighttime glitz. Soho and Covent Garden are thriving people zones with theaters, restaurants, pubs, and boutiques. And Regent and Oxford streets are the city's main shopping zones.

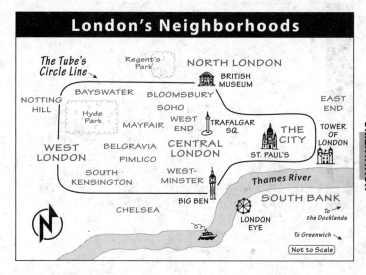

London's Neighborhoods

North London: Neighborhoods in this part of town—including Bloomsbury, Fitzrovia, and Marylebone—contain such major sights as the British Museum and the overhyped Madame Tussauds Waxworks. Nearby, along busy Euston Road, is the British Library, plus a trio of train stations (one of them, St. Pancras International, is linked to Paris by the Eurostar "Chunnel" train).

The City: Today's modern financial district, called simply "The City," was a walled town in Roman times. Gleaming skyscrapers are interspersed with historical landmarks such as St. Paul's Cathedral, legal sights (Old Bailey), and the Museum of London. The Tower of London and Tower Bridge lie at The City's eastern border.

East London: Just east of The City is the East End—the increasingly gentrified former stomping ground of Cockney ragamuffins and Jack the Ripper.

The South Bank: The South Bank of the Thames River offers major sights (Tate Modern, Shakespeare's Globe, London Eye) linked by a riverside walkway. Within this area, Southwark (SUTH-uck) stretches from the Tate Modern to London Bridge. Pedestrian bridges connect the South Bank with The City and Trafalgar Square.

West London: This huge area contains neighborhoods such as Mayfair, Belgravia, Pimlico, Chelsea, South Kensington, and Notting Hill. It's home to London's wealthy and has many trendy shops and enticing restaurants. Here you'll find a range of museums (Victoria and Albert Museum, Tate Britain, and more), my top hotel recommendations, lively Victoria Station, and the vast green expanses of Hyde Park and Kensington Gardens.

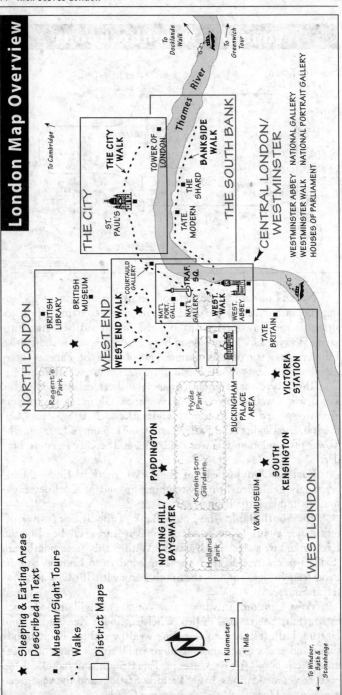

London Map Overview

Outside the Center: The Docklands, London's version of Manhattan, is farther east than the East End; Olympic Park is just north of the Docklands. Historic Greenwich is southeast of London and across the Thames. Kew Gardens and Hampton Court Palace are southwest of London. North of London is the Warner Bros. Studio Tour for Harry Potter fans.

PLANNING YOUR TIME

London is a super one-week getaway. Its sights can keep even the most fidgety traveler well entertained for seven days. After con-

sidering London's major tourist destinations, I've covered just my favorites in this book. You won't be able to see all of these, so don't try. You'll keep coming back to London. After dozens of visits myself, I still enjoy a healthy list of excuses to return.

For a one-week visit, buy the Seven-Day Travelcard (see page 23) and study up on "Affording London's Sights" (see page 70). Armed with this information and your Travelcard, you'll feel more like a Londoner, forget the high cost of sightseeing, and experience the city with a better attitude.

Here's a suggested schedule for London's best seven days:

Day 1

9:00	Tower of London (crown jewels first, then Beefeater tour and White Tower; note that on Sun-Mon, the Tower opens at 10:00).
13:00	Grab a picnic, catch a boat at Tower Pier, and relax with lunch on the Thames while cruising to Westminster Pier.
14:30	Tour Westminster Abbey, and consider their evensong service (usually at 17:00, at 15:00 on Sun and off-season Sat, never on Wed).
17:00 (or after evensong)	Follow my self-guided Westminster Walk. When you're finished, you could return to the Houses of Parliament and possibly pop into see the House of Commons in action (but check their schedule first—see page 45).

Day 2

8:30	Take a double-decker hop-on, hop-off London sightseeing bus tour (from Victoria Station or Green Park), and hop off for the Changing of the Guard.
11:00	Buckingham Palace (guards change most days May-

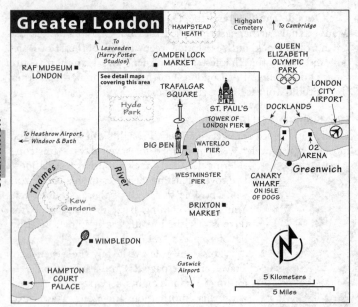

July at 11:30, alternate days Aug-April—confirm online).

12:00	Walk through St. James's Park to enjoy London's delightful park scene.
13:00	After lunch, tour the Churchill War Rooms.
16:00	Tour the National Gallery.
Evening	Have dinner—maybe at a pub?—before a play, concert, or evening walking tour. For ideas, see the Entertainment in London chapter; consider these activities for any evening over the following days.

Day 3

9:00	Follow the first two-thirds of my self-guided walk through The City (as far as St. Paul's), then follow my St. Paul's Cathedral Tour.
15:00	Cross London Bridge and follow my self-guided Bankside Walk along the South Bank of the Thames. Tour Shakespeare's Globe or the Tate Modern if you're interested (or, if it's a day that the Tate Modern is open late, circle back here later). Then walk the Jubilee Walkway from the Millennium Bridge to the London Eye.
Evening	Cap your day with South Bank sights and experiences that are open late (a ride on the London Eye—last ascent 20:30-21:00, depending on season and later on

weekends; a Shakespeare play at the Globe—usually at 19:30 in summer; or Tate Modern—open Fri-Sat until 22:00).

Day 4

10:00   Tour the British Museum, then have lunch.

14:00   Tube to Leicester Square to take my self-guided West End Walk to see Covent Garden and Soho, and browse the Regent Street shops.

17:00   Enjoy afternoon tea (at Fortnum & Mason, The Wolseley, or the Orangery at Kensington Palace).

Day 5

Spend the morning exploring a street market (try to make today coincide with the day that your market of choice is busiest—see the Shopping in London chapter for details).

Spend the rest of your day at your choice of major sights. Depending on your interests, choose from the British Library, Tate Britain, Museum of London, Imperial War Museum, or Kew Gardens (consider a cruise to Kew, return to London by Tube).

Day 6

10:00   Cruise from Westminster Pier to Greenwich.

11:15   Tour the salty sights of Greenwich.

16:00   Ride the Docklands Light Railroad (DLR) to the Docklands for a look at London's emerging "Manhattan."

18:30   Take the DLR or Tube back to London.

Day 7

10:00   Tour the Victoria and Albert Museum.

After lunch (or a picnic in the park), stroll through Hyde Park and visit Kensington Palace.

Spend the afternoon at Harrods or other shopping venues.

With More Time

To get a break from big-city London, you can easily spend a day or two side-tripping. Windsor, Cambridge, and Stonehenge each make a satisfying one-day visit.

Overview

TOURIST INFORMATION

For such a big and important city, it's amazing how hard it can be to find unbiased sightseeing information and advice in London. You'll see "Tourist Information" offices advertised everywhere, but most of them are private agencies that make a big profit selling tours and advance sightseeing and/or theater tickets; others are run by Transport for London (TFL) and are primarily focused on providing public-transit advice.

The **City of London Information Centre** next to St. Paul's Cathedral (to the right of the church) is the only publicly funded—and therefore impartial—"real" TI (Mon-Sat 9:30-17:30, Sun 10:00-16:00; Tube: St. Paul's, tel. 020/7332-1456, www.visitthecity.co.uk).

While officially a service of The City (London's financial district), this office also provides information about the rest of London. It sells Oyster cards, London Passes (see page 565), and advance "Fast Track" sightseeing tickets (described next), and stocks various free publications: *London Planner* (a free monthly that lists all the sights, events, and hours), some walking-tour brochures, the *Official London Theatre Guide*, a free Tube and bus map, the *Guide to River Thames Boat Services,* and brochures describing self-guided walks in The City (various themes, including Dickens, modern architecture, and film locations).

The TI plans to sell tour tickets for the Houses of Parliament—ask about these if you're interested. They give out a free map of The City, and sell several city-wide maps; ask if they have yet another, free map with a coupon good for 20 percent off admission to St. Paul's. I'd skip their room-booking service (charges a commission) and theater box office (may charge a commission).

Visit London, which serves the greater London area, doesn't have an office you can visit in person—but does operate a call center and website (tel. 0870-156-6366, www.visitlondon.com).

Fast Track Tickets: To skip the ticket-buying queues at certain London sights, you can buy Fast Track tickets in advance—and they can be cheaper than tickets sold right at the sight. They're particularly smart for the Tower of London, the London Eye, and Madame Tussauds Waxworks, all of which get very busy in high season. They're available through various sales outlets around London (including the City of London TI, souvenir stands, and faux-TIs scattered throughout touristy areas).

ARRIVAL IN LONDON

For more information on getting to or from London by train, bus, and plane, see the London Connections chapter.

By Train: London has nine major train stations, all connected by the Tube (subway). All have ATMs, and many of the larger stations also have shops, fast food, exchange offices, and luggage storage. From any station, you can ride the Tube or taxi to your hotel. For more info on train travel, see www.nationalrail.co.uk.

By Bus: The main intercity bus station is Victoria Coach Station, one block southwest of Victoria train/Tube station. For more on bus travel, see www.nationalexpress.com.

By Plane: London has six airports. Most tourists arrive at Heathrow or Gatwick airport, although flights from elsewhere in Europe may land at Stansted, Luton, Southend, or London City airport. For specifics on getting from London's airports to downtown, see the London Connections chapter; for hotels near Heathrow and Gatwick, see the Sleeping in London chapter.

HELPFUL HINTS

Theft Alert: Wear your money belt. The Artful Dodger is alive and well in London. Be on guard, particularly on public transportation and in places crowded with tourists, who, considered naive and rich, are targeted. The Changing of the Guard scene is a favorite for thieves. And more than 7,500 purses are stolen annually at Covent Garden alone.

Pedestrian Safety: Cars drive on the left side of the road—which can be as confusing for foreign pedestrians as for foreign drivers. Before crossing a street, I always look right, look left, then look right again just to be sure. Most crosswalks are even painted with instructions, reminding foreign guests to "Look right" or "Look left." While locals are champion jaywalkers, you shouldn't try it; jaywalking is treacherous when you're disoriented about which direction traffic is coming from.

Medical Problems: Local hospitals have good-quality 24-hour-a-day emergency care centers, where any tourist who needs help can drop in and, after a wait, be seen by a doctor. Your hotel has details. St. Thomas' Hospital, immediately across the river from Big Ben, has a fine reputation.

Getting Your Bearings: London is well-signed for visitors. Through an initiative called Legible London, the city has erected thoughtfully designed, pedestrian-focused maps around town. In this sprawling city—where predictable grid-planned streets are relatively rare—it's also smart to buy and use a good map. *Benson's London Street Map*, sold at many newsstands and bookstores, is my favorite for efficient sightseeing.

ORIENTATION

Daily Reminder

Sunday: The Tower of London and British Museum are both especially crowded today. Speakers' Corner in Hyde Park rants from early afternoon until early evening. These places are closed: Sir John Soane's Museum, and legal sights (Houses of Parliament, City Hall, and Old Bailey; the neighborhood called The City is dead). Westminster Abbey and St. Paul's are open during the day for worship but closed to sightseers. With all these closures, this morning is a good time to take a bus tour. Most big stores open late (around 11:30) and close early (18:00). Street markets are flourishing at Camden Lock, Spitalfields (at its best today), Petticoat Lane, Brick Lane, and Greenwich, but Portobello Road and Brixton markets are closed (though the Brixton farmers market is open 10:00-14:00). Because of all the market action, it's a good day to take the East End Walk (see page 79). Theaters are quiet, as most actors take today off. (There are a few exceptions, such as Shakespeare's Globe, which offers Sunday performances in summer, and theaters with family-oriented fare, including *The Lion King*, offered year-round.)

Monday: Virtually all sights are open, except Apsley House, Sir John Soane's Museum, Vinopolis, and a few others. The Houses of Parliament may be open as late as 22:00.

Tuesday: Virtually all sights are open, except Vinopolis and Apsley House. The British Library is open until 20:00, and the Houses of Parliament may be open as late as 22:00. On the first Tuesday of the month, Sir John Soane's Museum is open until 21:00.

Wednesday: Virtually all sights are open. Vinopolis is open until 21:30 and the Houses of Parliament may be open as late as 22:00.

Getting Online with a Mobile Device: In addition to the Wi-Fi that's likely available at your hotel, it's smart to get a free account with **The Cloud,** a Wi-Fi service found in many convenient spots around London, including most train stations and many museums, coffee shops, cafés, and shopping centers (though the connection can be slow). When you sign up at www.thecloud.net/free-wifi, you'll have to enter a street address and postal code; it doesn't matter which one (use your hotel's, or the Queen's: Buckingham Palace, SW1A 1AA).

Most **Tube stations** and trains have Wi-Fi, but it's free only to those with a British cellular account. However, the Tube's Wi-Fi always lets you access Transport for London's Journey Planner (www.tfl.gov.uk), making it easy to look up your city transit options—and get real-time updates on de-

Thursday: All sights are open, plus evening hours at the National Portrait Gallery (until 21:00) and Vinopolis (until 22:00).

Friday: All sights are open, except the Houses of Parliament. Sights open late include the British Museum (selected galleries until 20:30), National Gallery (until 21:00), National Portrait Gallery (until 21:00), Vinopolis (until 22:00), Victoria and Albert Museum (selected galleries until 22:00), and Tate Modern (until 22:00).

Saturday: Most sights are open, except legal ones (Old Bailey, City Hall; skip The City). The Houses of Parliament are open only with a tour. Vinopolis is open until 21:30 and the Tate Modern until 22:00. The Tower of London is especially crowded today. Today's the day to hit the Portobello Road street market; the Camden Lock and Greenwich markets are also good.

Notes: St. Martin-in-the-Fields church offers concerts at lunchtime (Mon, Tue, and Fri at 13:00) and in the evening (several nights a week at 19:30, jazz Wed at 20:00).

Evensong occurs nearly daily at St. Paul's (Sun at 15:15 and Tue-Sat at 17:00), Westminster Abbey (Sun at 15:00, Mon-Tue and Thu-Sat at 17:00 except Sat at 15:00 Sept-April), and Southwark Cathedral (Sun at 15:00, Tue-Fri 17:30, Sat at 16:00).

London by Night Sightseeing Tour buses leave from Victoria Station each evening (six departures 19:00-22:55; at 19:00, 20:45, and 22:10 in winter).

The London Eye spins nightly (last departure between 20:30 and 21:30, depending on the season).

In winter, Apsley House is open only on weekends (closed Mon-Fri).

lays—once you're in a station. To use the Tube's Wi-Fi, you can pay £2 for a one-day pass, or £5 for a one-week pass (http://my.virginmedia.com/wifi).

Useful Apps: Tube travelers might want to download the **MX Apps free Tube map** (www.mxapps.co.uk), which shows the easiest way to connect station A to station B. While you can always get Tube info online (with the "Transport for London's Journey Planner," www.tfl.gov.uk), the app works even when you're not online. When you are online, the app provides live updates about Tube delays and closures. (It doesn't, however, look up bus connections, and MX Apps' "Bus London" map isn't very useful offline.) The handy **Citymapper London** covers every mode of public transit in the city. **City Maps 2Go** lets you download searchable offline maps; their London version is quite good. **Time Out London's** free app has reviews and listings for theater, museums, movies, and more (download the "Things to Do" version, which is updated weekly, rather than the boilerplate "Travel Guide" version).

Travel Bookstores: Located between Covent Garden and Leicester Square, the very good **Stanfords Travel Bookstore** stocks current editions of many of my books (Mon-Fri 9:00-20:00, Sat 10:00-20:00, Sun 12:00-18:00, 12-14 Long Acre, second entrance on Floral Street, Tube: Leicester Square, tel. 020/7836-1321, www.stanfords.co.uk).

Two impressive **Waterstones** bookstores have the biggest collection of travel guides in town: on Piccadilly (Mon-Sat 9:00-22:00, Sun 11:30-18:00, Costa Café, great views from top-floor bar—see sidebar on page 86, 203 Piccadilly, tel. 0843-290-8549) and on Trafalgar Square (Mon-Sat 9:30-21:00, Sun 12:00-18:00, Costa Café on second floor, tel. 0843-290-8651).

Baggage Storage: Train stations have replaced lockers with more secure left-luggage counters. Each bag must go through a scanner (just like at the airport). Expect long waits in the morning to check in (up to 45 minutes) and in the afternoon to pick up (each item-£10.00/24 hours, most stations daily 7:00-23:00). You can also store bags at the airports (similar rates and hours, www.left-baggage.co.uk).

Updates to this Book: Check www.ricksteves.com/update for updates to this book.

GETTING AROUND LONDON

To travel smart in a city this size, you must get comfortable with public transportation. London's excellent taxis, buses, and subway (Tube) system make a car unnecessary (see page 33 for details on driving in London—and why it's a bad idea).

The helpful *Welcome to London* brochure, produced by the mayor's office and Transport for London (TFL), includes both a Tube map and a handy schematic map of the best bus routes (available free at TFL offices—such as the one in Victoria Station, the City of London TI, and at museums and hotels all over town). For specific directions on how to get from point A to point B on London's transit, call TFL's automated info line at 0843-222-1234.

Public-Transit Tickets and Passes

London has the most expensive public transit in the world—save money on your Tube rides using a multiride pass. You have two good options: Get a **Travelcard** for unlimited travel; these are available in one-day and seven-day versions. Or buy a £5 **Oyster**

card and top it up as needed to travel like a local for about £1-2 per ride.

The transit system has six zones. Since almost all of my recommended accommodations, restaurants, and sights are within Zones 1 and 2, those are the prices I've listed here; you'll pay more to go farther afield. Specific fares and other details change constantly; for a complete and updated list of prices, check www.tfl.gov.uk.

The Bottom Line

Wondering which pass works best for your trip? On a short visit (three days or fewer), if you think you'll be zipping around a lot, consider a One-Day Travelcard for each day you're here (or at least for your busiest days); if you'll be taking fewer rides, get an Oyster card (described later) and pay as you go. If you're in London for four days or longer, the Seven-Day Travelcard will likely pay for itself.

Individual Transit Tickets

Individual paper tickets are available, but they're so expensive (£4.70 per Tube ride) that you shouldn't buy one, unless you're literally taking just one ride your entire time in the city. Overall, a Travelcard or Oyster card offers far more value. If you do buy a single ticket, you can avoid ticket-window lines in Tube stations by using the coin-op machines; practice on the punchboard to see how the system works (hit "Adult Single" and your destination). These tickets are valid only on the day of purchase.

Travelcards

Travelcards are valid on the Tube, buses, Docklands Light Railway (DLR), and Overground. Travelcards let you ride as many times as you want within a one- or a seven-day period, for one fixed price. Like individual tickets, Travelcards become valid on the day of purchase (they should not be purchased in advance).

Before you buy a card, estimate where you'll be going; there's a card for Zones 1 and 2, and another for Zones 1-6 (which includes Heathrow Airport). If Heathrow is the only ride you're taking outside Zones 1-2 (which is likely), you can pay a small supplement to make the Zones 1-2 Travelcard stretch to cover that one ride.

The **One-Day Travelcard** gives you unlimited travel for a day (Zones 1-2: £9, off-peak version £8.90; Zones 1-6: £17, off-peak version £8.90; off-peak cards are good for travel after 9:30 on weekdays and anytime on weekends). This Travelcard works like a traditional paper ticket: Buy it at any Tube station ticket window or machine, then feed it into a turnstile (and retrieve it) to enter and exit the Tube. On a bus, just show it to the driver when you get on.

The **Seven-Day Travelcard** is a great option if you're staying four or more days and plan to use buses and the Tube a lot. It's issued as credit on your plastic Oyster card (described next), and gives you unlimited travel anytime, anywhere in Zones 1 and 2 for a week (£31.40 plus the refundable £5 deposit for the Oyster card). As with a standard Oyster card, you'll touch it to the yellow card reader when entering or exiting a Tube turnstile, or when boarding a bus. It's smart to keep an extra £5-6 worth of credit on your Oyster card on top of the Travelcard to cover travel outside zones 1-2 or after your Travelcard runs out.

Oyster Cards

A pay-as-you-go Oyster card (a plastic card embedded with a computer chip) allows you to economically ride the Tube, buses, Docklands Light Railway (DLR), and Overground (mostly suburban trains). On each type of transport, you simply lay the card flat against (or sufficiently near) the yellow card reader at the turnstile or entrance, it flashes green, and the fare is automatically deducted. (You'll also tap your card again to "touch out" as you exit the Tube and DLR turnstiles, but not to exit buses.)

With an Oyster card, rides cost about half the price of individual paper tickets (£2.20 or £2.80 per Tube ride—depending on

time of day, £1.45 per bus ride; the card is not shareable among companions taking the same ride). You buy the card itself at any Tube station ticket window for a refundable £5 deposit, then load it up with as much credit as you want. (For extra peace of mind, you could ask about registering your card against theft or loss.) When your balance gets low, simply add credit—or "top up"—at a ticket window or machine. A price cap on the pay-as-you-go Oyster card guarantees you'll never pay more than the One-Day Travelcard price within a 24-hour period.

You can see how much credit remains on your card by touching it to the pad at any ticket machine. Oyster card balances never expire (though they need reactivating at a ticket window every two years), so you can use the card whenever you're in London, or lend it to someone else.

When you're finished with the card (and if you don't mind a short wait), you should be able to reclaim your £5 deposit at any Underground ticket window. But you'll only be refunded any remaining balance if you have registered the card, and you must call TFL to request this refund. In short, it's easy to get the deposit back but not the balance, so ride away your remaining pounds.

Transfers: You can change from one Tube line to another on the same Oyster journey (as long as you don't leave the station);

however, if you change between buses, or change between bus and Tube, you'll pay a new fare.

Discounts

Families: A paying adult can take up to four kids (ages 10 and under) for free on the Tube, Docklands Light Railway (DLR), and Overground all day, every day (kids 10 and under are always free on buses). At the Tube station, use the manual gate, rather than the turnstiles, to be waved in. Other child and student discounts are explained at www.tfl.gov.uk/tickets. Or visit a Tube ticket window with your family; the clerk will tell you which deal is best.

River Cruises: A Travelcard gives you a 33 percent discount on most Thames cruises (see "Cruises," later). If you pay for Thames Clippers (including the Tate Boat museum ferry) with your pay-as-you go Oyster card, you'll get a 10 percent discount.

Sightseeing Deal: By buying a paper One-Day Travelcard at a train station, you can qualify for two-for-one discounts at many popular sights. If you and a companion will be visiting a pricey sight (such as the Tower of London, Churchill War Rooms, London Eye, or Madame Tussauds) and getting a One-Day Travelcard anyway, this is a smart move. But it only works if your paper Travelcard is issued through a National Rail train-station machine or ticket counter, and the sight discount must be used on the day the ticket is valid. Note that it doesn't get you in the Fast Track entrance. The deal doesn't work if your Travelcard is loaded onto an Oyster card, or if you get your Travelcard in a Tube station. Look for brochures with coupons at major train stations, or print vouchers at www.daysoutguide.co.uk.

By Tube

London's subway system is called the Tube or Underground (but never "subway," which, in Britain, refers to a pedestrian underpass). The Tube is one of this planet's great people-movers and usually the fastest long-distance transport in town (runs Mon-Sat about 5:00-24:00, Sun about 7:00-23:00; Central, Jubilee, Northern, Piccadilly, and Victoria lines run Fri-Sat 24 hours). Two other  commuter rail lines, while technically not part of the Tube, are tied into the network and use the same tickets: the Docklands Light Railway (called DLR, runs to the Docklands, Greenwich, and Olympic Park) and the Overground.

Get your bearings by studying a map of the system. At the front of this book, you'll find a Tube map of the city center, with color-coded lines and names. You can also pick up a free, more extensive Tube map at any station.

Each line has a name (such as Circle, Northern, or Baker-loo) and two directions (indicated by the end-of-the-line stops). Find the line that will take you to your destination, and figure out roughly which direction (north, south, east, or west) you'll need to go to get there.

You can use a Travelcard, Oyster card, or individual tickets (all explained earlier) to pay for your journey. At the Tube station, feed your Travelcard or regular paper ticket into the turnstile, reclaim it, and hang on to it—you'll need it later. If you have an Oyster card, touch it flat against the turnstile's yellow card reader, both when you enter and exit the station.

Find your train by following signs to your line and the (general) direction it's headed (such as Central Line: east). Since some

tracks are shared by several lines, double-check before boarding a train: First, make sure your destination is one of the stops listed on the sign at the platform. Also, check the electronic signboards that announce which train is next, and make sure the destination (the end-of-the-line stop) is the direction you want. Some trains, particularly on the Circle and District lines, split off for other directions, but each train has its final destination marked above its windshield.

Trains run about every 3-10 minutes. For a rough idea of how long it takes to get from point A to point B by Tube, estimate five minutes per stop (which includes time to walk into and out of stations, and to change trains). So a destination six stops away will take you about 30 minutes.

Rush hours (8:00-10:00 and 16:00-19:00) can be packed and sweaty. If one train is absolutely packed and another to the same destination is coming in three minutes, wait to avoid the sardine routine. Bring something to do to make your waiting time productive. If you get confused, ask for advice from a local, a blue-vested staff person, or at the information window located before the turnstile entry.

At most stations, you can't leave the system without touching your Oyster card to an electronic reader, or feeding your ticket or One-Day Travelcard into the turnstile. (If you have a single-trip paper ticket, the turnstile will eat your now-expired ticket; if it's a One-Day Travelcard, it will spit out your still-valid card.) Some stations, such as Hampton Court, do not have a turnstile, so you'll have to locate a reader to "touch out" your Oyster card. If you skip this step and leave the station, the system assumes you've ridden to the most remote station, and the highest fare will be deducted from your card. When leaving a station, save walking time by choosing the best street exit—check the maps on the walls or ask any station personnel.

The system can be fraught with construction delays and breakdowns (the Circle Line is notorious for problems). Most construction is scheduled for weekends. Closures are publicized in advance (online at www.tfl.gov.uk and with posters in the Tube; Google Maps also has real-time service alerts for the Tube, and TFL does a fine job of tweeting updates). Pay attention to signs and announcements explaining necessary detours. Closed Tube lines are often replaced by temporary bus service, but it can be faster to figure out alternate routes on the Tube; since the lines cross each other constantly, there are several ways to make any journey. For help, check out the "Journey Planner" at www.tfl.gov.uk, which is accessible (for free) on any mobile device within most Tube stations.

Tube Etiquette

- When your train arrives, stand off to the side and let riders exit before you try to board.
- Avoid using the hinged seats near the doors of some trains when the car is jammed; they take up valuable standing space.
- If you're blocking the door when the train stops, step out of the car and off to the side, let others off, then get back on.
- Talk softly in the cars. Listen to how quietly Londoners communicate and follow their lead.
- On escalators, stand on the right and pass on the left. But note that in some passageways or stairways, you might be directed to walk on the left (the direction Brits go when behind the wheel).
- Discreet eating and drinking are fine (nothing smelly); drinking alcohol and smoking are not.

By Bus

If you figure out the bus system, you'll swing like Tarzan through the urban jungle of London (see sidebar for a list of handy routes). Generally, the bus is much easier to use if you know where you are going—carry a good London map or pick up a free bus map; the most user-friendly is in the free *Welcome to London* brochure (download it at www.tfl.gov.uk). You can also find more in-depth maps of various sectors of the city (most useful is the Central London Bus Guide). Bus maps are available at Transport for London offices, the City of London TI, and other tourist spots around town.

With a mobile phone, you can find out the arrival time of the next bus by texting your bus stop's five-digit code (posted at the stop, above the timetable) to 87287 (if you're using your US phone's SIM card, text the code to 011-44-7797-800-287). Or try the helpful London Bus Checker app, with route maps and real-time bus info.

If you'd like more detailed instructions for a specific journey, use the journey planner at www.tfl.gov.uk (you can set it to show only bus options).

Buses are covered by Travelcards and Oyster cards, and you must have one of these to ride; there are no individual per-ride tickets available for buses. Any bus ride in downtown London costs £1.45 (with a cap of £4.40 per day).

The first step in mastering London's bus system is learning how to decipher the bus-stop signs found at major transfer points. For an example, see the accompanying photo, which shows a typical sign you might find at a bus stop. The sign lists the various buses that service that neighborhood and the destinations they go to. In the first column, find your destination on the list—e.g., to Paddington Tube/rail station. In the next column, find a bus that goes there— the #23 (routes marked "N" are night-only). In the final column, a letter within a circle (e.g., "H") tells you exactly which nearby bus stop is yours. After checking the accompanying bus-stop map, make your way

O		
Oakwood ⊖	N91	⑦ ⊗
Old Coulsdon	N68	Aldwych
Old Ford	N8	Oxford Circus
Old Kent Road Canal Bridge	53, N381	ⓟ
	453	Ⓐ ⓟ
	N21	Ⓖ
Old Street ⊖ ≋	243	Aldwych
Orpington ≋	N47	Ⓖ
Oxford Circus ⊖	Any bus	⑦
	N18	ⓢ

P		
Paddington ⊖ ≋	23, N15	Ⓗ ❷ ⑦
Palmers Green ≋	N29	❷
Park Langley	N3	Ⓐ Ⓜ
Peckham	12	Ⓐ ⓟ
	N89, N343	Ⓖ
	N136	Ⓐ Ⓝ
	N381	Ⓖ
Penge Pawleyne Arms	176	Ⓖ
	N3	Ⓐ Ⓜ
Petts Wood ≋	N47	Ⓖ
Pimlico Grosvenor Road	24	❷ Ⓝ
Plaistow Greengate	N15	❷ ⑦
Plumstead ≋	53	ⓟ
Plumstead Common	53	ⓟ

to that stop—you'll know it's yours because it will have the same letter on its pole—and wait for the bus with your number to arrive. If the sign says "request stop," hold your arm out when your bus approaches. Hop on and confirm your destination with the driver (often friendly and helpful).

As you board, show your Travelcard to the driver, or touch your Oyster card to the card reader. On "Heritage Routes" #9 and #15 (some of which use older double-decker buses), you may need to show your card to a conductor; take a seat, and he or she will come around. There's no need to show or tap your card when you hop off.

To alert the driver you want to get off, press one of the red buttons (on the poles between the seats) before your stop. In central London, stops are pretty close together, so if you do go past your destination, don't panic—it'll likely be only a short walk back.

If you have a Travelcard or an Oyster card, save your feet and get in the habit of hopping buses for quick little straight shots, even just to get to a Tube stop. During bump-and-grind rush hours (8:00-10:00 and 16:00-19:00), you'll usually go faster by Tube.

By Taxi

London is the best taxi town in Europe. Big, black, carefully regulated cabs are everywhere. (While historically known as "black cabs," some of London's official taxis are covered with wildly colored ads.) Some cabs now run on biofuels—a good way to dispose of all that oil used to fry fish-and-chips.

I've never met a crabby cabbie in London. They love to talk, and they know every nook and cranny in town. I ride in a taxi each day just to get my London questions answered (drivers must pass a rigorous test on "The Knowledge" of London geography to earn their license).

If a cab's top light is on, just wave it down. Drivers flash lights when they see you wave. They have a tight turning radius (on new cabs, the back tires actually pivot), so you can hail cabs going in either direction. If waving doesn't work, ask someone where you can find a taxi stand. Telephoning a cab will get you one in a few minutes, but costs a little more (tel. 0871-871-8710; £2 surcharge, plus extra fee to book ahead by credit card).

Rides start at £2.40. The regular tariff #1 covers most of the day (Mon-Fri 6:00-20:00), tariff #2 is during "unsociable hours" (Mon-Fri 20:00-22:00 and Sat-Sun 6:00-22:00), and tariff #3 is for nighttime (22:00-6:00) and holidays. Rates go up about 15-20 percent with each higher tariff. All extra charges are explained in writing on the cab wall. Tip a cabbie by rounding up (maximum 10 percent).

Handy Bus Routes

Ever since London instituted a congestion charge for cars, the bus system has gotten faster, easier, and cheaper. Tube-oriented travelers need to get over their tunnel vision, learn the bus system, and get around fast and easy. The best views are upstairs on a double-decker.

Here are some of the most useful routes:

Route #9: High Street Kensington to Knightsbridge (Harrods) to Hyde Park Corner to Piccadilly Circus to Trafalgar Square. This is one of two "Heritage Routes," using some old-style double-decker buses.

Route #11: Victoria Station to Westminster Abbey to Trafalgar Square to St. Paul's and Liverpool Street Station and the East End.

Route #15: Regent Street to Piccadilly Circus to Trafalgar Square to St. Paul's to Tower of London. This is the other "Heritage Route," also with old-style double-decker buses.

Routes #23 and #159: Paddington Station to Oxford Circus to Piccadilly Circus to Trafalgar Square; from there, #23 heads east to St. Paul's and Liverpool Street Station, while #159 heads to Westminster and the Imperial War Museum.

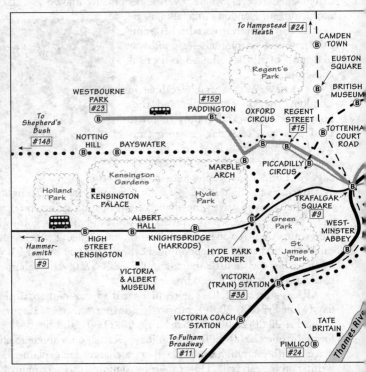

In addition, several buses (including #6, #13, and #139) also make the corridor run between Marble Arch, Oxford Circus, Piccadilly Circus, and Trafalgar Square.

Route #24: Pimlico to Victoria Station to Westminster Abbey to Trafalgar Square to Euston Square, then all the way north to Camden Town (Camden Lock Market) and Hampstead Heath.

Route #38: Victoria Station to Hyde Park Corner to Piccadilly Circus to British Museum.

Route #RV1 (a scenic South Bank joyride): Tower of London to Tower Bridge to Southwark Street (five-minute walk behind Tate Modern/Shakespeare's Globe) to London Eye/Waterloo Station, then over Waterloo Bridge to Aldwych and Covent Garden.

Route #148: Westminster Abbey to Victoria Station to Notting Hill and Bayswater (by way of the east end of Hyde Park and Marble Arch).

Check the bus stop closest to your hotel—it might be convenient to your sightseeing plans.

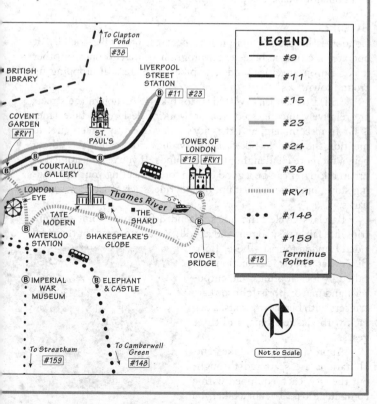

Connecting downtown sights is quick and easy, and will cost you about £6-10 (for example, St. Paul's to the Tower of London, or between the two Tate museums). For a short ride, three adults in a cab generally travel at close to Tube prices—and groups of four or five adults should taxi everywhere. All cabs can carry five passengers, and some take six, for the same cost as a single traveler.

Don't worry about meter cheating. Licensed British cab meters come with a sealed computer chip and clock that ensures you'll get the correct tariff. The only way a cabbie can cheat you is by taking a needlessly long route. One serious pitfall, however, is taking a cab when traffic is bad to a destination efficiently served by the Tube. On one trip to London, I hopped in a taxi at South Kensington for Waterloo Station and hit bad traffic. Rather than spending 20 minutes and £2 on the Tube, I spent 40 minutes and £16 in a taxi.

If you overdrink and ride in a taxi, be warned: Taxis charge £40 for "soiling" (a.k.a., pub puke).

If you forget this book in a taxi, call the Lost Property office and hope for the best (tel. 0845-330-9882).

By Bike

London is keeping up its push to become more bike-friendly. It operates a citywide bike-rental program similar to ones in other major European cities, and new bike lanes are still cropping up around town.

Still, London isn't (yet) ideal for biking. Although the streets are relatively uncongested, the network of designated bike lanes is far from complete, and the city's many one-way streets (not to mention the need to bike on the "wrong" side) can make biking here a bit more challenging than it sounds. If you're accustomed to urban biking, it can be a good option for connecting your sightseeing stops, but if you're just up for a joyride, stick to London's large parks.

Barclays Cycle Hire bikes, intended for quick point-to-point trips, are fairly easy to rent and a giddy joy to use, even for the most jaded London tourist. These "Boris Bikes" (as they are affectionately called by locals, after cycle enthusiast and mayor Boris Johnson) are cruisers with big, cushy seats, a bag rack with elastic straps, and three gears.

Approximately 600 bike-rental stations are scattered throughout the city, each equipped with a computer kiosk. To rent a bike, you need to pay an access fee (£2/day or £10/week). The first 30 minutes are free; if you hang on to the bike for longer, you'll be charged (£1 for 1 hour, £4 for 1.5 hours, £6 for 2 hours, and much steeper beyond that).

When you're ready to ride, press "Hire a Cycle" and insert your credit card when prompted. You'll then get a ticket with a five-digit code. Take the ticket to any bike, then wake the machine up by pressing any button on the panel near the front tire. When the light comes on, punch in the number. After the yellow light blinks, a green light will appear: Now you can (firmly) pull the bike out of the slot.

When your ride is over, find a station with an empty slot, then push your bike in until it locks and the green light flashes.

You can hire bikes as often as you like (which will start your free 30-minute period over again), as long as you wait five minutes between each use. There can be problems, of course—stations at popular locations (such as entrances to parks) can temporarily run out of bikes, and you may have trouble finding a place to return a bike—but for the most part, this system works great. To make things easier, get a map of the docking stations—pick one up at any major Underground station. It's also available online at www.tfl.gov.uk (click on "Barclays Cycle Hire") and as a free smartphone app (http://cyclehireapp.com).

Helmets are not provided, so ride carefully. Stay to the far-left side of the road and watch closely at intersections for *left*-turning cars. Be aware that in most parks (including Hyde Park/Kensington Gardens) only certain paths are designated for bike use—you can't ride just anywhere. Maps posted at park entrances identify bike paths, and non-bike paths are generally clearly marked.

Some bike tour companies also rent bikes—for details, see page 39.

By Car

If you have a car, stow it—you don't want to drive in London. If you need convincing, here's one more reason: A £10 **congestion charge** is levied on any private car entering the city center during peak hours (Mon-Fri 7:00-18:00, no charge Sat-Sun and holidays, fee payable at gas stations, convenience stores, and self-service machines at public parking lots, or online at www.cclondon.com). Traffic cameras photograph and identify every vehicle that enters the fee zone; if you get spotted and don't pay up by midnight that day (or pay £12 before midnight of the following day), you'll get socked with a penalty of at least £60. The system has been effective in cutting down traffic jam delays and bolstering London's public transit. The revenue that's raised subsidizes the buses, which are now cheaper, more frequent, and even more user-friendly than before. Today, the vast majority of vehicles in the city center are buses, taxis, and service trucks.

Tours in London

To sightsee on your own, download my series of free audio tours that illuminate some of London's top sights and neighborhoods (see sidebar on page 8 for details).

▲▲▲BY HOP-ON, HOP-OFF DOUBLE-DECKER BUS TOURS

Two competitive companies (Original and Big Bus) offer essentially the same two tours of the city's sightseeing highlights, with nearly 30 stops on each route. Big Bus tours are a little more expensive (£30), while Original tours are cheaper (£25 with this book).

These two-to-three hour, once-over-lightly bus tours drive by all the famous sights, providing a stress-free way to get your bearings and see the biggies. They stop at the same core group of sights regardless of which overview tour you're on: Piccadilly Circus, Trafalgar Square, Big Ben, St. Paul's, the Tower of London, Marble Arch, Victoria Station, and elsewhere. With a good guide and nice weather, I'd sit back and enjoy the entire tour. (If you don't like your guide, you can hop off and try your luck with the next departure.) On a recent trip, I had a livelier, more informative guide on the Original tour than the Big Bus tour, though guides can vary even within the same company.

Each company offers at least one route with live (English-only) guides, and a second (sometimes slightly different route) comes with recorded, dial-a-language narration. In addition to the overview tours, both Original and Big Bus include the Thames River boat trip by City Cruises (between Westminster and the Tower of London) and three 1.5-hour walking tours.

Pick up a map from any flier rack or from one of the countless salespeople, and study the color-coded system. Sunday morning—when the traffic is light and many museums are closed—is a fine time for a tour. Traffic is at its peak around lunch and during the evening rush hour (around 17:00). Unless you're using the bus tour mainly for hop-on, hop-off transportation, consider saving time and money by taking a night tour (described below).

Buses run daily about every 10-15 minutes in summer, every 10-20 minutes in winter. They start at about 8:00 or 8:30 and run until early evening in summer or late afternoon in winter. The last full loop usually leaves Victoria Station at about 19:00 in summer, and at about 17:00 in winter (confirm by checking the schedule or asking the driver).

You can buy tickets from drivers or from staff at street kiosks

Combining a London Bus Tour and the Changing of the Guard

For a grand and efficient intro to London, consider catching an 8:30 departure of a hop-on, hop-off overview bus tour, riding 90 percent of the loop (which takes just over two hours, depending on traffic), and hopping off at Buckingham Palace in time to find a good spot to watch the Changing of the Guard ceremony at 11:30. You could start the tour as early as 8:00 if you take the Big Bus tour (catch it at Victoria Station); the Original tour starts at 8:30 (at Grosvenor Gardens a block from Victoria Station). If you miss the first bus, you could take the next one (generally about 20 minutes later), though it may get you to the ceremony late (check with the driver).

(credit cards accepted at kiosks at major stops such as Victoria Station, ticket good for 24 hours, or 48 hours in winter).

Original London Sightseeing Bus Tour

They offer two versions of their basic highlights loop: **The Original Tour** (live guide, marked with a yellow triangle on the front of the bus) and the **City Sightseeing Tour** (essentially the same route but with recorded narration, a kids' soundtrack option, and a stop at Madame Tussauds; bus marked with a red triangle). Other routes include the blue-triangle **Museum Tour** (connecting far-flung museums and major shopping stops), and green, black, and purple triangle routes (linking major train stations to the central route). All routes are covered by the same ticket. Keep it simple and just take one of the city highlights tours (£29, £4 less with this book, limit four discounts per book, they'll rip off the corner of this page—raise bloody hell if the staff or driver won't honor this discount; also online deals, info center at 17 Cockspur Street, tel. 020/8877-1722, www.theoriginaltour.com).

Big Bus London Tours

For £30 (up to 30 percent discount online—print tickets or have them delivered to your phone), you get the same basic overview tours: Red buses come with a live guide, while the blue route has a recorded narration and a one-hour longer path that goes around Hyde Park. These pricier Big Bus tours tend to have more departures—meaning shorter waits for those hopping on and off; they also have an early starting departure from Victoria Station at 8:00 (daily 8:00-18:00, winter until 16:30, tel. 020/7233-9533, www.bigbustours.com).

BY BUS OR CAR
London by Night Sightseeing Tour

This tour offers a 1.5-hour circuit, but after hours, with no extras (e.g., walks, river cruises), and at a lower price. While the narration can be pretty lame, the views at twilight are grand—though note that it stays light until late on summer nights, and London just doesn't do floodlighting as well as, say, Paris (£19, £15 online). From June through late September, open-top buses depart at 19:00, 20:00, 20:45, 21:30, 22:10, and 22:55 from Victoria Station (Jan-May and late Sept-late Dec departs at 19:00, 20:45, and 22:10 only with closed-top bus, no tours between Christmas and New Year). Buses leave from near Victoria Station (in front of Grosvenor Hotel on Buckingham Palace Road; or you can board at any stop, such as Marble Arch, Trafalgar Square, London Eye, or Tower of London; tel. 020/8545-6110, www.london-by-night.net). For a memorable and economical evening, munch a scenic picnic dinner on the top deck. (There are plenty of take-away options within the train stations and near the various stops.)

Land and Sea Tours

A bright-yellow amphibious WWII-vintage vehicle (the model that landed troops on Normandy's beaches on D-Day) takes a gang of 30 tourists past some famous sights on land—Big Ben, Trafalgar Square, Piccadilly Circus—then splashes into the Thames for a cruise. All in all, it's good fun at a rather steep price. The live guide works hard, and it's kid-friendly to the point of goofiness. Beware: These book up in advance (£21, April-Sept daily, first tour 9:30 or 10:00, last tour usually 15:00, shorter hours Oct-March, 1-4/hour, 1.25 hours—45 minutes on land and 30 minutes in the river, £3 booking fee by phone or online, departs from Chicheley Street—you'll see the big, ugly vehicle parked 100 yards behind the London Eye, Tube: Waterloo or Westminster, tel. 020/7928-3132, www.londonducktours.co.uk).

Driver-Guides

These three guides have cars or a minibus (particularly helpful for travelers with limited mobility), and they also do walking-only tours: **Robina Brown** (£330/half-day, £475/day, £660 outside London, £40 more for groups of 4-6 people, also does overnight tours farther afield, tel. 020/7228-2238, www.driverguidetours.com, robina@driverguidetours.com), **Janine Barton** (£350/half-day, £470/day within London, £550 outside London, tel. 020/7402-4600, http://seeitinstyle.synthasite.com, jbsiis@aol.com), and **David Stubbs** (£195/half-day, £245/day, about £50 more for groups of 4-6 people, also does tours to the Cotswolds, Stonehenge, and

Stratford, mobile 07775-888-534, www.londoncountrytours. co.uk, info@londoncountrytours.co.uk).

▲▲ON FOOT

Several times a day, top-notch local guides lead (sometimes big) groups through specific slices of London's past. Look for brochures at TIs or ask at hotels, although the latter usually push higher-priced bus tours. *Time Out,* the weekly entertainment guide, lists some, but not all, scheduled walks. Check with the various tour companies by phone or online to get their full picture.

To take a walking tour, simply show up at the announced location and pay the guide. Then enjoy two chatty hours of Dickens, Harry Potter, the Plague, Shakespeare, Legal London, the Beatles, Jack the Ripper, or whatever is on the agenda.

London Walks

This leading company lists its extensive and creative daily schedule on their amusing website, as well as in a beefy, plain *London Walks* brochure (available at St. Martin-in-the-Fields' Café in the Crypt on Trafalgar Square and at the City of London TI). Just perusing their fascinating lineup of tours inspires me to stay longer in London. Their two-hour walks, led by top-quality professional guides (ranging from archaeologists to actors), cost £9 (cash only, walks offered year-round, private tours for groups-£130, tel. 020/7624-3978 for a live person, tel. 020/7624-9255 for a recording of today's or tomorrow's walks and the Tube station they depart from, www. walks.com).

London Walks also offers day trips into the countryside, a good option for those with limited time and transportation (£16 plus £10-50 for transportation and any admission costs, cash only: Stonehenge/Salisbury, Oxford/Cotswolds, Cambridge, Bath, and so on). These are economical in part because everyone gets group discounts for transportation and admissions.

Sandemans New London "Free Royal London Tour"

This company employs students (rather than licensed guides) who recite three-hour spiels covering the basic London sights. While the fast-moving, youthful tours are light and irreverent, and can be both entertaining and fun, it's misleading to call the tours "free," as tips are expected (the guides actually pay the company for the privilege of asking for tips). Given that London Walks offers daily tours at a reasonable price, taking this "free" tour makes no sense to me (daily at 11:00 and 13:00, meet at Covent Garden Piazza by the Apple Store, Tube: Covent Garden). Sandemans also has other guided tours for a charge, including a Pub Crawl (£18, nightly at 19:30, meet at Belushi's Bar in Covent Garden, Tube: Leicester Square, www.newlondon-tours.com).

Beatles Walks

Fans of the still-Fab Four can take one of three Beatles walks (London Walks has two that run 6 days/week; for more on Beatles sights, see page 69).

Jack the Ripper Walks

Each walking tour company seems to make most of its money with "haunted" and Jack the Ripper tours. Many guides are historians and would rather not lead these lightweight tours—but, in tourism as in journalism, "if it bleeds, it leads" (which is why the juvenile London Dungeon is one of the city's busiest sights).

Back in 1888—in the decade of Sherlock Holmes and Dr. Jekyll and Mr. Hyde, when London was still a Dickensian Tale of Two Cities—locals were terrorized by the murder of five prostitutes within a few weeks. In the wee hours, the murderer (who was given his name by local newspapers, which made a fortune on this sensational series of events) slit the throats and cut out the guts of his victims in the poor and wretched side of town. These were desperate women—so desperate they took their customers not to a bed, but up against a wall for a "four-penny knee trembler." While almost no hint of the dark and scary London of that period survives, guides do a good job of spinning the story. Think of this mile-long walk, starting at the Tower of London, as a cheap night out with a few laughs. It's still light out in summer, so the scary factor is limited to the tales of the victims' miserable lot in life and the gory way in which they were killed.

Two reliably good two-hour tours start every night at the Tower Hill Tube station exit. **London Walks** leaves nightly at 19:30 (£9, pay at the start, tel. 020/7624-3978, recorded info tel. 020/7624-9255, www.jacktheripperwalk.com). **Ripping Yarns,** which leaves earlier, is guided by off-duty Yeoman Warders—the Tower of London "Beefeaters" (£8, pay at end, nightly at 18:45, no tours between Christmas and New Year, mobile 07813-559-301, www.jack-the-ripper-tours.com). After taking both, I found the London Walks tour more entertaining, informative, and with a better route (along quieter, once hooker-friendly lanes, with less traffic), starting at Tower Hill and ending at Liverpool Street Station. Groups can be huge for both, and one group can be nearly on top of another, but there's always room—just show up.

Private Walks with Local Guides

Standard rates for London's registered Blue Badge guides are about £150-165 for four hours and £250 or more for nine hours (tel. 020/7611-2545, www.guidelondon.org.uk or www.britainsbestguides.org). I know and like four fine local guides: **Sean Kelleher** (tel. 020/8673-1624, mobile 07764-612-770, sean@seanlondonguide.com), **Britt Lonsdale** (£220/half-day, £320/day, great with families, tel. 020/7386-9907, mobile 07813-278-077, brittl@btinternet.com), and two others who work in London when they're not on the road leading my Britain tours, **Tom Hooper** (mobile 07986-048-047, tomh@ricksteves.net) and **Gillian Chadwick** (mobile 07889-976-598, gillychad@hotmail.co.uk).

BY BIKE

London is committed to creating more bike paths, and many of its best sights can be laced together with a pleasant pedal through its parks. A bike tour is a fun way to see the sights and enjoy the city on two wheels.

London Bicycle Tour Company

Three tours covering London are offered daily from their base at Gabriel's Wharf on the South Bank of the Thames. Sunday is the best, as there is less car traffic (**Central Tour**—£24, daily at 10:30, 6 miles, 3 hours, includes Westminster, Buckingham Palace, Covent Garden, and St. Paul's; **West End Tour**—£24, April-Oct daily at 14:30, Nov-March daily at 12:00 as long as at least 4 people show up, 7 miles, 3 hours, includes Westminster, Buckingham Palace, Hyde Park, Soho, and Covent Garden; **East Tour**—£27.50, April-Oct Sat-Sun at 14:00, Nov-March only on Sat-Sun at 12:00, 9 miles, 3.5 hours, includes south side of the river to Tower Bridge, then The City to the East End; book ahead for off-season tours). They also rent bikes (£3.50/hour, £20/day; office open daily April-Oct 9:30-18:00, Nov-March 10:00-16:00, west of Blackfriars Bridge on the South Bank, 1 Gabriel's Wharf, tel. 020/7928-6838, www.londonbicycle.com).

Fat Tire Bike Tours

Daily bike tours cover the highlights of downtown London, on two different itineraries (£2 discount with this book): **Royal London** (£20, daily March-Nov at 11:00, mid-May-mid-Sept also at 15:30, 7 miles, 4 hours, meet at Queensway Tube station; includes Parliament, Buckingham Palace, Hyde Park, and Trafalgar Square) and **River Thames** (£28, March-Nov Thu-Sat at 10:30, nearly daily in summer, 4.5 hours, meet just outside Southwark Tube Station; includes London Eye, St. Paul's, Tower of London, and London Bridge). Their guiding style wears its learning lightly, mixing history with humor. Reservations are easy online, and required for River Thames tours and kids' bikes (off-season tours can be arranged, mobile 078-8233-8779, www.fattirebiketourslondon.com). Confirm the schedule online or by phone. They also offer a range of walking tours that include a fish-and-chips dinner, a beer-tasting pub tour, and theater packages (details online or by phone).

ORIENTATION

▲▲BY CRUISE BOAT

London offers many made-for-tourist cruises, most on slow-moving, open-top boats accompanied by entertaining commentary about passing sights. Several companies offer essentially the same trip. Generally speaking, you can either do a **short city-center cruise** by riding a boat 30 minutes from Westminster Pier to Tower Pier (particularly handy if you're interested in visiting the Tower of London anyway), or take a **longer cruise** that includes a peek at the East

End, riding from Westminster all the way to Greenwich (save time by taking the Tube back).

Each company runs cruises daily, about twice hourly, from morning until dark; many reduce frequency off-season. Boats come and go from various docks in the city center (see sidebar). The most popular places to embark are Westminster Pier (at the base of Westminster Bridge across the street from Big Ben) and Waterloo Pier (at the London Eye, across the river).

A one-way trip within the city center costs about £10; going all the way to Greenwich costs about £2 more. Most companies charge around £3 more for a round-trip ticket, and others sell hop-on, hop-off day tickets (around £19). But I'd rather just savor one cruise, then zip home by Tube—making these return tickets not usually worthwhile.

You can buy tickets at kiosks on the docks. A Travelcard can snare you a 33 percent discount on most cruises (just show the card when you pay for the cruise); the pay-as-you-go Oyster card nets you a discount only on Thames Clippers. Because companies vary in the discounts they offer, always ask. Children and seniors generally get discounts. You can purchase drinks and scant, overpriced snacks on board. Clever budget travelers pack a picnic and munch while they cruise.

The three dominant companies are **City Cruises** (handy 30-minute cruise from Westminster Pier to Tower Pier; www.citycruises.com), **Thames River Services** (fewer stops, classic boats, friendlier and more old-fashioned feel; www.thamesriverservices.co.uk), and **Circular Cruise** (full cruise takes about an hour, operated by Crown River Services, www.crownriver.com). I'd skip the **London Eye's** River Cruise from Waterloo Pier—it's about the same price as Circular Cruise, but 20 minutes shorter. The speedy **Thames Clippers** (described later) are designed more for no-nonsense transport than lazy sightseeing.

Thames Boat Piers

While Westminster Pier is the most popular, it's not the only dock in town. Consider all the options (listed from west to east, as the Thames flows—see the color maps in the front of this book):

Millbank Pier (North Bank), at the Tate Britain Museum, is used primarily by the Tate Boat service (express connection to Tate Modern at Bankside Pier).

Westminster Pier (North Bank), near the base of Big Ben, offers round-trip sightseeing cruises and lots of departures in both directions (though the Thames Clippers boats don't stop here). Nearby sights include Parliament and Westminster Abbey.

Waterloo Pier (a.k.a. **London Eye Pier,** South Bank), right at the base of the London Eye, is a good, less-crowded alternative to Westminster, with many of the same cruise options (Waterloo Station is nearby).

Embankment Pier (North Bank) is near Covent Garden, Trafalgar Square, and Cleopatra's Needle (the obelisk on the Thames). This pier is used mostly for special boat trips (such as some RIB—rigid inflatable boat—trips, and lunch and dinner cruises).

Festival Pier (South Bank) is next to the Royal Festival Hall, just downstream from the London Eye.

Blackfriars Pier (North Bank) is in The City, not far from St. Paul's.

Bankside Pier (South Bank) is directly in front of the Tate Modern and Shakespeare's Globe.

London Bridge Pier (a.k.a. **London Bridge City Pier,** South Bank) is near the HMS *Belfast* and the start of my Bankside Walk.

Tower Pier (North Bank) is at the Tower of London, at the east edge of The City and near the East End.

St. Katharine's Pier (North Bank) is just downstream from the Tower of London.

Canary Wharf Pier (North Bank) is at the Docklands, London's new "downtown."

In outer London, you might also use the piers at **Greenwich, Kew Gardens,** and **Hampton Court.**

For details—including prices, schedules, and exactly which piers each company uses—check their websites or look for ticket kiosks at the docks. If you'd like to compare all of your options in one spot, head to Westminster Pier, which has a row of kiosks for all of the big outfits.

Cruising Downstream, to Greenwich: Both **City Cruises** and **Thames River Services** head from Westminster Pier to Greenwich. The cruises are usually narrated by the captain, with most commentary given on the way to Greenwich. The companies' prices are the same, though their itineraries are slightly different (Thames River Services makes only one stop en route and takes just an hour, while City Cruises makes two stops and adds about 10 minutes). The **Thames Clippers** boats, described later, are cheaper and faster (about 20-45 minutes to Greenwich), but have no commentary and no seating up top. To maximize both efficiency and sightseeing, I'd take a narrated cruise to Greenwich one way, and go the other way on the DLR (Docklands Light Railway), with a stop in the Docklands (Canary Wharf station; ✪ see The Docklands Walk chapter).

Cruising Upstream, to Kew Gardens and Hampton Court Palace: Boats operated by the Westminster Passenger Service Association leave for Kew Gardens from Westminster Pier (£12 one-way, £18 round-trip, cash only, discounts with Travelcard, 2-4/day depending on season, 1.5 hours, boats sail April-Oct, about half the trip is narrated, www.wpsa.co.uk). Most boats continue on to Hampton Court Palace for an additional £3 (and another 1.5 hours). Because of the river current, you can save 30 minutes cruising from Hampton Court back into town (depends on the tide—ask before you commit to the boat). Romantic as these rides sound, it can be a long trip...especially upstream.

Commuting by Clipper

The sleek, 220-seat catamarans used by **Thames Clippers** are designed for commuters rather than sightseers. Think of the boats as express buses on the river—they zip through London every 20-30 minutes, stopping at most of the major docks en route (including Canary Wharf/Docklands and Greenwich). They're fast: roughly 20 minutes from Embankment to Tower, 10 more minutes to Docklands, and 10 more minutes to Greenwich. However, the boats are less pleasant for joyriding than the cruises described earlier, with no commentary and no open deck up top (the only outside access is on a crowded deck at the exhaust-choked back of the boat, where you're jostling for space to take photos). Any one-way ride costs £6.50, and a River Roamer all-day ticket costs £15 (discounts with Travelcard and Oyster card, www.thamesclippers.com).

Thames Clippers also offers two express trips. The **Tate Boat** ferry service, which directly connects the Tate Britain (Millbank Pier) and the Tate Modern (Bankside Pier), is made for art lovers (£6.50 one-way, covered by River Roamer day ticket; buy ticket at gallery desk or on board; for frequency and times, see the Tate Britain and Tate Modern tour chapters or www.tate.org.uk/visit/tate-boat). The **O2 Express** runs only on nights when there are events at the O2 arena (departs from Waterloo Pier).

Other Cruise Options

Careening at Top Speed Along the Thames: Two competing companies invite you aboard a small, 12-person, high-speed rigid inflatable boat (RIB—similar to a Zodiac) for a pricey, adrenaline-fueled tour of the city (**London RIB Voyages** departs Waterloo Pier, www.londonribvoyages.com; **Thames RIB Experience** boats depart Embankment Pier, www.thamesribexperience.com).

Away from the Thames, on Regent's Canal: Consider exploring London's canals by taking a cruise on historic Regent's Canal in north London. The good ship *Jenny Wren* offers 1.5-hour guided canal boat cruises from Walker's Quay in Camden Town through scenic Regent's Park to Little Venice (£10.75; 2-3/day April-Oct, weekends only in March, Walker's Quay, 250 Camden High Street, 3-minute walk from Tube: Camden Town; tel. 020/7485-4433, www.walkersquay.com). While in Camden Town, stop by the popular, punky Camden Lock Market to browse through trendy arts and crafts (open daily, busiest on weekends, a block from Walker's Quay, www.camdenlockmarket.com; for more on the market, see page 448).

TOUR PACKAGES FOR STUDENTS

Andy Steves (my son) runs **WSA Europe,** offering three-day and longer guided and unguided packages—including accommodations, sightseeing, and unique local experiences—for budget travelers across 11 top European cities, including London (from €99, see www.wsaeurope.com for details).

ORIENTATION

SIGHTS IN LONDON

These sights are arranged by neighborhood for handy sightseeing. When you see a ✪ in a listing, it means the sight is covered in much more depth in a self-guided walk or in one of the tours.

Check www.ricksteves.com/update for any significant changes that have occurred since this book was published. For money-saving tips, see "Affording London's Sights" on page 70.

"Voluntary Donations": Some London sights automatically add a "voluntary donation" of about 10 percent to their admission fees. The prices posted and quoted in this book include the donation, though it's perfectly fine to pay the base price without the donation. Some of London's free museums also ask for donations as you enter, but again, it's completely optional.

Central London

WESTMINSTER

These sights are listed in roughly geographical order from Westminster Abbey to Trafalgar Square, and are linked in the ✪ Westminster Walk chapter.

▲▲▲Westminster Abbey

The greatest church in the English-speaking world, Westminster Abbey is the place where England's kings and queens have been crowned and buried since 1066. Like a stony refugee camp huddled outside St. Peter's Pearly Gates, Westminster Abbey has many stories to tell. The steep admission includes a fine audioguide, worthwhile if you have the time and interest. To experience the church more vividly, take a live tour, or attend evensong or an organ concert.

Cost and Hours: £18, £36 family ticket (covers 2 adults and

1 child), includes cloisters, audioguide, and Abbey Museum; abbey—Mon-Fri 9:30-16:30, Wed until 19:00 (main church only), Sat 9:30-14:30, last entry one hour before closing, closed Sun to sightseers but open for services, guided tours available; museum—daily 10:30-16:00; cloisters—daily 8:00-18:00; Tube: Westminster or St. James's Park, tel. 020/7222-5152, www.westminster-abbey.org.

Music: The church hosts evensong performances daily except Wednesday (Sun at 15:00, Mon-Tue and Thu-Sat at 17:00 except Sat at 15:00 Sept-April). A free 30-minute organ recital is usually held on Sunday at 17:45.

○ See the Westminster Abbey Tour chapter.

▲▲Houses of Parliament (Palace of Westminster)

This Neo-Gothic icon of London, the royal residence from 1042 to 1547, is now the meeting place of the legislative branch of government. Like the US Capitol in Washington, DC, the complex

is open to visitors. You can view parliamentary sessions from the public galleries in either the bickering House of Commons or the sleepy House of Lords. Or you can tour the historic building on your own or with a guide (through a few closely monitored rooms).

Even if you don't take a tour, you can grab a look at the public spaces—the cavernous and historic Westminster Hall, St. Stephen's Hall, and the Central Lobby—before queuing up for either (or both) of the two chambers (the House of Lords has the grander space and usually has a shorter wait).

Cost and Hours (House Galleries): Free, open only when parliament is in session; House of Commons—Oct-July Mon 14:30-22:00, Tue-Wed 11:30-19:00, Thu 9:30-17:30; House of Lords—Oct-July Mon-Tue 14:30-22:00, Wed 15:00-22:00, Thu 11:00-19:00; last entry usually around 20:00; get the exact schedule at www.parliament.uk. Both houses are closed Fri-Sun, and during the Aug-Sept recess, except by guided tour.

Tours: On Saturdays year-round (9:15-16:30) and most days during recess (Aug-Sept, generally Mon-Sat—times vary), the only

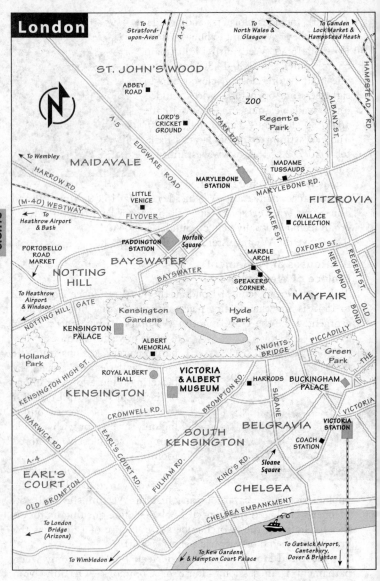

London

To Stratford-upon-Avon

To North Wales & Glasgow

To Camden Lock Market & Hampstead Heath

ST. JOHN'S WOOD

ABBEY ROAD

ZOO

Regent's Park

LORD'S CRICKET GROUND

To Wembley

MAIDAVALE

HARROW RD.

EDGWARE ROAD

MADAME TUSSAUDS

MARYLEBONE STATION

MARYLEBONE RD.

FITZROVIA

LITTLE VENICE

(M-40) WESTWAY

To Heathrow Airport & Bath

FLYOVER

WALLACE COLLECTION

OXFORD ST.

PADDINGTON STATION

Norfolk Square

PORTOBELLO ROAD MARKET

BAYSWATER

MARBLE ARCH

NEW BOND ST.

NOTTING HILL

BAYSWATER

SPEAKERS' CORNER

MAYFAIR

OLD BOND

To Heathrow Airport & Windsor

NOTTING HILL GATE

Kensington Gardens

Hyde Park

KNIGHTS-BRIDGE

PICCADILLY

Green Park

KENSINGTON PALACE

Holland Park

ALBERT MEMORIAL

ROYAL ALBERT HALL

VICTORIA & ALBERT MUSEUM

HARRODS

BUCKINGHAM PALACE

KENSINGTON HIGH ST.

KENSINGTON

CROMWELL RD.

BROMPTON RD.

SLOANE

BELGRAVIA

VICTORIA STATION

VICTORIA

WARWICK RD.

SOUTH KENSINGTON

COACH STATION

A-4

EARL'S COURT

EARL'S COURT RD.

FULHAM RD.

KING'S RD.

Sloane Square

OLD BROMPTON

CHELSEA

To London Bridge (Arizona)

CHELSEA EMBANKMENT

To Wimbledon

To Kew Gardens & Hampton Court Palace

To Gatwick Airport, Canterbury, Dover & Brighton

way you can get inside is with a tour—either with an audioguide (£17.50) or a live guide (£25, 1.5 hours). Confirm the tour schedule at www.parliament.uk. Book ahead by calling 0844-847-1672 or through www.ticketmaster.co.uk. The on-site ticket office (open 8:45-16:45 on tour days only) is located next to the Jewel Tower, opposite the southern end of the Houses of Parliament. The TI across from St. Paul's Cathedral plans to sell tour tickets as well.

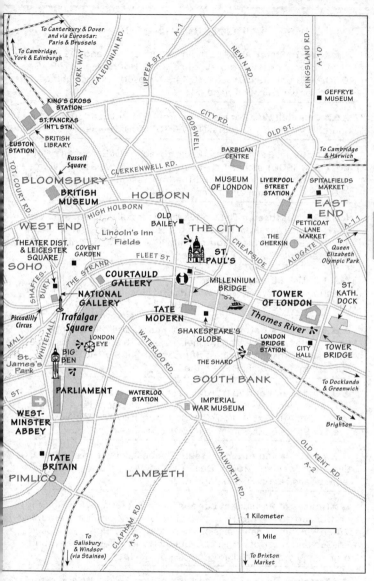

Crowd-Beating Tips: Lines tend to be longest at the start of each session, particularly on Wednesdays; for the shortest wait, try to show up later in the afternoon (but don't push it, as things sometimes close down early).

✪ See the Houses of Parliament Tour chapter.

Nearby: Across the street from the Parliament building's St. Stephen's Gate, the **Jewel Tower** is a rare remnant of the old Palace

London at a Glance

▲▲▲**Westminster Abbey** Britain's finest church and the site of royal coronations and burials since 1066. **Hours:** Mon-Fri 9:30-16:30, Wed until 19:00, Sat 9:30-14:30, closed Sun to sightseers except for worship. See page 44.

▲▲▲**Churchill War Rooms** Underground WWII headquarters of Churchill's war effort. **Hours:** Daily 9:30-18:00. See page 50.

▲▲▲**National Gallery** Remarkable collection of European paintings (1250-1900), including Leonardo, Botticelli, Velázquez, Rembrandt, Turner, Van Gogh, and the Impressionists. **Hours:** Daily 10:00-18:00, Fri until 21:00. See page 54.

▲▲▲**British Museum** The world's greatest collection of artifacts of Western civilization, including the Rosetta Stone and the Parthenon's Elgin Marbles. **Hours:** Daily 10:00-17:30, Fri until 20:30 (selected galleries only). See page 64.

▲▲▲**British Library** Fascinating collection of important literary treasures of the Western world. **Hours:** Mon-Fri 9:30-18:00, Tue until 20:00, Sat 9:30-17:00, Sun 11:00-17:00. See page 64.

▲▲▲**St**. **Paul's Cathedral** The main cathedral of the Anglican Church, designed by Christopher Wren, with a climbable dome and daily evensong services. **Hours:** Mon-Sat 8:30-16:30, closed Sun except for worship. See page 73.

▲▲▲**Tower of London** Historic castle, palace, and prison housing the crown jewels and a witty band of Beefeaters. **Hours:** March-Oct Tue-Sat 9:00-17:30, Sun-Mon 10:00-17:30; Nov-Feb Tue-Sat 9:00-16:30, Sun-Mon 10:00-16:30. See page 77.

▲▲▲**Victoria and Albert Museum** The best collection of decorative arts anywhere. **Hours:** Daily 10:00-17:45, Fri until 22:00 (selected galleries only). See page 100.

▲▲**Houses of Parliament** London landmark famous for Big Ben and occupied by the Houses of Lords and Commons. **Hours:** When Parliament is in session, generally open Mon-Thu, closed Fri-Sun and most of Aug-Sept. Guided tours offered year-round on Sat and most days during Aug-Sept. See page 45.

▲▲**Trafalgar Square** The heart of London, where Westminster, The City, and the West End meet. **Hours:** Always open. See page 53.

▲▲**National Portrait Gallery** A *Who's Who* of British history, featuring portraits of this nation's most important historical figures. **Hours:** Daily 10:00-18:00, Thu-Fri until 21:00, first and second floors open Mon at 11:00. See page 54.

▲▲**Covent Garden** Vibrant people-watching zone with shops, cafés, street musicians, and an iron-and-glass arcade that once hosted a produce market. **Hours:** Always open. See page 58.

▲▲**Changing of the Guard at Buckingham Palace** Hour-long spectacle at Britain's royal residence. **Hours:** Generally May-July daily at 11:30, Aug-April every other day. See page 62.

▲▲**London Eye** Enormous observation wheel, dominating—and offering commanding views over—London's skyline. **Hours:** Daily April-Aug 10:00-21:00, Sept-March 10:00-20:30, later on weekends. See page 82.

▲▲**Imperial War Museum** Exhibits examining the military history of the bloody 20th century. **Hours:** Daily 10:00-18:00. See page 83.

▲▲**Tate Modern** Works by Monet, Matisse, Dalí, Picasso, and Warhol displayed in a converted powerhouse. **Hours:** Daily 10:00-18:00, Fri-Sat until 22:00. See page 88.

▲▲**Shakespeare's Globe** Timbered, thatched-roofed reconstruction of the Bard's original "wooden O." **Hours:** Theater complex, museum, and actor-led tours generally daily 9:00-17:00; in summer, morning theater tours only. Plays are also staged here. See page 88.

▲▲**Tate Britain** Collection of British painting from the 16th century through modern times, including works by William Blake, the Pre-Raphaelites, and J. M. W. Turner. **Hours:** Daily 10:00-18:00. See page 93.

▲▲**Kensington Palace** Recently restored former home of British monarchs, with appealing exhibits on Queen Victoria, as well as William and Mary. **Hours:** Daily 10:00-18:00, until 17:00 Nov-Feb. See page 97.

▲▲**Natural History Museum** A Darwinian delight, packed with stuffed creatures, engaging exhibits, and enthralled kids. **Hours:** Daily 10:00-17:50. See page 101.

▲▲ **Greenwich** Seafaring borough just east of the city center, with *Cutty Sark* tea clipper, Royal Observatory, other maritime sights, and a pleasant market. **Hours:** Most sights open daily, typically 10:00-17:00; market closed Mon. See page 351.

▲**Courtauld Gallery** Fine collection of paintings filling one wing of the Somerset House, a grand 18th-century palace. **Hours:** Daily 10:00-18:00. See page 59.

SIGHTS

Winston Churchill (1874-1965)

As the 20th century dawned, 25-year-old Winston Churchill was making a name for himself in Britain. Working as a newspaper reporter embedded with British troops in South Africa, his train was attacked by Boers. Churchill was captured and held as a POW. Meanwhile, back home, the London papers were praising the young man's heroism for saving fellow train passengers. After

two weeks, Churchill escaped from the Boer camp—he slipped through a bathroom window, scaled a wall, walked nonchalantly through an enemy town, hopped a freight train, and was smuggled out of the country. He emerged to find himself famous.

Churchill later entered politics. He first followed in his father's (Lord Randolph Churchill) Conservative Party footsteps, but his desire for social reform drove him to switch to the Liberal Party. (He would later flip back to Conservative.) For three decades, Churchill held numerous government posts, serving as Chancellor of This, Undersecretary of That, and Minister of The Other. He earned

praise for prison reform and for developing newfangled airplanes for warfare; he was criticized for the heavy-handed way he broke labor strikes and for bungling the pacification of Iraq. During World War I, he took a break from politics to personally command British troops on the Western Front.

of Westminster, used by kings until Henry VIII. The crude stone tower (1365-1366) was a guard tower in the palace wall, overlooking a moat. It contains a fine exhibit on the medieval Westminster Palace and the tower (£4, April-Oct daily 10:00-17:00; Nov-March Sat-Sun 10:00-16:00, closed Mon-Fri; tel. 020/7222-2219). Next to the tower (and free) is a quiet courtyard with picnic-friendly benches.

Big Ben, the 315-foot-high clock tower at the north end of the Palace of Westminster is named for its 13-ton bell, Ben. The light above the clock is lit when Parliament is in session. The face of the clock is huge—you can actually see the minute hand moving. For a good view of it, walk halfway over Westminster Bridge.

▲▲▲Churchill War Rooms

This excellent sight offers a fascinating walk through the underground headquarters of the British government's fight against the Nazis in the darkest days of the Battle for Britain. It has two parts: the war rooms themselves, and a top-notch museum dedicated to the man who steered the war from here, Winston Churchill. For

In 1929, Churchill-the-career-bureaucrat retired from politics. He wrote books *(History of the English-Speaking Peoples)* and spoke out about the growing threat of fascist Germany. When World War II broke out, Prime Minister Chamberlain's appeasement policies were discredited, and—on the day that Germany invaded the Netherlands—the king appointed Churchill as prime minister. Churchill guided the nation through its darkest hour (see sidebar on page 274). His greatest contribution may have been his stirring radio speeches that galvanized the will of the British people.

Despite the Allies' victory over the Nazis, Churchill lost the 1945 election. Though considered the ideal man to lead Britain during war, many believed that he and his Conservative Party colleagues were not the best choice to lead the country in peace and during rebuilding. Never one to be idle, he remained active in politics (especially in world affairs) as Leader of the Opposition. In 1946, he gave a speech at a Missouri college, which included the famous Cold War line, "From Stettin in the Baltic to Trieste in the Adriatic, an Iron Curtain has descended across the Continent." In 1951, Churchill was again elected prime minister and served for four years before he retired in 1955. When he died at the age of 90 in 1965, his state funeral in St. Paul's attracted leaders from around the world. Churchill, a legend in his own time, was buried in the family plot at Bladon, a mile from Blenheim Palace, the place of his birth.

details on all the blood, sweat, toil, and tears, pick up the excellent, essential, and included audioguide at the entry, and dive in. Allow yourself 1-2 hours for this sight.

Cost and Hours: £17.50 includes audioguide (and 10 percent optional donation), £5 guidebook, daily 9:30-18:00, last entry one hour before closing; on King Charles Street, 200 yards off Whitehall, follow the signs, Tube: Westminster, tel. 020/7930-6961, www.iwm.org.uk/churchill. The museum's gift shop is great for anyone nostalgic for the 1940s.

Cabinet War Rooms: The 27-room, heavily fortified nerve center of the British war effort was used from 1939 to 1945. Churchill's room, the map room, and other rooms are just as they were in 1945. As you follow the one-way route, be sure to take advantage of the audioguide, which explains each room and offers first-person accounts of wartime happenings here. Be patient—it's well worth it. While the rooms are spartan, you'll see how British gentility survived even as the city was bombarded—posted signs informed those working underground what the weather was like outside, and a cheery notice reminded them to turn off the light switch to conserve electricity.

Churchill Museum: Don't bypass this museum, which occupies a large hall amid the war rooms. It dissects every aspect of the man behind the famous cigar, bowler hat, and V-for-victory sign. It's extremely well-presented and engaging, using artifacts, quotes, political cartoons, clear explanations, and high-tech interactive exhibits to bring the colorful statesman to life. You'll get a taste of Winston's wit, irascibility, work ethic, passion for painting, American ties, writing talents, and drinking habits. The exhibit shows Winston's warts as well: It questions whether his party-switching was just political opportunism, examines the basis for his opposition to Indian self-rule, and reveals him to be an intense taskmaster who worked 18-hour days and was brutal to his staffers (who deeply respected him nevertheless).

A long touch-the-screen timeline lets you zero in on events in his life from birth (November 30, 1874) to his first appointment as prime minister in 1940. Many of the items on display—such as a European map divvied up in permanent marker, which Churchill brought to England from the postwar Potsdam Conference—drive home the remarkable span of history this man lived through. Imagine: Churchill began his military career riding horses in the cavalry and ended it speaking out against the proliferation of nuclear armaments. It's all the more amazing considering that, in the 1930s, the man who would become my vote for greatest statesman of the 20th century was considered a washed-up loony ranting about the growing threat of fascism.

Eating: Get your rations at the Switch Room café (until 17:00, in the museum), or for a nearby pub lunch, try Westminster Arms (food served downstairs, on Storey's Gate, a couple of blocks south of the museum).

Horse Guards

The Horse Guards change daily at 11:00 (10:00 on Sun), and a colorful dismounting ceremony takes place daily at 16:00. The rest of the day, they just stand there—terrible for video cameras (at Horse Guards Parade on Whitehall, directly across from the Banqueting House,

between Trafalgar Square and 10 Downing Street, Tube: West-
minster, www.royal.gov.uk—search "Changing the Guard").
Buckingham Palace pageantry is canceled when it rains, but the
Horse Guards change regardless of the weather.

▲Banqueting House

England's first Renaissance building (1619-1622) is still standing.
Designed by Inigo Jones, built by King James I, and decorated by
his son Charles I, the Banqueting House came to symbolize the
Stuart kings' "divine right" management style—the belief that
God himself had anointed them to rule. The house is one of the
few London landmarks spared by the 1698 fire and the only surviving part of the original Palace of Whitehall. Today it opens its
doors to visitors, who enjoy a restful 15-minute audiovisual history,
a 30-minute audioguide, and a look at the exquisite banqueting
hall itself. As a tourist attraction, it's basically one big room, with
sumptuous ceiling paintings by Peter Paul Rubens. At Charles I's
request, these paintings drove home the doctrine of the legitimacy
of the divine right of kings. Ironically, in 1649—divine right ignored—King Charles I was famously executed right here.

Cost and Hours: £6 includes audioguide (and 10 percent optional donation), daily 10:00-17:00, last entry at 16:30, may close
for government functions—though it promises to stay open at least
until 13:00 (call ahead for recorded information about closures),
aristocratic WC, immediately across Whitehall from the Horse
Guards, Tube: Westminster, tel. 020/3166-6150, www.hrp.org.uk.

For a brief self-guided tour of the Banqueting House—and
more details about the history of the place—see page 121 in the
Westminster Walk.

ON TRAFALGAR SQUARE
▲▲Trafalgar Square

London's renovated central square, the climax of most marches
and demonstrations, is a thrilling place to simply hang out. Lord
Nelson stands atop his
185-foot-tall fluted granite column, gazing out
toward Trafalgar, where
he lost his life but defeated the French fleet. Part
of this 1842 memorial is
made from his victims'
melted-down cannons.
He's surrounded by spray-
ing fountains, giant lions, hordes of people, and—until recently—
even more pigeons. A former London mayor decided that London's

SIGHTS

"flying rats" were a public nuisance and evicted Trafalgar Square's venerable seed salesmen (Tube: Charing Cross).

For more on Trafalgar Square, see page 125 in the Westminster Walk.

▲▲▲National Gallery

Displaying an unsurpassed collection of European paintings from 1250 to 1900—including works by Leonardo, Botticelli, Velázquez, Rembrandt, Turner, Van Gogh, and the Impressionists—this is one of Europe's great galleries. The collection is huge; following the route suggested in my self-guided tour will give you the best quick visit. For a more thorough tour, use the gallery's excellent audioguide. Or pick out just one masterpiece or a handful of great artists using the gallery's online "Short of Time" suggestions. Whatever time you spend here is worth it.

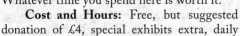

Cost and Hours: Free, but suggested donation of £4, special exhibits extra, daily 10:00-18:00, Fri until 21:00, last entry to special exhibits 45 minutes before closing; free guided tours available, worthwhile audioguide-£3.50, floor plan-£1; on Trafalgar Square, Tube: Charing Cross or Leicester Square, recorded info tel. 020/7747-2885, switchboard tel. 020/7839-3321, www.nationalgallery.org.uk. The excellent-but-pricey museum restaurant called the National Dining Rooms is a good spot to split afternoon tea (see page 434); the museum has cheaper eateries as well.

✪ See the National Gallery Tour chapter.

▲▲National Portrait Gallery

Cut off by halls of 19th-century characters who meant nothing to me, I used to call this "as interesting as someone else's yearbook." But a selective walk through this 500-year-long *Who's Who* of British history is quick and free, and puts faces on the story of England.

Some highlights: Henry VIII and wives; portraits of the "Virgin Queen" Elizabeth I, Sir Francis Drake, and Sir Walter Raleigh; the only real-life portrait of William Shakespeare; Oliver Cromwell and Charles I with his head on; portraits by Gainsborough and Reynolds; the Romantics (William Blake, Lord Byron, William Wordsworth, and company); Queen Victoria and her era; and the present royal family, including the late Princess Diana.

The collection is well-described, not huge, and in historical sequence, from the 16th century on the second floor to today's royal family on the ground floor.

Cost and Hours: Free, but suggested donation of £5, special exhibits extra; daily 10:00-18:00, Thu-Fri until 21:00, first and second floors open Mon at 11:00, last entry to special exhibits one hour before closing; audioguide-£3, floor plan-£1; entry 100 yards off Trafalgar Square (around the corner from National Gallery, opposite Church of St. Martin-in-the-Fields), Tube: Charing Cross or Leicester Square, tel. 020/7306-0055, recorded info tel. 020/7312-2463, www.npg.org.uk.

○ See the National Portrait Gallery Tour chapter.

▲St. Martin-in-the-Fields

The church, built in the 1720s with a Gothic spire atop a Greek-type temple, is an oasis of peace on wild and noisy Trafalgar Square. St. Martin cared for the poor. "In the fields" was where the first church stood on this spot (in the 13th century), between Westminster and The City. Stepping inside, you still feel a compassion for the needs of the people in this neighborhood—the church serves the homeless and houses a Chinese community center. The modern east window—with grillwork bent into the shape of a warped cross—was installed in 2008 to replace one damaged in World War II.

A freestanding glass pavilion to the left of the church serves as the entrance to the church's underground areas. There you'll find

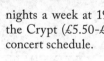

the concert ticket office, a gift shop, brass-rubbing center, and the recommended support-the-church Café in the Crypt.

Cost and Hours: Free, but donations welcome; hours vary but generally Mon-Fri 8:30-13:00 & 14:00-18:00, Sat 9:30-18:00, Sun 15:30-17:00; £3.50 audioguide at shop downstairs, Tube: Charing Cross, tel. 020/7766-1100, www.smitf.org.

Music: The church is famous for its concerts. Consider a free lunchtime concert (suggested £3 donation; Mon, Tue, and Fri at 13:00), an evening concert (£8-28, several nights a week at 19:30), or Wednesday night jazz at the Café in the Crypt (£5.50-£12 at 20:00). See the church's website for the concert schedule.

THE WEST END AND NEARBY

The following areas are linked (and further described) in the ○ West End Walk chapter.

▲Piccadilly Circus

Although this square is slathered with neon billboards and tacky attractions (think of it as

SIGHTS

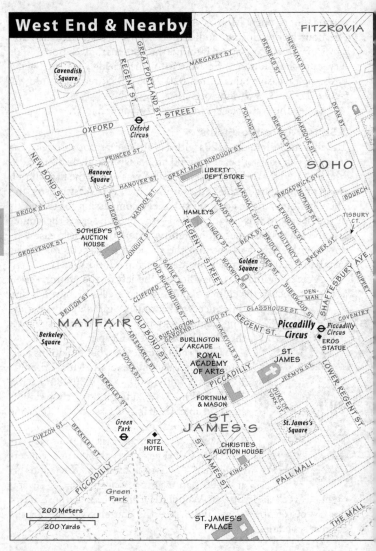

West End & Nearby

FITZROVIA

Cavendish Square

REGENT ST.

GREAT PORTLAND ST.

MARGARET ST.

BERNERS ST.

NEWMAN ST.

OXFORD   STREET

Oxford Circus

PRINCES ST.

POLAND ST.

BERWICK ST.

WARDOUR ST.

DEAN ST.

SOHO

NEW BOND ST.

Hanover Square

HANOVER ST.

GREAT MARLBOROUGH ST.

LIBERTY DEP'T STORE

BROADWICK ST.

HOPKINS ST.

BOURCH

BROOK ST.

ST. GEORGE ST.

MADDOX ST.

HAMLEYS

CARNABY ST.

MARSHALL ST.

LEXINGTON ST.

BREWER ST.

TISBURY CT.

SOTHEBY'S AUCTION HOUSE

CONDUIT ST.

REGENT STREET

KINGLY ST.

BEAK ST.

G. PULTENEY ST.

BRIDLE CT.

GROSVENOR ST.

SAVILE ROW

Golden Square

JAMES ST.

SHAFTESBURY AVE.

CLIFFORD ST.

WARWICK ST.

SHERWOOD ST.

RUPERT

BRUTON ST.

OLD BURLINGTON ST.

GLASSHOUSE ST.

DEN-MAN

COVENTRY

MAYFAIR

OLD BOND ST.

BURLINGTON GARDENS

VIGO ST.

REGENT ST.

Piccadilly Circus

Piccadilly Circus

Berkeley Square

ALBEMARLE ST.

SACKVILLE ST.

EROS STATUE

BURLINGTON ARCADE

ROYAL ACADEMY OF ARTS

DOVER ST.

ST. JAMES

PICCADILLY

JERMYN ST.

LOWER REGENT ST.

BERKELEY ST.

FORTNUM & MASON

DUKE OF YORK ST.

CURZON ST.

Green Park

ST. JAMES'S

St. James's Square

RITZ HOTEL

CHRISTIE'S AUCTION HOUSE

PICCADILLY

ST. JAMES'S ST.

KING ST.

PALL MALL

Green Park

200 Meters

200 Yards

ST. JAMES'S PALACE

THE MALL

the Times Square of London), the surrounding streets are packed with great shopping opportunities and swimming with youth on the rampage.

Nearby Shaftesbury Avenue and Leicester Square teem with fun-seekers, theaters, Chinese restaurants, and street singers. To the northeast is London's Chinatown and, beyond that, the funky Soho neighborhood (described next). And curling to the northwest from Piccadilly Circus is genteel Regent Street, lined with exclusive shops.

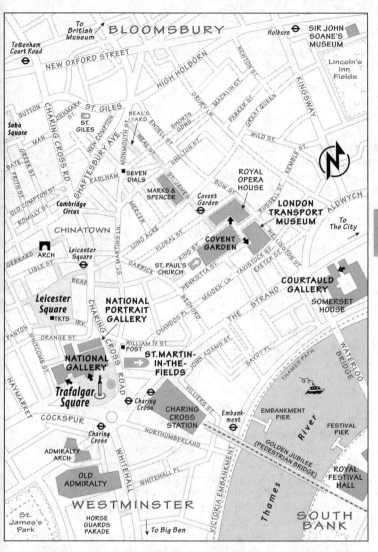

▲Soho

North of Piccadilly, seedy Soho has become trendy—with many recommended restaurants—and is well worth a gawk (❂ see the West End Walk chapter). It's the epicenter of London's thriving, colorful youth scene, a fun and funky *Sesame Street* of urban diversity.

Soho is also London's red light district (especially near Brewer and Berwick Streets), where "friendly models" wait in tiny rooms up dreary stairways, voluptuous con artists sell strip shows, and eager male tourists are frequently ripped off. But it's easy to avoid trouble if you're not looking for it. In fact, the sleazy joints share the block with respectable pubs and restaurants, and elderly couples stroll past neon signs that flash *Licensed Sex Shop in Basement.*

▲▲Covent Garden

The centerpiece of this boutique-ish shopping district is an iron-and-glass arcade. The "Actors' Church" of St. Paul, the Royal Opera House, and the London Transport Mu-seum (described next) all border the square, and theaters are nearby. The area is a people-watcher's delight, with cigarette eaters, Punch-and-Judy acts, food that's good for you (but not your wallet), trendy crafts, and row after row of boutique shops and market stalls. For more on this square, see page 184. Better Covent Garden lunch deals can be found by walking a block or two away from the eye of this touris-tic hurricane (check out the places north of the Tube station, along Endell and Neal Streets, and see my suggestions on page 425).

▲London Transport Museum

This modern, well-presented museum, located right at Covent Garden, is fun for kids and thought-provoking for adults (if a bit overpriced). Whether you're cursing or marveling at the buses and Tube, the growth of Europe's third-biggest city (after Moscow and Istanbul) has been made possible by its public transit system. Kids enjoy picking up the "stamp card," then punching it with old-fash-ioned ticket punchers at the different exhibits.

Cost and Hours: £15, ticket good for one year, kids under 18 free, Sat-Thu 10:00-18:00, Fri 11:00-18:00, last entry 45 minutes before closing; pleasant upstairs café with Covent Garden view; in southeast corner of Covent Garden courtyard, Tube: Covent Gar-den, switchboard tel. 020/7379-6344, recorded info tel. 020/7565-7299, www.ltmuseum.co.uk.

Visiting the Museum: After you enter, take the elevator up to the top floor...and the year 1800, when horse-drawn vehicles ruled the road. London invented the notion of a public bus traveling a set route that anyone could board without a reservation. Next, you descend to the first floor and the world's first underground Metro system, which used steam-powered locomotives (the Circle Line, c. 1865). On the ground floor, horses and trains are replaced by motorized vehicles (cars, taxis, double-decker buses, streetcars), re-sulting in 20th-century congestion. How to deal with it? In 2003, car drivers in London were slapped with a congestion charge, and today, a half-billion people ride the Tube every year. Learn how city planners hope to improve efficiency with better tracks and more coverage of the expanding East End. Finally, an exhibit lets you imagine four different scenarios for the year 2055 depending on the choices you make today. Will fresh strawberries in December destroy the planet?

▲Courtauld Gallery

This wonderful and compact collection of paintings is a joy. The gallery is part of the Courtauld Institute of Art, and the thoughtful description of each piece of art reminds visitors that the gallery is still used for teaching. You'll see medieval European paintings and works by Rubens, the Impressionists (Manet, Monet, and Degas), Post-Impressionists (Cézanne and an intense Van Gogh self-portrait), and more. Besides the permanent collection, a quality selection of loaners and special exhibits are often included in the entry fee. The gallery is located within the grand Somerset House; enjoy the riverside eateries and the courtyard featuring a playful fountain.

Cost and Hours: £6 (£3 on Mon); open daily 10:00-18:00, last entry 30 minutes before closing, occasionally open Thu until 21:00—check website; in Somerset House on the Strand, Tube: Temple or Covent Garden, recorded info tel. 020/7848-2526, www.courtauld.ac.uk.

○ See the Courtauld Gallery Tour chapter.

BUCKINGHAM PALACE AREA

The working headquarters of the British monarchy, Buckingham Palace is where the Queen carries out her official duties as the head

of state. She and other members of the royal family also maintain apartments here. The property hasn't always been this grand—James I (1603-1625) first brought the site under royal protection as a place for his mulberry plantation, for rearing silkworms.

Ticketing Options: Three palace sights require admission—the State Rooms (Aug-Sept only), Queen's Gallery, and Royal Mews. You can pay for each separately (prices below), or buy a combo-ticket: A £34.50 combo-ticket admits you to all three sights; a £16.75 version covers the Queen's Gallery and Royal Mews. For more information or to book tickets online, see www.royalcollection.org.uk. Many tourists are more interested in the Changing of the Guard, which costs nothing at all to view (see page 62). For locations, see map on page 60.

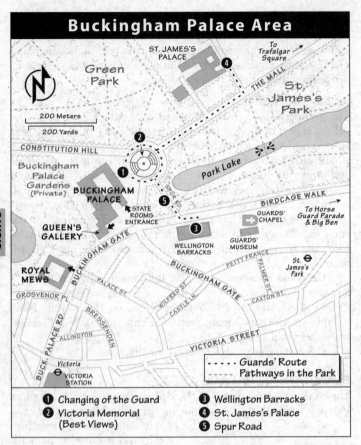

Buckingham Palace Area

Green Park

ST. JAMES'S PALACE

To Trafalgar Square

THE MALL

St. James's Park

200 Meters
200 Yards

CONSTITUTION HILL

Buckingham Palace Gardens (Private)

BUCKINGHAM PALACE

Park Lake

BIRDCAGE WALK

STATE ROOMS ENTRANCE

QUEEN'S GALLERY

GUARDS' CHAPEL

To Horse Guard Parade & Big Ben

WELLINGTON BARRACKS

GUARDS' MUSEUM

BUCKINGHAM GATE

ROYAL MEWS

PETTY FRANCE

St. James's Park

PALACE ST.

WILFRED ST.

BUCKINGHAM GATE

PALMER ST.

BUCK PALACE RD.

GROSVENOR PL.

BRESSENDEN

CASTLE LN.

CAXTON ST.

ALLINGTON

VICTORIA STREET

Victoria

VICTORIA STATION

····· Guards' Route
– – – Pathways in the Park

❶ Changing of the Guard
❷ Victoria Memorial (Best Views)
❸ Wellington Barracks
❹ St. James's Palace
❺ Spur Road

▲State Rooms at Buckingham Palace

This lavish home has been Britain's royal residence since 1837, when the newly ascended Queen Victoria moved in. When to-day's Queen is at home, the royal standard flies (a red, yellow, and blue flag); otherwise, the Union Jack flaps in the wind. The Queen opens her palace to the public—but only in August and September, when she's out of town.

Cost and Hours: £19.75 for lavish State Rooms and throne room, includes audioguide; Aug-Sept only, daily 9:30-18:30, until 19:00 in Aug, last admission 16:45 in Aug, 15:45 in Sept; limited to 8,000 visitors a day by timed entry; come early to the palace's Visitor Entrance (opens 9:15), or book ahead in person, by phone, or online (£2.50 extra); Tube: Victoria, tel. 020/7766-7300.

Changing of the Guard Timeline

When	What	Where
10:30	Tourists begin to gather (arrive now for a spot front and center by the fence)	Fence outside the palace
11:00	Victoria Monument gets crowded	Middle of traffic circle in front of palace
11:00-11:15	"New Guard" gathers for inspection	Wellington Barracks
11:00 (10:00 Sun)	Changing of the Horse Guard	Horse Guards Parade (opposite end of St. James's Park)
11:15-11:30	Tired St. James's Palace guards and Horse Guard both head for the palace	Down the Mall
11:15-11:30	Fresh replacement troops head from Wellington Barracks to Buckingham Palace	Down Spur Road
11:30-11:45	All guards gradually converge	Around Victoria Monument in front of the palace
11:45-12:00	The Changing of the Guard ceremony	Inside fenced courtyard of Buckingham Palace
12:00-12:10	Tired guards head for Wellington Barracks	Up the Mall
12:00-12:10	Fresh guards head for St. James's Palace	Up Spur Road
12:15	Smaller changing of the guard ceremony	In front of St. James's Palace

Queen's Gallery at Buckingham Palace

A small sampling of Queen Elizabeth's personal collection of art is on display in five rooms in a wing adjoining the palace. Her 7,000 paintings, one of the largest private art collections in the world, are actually a series of collections built upon by each successive monarch since the 16th century. The Queen rotates the paintings, enjoying some privately in her many palatial residences while sharing others with her subjects in public galleries in Edinburgh and London. The exhibits change two or three times a year and are lovingly described by the included audioguide.

Because the gallery is small and security is tight (involving lines), I'd suggest visiting this gallery only if you're a patient art lover interested in the current exhibit.

Cost and Hours: £9.75 but can change depending on exhibit, £16.75 combo-ticket with Royal Mews, daily 10:00-17:30, opens at 9:30 Aug-Sept, last entry one hour before closing, Tube: Victoria, tel. 020/7766-7301—but Her Majesty rarely answers. Men shouldn't miss the mahogany-trimmed urinals.

Royal Mews

A visit to the Queen's working stables is likely to be disappointing unless you follow the included audioguide or the hourly guided tour (April-Oct only, 45 minutes), in which case it's fairly entertaining—especially if you're interested in horses and/or royalty. You'll see a few of the Queen's 30 horses (most active between 10:00 and 12:00), a fancy car, and a bunch of old carriages, finishing with the Gold State Coach (c. 1760, 4 tons, 4 mph). Queen Victoria said absolutely no cars. When she died, in 1901, the mews got its first Daimler. Today, along with the hay-eating transport, the stable is home to five Bentleys and Rolls-Royce Phantoms, with one on display.

Cost and Hours: £8.75, £16.75 combo-ticket with Queen's Gallery, April-Oct daily 10:00-17:00, Nov-March Mon-Sat 10:00-16:00, closed Sun, last entry 45 minutes before closing, guided tours on the hour in summer, Buckingham Palace Road, Tube: Victoria, tel. 020/7766-7302.

▲▲Changing of the Guard at Buckingham Palace

This is the spectacle every visitor to London has to see at least once: stone-faced, red-coated (or in winter, gray-coated), bearskin-hatted guards changing posts with much fanfare, in an hour-long ceremony accompanied by a brass band.

It's 11:00 at Buckingham Palace, and the on-duty guards (the "Queen's Guard") are ready to finish their shift. Nearby at St. James's Palace (a half-mile northeast), a second set of guards is also ready for a break. Meanwhile, fresh replacement guards (the "New Guard") gather for a review and inspection at Wellington Barracks, 500 yards east of the palace (on Birdcage Walk).

At 11:15, the tired St. James's guards head out to the Mall, and then take a right turn for Buckingham Palace. At 11:30, the replacement troops, led by the band, also head for Buckingham Palace. Meanwhile, a fourth group—the Horse Guard—passes by along the Mall on its way back to Hyde Park Corner from its own changing-of-the-guard ceremony on Whitehall (which just took place at Horse Guards Parade at 11:00, or 10:00 on Sun).

At 11:45, the tired and fresh guards converge on Buckingham Palace in a perfect storm of red-coat pageantry. Everyone parades around, the guard changes (passing the regimental flag, or "colour") with much shouting, the band plays a happy little concert, and then they march out. At noon, two bands escort two detachments of guards away: the tired guards to Wellington Barracks and the fresh guards to St. James's Palace. As the fresh guards set up at St. James's Palace and the tired ones dress down at the barracks, the tourists disperse.

Cost and Hours: Free, daily May-July at 11:30, every other day Aug-April, no ceremony in very wet weather; exact schedule subject to change—call 020/7766-7300 for the day's plan, or check www.royal.gov.uk (search "Changing the Guard"); Buckingham Palace, Tube: Victoria, St. James's Park, or Green Park. Or hop into a big black taxi and say, "Buck House, please."

Sightseeing Strategies: Most tourists just show up and get lost in the crowds, but those who know the drill will enjoy the event more. The action takes place in stages over the course of an hour, at several different locations. The main event is in the forecourt right in front of Buckingham Palace (between Buckingham Palace and the fence) from 11:30 to 12:00. To see it close up, you'll need to get here no later than 10:30 to get a place front and center, next to the fence.

But there's plenty of pageantry elsewhere. Get out your map and strategize. You could see the guards mobilizing at Wellington Barracks or St. James's Palace (11:00-11:15). Or watch them parade with bands down The Mall and Spur Road (11:15-11:30). After the ceremony at Buckingham Palace is over (and many tourists have gotten bored and gone home), the parades march back along those same streets (12:10).

Pick one event and find a good, unobstructed place from which to view it. The key is to get either right up front along the road or fence, or find some raised elevation to stand or sit on—a balustrade or a curb—so you can see over people's heads.

If you get there too late to score a premium spot right along the fence, head for the high ground on the circular Victoria Memorial, which provides the best overall view (come before 11:00 to get a place). From the memorial, you have good (if more distant) views of the palace as well as the arriving and departing parades along The Mall and Spur Road. The actual Changing of the Guard in front of the palace is a nonevent. It is interesting, however, to see nearly every tourist in London gathered in one place at the same time.

If you arrive too late to get any good spot at all, or you just don't feel like jostling for a view, stroll down to St. James's Palace and wait near the corner for a great photo-op. At about 12:15, the parade marches up The Mall to the palace and performs a smaller changing ceremony—with almost no crowds. Afterward, stroll through nearby St. James's Park.

North London

▲▲▲British Museum

Simply put, this is the greatest chronicle of civilization...anywhere. A visit here is like taking a long hike through *Encyclopedia Britannica* National Park. The vast British Museum wraps around its Great Court (the huge entrance hall), with the most popular sections filling the ground floor: Egyptian, Assyrian, and ancient Greek, with the famous frieze sculptures from the Parthenon in Athens. The museum's stately Reading Room—famous as the place where Karl Marx hung out while formulating his ideas on communism and writing *Das Kapital*—sometimes hosts special exhibits.

Cost and Hours: Free but a £5 donation requested, special exhibits usually extra (and with timed ticket); daily 10:00-17:30, Fri

until 20:30 (selected galleries only), least crowded weekday late afternoons; free guided tours offered, multimedia guide-£5, free Rick Steves audio tour available—see page 8; Great Russell Street, Tube: Tottenham Court Road, general info tel. 020/7323-8000, ticket desk tel. 020/7323-8181, www.britishmuseum.org.

✪ See the British Museum Tour chapter.

▲▲▲British Library

Here, in just two rooms, are the literary treasures of Western civilization, from early Bibles, to the Magna Carta, to Shakespeare's

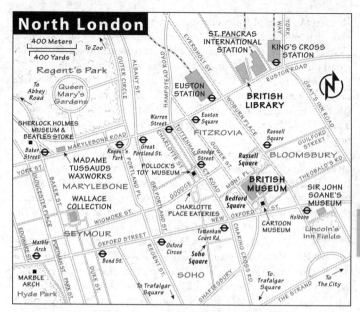

North London

400 Meters
400 Yards

To Zoo

Regent's Park

To Abbey Road

Queen Mary's Gardens

SHERLOCK HOLMES MUSEUM & BEATLES STORE

Baker Street

MADAME TUSSAUDS WAXWORKS

WALLACE COLLECTION

MARYLEBONE

SEYMOUR

Marble Arch

MARBLE ARCH

Hyde Park

OUTER CIRCLE
ALBANY ST.
HAMPSTEAD ROAD
EVERSHOLT ST.
YORK WAY

ST. PANCRAS INTERNATIONAL STATION

KING'S CROSS STATION

EUSTON STATION

BRITISH LIBRARY

EUSTON ROAD

GRAY'S INN ROAD

Warren Street

Euston Square

Great Portland St.

FITZROVIA

Russell Square

GUILFORD STREET

Regent's Park

Goodge Street

Russell Square

BLOOMSBURY

THEOBALD'S RD.

POLLOCK'S TOY MUSEUM

BRITISH MUSEUM

SIR JOHN SOANE'S MUSEUM

CHARLOTTE PLACE EATERIES

Bedford Square

Holborn

Lincoln's Inn Fields

CARTOON MUSEUM

WIGMORE ST.

OXFORD STREET

Oxford Circus

Bond St.

Tottenham Court Rd.

Soho Square

SOHO

To Trafalgar Square

To Trafalgar Square

To The City

THE STRAND

To Trafalgar Square

Hamlet, to Lewis Carroll's *Alice's Adventures in Wonderland.* You'll see the Lindisfarne Gospels transcribed on an illuminated manuscript, as well as Beatles lyrics scrawled on the back of a greeting card. The British Empire built its greatest monuments out of paper; it's through literature that England made her most lasting and significant contribution to civilization and the arts.

Cost and Hours: Free, but £5 suggested donation, admission charged for some special exhibits; Mon-Fri 9:30-18:00, Tue until 20:00, Sat 9:30-17:00, Sun 11:00-17:00; guided tours offered, free Rick Steves audio tour available—see page 8; 96 Euston Road, Tube: King's Cross St. Pancras or Euston, tel. 019/3754-6060 or 020/7412-7676, www.bl.uk.

✪ See the British Library Tour chapter.

▲Wallace Collection

Sir Richard Wallace's fine collection of 17th-century Dutch Masters, 18th-century French Rococo, medieval armor, and assorted aristocratic fancies fills the sumptuously furnished Hertford House on Manchester Square. From the rough and intimate Dutch lifescapes of Jan Steen to the pink-cheeked

Rococo fantasies of François Boucher, a wander through this little-visited mansion makes you nostalgic for the days of the empire. While this collection would be a big deal in a mid-sized city, it's small potatoes here in London...but thoroughly enjoyable.

Cost and Hours: Free, daily 10:00-17:00, audioguide-£3, free guided tours or lectures almost daily at 11:30 and 14:30—call to confirm times, just north of Oxford Street on Manchester Square, Tube: Bond Street. Tel. 020/7563-9500, www.wallacecollection. org.

Visiting the Museum: The manageable collection is displayed on three floors. As you enter the ground floor, on the right you'll find drawing rooms filled with medieval relics, and to the left (through the gift shop) are the collections of Oriental and European armor. Then head up the red-carpeted grand staircase to the upper floor, devoted mostly to artwork.

In the Oval Drawing Room, look for the small but symbolism-packed Rococo masterpiece *The Swing* (1767), by Jean-Honoré Fragonard. The woman is being pulled on the swing by her husband. He's on the right, hidden in shadows, literally "in the dark"—unaware that his wife is having an affair with the man hiding in the bushes on the left. The rascal holds his arm erect as he peeps up this swinging lady's skirt and watches her shoe fly off, symbolizing sexual abandon.

In the Great Gallery, find one of the museum's best-known paintings, *The Laughing Cavalier* (1624), by Frans Hals. With his hat perched at a jaunty angle, the man smirks enigmatically with unhappy eyes...more of a polite chuckle or a bemused snort. As you view the canvas from multiple angles, notice his eyes following you.

Then head back down to the main floor and go out the door behind the staircase, into the building's gorgeous, glassed-in atrium, filled with light and a restaurant (with slow service and overpriced food).

Downstairs from the atrium, you'll find a tiny gallery displaying methods of restoration and, often, a revolving exhibit.

▲Madame Tussauds Waxworks

This waxtravaganza is gimmicky, crass, and crazily expensive, but dang fun...a hit with the kind of tourists who skip the British Museum. The original Madame Tussaud did wax casts of heads lopped off during the French Revolution (such as Marie-Antoinette's). She took her show on the road and ended up in London in 1835. These days, they've dumped anything really historical (except for

what they claim is the blade that beheaded Marie-Antoinette) because "there's no money in it and we're a business." Now it's all about squeezing Leonardo DiCaprio's bum, singing with Lady Gaga, and partying with Beyoncé, Brangelina, and the Beatles. The gallery, which sprawls through several rooms of a huge building, is one giant photo-op—the whole point is jockeying for position to snap the best picture of your travel buddy with a famous "person." It's extremely crowded and chaotic, as everyone clamors to press the wax with their heroes, while dodging tourist trinket kiosks and photographers standing by to overcharge you for a print. These dummies are eerily realistic—count how many times you say "excuse me" after bumping into a wax figure.

Cost: £30, up to 25 percent discount and shorter lines if you buy tickets on their website (also consider combo-deal with London Eye, sold cheaper online; see page 565); often even bigger discount—up to 50 percent—if you get "Late Saver" tickets at the door after 17:30, but be aware that some experiences close at 18:00; two-for-one rail vouchers accepted (see page 25). Kids also get a discount of about £4, and those under 5 are free.

Hours: Mid-July-Aug and school holidays daily 9:00-19:00, Sept-mid-July Mon-Fri 9:30-17:30, Sat-Sun 9:00-18:00, these are last entry times—place stays open roughly two hours later; Marylebone Road, Tube: Baker Street, tel. 0871-894-3000, www.madametussauds.com.

Crowd-Beating Tips: This popular attraction can be swamped with people. To avoid the ticket line, buy an Online Saver and reserve a time slot at least a day in advance. If you wait to buy tickets at the attraction, you'll discover that the ticket-buying line is often halfway down the block, and once inside it continues to twist endlessly (believe the posted signs about the wait—an hour or more is not unusual at busy times). If you buy your tickets at the door, try to arrive after 15:00—a smart move even with advance tickets, as the crowds inside thin out later in the day.

Visiting the Waxworks: First you'll join the paparazzi on the red carpet with A-list stars, then you'll head through several themed sections, featuring Hollywood stars new and old, sports heroes (including some unfamiliar-to-Americans cricket players and footballers), the royal family (pose with the Queen, Will, and Kate...or settle for Charles and Camilla), scientists, artists, writers, musicians, and world leaders. Britain's previous prime minister, the unpopular Gordon Brown, was the first British PM in 150 years not to be immortalized in wax. His successor, David Cameron, got the wax treatment within a few weeks of his 2010 election. Even Hitler has a wax figure. Ouch.

Downstairs is a hokey but gory haunted-house exhibit called "Scream!" where you'll walk through a dark hallway while actors jump out and grab at you (a lame mini-version of the also-lame London Dungeon). A small exhibit explains the history of Madame Tussaud and her waxy army, along with the process for casting a person in wax. Then you'll board a Disney-type people-mover and cruise through a kid-pleasing "Spirit of London" time trip, with a fun, once-over-lightly history of this city. The finale is the Marvel Super Heroes section, which ends with a silly, crowd-pleasing nine-minute "4-D" show—a 3-D movie heightened by wind, "back ticklers," and other special effects (not worth a long wait in line).

▲Sir John Soane's Museum

Architects love this quirky place, as do fans of interior decor, eclectic knickknacks, and Back Door sights. Tour this furnished home on a bird-chirping square and see 19th-century chairs, lamps, wood-paneled nooks and crannies, sculptures, and stained-glass skylights. (Some sections may be closed for restoration through 2015, but the main part of the house will be open.) As professor of architecture at the Royal Academy, Soane created his home to be a place of learning, cramming it floor to ceiling with ancient relics, curios, and famous paintings, including several excellent Canalettos and Hogarth's series on *The Rake's Progress*

(which is hidden behind a panel in the Picture Room and opened randomly at the museum's discretion, usually twice an hour). In 1833, just before his death, Soane established his house as a museum, stipulating that it be kept as nearly as possible in the state he left it. If he visited today, he'd be entirely satisfied by the diligence with which the staff safeguards his treasures. You'll leave wishing you'd known the man.

Cost and Hours: Free, but donations much appreciated; Tue-Sat 10:00-17:00, open and candlelit the first Tue of the month 18:00-21:00, closed Sun-Mon, last entry 30 minutes before closing, long entry lines on Sat; guidebook-£5, guided tour-£10—includes guidebook—Tue and Fri 11:30, Wed and Thu 3:30; 13 Lincoln's Inn Fields, quarter-mile southeast of British Museum, Tube: Holborn, tel. 020/7405-2107, www.soane.org.

Cartoon Museum

This humble but interesting museum is located in the shadow of the British Museum. While its three rooms are filled with British cartoons unknown to most Americans, the satirical takeoffs on famous bigwigs and politicians—including Napoleon, Margaret Thatcher, the Queen, and Tony Blair—show the power of parody to deliver social commentary. Upstairs are panels of well-known comics that will interest only diehard fans.

Cost and Hours: £7, Mon-Sat 10:30-17:30, Sun 12:00-17:30, 35 Little Russell Street—go one block south of the British Museum on Museum Street and turn right, Tube: Tottenham Court Road, tel. 020/7580-8155, www.cartoonmuseum.org.

Pollock's Toy Museum

This rickety old house, with glass cases filled with toys and games lining its walls and halls, is a time-warp experience that brings back childhood memories to people who grew up without batteries or computer chips. It also gives a sense of the history of childhood itself, starting from when "childhood" as we know it now first came to be. Though the museum is small, you could spend a lot of time here, squinting at the fascinating toys and well-loved dolls that entertained the children of 19th- and early 20th-century England.

The included information is great. The story of Theodore Roosevelt refusing to shoot a bear cub while on a hunting trip was celebrated in 1902 cartoons, resulting in a new, huggable toy: the Teddy Bear. It was popular for good reason: It could be manufactured during World War I without rationed products; it coincided with the new belief that soft toys were good for a child's development; it was an acceptable "doll for boys"; and it was *the* toy children kept long after they'd grown up.

Cost and Hours: £6, kids-£3, Mon-Sat 10:00-17:00, closed Sun, last entry 30 minutes before closing, 1 Scala Street, Tube: Goodge Street, tel. 020/7636-3452, www.pollockstoymuseum. com. A fun retro toy shop is attached.

Beatles Sights

London's city center is surprisingly devoid of sights associated with the famous '60s rock band. To see much of anything, consider taking a guided walk (see page 38).

Affording London's Sights

London is one of Europe's most expensive cities, with the dubious distinction of having some of the world's steepest admission prices. Fortunately, many sights are free.

Free Museums: Many of the city's biggest and best museums won't charge you a dime. Free sights include the British Museum, British Library, National Gallery, National Portrait Gallery, Tate Britain, Tate Modern, Wallace Collection, Imperial War Museum, Victoria and Albert Museum, Natural History Museum, Science Museum, National Army Museum, Sir John Soane's Museum, the Museum of London, the Geffrye Museum, and on the outskirts of town, the Royal Air Force Museum London.

About half of these museums request a donation of a few pounds, but whether you contribute or not is up to you. If I spend money for an audioguide, I feel fine about not otherwise donating. If you can afford it, donate.

Free Churches: Smaller churches let worshippers (and tourists) in free, although they may ask for a donation. The big sightseeing churches—Westminster Abbey and St. Paul's—charge higher admission fees, but offer free evensong services nearly daily (though you can't stick around afterward to sightsee). Westminster Abbey also offers free organ recitals most Sundays.

Other Freebies: London has plenty of free performances, such as lunch concerts at St. Martin-in-the-Fields (see page 461) and summertime movies at The Scoop amphitheater near City Hall (see page 464). For other freebies, check out www.whatsfreeinlondon.co.uk. There's no charge to enjoy the pageantry of the Changing of the Guard, rants at Speakers' Corner in Hyde Park (on Sun afternoon), displays at Harrods, the people-watching scene at Covent Garden, and the colorful streets of the East End. It's free to view the legal action at the Old Bailey and the legislature at work in the Houses of Parliament. And you can get into a bit of the Tower of London and Windsor Castle by attending Sunday services in each place's chapel (chapel access only).

Greenwich makes for an inexpensive outing. Many of its sights are free, and the journey there is covered by a cheap Zones 1-2 Tube ticket or pass.

Sightseeing Deals: If you buy a paper One-Day Travelcard at a National Rail station (such as Paddington or Victoria), you may be eligible for two-for-one discounts at many popular sights, such as the Churchill War Rooms, London Eye, Tower of London, and Madame Tussauds. (This also works with paper train tickets bought in person at the station—if you'll be riding into London and visiting one of these sights later in the day.) See page 25 for details.

Good-Value Tours: The city walking tours with professional guides (£9) are one of the best deals going. (Note that the guides for the "free" walking tours are unpaid by their companies, and they expect tips—I'd pay up front for an expertly guided tour instead.) Hop-on, hop-off big-bus tours, while expensive (£25-30), provide a great overview and include free boat tours as well as city walks. (Or, for the price of a transit ticket, you could get similar views from the top of a double-decker public bus.) A one-hour Thames ride to Greenwich costs £12 one-way, but most boats come with entertaining commentary. A three-hour bicycle tour is about £20.

Pricey...but Worth It? Big-ticket sights worth their hefty admission fees (£14-18) are Kew Gardens, Shakespeare's Globe, the Churchill War Rooms, and Kensington Palace.

The London Eye has become a London must-see—though if you're on a tight budget, it's difficult to justify its very high cost (£20). While Hampton Court Palace (£18.20) is expensive, it is well presented and a reasonable value if you have an interest in royal history. The Queen charges royally for a peek inside Buckingham Palace (£19.75, open Aug-Sept only), and her art gallery and carriage museum (adjacent to the palace, about £9 each) are expensive but interesting. Madame Tussauds Waxworks is pricey but still hard for many to resist (£30, see page 67 for info on discounts). Harry Potter fans gladly pay the Hagrid-sized £30 fee to see the sets and props at the Warner Bros. Studio Tour (but those who wouldn't know a wizard from a Muggle shouldn't waste the time or money).

Many smaller museums charge relatively low admission (under £8). My favorites include the Courtauld Gallery and the Wellington Museum at Apsley House.

Totally Pants (Brit-speak for Not Worth It): The London Dungeon, at £25.20, is gimmicky, overpriced, and a terrible value...despite the long line at the door.

Theater: Compared with Broadway's prices, London's theater is a bargain. Seek out the freestanding TKTS booth at Leicester Square to get discounts from 25 to 50 percent on good seats (and full-price tickets to the hottest shows with no service charges; see page 455). Buying direct at the theater box office can score you a great deal on same-day tickets, and even the most popular shows generally have some seats under £20 (possibly with obstructed views)—ask. A £5 "groundling" ticket for a play at Shakespeare's Globe is the best theater deal in town (see page 459). Tickets to the Open Air Theatre at north London's Regent's Park start at £15 (see page 461).

London doesn't come cheap. But with its many free museums and affordable plays, this cosmopolitan, cultured city offers days of sightseeing thrills without requiring you to pinch your pennies (or your pounds).

For a photo op, go to **Abbey Road** and walk the famous cross-walk pictured on the *Abbey Road* album cover (Tube: St. John's Wood, get information and buy Beatles memorabilia at the small kiosk in the station). From the Tube station, it's a five-minute walk west down Grove End Road to the intersection with Abbey Road. The Abbey Road recording studio is the low-key, white building to the right of Abbey House (it's still a working studio, so you can't go inside). Ponder the graffiti on the low wall outside, and...imagine. To re-create the famous cover photo, shoot the crosswalk from the roundabout as you face north up Abbey Road. Shoes are optional.

Nearby is **Paul McCartney's current home** (7 Cavendish Avenue): Continue down Grove End Road, turn left on Circus Road, and then right on Cavendish. Please be discreet.

The **Beatles Store** is at 231 Baker Street (Tube: Baker Street). It's small—some Beatles-logo T-shirts, mugs, pins, and old vinyl like you might have in your closet—and has nothing of historic value (open eight days a week, 10:00-18:30, tel. 020/7935-4464, www.beatlesstorelondon.co.uk; another rock memorabilia store is across the street).

Sherlock Holmes Museum

A few doors down from the Beatles Store, this meticulous re-creation of the (fictional) apartment of the (fictional) detective sits at the (real) address of 221b Baker Street. The first-floor replica (so to speak) of Sherlock's study delights fans with the opportunity to play Holmes and Watson while sitting in authentic 18th-century chairs. The second and third floors offer fine exhibits on daily Victorian life, showing off furniture, clothes, pipes, paintings, and chamber pots; in other rooms, models are posed to enact key scenes from Sir Arthur Conan Doyle's famous books.

Cost and Hours: £10, daily 9:30-18:00, last entry at least 30 minutes before closing, expect to wait 15 minutes or more, large gift shop for Holmes connoisseurs, Tube: Baker Street, tel. 020/7935-8866, www.sherlock-holmes.co.uk.

The City

When Londoners say "The City," they mean the one-square-mile business center in East London that 2,000 years ago was Roman Londinium. The outline of the Roman city walls can still be seen in the arc of roads from Blackfriars Bridge to Tower Bridge. Within The City are 23 churches designed by Sir Christopher Wren, mostly just ornamentation around St. Paul's Cathedral. Today, while home to only 7,000 residents, The City thrives with nearly 300,000 office workers coming and going daily. It's a fascinating district to wander on weekdays, but since almost nobody actually lives there, it's dull in the evenings and on Saturday and Sunday.

○ See The City Walk chapter.

ST. PAUL'S CATHEDRAL AND NEARBY
▲▲▲St. Paul's Cathedral

Wren's most famous church is the great St. Paul's, its elaborate interior capped by a 365-foot dome. Since World War II, St. Paul's has been Britain's symbol of resilience. Despite 57 nights of bombing, the Nazis failed to destroy the cathedral, thanks to St. Paul's volunteer fire watchmen, who stayed on the dome. Today you can climb the dome for a great city view. The crypt (included with admission) is a world of historic bones and memorials, including Admiral Nelson's tomb and interesting cathedral models.

Cost and Hours: £16, includes church entry, dome climb, crypt, tour, and audioguide; Mon-Sat 8:30-16:30, last entry for sightseeing 16:00 (dome opens at 9:30, last entry at 16:15), closed Sun except for worship; guided tours offered, free Rick Steves audio tour available—see page 8; Tube: St. Paul's, recorded info tel. 020/7236-4128, reception tel. 020/7246-8350, www.stpauls.co.uk.

Music: The evensong services are free (Sun 15:15, Tue-Sat 17:00, not on Mon), but nonpaying visitors are not allowed to linger afterward (see page 264 for details).

Cheap Trick: To get a free cityscape view nearly as good as the expensive view from St. Paul's dome, head for a terrace just behind the church. To reach it, walk through the churchyard (to the left of the church as you face it), cross the busy street to the modern shopping mall, and ride its glass elevator to the top floor.

○ See the St. Paul's Cathedral Tour chapter.

▲Old Bailey

To view the British legal system inaction—lawyers in little blond wigs speaking legalese with an upper-crust accent—spend a few minutes in the visitors' gallery at the Old Bailey courthouse, called the "Central Criminal Court." Don't enter under the dome; continue down the block about halfway to the modern part of the building—the entry is at Warwick Passage.

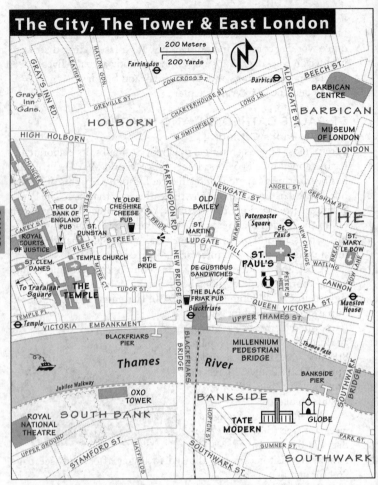

The City, The Tower & East London

200 Meters
200 Yards

Farringdon

Barbican

BARBICAN CENTRE

BARBICAN

MUSEUM OF LONDON

LONDON

GRAY'S INN RD.

LEATHER LN.

HATTON GDN.

COWCROSS ST.

ALDERGATE ST.

BEECH ST.

Gray's Inn Gdns.

GREVILLE ST.

CHARTERHOUSE ST.

LONG LN.

HIGH HOLBORN

HOLBORN

W. SMITHFIELD

CHANCERY LN.

NEWGATE ST.

ANGEL ST.

GRESHAM ST.

THE

OLD BAILEY

Paternoster Square

St. Paul's

ST. MARY LE BOW

NEW CHANGE

BREAD ST.

BOW LANE

CAREY ST.

YE OLDE CHESHIRE CHEESE PUB

THE OLD BANK OF ENGLAND PUB

ST. MARTIN

ROYAL COURTS OF JUSTICE

ST. DUNSTAN

STREET

LUDGATE

ST. PAUL'S

WATLING

FETTER LN.

ST. BRIDE

ST. CLEM. DANES

FLEET

TEMPLE CHURCH

ST. BRIDE

DE GUSTIBUS SANDWICHES

CANNON

Mansion House

To Trafalgar Square

THE TEMPLE

MITRE CT.

TUDOR ST.

NEW BRIDGE ST.

FARRINGDON RD.

THE BLACK FRIAR PUB

QUEEN VICTORIA ST.

PETER'S HILL

TEMPLE PL.

VICTORIA EMBANKMENT

Blackfriars

UPPER THAMES ST.

Temple

BLACKFRIARS PIER

BLACKFRIARS BRIDGE

Thames River

MILLENNIUM PEDESTRIAN BRIDGE

Thames Path

BANKSIDE PIER

SOUTHWARK BRIDGE

Jubilee Walkway

OXO TOWER

BANKSIDE

ROYAL NATIONAL THEATRE

SOUTH BANK

TATE MODERN

GLOBE

PARK ST.

UPPER GROUND

HOPTON ST.

SOUTHWARK ST.

SUMNER ST.

SOUTHWARK

STAMFORD ST.

HATFIELDS

Cost and Hours: Free, generally Mon-Fri 10:00-13:00 & 14:00-16:30 depending on caseload, last entry at 12:30 and 15:45 but often closes an hour or so earlier, closed Sat-Sun, fewer cases in Aug; no kids under 14; no bags, mobile phones, cameras, iPods, or food, but small purses OK; you can check bags at the Capable Travel agency just down the street at Old Bailey 4—£5/bag, £1 per phone or camera; 2 blocks northwest of St. Paul's on Old Bailey Street, follow signs to public entrance, Tube: St. Paul's, tel. 020/7248-3277 www.cityoflondon.gov.uk.

▲Museum of London

This museum tells the fascinating story of London, taking you on a walk from its pre-Roman beginnings to the present. It features London's distinguished citizens through history—from Nean-

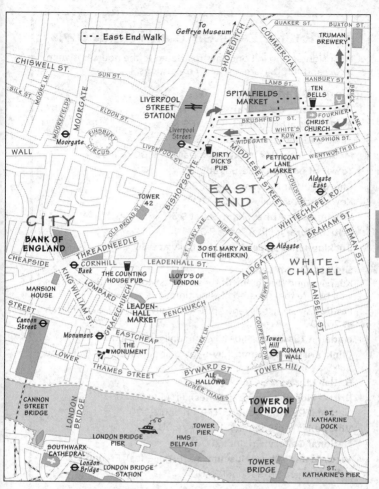

derthals, to Romans, to Elizabethans, to Victorians, to Mods, to today. The displays are chronological, spacious, and informative without being overwhelming. Scale models and costumes help you visualize everyday life in the city at different periods. There are enough whiz-bang multimedia displays (including the Plague and the Great Fire) to spice up otherwise humdrum artifacts. This regular stop for the local school kids gives the best overview of London history in town.

Cost and Hours: Free, daily 10:00-18:00, galleries shut down 30 minutes before closing, see the day's events board for special talks and tours, café, £1 lockers, 150 London Wall at Aldersgate Street, Tube: Barbican or St. Paul's plus a five-minute walk, tel. 020/7001-9844, www.museumoflondon.org.uk.

London for Early Birds and Night Owls

Most sightseeing in London is restricted to the hours between 10:00 and 18:00. Here are a few exceptions:

Sights Open Early

Westminster Cathedral: Daily at 7:00

St. Paul's Cathedral: Mon-Sat at 8:30

Shakespeare's Globe: Daily at 9:00

Madame Tussauds Waxworks: Daily at 9:00 or 9:30

Tower of London: Tue-Sat at 9:00

Churchill War Rooms: Daily at 9:30

Kew Gardens: Daily at 9:30

Westminster Abbey: Mon-Sat at 9:30

British Library: Mon-Sat at 9:30

Buckingham Palace: Aug-Sept daily at 9:30

Sights Open Late

Keep in mind that many of these sights stop admitting visitors well before their posted closing times.

London Eye: Last ascent April-Aug daily at 21:00, Sept-March at 20:30

Madame Tussauds: Mid-July-Aug daily until 19:00

Clink Prison Museum: July-Sept daily until 21:00, Oct-June Sat-Sun until 21:00

British Library: Tue until 20:00

British Museum (some galleries): Fri until 20:30

National Portrait Gallery: Thu-Fri until 21:00

Vinopolis: Thu-Sat until 21:30 or 22:00

National Gallery: Fri until 21:00

Victoria and Albert Museum (some galleries): Fri until 22:00

Tate Modern: Fri-Sat until 22:00

Visiting the Museum: The first part of the tour zips quickly through a half-million years, when Britain morphed from peninsula to island, Neanderthals speared mammoths, and Stone Age humans huddled in crude huts on the South Bank of the Thames.

In 54 B.C., Julius Caesar invaded, and the Romans built "Londinium" on the north bank. The settlement quickly became the hub of Britain and a river-trade town, complete with arenas, forums, baths, a bridge across the Thames, and a **city wall.** That wall—arcing from the present Tower of London to St. Paul's—defined the city's boundaries for the next 1,500 years. The Museum of London sits on the northwest perimeter of the city wall—look out the windows to see a crumbling remnant along the street, now called "London Wall."

When Rome could no longer defend the city (A.D. 410), it fell to the Saxons (becoming "Lundenburg") and, later, the Normans (in 1066), who built the Tower of London. Medieval London was devastated by the Black Death plague of 1348. As the city recovered and grew even bigger, it became clear to wannabe kings that whoever controlled London controlled Britain.

When Queen Elizabeth I brought peace to the land, London thrived as a capital of theaters (the Globe and Rose), arts, and ideas. Then, just when things were going so well, the Great Fire of 1666 destroyed the city, leaving London a blank slate.

Next head downstairs to stroll through a multimedia **"plea-sure garden"** and take a **"Victorian walk"** through a re-creation of a London street, experiencing what it was like to live in the world's greatest city. The interesting costume section helps humanize all the history.

Two world wars and the car changed 20th-century London into a concrete jungle. But it remained a cultural capital of elegance (see an Art Deco elevator from Selfridge's) and a global trendsetter (Beatles-era memorabilia).

In the last room, you'll see the museum's prized possession—an example of the opulence of rebuilt Georgian London. The **Lord Mayor's Coach,** a golden carriage pulled by six white horses, looks as if it pranced right out of the pages of *Cinderella*. At the back of this room, a touching memorial to the victims of the terrorist bombings of July 7, 2005, weaves contemporary London into the tapestry of history.

The Monument
Wren's 202-foot-tall tribute to London's 1666 Great Fire was recently restored. Climb the 331 steps inside the column for a monumental view of The City.

Cost and Hours: £3, £10.50 combo-ticket with Tower Bridge, daily 9:30-18:00, until 17:30 Oct-March, last entry 30 minutes before closing, junction of Monument Street and Fish Street Hill, Tube: Monument, tel. 020/7626-2717, www.themonument.info.

TOWER OF LONDON AND NEARBY
▲▲▲Tower of London
The Tower has served as a castle in wartime, a king's residence in peacetime, and, most notoriously, as the prison and execution site of rebels. You can see the crown jewels, take a witty Beefeater tour, and ponder the executioner's block that dispensed with troublesome heirs to the throne and a couple of Henry VIII's wives.

Note that lines can be long for this sight; see page 276 for tips on getting in quickly. After your visit, consider taking the boat to Greenwich from here (see cruise info on page 40).

Cost and Hours: £22, family-£57 (prices include a 10 percent optional donation); March-Oct Tue-Sat 9:00-17:30, Sun-Mon 10:00-17:30; Nov-Feb Tue-Sat 9:00-16:30, Sun-Mon 10:00-16:30; last entry 30 minutes before closing; free Beefeater tours available, skippable audioguide-£4, Tube: Tower Hill, switchboard tel. 0844-482-7777, www.hrp.org.uk.

○ See the Tower of London Tour chapter.

Tower Bridge

The iconic Tower Bridge (often mistakenly called London Bridge) has been recently painted and restored. The hydraulically powered drawbridge was built in 1894 to accommodate the growing East End. While fully modern, its design was a retro Neo-Gothic look.

The bridge is most interesting when the drawbridge lifts to let ships pass, as it does a thousand times a year, but it's best viewed from outside the museum. For the bridge-lifting schedule, check the website or call.

You can tour the bridge at the **Tower Bridge Exhibition,** with a history display and a peek at the Victorian engine room that lifts the span. It's overpriced, though the city views from the walkways are spectacular.

Cost and Hours: £9, £10.50 combo-ticket with Monument, daily 10:00-18:00 in summer, 9:30-17:30 in winter, last entry 30 minutes before closing, enter at northwest tower, Tube: Tower Hill, tel. 020/7403-3761, www.towerbridge.org.uk.

Nearby: The best remaining bit of London's **Roman Wall** is just north of the Tower (at the Tower Hill Tube station). The chic **St. Katharine Dock,** just east of Tower Bridge, has private yachts, mod shops, the recommended medieval banquet, and the classic Dickens Inn, fun for a drink or pub lunch. Across the bridge, on the South Bank, is the upscale Butlers Wharf area, as well as City Hall, museums, the Jubilee Walkway, and, towering overhead, the Shard. Or you can head north to Liverpool Street Station, and follow my **East End Walk** (described next).

East London

▲East End Walk: Markets, Banglatown, and Jack the Ripper

The East End has a long history as London's poorer side of town—even in medieval times, this was the less desirable end, in part because it was downwind from the noxious hide-tanning district. London's east/west disparity was exacerbated in Victorian times, when the wind carried the pollution of a newly industrialized London. These days, it still lacks the posh refinement of the West End—but the area just beyond Liverpool Street Station is now one of London's hippest, most fun spots. Take a walk around the Spitalfields Market neighborhood to see the colorful mix of bustling markets, late-night dance clubs, the Bangladeshi ghetto, and tenements of Jack the Ripper's London, all in the shadow of glittering new skyscrapers. This walk—which takes about an hour without stopping to slurp a curry or shop the markets—is best on Sunday afternoons, when the Spitalfields, Petticoat Lane, and Backyard markets thrive (for more on these markets, see page 449).

Getting There: Ride the Tube to Liverpool Street, and head into the train station. Exit the busy station through the Bishopsgate exit (with your back to the train tracks, it's on your left and up the stairs/escalators).

◐Self-Guided Walk: Outside the train station, cross Bishopsgate street and turn left—you'll pass Dirty Dick's Pub on the right (this is where we'll end our walk). Continue two blocks ahead to the glassy, modern RBS building, then turn right on Brushfield Street; from here you can see the steeple of Christ Church (described later).

On the left side of the street, veer left through the small plaza and into a covered arcade that leads to **Spitalfields Market.** Explore this lively, inviting, modern-feeling market hall, boasting a combination of colorful restaurants, shops, and—on many days—market stalls selling upscale crafts. While the eateries here are tempting, consider waiting for the Bangladeshi curry joints coming up soon on this walk.

Exit the market at the far eastern end through the "Spitfire" gate. Across busy Commercial Street (at the intersection with Brushfield/Fournier Street) is the working-class **Ten Bells Pub.** Established in 1753, it was the hangout of one of Jack the Ripper's victims. Across the street from the pub is **Christ Church,** with its towering 225-foot steeple. Many

Ripper witnesses could help pinpoint the time of the crimes by remembering the church bells' chimes.

From the pub, cross the street and continue east along the left side of the church, heading one long block down **Fournier Street,** which is lined with classic brick tenement houses (though "tenement" now carries a negative connotation, it originally just described any urban apartment building). With the old lampposts and few signs of modern life, it's not hard to imagine how this gaslit street would have looked on a foggy night in Jack the Ripper's time. Keep going toward the end of the street.

When you reach Brick Lane, you're suddenly immersed in **"Banglatown,"** London's highest concentration of Bangladeshi residents. Immediately on your left is the neighborhood mosque, **Jamme Masjid**—also called the Great London Mosque. This building has a history as dynamic as London itself: It was built as a Huguenot chapel and then used as a Methodist chapel and a Jewish synagogue before being converted into a mosque in 1976. Notice the slender, new, metallic minaret.

Wander north (to the left) up **Brick Lane,** window-shopping for lunch or dinner. Here in "the curry capital of Europe," neon signs advertise cheap meals, and out front, pitchmen jockey for your business. The slightest hesitation on your part will result in an offer of a 20 percent discount. This is a great place to sample "Ruby Murray" (Cockney rhyming slang for "curry"—see page 258).

After two blocks is the former **Truman Brewery,** which now houses a Sunday market, trendy shops, and Café 1001 (good coffee). A half-block farther north, you'll find the old brewery smokestack. This is the epicenter of a youthful, trendy scene with several lively pub/café/nightclubs (including Vibe Bar and 93 Feet East).

Now turn around and backtrack south on Brick Lane, passing the mosque at Fournier Street (where you entered this street); continue another block and turn right (west) on **Fashion Street.** Though it twists around and changes names several times, this road leads straight back to the Liverpool Street Station. Along the way (on the left just after you start down Fashion Street), you'll pass the Islamic-looking **Abraham Davis' Moorish Market,** now housing high-tech businesses.

When you hit busy Commercial Street, cross it, then veer left, and detour a block south on Toynbee Street—past a hair salon called "Jack the Clipper"—then right on **Brune Street.** Here you'll see more Industrial Age tenements, the "Soup Kitchen for the Jewish Poor" (see engraved sign on building on right, at #9), and, to the left, a peek-a-boo view of the modern, bullet-shaped building known around here as "the Gherkin." Modernization is changing this neighborhood. At the end of the block, turn right onto Tenter Ground, the street where weavers once dried cloth "on tenterhooks," giving us the phrase that means "uneasy."

Tenter Ground leads you back to White's Row (at the parking garage). Turn left onto narrow **Artillery Lane,** which soon becomes the atmospheric **Artillery Passage,** lined with tiny eateries—giving you an idea of how densely packed this neighborhood was when it was filled with grimy-faced 19th-century factory workers.

At the intersection with Sandy's Row are the **bollards** (black-white-red stakes in the pavement), alerting you that you're officially leaving the East End and entering the City of London.

Continue west one block on Widegate Street to busy Middlesex Street. Just to the left, along Middlesex Street, is the start of **Petticoat Lane Market.** One of the oldest markets in Britain, this one has existed here in some form for more than 400 years.

Continuing straight on Middlesex Street, you'll again see **Dirty Dick's Pub** on the corner (although the name has a history, the pub itself doesn't). Turn left and cross the street to return to the **Liverpool Street** train and Tube stations. At 8:45 on July 7, 2005, a Tube train had just pulled out of Liverpool Street Station when it was rocked by a terrorist bomb—the first of four to hit London that day. But the next day, Londoners were back on the Tube.

▲Geffrye Museum

This low-key but well-organized museum—housed in an 18th-century almshouse—is located north of Liverpool Street Station in the hip Shoreditch area. Its displays give a historical overview of the "middling sort" (middle class), as seen through the prism of home decor. Walk past 11 English living rooms, furnished and decorated in styles from 1600 to 2000, then descend the circular stairs to see changing exhibits. In summer, explore the fragrant herb garden.

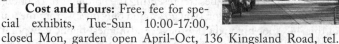

Cost and Hours: Free, fee for special exhibits, Tue-Sun 10:00-17:00, closed Mon, garden open April-Oct, 136 Kingsland Road, tel. 020/7739-9893, www.geffrye-museum.org.uk.

Getting There: Take the Tube to Liverpool Street, then ride the bus 10 minutes north (bus #149 or #242—leave station through

Bishopsgate exit and head left a few steps to find stop; hop off at the Hoxton Station stop, just after passing the brick museum on the right). Or take the East London line on the Overground to the Hoxton stop, which is right next to the museum (Tube tickets and Oyster cards also valid on Overground).

The South Bank

The South Bank of the Thames is a thriving arts and cultural center, tied together by the riverfront Jubilee Walkway.

▲Jubilee Walkway

This riverside path is a popular, pub-crawling pedestrian promenade that stretches all along the South Bank, offering grand views of the Houses of Parliament and St. Paul's. On a sunny day, this is the place to see Londoners out strolling. The Walkway hugs the river except just east of London Bridge, where it cuts inland for a couple of blocks. It has been expanded into a 60-mile "Greenway" circling the city, including the 2012 Olympics site.

▲▲London Eye

This giant Ferris wheel, towering above London opposite Big Ben, is one of the world's highest observational wheels and London's

answer to the Eiffel Tower. Riding it is a memorable experience, even though London doesn't have much of a skyline, and the price is borderline outrageous. Whether you ride or not, the wheel is a sight to behold.

Designed like a giant bicycle wheel, it's a pan-European undertaking: British steel and Dutch engineering, with Czech, German, French, and Italian mechanical parts. It's also very "green," running extremely efficiently and virtually silently. Twenty-five people ride in each of its 32 air-conditioned capsules (representing the boroughs of London) for the 30-minute rotation (you go around only once). From the top of this 443-foot-high wheel—the second-highest public viewpoint in the city—even Big Ben looks small. Built to celebrate the new millennium, the Eye has become a permanent fixture on the London skyline.

After buying your ticket inside, you'll be aggressively ushered

into the *London Eye 4-D Experience*, a brief (four-minute) and engaging show combining a 3-D movie with wind and water effects. This bombastic ad for the attraction you already bought a ticket for, in some ways, is more exciting than riding the Eye itself. You can politely skip the show if you just want to get on the wheel, and you have the option of coming back later to see the movie (which is free to enter, even if you don't buy a ticket for the Eye).

Cost: £20, family ticket available, about 10 percent cheaper if bought online. Buy tickets in advance at www.londoneye.com, by calling 0870-500-0600, or in person at the box office (in the corner of the County Hall building nearest the Eye). A combo-ticket that also covers Madame Tussauds Waxworks is also cheaper online.

Hours: Daily April-Aug 10:00-21:00, Sept-March 10:00-20:30, these are last-ascent times, open later on weekends, closed Dec 25 and a few days in Jan for annual maintenance, Tube: Waterloo or Westminster. Thames boats come and go from Waterloo Pier at the foot of the wheel.

Crowd-Beating Tips: The London Eye is busiest between 11:00 and 17:00, especially on weekends year-round and every day in July and August. You might have to wait up to 30 minutes to buy your ticket, then another 30-45 minutes to board your capsule—it's best to call ahead or go online to prebook your ticket during these times. To retrieve your ticket at the sight, punch your confirmation code into the machine in the ticket office (or pick it up in the short "Groups and Ticket Collection" line at desk #5). Even if you pre-reserve, you still have to wait a bit to board the wheel. You can pay an extra £10 for a Fast Track ticket that lets you jump the queue, but it's probably not worth the expense.

By the Eye: The area next to the London Eye has developed a cotton-candy ambience of kitschy, kid-friendly attractions. There's an aquarium, game arcade, and London Film Museum dedicated to movies filmed in London, from *Harry Potter* to *Star Wars* (not to be confused with the far superior British Film Institute, a.k.a. the BFI Southbank, just to the east).

▲▲Imperial War Museum

This impressive museum covers the wars of the last century—from World War I biplanes, to the rise of fascism, to Montgomery's Africa campaign tank, to the Cold War, the Cuban Missile Crisis, the Troubles in Northern Ireland, the wars in Iraq and Afghanistan, and terrorism. Rather than glorify war, the museum encourages an

The South Bank

THE TEMPLE

Temple

Blackfriars

COURTAULD GALLERY

VICTORIA EMBANKMENT

SOMERSET HOUSE

BLACKFRIARS PIER

BLACKFRIARS BRIDGE

THE STRAND

Thames River

Jubilee Walkway

OXO TOWER

BANK

Trafalgar Square

CHARING CROSS STATION

WATERLOO BRIDGE

Charing Cross

Embank-ment

EMBANKMENT PIER

BFI SOUTHBANK

UPPER GROUND

STAMFORD ST.

SOUTHWARK ST.

FESTIVAL PIER

SOUTH BANK

WHITEHALL

VICTORIA EMBANKMENT

GOLDEN JUBILEE BRIDGE

BELVEDERE RD.

LONDON EYE

Jubilee Gardens

Waterloo

Southwark

BLACKFRIARS RD.

WATERLOO PIER

YORK RD.

WATERLOO STATION

WATERLOO RD.

PARK ST.

WEST-MINSTER PIER

FORMER COUNTY HALL

THE BOROUGH

West-minster

WESTMINSTER

BIG BEN & PARLIAMENT

WESTMINSTER BR. RD.

Lambeth North

BOROUGH

ST. THOMAS' HOSPITAL

LONDON RD.

WEST-MINSTER ABBEY

SOUTH PALACE RD.

Arch-bishop's Park

ST. GEORGE'S RD.

MILLBANK

To Tate Britain

LAMBETH RD.

IMPERIAL WAR MUSEUM

Harmsworth Park

Elephant & Castle

SIGHTS

understanding of the history of modern warfare and the wartime experience, including the effect it has on the everyday lives of peo-

ple back home. The museum's coverage never neglects the human side of one of civilization's more uncivilized, persistent traits.

Allow plenty of time, as this powerful museum—with lots of artifacts and video clips—can be engrossing. The highlights are the new WWI galleries (renovated to commemorate the 100-year anniversary of that conflict) and the WWII area, the "Secret War" section, and the Holocaust exhibit. War wonks love the place, as do general history buffs who enjoy patiently reading displays. For the rest, there are enough interactive experiences and multimedia exhibits and submarines for the kids to climb in to keep it interesting.

The museum (which sits in an inviting park equipped with an equally inviting café) is housed in what had been the Royal Bethlam Hospital. Also known as "the Bedlam asylum," the place

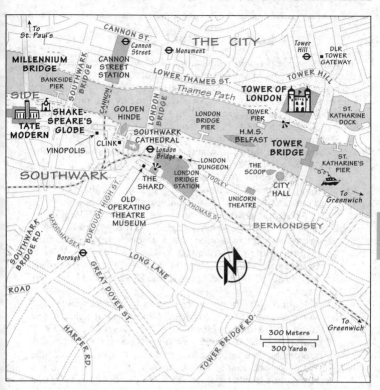

was so wild that it gave the world a new word for chaos. Back in Victorian times, locals—without reality shows and YouTube—paid admission to visit the asylum on weekends for entertainment.

Cost and Hours: Free, daily 10:00-18:00, last entry 17:45, special exhibits extra, audioguide-£3.50, guided tours usually Sat-Sun at 11:30 and 13:30—confirm at info desk, Tube: Lambeth North or Elephant and Castle; buses #3, #12, and #159 come here from Westminster area; tel. 020/7416-5000, www.iwm.org.uk.

Visiting the Museum: Start with the museum's latest pride and joy: the recently renovated WWI galleries. Comprehensive exhibits narrate the war's history through the lives of those on the front lines and on the home front. Displays include a simulated supply line—showing what it took to keep the troops fed and ready to fight—and a re-created trench, complete with sound effects.

Then head into the WWII section that explains the Blitzkrieg and its effects, and visit the Family in Wartime exhibit, which tells the story of one London family during the war.

The **cinema** on the ground floor shows a rotating selection of films. Up on the first floor, you'll get the best view of the entry hall's **large exhibits**—including an awesome 50-foot V-2 rocket

London's Best Views

Though London is a height-challenged city, you can get lofty perspectives on it from several high-flying places. For some viewpoints, you need to pay admission (cheapest at The Monument), and at the bars or restaurants, you'll need to buy a drink; the only truly free spots are Primrose Hill, the rooftop terrace of a shopping mall next to St. Paul's Cathedral, and the viewpoint in front of Greenwich's Royal Observatory.

London Eye: Ride the giant Ferris wheel for stunning London views. See page 82.

St. Paul's Dome: You'll earn a striking, unobstructed view by climbing hundreds of steps to the cramped balcony of the church's cupola. See the St. Paul's Cathedral Tour chapter.

City Rooftop Terrace: Get fine, free views of St. Paul's Cathedral and surroundings—nearly as good as those from St. Paul's Dome—from the rooftop terrace of the shopping mall just behind and east of the church. See page 73.

Tate Modern: Take in a classic vista across the Thames from the museum's level-6 restaurant and bar. See the Tate Modern Tour chapter.

The Monument: Though surrounded by modern buildings in the financial district, this 202-foot column memorializing the Great Fire of 1666 affords a nice view of The City. See page 77.

National Portrait Gallery: A mod top-floor restaurant peers over Trafalgar Square and the Westminster neighborhood. See the National Portrait Gallery Tour chapter.

Waterstones Bookstore: Its hip, low-key, top-floor café/bar has reasonable prices and sweeping views of the London Eye,

SIGHTS

(towering up from the ground floor)—the kind the Nazis rained down on London, which could arrive silently and destroy a city block.

The **Secret War** exhibit peeks into the intrigues of espionage in World Wars I and II and in conflicts since. You'll learn about MI5 (Britain's domestic spy corps), MI6 (their international spies—like the CIA), and the Special Operations Executive (SOE), who led espionage efforts during World War II. The exhibit features actual surveillance equipment and poses challenging questions about the role of secrecy in government.

The second floor has the **John Singer Sargent room,** an art gallery of military-themed works; hiding behind the entryway is Sargent's *Gassed* (1919), showing besieged troops in World War I, and other giant canvases. The third-floor section on the **Holo-**

Big Ben, and the Houses of Parliament (see page 22, on Sun bar closes one hour before bookstore, www.5thview.co.uk).

OXO Tower: Perched high over the Thames River, the building's upscale restaurant/bar boasts views over London and St. Paul's, with al fresco dining in good weather (Barge House Street, Tube: Blackfriars, tel. 020/7803-3888, www.harveynichols.com/restaurants/oxo-tower-london).

London Hilton, Park Lane: You'll spot Buckingham Palace, Hyde Park, and the London Eye from Galvin at Windows, a 28th-floor restaurant/bar in an otherwise nondescript hotel (22 Park Lane, Tube: Hyde Park Corner, tel. 020/7208-4021, www.galvinatwindows.com).

The Shard: The observation decks that cap this 1,020-foot-tall skyscraper offer London's most commanding views, but at an outrageously high price. See page 92.

Primrose Hill: For dramatic 360-degree city views, head to the huge grassy expanse at the summit of Primrose Hill, just north of Regent's Park (off Prince Albert Road, Tube: Chalk Farm or Camden Town, www.royalparks.gov.uk/parks/the-regents-park).

The Thames River: Various companies run boat trips on the Thames, offering a unique vantage point and unobstructed, ever-changing views of great landmarks (see page 40).

Royal Observatory Greenwich: Enjoy sweeping views of Greenwich's grand buildings in the foreground, the Docklands' skyscrapers in the middle ground, and The City and central London in the distance.

SIGHTS

caust, one of the best on the subject anywhere, tells the story of Nazi persecution of the Jews and other groups, with powerful videos, artifacts, and fine explanations.

FROM TATE MODERN TO CITY HALL

These sights are in Southwark (SUTH-uck), the core of the tourist's South Bank. Southwark was for centuries the place Londoners would go to escape the rules and decency of the city and let their hair down. Bearbaiting, brothels, rollicking pubs, and theater—you name the dream, and it could be fulfilled just across the Thames. A run-down warehouse district through the 20th century, it's been gentrified with classy restaurants, office parks, pedestrian promenades, major sights (such as the Tate Modern and Shakespeare's Globe), and a colorful collection of lesser sights. The area is easy on foot and a scenic—though circuitous—way to connect the Tower of London with St. Paul's. You'll find more information on these sights in the ○ Bankside Walk chapter.

SIGHTS

▲▲Tate Modern

Dedicated in the spring of 2000, the striking museum across the river from St. Paul's opened the new century with art from the previous one. Its powerhouse collection of Monet, Matisse, Dalí, Picasso, Warhol, and much more is displayed in a converted powerhouse. Of equal interest are the many temporary exhibits featuring more current, cutting-edge art. Each year, the main hall features a different monumental installation by a prominent artist.

Cost and Hours: Free, but £4 donation appreciated, fee for special exhibitions, open daily 10:00-18:00, Fri-Sat until 22:00, last entry to special exhibits 45 minutes before closing, especially crowded on weekend days (crowds thin out on Fri and Sat evenings), guided tours available, videoguide-£4, view restaurant on top floor, cross the Millennium Bridge from St. Paul's; Tube: Southwark, London Bridge, St. Paul's, or Mansion House plus a 10-15-minute walk; or connect by Tate Boat museum ferry from Tate Britain—see page 42; tel. 020/7887-8888, www. tate.org.uk.

● See the Tate Modern Tour chapter.

▲Millennium Bridge

The pedestrian bridge links St. Paul's Cathedral and the Tate Modern across the Thames. This is London's first new bridge in a century. When it opened, the $25 million bridge wiggled when people walked on it, so it promptly closed for repairs; 20 months and $8 million later, it reopened. Nicknamed the "blade of light" for its sleek minimalist design (370 yards long, four yards wide, stainless steel with teak planks), its clever aerodynamic handrails deflect wind over the heads of pedestrians.

▲▲Shakespeare's Globe

This replica of the original Globe Theatre was built, half-timbered and thatched, as it was in Shakespeare's time. (This is the first thatched roof constructed in London since they were outlawed after the Great Fire of 1666.) The Globe originally accommodated 2,200 seated and another 1,000 standing. Today, slightly smaller and leaving space for reasonable aisles, the theater holds 800 seated and 600 groundlings. Its promoters brag that the theater melds "the three A's"—actors, audience, and architecture—with each contributing to the play. The working theater hosts authentic performances of Shakespeare's plays with actors in period costumes, modern interpretations of his works, and some works by other playwrights. For details on attending a play, see page 460.

The Globe complex has four parts: the Globe theater itself, the box office, a museum (called the Exhibition), and the new Sam Wanamaker Playhouse. This indoor Jacobean theater, which is attached to the back of the Globe complex, allows performances to continue through the winter. The horseshoe-shaped venue, seating fewer than 350, uses authentic candle-lighting for period performances. The repertoire focuses less on Shakespeare and more on the work of his contemporaries (Jonson, Marlow, Fletcher), as well as concerts. (For details on getting tickets, see page 460.)

Cost: £13.50 ticket (good all day) includes Exhibition, audioguide, and 40-minute tour of the Globe; when theater is in use, you can tour the Exhibition only for £10.

Hours: The complex is open daily 9:00-17:00. Tours start every 30 minutes; during Globe theater season (late April-early Oct), last tour Mon at 17:00, Tue-Sat at 12:30, Sun at 11:30; located on the South Bank directly across Thames over Southwark Bridge from St. Paul's, Tube: Mansion House or London Bridge plus a 10-minute walk; tel. 020/7902-1400, box office tel. 020/7401-9919, www. shakespearesglobe.com.

Visiting the Globe: You browse on your own in the **Exhibition** (with the included audioguide) through displays of Elizabethan-era costumes and makeup, music, script-printing, and special ef-

fects (the displays change). There are early folios and objects that were dug up on site. Videos and scale models help put Shakespearean theater within the context of the times. (The Globe opened one year after England mastered the seas by defeating the Spanish Armada. The debut play was Shakespeare's *Julius Caesar*.) You'll also learn how they built the replica in modern times, using Elizabethan materials and techniques. Take advantage of the touch screens to delve into specific topics.

You must **tour the theater** at the time stamped on your ticket, but you can come back to the Exhibition museum afterward. A guide (usually an actor) leads you into the theater to see the stage and

the various seating areas for the different classes of people. You take a seat and learn how the new Globe is similar to the old Globe (open-air performances, standing-room by the stage, no curtain) and how it's different (female actors today, lights for night performances, concrete

floor). It's not a backstage tour—you don't see dressing rooms or costume shops or sit in on rehearsals—but the guides are energetic, theatrical, and knowledgeable, bringing the Elizabethan period to life.

Eating: The Swan at the Globe café offers a sit-down restaurant (for lunch and dinner, reservations recommended, tel. 020/7928-9444), a drinks-and-plates bar, and a sandwich-and-coffee cart (daily 9:00-closing, depending on performance times).

Vinopolis

While it seems illogical to have a huge wine museum in beer-loving London, Vinopolis makes a good case. Built over a Roman wine store and filling the massive vaults of an old wine warehouse, the museum offers interactive exhibits that give a light yet earnest history of wine to accompany your sips of various mediocre reds and whites, ports, and champagnes. A few varieties of spirits help keep it interesting. Your visit starts with a 15-minute wine-tasting lesson, then you're let loose.

Ticket prices vary according to how many virtual "tokens" you load onto a card, which you use to dispense your samples through their "enomatic" machines (most wines cost 1-4 tokens). Tapas-style snacks are available, in addition to the three restaurants on site. Booking ahead for Friday and Saturday nights is smart.

Cost and Hours: Self-guided tour options range from £27 (7 tokens) to £38 (16 tokens); also offer packages that include a meal, Wed 18:00-21:30, Thu-Fri 14:00-22:00, Sat 12:00-21:30, Sun 12:00-18:00, closed Mon-Tue, last entry 2 hours before closing (4 hours on Sun), between Shakespeare's Globe and Southwark Cathedral at 1 Bank End, Tube: London Bridge, tel. 020/7940-8300, www.vinopolis.co.uk.

The Clink Prison Museum

Proudly the "original clink," this was, until 1780, where law-abiding citizens threw Southwark troublemakers. Today, it's a low-tech torture museum filling grotty old rooms with papier-mâché gore. There are storyboards about those unfortunate enough to be thrown in the Clink, but little that seriously deals with the fascinating problem of law and order in Southwark, where 18th-century Londoners went for a good time.

Cost and Hours: Overpriced at £7.50; July-Sept daily 10:00-21:00; Oct-June Mon-Fri 10:00-18:00, Sat-Sun until 21:00, last entry 30 minutes before closing; 1 Clink Street, Tube: London Bridge, tel. 020/7403-0900, www.clink.co.uk.

Crossing the Thames on Foot

You can cross the Thames on any of the bridges that carry car traffic over the river, but London's two pedestrian bridges are more fun. The Millennium Bridge (see photo) connects the sedate St. Paul's Cathedral with the great Tate Modern. The Golden Jubilee Bridge, well-lit and with a sleek, futuristic look, links bustling Trafalgar Square on the North Bank with the London Eye and Waterloo Station on the South Bank.

Golden Hinde Replica

This is a full-size replica of the 16th-century warship in which Sir Francis Drake circumnavigated the globe from 1577 to 1580. Commanding the original ship (now long gone), Drake earned his reputation as history's most successful pirate. This replica, however, has logged more than 100,000 miles, including a voyage around the world. While the ship is fun to see, its interior is not worth touring.

Cost and Hours: £6, daily 10:00-17:00, last entry at 16:15, sometimes closed for private events, Tube: London Bridge, ticket office just up Pickfords Wharf from the ship, tel. 020/7403-0123, www.goldenhinde.com.

▲Southwark Cathedral

While made a cathedral only in 1905, it's been the neighborhood church since the 13th century, and comes with some interesting history. The enthusiastic docents give impromptu tours if you ask.

Cost and Hours: Free, but £4 donation requested (you'll likely be approached about the donation, so be prepared with at least £1 or a simple "No"), Mon-Fri 8:00-18:30, Sat-Sun 8:30-18:00—though during frequent services only the back of the nave is open to discreet sightseers, last entry 30 minutes before closing, £4.50 guidebook, no photos without permission (£2), Tube: London Bridge. Tel. 020/7367-6700, http://cathedral.southwark.anglican.org.

Music: The cathedral hosts evensong Sun at 15:00, Tue-Fri 17:30, Sat at 16:00; they also host organ recitals Mon at 13:00 and music recitals Tue at 15:15 (call or check website to confirm times of evensong and recitals).

▲Old Operating Theatre Museum and Herb Garret

Climb a tight and creaky wooden spiral staircase to a church attic where you'll find a garret used to dry medicinal herbs, a fascinating exhibit on Victorian surgery, cases of well-described 19th-century medical paraphernalia, and a special look at "anesthesia, the defeat of pain." Then you stumble upon Britain's oldest operating theater, where limbs were sawed off way back in 1821. (See page 297 for a full description.)

Cost and Hours: £6.50, cash only, borrowable laminated descriptions, daily 10:30-16:45, closed Dec 15-Jan 5, £1 audioguide tries hard but not quite worthwhile, 9a St. Thomas Street, Tube: London Bridge, tel. 020/7188-2679, www.thegarret.org.uk.

The Shard

Rocketing dramatically 1,020 feet above the south end of the London Bridge, this recent addition to London's skyline is by far the tallest building in Western Europe. Designed by Renzo Piano (best known as the co-architect of Paris' Pompidou Center), the glass-clad pyramid shimmers in the sun and its prickly top glows like the city's nightlight after dark. Its uppermost floors are set aside as public viewing galleries, but the ticket price is as outrageously high as the building itself, especially given that it's a bit far from London's most exciting landmarks. For a list of cheaper view opportunities in London, see the sidebar on page 86.

Cost and Hours: £25 if booked at least a day in advance, £30 for same-day reservations, book as soon as you have reasonable chance of assuring decent weather, least crowded on weekday mornings, daily 10:00-22:00, last entry slot at 20:30, Tube: London Bridge—use London Bridge exit, tel. 0844-499-7111, www.theviewfromtheshard.com.

Visiting the Shard: From the entrance on Joiner Street (just off St. Thomas Street) you'll take a two-part elevator ride up to the 68th floor, then climb up one story to the main observation platform. It's equipped with cool telescopes that label major landmarks, and even let you see how the view from here would appear at other times of the day. From here you've got great views of St. Paul's, the Tower of London, Southwark Cathedral (straight down), and, in the distance, the 2012 Olympic stadium in one direction, and the Houses of Parliament in the other (find Buckingham Palace, just left of the Eye). On the clearest days, you can see 40 miles out, and a few people say they've been able to make out ships on the North Sea. Even in bad weather it's mesmerizing to watch the constant movement of the city's transit system, which looks like a model-train set from this height. Climbing up to the 72nd floor gets you to the open-air deck, where the wind roars over the glass enclosure. As you look up, try to picture Prince Andrew rappelling off the very top, which he and 40 others did in 2012 as a charity fundraising stunt.

HMS *Belfast*

The last big-gun armored warship of World War II clogs the Thames just upstream from the Tower Bridge. This huge vessel—now manned with wax sailors—thrills kids who always dreamed of sitting in a turret shooting off their imaginary guns. If you're into WWII warships, this is the ultimate. Otherwise, it's just lots of exercise with a nice view of the Tower Bridge.

Cost and Hours: £16 including 9 percent voluntary donation, includes audioguide, kids under 16 free, daily March-Oct 10:00-18:00, Nov-Feb 10:00-17:00, last entry one hour before closing, Tube: London Bridge, tel. 020/7940-6300, www.iwm.org.uk/visits/hms-belfast.

City Hall

The glassy, egg-shaped building near the south end of Tower Bridge is London's City Hall, designed by Sir Norman Foster, the architect who worked on London's Millennium Bridge and Berlin's Reichstag. Nicknamed "the Armadillo," City Hall houses the office of London's mayor—the blond, flamboyant, conservative former journalist and author Boris Johnson. He consults here with the Assembly representatives of the city's 25 districts. An interior spiral ramp allows visitors to watch and hear the action below in the Assembly Chamber—ride the lift to floor 2 (the highest visitors can go) and spiral down. On

the lower ground floor is a large aerial photograph of London and a handy cafeteria. Next to City Hall is the outdoor amphitheater called The Scoop (see page 464 for info on performances).

Cost and Hours: Free, open to visitors Mon-Thu 8:30-18:00, Fri 8:30-17:30, closed Sat-Sun; Tube: London Bridge station plus 10-minute walk, or Tower Hill station plus 15-minute walk; tel. 020/7983-4000, www.london.gov.uk.

West London

▲▲Tate Britain

One of Europe's great art houses, Tate Britain specializes in British painting from the 16th century through modern times. The recently renovated museum has a good representation of William Blake's religious sketches, the Pre-Raphaelites' naturalistic and detailed art, Gainsborough's aristocratic ladies, and the best collection anywhere of J. M. W. Turner's swirling works.

Cost and Hours: Free but £4 donation requested, admission fee for special exhibits; daily 10:00-18:00, last entry 45 minutes before closing; free tours generally daily; on the Thames River, south of Big Ben and north of Vauxhall Bridge, Tube: Pimlico, Tate Boat museum ferry goes directly to the museum from Tate Modern—see page 42; switchboard tel. 020/7887-8888, www.tate.org.uk.

❂ See the Tate Britain Tour chapter.

Victoria Station

From underneath this station's iron-and-glass canopy, trains depart for the south of England and Gatwick Airport. While Victoria Station is famous and a major Tube stop, few tourists actually take trains from here—most just come to take in the exciting bustle. It's a fun place to just be a "rock in a river" teeming with commuters and services. The station is surrounded by big red buses and taxis, travel agencies, and lousy eateries. It's next to the main intercity bus station (Victoria Coach Station) and the best inexpensive lodgings in town.

Westminster Cathedral

This cathedral, the largest Catholic church in England and just a block from Victoria Station, is strikingly Neo-Byzantine, but not very historic or important to visit. Opened in 1903, the church has an unfinished interior, with a spooky, blackened ceiling waiting for the mosaics that are supposed to be placed there. While it's definitely not Westminster Abbey, half the tourists wandering around inside seem to think it is. Take the lift to the top of the 273-foot bell tower for a view of the glassy office blocks of Victoria Station.

Cost and Hours: Free entry, £5 for the lift; church—daily 7:00-19:00; tower—daily 9:30-17:00, Sat-Sun until 18:00, last trip 30 minutes earlier; 5-minute walk from bus terminus in front of Victoria Station, just off Victoria Street at 42 Francis Street, Tube: Victoria, www.westminstercathedral.org.uk.

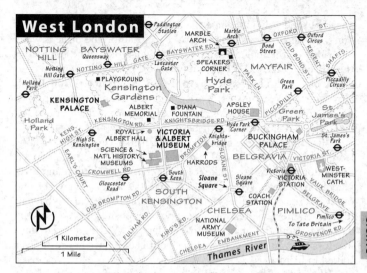

National Army Museum

This museum—which is closed for a major renovation until summer 2016—tells the story of the British army from 1415 through the Bosnian conflict and Iraq, with lots of Redcoat lore and a good look at Waterloo. Kids enjoy trying on a Cromwellian helmet, seeing the skeleton of Napoleon's horse, and peering out from a World War I trench through a working periscope.

Cost and Hours: When it reopens, it will likely be free, daily 10:00-17:30, Royal Hospital Road, Chelsea, Tube: Sloane Square, tel. 020/7730-0717, www.national-army-museum.ac.uk.

HYDE PARK AND NEARBY

A number of worthwhile sights border this grand park, from Apsley House on the east to Kensington Palace on the west.

▲Apsley House (Wellington Museum)

Having beaten Napoleon at Waterloo, Arthur Wellesley, the First Duke of Wellington, was once the most famous man in Europe.

He was given a huge fortune, with which he purchased London's ultimate address, Number One London. His refurbished mansion offers a nice interior, a handful of world-class paintings, and a glimpse at the life of the great soldier and two-time prime minister. Those who know something about Wellington

ahead of time will appreciate the place much more than those who
don't, as there's scarce biographical background. The place is well-
described by the included audioguide, which has sound bites from
the current Duke of Wellington (who still lives at Apsley).

Cost and Hours: £7, April-Oct Wed-Sun 11:00-17:00,
Nov-March Wed-Sun 11:00-16:00, closed Mon-Tue year-round;
no photos, 20 yards from Hyde Park Corner Tube station, tel.
020/7499-5676, www.english-heritage.org.uk.

Visiting the House: An 11-foot-tall marble statue of Napoleon, clad only in a fig leaf, greets you. Napoleon commissioned
the sculptor Canova to make it for him but didn't like it, and after
Napoleon's defeat, Wellington acquired it as a war trophy. It's one
of several images Wellington acquired of his former foe to have in
his home. The two great men were polar opposites—Napoleon the
daring general and champion of revolution, Wellington the play-
it-safe strategist and conservative politician—but they're forever
linked in history.

The core of the collection is a dozen first-floor rooms decorated with fancy wallpaper, chandeliers, a few pieces of furniture,

and wall-to-wall paintings from Wellington's collection. You'll see fancy dinnerware and precious objects given to the
Irish-born general by the crowned heads
of Europe, who were eternally grateful
to him for saving their necks from the
guillotine. The highlight is the large ballroom, the Waterloo Gallery, decorated
with Anthony van Dyck's *Charles I on
Horseback* (over the main fireplace), Diego
Velázquez's earthy *Water-Seller of Seville*
(to the left of Van Dyck), Jan Steen's
playful *Dissolute Household* (to the right). Just outside the door, in
the Portico Room, is a large portrait of Wellington by Francisco
Goya.

Downstairs is a small gallery of Wellington memorabilia, including a pair of Wellington boots, which the duke popularized—
Brits today still call rubber boots "wellies."

Nearby: Hyde Park's pleasant rose garden is picnic-friendly.
Wellington Arch, which stands just across the street, is open to
the public but not worth the £4 charge (or £8.60 combo-ticket with
Apsley House; elevator up, lousy views and boring exhibits).

▲Hyde Park and Speakers' Corner

London's "Central Park," originally Henry VIII's hunting grounds,
has more than 600 acres of lush greenery, "Boris Bikes" rental stations, the huge man-made Serpentine Lake (with rental boats and

a lakeside swimming pool), the royal Kensington Palace (described next), and the ornate Neo-Gothic Albert Memorial across from the Royal Albert Hall (for more about the park, see www.royalparks. org.uk/parks/hyde-park). The western half of the park is known as Kensington Gardens. The park is huge—study a Tube map to choose the stop nearest to your destination.

On Sundays, from just after noon until early evening, **Speakers' Corner** offers soapbox oratory at its best (northeast corner of

the park, Tube: Marble Arch). Characters climb their stepladders, wave their flags, pound emphatically on their sandwich boards, and share what they are convinced is their wisdom. Regulars have resident hecklers who know their lines and are always ready with a verbal jab or barb. "The grass roots of democracy" is actually a holdover from when the gallows stood here and the criminal was allowed to say just about anything he wanted to before he swung. I dare you to raise your voice and gather a crowd—it's easy to do.

The **Princess Diana Memorial Fountain** honors the "People's Princess," who once lived in nearby Kensington Palace. The low-key circular stream, great for cooling off your feet on a hot day, is in the south-central part of the park, near the Albert Memorial and Serpentine Gallery (Tube: Knightsbridge). A similarly named but different sight, the **Diana, Princess of Wales Memorial Playground,** in the park's northwest corner, is loads of fun for kids (Tube: Queensway).

▲▲Kensington Palace

For nearly 150 years (1689-1837), Kensington was the royal residence, before Buckingham Palace became the official home of the monarch. Sitting primly on its pleasant parkside grounds, the palace is immaculately restored and creatively presented, with exhibits designed to appeal to adults and kids alike. It gives a fun glimpse into the lives of several important residents, especially Queen Victoria, who was born and raised here. It's strange to think that, in this city that was so shaped by Victoria, this is London's first and only museum that's truly *about* Victoria. (For more on Victoria's life and times, see the sidebar on page 534.)

After Queen Victoria moved the monarchy to Buckingham

Palace, lesser royals bedded down at Kensington. Princess Diana lived here both during and after her marriage to Prince Charles (1981-1997). More recently, Will and Kate moved into a thoroughly renovated Apartment 1A (the southern flank of the palace complex, with four stories and 20 rooms). And Prince Harry lives in their old digs, a "cottage" on the other side of the main building. However—as many disappointed visitors discover—none of these more recent apartments are open to the public.

Cost and Hours: £16.50 (includes 10 percent optional donation), save £1 by booking online, daily 10:00-18:00, until 17:00 Nov-Feb, last entry one hour before closing, least crowded in mornings, £5 guidebook but friendly and knowledgeable "explainers" will answer questions for free, cloakroom available for bags and luggage, a 10-minute stroll through Kensington Gardens from either High Street Kensington or Queensway Tube stations, tel. 0844-482-7788, www.hrp.org.uk.

➲ **Self-Guided Tour:** Before entering the building, notice the statue of Queen Victoria welcoming you to her birth palace. (The queen's daughter, the feminist bohemian Princess Louise, carved it.) After buying your ticket, head into the vestibule. From here, you can reach any of the three main exhibits. To see them chronologically, head to the right, to start with the...

Queen's State Apartments: This highly conceptual exhibit focuses on the palace's first royal residents, William and Mary. It's 1689, and an optimistic England welcomes King William, a Protestant from the Netherlands, to take the British throne. The grand entrance stairway is decorated to evoke the king's voyage to his new home. Entering the Big Hall, you get a sense of the grandeur of the palace—the dances and banquets held here, with expansive views over landscaped gardens. Sir Christopher Wren built the palace in what was then the peaceful village of Kensington, as an escape from grimy central London. The birds overhead evoke a time when Queen Mary kept songbirds in this room. Find portraits of William and Mary. Parliament had recently overthrown the Catholic King James II in the "Glorious Revolution," and William and Mary represented a new, more democratic start.

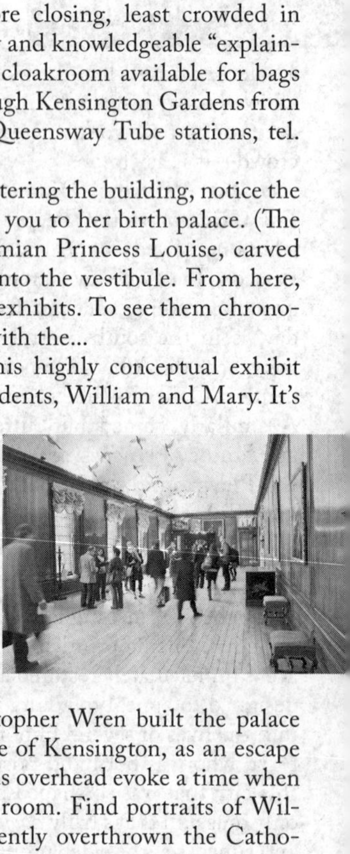

But things would not end well. As you head into the "Whispering Room," the multimedia exhibits murmur rumors of Mary's impending death from smallpox. (The displays were conceived by a theatrical-design company; the helpful staff in each room can explain what's going on.)

When Mary died—childless—she was eventually succeeded by her sister, Anne. In the next room, you're faced with 18 little, empty chairs, representing the 18 failed pregnancies Queen Anne suffered in her desperate attempts to bear an heir. Continuing to the next room, a dreamlike film (projected overhead) shows how Anne finally had one child who survived. But on his 11th birthday, he danced so heartily that he came down with a fever and dropped dead. Who would rule after Anne? In the last room, the 43 tree houses represent the convoluted family tree of would-be kings and queens. Parliament solved the dilemma by inviting the German-born Hanover dynasty (the "King Georges")—whose apartments we see next.

• *Retrace your steps back down to the vestibule hall, then up the grand King's Staircase to the...*

King's State Apartment: These more lavishly decorated rooms give the best look at royal life in the palace. After climb-

ing the staircase (with its colorful murals of courtiers gazing down at you), you enter Room 2, where the king would receive visitors on a raised throne. The next rooms showcase court life during the palace's heyday in the 1700s—the salons attended by wits and intellectuals (held in Room 3); the parties, music, and dancing (in the impressive Room 4); and card games in the drawing room (Room 5). Mannequins in Room 6 wear clothes of the day—men in ruffled sleeves, ladies in wi-i-ide skirts, and the elaborate costume of the prestigious Order of the

Garter. Room 7 has "Mad" King George III's red-and-white, velvet-and-ermine coronation robe, with its 10-foot train. The large Room 8 ends the visit with world-class paintings by Tintoretto *(Esther Before Ahaserus)* and Veronese *(Adoration of the Kings).*

• *Now head back downstairs to the vestibule, and up the stone stairs to the third main exhibit...*

Victoria Revealed: The artifacts here tell the story of Queen Victoria's life, displayed in the very rooms where she grew up. As Victoria was an avid journaler, you'll see excerpts from her own accounts all over the place.

The Red Saloon re-creates her 1837 inauguration day and the

first meeting with her Privy Council. You see the once black but now faded dress the 4'11," 18-year-old monarch wore. A painting on the wall shows the young queen (now dressed in white) facing down a room full of nobility assigned to advise her. Standing at the far right end of the table, find Robert "Bobbie" Peel, who's credited with starting the first professional police force—the "bobbies." As you can see from the painting, the meeting took place in this very room.

The next room commemorates Victoria's marriage to her beloved Prince Albert (see their portraits). The carpets, mirrors, and screen are decorated with passages from their love letters, and Victoria's wedding gown is on display (she began the fashion of brides wearing white). The room to the left is where, most likely, Victoria was born. It has objects from her own childhood (such as her original doll collection) and portraits of her nine children. Continue on to Room 6, which celebrates Prince Albert's Great Exhibition of 1851, including a model of the Crystal Palace—the wonder of its age—that once stood in the park just in front of you.

The room shrouded in dark drapes evokes Albert's sudden and tragic death from typhoid fever: You see the heart-shaped locket that holds a lock of Albert's hair, and the book that his family read to him in his final hours. Victoria would dress in black for the rest of her life. She lived to be 82, and you can watch footage of her Diamond Jubilee celebration. Finally, the exhibit ends with an eclectic collection of items belonging to the royal couple, including Albert's dressing case (with his tongue scraper), and Victoria's watercolor box and Transylvanian jewelry. Before you exit, stand on the balcony, in the footsteps of the 16-year-old princess, and imagine her thoughts as she watched the young Prince Albert stride through the doors below for the first time.

Outside: Garden enthusiasts enjoy popping into the secluded Sunken Garden, 50 yards from the exit. Consider afternoon tea at the nearby Orangery (see page 434), built as a greenhouse for Queen Anne in 1704. On the south side of the palace are the golden gates that became famous in 1997 as the backdrop to the sea of flowers left here by Princess Diana's mourners.

▲▲▲Victoria and Albert Museum

The world's top collection of decorative arts encompasses 2,000 years of art and design (ceramics, stained glass, fine furniture, clothing, jewelry, carpets, and more), displaying a surprisingly interesting and diverse assortment of crafts from the West, as well as Asian and Islamic cultures. There's much to see, including Raphael's tapestry cartoons, five of Leonardo da Vinci's notebooks, the huge Islamic Ardabil Carpet (4,914 knots in every 10 square centimeters), and a cast of Trajan's Column that depicts the emperor's conquests—not to mention the catsuit Mick Jagger wore for the Rolling Stones' 1972 world tour.

Cost and Hours: Free, but £3 donation requested, extra for some special exhibits, daily 10:00-17:45, some galleries open Fri until 22:00, free tours daily, on Cromwell Road in South Kensington, Tube: South Kensington, from the Tube station a long tunnel leads directly to museum, tel. 020/7942-2000, www.vam.ac.uk.

✪ See the Victoria and Albert Museum Tour chapter.

▲▲Natural History Museum

Across the street from the Victoria and Albert, this mammoth museum is housed in a giant and wonderful Victorian, Neo-

Romanesque building. In the main hall, above a big dinosaur skeleton and under a massive slice of sequoia tree, Charles Darwin sits as if upon a throne overseeing it all. Built in the 1870s specifically for the huge collection (50 million specimens), the building has several color-coded "zones" that cover everything from life ("creepy crawlies," human biology, "our place in evolution," and awe-inspiring dinosaurs) to earth science (meteors, volcanoes, earthquakes, and so on). Pop in, if only for the wild collection of dinosaurs—including a realistic animatronic T-rex—and to hear English children exclaim, "Oh, my goodness!"

Cost and Hours: Free, but £3 donation requested, fees for (optional) special exhibits, daily 10:00-17:50, open later last Fri of the month, last entry 20 minutes before closing, long tunnel leads directly from South Kensington Tube station to museum, tel. 020/7942-5000, exhibit info and reservations tel. 020/7942-5011, www.nhm.ac.uk.

Visiting the Museum: Use the helpful map (£1 suggested donation) to find your way through the collection. Exhibits are wonderfully explained, with lots of creative, interactive displays. Get oriented by talking with one of the many helpful guides scattered throughout the museum, review the "What's on Today" board for special events and tours, and note which sections are closed (according to the signs, these sections aren't being "renovated," but are "evolving"). While the dinosaur hall might have a long line, everything else is wide open. Up the main stairs, above and behind Darwin, is the Treasures Gallery, housing a rotating display of the museum's greatest hits, including a dodo skeleton, moon rock, stuffed specimen of the extinct great auk, and the iguanodon tooth that kicked off human awareness of dinosaurs.

Way over in the red zone, you can ride a dramatic escalator up one floor to experience an earthquake. Don't miss the vault in the mineralogy section (top floor of the green zone), with rare and precious stones, including a meteorite from Mars, the Aurora Pyramid of Hope—displaying 296 diamonds showing their full range of natural colors—and this description of some microscopic cosmic diamonds: "These are the oldest things you will ever see."

▲Science Museum

Next door to the Natural History Museum, this sprawling wonderland for curious minds is kid-perfect, with themes such as measuring time, exploring space, climate change, and the evolution of modern medicine. It offers hands-on fun, from moonwalks to deep-sea exploration, with trendy technology exhibits, a state-of-the-art IMAX theater (shows-£10, £8 for kids, £27 family ticket), and the Garden, a cool play area for children up to age seven.

Cost and Hours: Free, daily 10:00-18:00, until 19:00 during school holidays, last entry 45 minutes before closing, Exhibition Road, Tube: South Kensington, tel. 0870-870-4868, www.sciencemuseum.org.uk.

Greater London

EAST OF LONDON

▲▲Greenwich

This borough of London—an easy boat trip or DLR (light rail) journey from downtown—combines majestic, picnic-perfect parks; the stately trappings of Britain's proud nautical heritage (the newly restored *Cutty Sark* clipper; the over-the-top-ornate retirement home for sailors at the **Old Royal Naval College;** and the comprehensive **National Maritime Museum**); and the **Royal Observatory Greenwich,** with a fine museum on the evolution of seafaring and a chance to straddle the eastern and western hemispheres at the Prime Meridian. An affordable jaunt from central London, and boasting several top-notch museums (including some free ones), Greenwich is worth considering and easy to combine with a look at the Docklands (described next).

❂ See the Greenwich Tour chapter.

▲▲The Docklands

Once the primary harbor for the Port of London, the Docklands has been transformed into a vibrant business center, with ultra-tall skyscrapers, subterranean supermalls, trendy pubs, and peaceful parks with pedestrian bridges looping over canals. It also boasts the very good **Museum of London Docklands,** which illuminates the gritty and fascinating history of the port. While not full of the touristy sights that many are seeking in London, the Docklands offers a refreshing look at the British version of a 21st-century city. It's best at the end of the workday, when it's lively with office workers. It's ideal to see on your way back from Greenwich, since both line up on the same train tracks.

✪ See The Docklands Walk chapter.

Queen Elizabeth Olympic Park

London refashioned this park—the biggest new park to open in the city in a century—from the site of the 2012 Olympic Games. You'll find miles of parkland trails and waterways, kids' play areas, an array of sporting venues (London Aquatics Centre, Lee Valley VeloPark, Copper Box Arena), quirky sculpture, and places to eat. The park is huge—bigger than Hyde Park/Kensington Gardens. It's also quite beautiful, laced with canals and tributaries of the Lea River. The best overview of the park is along a 500-yard-long berm called the **Greenway,** which sits at the park's southern perimeter. The easiest landmark to head for is the **View Tube,** a covered shelter with a free lookout tower, café, WC, and maps. There's also the hard-to-miss red, 350-foot viewing tower called the **Orbit,** which was designed as an Eiffel-Tower-like landmark for London and has been compared to a vertical roller coaster and a giant hookah. For help in planning your visit, drop by the "Information Point" near the Aquatics Centre, where you can also ask about a tour with a Blue Badge guide (£10, Thu and Sat at 11:00).

Cost and Hours: Free and always open, toll-free tel. 0800-0722-110, www.queenelizabetholympicpark.co.uk.

Getting There: From central London by Tube, it's a 30-minute ride to the Stratford station. Take the escalator up to street level (which is actually the outdoor part of a shopping center), bear left past The Cow pub, and the park is directly ahead of you, across the road.

WEST OF LONDON
▲▲Kew Gardens

For a fine riverside park and a palatial greenhouse jungle to swing through, take the Tube or the boat to every botanist's favorite escape, Kew Gardens. While to most visitors the Royal Botanic Gardens of Kew are simply a delightful opportunity to wander among 33,000 different types of plants, to the hardworking organization that runs them, the gardens are a way to promote the understanding and preservation of the botanical diversity of our planet.

SIGHTS

Cost and Hours: £16.50 (includes £2 suggested donation), discounted to £12.50 45 minutes before glasshouses close, kids under 17 free; April-Aug Mon-Fri 9:30-18:30, Sat-Sun 9:30-19:30, closes earlier Sept-March—check schedule online, last entry to gardens 30 minutes before closing, glasshouses close at 17:30 in high season—earlier off-season, free one-hour walking tours daily at 11:00 and 13:30, Tube: Kew Gardens, boats run April-Oct between Kew Gardens and Westminster Pier—see page 40, switchboard tel. 020/8332-5000, recorded info tel. 020/8332-5655, www.kew.org.

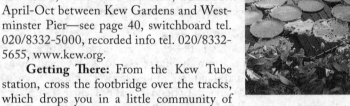

Getting There: From the Kew Tube station, cross the footbridge over the tracks, which drops you in a little community of plant-and-herb shops, a two-block walk from Victoria Gate (the main garden entrance).

Visiting the Gardens: Pick up a map brochure and check at the gate for a monthly listing of the best blooms. Garden lov-

ers could spend days exploring Kew's 300 acres. For a quick visit, spend a fragrant hour wandering through three buildings: the Palm House, a humid Victorian world of iron, glass, and tropical plants that was built in 1844; a Waterlily House that Monet would swim for (see photo below); and the Princess of Wales Conservatory, a meandering modern greenhouse with many different climate zones growing countless cacti, bug-munching carnivorous plants, and more. With extra time, check out the Xstrata Treetop Walkway, a 200-yard-long scenic steel walkway that puts you high in the canopy 60 feet above the ground. Young kids will love the Climbers and Creepers indoor/outdoor playground and little zip line, as well as a slow and easy ride on the hop-on, hop-off Kew Explorer tram (£4 for narrated 40-minute ride, departs on the hour from 11:00 from near Victoria Gate, 2/hour in summer).

Eating: For a sun-dappled lunch or snack, walk 10 minutes from the Palm House to the Orangery Cafeteria (£4 sandwiches, £8-12 lunches, daily 10:00-17:30, until 15:15 in winter, closes early for events).

▲Hampton Court Palace

Fifteen miles up the Thames from downtown, the 500-year-old palace of Henry VIII is worth ▲▲ for palace aficionados. Actually, it was originally the palace of his minister, Cardinal Wolsey. When Wolsey, a clever man, realized Henry VIII was experiencing a little palace envy, he gave the mansion to his king. The Tudor palace was also home to Elizabeth I and Charles I. Sections were updated by Christopher Wren for William and Mary. The stately palace stands overlooking the Thames and includes some fine Tudor rooms, including a Great Hall with a magnificent hammer-beam ceiling. The industrial-strength Tudor kitchen was capable of keeping 600 schmoozing courtiers thoroughly—if not well—fed. The sculpted garden features a rare Tudor tennis court and a popular maze.

The palace tries hard to please, but it doesn't quite sparkle. From the information center in the main courtyard, you can pick

SIGHTS

up audioguides for self-guided tours of various wings of the palace (free but slow, aimed mostly at school-aged children). For more in-depth information, strike up a conversation with the costumed characters or docents posted in each room. The Tudor portions of the castle, including the rooms dedicated to the young Henry, are most interesting; the Georgian rooms are pretty dull. The maze in the nearby garden is a curiosity some find fun (maze free with palace ticket, otherwise £5).

Cost and Hours: £18.20, family-£46.80 (both prices include a 10 percent optional donation); online discounts, daily April-Oct 10:00-18:00, Nov-March 10:00-16:30, last entry one hour before closing, café, tel. 0844-482-7777 or 020/3166-6000, www.hrp.org.uk.

Getting There: The train (2/hour, 35 minutes, Oyster cards OK) from London's Waterloo Station drops you across the river from the palace (just walk across the bridge). Consider arriving at or departing from the palace by boat (connections with London's Westminster Pier, see page 40); it's a relaxing and scenic three- to four-hour cruise past two locks and a fun new/old riverside mix.

Kew Gardens/Hampton Court Blitz: Because these two sights are in the same general direction (about £20 for a taxi between the two), you can visit both in one day. Here's a game plan: Start your morning at Hampton Court, tour the palace and garden, and have a Tudor-style lunch in the atmospheric dining hall. After lunch, take bus #R68 from Hampton Court Station to Richmond (40 minutes), then transfer to bus #65, which will drop you off at the Kew Gardens gate (5 minutes). After touring the gardens, have tea in the Orangery, then Tube or boat back to London.

NORTH OF LONDON
Royal Air Force Museum London
A hit with aviation enthusiasts, this huge aerodrome and airfield contain planes from World War II's Battle of Britain up through the Gulf War. You can climb inside some of the planes, try your luck in a cockpit, and fly with the Red Arrows in a flight simulator.

Cost and Hours: Free, daily 10:00-18:00, last entry 30 minutes before closing, café, shop, parking-£2.50 for up to 3 hours, Grahame Park Way, 30-minute ride from downtown London, Tube: Colindale—top of Northern Line Edgware branch, tel. 020/8205-2266, www.rafmuseum.org.uk.

Hampstead Heath
This surprisingly vast expanse of greenery sprawls over a square mile and a quarter at the northern edge of downtown London. It features rolling, scrubby pastures ("heath") as well as tranquil wooded areas. Its most popular viewpoint, Parliament Hill, offers distant views of London's fast-growing skyline. At the northeast corner of the park is a chunk of land owned by English Heritage, where a stately palace called Kenwood House overlooks a pasture, pond, and gentle wood; inside is  a fine art collection, plus an inviting café (and WCs). Maps posted at each entrance to the park help get you oriented. On a sunny day, the park is crammed with Londoners communing with nature—relieved to escape from their bustling burg. The adjoining village of Hampstead is quaint and cute; a stroll through here is almost as pleasant as the park itself.

Getting There: Hampstead Heath is just a 20-minute Tube ride from downtown London. The handiest Tube stop is the one called Hampstead (on the convenient Northern line/Edgware branch, which runs north to south through London's city center). This stop is in the middle of the charming village of Hampstead, from which it's about a 10-minute, gently uphill walk—passing pubs and homes—to the park. The station called Hampstead Heath, directly at the southern tip of the park, is on the less convenient Overground line; however, bus #24 easily (though slowly) connects Victoria Station and downtown London (including Trafalgar Square) with the Hampstead Heath stop.

Hampstead Heath combines well with a visit to the fun and funky Camden Lock Market (see page 448), which is on both the Northern Tube line and the bus #24 route.

Highgate Cemetery

Located in the tea-cozy-cute village of Highgate, north of the city, this Victorian cemetery represents a fascinating, offbeat piece of London history. Built as a private cemetery, this was the fashionable place to bury the wealthy dead in the late 1800s. It has themed mausoleums, professional mourners, and several high-profile residents in its East Cemetery, including Karl Marx, George Eliot, and Douglas Adams. The tomb of "Godfather of Punk" Malcolm McLaren (former manager of the Sex Pistols) is often covered with rotten veggies.

Cost and Hours: East Cemetery—£4, Mon-Fri 10:00-17:00, Sat-Sun 11:00-17:00, last entry 30 minutes before closing; older, creepier West Cemetery—viewable by £12 guided tour only, Mon-Fri at 14:00—arrive by 13:45, Sat-Sun hourly 11:00-15:00, call ahead or reserve online for weekday tours; Tube: Archway (Northern Line/High Barnet branch) or—slower—bus #C2 from Victoria Station or Oxford Circus, tel. 020/8340-1834, www.highgatecemetery.org.

The Making of Harry Potter:
Warner Bros. Studio Tour London

While you can visit several real-life locations in Britain where the Harry Potter movies were filmed (see sidebar on page 108), there's only one way to see imaginary places like Hogwarts' Great Hall, Diagon Alley, Dumbledore's office, and the interior of #4 Privet Drive: by visiting the Warner Bros. studios in Leavesden, where Daniel Radcliffe and company brought the tale of the boy wizard to life. You'll begin with a brief guided tour, then be set free to explore on your own.

Attractions include the actual sets used for the films, several familiar costumes and props (such as the Nimbus 2000, the Sorting Hat, the Sword of Gryffindor, and Hagrid's motorcycle), video interviews with the actors and filmmakers, and exhibits about how the films' special effects were created. As this attraction is understandably popular, it's essential to reserve your visit online as far ahead as you can (entrance possible only with reserved time slot). Allowing about three hours for your time at the studio, plus the time it takes to get there and back, this experience will eat up the better part of a day.

Cost and Hours: £30, kids ages 5 to 15-£22.50, family ticket for 2 adults and 2 kids-£89, £5 extra for audio/videoguide; opening hours flex with season—first tour at 9:00 or 10:00, last tour as early as 16:00 or as late as 18:30; café, still photography allowed, tel. 0845-084-0900, www.wbstudiotour.co.uk.

Getting There: Leavesden is about 20 miles northwest of London. Reaching the studio requires a **train and shuttle bus**

Harry Potter's London

Harry Potter's story is set in a magical Britain, and all of the places mentioned in the books, except London, are fictional, but you can visit many real film locations. Many of the locations are closed to visitors, though, or are an un-magical disappointment in person, unless you're a huge fan. For those diehards, here's a sampling.

Spoiler Warning: The information below will ruin surprises for the three of you who haven't yet read or seen the Harry Potter series.

Harry's story begins in suburban London, in the fictional town of Little Whinging. In the first film, *The Sorcerer's Stone* (2001), the gentle giant Hagrid touches down on his flying motorcycle at #4 Privet Drive. There, baby Harry—who was orphaned by the murder of his wizard parents—is left on the doorstep to be raised by an anti-magic aunt and uncle. The scene was shot in the town of **Bracknell** (pop. 50,000, 10 miles west of Heathrow) on a street of generic brick rowhouses called Picket Close. Later, 10-year-old Harry first realizes his wizard powers when talking with a boa constrictor, filmed at the **London Zoo's Reptile House** in Regent's Park (Tube: Great Portland Street). Harry soon gets invited to Hogwarts School of Witchcraft and Wizardry, where he'll learn the magical skills he'll need to eventually confront his parents' murderer, Lord Voldemort.

Big Ben and **Parliament,** along the Thames, welcome Harry to the modern city inhabited by Muggles (nonmagic folk). London bustles along oblivious to the parallel universe of wizards. Hagrid takes Harry shopping for school supplies. They enter the glass-roofed **Leadenhall Market** (Tube: Bank) and approach the **storefront** at 42 Bull's Head Passage—the entrance to The Leaky Cauldron pub (which, in the books, is placed among the bookshops of Charing Cross Road). The pub's back wall parts, opening onto the magical Diagon Alley, where Harry shops for wands, cauldrons, and wizard textbooks. He pays for them with gold Galleons from goblin-run Gringotts Wizarding Bank, filmed in the marble-floored and chandeliered Exhibition Hall of **Australia House** (Tube: Temple), home of the Australian Embassy.

Harry catches the train to Hogwarts at **King's Cross Station.** (The fanciful exterior shot in *The Chamber of Secrets* (2002) is actually nearby **St. Pancras International Station.**) Inside the glass-roofed train station, on a **pedestrian sky bridge** over the tracks, Hagrid gives Harry a train ticket. Harry heads to platform 9¾, where he and his new buddy Ron magically push their luggage carts through a brick pillar between the platforms, emerging onto a hidden platform. (For a fun photo-op, head to the station's track 9 to find the *Platform 9¾* sign, the luggage cart that looks like it's disappearing into the wall, and a Harry Potter gift shop.)

A red steam train—the Hogwarts Express—speeds the boys through the (Scottish) countryside to Hogwarts, where Harry will spend the next seven years. Harry is taught how to wave his wand by tiny Professor Flitwick in a wood-paneled classroom filmed at **Harrow School** in Harrow on the Hill, eight miles northwest of London (Tube: Harrow on the Hill).

In *The Prisoner of Azkaban* (2004), Harry careens through London's lamp-lit streets on a purple three-decker bus that dumps him at The Leaky Cauldron pub. In this film, the pub's exterior was shot on rough-looking Stoney Street at the southeast edge of **Borough Street Market,** by The Market Porter pub, with trains rumbling overhead (Tube: London Bridge).

In *The Order of the Phoenix* (2007), the Order takes to the night sky on broomsticks, zooming down the Thames and over London, passing over plenty of identifiable landmarks, including the **Tower Bridge, London Eye, Big Ben,** and **Buckingham Palace.** They arrive at Sirius Black's home at "Twelve Grimmauld Place," filmed at a park-like square called Lincoln's Inn Fields, near Sir John Soane's Museum (Tube: Holborn).

The **Millennium Bridge** is attacked by Death Eaters and collapses into the Thames in the dramatic finale to *The Half-Blood Prince* (2009).

For *Order of the Phoenix* and the first *Deathly Hallows* (2010), the real government offices of Whitehall serve as exteriors for the Ministry of Magic. Also for the first *Deathly Hallows,* Harry, Ron, and Hermione fight off disguised Death Eaters in a Muggle café, filmed in the West End's bustling **Piccadilly Circus.** Other London settings, like Diagon Alley, only exist at **Leavesden Film Studios** (20 miles north of London), where most of the films' interiors were shot. Leavesden recently opened its doors to Harry Potter pilgrims, who come to see many of the original sets and props.

Finally, cinema buffs can visit **Leicester Square** (Tube: Leicester Square), where Daniel Radcliffe and other stars have strolled past paparazzi and down red carpets to the Odeon Theater to attend the movies' premieres.

connection. First, take the frequent train from London Euston to Watford Junction (about 5/hour, 15-20 minutes). From there, you can take a Mullany's Coaches shuttle bus to the studio tour (2-4/hour, 15 minutes, arrive at Watford Junction at least 45 minutes before your tour entrance time, £1.50 one-way, £2 round-trip).

More direct (and more expensive), Golden Tours runs three **buses** per day between their office near Victoria Station in central London and the studio (price includes round-trip bus and studio entrance: adults-£59, kids-£54; leaves London at 8:00, 11:00, and 14:00, tour begins 2 hours after bus departs, reserve ahead at www.goldentours.com).

SIGHTS

WESTMINSTER WALK

From Big Ben to Trafalgar Square

Just about every visitor to London strolls along historic Whitehall from Big Ben to Trafalgar Square. This quick nine-stop walk gives meaning to that touristy ramble. Under London's modern traffic and big-city bustle lie 2,000 fascinating years of history. You'll get a whirlwind tour as well as a practical orientation to London.

Orientation

Length of This Walk: Allow one hour for a leisurely walk, and add more time if you drop by the Churchill War Rooms (1-2 hours) and the Banqueting House (30-60 minutes). Other nearby sights include the Houses of Parliament, Westminster Abbey, National Gallery, National Portrait Gallery, and St. Martin-in-the-Fields.

Getting There: Take the Tube to Westminster, then take the Westminster Pier exit. The walk ends at Trafalgar Square (nearest Tube stop: Charing Cross).

Churchill War Rooms: £17.50 (includes 10 percent optional donation), daily 9:30-18:00, last entry one hour before closing.

Supreme Court: Free, Mon-Fri 9:30-16:30, closed Sat-Sun, £2 guidebooklet, requires security check, tel. 020/7960-1900, www.supremecourt.gov.uk.

Banqueting House: £6 (includes 10 percent optional donation), includes audioguide, daily 10:00-17:00, last entry 30 minutes before closing; may close for government functions—though it always stays open at least until 13:00; aristocratic WC.

Horse Guards: Free to see Changing of the Guard Mon-Sat at 11:00, Sun at 10:00, dismounting ceremony daily at 16:00.

Audio Tour: You can download this chapter as a free Rick Steves audio tour (see page 8).

WCs: You'll find several WCs along this walk: at Westminster Pier (50p), at the intersection of Bridge Street and Whitehall (underground, 50p), and at Trafalgar Square (free WCs located in square, at National Gallery, and downstairs at St. Martin-in-the-Fields).

Eateries: See page 422 for a list of recommended eateries near Trafalgar Square, and page 129 for recommendations near Westminster Abbey.

The Walk Begins

• *Start halfway across Westminster Bridge.*

❶ On Westminster Bridge
Views of Big Ben and Parliament
• *First look upstream, toward the Parliament.*

Ding dong ding dong. Dong ding ding dong. Yes, indeed, you are

in London. **Big Ben** is actually "not the clock, not the tower, but the bell that tolls the hour." However, since the 13-ton bell is not visible, everyone just calls the whole works Big Ben. Named for a fat bureaucrat, Ben is scarcely older than my great-grandmother, but it has quickly become the city's symbol. The tower—officially named the "Elizabeth Tower" in honor of Queen Elizabeth II's Diamond Jubilee—is 315 feet high. The clock faces are 23 feet across, and the 13-foot-long minute hand sweeps the length of your body every five minutes. For fun, call home from near Big Ben at about three minutes before the hour to let your loved one hear the bell ring.

Big Ben hangs out in the north tower of a long building (the Houses of Parliament) that stretches along the Thames. Britain is ruled from this building, which for five centuries was the home of kings and queens. Then, as democracy was foisted on tyrants, a parliament of nobles was allowed to meet in some of the rooms. Soon, commoners were elected to office, the neighborhood was shot, and the royalty moved to Buckingham Palace. While most of the current building looks medieval with its prickly flamboyant spires, it was actually built after a fire gutted the old Westminster Palace in 1834.

Today, the House of Commons meets in one end of the building. The rubber-stamp House of Lords grumbles and snoozes in

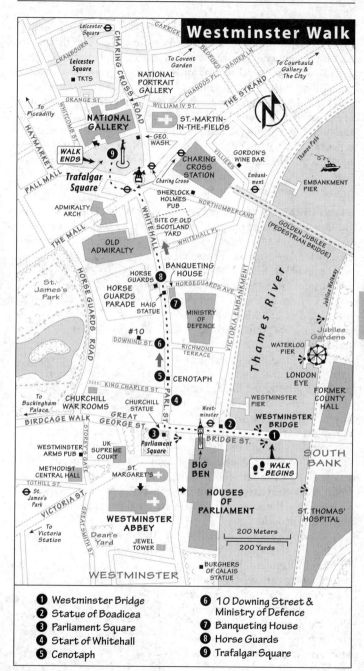

Westminster Walk

- ❶ Westminster Bridge
- ❷ Statue of Boadicea
- ❸ Parliament Square
- ❹ Start of Whitehall
- ❺ Cenotaph
- ❻ 10 Downing Street & Ministry of Defence
- ❼ Banqueting House
- ❽ Horse Guards
- ❾ Trafalgar Square

WESTMINSTER

the other end of this 1,000-room complex, and provides a tempering effect on extreme governmental changes. The two houses are very much separate: Notice the riverside tea terraces with the color-coded awnings—royal red for lords, common green for commoners. Alluding to the traditional leanings of the two chambers, locals say, "Green for go...red for stop" (for tips on visiting the Houses of Parliament, see page 139). The modern Portcullis Building (with the tube-like chimneys), across Bridge Street from Big Ben, holds offices for the 650 members of the House of Commons. They commute to the Houses of Parliament by way of an underground passage.

• *Now look north (downstream).*

Views of the London Eye, The City, and the Thames

Built in 2000 to celebrate the millennium, the London Eye—originally nicknamed "the London Eyesore," but now generally appreciated by locals—is a giant Ferris wheel standing 443 feet tall. It slowly spins 32 capsules (also the number of boroughs in London), each filled with a maximum of 25 visitors, up to London's best viewpoint (with up to 25 miles' visibility on a rare clear day). Aside from Big Ben, Parliament, St. Paul's Cathedral (not visible from here), and the wheel itself, London's skyline is not overwhelming; it's a city that wows from within.

Next to the wheel sprawls the huge former County Hall building, now a hotel and tourist complex. The London Eye marks the start of the Jubilee Walkway, a pleasant one-hour riverside promenade along the South Bank of the Thames, through London's vibrant, gentrified arts-and-cultural zone. Along the way, you have views across the river of St. Paul's stately dome and the financial district, called The City.

London's history is tied to the **Thames,** the 210-mile river linking the interior of England with the North Sea. The city got its start in Roman times as a trade center along this watery highway. As recently as a century ago, large ships made their way upstream to the city center to unload. Today, the major port is 25 miles downstream, and tourist cruise boats ply the waters.

Look for the **boat piers** on

WESTMINSTER

either bank of the Thames. Several tour-boat companies offer regular departures from Westminster Pier (on the left) or Waterloo Pier (on the right, near the London Eye). This is an efficient, scenic way to get from here to the Tower of London or Greenwich (downstream) or Kew Gardens (upstream). For details, see page 40.

Lining the river, beneath the lampposts, are little green copper **lions' heads** with rings for tying up boats. Before the construction of the Thames Barrier in 1982 (the world's largest movable flood barrier, downstream near Greenwich), high tides from the nearby North Sea made floods a recurring London problem. The police kept an eye on these lions: "When the lions drink, the city's at risk."

Until 1750, only London Bridge crossed the Thames. Then a bridge was built here. Early in the morning of September 3, 1802, William Wordsworth stood where you're standing and described what he saw:

> *This City now doth, like a garment, wear*
> *The beauty of the morning; silent, bare,*
> *Ships, towers, domes, theatres, and temples lie*
> *Open unto the fields, and to the sky;*
> *All bright and glittering in the smokeless air.*

• *Near Westminster Pier is a big statue of a lady on a chariot (nicknamed "the first woman driver"...no reins).*

❷ Statue of Boadicea, Queen of the Iceni

Riding in her two-horse chariot, daughters by her side, this Celtic Xena leads her people against Roman invaders. Julius Caesar was

the first Roman general to cross the Channel, but even he was weirded out by the island's strange inhabitants, who worshipped trees, sacrificed virgins, and went to war painted blue. Later, Romans subdued and civilized them, building roads and making this spot on the Thames—"Londinium"—into a major urban center.

But Boadicea refused to be Romanized. In A.D. 60, after Roman soldiers raped her daughters, she rallied her people and "liberated" London, massacring its 60,000 Romanized citizens. However, the brief revolt was snuffed out, and she and her family took poison to avoid surrender.

• *There's a civilized public toilet down the stairs behind Boadicea. Cross the street to just under Big Ben and continue one block inland to the busy intersection of Parliament Square. Pause here for the view.*

❸ Parliament Square

To your left are the sandstone-hued **Houses of Parliament.** If Parliament is in session, the entrance (midway down the building) is lined with tourists, enlivened by political demonstrations, and staked out by camera crews interviewing Members of Parliament (MPs) for the evening news. Only the core part, Westminster Hall, survives from the circa-1090s original. While the Houses of Parliament are commonly described as "Neo-Gothic" (even in this book), this uniquely English style is more specifically called Neo-Perpendicular Gothic. For a peek at genuine Perpendicular Gothic (the fanciest and final stage of that style), simply look across the street at the section of Westminster Abbey closest to the Houses of Parliament—it dates from 1484.

Kitty-corner across the square, the two white towers of **Westminster Abbey** rise above the trees. The broad boulevard of Whitehall (here called Parliament Street) stretches to your right up to Trafalgar Square.

This square is the heart of what was once a suburb of London—the medieval City of Westminster. Like Buda and Pest (later Budapest), London is two cities that grew into one. In Roman and medieval times, the city was centered farther east, near St. Paul's Cathedral. But in the 11th century, King Edward the Confessor moved his court here, and the center of political power shifted to this area. Edward built a palace and a church (minster) here in the west, creating the city of

"West Minster." Over time, the palace evolved into a meeting place for debating public policy—a parliament. Today's Houses of Parliament sit atop the remains of Edward's original palace. To this day, the Houses of Parliament are known to Brits as the "Palace of Westminster."

Across from Parliament, the cute little church with the blue sundials, snuggling under the Abbey "like a baby lamb under a ewe," is **St. Margaret's Church.** Since 1480, this has been *the* place for politicians' weddings, including Winston and Clementine Churchill's.

Parliament Square, the expanse of green between Westminster Abbey and Big Ben, is filled with statues of famous Brits (and sometimes with protesters). The statue of **Winston Churchill,** the man who saved Britain from Hitler, shows him in the military overcoat he was fond of wearing. According to tour guides, the statue has a current of electricity running through it to honor Churchill's wish that if a statue were made of him, his head wouldn't be soiled by pigeons. Most of the other statues are Commonwealth politicians that few Americans would recognize. There are also a few non-Brits, honored not for their contributions to Britain but to mankind. At the oppo-

site corner of the square from Churchill, look for the newer statue of the leader who battled South African apartheid, **Nelson Mandela** (erected in 2007). And across the street and a bit to the right stands a man who opposed American slavery, **Abraham Lincoln** (erected in 1920, patterned after a similar statue in Chicago's Lincoln Park).

The white building (flying the Union Jack) at the far end of the square houses Britain's **Supreme Court.** You can wander the building after going through security, see a small exhibit on this recently sanctioned legal body, and observe any courts currently in session (it also has a café and WCs).

In 1868, the world's first traffic light was installed on the corner where Whitehall now spills double-decker buses into the square. Another reminder of a bygone era is the little yellow "Taxi" lantern atop the fence on the street corner closest to Parliament. In pre-mobile phone days, when an MP needed a taxi, this lit up to hail one. And here's one more ancient artifact: Along the north side of Parliament Square are nearly obsolete remnants of 20th-century technology—red phone booths, mainly used today by tourists wanting a photo-op with Big Ben.

• *Consider touring Westminster Abbey (✪ see the Westminster Abbey Tour chapter). Otherwise, turn right (north), walk away from the Houses of Parliament and the Abbey, and continue up Parliament Street, which becomes Whitehall.*

❹ Walking Along Whitehall

Today, Whitehall is choked with traffic, but imagine the effect this broad street must have had on out-of-towners a century ago.

In your horse-drawn carriage, you'd clop along a tree-lined boulevard past well-dressed lords and ladies, dodging street urchins. Gazing left, then right, you'd try to take it all in, your eyes dazzled by the bone-white walls of this man-made marble canyon.

Whitehall is now the most important street in Britain, lined with the ministries of finance, treasury, and so on. You may see limos and camera crews as important dignitaries enter or exit. Political demonstrators wave signs and chant slogans—sometimes about issues foreign to most Americans (Britain's former colonies still resent the empire's continuing influence), and sometimes about issues very familiar to us (the wars in the Middle East and the troubled economy). Notice the security measures. Iron grates seal off the concrete ditches between the buildings and sidewalks for protection against explosives.

The black, ornamental arrowheads topping the iron fences were once colorfully painted. In 1861, Queen Victoria ordered them all painted black when her beloved Prince Albert ("the only one who called her Vickie") died. Possibly the world's most determined mourner, Victoria wore black for the standard two years of mourning—and then tacked on 38 more. (For more on Victoria, see the sidebar on page 534.)

• *Continue down Whitehall. On your right is a colorful pub, the Red Lion. Across the street, a 700-foot detour down King Charles Street leads to the Churchill War Rooms, the underground bunker of 27 rooms that was the nerve center of Britain's campaign against Hitler (see page 50 for details). Farther along, you reach a tall, square, stone monument in the middle of the boulevard.*

❺ Cenotaph

This monument honors those who died in the two events that most shaped modern Britain—World Wars I and II. The monumental devastation of these wars helped turn a colonial superpower into a cultural colony of an American superpower.

The actual cenotaph is the slab that sits atop the pillar—a tomb. You'll notice no religious symbols on this memorial. The dead honored here came from many creeds and all corners of Britain's empire. It looks lost in a sea of noisy cars, but on each Remembrance Sunday (closest to November 11), Whitehall is closed to traffic, the royal family fills the balcony overhead in the foreign ministry, and a memorial service is held around the cenotaph.

The year 2014 marked the centennial of the start of what Brits call "the Great War"—World War I. It's hard for an American to understand the war's long-term impact on Europe. On a single day (at the Battle of the Somme, 1916), the British suffered nearly 60,000 casualties. It's said that if the roughly one million WWI dead from the British Empire were to march four abreast past the cenotaph, the sad parade would last for seven days.

Eternally pondering the cenotaph (from *way* up the street—

barely visible from here) is an equestrian statue. **Field Marshal Douglas Haig** (marked with his honorary title, *Earl Haig*) was commander-in-chief of the British army from 1916 to 1918. He was responsible for ordering so many brave and not-so-brave British boys out of the trenches and onto the killing fields of World War I.

• *Just past the cenotaph, on the other (west) side of Whitehall, is an iron security gate guarding the entrance to Downing Street.*

❻ 10 Downing Street and the Ministry of Defence

Britain's version of the White House is where the prime minister and his family live, at #10 (in the black-brick building 300 feet

down the blocked-off street, on the right; there's a lantern and usually a security guard).

Like the White House's Rose Garden, the black door marked #10 is a highly symbolic point of power, popular for photo ops to mark big occasions. This is where suffragettes protested in the early 20th century, where Neville Chamberlain showed off his regrettable peace treaty with Hitler, and where Winston Churchill made famous the V-for-Victory sign. It's where President Barack Obama came to discuss global economic issues with the previous prime minister, and where Prime Minister David Cameron and his wife Samantha try to raise their young family like normal people.

It looks modest, but #10's entryway does open up into fairly impressive digs—the prime minister's offices (downstairs), his residence (upstairs), and two large formal dining rooms. The PM's staff has offices here. Many on the staff are permanent bureaucrats, staying on to serve as prime ministers come and go. The cabinet meets at #10 on Tuesday mornings. This is where foreign dignitaries come for official government dinners, where the prime minister receives honored school kids and victorious soccer teams, and where he gives monthly addresses to the nation. Next door, at #11, the chancellor of the exchequer (finance minister) lives with his family, and #12 houses the PM's press office.

This has been the traditional home of the prime minister since the position was created in the early 18th century. But even before that, the neighborhood (if not the building itself) was a center of power, where Edward the Confessor and Henry VIII had palaces. The facade is, frankly, quite cheap, having been built as part of a middle-class cul-de-sac of homes by American-born George Downing in the 1680s. When the first PM moved in, the humble interior was combined with a mansion in back. During a major

Prime Minister David Cameron

David Cameron succeeded Gordon Brown as prime minister in May of 2010, and lives at 10 Downing Street with his wife, Samantha, and their young children. Elected at age 43, Cameron was the youngest PM in two centuries. He heads the Conservative Party (the "Tories"), but has never quite fit the stodgy Conservative image. Rumors still swirl of wild parties and illicit drugs in his student days at Oxford. He's known as "Dave" to his friends, and he developed a habit of riding his bike to work. Cameron rose quickly through the political ranks: He worked to re-elect Conservative PM John Major (1992), assisted the finance minister at 11 Downing Street (1992-1994), and was himself elected to Parliament in 2001, becoming head of the Conservative Party in 2005. By 2008, he was on the cover of *Time* magazine, which hailed him as the future of conservatism.

In 2010, Cameron's Conservative Party came to power, but it was hardly a sweeping Conservative mandate: Three parties split the vote, forcing Cameron's Conservatives to form a coalition with the (more left-leaning) Liberal Democrat Party. The Labour Party, which had held power in Britain for 13 years under Gordon Brown and Tony Blair, is the coalition's chief opposition.

Politically, Cameron is a moderate Conservative who is more pragmatic than ideological. Socially, he's "liberal" in the classical sense, advocating for personal freedoms—gay rights, decriminalization of drugs, allowing hunting and smoking, and ensuring citizens' privacy against government intrusion. Fiscally, he rails against big-government waste. His fiscal policies have emphasized austerity and belt-tightening in order to get the budget under control. The immediate result was a double-dip recession. His most right-of-center stance is his support for distancing Britain from the euro and the European Union; his veto of EU treaty amendments during the euro crisis led some to predict "the beginning of the end" of Britain's EU membership.

Despite his personal appeal, Cameron can't quite shake the Conservatives' image as the party of the upper class. Cameron was born rich, married rich, and has worked within the corporate culture. His colleagues form an old boys' network from his days at Eton, England's most exclusive prep school. The mayor of London, Boris Johnson, is not only an old Oxford frat buddy but also a distant cousin. Cameron's reputation has been tarnished by his links to discredited media mogul Rupert Murdoch, and some have questioned his handling of riots in London and other urban centers in the summer of 2011.

As the Conservatives try to unite the country to solve Britain's severe economic and cultural problems, it remains to be seen whether David Cameron has brought a fresh enough approach to #10. The people of Britain will get a chance to weigh in on May 7, 2015, when Cameron's party is up for re-election.

upgrade in the 1950s, they discovered that the facade's black bricks were actually yellow—but had been stained by centuries of Industrial Age soot. To keep with tradition, they now paint the bricks black.

The guarded metal gates were installed in 1989 to protect against Irish terrorists. Even so, #10 was hit and partly damaged in 1991 by an Irish Republican Army mortar launched from a van. These days, there's typically not much to see unless a VIP happens to drive up. Then the bobbies snap to and check credentials, the gates open, the car is inspected for bombs, the traffic barrier midway down the street drops into its bat cave, the car drives in, and... the bobbies go back to mugging for the tourists.

The huge building across Whitehall from Downing Street is the **Ministry of Defence** (MOD), the "British Pentagon." This

THE WOMEN OF WORLD WAR II

bleak place looks like a Ministry of Defence should. In front are statues of illustrious defenders of Britain. "Monty" is **Field Marshal Bernard Law Montgomery** of World War II, who beat the Nazis in North Africa (defeating Erwin "The Desert Fox" Rommel at El Alamein), giving the Allies a jumping-off point to retake Europe. Along with Churchill, Monty breathed confidence back into a demoralized British army, persuading them they could ulti-

mately beat Hitler. A **memorial** honoring the women who fought and died in World War II stands in the middle of the street. Its empty uniforms evoke the often-overlooked sacrifices of Britain's female war heroes.

You may be enjoying the shade of London's **plane trees.** They do well in polluted London: roots that work well in clay, waxy leaves that self-clean in the rain, and bark that sheds and regenerates so the pollution doesn't get into the trees' vascular systems.

• *At the equestrian statue of Haig (described earlier), you'll be flanked by the Welsh and Scottish government offices. At the corner (same side as the Ministry of Defence), you'll find the...*

❼ Banqueting House

This two-story building is just about all that remains of what was

once the biggest palace in Europe—Whitehall Palace, which once stretched from Trafalgar Square to Big Ben. Henry VIII started building it when he moved out of the Palace of Westminster (now the Parliament) and into the

residence of the archbishop of York. Queen Elizabeth I and other monarchs added on as England's worldwide prestige grew.

Today, the exterior of Greek-style columns and pediments looks rather ho-hum, much like every other white, marble building in London. But in 1620, it was a one-of-a-kind wonder—a big, white temple rising above small, half-timbered huts. Built by architect Inigo Jones, it sparked London's interest in the classical style. Within a century, London was awash in Georgian-style architecture, the English version of Neoclassical.

Facing the Banqueting House, look at the first-floor windows (with the balustrade)—the site of one of the pivotal events of English history. On January 30, 1649, a man dressed in black appeared at one of the windows and looked out at a huge crowd that surrounded the building. He stepped out the window and onto a wooden platform. It was King Charles I. He gave a short speech to the crowd, framed by the magnificent backdrop of the Banqueting House. His final word was "Remember." Then he knelt and laid his neck on a block as another man in black approached. It was the executioner—who cut off the king's head.

Plop—the concept of divine monarchy in Britain was decapitated. But there would still be kings after Oliver Cromwell, the Protestant anti-monarchist who brought about Charles I's death and then became England's leader. Soon after Cromwell's death, royalty was restored, and Charles' son, Charles II, got his revenge here in the Banqueting Hall...by living well. But, from then on, every king knew that he ruled by the grace of Parliament.

Charles I is remembered today with a statue at one end of Whitehall (in Trafalgar Square at the base of the tall column), while his enemy, Oliver Cromwell, is given equal time with a statue at the other end (at the Houses of Parliament).

• *You can pop into the Banqueting House, following the self-guided tour below. Otherwise, skip to "Horse Guards."*

Banqueting House Interior

Start with the 15-minute video on the history of the House, which shows the place in banqueting action. History buffs might consider the included, 30-minute audioguide. The low-ceilinged ground floor, a.k.a. the Undercroft, was King James I's personal wine cellar and tasting room. Climb to the first floor to find a portrait of the doomed king.

The main hall is impressive—two stories high, white with gold trim, full of light, and topped with colorful paintings in a gold-coffered ceiling. At 55 feet wide, 55 feet high, and 110 feet long, it's a perfect double cube. The chandeliers can be raised and lowered to accommodate any event. The throne is a modern reconstruction, but it gives an idea of the king's canopied throne that once stood here.

Ceiling Paintings: Charles I, who inherited the Banqueting House from his father, commissioned the famed Peter Paul Rubens to complete the decor. The paintings glorify Charles' dad, James I, the man who built the Banqueting House and who once told Parliament: "Kings are called gods...even by God himself."

To view the large oval painting in the center, *The Apotheosis of James I,* approach from the entrance, like a visiting ambassador, and watch the scene unfold. King James I (in red robe, with gray beard) rests his foot on a globe, as king of the whole world. Lady Faith (with a torch) and Miss Justice (with scales) lead him up into heaven, where baby angels blow trumpets and the goddess Minerva crowns him with the laurel wreath of wisdom. Minerva sticks her foot in our face, a triumph of illusion three centuries before 3-D glasses.

The painting above the throne, *The Peaceful Reign of King James,* shows wise King James seated on his throne, flanked by corkscrew columns from the temple of wise King Solomon. To the left, Peace embraces Plenty. Two angels swoop down at dramatic angles to adorn James with laurels, while a cherub holds his royal crown. Below, the Roman gods—Mercury, Mars, Minerva—arrive to help James subdue the serpents of rebellion.

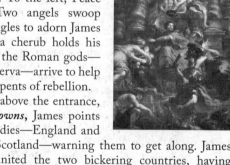

In the painting above the entrance, *The Union of the Crowns,* James points his scepter at two ladies—England and

Scotland—warning them to get along. James united the two bickering countries, having been crowned both King of Scots (in 1567) and King of England (1603). Smoke clouds of peace rise in the background as Cupid (bottom left corner) torches the weapons of war. The ladies place a crown on a baby's head and lead him to the throne. It's James' son, the future Charles I. When Charles grew up, he had this painting hung so that he could see it (right-side up) while seated on the Banqueting House throne.

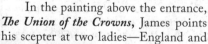

WESTMINSTER

The Banqueting House Through History

Imagine the many events this place has hosted over the centuries. Originally built as the royal dining hall for the sprawling Whitehall Palace, the Banqueting House also served as its de facto throne room. Picture ambassadors arriving here and walking the length of this hall lined with courtiers to pay homage to the king on his canopied throne. Loyal subjects knelt here to be made knights and nobles.

In the 1600s, the hall was famous throughout Europe as an occasional theater. Plays called "masques" were performed by torchlight and featured mask-wearing actors, singers and dancers, and elaborate costumes, sets, and special effects.

Picture the scene in 1622, when the brand-new Banqueting House was inaugurated with a performance of *The Masque of Augurs*, by Shakespeare protégé Ben Jonson (with set design by the hall's architect, Inigo Jones). King James and his courtiers crowded the balcony and tiered seats, and watched in awe as a parade of goofy commoners in masks entered the hall, singing and reveling, accompanied by two dancing bears. The comic chaos was suddenly interrupted by Greek gods who descended magically from the ceiling, eventually bringing harmony to the realm—just as a wise king does. And behind one of the masks, one of the actors was none other than 21-year-old Prince "I just can't wait to be king" Charles.

In 1649, the Banqueting House served a much more serious purpose—as an execution site for the public beheading of Charles I. Oliver Cromwell subsequently used this symbolic spot to legitimize his own leadership as Lord Protector. When Charles' son, Charles II, restored the monarchy in 1660, it was here that they celebrated.

In 1698, a massive fire destroyed Whitehall Palace, leaving only the name and the Banqueting House. The monarchs moved their residence elsewhere, eventually to Buckingham Palace. The Banqueting House became the Royal Chapel, complete with organ and pews.

Today, besides being a museum, the Banqueting House still functions much as it did in its heyday—hosting government receptions for foreign dignitaries or for parliament. World-renowned classical musicians perform for the paying public. And it's a rent-a-hall for parties and dinners. You could hold your daughter's wedding reception here, with 400 guests and full catering, for as little as $100,000.

• *When you're finished ogling the paintings, head back outside. Continue up Whitehall on the left (west) side, where you'll see (and smell) the building known as Horse Guards, guarded by traditionally dressed soldiers—who are also called Horse Guards.*

❽ Horse Guards

For 200 years, soldiers in cavalry uniforms have guarded this arched entrance along Whitehall that leads to Buckingham Palace and its predecessor as royal residence, St. James's Palace.

Two different squads alternate, so depending on the day you visit, you'll see soldiers in either red coats with white plumes in their helmets (the Life Guards), or blue coats with red plumes (the Blues and Royals). Together, they constitute the Queen's personal bodyguard. Besides their ceremonial duties here in old-time uniforms, these elite troops have fought in Iraq and Afghanistan. Both Prince William and Prince Harry have served in the Blues and Royals.

The Horse Guards building was the headquarters of the British army from the time of the American Revolution until the Ministry of Defence was created in World War II. Back when this archway was the only access point to The Mall (the street leading to Buckingham Palace), it was a security checkpoint. Anyone on horseback had to dismount before passing through. Today, by tradition, you must dismount your bicycle, Vespa, or Segway and walk it through. During the 2012 Olympics, the broad expanse of Horse Guards Parade was covered in sand to host the beach volleyball matches.

The Horse Guards Museum offers a glimpse at the stables and a collection of uniforms and weapons.

• *Continue up Whitehall, passing the Old Admiralty (#26, on left), headquarters of the British navy that once ruled the waves. Across the street, behind the old Clarence Pub, stood the original Scotland Yard, headquarters of London's crack police force in the days of Sherlock Holmes. Finally, Whitehall opens up into the grand, noisy, traffic-filled Trafalgar Square.*

To reach the center of the square, cross a few streets at the crosswalks.

❾ Trafalgar Square

London's central meeting point bustles around the world's biggest Corinthian column, where **Admiral Horatio Nelson** stands 170 feet off the ground, looking over London in the direction of one of the greatest naval battles in history. Nelson saved England at a time as dark as World War II. In 1805, Napoleon was poised

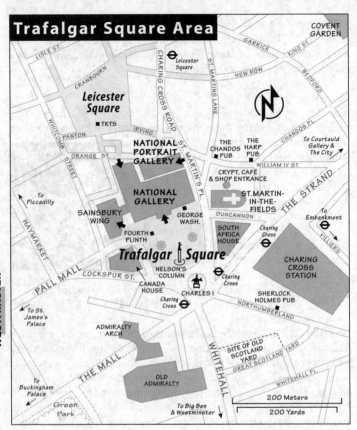

Trafalgar Square Area

COVENT GARDEN

LISLE ST.

GARRICK   KING ST.

CRANBOURN

Leicester Square

NEW ROW

BEDFORD

WHITCOMB

PANTON

Leicester Square

CHARING CROSS ROAD

ST. MARTINS LANE

CHANDOS PL.

To Courtauld Gallery & The City

TKTS

IRVING

THE CHANDOS PUB

THE HARP PUB

ORANGE ST.

NATIONAL PORTRAIT GALLERY

ST. MARTIN'S PL.

WILLIAM IV ST.

To Piccadilly

NATIONAL GALLERY

CRYPT, CAFÉ & SHOP ENTRANCE

ST. MARTIN-IN-THE-FIELDS

THE STRAND

SAINSBURY WING

GEORGE WASH.

DUNCANNON

To Embankment

FOURTH PLINTH

SOUTH AFRICA HOUSE

Charing Cross

VILLIERS

Trafalgar Square

HAYMARKET

NELSON'S COLUMN

Charing Cross

CHARING CROSS STATION

PALL MALL

COCKSPUR ST.

CANADA HOUSE

CHARLES I

SHERLOCK HOLMES PUB

To St. James's Palace

Charing Cross

NORTHUMBERLAND

ADMIRALTY ARCH

SITE OF OLD SCOTLAND YARD

GREAT SCOTLAND YARD

WHITEHALL

WHITEHALL PL.

THE MALL

OLD ADMIRALTY

To Buckingham Palace

Green Park

To Big Ben & Westminster

200 Meters

200 Yards

WESTMINSTER

on the other side of the Channel, threatening to invade England. Meanwhile, more than 900 miles away, the one-armed, one-eyed, and one-minded Lord Nelson attacked the French fleet off the coast of Spain at Trafalgar. The French were routed, Britannia ruled the waves, and the once-invincible French army was slowly worn down, then defeated at Waterloo. Nelson, while victorious, was shot by a sniper in the battle. He died, gasping, "Thank God, I have done my duty."

At the top of Trafalgar Square (north) sits the domed **National Gallery** with its grand staircase, and, to the right, the steeple of **St. Martin-in-the-Fields,** built in 1722, inspiring the steeple-over-the-entrance style of many town churches in New England (free lunch concerts—see page 461).

At the base of Nelson's column are bronze

reliefs cast from melted-down enemy cannons, and four huggable lions dying to have their photo taken with you. In front of the column, Charles I sits on horseback, with his head still on his shoulders. In the pavement just behind the statue is a plaque marking the center of London, from which all distances are measured. Of the many statues that dot the square, the pedestal on the northwest corner (the "fourth plinth") is periodically topped with contemporary art. The fountains, lit by colored lights, can shoot water 80 feet in the air.

Trafalgar Square is the center of modern London, connecting Westminster, The City, and the West End. A 2003 remodeling

of the square rerouted car traffic, helping reclaim the area for London's citizens. Spin clockwise 360 degrees and survey the city:

To the south (down Whitehall) is the center of government, Westminster. Looking southwest, down the broad boulevard called The Mall, you see Buckingham Palace in the distance. (Down Pall Mall is St. James's Palace and Clarence House, where Prince Charles lives when in London.) A few blocks northwest of Trafalgar Square is Piccadilly Circus. Directly north (a block behind the National Gallery) sits Leicester Square, the jumping-off point for Soho, Covent Garden, and the West End theater district (❂ see the West End Walk chapter).

The boulevard called the Strand takes you past Charing Cross Station, then eastward to The City, the original walled town of London and today's financial center. In medieval times, when people from The City met with the Westminster government, it was here. And finally, Northumberland Street leads southeast to the Golden Jubilee pedestrian bridge over the Thames. Along the way, you'll pass the Sherlock Holmes Pub (just off Northumberland Street, on Craven Passage), housed in Sir Arthur Conan Doyle's favorite watering hole, with an upstairs replica of 221b Baker Street.

Soak it in. You're smack-dab in the center of London, a thriving city atop two millennia of history.

WESTMINSTER

WESTMINSTER ABBEY TOUR

Westminster Abbey is more than just an "abbey"—it's the most famous English church in Christendom, where royalty has been wedded, crowned, and buried since the 11th century. Indeed, the histories of Westminster Abbey and England are almost the same. A thousand years of English history—3,000 tombs, the remains of 29 kings and queens, and hundreds of memorials to poets, politicians, scientists, and warriors—lie within its stained-glass splendor and under its stone slabs.

Orientation

Cost: £18, £36 family ticket (covers 2 adults and 1 child), cash or credit cards accepted (line up in the correct queue to pay; if the situation is unclear, ask an Abbey attendant for help), includes fine audioguide and entry to the cloisters and Abbey Museum. Praying is free, thank God. It's also free to enter just the cloisters and Abbey Museum (through Dean's Yard, around the right side as you face the main entrance), but if it's too crowded inside, the marshal at the cloister entrance may not let you in.

Hours: Abbey—Mon-Fri 9:30-16:30, Wed until 19:00 (main church only), Sat 9:30-14:30, last entry one hour before closing, closed Sun to sightseers but open for services; Abbey Museum—daily 10:30-16:00; cloisters—daily 8:00-18:00. Special events can shut down all or part of the Abbey.

When to Go: The place is most crowded every day at midmorning and all day Saturdays and Mondays. Visit early, during lunch, or late to avoid tourist hordes. Weekdays after 14:30 are less congested; come after that time and stay for the 17:00 evensong. The main entrance, on the Parliament Square side, often has a sizable line.

Dress Code: There is none, even for services.

Getting There: Near Big Ben and the Houses of Parliament (Tube: Westminster or St. James's Park).

Information: Because special events and services can shut out sightseers, check the website or call ahead to confirm that the Abbey is open, and get the latest schedule for guided tours, concerts, or services (tel. 020/7222-5152, www.westminster-abbey.org). If you have questions about the cathedral, ask any marshal in red or volunteer verger in green. There's surprisingly little posted information on the Abbey's sights, so you must rely on the audioguide, the vergers, or this book.

Music and Church Services: Mon-Fri at 7:30 (prayer), 8:00 (communion), 12:30 (communion), 17:00 evensong (except on Wed, when the evening service is generally spoken—not sung); **Sat** at 8:00 (communion), 9:00 (prayer), 15:00 (evensong; May-Aug it's at 17:00); **Sun** services generally come with more music: at 8:00 (communion), 10:00 (sung Matins), 11:15 (sung Eucharist), 15:00 (evensong), 18:30 (evening service). Services are free to anyone, though visitors who haven't paid church admission aren't allowed to linger afterward. Free **organ recitals** are usually held Sun at 17:45 (30 minutes). For a schedule of services or recitals on a particular day, look for posted signs with schedules or check the Abbey's website.

Tours: The included **audioguide** is excellent, taking some of the sting out of the steep admission fee. To add to the experience, you can take an entertaining **guided tour** from a verger—the church equivalent of a museum docent (£3, schedule posted both outside and inside entry, up to 5/day in summer, 4/day in winter, 1.5 hours).

Length of This Tour: Allow 1.5 hours. If you have less time, focus on the main part of the church, skipping the cloisters and Abbey Museum.

Services: WCs are inside the abbey, near Poets' Corner. Outside the abbey, the nearest public WCs (50p) are in front of Methodist Central Hall, the grand domed building across the street from the Abbey's west entrance.

Photography: Photos are prohibited, except in the Little Cloister and College Garden.

Eating: A **café** with table service and simple fare (£7 sandwiches, £24 afternoon tea) is in the abbey's cellar; enter through the cloisters. Other options are nearby: **Wesley's Café,** the cafeteria in the basement of Methodist Central Hall across the street, serves £7-9 lunches (Mon-Fri 8:00-16:00, Sat-Sun 9:00-16:00, good free WC). The **Supreme Court** building on Parliament Square has a basic basement café and free WCs (but you have to go through a security checkpoint to get there;

Mon-Fri 9:30-16:30, closed Sat-Sun). The **Westminster Arms** pub is just past the Methodist Central Hall on Storey's Gate (£9-10 pub grub including fish-and-chips, food served daily 12:00-20:00, eat downstairs). Picnickers can find benches at the nearby Jewel Tower, a half-block south of the Abbey.
Starring: Edwards, Elizabeths, Henrys, Annes, Marys, and poets.

The Tour Begins

You'll have no choice but to follow the steady flow of tourists through the church, following the route laid out for the audioguide. It's all one-way, and most days the crowds can be a real crush. Here are the Abbey's top 10 (plus one) stops.

• *Walk straight in, entering the north transept. Pick up the map flier that locates the most illustrious tombs and borrow the included audioguide. Follow the crowd flow to the right, passing through "Scientists' Corner," with memorials to Isaac Newton (left of altar), Michael Faraday, Charles Darwin (on the floor), and others. Enter the spacious...*

❶ Nave

Look down the long and narrow center aisle of the church. Lined with the praying hands of the Gothic arches, glowing with light from the stained glass, it's clear that this is more than a museum. With saints in stained glass, heroes in carved stone, and the bodies of England's greatest citizens under the floor stones, Westminster Abbey is the religious heart of England.

The Abbey was built in 1065. Its name, Westminster, means Church in the West (west of St. Paul's Cathedral). The king who built the Abbey was Edward the Confessor. Find him in the stained glass windows on the left side of the nave ("left" as you face the altar). He's in the third bay from the end (marked *S: Edwardus rex...*), with his crown, scepter, and ring. Take some time to thank him for this Abbey.

For the next 250 years, the Abbey was redone and remodeled to become essentially the church you see today, notwithstanding an extensive resurfacing in the 19th century. Thankfully, later architects—ignoring building trends of their generation—honored the vision of the original planner, and the building was completed in one relatively harmonious style.

The Abbey's 10-story nave is the tallest in England. The chan-

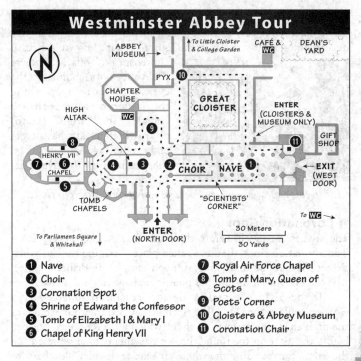

Westminster Abbey Tour

1 Nave
2 Choir
3 Coronation Spot
4 Shrine of Edward the Confessor
5 Tomb of Elizabeth I & Mary I
6 Chapel of King Henry VII

7 Royal Air Force Chapel
8 Tomb of Mary, Queen of Scots
9 Poets' Corner
10 Cloisters & Abbey Museum
11 Coronation Chair

WESTMINSTER ABBEY

deliers, 10 feet tall, look small in comparison (16 were given to the Abbey by the Guinness family).

On the floor near the west entrance of the Abbey is the flower-lined **Grave of the Unknown Warrior,** one ordinary WWI soldier buried in soil from France with lettering made from melted-down weapons from that war. As 2014 was the centennial of the start of the war, take time to contemplate the million-man army from the British Empire, and all those who gave their lives. Their memory is so revered that, when Kate Middleton walked up the aisle on her wedding day, by tradition she had to step around the tomb (and her wedding bouquet was later placed atop this tomb, also in accordance with tradition). Hanging on a column next to the tomb is the US Medal of Honor, presented by General John J. Pershing in 1921 to honor England's WWI dead. Closer to the door, also on the floor, is a memorial to a hero of World War II, Winston Churchill.

• *Now walk straight up the nave toward the altar. This is the same route every future monarch walks on the way to being crowned. Midway up the nave, you pass through the colorful screen of an enclosure known as the...*

❷ Choir

These elaborately carved wood and gilded seats are where monks once chanted their services in the "quire"—as it's known in British churchspeak. Today, it's where the Abbey boys' choir sings the evensong. You're approaching the center of a cross-shaped church. The **"high" (main) altar** (which usually has a cross and candlesticks atop it) sits on the platform up the five stairs in front of you.

• *It's on this platform—up the five steps—that the monarch is crowned.*

❸ Coronation Spot

The area immediately before the high altar is where every English coronation since 1066 has taken place. Imagine the day when Prince William becomes king. (Or you can picture Prince Charles, who'll come first if his mother doesn't manage to outlive him.)

The nobles in robes and powdered wigs look on from the carved wooden stalls of the choir. The Archbishop of Canterbury stands at the high altar. The coronation chair (which we'll see later) is placed before the altar on the round, brown pavement stone representing the earth. Surrounding the whole area are temporary bleachers for 8,000 VIPs, going halfway up the rose windows of each transept, creating a "theater."

Long silver trumpets hung with banners sound a fanfare as the monarch-to-be enters the church. The congregation sings, "I will go into the house of the Lord," as William parades slowly down the nave and up the steps to the altar. After a church service, he sits in the chair, facing the altar, where the crown jewels are placed. William is anointed with holy oil, then receives a ceremonial sword, ring, and cup. The royal scepter is placed in his hands, and—dut, dutta dah—the archbishop lowers the Crown of St. Edward the Confessor onto his royal head. Finally, King William V stands up, descends the steps, and is presented to the people. As cannons roar throughout the city, the people cry, "God save the king!"

Royalty are also given funerals here. Princess Diana's coffin was carried to this spot for her funeral service in 1997. The "Queen Mum" (mother of Elizabeth II) had her funeral here in 2002. This is also where most of the last century's royal weddings have taken place, including the unions of Queen Elizabeth II and Prince Philip (1947), her parents (1923), her sister Princess Margaret (1973), and her son Prince Andrew (to Sarah Ferguson, 1986). Most recently, of course, in April 2011, Prince William and Kate Middleton strolled up the nave, passed through the choir, climbed the five steps to the high altar, and became husband and wife—and the future King and Queen of the United Kingdom and its Commonwealth. Though royal marriages and funerals can happen anywhere, only one church can hold a coronation—the Abbey.

• *Now veer left and follow the crowd. You'll walk past the statue of Robert ("Bob") Peel, the prime minister whose policemen were nicknamed "bobbies." Stroll a few yards into the land of dead kings and queens. Use the audioguide to explore the **side chapels**—the Chapel of St. John the Baptist and Chapel of St. Michael. There you'll see effigies of the dead lying atop their tombs of polished stone. They lie on their backs or recline on their sides. Dressed in ruffed collars, they relax on pillows, clasping their hands in prayer, many buried side by side with their spouses.*

After exploring the chapels, pause at the wooden staircase on your right.

❹ Shrine of Edward the Confessor

The holiest part of the church is the raised area behind the altar (where the wooden staircase leads—sorry, no tourist access except with verger tour). Step back and peek over the dark coffin of Edward I to see the tippy-top of the green-and-gold wedding-cake tomb of King Edward the Confessor—the man who built Westminster Abbey.

God had told pious Edward to visit St. Peter's Basilica in Rome. But with the Normans thinking conquest, it was too dangerous for him to leave England. Instead, he built this grand church and dedicated it to St. Peter. It was finished just in time to bury Edward and to crown his foreign successor, William the Conqueror, in 1066. After Edward's death, people prayed at his tomb, and, after getting good results, Pope Alexander III canonized him. This elevated, central tomb—which lost some of its luster when Henry VIII melted down the gold coffin-case—is surrounded by the tombs of eight kings and queens.

• *Continue on. At the top of the stone staircase, veer left into the private burial chapel of Queen Elizabeth I.*

❺ Tomb of Queens Elizabeth I and Mary I

Although only one effigy is on the tomb (Elizabeth's), there are actually two queens buried beneath it, both daughters of Henry VIII (by different mothers). Bloody Mary—meek, pious, sickly, and Catholic—enforced Catholicism during her short reign (1553-1558) by burning "heretics" at the stake.

Elizabeth—strong, clever, and Protestant—steered England on an Anglican course. She holds a royal orb symbolizing that she's queen of the whole globe. When 26-year-old Elizabeth was crowned in the Abbey, her right to rule was questioned (especially by her Catholic subjects) because she was considered the bastard seed of Henry VIII's unsanctioned marriage to Anne Boleyn. But Elizabeth's long reign (1559-1603) was one of the greatest in English history, a time when England ruled the seas and Shakespeare explored human emotions. When she died, thousands turned out for her funeral in the Abbey. Elizabeth's face on the tomb, modeled after her death mask, is considered a very accurate take on this hook-nosed, imperious "Virgin Queen."

The two half-sisters disliked each other in life—Mary even had Elizabeth locked up in the Tower of London for a short time. Now they lie side by side for eternity. The Latin inscription ends, "Here we lie, two sisters in hope of one resurrection."

• *Continue into the ornate, flag-draped room up a few more stairs, directly behind the main altar.*

❻ Chapel of King Henry VII (The Lady Chapel)

The light from the stained-glass windows; the colorful banners overhead; and the elaborate tracery in stone, wood, and glass give

this room the festive air of a medieval tournament. The prestigious Knights of the Bath meet here, under the magnificent ceiling studded with gold pendants. The ceiling—of carved stone, not plaster (1519)—is the finest English Perpendicular Gothic and fan vaulting you'll see (unless you're going to King's College Chapel in Cambridge). The ceiling was sculpted on the floor in pieces, then jigsaw-puzzled into place. It capped the Gothic period and signaled the vitality of the coming Renaissance.

The knights sit in the wooden stalls with their coats of arms on the back, churches on their heads, their banner flying above, and the graves of dozens of kings beneath their feet. When the Queen worships here, she sits in the southwest corner chair under the carved wooden throne with the lion crown (immediately to the left as you enter).

Behind the small altar is an iron cage housing tombs of the old warrior Henry VII of Lancaster and his wife, Elizabeth of York. Their love and marriage finally settled the Wars of the Roses between the two clans. The combined red-and-white rose symbol decorates the top band of the ironwork. Henry VII, the first Tudor king, was the father of Henry VIII and the grandfather of Elizabeth I. This exuberant chapel heralds a new optimistic, postwar era as England prepares to step onto the world stage.

• *Go to the far end of the chapel and stand at the banister in front of the modern set of stained-glass windows.*

❼ Royal Air Force Chapel

Saints in robes and halos mingle with pilots in parachutes and bomber jackets. This tribute to WWII flyers is for those who earned their angel wings in the Battle of Britain (July-Oct 1940). Hitler's air force ruled the skies in the early days of the war, bombing at will, and threatening to snuff Britain out without a fight. But while determined Londoners hunkered down underground, British pilots in their Spitfires and Hurricanes took advantage of newly invented radar to get the jump on the more powerful Luftwaffe. These were the fighters about whom Churchill said, "Never...was so much owed by so many to so few."

The Abbey survived the Battle and the Blitz, but this window did not. As a memorial, a bit of bomb damage has been preserved—the little glassed-over hole in the wall below the windows in the lower left-hand corner. The book of remembrances lists each of the 1,497 airmen (including one American) who died in the Battle of Britain.

You're standing on the grave of Oliver Cromwell, leader of the rebel forces in England's Civil War. Or, rather, what had been his grave, when Cromwell was buried here from 1658 to 1661. Then his corpse was exhumed, hanged, drawn, quartered, and decapitated, and the head displayed on a stake as a warning to anarchists.

• *Exit the Chapel of Henry VII. Turn left into a side chapel with the tomb (the central one of three in the chapel).*

❽ Tomb of Mary, Queen of Scots

Historians get dewy-eyed over the fate of Mary, Queen of Scots (1542-1587). The beautiful, French-educated queen was held under house arrest for 19 years by Queen Elizabeth I, who considered her a threat to her sovereignty. Elizabeth got wind of an assassination plot, suspected Mary was behind it, and had her first cousin (once removed) beheaded. When Elizabeth—who was called the "Virgin Queen"—died heirless, Mary's son, James VI, King of Scots, also became King James I of England and Ireland. James buried his mum here (with her head sewn back on) in the Abbey's most sumptuous tomb.

• *Exit Mary's chapel. Ahead of you, again, is the tomb of the church's founder, Edward the Confessor. Continue on, until you emerge in the south transept. You're in...*

❾ Poets' Corner

England's greatest artistic contributions are in the written word. Here the masters of arguably the world's most complex and expressive language are remembered. (Many writers are honored with plaques and monuments; relatively few are actually buried here.)

• *Start with Chaucer, buried in the wall under the blue windows, marked with a white plaque reading* Qui Fuit Anglorum...

Geoffrey Chaucer (c. 1343-1400) is often considered the father of English literature. Chaucer's *Canterbury Tales* told of earthy people speaking everyday English, not French or Latin. He was the first great writer buried in the Abbey (thanks to his job as a Westminster clerk). Later, it became a tradition to bury other writers here, and Poets' Corner was built around his tomb. The blue windows have blank panels awaiting the names of future poets.

• *The plaques on the floor before Chaucer are gravestones and memorials to other literary greats.*

Lord Byron, the great lover of women and adventure: "Though the night was made for loving, / And the day returns too soon, / Yet we'll go no more a-roving / By the light of the moon."

Dylan Thomas, alcoholic master of modernism, with a Romantic's heart: "Oh as I was young and easy in the mercy of his means, / Time held me green and dying / Though I sang in my chains like the sea."

W. H. Auden, Brit-turned-American modernist on love, politics, and religion: "He was my North, my South, my East and West / My working week and Sunday rest / My noon, my midnight, my talk, my song / I thought that love would last forever: I was wrong."

Lewis Carroll, creator of *Alice's Adventures in Wonderland* and *Through the Looking-Glass:* "'Twas brillig, and the slithy toves / Did gyre and gimble in the wabe..."

T. S. Eliot, American-turned-British author of the influential *Waste Land:* "April is the cruellest month, breeding / Lilacs out of the dead land, mixing / Memory and desire, stirring / Dull roots with spring rain."

Alfred, Lord Tennyson, conscience of the Victorian era: "'Tis better to have loved and lost / Than never to have loved at all."

Robert Browning: "Oh, to be in England / Now that April's there."

• *Farther out in the south transept, you'll find a statue of...*

William Shakespeare: Although he's not buried here, this greatest of English writers is honored by a fine statue that stands near the end of the transept, overlooking the others: "Life's but a walking shadow, a poor player that struts and frets his hour upon the stage and then is heard no more."

George Frideric Handel: High on the wall opposite Shakespeare is the German immigrant famous for composing the *Messiah* oratorio: "Hallelujah, hallelujah, hallelujah." The statue's features are modeled on Handel's death mask. Musicians can read the vocal score in his hands for "I Know That My Redeemer Liveth." His actual tomb is on the floor, next to...

Charles Dickens, whose serialized novels brought literature to the masses: "It was the best of times, it was the worst of times."

On the floor near Shakespeare, you'll also find the tombs of **Samuel Johnson** (who wrote the first English dictionary) and the great English actor **Laurence Olivier.** (Olivier disdained the "Method" style of experiencing intense emotions in order to portray them. When co-star Dustin Hoffman stayed up all night in order to appear haggard for a scene, Olivier said, "My dear boy, why don't you simply try acting?")

And finally, near the center of the transept, find the small, white floor plaque of **Thomas Parr** (marked *THO: PARR*). Check the dates of his life (1483-1635) and do the math. In his (reputed) 152 years, he served 10 sovereigns and was a contemporary of Columbus, Henry VIII, Elizabeth I, Shakespeare, and Galileo.

• *Exit the church (temporarily) at the south door, which leads to the...*

❿ Cloisters and Abbey Museum

The buildings that adjoin the church housed the monks. (The church is known as the "abbey" because it was the headquarters of the Benedictine Order until Henry VIII kicked them out in 1540.) Cloistered courtyards gave them a place to meditate on God's creations.

The **Chapter House** is where the monks had daily meetings. It features fine architecture and stained glass, some faded but well-described medieval paintings and floor tiles, and—in the corridor—Britain's oldest door. A few steps farther down the hall is the **Pyx Chamber.** This old, thick-walled room once safeguarded the coins used to set the silver standard of the realm (a pyx is a small box that held gold and silver coins).

The small **Abbey Museum,** formerly the monks' lounge, is worth a peek for its fascinating and well-described exhibits. Look into the impressively realistic eyes of Elizabeth I, Charles II, Admiral Nelson, and a dozen others, part of a compelling series of wax-and-wood statues that, for three centuries, graced coffins during funeral processions. Also see exhibits on royal coronations, funerals, Abbey history, a close-up look at medieval stained glass, and replicas of the crown jewels used for coronation practice. The once-exquisite, now-fragmented Westminster Retable, which decorated the high altar in 1270, is the oldest surviving altarpiece in England. The image of Christ in the central panel is time-worn, but it retains the essentials: his face, the orb of power, and his blessing hand. Beyond the Abbey Museum, passageways lead to the Little Cloister and picturesque College Garden (open Tue-Thu).

As you return to the church, look back through the cloister courtyard to the church exterior, and meditate on the **flying but-tresses.** These stone bridges that push in on the church walls allowed Gothic architects to build so high.

If you need a bite or drink, or the WC, head for the abbey café.
• *Go back into the church for the last stop.*

⓫ Coronation Chair

A gold-painted oak chair waits here under a regal canopy for the next coronation. For every English coronation since 1308 (except two), it's been moved to its spot before the high altar to receive the royal buttocks. The chair's legs rest on lions, England's symbol. The space below the chair originally held a big sandstone rock from Scotland called the Stone of Scone (pronounced "skoon"), symbolizing Scotland's unity with England's monarch. But in the 1990s, Britain gave Scotland more sovereignty, its own Parliament, and the Stone, which Scotland has agreed to loan to Britain for future coronations (the rest of the time, it's on display in Edinburgh Castle).

Next to the chapel with the chair hangs a 600-year-old portrait of King Richard II. The boy king is holding the royal orb and scepter, wearing the crown, and seated upon this very chair.

Finally, take one last look down the nave. Listen to and ponder this place, filled with the remains of the people who made Britain a world power—saints, royalty, poets, musicians, scientists, soldiers, politicians. Now step back outside into a city filled with the modern-day poets, saints, and heroes who continue to make Britain great.

HOUSES OF PARLIAMENT TOUR

With an epic history, the Houses of Parliament (home to the House of Commons and the House of Lords) remains the site of fierce verbal tussles among members of the UK's Conservative, Labour, and smaller parties. "Westminster" (as Brits call the place) appears almost nightly on TV, as the impressive backdrop to the latest political news. A visit here gives both UK residents and foreign tourists alike a chance to tour a piece of living history and see the British government inaction.

Orientation

Cost: Free.

Hours: The public galleries of both houses are open for visitors only when Parliament is in session—generally October to July, Monday through Thursday. If you see a light above Big Ben's clock, then Parliament is in session.

More specifically, the **House of Commons** is in session Oct-July Mon 14:30-22:00, Tue-Wed 11:30-19:00, Thu 9:30-17:30; **House of Lords** is in session Oct-July Mon-Tue 14:30-22:00, Wed 15:00-22:00, Thu 11:00-19:00; last entry usually around 20:00, both houses closed Fri-Sun except for Sat tours.

During the Aug-Sept recess and on Sat year-round, the only way to visit is on a guided tour (see "Tours," later).

Getting There: You can't miss this gigantic, riverside, Neo-Gothic temple of government—it's London's most recognized symbol. The visitor's entrance is around the back side (away from the river), facing the buttresses of Westminster Abbey. Tube: Westminster.

Information: Tel. 020/7219-4272 or 020/7219-3107. See www.parliament.uk for schedule, or visit www.parliamentlive.tv for a preview. To preview a debate from home, tune into "Prime Minister's Questions"; in the US, the 30-minute broadcast airs live Wed mornings at 7:00 (ET) on C-SPAN2, re-airing Sun at 21:00 (ET) on regular C-SPAN (www.c-span.org).

Crowd-Beating Tips: Expect lines—it may take a while to get through security, plus another 20-60 minutes once inside to be admitted to the house chambers. Lines are longest at the start of each day's session (when the most fiery debate often occurs), and usually enormous on Wednesdays, when the prime minister normally attends. The later in the day you enter, the less crowded (and less exciting) it is. Visiting after 18:00 is risky, as sessions tend to end well before their official closing time, and visitors aren't allowed in after the politicians call it a day.

Choosing a House: If you only visit one of the bicameral legislative bodies, I'd choose the House of Lords. Though less important politically, the Lords meet in a more ornate room, and the waiting time is shorter (likely less than 30 minutes). The House of Commons is where major policy is made, but the room itself is sparse, and waiting times are longer (30-60 minutes or more). If you just want to see the grand halls of this majestic building (without visiting either of the legislative chambers), you won't have any waiting once you're through security.

Tours: On Saturdays year-round and when Parliament is in recess (during much of Aug and Sept), you can get a behind-the-scenes peek at the chambers of both houses by taking a tour—either with an audioguide or a live guide. The advantage of a tour is that you can linger and see a few more rooms (audioguide-£17.50, guided tour-£25, 1.5 hours, Saturdays 9:15-16:30 and selected days during recess, generally Mon-Sat—but days and times vary, so confirm exact schedule on the Parliament website at www.parliament.uk). Book ahead by calling 0844-847-1672 or through www.ticketmaster.co.uk; the on-site ticket office (open 8:45-16:45 on tour days only) is located next to the Jewel Tower, opposite the south end of the Houses of Parliament. The TI across from St. Paul's Cathedral plans to sell tour tickets, too.

Length of This Tour: Aside from the sometimes lengthy lines and security rigmarole (which can eat up an hour or more), it takes less than an hour to tour the interior and drop in—briefly—on a parliamentary session.

Starring: A grand building and a gaggle of chattering parliamentarians.

BACKGROUND

The Palace of Westminster has been the center of political power in England for nearly a thousand years. Around 1050, King Edward the Confessor moved here to be next to his newly constructed "minster" (church) in the "west"—Westminster Abbey. The Palace became the monarch's official residence, the meeting place of his noble advisors (or parliament), and the supreme court of the land. In the 1500s, Henry VIII moved down the block to Whitehall Palace (now destroyed, see page 124), and later monarchs chose to live at Kensington and Buckingham Palaces. But Westminster Palace remained home to the increasingly powerful Parliament.

In 1834, a horrendous fire gutted the Palace. It was rebuilt in a retro, Neo-Gothic style that recalled England's medieval Christian roots—pointed arches, stained-glass windows, spires, and saint-like statues. At the same time, Britain was also retooling its government. Democracy was on the rise, the queen became a constitutional monarch, and Parliament emerged as the nation's ruling body. The Palace of Westminster became a symbol—a kind of cathedral—of democracy.

The Tour Begins

• *Enter midway along the west side of the building (across the street from Westminster Abbey), where a tourist ramp leads to the...*

Visitor's Entrance
As you enter, you'll be asked if you want to visit the House of Commons or the House of Lords. I choose "Lords" (because the line is shorter), but it really doesn't matter. Once inside the building, you'll be able to see all the public spaces described in this tour as you transit to the chamber you intend to visit. If you have questions, the attendants are extremely helpful.

• *At the airport-style security, you're photographed and given a badge (Lords or Commons). Continue past the Jubilee Café (which has live video feeds of Parliament in session), pick up helpful brochures at the information desk, and take in the cavernous...*

Westminster Hall
This vast hall—covering 16,000 square feet—survived the 1834 fire, and is one of the oldest and most important buildings in England. Begun in 1097, the hall was greatly remodeled around 1390 by Richard II, who made it the grandest space in Europe. His self-supporting oak-timber roof (1397) wowed everyone. Unlike earlier roofs that spanned the hall with long

HOUSES OF PARLIAMENT

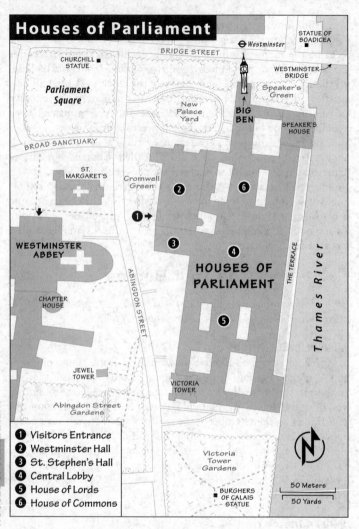

Houses of Parliament

STATUE OF BOADICEA

Westminster

BRIDGE STREET

CHURCHILL STATUE

Parliament Square

New Palace Yard

WESTMINSTER BRIDGE

Speaker's Green

BIG BEN

BROAD SANCTUARY

ST. MARGARET'S

Cromwell Green

SPEAKER'S HOUSE

1 →

2

6

WESTMINSTER ABBEY

3

4

HOUSES OF PARLIAMENT

THE TERRACE

Thames River

ABINGDON STREET

CHAPTER HOUSE

5

JEWEL TOWER

Abingdon Street Gardens

VICTORIA TOWER

N

Victoria Tower Gardens

1 Visitors Entrance
2 Westminster Hall
3 St. Stephen's Hall
4 Central Lobby
5 House of Lords
6 House of Commons

BURGHERS OF CALAIS STATUE

50 Meters
50 Yards

HOUSES OF PARLIAMENT

beams, this "hammer-beam" roof uses short beams that jut horizontally out from the walls. They're part of a complex system of curved braces and arches that distribute the weight of the roof outward to the walls, not downward to the floor, so there's no need for supporting pillars. The 26 carved angels also do their part to hold up the 650-ton roof.

Stroll the room to read various plaques about the hall's history. The King's Table (c.1250) originally sat on a raised platform at the south end of the hall. Here the king presided—dispensing justice, welcoming ambassadors, hosting his coronation banquet, toasting revelers.

England's vaunted legal system was invented in this hall, as this was the major court of the land for 700 years. King Charles I was tried and sentenced to death here. Guy Fawkes was condemned for plotting to blow up the Halls of Parliament in 1605. (He's best remembered today for the sly-smiling "Guy Fawkes mask" that has become the symbol of 21st-century anarchists.)

In more recent times, the hall has hosted the lying-in-state of Winston Churchill, G-G-G-George VI, and the Queen Mother. And in 2011, Britain's bigwigs gathered here for a speech by Barack Obama.

• *Walking through the hall and up the stairs, you'll enter the busy world of today's government. You soon reach St. Stephen's Hall, where visitors wait to enter the House of Commons Chamber.*

St. Stephen's Hall

This long, beautifully lit room was the original House of Commons for three centuries (from 1550 until the fire of 1834). MPs sat in church pews on either side of the hall—the ruling party on one side, the opposition on the other—a format they'd keep when they moved into the new chambers.

It was here that British history turned forever. On January 4, 1642, King Charles I marched into this room with 400 soldiers and demanded that Parliament turn over five rebels. The Speaker bluntly refused. The standoff between King and Parliament eventually snowballed into the English Civil War, the king was decapitated, and Parliament emerged triumphant.

After the fire of 1834, the hall was rebuilt. The stained glass windows—forming a tall, rectangular grid—are a textbook example of the "Perpendicular" Gothic style used by architect Charles Barry.

• *Next, you reach the...*

Central Lobby

This ornate, octagonal, high-vaulted room is often called the "heart of British government," because it sits in the geographical center of the Palace, midway between the House of Commons (to the left) and House of Lords (right). Clerks bustle about. Constituents come to this lobby to petition, or "lobby," their MPs (from which the term may derive). Video monitors list the schedule of meetings and events going on in this 1,100-room governmental hive.

This is the best place to admire the Palace's interior decoration—carved wood, chandeliers, statues, and floor tiles—designed by Barry's partner, Augustus Pugin.

• *This lobby marks the end of the public space where you can wander freely. To see the House of Lords or House of Commons you must wait in line. You must also check your belongings—bag, camera, phone, even this guidebook. While you wait, ask the attendant for any brochures.*

House of Lords

When you're called, you'll walk to the Lords Chamber by way of the long Peers' Corridor. Paintings on the corridor walls depict the anti-authoritarian spirit brewing under the reign of Charles I: you'll see Parliament rebuffing Charles' demands for the five MPs, and the freedom-seeking Pilgrims leaving England for America on the Mayflower. When you reach the House of Lords Chamber, you watch the proceedings from an upper-level gallery.

The House of Lords consists of around 800 members, called "Peers." They are not elected by popular vote. Some are nobles who've inherited the position; others are appointed by the Queen. These days, their role is largely advisory. They can propose, revise, and filibuster laws, but they have no real power to pass laws on their own. On any typical day, only a handful of the lords actually shows up to debate.

The Lords Chamber is church-like and impressive, with stained glass and intricately carved walls. At the far end is the Queen's gilded throne. She's the only one who may sit there, and only once a year, when she gives a speech to open Parliament.

The benches where the Lords sit are always upholstered red. (The House of Commons is green.) Notice the seating arrangement: ruling party on one side, opposition on the other, and un-affiliated "crossbenchers" in between. In the center of the room sits the "Woolsack"—a cushion stuffed with wool. Here the Lord Speaker presides, with his/her ceremonial mace placed behind the backrest.

House of Commons

On the way to the House of Commons Chamber, you first pass through the long Commons Corridor, which spills into the Members' Lobby. In the lobby, MPs check their message box with its state-of-the-art 1960s technology; they enter the chamber through a stone archway that still bears bomb damage from the Nazi Blitz; and as they enter, many rub the Churchill statue's golden toe for good luck, though visitors are asked not to touch.

The Commons Chamber may be much less grandiose than the Lords', but this is where the sausage gets made. The House of Commons is as powerful as the Lords, prime minister, and Queen combined.

This seat of power is surprisingly small—barely 3,000 square feet. The chamber was destroyed in the Blitz, and Churchill rebuilt it with the same cube-shaped floor plan. Of today's 650-plus MPs, only 450 can sit—the rest have to stand at the ends. On any given day, most MPs are in their offices, located elsewhere in the complex or in nearby, modern buildings.

As in the House of Lords, the ruling party sits on the left, opposition on the right. Keep an eye out for two red lines on the floor, which cannot be crossed when debating the other side. (They're supposedly two sword-lengths apart, to prevent a literal clashing of swords.) Between the benches is the canopied Speaker's Chair, for the chairman who keeps order and chooses who can speak next. The clerks sit at a central table that holds the ceremonial mace, a symbol of the power given Parliament by the monarch. Also on the table are the two "dispatch boxes"—old wooden chests that serve as lecterns, one for each side.

The Queen is not allowed in the Commons Chamber. The last monarch to enter a Commons Chamber was Charles I, and you know what happened to him. When the prime minister visits, he speaks from one of the boxes. His ministers (or cabinet) join him on the front bench, while lesser MPs (the "backbenchers") sit behind. It's often a fiery spectacle, as the prime minister defends his policies, while the opposition grumbles and harrumphs in displeasure. It's not unheard-of for MPs to get out of line and be escorted out by the Serjeant at Arms. One furious MP even grabbed the Serjeant's hallowed mace and threw it to the ground. His career was over.

• *And so is our tour. Heading back out of the sprawling complex, be sure to get a good look at—if you haven't already—the Houses of Parliament's best-known symbol, its giant clock tower. For a full description on what tourists call "Big Ben," see the start of the ✪ Westminster Walk.*

HOUSES OF PARLIAMENT

NATIONAL GALLERY TOUR

The National Gallery lets you tour Europe's art without ever crossing the Channel. With so many exciting artists and styles, it's a fine overture to art if you're just starting a European trip, and a pleasant reprise if you're just finishing. The "National Gal"—with Britain's greatest collection of paintings—is always a welcome interlude from the bustle of London sightseeing.

This tour gives you a quick chronological sweep through art history: medieval holiness, Renaissance realism, Dutch detail, Baroque excess, British restraint, and the colorful French Impressionism that leads to the modern world. Cruise like an eagle with wide eyes for the big picture, seeing how each style progresses into the next. Enjoy the biggies quickly, leaving yourself with enough time to circle back and browse.

Orientation

Cost: Free, but suggested donation of £4 (consider depositing your loose change here). Special exhibits require an admission fee.

Hours: Daily 10:00-18:00, Fri until 21:00, last entry to special exhibits 45 minutes before closing.

Getting There: It's as central as can be, overlooking Trafalgar Square, a 15-minute walk from Big Ben and 10 minutes from Piccadilly. The closest Tube stop is Charing Cross or Leicester Square. Handy buses #9, #11, #15, and #24 (among others) pass by (see page 30).

Information: The information desk in the lobby has a £1 floor plan (similar to this book's map, but with a few masterpieces highlighted) and a schedule of upcoming events and lunchtime lectures. The National Gallery loans out many paintings, so some of the canvases mentioned in this tour may not be on display.

Special exhibitions sometimes force paintings in the permanent collection to be moved, usually temporarily. If you can't
find a particular piece, ask the attendants stationed in each
room. Info tel. 020/7747-2885, switchboard tel. 020/7839-
3321, www.nationalgallery.org.uk.

Tours: Free one-hour **overview tours** leave from the Sainsbury
Wing info desk daily at 11:30 and 14:30, plus Fri at 19:00 and
Sat-Sun at 16:00. Ask the info desk about 10-minute talks on
individual paintings, Mon-Fri at 16:00.

The **audioguides** are excellent. Choose from the one-
hour highlights tour, several theme tours, or a tour option that
lets you dial up info on any painting in the museum (£3.50).

The Gallery's **ArtStart** computer terminals help you
study any artist, style, or topic in the museum, and print out
a tailor-made tour map. You'll find plenty of terminals in the
comfy Espresso Bar on the ground floor of the main building
(described below); a few more (but without the ability to print)
are just inside the entrance of the Sainsbury Wing, and also
hiding behind a partition upstairs in the passage between the
Sainsbury Wing and the main building.

The museum is surprisingly family-friendly (especially on
Sunday mornings). Check their website for a variety of **kids'
activities.**

Length of This Tour: Allow 1.5 hours. If you have less time, the
can't-miss pieces are Van Eyck's *Arnolfini Portrait,* Leonardo's *Virgin and Child with St. Anne and St. John the Baptist,*
Rembrandt's *Belshazzar's Feast* and self-portraits, Velázquez's
Rokeby Venus, Turner's *Fighting Téméraire,* the Impressionists,
and Van Gogh's *Sunflowers.*

Cloakroom: Cloakrooms are at each entrance (free, but £1 suggested donation). You can take a small bag into the museum.

Photography: Photos are strictly forbidden.

Cuisine Art: There are three eateries in the Gallery. The National Dining Rooms, located on the first floor of the Sainsbury
Wing, has a classy, table-service restaurant (£13-20 main
dishes) and cheaper bakery next door (£8-12 meals). The National Café, located near the Getty Entrance, has a table-service restaurant (£15-20 entrées) and an adjoining sandwich/
soup/salad/pastry café (£4-5). Both places offer afternoon tea
(see page 434). Seek out the Espresso Bar, near the Portico and
Getty entrances, for soft couches, sandwiches, and ArtStart
computers. Outside the Gallery, several options are on or near
Trafalgar Square (see page 422).

Starring: You name it—Leonardo, Raphael, Titian, Rembrandt,
Monet, and Van Gogh.

The Tour Begins

The National Gallery has three entrances facing Trafalgar Square: The main Portico Entrance (under the dome, in the center), the low-key Getty Entrance (to the right as you face the building), and the Sainsbury Entrance (in the smaller building to the left of the main entrance).

• *Enter through the Sainsbury Entrance. Pick up the handy map (£1) and climb the stairs. At the top, turn left, then left again through Room 51, and enter Room 52.*

MEDIEVAL AND EARLY RENAISSANCE (1260-1440)

In Rooms 52 and 53, shiny gold paintings of saints, angels, Madonnas, and crucifixions float in an ethereal gold never-never land. One thing is very clear: Medieval heaven was different from medieval earth. The holy wore gold plates on their heads. Faces were serene and generic. People posed stiffly, facing either directly out or to the side, never in between. Saints are recognized by the symbols they carry (a key, a sword, a book), rather than by their human features.

Art in the Middle Ages was religious, dominated by the Church. The illiterate faithful could meditate on an altarpiece and visualize heaven. It's as though they couldn't imagine saints and angels inhabiting the dreary world of rocks, trees, and sky they lived in.

• *One of the finest medieval altarpieces is in a glass case in Room 53.*

Anonymous—*The Wilton Diptych* (c. 1395-1399)

Two saint/kings and St. John the Baptist present King Richard II (left panel) to the Virgin Mary and her rosy-cheeked baby (right panel), who are surrounded by angels with flame-like wings. Despite the gold-leaf background, a glimmer of human realism peeks through. The kings have distinct, down-to-earth faces. And the outside shows not a saint, not a god, but a real-life deer lying down in the grass of this earth.

But the anonymous artist is struggling with reality. John the Baptist is holding a "lamb of God" that looks more like a Chihuahua. Nice try. Mary's exquisite fingers hold an anatomically impossible little foot. The figures are flat, scrawny, and sinless, with cartoon features—far from flesh-and-blood human beings. Still, Richard II himself (king of England from 1377 to 1399) knelt before this portable altarpiece to inspire his personal devotions to the Virgin.

• *Continuing into Room 54, you'll leave this gold-leaf peace and find...*

Uccello—*Battle of San Romano* (c. 1438-1440)

This colorful battle scene shows the victory of Florence over Siena in 1432—and the battle for literal realism on the canvas. It's an

early Renaissance attempt at a realistic, nonreligious, three-dimensional scene.

Uccello challenges his ability by posing the horses and soldiers at every conceivable angle. The background of farmyards, receding hedges, and tiny soldiers creates an illusion of distance. The artist actually constructs a grid of fallen lances in the foreground, then places the horses and warriors within it. Still, Uccello hasn't quite worked out the bugs—the figures in the distance are far too big, and the fallen soldier on the left isn't much larger than the fallen shield on the right.

• *In Room 56, you'll find...*

Van Eyck—*The Arnolfini Portrait* (1434)

Called by some "The Shotgun Wedding," this painting was once thought to depict a wedding ceremony forced by the lady's swelling

belly. Today it's understood as a portrait of a solemn, well-dressed, well-heeled couple, the Arnolfinis of Bruges, Belgium. It is a masterpiece of down-to-earth details.

Van Eyck has built a medieval dollhouse, inviting us to linger over the furnishings. Feel the texture of the fabrics, count the terrier's hairs, trace the shadows generated by the window. Each object is painted at an ideal angle, with the details you'd see if you were standing directly in front of it. So the strings of beads hanging on the back wall are as crystal clear as the bracelets on the woman.

To top it off, look into the round mirror on the far wall—the whole scene is reflected backward in miniature, showing the loving couple and a pair of mysterious visitors. Is one of them Van Eyck himself at his easel? Or has the artist painted you, the home viewer, into the scene?

NATIONAL GALLERY

MEDIEVAL & EARLY RENAISSANCE
1 ANONYMOUS – The Wilton Diptych
2 UCCELLO – Battle of San Romano
3 VAN EYCK – The Arnolfini Portrait

ITALIAN RENAISSANCE
4 LEONARDO – The Virgin of the Rocks
5 BOTTICELLI – Venus and Mars
6 CRIVELLI – The Annunciation, with Saint Emidius
7 LEONARDO – Virgin and Child with St. Anne and St. John the Baptist

VENETIAN RENAISSANCE
8 TITIAN – Bacchus and Ariadne
9 TINTORETTO – The Origin of the Milky Way

HIGH RENAISSANCE
10 MICHELANGELO – The Entombment
11 RAPHAEL – Pope Julius II
12 BRONZINO – An Allegory with Venus and Cupid
13 HOLBEIN – The Ambassadors

NORTHERN PROTESTANT ART
14 VERMEER – A Young Woman Standing at a Virginal
15 VAN HOOGSTRATEN – A Peepshow with Views of the Interior of a Dutch House
16 REMBRANDT – Belshazzar's Feast
17 REMBRANDT – Self-Portrait at the Age of 63

BAROQUE & FRENCH ROCOCO
18 RUBENS – The Judgment of Paris
19 VELÁZQUEZ – The Rokeby Venus
20 VAN DYCK – Equestrian Portrait of Charles I
21 CARAVAGGIO – The Supper at Emmaus
22 BOUCHER – Pan and Syrinx

BRITISH ROMANTIC ART
23 CONSTABLE – The Hay Wain
24 TURNER – The Fighting Téméraire
25 DELAROCHE – The Execution of Lady Jane Grey

To Leicester Square (5 min. walk)

SAINSBURY WING

ENTRANCE ON LEVEL 0

SELF-GUIDED TOUR STARTS ON LEVEL 2

TOUR BEGINS

SAINSBURY ENTRANCE

NATIONAL GALLERY

The surface detail is extraordinary, but the painting lacks true Renaissance depth. The tiny room looks unnaturally narrow, cramped, and claustrophobic.

In medieval times (this was painted only a generation after *The Wilton Diptych*), everyone could read the hidden meaning of certain symbols—the chandelier with its one lit candle (love), the fruit on the windowsill (fertility), the dangling whisk broom (the woman's domestic responsibilities), and the terrier (Fido—fidelity).

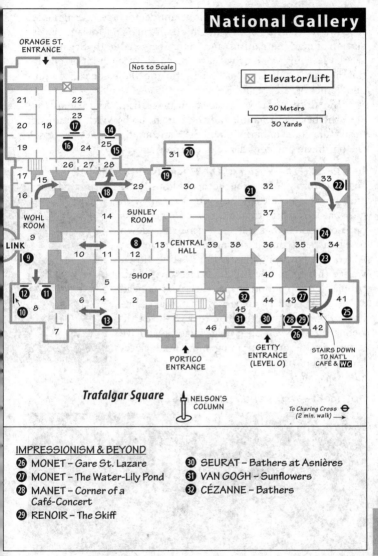

National Gallery

ORANGE ST. ENTRANCE

Not to Scale

⊠ Elevator/Lift

30 Meters
30 Yards

WOHL ROOM 9

LINK

SUNLEY ROOM

CENTRAL HALL

SHOP

PORTICO ENTRANCE

GETTY ENTRANCE (LEVEL 0)

STAIRS DOWN TO NAT'L CAFÉ & WC

Trafalgar Square

NELSON'S COLUMN

To Charing Cross ⊖
(2 min. walk) →

IMPRESSIONISM & BEYOND

㉖ MONET – Gare St. Lazare
㉗ MONET – The Water-Lily Pond
㉘ MANET – Corner of a Café-Concert
㉙ RENOIR – The Skiff

㉚ SEURAT – Bathers at Asnières
㉛ VAN GOGH – Sunflowers
㉜ CÉZANNE – Bathers

By the way, the woman likely is not pregnant. The fashion of the day was to gather up the folds of one's extremely full-skirted dress. At least, that's what they told her parents.

• *Return to Room 55, turn left into Room 57, and enter the...*

ITALIAN RENAISSANCE (1400-1550)

The Renaissance—or "rebirth" of the culture of ancient Greece and Rome—was a cultural boom that changed people's thinking about every aspect of life. In politics, it meant democracy. In religion, it meant a move away from Church dominance and toward the assertion of man (humanism) and a more personal faith. Science and secular learning were revived after centuries of superstition and ignorance. In architecture, it was a return to the balanced columns and domes of Greece and Rome.

In painting, the Renaissance meant realism. Artists rediscovered the beauty of nature and the human body. With pictures of beautiful people in harmonious, 3-D surroundings, they expressed the optimism and confidence of this new age.

Leonardo—*The Virgin of the Rocks* (c. 1491-1508)

In this painting, Mary, the mother of Jesus, plays with her son and little Johnny the Baptist (with cross, at left) while an androgynous angel looks on. Leonardo brings this holy scene right down to earth by setting it among rocks, stalactites, water, and flowering plants. But looking closer, we see that Leonardo has deliberately posed his people into a pyramid shape, with Mary's head at the peak, creating an oasis of maternal stability and serenity amid the hard rock of the earth. Leonardo, who was born illegitimate, may have sought in his art the young mother he never knew. Freud thought so.

• *In Room 58 is...*

Botticelli—*Venus and Mars* (c. 1485)

Mars takes a break from war, succumbing to the delights of love (Venus), while impish satyrs play innocently with the discarded tools of death. In the early spring of the Renaissance, there was an optimistic mood in the air—the feeling that enlightened Man could solve all problems, narrowing the gap between mortals and the Greek gods. Artists felt free to use the pagan Greek gods as symbols of human traits, virtues, and vices. Venus has sapped man's medieval stiffness; the Renaissance has arrived.

NATIONAL GALLERY

• *Continue to Room 59.*

Crivelli—*The Annunciation, with Saint Emidius* (1486)

Mary, in green, is visited by the dove of the Holy Spirit, who beams down from the distant heavens in a shaft of light.

Like Van Eyck's wedding, this is a brilliant collection of realistic details. Notice the hanging rug, the peacock, the architectural minutiae that lead you way, way back, then bam!—you have a giant pickle in your face.

It combines meticulous detail with Italian spaciousness. The floor tiles and building bricks recede into the distance. We're sucked right in, accelerating through the alleyway, under the arch, and off into space. The Holy Spirit spans the entire distance, connecting heavenly background with earthly foreground.

Crivelli creates an Escheresque labyrinth of rooms and walkways that we want to walk through, around, and into—or is that just a male thing?

Renaissance Italians were interested in—even obsessed with—portraying 3-D space. Perhaps they focused their spiritual passion away from heaven and toward the physical world. With such restless energy, they needed lots of elbow room. Space, the final frontier.

• *Walk straight ahead into Room 60, then turn right into Room 51, where we first entered. Tucked in an adjoining room labeled* The Leonardo Cartoon *is...*

Leonardo—*Virgin and Child with St. Anne and St. John the Baptist* (c. 1499-1500)

At first glance, this chalk cartoon (a full-size preparatory drawing for a painting) looks like a simple snapshot of two loving moms and two playful kids. The two children play—oblivious to the violent deaths they'll both suffer—beneath their mothers' Mona Lisa smiles.

But follow the eyes: Shadowy-eyed Anne turns toward Mary, who looks tenderly down to Jesus, who blesses John, who gazes back dreamily. As your eyes follow theirs, you're led back to the literal and psychological center of the composition—Jesus—the Alpha and Omega. Without resorting to heavy-handed medieval symbolism, Leonardo drives home a theological concept in a natural, human way. Leonardo the perfectionist rarely finished paintings. This sketch—pieced together from two separate papers (see the line down the middle)—gives us an inside peek at his genius.

• *From Room 51, cross to the main building (the West Wing) and enter the large Room 9, filled with big, colorful canvases.*

VENETIAN RENAISSANCE (1510-1600)

The Renaissance was born in Florence, but it flowered in Venice. The Venetians had become wealthy by trading with the luxurious and exotic East, and their artists forged a happy-go-lucky art style that shows a taste for the finer things in life. Madonnas and saints were replaced by smooth-skinned, sexy, golden centerfolds. Venetian artists revived the classical world in all its pagan glory, creating beautiful scenes of sensuous Nature. Be aware that the following works may be moved around among Rooms 9-12.

• *Walk from Room 9 (through Rooms 10 and 11) to Room 12, and look for...*

Titian—*Bacchus and Ariadne* (1520-1523)

Bacchus, the god of wine, leaps from his leopard-drawn chariot, his red cape blowing behind him, to cheer up Ariadne (far left), who has been jilted by her lover. Bacchus' motley entourage rattles cymbals, bangs on tambourines, and literally shakes a leg.

Man and animal mingle in this pre-Christian orgy, with leopards, a snake, a dog, and the severed head and leg of an ass ready for the barbecue. Man and animal also literally "mix" in the satyrs—part man, part goat. The fat, sleepy guy in the background has had too much.

Titian (see his "Ticianus" signature on the gold vase, lower left) uses a pyramid composition to balance an otherwise chaotic scene. Follow Ariadne's gaze up to the peak of Bacchus' flowing cape, then down along the snake handler's spine to the lower-right corner. In addition, the artist balances the picture with harmonious colors—blue sky on the left, green trees on the right, while the two main figures stand out with loud splotches of red.

• *Head back to Room 9, (checking Rooms 12 and 10 on the way, in case the Tintoretto painting has been moved) where you should find...*

Tintoretto—*The Origin of the Milky Way* (c. 1575)

In this scene from a classical myth, the god Jupiter places his illegitimate son, baby Hercules, at his wife's breast. Juno says, "Wait

a minute. That's not my baby!" Her milk spurts upward, becoming the Milky Way.

Tintoretto places us right up in the clouds, among the gods, who swirl around at every angle. Jupiter appears to be flying almost right at us. An X composition unites it all—Juno slants one way while Jupiter tilts the other.

• *From Room 9, exit at the near end, entering Room 8.*

HIGH RENAISSANCE (1500)

The "Big Three" of the High Renaissance—Leonardo (whom we saw earlier), Michelangelo, and Raphael—were the painters who finally conquered realism. But these three Florence-trained artists weren't content just to copy nature, cranking out photographs-on-canvas. Like Renaissance architects (which they also were), they carefully composed their figures on the canvas, "building" them into geometrical patterns that reflected the balance and order they saw in nature.

Michelangelo—*The Entombment* (c. 1500-1501)

Michelangelo, the greatest sculptor ever, proves it here in this "painted sculpture" of the crucified Jesus being carried to the tomb.

Florentine artists like Michelangelo were inspired by ancient statues of balanced, anatomically perfect, nude Greek gods. Like a chiseled Greek god, this musclehead in red ripples beneath his clothes. Christ's naked body, shocking to the medieval Church, was completely acceptable in the Renaissance world, where classical nudes were admired as an expression of the divine.

Renaissance balance and symmetry reign. Christ is the center of the composition, flanked by two equally leaning people who support his body with strips of cloth. They, in turn, are flanked by two others.

The painting is not damaged, but it is unfinished. Michelangelo, 25 years old at the time, moved on to other projects before he got around to adding crucial details, even leaving a blank space in the lower right where Mary would have been.

Regardless of the lack of detail, Michelangelo lets the bodies do the talking. The two supporters strain to hold up Christ's body, and in their tension we, too, feel the great weight and tragedy of their dead god. Michelangelo expresses the divine through the human form.

Raphael—*Pope Julius II* (1511)

The new worldliness of the Renaissance even reached the Church. Pope Julius II, who was more a swaggering conquistador than a

pious pope, set out to rebuild Rome in Renaissance style, hiring Michelangelo to paint the ceiling of the Vatican's Sistine Chapel.

Raphael gives a behind-the-scenes look at this complex leader. On the one hand, the pope is an imposing pyramid of power, with a velvet shawl, silk shirt, and fancy rings boasting of wealth and success. But at the same time, he's a bent and broken man, his throne backed into a corner, with an expression that seems

to say, "Is this all there is?"

• *And now for something completely different. In Room 8, find...*

Bronzino—*An Allegory with Venus and Cupid* (c.1545)

You may not recognize this painting, but you might recognize a foot. Look closely at the figure of boy Cupid, on the left. His right foot became famous on TV in the 1970s and 1980s in the comedy show *Monty Python's Flying Circus*. As the show opened and circus music played, the credits would come to an end on the last note, with Cupid's giant foot coming down from above to squash the scene with a flatulent *ffft!* The Pythons used collage-style graphics to end sketches abruptly (rather than fumble for a punch line), thus making a seamless (if surreal) transition to the next bit.

• *Exit Room 8 (turn left from where you entered), and pass through Room 6 to reach Room 4.*

Holbein—*The Ambassadors* (1533)

Italian 3-D even shows up in this work by German-born Hans Holbein the Younger, who settled in England to create portraits for Henry VIII. Two well-dressed, suave men flank a shelf

Painting: From Tempera to Tubes

The technology of painting has evolved over the centuries.

1400s Artists used tempera (pigments dissolved in egg yolk) on wood.

1500s Still painting on wood, artists mainly used oil (pigments dissolved in vegetable oil, such as linseed, walnut, or poppy).

1600s Artists applied oil paints to canvases stretched across wooden frames.

1850 Paints in convenient, collapsible tubes are invented, making open-air painting feasible.

The Frames: Although some frames are original, having been chosen by the artist, most are selected by museum curators. Some are old frames from other paintings, others are Victorian-era reproductions in wood, and still others are recent reproductions made of a composite substance to look like gilded wood.

full of books, globes, navigational tools, and musical instruments—objects that symbolize the secular knowledge of the Renaissance. Almost forgotten is the tiny crucifix in the upper-left corner. So what's with the gray, slanting blob at the bottom? If you view the blob from the right-hand edge of the painting (get real close, right up to the frame), the blob suddenly becomes...a skull. In painting terms, the optical illusion is called an anamorphic projection. (For another example, see page 158.) Symbolically, the skull is a memento mori, a reminder that—despite the fine clothes, proud poses, and worldly knowledge—we will all die.

• *Backtrack through Rooms 6 and 8, returning to the big Room 9. Exit this room at the far end and turn right, entering the long Room 29 (with forest-green wallpaper). Midway through Room 29, turn left and find Room 25.*

NORTHERN PROTESTANT ART (1600-1700)

We switch from CinemaScope to a tiny TV—smaller canvases, subdued colors, everyday scenes, and not even a bare shoulder.

Money shapes art. While Italy had wealthy aristocrats and the powerful Catholic Church to purchase art, the North's patrons were middle-class, hardworking, Protestant merchants. They wanted simple, cheap, no-nonsense pictures to decorate their homes and offices. Greek gods and Virgin Marys were out, hometown folks and hometown places were in—portraits, landscapes, still lifes, and slice-of-life scenes. Painted with great attention to detail, this is art meant not to wow or preach at you, but to be enjoyed and lingered over. Sightsee.

Vermeer—*A Young Woman Standing at a Virginal* (c. 1670)

Inside a simple but wealthy Dutch home, a prim virgin plays an early piano called a "virginal." We've surprised her, and she pauses

to look up at us.

By framing off such a small world to look at—from the blue chair in the foreground to the wall in back—Vermeer forces us to appreciate the tiniest details, the beauty of everyday things. We can meditate on the tiles lining the floor, the subtle shades of the white wall, and the pale, diffused light that seeps in from the window. Amid straight lines and rectangles, the woman's billowing dress adds a soft touch. The painting of a nude cupid on the back wall only strengthens this virgin's purity.

• *Also in Room 25, you'll find...*

Van Hoogstraten—*A Peepshow with Views of the Interior of a Dutch House* (c. 1655-1660)

Look through the open end of this ingenious device to make the painting of a house interior come to three-dimensional life. Compare the twisted curves of the painting with the illusion it creates and appreciate the painstaking work of the dedicated artist. Painted on the top of the box is another anamorphic projection.

• *Enter the adjoining Room 24.*

Rembrandt—*Belshazzar's Feast* (c. 1635)

Belshazzar, the wicked king of Babylon, has been feasting with God's sacred dinnerware when the meal is interrupted. The king turns to see the hand of God, burning an ominous message into

the wall that Belshazzar's number is up. As he turns, he knocks over a goblet of wine. We see the jewels and riches of his decadent life.

Rembrandt captures the scene at the most ironic moment. Belshazzar is about to be ruined. We know it, his guests know it, and, judging by the look on his face, he's coming to the same conclusion.

Rembrandt's flair for the dramatic is accentuated by the strong contrast between light and dark. Most of his canvases are a rich, dark brown, with a few crucial details highlighted by a bright light.

Before leaving this room, notice the self-portrait of Rembrandt at age 34, just to the left. Remember this face.

• *Enter the adjoining Room 23.*

Rembrandt—*Self-Portrait at the Age of 63* (1669)

Rembrandt throws the light of truth on...himself. He made this craggy self-portrait in the year he would die, at age 63. Contrast it with one done three decades earlier (which we just saw in the previous room).  Rembrandt, the greatest Dutch painter, started out as the successful, wealthy young genius of the art world. But he refused to crank out commercial works. Rembrandt painted things that he believed in but no one would invest in—family members, down-to-earth Bible scenes, and self-portraits like these.

Here, Rembrandt surveys the wreckage of his independent life. He was bankrupt, his mistress had just died, and he had also buried several of his children. We see a disillusioned, well-worn, but proud old genius.

• *Backtrack to the long, forest-green Room 29.*

BAROQUE (1600-1700)
Paintings by Peter Paul Rubens

This room holds big, colorful, emotional works by Peter Paul Rubens and others from Catholic Flanders (Belgium). While Protestant and democratic Europe painted simple scenes, Catholic and aristocratic countries turned to the style called Baroque. Baroque art took what was flashy in Venetian art and made it flashier, what was gaudy and made it gaudier, what was dramatic and made it shocking.

Rubens painted anything that would raise your pulse— battles, miracles, hunts, and, especially, fleshy women with dimples on all four cheeks. For instance, *The Judgment of Paris* (one of two versions by Rubens in this museum) is little more than an excuse for a study of  the female nude, showing front, back, and profile all on one canvas.

• *Exit Room 29 at the far end. In Room 30 (with red wallpaper), on the left-hand wall, you'll find...*

Velázquez—*The Rokeby Venus* (c. 1647-1651)

Like a Venetian centerfold, Venus lounges diagonally across the canvas, admiring herself, with flaring red, white, and gray fabrics to highlight her rosy white skin and inflame our passion. Horny

Spanish kings loved Titianesque nudes despite Spain's strict Inquisition, the Church tribunal that rooted out bad behavior. This work by the king's personal court painter is a rare Spanish nude from that ultra-Catholic country. About the sole concession to Spanish modesty is the false reflection in the mirror—if it really showed what the angle should show, Velázquez would have needed two mirrors...and a new job.

• *From Room 30, turn left into the big, red Room 31, where you'll see a large canvas.*

Van Dyck—*Equestrian Portrait of Charles I* (c. 1637-1638)

King Charles sits on a huge horse, accentuating his power. The horse's small head makes sure that little Charles isn't dwarfed.

Charles was a soft-on-Catholics king in a hard-core Protestant country until England's Civil War (1648), when his genteel head was separated from his refined body by Cromwell and company.

Kings and bishops used the grandiose Baroque style to impress the masses with their power. Van Dyck's portrait style set the tone for all the stuffy, boring portraits of British aristocrats who wished to be portrayed as sophisticated gentlemen—whether they were or not.

• *Return to Room 30 and turn left, exiting at the far end, and entering Room 32. On the right wall, find...*

Caravaggio—*The Supper at Emmaus* (1601)

After Jesus was crucified, he rose from the dead and appeared without warning to some of his followers. Jesus just wants a quiet meal, but the man in green, suddenly realizing who he's eating with, is about to jump out of his chair in shock. To the right, a man spreads his hands in amazement, bridging the distance between Christ and us by sticking his hand in our faces.

The Baroque took reality and exaggerated it. Most artists amplified prettiness, but Caravaggio exaggerated grittiness, using real, ugly, unhaloed people in Bible scenes. Caravaggio's paintings look like how a wet dog smells. Reality.

We've come a long way since the first medieval altarpieces that wrapped holy people in gold foil. From the torn shirts to the five

o'clock shadows, from the blemished apples to the uneven part in Jesus' hair, we are witnessing a very human miracle.
• *Leave Room 32 at the far end, and enter Room 33.*

FRENCH ROCOCO (1700-1800)

As Europe's political and economic center shifted from Italy to France, Louis XIV's court at Versailles became its cultural hub. Every aristocrat spoke French, dressed French, and bought French paintings. The Rococo art of Louis' successors was as frilly, sensual, and suggestive as the decadent French court. We see their rosy-cheeked portraits and their fantasies: lords and ladies at play in classical gardens, where mortals and gods cavort together.
• *One of the finest examples is the tiny...*

Boucher—*Pan and Syrinx* (1759)

Curious Pan seeks a threesome, but to elude him, Syrinx eventually changes into reeds, leaving him all wet.

Rococo art is like a Rubens that got shrunk in the wash—smaller, lighter pastel colors, frillier, and more delicate than the Baroque style. Same dimples, though.
• *Enter Room 34. Take a hike around and enjoy the English country-garden ambience.*

BRITISH ROMANTIC ART (1800-1850)
Constable—*The Hay Wain* (1821)

The reserved British were more comfortable cavorting with nature

than with the lofty gods. Come-as-you-are poets like Wordsworth found the same ecstasy just in being outside.

John Constable set up his easel out-of-doors, making quick sketches to capture the simple majesty of billowing clouds, spreading trees, and everyday rural life. Even British portraits (by Thomas Gainsborough and others) placed refined lords and ladies amid idealized greenery.

This simple style—believe it or not—was considered shocking in its day. The rough, thick, earth-toned paint and crude country settings scandalized art lovers used to the highfalutin, prettified sheen of the Baroque and Rococo.

Turner—*The Fighting Téméraire* (1839)

Constable's landscape was about to be paved over by the Industrial Revolution. Soon, machines began to replace humans, factories belched smoke over Constable's hay cart, and cloud-gazers had to punch the clock. Romantics tried to resist it, lauding the forces of nature and natural human emotions in the face of technological "progress." But alas, here a modern steamboat symbolically drags a famous but obsolete sailing battleship off into the sunset to be destroyed.

Turner's messy, colorful style gives us our first glimpse into the modern art world—he influenced the Impressionists. Turner takes an ordinary scene (like Constable), captures the play of light with messy paints (like Impressionists), and charges it with mystery (like, wow).

• *To view more Constables, an enormous collection of Turners, and other British art, visit London's Tate Britain (❷ see the Tate Britain Tour). For now, continue ahead to Room 41.*

Delaroche—*The Execution of Lady Jane Grey* (1833)

It's 1554. The teenage queen's nine-day reign has reached its curfew. This innocent girl, manipulated into power politics by cunning ad-

visors, is now sent to the execution site in the Tower of London. As her friends swoon with grief, she's blindfolded and forced to kneel at the block. Legend has it that the confused, humiliated girl was left kneeling on the scaffold. She crawled around, groping for the chopping block, crying out, "Where is it? What am I supposed to do?" The executioner in scarlet looks on with as much compassion as he can muster.

Britain's distinct contribution to art history is this Pre-Raphaelite style, showing medieval scenes in luminous realism with a mood of understated tragedy.

• *Exit Room 41 and enter Room 43. The Impressionist paintings are scattered throughout Rooms 43-46.*

IMPRESSIONISM AND BEYOND (1850-1910)

For 500 years, a great artist was someone who could paint the real world with perfect accuracy. Then along came the camera, and, click, the artist was replaced by a machine. But unemployed artists refused to go the way of *The Fighting Téméraire.*

They couldn't match the camera for painstaking detail, but they could match it—even beat it—in capturing color, the fleeting moment, the candid pose, the play of light and shadow, the quick impression. A new breed of artists burst out of the stuffy confines of the studio. They donned scarves and berets and set up their canvases in farmers' fields or carried their notebooks into crowded cafés, dashing off quick sketches in order to catch a momentary... impression.

• *Start with the misty Monet train station.*

Monet—*Gare St. Lazare* (1877)

Claude Monet, the father of Impressionism, was more interested in the play of light off his subject than the subject itself. He uses smudges of white and gray paint to capture how sun filters through the glass roof of the train station and is refiltered through the clouds of steam.

Monet—*The Water-Lily Pond* (1899)

We've traveled from medieval spirituality to Renaissance realism to Baroque elegance and Impressionist colors. Before you spill out into the 21st-century hubbub of London, relax for a second in Monet's garden at Giverny, near Paris. Monet planned an artificial garden, rechanneled a stream, built a bridge, and planted these water lilies—a living work of art, an oasis of order and calm in a hectic world.

Manet—*Corner of a Café-Concert* (1878-1880)

Imagine just how mundane (and therefore shocking) Manet's quick "impression" of this café must have been to a public that was raised on Greek gods, luscious nudes, and glowing Madonnas.

Renoir—*The Skiff* (1875)

It's a nice scene of boats on sun-dappled water. Now move in close. The "scene" breaks up into almost random patches of bright colors. The "blue" water is actually separate brushstrokes of blue, green, pink, purple, gray, and white. The rower's hat is a blob of green, white, and blue. Up close, it looks like a mess, but when you back up to a proper distance, *voilà!* It shimmers. This kind of rough, coarse brushwork (where you can actually see the brushstrokes) is one of the telltale signs of Impressionism. Renoir was not trying to paint the water itself, but the reflection of sky, shore, and boats off its surface.

NATIONAL GALLERY

• *In Room 44, you'll find...*

Seurat—*Bathers at Asnières* (1884)

Viewed from about 15 feet away, this is a bright, sunny scene of people lounging on a riverbank. Up close it's a mess of dots, show-

ing the Impressionist color technique taken to its logical extreme. The "green" grass is a shag rug of green, yellow, red, brown, purple, and white brushstrokes. The boy's "red" cap is a collage of red, yellow, and blue.

Seurat has "built" the scene dot by dot, like a newspaper photo, using small points of different, bright colors. Only at a distance do the individual brushstrokes blend. Impressionism is all about color. Even people's shadows are not dingy black, but warm blues, greens, and purples.

• *In Room 45, you'll see...*

Van Gogh—*Sunflowers* (1888)

In military terms, Van Gogh was the point man of his culture. He went ahead of his cohorts, explored the unknown, and caught a bullet young. He added emotion to Impressionism, infusing his love of life even into inanimate objects. These sunflowers, painted with characteristic swirling brushstrokes, shimmer and writhe in either agony or ecstasy—depending on your own mood.

Van Gogh painted these during his stay in southern France, a time of frenzied creativity, when he hovered between despair and delight, bliss and madness. A year later, he shot himself.

In his day, Van Gogh was a penniless nobody, selling only one painting in his whole career. In 1987, a different *Sunflowers* painting (he did a half-dozen versions) sold for $40 million (a salary of about $2,500 a day for 45 years), and that's not even his highest-priced painting. Hmm.

Cézanne—*Bathers* (c. 1894-1905)

These bathers are arranged in strict triangles à la Leonardo—the five nudes on the left form one triangle, the seated nude on the right forms another, and even the background trees and clouds are triangular patterns of paint.

Cézanne uses the Impressionist technique of building a figure with dabs of paint (though his "dabs" are often larger-sized "cube"

shapes) to make solid, 3-D geometrical figures in the style of the Renaissance. In the process, his cube shapes helped inspire a radical new style—Cubism—bringing art into the 20th century.

• *Exiting Room 45, you find yourself in the stairwell of the Gallery's main entrance (under the dome) on Trafalgar Square. If you want to return to the Sainsbury Entrance, cross the stairwell and pass through several familiar rooms (with* The Ambassadors, *Michelangelo, etc.). When you reach Room 9, turn left to reach the Sainsbury Wing.*

After perusing 700 years of art—from gold-backed Madonnas to Cubistic bathers—you've earned a well-deserved break.

NATIONAL PORTRAIT GALLERY TOUR

Rock groupies, book lovers, movie fans, gossipmongers, and even historians all can find at least one favorite celebrity here. From Elizabeth I to Elizabeth II, Byron to Bowie, the National Portrait Gallery puts a face on 500 years, making "history" the simple story of flesh-and-blood people. Consider that, for the most part, these portraits were painted in the presence of their subjects—providing us with a tangible link to the real person in the painting. The Gallery is a great rainy-day museum for serious students, or a quick (and free) peek at the eccentric inhabitants of the British Isles.

Orientation

Cost: Free, but suggested donation of £5; temporary (optional) exhibits require an admission fee.

Hours: Daily 10:00-18:00, Thu-Fri until 21:00—often with music and drinks offered in the evening, first and second floors open Mon at 11:00, last entry to special exhibits 1 hour before closing.

Getting There: It's at St. Martin's Place, 100 yards off Trafalgar Square (around the corner from the National Gallery and opposite the Church of St. Martin-in-the-Fields). The closest Tube stops are Charing Cross and Leicester Square.

Information: A floor plan costs £1. The cozy "Digital Space" lounge on the first-floor mezzanine level (just up the stairs from the main lobby) is filled with comfy chairs and computers that let you tailor your own printable tour route through the collection. Tel. 020/7306-0055, recorded info tel. 020/7312-2463, www.npg.org.uk.

Tours: The well-done £3 audioguide lets you choose among several theme tours, or you can dial up any of 300 individual works.

"Portrait Explorer" computers on the mezzanine give info on virtually any portrait or artist in the extensive collection.

Length of This Tour: Allow 1.5 hours. If you're in a rush, focus on your favorite Brits through history.

Photography: Photos aren't allowed.

Cloakroom: Stuff your stuff in a £1 locker, or pay a £2 donation at the coat check (both downstairs from the entry).

Cuisine Art: The elegant Portrait Restaurant on the top floor is pricey but offers afternoon tea, and has a fine view over the rooftops of Westminster (£15-20 entrées, reservations wise, tel. 020/7312-2490); you can also just enjoy a drink at the bar with the same view. The Portrait Café in the basement (take the elevator down) is cheaper and offers sandwiches, salads, and pastries. For more eateries near Trafalgar Square, see page 422.

Starring: Royalty (Henry VIII, Elizabeth I, Victoria), writers (Shakespeare, the Brontës), scientists (Newton, Darwin), politicians (Churchill), and musicians (Handel, McCartney).

OVERVIEW

The Gallery covers 500 years of history from top to bottom—literally. Start on the top (second) floor and work chronologically down to modern times on the ground floor. Historians should linger at the top; celebrity hunters will lose elevation quickly and head to the contemporary section. There are many, many famous people from all walks of life, so use this chapter as an overview, then follow your interests, either with an audioguide or by reading the museum's informative labels.

The Tour Begins

• *From the lobby (which is up on the first floor), ride the long escalator up to the second floor and start in Room 1, marked* The Early Tudors.

Second Floor

1500s—DEBUT

The small, isolated island of Britain (pop. four million) enters the world stage. The Tudor kings—having already settled family feuds (the Wars of the Roses), balanced religious factions, and built England's navy—bring wealth from abroad.

• *Find the large black-and-white sketch (cartoon) of Henry VIII with his hands on his hips.*

National Portrait Gallery— Second Floor

To Room 20

ORANGE STREET ENTRANCE (BELOW)

19 18 16 14 **14** **12** 12 11
        16 **15** 15 **13** 13 **11**
        17 ✕REST **8** **9** 9 **10** 10
STAIRS TO FIRST FLOOR **8** 7 6 **7** 5 **6** **4** 4 **5**
📱 TOUR BEGINS **1** 1 2 **3** 3 ELEV. ✕
        2

Not to Scale

ST. MARTIN'S PLACE ENTRANCE (BELOW)

- **1** Henry VIII & Wives
- **2** Edward VI
- **3** Elizabeth I (3 Versions)
- **4** William Shakespeare
- **5** James I
- **6** Charles I
- **7** Oliver Cromwell
- **8** Charles II
- **9** Isaac Newton & John Locke
- **10** Christopher Wren
- **11** George Frideric Handel
- **12** James Watt
- **13** George III
- **14** George Washington
- **15** Admiral Horatio Nelson & Emma, Lady Hamilton
- **16** The Romantics

❶ Henry VIII (1491-1547), The Whitehall Mural Cartoon

Young, athletic, intense, and charismatic, with jeweled hands, gold dagger, and bulging codpiece (the very image of kingly power), Henry VIII carried England on his broad shoulders from political isolation to international power.

In middle age, he divorced his older, dull-eyed, post-childbearing queen, Catherine of Aragon (see her portrait on the nearby wall), for the younger, shrewd, sparkling-eyed Anne Boleyn (near Catherine; see photo, next page), in search of love, sex, and a male heir. Nine months later, the future Elizabeth I was born, and the pope excommunicated adulterous Henry. Defiant, Henry started the (Protestant) Church of England, sparking a century-plus of religious strife between the country's Protestants and Catholics.

By the time Henry died—400

NATIONAL PORTRAIT GALLERY

pounds of stinking, pus-ridden paranoia—he had wed six wives (see the
sixth, sweet young Catherine Parr, opposite her predecessors), executed several
of them (including Anne Boleyn), killed
trusted advisors, pursued costly wars,
and produced one male heir, Edward
VI (for more on Henry, see the sidebar,
later).

• *Opposite Henry is the looooong picture of...*

❷ Edward VI (1537-1553)

Nine-year-old Edward (son of Henry's third wife, Jane Seymour)
ruled for only six years before dying young, leaving England in
religious and economic turmoil. (View the optical illusion through
the hole at the right end to put the enigmatic boy king into perspective.)

• *Go to Room 2.*

❸ Elizabeth I (1533-1603) in Three Different Portraits

Elizabeth I was pale, stern-looking, red-haired (like her father,
Henry VIII), and wore big-shouldered power dresses. During

her reign, she kept Protestant/Catholic
animosity under control and made England a naval power and cultural capital.
Find three different portraits that span
her life. The one with the most elaborate
frame with a crown on the top shows her
coronation at age 26, with the crown,
scepter, and orb. At age 42 (see photo),
she exudes a regal bearing. The largest
painting *(The Ditchley Portrait)* captures
her standing on a map of England, age
60. She looks ageless, always aware of
her public image, resorting to makeup,

dye, wigs, showy dresses, and pearls to dazzle courtiers.

The "Virgin Queen" was married only to her country, but she
flirtatiously wooed opponents to her side. ("I know I have the body
of a weak and feeble woman," she'd coo, "but I have the heart and
stomach of a king.") When England's navy sank 72 ships of the
Spanish Armada in a single, power-shifting battle (1588), Britannia ruled the waves, feasting on New World spoils. Elizabeth surrounded herself with intellectuals, explorers, and poets.

• *Pass through Room 3, through the stairwell, and into Room 4.*

Henry VIII (1491-1547)

The notorious king who single-handedly transformed England was a true Renaissance Man—six feet tall, handsome, charismatic, well-educated, and brilliant. He spoke English, Latin, French, and Spanish. A legendary athlete, he hunted, played tennis, and jousted with knights and kings. He played the lute and wrote folk songs; his "Pastime with Good Company" is still being performed. When 17-year-old Henry, the second monarch of the House of Tudor, was crowned king in Westminster Abbey, all of England rejoiced.

Henry left affairs of state in the hands of others, and filled his days with sports, war, dice, women, and the arts. But in 1529, Henry's personal life became a political atom bomb, and it changed the course of history. Henry wanted a divorce, partly because his wife had become too old to bear him a son, and partly because he'd fallen in love with Anne Boleyn, a younger woman who stubbornly refused to be just the king's mistress. Henry begged the pope for an annulment, but—for political reasons, not moral ones—the pope refused. Henry went ahead and divorced his wife anyway, and he was excommunicated.

The event sparked the English Reformation. With his defiance, Henry rejected papal authority in England. He forced monasteries to close, sold off some church land, and confiscated everything else for himself and the Crown. Within a decade, monastic institutions that had operated for centuries were left empty and gutted (many ruined sites can be visited today, including the abbeys of Glastonbury, St. Mary's at York, Rievaulx, and Lindisfarne). Meanwhile, the Catholic Church was reorganized into the (Anglican) Church of England, with Henry as its head. Though Henry himself basically adhered to Catholic doctrine, he discouraged the veneration of saints and relics, and commissioned an English translation of the Bible. Hard-core Catholics had to assume a low profile. Many English welcomed this break from Italian religious influence, but others rebelled. For the next few generations, England would suffer through bitter Catholic-Protestant differences.

Henry famously had six wives. The issue was not his love life (which could have been satisfied by his numerous mistresses), but the politics of royal succession. To guarantee the Tudor family's dominance, he needed a male heir born by a recognized queen.

Henry's first marriage, to Catherine of Aragon, had been arranged to cement an alliance with her parents, Ferdinand and Isabel of Spain. Catherine bore Henry a daughter, but no sons. Next came Anne Boleyn, who also gave birth to a daughter. After a turbulent few years with Anne and several miscarriages, a frustrated

Henry had her beheaded at the Tower of London. His next wife, Jane Seymour, finally had a son (but Jane died soon after giving birth). A blind-marriage with Anne of Cleves ended quickly when she proved to be both politically useless and ugly—the "Flanders Mare." Next, teen bride Catherine Howard ended up cheating on Henry, so she was executed. Henry finally found comfort—but no children—in his later years with his final wife, Catherine Parr.

In 1536 Henry suffered a serious accident while jousting. His health would never be the same. Increasingly, he suffered from festering boils and violent mood swings, and he became morbidly obese, tipping the scales at 400 pounds with a 54-inch waist.

Henry's last years were marked by paranoia, sudden rages, and despotism. He gave his perceived enemies the pink slip in his signature way—charged with treason and beheaded. (Ironically, Henry's own heraldic motto was "Coeur Loyal"—true heart.) Once-wealthy England was becoming depleted, thanks to Henry's expensive habits, which included making war on France, building and acquiring palaces (he had 50), and collecting fine tapestries and archery bows.

Henry forged a large legacy. He expanded the power of the monarchy, making himself the focus of a rising, modern nation-state. Simultaneously, he strengthened Parliament—largely because it agreed with his policies. He annexed Wales, and imposed English rule on Ireland (provoking centuries of resentment). He expanded the navy, paving the way for Britannia to soon rule the waves. And—thanks to Henry's marital woes—England would forever be a Protestant nation.

When Henry died at age 55, he was succeeded by his nine-year-old son by Jane Seymour, Edward VI. Weak and sickly, Edward died six years later. Next to rule was Mary, Henry's daughter from his first marriage. A staunch Catholic, she tried to brutally reverse England's Protestant Reformation, earning the nickname "Bloody Mary." Finally came Henry's daughter with Anne Boleyn—Queen Elizabeth I, who ruled a prosperous, expanding England, seeing her father's seeds blossom into the English Renaissance.

London abounds with "Henry" sights. He was born in Greenwich (at today's Old Royal Naval College) and was crowned in Westminster Abbey. He built a palace along Whitehall and enjoyed another at Hampton Court. At the National Portrait Gallery, you can see portraits of some of Henry's wives, and at the Tower you can see where he executed them. Henry is buried alongside his final wife at Windsor Castle.

❹ William Shakespeare (1564-1616)

Though famous in his day, Shakespeare's long hair, beard, ear-ring, untied collar, and red-rimmed eyes make him look less the celebrity and more the bohemian barfly he likely was (for more on Shakespeare's life and influence, see the sidebar on page 236). This unassuming portrait captures 45-year-old Shakespeare just before he retired from his career as actor, poet, and world's greatest play-wright. The shiny, domed forehead is a beacon of intelligence. (I suspect Shakespeare liked this plain-spoken portrait.)

The museum attributes this portrait to a Shakespeare contemporary, John Taylor, and claims it's the only one that could have been painted during the Bard's lifetime. But other scholars insist it was done long after the writ-er's death. Compare this version with the one you can see in the British Library (see page 238.) One recently discovered portrait (not in the museum) depicts a 46-year-old Shake-speare looking like a matinee idol, with a full head of hair. The search goes on for the "real" Will.

• *Also in Room 4, find the portrait of James I that marks the end of the Elizabethan Age and the beginning of the...*

1600s—RELIGIOUS AND CIVIL WARS

Catholic kings bickered with an increasingly vocal Protestant Par-liament until Civil War erupted (1642-1651), killing thousands, decapitating the king, and eventually establishing Parliament as the main power.

❺ James I of England and VI of Scotland (1566-1625)

When the "Virgin Queen" died childless, her cousin—an arrogant Scotsman—moved to genteel London and donned the royal robes. Deeply religious, he launched the "King James" translation of the Bible, but he alien-ated Anglicans (Church of England), harder-line Protestants (Puritans), and democrats ev-erywhere by insisting that he ruled by divine right, directly from God. He passed on this attitude to his son, Charles.

• *Enter Room 5, with portraits of Civil War vet-erans.*

❻ Charles I (1600-1649)

Picture Charles' sensitive face (with scholar's eyes and artist's long hair and beard) severed from his elegant body (in horse-riding finery), and you've arrived quickly at the heart of the Civil War.

The short, shy, stuttering Charles angered Protestants and democrats by dissolving Parliament, raising taxes, and marrying a Catholic. Parliament formed an army, fought the king's supporters, arrested and tried Charles, and—outside the Banqueting House on Whitehall—beheaded him.

• *The man responsible was...*

❼ Oliver Cromwell (1599-1658)

Cromwell, with armor, sword, command baton, and a determined look, was the Protestant champion and military leader. The Civil

War pitted Parliamentarians (Parliament, Protestant Puritans, industry, and urban areas) against Royalists (King, Catholics, nobles, traditionalists, and rural areas). After Charles' execution, Cromwell led kingless England as "Lord Protector."

Stern Cromwell hated luxury and ordered a warts-and-all portrait (see wart on his left temple and scar between his eyebrows). He has a simple, bowl-cut hairstyle adorning his 82-ounce brain (49 is average). Speaking of heads, three years after Cromwell's death, vengeful Royalists exhumed his body, cut off the head, stuck it on a stick, and placed it outside Westminster Abbey, where it rotted publicly for 24 years.

• *Pass through Room 6 and into Room 7. Facing you is...*

❽ Charles II (1630-1685)

After two decades of wars, Cromwell's harsh rule, and Puritanical excesses (no dancing, theater, or political incorrectness), Parliament welcomed the monarchy back (with tight restrictions) under Charles II. England was ready to party.

Looking completely ridiculous, with splayed legs, puffy face, big-hair wig, garters, and ribbons on his shoes, Charles II became a king with nothing to do, and he did it with grace and a sense of humor. Charles' picture is sandwiched between portraits of his devoted wife,

Catherine of Braganza, and one of his well-known mistresses, the actress Nell Gwyn.

• *Make a U-turn right, entering Room 8. In the right corner are the bewigged and unamused...*

❾ Isaac Newton (1642-1727) and John Locke (1632-1704)

The 1600s, the Age of Enlightenment, saw scientific discoveries suggesting that the world operates in an orderly, rational way. Isaac Newton explained the universe's motion with the simplest of formulas (f = ma, etc.), and John Locke used human reason to plan a democratic utopia, coining phrases like "life, liberty..." that would inspire America's revolutionaries.

• *Walk straight ahead (through Room 9) to Room 10. Along the right wall, find...*

❿ Christopher Wren (1632-1723)

Christopher Wren—leaning on blueprints with a compass in hand—designed St. Paul's Cathedral, a glorious demonstration of mathematics in stone.

• *In Room 11, make a U-turn left, entering Room 12, with painters, writers, actors, and musicians of the 1700s.*

1700s—DOMESTIC STABILITY, WARS WITH FRANCE

Blossoming agriculture, the first factories, overseas colonization, and political stability from German-born kings (George I, II, III) allowed the arts to flourish. Overseas, England financed wars against Europe's No. 1 power, France.

⓫ George Frideric Handel (1685-1759)

In London, an old form of art became something new—modern theater. Handel, a German who wrote Italian operas in England, had several smash hits in London (especially with the oratorio *Messiah*, on his desk), making musical theater popular with ordinary folk. Hallelujah.

• *Walk on, to Room 13, for the portrait of...*

⓬ James Watt (1736-1819)

Deep-thinking Watt pores over plans to turn brainpower into work power. His steam engines (with a separate condenser to capture formerly wasted heat energy) soon powered gleaming machines, changing the focus of England's economy from grain and ships to iron and coal.

• *Head to Room 14, where you'll find George III over your left shoulder and George Washington along the right wall.*

⓭ George III (1738-1820) and
⓮ George Washington (1732-1799)

Just crowned at 23, King George III gives little hint in this portrait that he will lead England into the drawn-out, humiliating "Ameri-

can War" (Revolutionary War) against a colony demanding independence. George III, perhaps a victim of an undiagnosed disease, closed out the stuffy "Georgian" era (in Percy Shelley's words) "an old, mad, blind, despised, dying king."

Perhaps it was the war that drove him mad, or perhaps it was that his enemy, George Washington (portrait nearby), had the same hairdo. Washington was born in British-ruled Virginia and fought for Britain in the French and Indian War, but sided with the colonies in what the British called the "American War." This famous portrait of Washington is one of several versions of a 1796 portrait by Gilbert Stuart.

1800s—COLONIAL AND INDUSTRIAL GIANT

Britain defeated France (Napoleon) and emerged as the world's top power. With natural resources from overseas colonies (Australia, Canada, India, West Indies, China), good communications, and a growing population of seven million, Britain became the first industrial powerhouse, dotted with smoke-belching factories and laced with railroads.

• *Exit Room 14 into Room 8 and turn right, ending up in the bright aqua Room 17, featuring a red-jacketed man flanked by portraits of brave Brits who battled Napoleon.*

⓯ Admiral Horatio Nelson (1758-1805) and
Emma, Lady Hamilton (1761-1815)

While the Duke of Wellington fought Napoleon on land (the final victory at Waterloo, near Brussels, 1815), Admiral Nelson battled France at sea (Battle of Trafalgar, off Spain, 1805).

At Nelson's side is Emma, Lady Hamilton, dressed in white, with her famously beautiful face turned coyly. She first met dashing Nelson on his way to fight the French in Egypt. She used the influence of her husband, Lord Hamilton, to restock Nelson's ships. Nelson's daring victory at the Battle of the Nile made him an instant celebrity, though the battle cost him an arm and an eye. The hero—a married man—returned home to woo, bed, and impregnate Lady H., with sophisticated Lord Hamilton's patriotic tolerance.

NATIONAL PORTRAIT GALLERY

• *Go to Room 18.*

⓰ The Romantics

Not everyone worshipped industrial progress. Romantics questioned the clinical detachment of science, industrial pollution, and the personal restrictions of modern life. They reveled in strong emotions, non-Western cultures, personal freedom, opium, and the beauties of nature.

• *Scattered around the room, you'll see...*

John Keats (1795-1821) broods over his just-written "Ode to a Nightingale." ("My heart aches, and a drowsy numbness pains/My sense, as though of hemlock I had drunk.")

Samuel Taylor Coleridge (1772-1834), at 23, is open-eyed, open-mouthed, and eager. ("And all should cry, Beware! Beware!/His flashing eyes, his floating hair!/...For he on honey-dew hath fed,/And drunk the milk of Paradise."—"Kubla Khan")

Mary Wollstonecraft Shelley (1797-1851), in telling ghost stories with husband Percy Shelley and friend Lord Byron, conceived a tale of science run amok—*Frankenstein*—imitated by many. ("Ahhhhhhh, sweet mystery of life, at last I've found you!")

William Wordsworth (1770-1850): "The world is too much with us.../Little we see in Nature that is ours;/We have given our hearts away, a sordid boon!"

Percy Bysshe Shelley (1792-1822), political radical, sexual explorer (involving Mary and Claire Clairmont), traveler, and poet. ("O wild West Wind, thou breath of Autumn's being,.../If Winter comes, can Spring be far behind?")

George Gordon, **Lord Byron** (1788-1824), was athletic, exotic, and passionate about women and freedom. Famous and scandalous in his day, he became a Kerouacian symbol of the Romantic movement. ("She walks in beauty, like the night/Of cloudless climes and starry skies...")

Jane Austen (1775-1817) wrote of her surrounding landed-gentry class—its manners, love lives, and lifestyle. ("The person, be it gentleman or lady, who has not pleasure in a good novel, must be intolerably stupid.")

• *After browsing Rooms 19 and 20, backtrack to Room 15 and head downstairs one flight to the **first floor**. Turn right at the bottom of the stairs, pass through the long hall lined with busts (Room 22), and enter Room 21.*

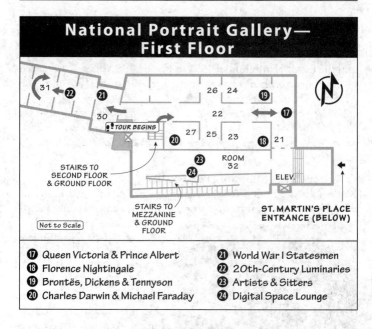

National Portrait Gallery— First Floor

31 22 21
30 TOUR BEGINS
20 27 25 23 18 21
26 24 19
22 17
23 ROOM 32
24 ELEV.

STAIRS TO
SECOND FLOOR
& GROUND FLOOR

STAIRS TO
MEZZANINE
& GROUND
FLOOR

Not to Scale

ST. MARTIN'S PLACE
ENTRANCE (BELOW)

17 Queen Victoria & Prince Albert
18 Florence Nightingale
19 Brontës, Dickens & Tennyson
20 Charles Darwin & Michael Faraday

21 World War I Statesmen
22 20th-Century Luminaries
23 Artists & Sitters
24 Digital Space Lounge

First Floor

1837-1901—THE VICTORIANS

As the wealthiest nation on earth with a global colonial empire, Britain during Queen Victoria's long reign embraced modern technology, contributing to the development of power looms, railroads, telephones, motorcars, and electric lights. It was a golden age of science, literature, and middle-class morality, though pockets of extreme poverty and vice lurked in the heart of London itself.

• *Find a statue of a happy couple, titled* Queen Victoria and Prince Albert in Anglo-Saxon Dress. *Flanking the statue are paintings of...*

17 Queen Victoria (1819-1901) and Prince Albert (1819-1861)

Crowned at 18, the short (5 feet), plump, bug-eyed, quiet girl in-

herited a world empire. The next year, she proposed marriage (the custom) to the German Prince Albert. They were a perfect match—lovers, friends, and partners—a model for middle-class couples.

(See the white statue of the pair as genteel knight and adoring lady.) Albert co-ruled, especially when "Vickie" was pregnant with their nine kids. "Bertie" promoted education, science, public works, and the Great Exhibition of 1851 in Hyde Park. When Albert died at 42, a heartbroken Victoria moped for 40 years. (For more on Victoria, see the sidebar on page 534.)

• *Double back through the long hall lined with stuffy busts of starched shirts (Room 22), browsing around the rooms branching off it. These rooms are filled with many prominent Victorians. Start with Room 23 and...*

⓲ Florence Nightingale (1820-1910)

Known as "the Lady with the Lamp" for her nightly nursing visits (though in this detail from a larger painting, she's standing lamp-

less, in the center, with a piece of paper), Nightingale traveled to Turkey in 1854 to tend to Crimean War victims. In fact, her forte was not hands-on nursing but efficient hospital administration (sanitation, keeping supplies stocked, transporting wounded), which ended up saving lives and raising public awareness about health issues. To learn more about her, you can visit the Florence Nightingale Museum, just across the Thames from Big Ben (in Gassiot House at 2 Lambeth Palace Road, Tube: Westminster, Waterloo, or Lambeth North).

• *Across the hall, in Room 24, you'll find several...*

⓳ Writers

Anne, Emily, and Charlotte Brontë (left to right, youngest to oldest, painted by brother Branwell), three teenage country girls, grew up to write novels such as *Wuthering Heights* (Emily, 1818-1848) and *Jane Eyre* (Charlotte, 1816-1855), about the complex family and love lives of England's rural gentry.

To the left of the Brontës is a youthful **Charles Dickens** (1812-1870). He was only 12 years old when his dad was sent to a debtor's prison, forcing young Charles to work in a factory. The experience gave him a working-class perspective on British society. He became phenomenally successful writing popular novels *(Oliver Twist, A Tale of Two Cities, A Christmas Carol)* for Britain's educated middle class.

To the right of the Brontës is **Alfred, Lord Tennyson** (1809-1892), the poet laureate of Victorian earnestness. ("Theirs not to reason why,/Theirs but to do and die;/Into the Valley of Death/ Rode the six hundred.")

• *Head to Room 27.*

⓴ Science and Technology

Charles Darwin (1809-1882), with basset-hound eyes and long white beard, looks tired after a lifetime of reluctantly defending his

controversial theory of evolution, which shocked an entire generation. **Michael Faraday** (1791-1867), across from Darwin, shocked himself from time to time, harnessing electricity as the work force of the next century.

• *The long hall (Room 22) leads into Room 30, dedicated to World War I.*

1900s—WORLD WARS

Two devastating world wars and an emerging US superpower shrank Britain from global empire to island nation. But the country remained a cultural giant, producing writers, actors, composers, painters, and Beatles.

㉑ World War I Statesmen

Fighting Germans from trenches in France and Belgium, the British Army lost nearly a million men. In the big group portrait titled *Some Statesmen of the Great War,* find a bored-looking Winston Churchill.

• *The large Room 31 contains 20th-century portraits. These exhibits change frequently, and some of the portraits mentioned here may not be on display during your visit. Be prepared to put the book aside and browse.*

㉒ 20th-Century Luminaries

Find the painting of the **Duchess of Windsor** (see photo) and the small statue of **Edward, Duke of Windsor.** The Duchess' smug smile tells us she got her man.

Edward VIII (1894-1972), great-grandson of Queen Victoria, became king in 1936 as a bachelor dating a common-born (gasp),

twice-divorced (double gasp) American (oh no!) named Wallis Simpson (1896-1986). Rather than create a constitutional stink, Edward quietly abdicated, married Wallis, and the two moved to the Continent, living happily ever after. They hosted cocktail parties, played golf, and listened to servants call them "Your Majesty"—though they were now just plain Duke and Duchess of Windsor. (His brother "Bertie" took over as King George VI, and George VI's daughter became Queen Elizabeth II. Elizabeth—and all the other royals—essentially snubbed their disgraced aunt and uncle for the rest of their lives.)

George Bernard Shaw (1856-1950)—playwright, critic, and political thinker—brought socialist ideas into popular discussion with plays such as *Man and Superman* and *Major Barbara*. **Virginia Woolf** (1882-1941) wrote feminist essays ("A woman must have money and a room of her own if she is to write fiction") and experimental novels (*Mrs. Dalloway* jumps back and forth in time) before filling her pockets with stones and drowning herself in a river to silence the voices in her head.

In the darkest days at the beginning of World War II, with Nazi bombs raining on a wounded London, Sir **Winston Churchill** (1874-1965) rallied his people with stirring speeches from the Houses of Parliament. ("We shall fight on the beaches... We shall never surrender!") Britain's military chief, Field Marshall **Bernard Montgomery, 1st Viscount** (1887-1976, known as "Monty") points out the D-Day beaches of the decisive Allied assault.

Sir **Laurence Olivier** (1907-1989), movie and stage actor, played everything from romantic leads and Shakespeare heavies to character parts with funny accents. Sir **Noel Coward** (1899-1973) continued the British tradition of writing witty, sophisticated comedies about the idle rich. **Henry Moore** (1898-1986), the most famous 20th-century sculptor, combined the grandeur of Michelangelo, the raw stone of primitive carvings, and the simplified style of abstract art. **Dylan Thomas** (1914-1953) wrote abstract imagery with a Romantic's heart ("Do not go gentle into that good night..."). American-born poet **T. S. Eliot** (1888-1965; see photo) captured the quiet banality of modern life: "This is the way the world ends/Not with a bang but a whimper."

• *Backtrack to the stairs. Just before you reach them, the long Room 32 is filled with an exhibit called...*

㉓ Artists and Sitters: Britain 1960-1990

This ever-changing collection highlights the relationship between portraitist and subject. Often included in this section are contemporary royals (including Queen Elizabeth II, Prince Charles, and the late Princess Di), politicians (Margaret Thatcher), and fixtures of British popular culture. Look for iconic Andy Warhol portraits of Mick Jagger, Joan Collins, and Elizabeth Taylor (London-born to American parents).

• *Now head down to the **ground floor**.*

1990 TO THE PRESENT

London since the Swinging '60s has been a major exporter of pop culture. The contemporary collection, located in Rooms 32-42, changes often depending on who's hot, but you may find royal youngsters (William and Harry, plus a famously creepy-looking Kate), politicians (Tony Blair), entrepreneurs (Sir Richard Branson), classic-rock geezers (Sir Paul McCartney, Sir Elton John, David Bowie), and actors (Sir Michael Caine, Dame Judi Dench), as well as those in lower-profile professions—writers (Sir Salman Rushdie, Doris Lessing, Germaine Greer), scientists (Stephen Hawking), composers, painters, and intellectuals.

We've gone from battles to Beatles, seeing Britain's history in the faces of its major players.

WEST END WALK

From Leicester Square to Piccadilly Circus

The West End, the area just west of the original walled City of London, is London's liveliest neighborhood. It's easy to get caught up in fantasies of jolly olde England, but the West End is where you'll feel the pulse of the living, breathing London of today, from genteel shopping to raunchy red light districts, and everything in between. Theaters, pubs, restaurants, bookstores, ethnic food, markets, and boutiques attract rock stars, punks, tourists, and ladies and gentlemen stepping from black cabs for a night on the town.

Most of this book's walks and tours focus on history, art, and museums. But this walk is about appreciating the London lifestyle: the entertainment energy at Leicester Square; the thriving popular hum of Covent Garden; the rock-and-roll history of Denmark Street; the bohemian, creative, hedonistic groove of Soho; the once-swingin', now corporate Carnaby Street; the bustling neon hub of Piccadilly Circus; and the distinctive shopping boulevards of Regent Street and Piccadilly Street.

The walk is divided into two parts. The first takes you through the colorful heart of this area (lively and a bit seedy), while the second part—for those who still have energy (and pounds) left—is more focused on swanky shopping (or window-shopping) zones.

Orientation

Length of This Walk: Allow three hours to lace together these highlights (or much more if you go beyond window-shopping). To trim about an hour off this walk, do just Part 1 (trim more by skipping some window-shopping).

When to Go: Take your pick—shopping by day, or nightlife after dark. The many shops in this walk are generally open Mon-Sat 10:00-18:00 or 20:00, and Sun 12:00-18:00. If you'd like to have afternoon tea at The Wolseley or Fortnum & Mason, plan on arriving at either place between 15:30 and 18:30 (though The Wolseley closes earlier on Sat, and F&M closes earlier on Sun—see page 433). Early evenings are ideal, since most shops stay open at least until 18:00 (and many later). After that, you join the bustle of people grabbing dinner or a show.

Getting There: Take the Tube to the Leicester Square stop, which is a block from the square itself.

Finding Your Way: If you have a more detailed map than the one provided here, it may help you find your way more quickly through the maze of irregular streets.

The Walk Begins

• *Start at Leicester Square. Stand at the top of the square and take in the scene.*

PART 1: LEICESTER SQUARE, COVENT GARDEN, AND SOHO
❶ Leicester Square

Leicester (LESS-ter) Square is a small park surrounded by glitzy cinema houses. This space was modernized and spiffed up in anticipation of the 2012 Olympics crowds. It sits smack in the middle of the theater district—ground zero for London's enticing offerings of flashy musicals, intimate plays starring big-name actors, and much more (for details, see the Entertainment in London chapter). Here, at the entertainment center of London, a statue of Shakespeare looks out, as if pondering the quote chiseled into his pedestal: "There is no darkness but ignorance." Charlie Chaplin, facing the bard, was a Londoner, the child of music-hall performers.

The square's **movie theaters**—the Odeon (Britain's largest cinema), Empire, and Vue—are famous for hosting red-carpet

movie premieres. When Tom Cruise, Angelina Jolie, or Brad Pitt needs a publicity splash, it'll likely be here. (Search online for "London film premieres" to find upcoming events.) On any given night, this entire area is a mosh-pit of clubs and partying teens in town from the suburbs.

Leicester Square is the central clearinghouse for daytime theater ticket sales. Check out the **TKTS booth** (see page 455) and ignore all the other establishments that bill themselves as "half-price" (they're just normal booking agencies). It's usually cheaper still to buy tickets directly from one of the theaters we'll pass on this walk.

Capital Radio London (next to the Odeon) plays a role in British rock-and-roll history. Back in the 1960s, the BBC was the only radio station in town, and it was mostly talk and Bach, with a smattering of pop. The British Invasion was in full swing—Beatles, Rolling Stones, The Who—but Brits couldn't hear much of it on the BBC. They had to resort to "pirate" radio stations, beamed from Luxembourg or from ships at sea. Capital Radio was one of the first commercial stations allowed to play rock and roll—and that was in 1973! Ironically, within a few years, Capital had itself become mainstream, refusing to play punk acts like the Clash or Ramones. The Clash struck back with their song "Capital Radio," which starts, "Yes, it's time for the Dr. Goebbels Show..." Today, FM 95.8 carries on as a major top-40 broadcasting power.

• *Exit Leicester Square from its top corner, heading east (past the Vue cinema) on Cranbourn Street. Cross Charing Cross Road and continue along Cranbourn to the six-way intersection, then angle right onto Garrick Street.*

Shortly afterward, turn left onto calm, brick-lined Floral Street. Soon you'll pass (on the left) the back door of Stanfords, an excellent travel book and map shop (see page 22). Farther along Floral Street, you'll be immersed in a scintillating array of fashion boutiques. (Lovers of couture may want to pace themselves—there are plenty of shopping opportunities coming up.) When Floral Street opens onto traffic-free James Street, turn right and head for...

❷ Covent Garden

Covent Garden (only tourists pluralize the name) is a large square teeming with people and street performers—jugglers, sword swallowers, and guitar players. London's buskers (including those in the Tube) are auditioned, licensed, and assigned times and places where they are allowed to perform.

The square's centerpiece is a covered marketplace. A market has been here since medieval times, when it was the "convent" garden owned by Westminster Abbey. In the 1600s, it became a housing development with this courtyard as its center, done in the Palladian style by Inigo Jones. Today's fine iron-and-glass structure was built in 1830 (when such buildings were all the Industrial Age rage) to house the stalls of what became London's chief produce market.

A market still thrives here today (for details, see page 450). Go inside the market hall and poke around. As you enter through the brick passage, notice the posted diagram on the right identifying shops. Inside the market, you'll hit the so-called Apple Market zone. Picture it in full Dickensian color, lined with fruit and vegetable stalls. Covent Garden remained a produce market until 1973, when its venerable arcades were converted to boutiques, cafés, and antique shops.

Back out on Covent Garden square, across from the west end of the market hall, stands **St. Paul's Church** (not the famous cathedral), with its Greek temple-like facade and blue clock face (notice the 50p WCs just to the left). Known as the Actors' Church, it's long been a favorite of nervous performers praying for success. To go inside, pass through one of the gates on either side of the facade, and find the entrance around back. If the gates are closed, you can duck down the streets on either side of the church and look for the passage leading to the tranquil churchyard—a nice escape from the busker bustle on Covent Garden. Inside, the walls are lined with memorials to theater folk, some of whom (Chaplin, Karloff) you might recognize (irregular hours, generally daily 8:30-17:30, often later for special events, sometimes closed Mon in winter).

At the bottom (southeast) corner of the square is the **London Transport Museum,** which gives a well-presented look at the evolution of this city's famously well-planned mass transit system (see page 58).

Tucked into the top (northeast) corner of the square is the **Royal Opera House,** which showcases top-notch opera and ballet. For such a high-profile building, it has a surprisingly low-profile entrance (through the revolving door in the corner of the square).

• *Now browse your way northwest, along some lively and colorful streets.*

❸ From Covent Garden to Charing Cross Road

First backtrack two blocks up James Street, then continue straight (along the side of Marks & Spencer) up narrow Neal Street. Head two blocks up Neal Street, passing through an up-and-coming shopping zone. Turn left on Short's Gardens, and find the tight alley (on the right) leading to the cozy, funky, psychedelically painted courtyard called **Neal's Yard,** with a thriving veggie restaurant scene (see page 425 in the Eating in London chapter).

WEST END

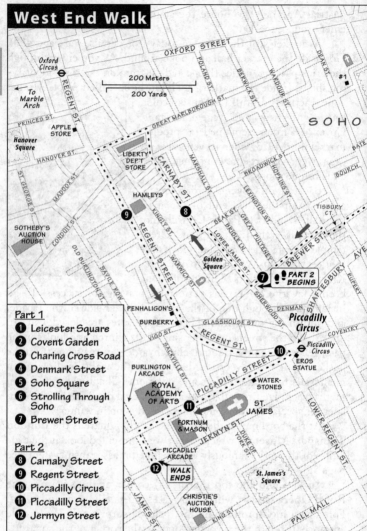

West End Walk

Part 1
1. Leicester Square
2. Covent Garden
3. Charing Cross Road
4. Denmark Street
5. Soho Square
6. Strolling Through Soho
7. Brewer Street

Part 2
8. Carnaby Street
9. Regent Street
10. Piccadilly Circus
11. Piccadilly Street
12. Jermyn Street

Back on Short's Gardens, Neal's Yard Dairy (at #17) sells a wide variety of cheeses from the British Isles. This is the original shop of what is now a thriving chain. Everything is well-described, and they'll slice off a sample if you ask nicely (Mon-Sat 10:00-19:00, closed Sun).

Continue along Short's Gardens to the next intersection—called **Seven Dials**—where seven sundials atop a pole mark the meeting of seven small streets. Continue more or less straight ahead onto Earlham Street.

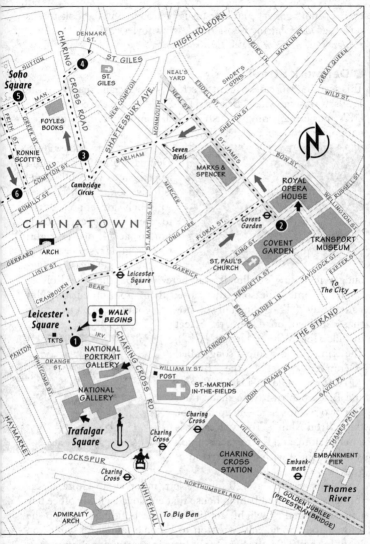

Then, bearing left, you'll spill out into **Cambridge Circus**—the busy intersection of Shaftesbury Avenue and Charing Cross Road—with its fine red-brick Victorian architecture and classic theaters. **Charing Cross Road** is the traditional home of London's bookstores. Turn right up Charing Cross and walk two blocks to reach one of the biggest, **Foyles Books,** which puts on free events several nights a week—from book signings to jazz in

their upstairs gallery and café (usually around 18:00, bookstore is on left at 113 Charing Cross Road, www.foyles.co.uk).

• *A few steps up from Foyles, turn right onto...*

❹ Denmark Street

This seemingly nondescript little street is a musician's mecca. In the 1920s, it was known as "Britain's Tin Pan Alley"—the center of the UK's music-publishing industry, when songwriters here cranked out popular tunes printed as sheet music.

Later, in the 1960s, Denmark Street was ground zero for rock and roll's British Invasion, which brought so much great pop music to the US. Regent Sounds Studio (at #4, on the right, now a guitar store with a similar name) was a low-budget recording studio. It was here in 1964 that the Rolling Stones recorded the song that raised them from obscurity, "Not Fade Away" ("I'm gonna tell you how it's gonna be..."). Other acts that recorded on Denmark Street include The Who ("Happy Jack"), The Kinks (who wrote a song called "Denmark Street"), the Beatles ("Fixing a Hole"), David Bowie, and Black Sabbath (who made their first two records here—including the track "Iron Man"). Today, Regent is a music store, and the former studio's walls are lined with a wonderland of guitars.

The storefront at #20 (on the left, now Wunjo Guitars) was formerly a music publishing house that employed a lowly office boy named Reginald Dwight. In 1969, on the building's rooftop, he wrote "Your Song" and went on to become famous as Sir Elton John. In the 1970s, the Sex Pistols lived in apartments above #6 (on the right). The 12 Bar Café (at #25, on the left) features live music, and helped launch the careers of more recent acts: Damien Rice, KT Tunstall, Jeff Buckley, and Keane.

Today, Denmark Street offers one-stop shopping for the modern musician. Without leaving this short street, you could buy a vintage Rickenbacker guitar, get your sax repaired, take piano lessons, lay down a bass track, have a few beers, or tattoo your name across your fist like Ozzy Osbourne. Notice the bulletin board in the alley alongside the 12 Bar Café (through the doorway marked

#27). If you're a musician looking for a band to play in, this could be your connection.

• *From Denmark Street, go back across Charing Cross Road and head down Manette Street (alongside Foyles). After a short block, on the right (down the lane called Orange Yard) you'll see The Borderline, where R.E.M. and Oasis have played. Continue down Manette Street and under the "Pillars of Hercules" passage, then turn right up Greek Street to...*

❺ Soho Square

The Soho neighborhood is London's version of New York City's Greenwich Village. It's a ritzy, raffish, edgy, and colorful area. Because of its eccentric 1970s landlord, porn publisher Paul Raymond, the Soho district escaped late 20th-century development. So, rather than soulless office towers, it retains its characteristic charm. And because the square has no real through-roads, it's almost traffic-free—strangely quiet and residential-feeling for being in the center of such a huge city.

Soho Square Gardens is a favorite place on a sunny afternoon. The little house in the middle of the square is the gardener's hut. At #1, on the west (left) side of the square, the MPL building (McCartney Publishing Limited) houses offices of Britain's richest musician, Sir Paul McCartney.

• *At the bottom of the square, wander down Frith Street (which runs parallel to Greek Street).*

❻ Strolling Through Soho

The restaurants and boutiques here and on adjoining streets (such as Greek, Dean, and Wardour streets) are trendy and creative, the kind that attract high society when they feel like slumming it. Bars with burly, well-dressed bouncers abound. Private clubs, like the low-profile Groucho Club (a block over, at #45 Dean Street), cater to the late-night rock crowd.

Ronnie Scott's Jazz Club (#47 Frith Street) has featured big-name acts for more than 50 years. In 1970, Jimi Hendrix jammed here with Eric Burdon and War; it was the last performance before his death in a London apartment a few days later.

Frith Street hits **Old Compton Street** at the center of the neighborhood. This street is a fixture of London's gay scene. Stroll a block to the right on Old Compton Street to take in the eclectic variety of people going by. You're surrounded by the buzz of Soho.

At the corner of Dean Street, look for the pagoda-style arch down the street. South of here, on the other side of Shaftesbury

Avenue, is London's underwhelming **Chinatown.** With Gerrard Street as its spine, it occupies what was once just more of Soho, with the same Soho artsy vibe. In the 1960s, the Chinese community gathered here, eventually dominated this zone, and non-Asian businesses moved out. The Chinese population swelled when the former British colony of Hong Kong was returned to China in 1997, but the neighborhood's identity is now threatened by developers eyeing this high-rent real estate.

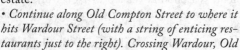

• *Continue along Old Compton Street to where it hits Wardour Street (with a string of enticing restaurants just to the right). Crossing Wardour, Old Compton squeezes down into a narrow alley (Tisbury Court). Penetrate this sleazy passage of sex shows and blue-video shops, tolerate the barkers' raunchy come-ons, then jog a half-block right and turn left on Brewer Street.*

❼ Brewer Street: Sleaze, Porn Shops, and Prostitutes

Soho was a bordello zone in the 19th century. A bit of that survives today in this area. Sex shops, video arcades, and prostitution mingle with upscale restaurants here in west Soho. While it's il-

legal in Britain to sell sex on the street, well-advertised "models" entertain (profitably) in their tiny apartments. Berwick Street hosts a daily produce market.

• *The first half of our walk is nearly finished. Continue a few short blocks along Brewer Street, observing the fascinating metamorphosis of a neighborhood from sleaze to gentrification. When you reach The Crown Tavern, at the intersection of Brewer Street and Sherwood Street (also called Lower James Street), it's time to plan your next move.*

If you're ready to call it quits, you could turn left onto Sherwood Street, walk one block, and turn to page 192 to finish up at Piccadilly Circus.

Better yet, stick with me for...

PART 2: SHOPPING STREETS AND PICCADILLY CIRCUS

The mile-long second half of this walk—along Regent Street to Piccadilly Circus, then up the street called Piccadilly and down Jermyn Street—takes you by the most typically London stores and shops. While useful for true shoppers, this walk is also a lot of fun for window-shoppers.

• *At Sherwood/Lower James Street, turn right (north on Upper James Street) and walk two blocks, passing the park-like Golden Square. Then jog left at Beak Street to find...*

❽ Carnaby Street

In the Swinging '60s, when Pete Townshend needed a paisley shirt, John Lennon a Nehru jacket, or Twiggy a miniskirt, they came here—where those mod fashions were invented. Today, there's not

a hint of hippie. For the most part, Carnaby Street looks like everything else from the '60s does now—sanitized and co-opted by upscale franchises. At least the upper end of the street retains a whiff of funkiness.

Walk north, the length of Carnaby Street, which leads to the back entrance of the venerable **Liberty** department store. Pop in. Liberty is a big, stately, local-favorite department store established in 1875, now housed in this distinctive faux-Tudor building (built in the 1920s from the timbers of two Royal Navy ships). Liberty is known for its fine design and "Liberty Print" patterned cloth.

• *From Liberty, continue west (hook left on Great Marlborough Street), then left again onto...*

❾ Regent Street

You're in the heart of London's shopping neighborhood. This intersection also marks a sort of class divide among London shoppers. (A couple of blocks to the north is the mid-range shopping area, **Oxford Street,** which is lined by less-distinguished chains and department stores and seems scruffier than Regent Street).

But this walk focuses on **Regent Street,** with London's high-class, top-dollar shopping outlets. This street has wide sidewalks, fine architecture, and royal-family connections. Most of its shops call the Queen their landlord, as she owns much of the land here.

While it's the local shops and boutiques that make Regent Street famous, American chains are certainly part of the scene. For example, the **Apple Store**—a half-block up from Liberty at #235 Regent Street—is in a building that looks more like a palace. It's popular with Londoners, who are astounded by its service. The English are capable of good service too, but, as a Londoner put it to me, "not the obsequious butt-kissing some Americans expect, because that makes you feel like a servant."

Also on Regent Street (just downhill from Liberty, left side, at #188-196), follow the giddy kids to **Hamleys,** Britain's biggest toy store. In 2010 it marked its 250th anniversary of delighting children. Seven floors buzz with 28,000 toys, managed by a staff of 200. Employees, some dressed in playful costumes, give demos of the latest gadgets. It was here at Hamleys that the world first got to know the Build-a-Bear Workshop (now a fixture at malls everywhere) and London's genteel Paddington Bear.

On this stretch of Regent Street, fine bits of old England class dominate. **Hackett** (right, at #143-147) is the place to go for preppy young English menswear. **Mappin and Webb** (left, at #132) is the Queen's jeweler. **Penhaligon's** (right, at #125) is the quintessential English perfumery, where royals shop (note the coat of arms at the door) for classic English scents like lavender and rose (fine sampler gift packs and free sniff samples). Once dowdy—it's a clothier of the royal family—**Burberry** (on the right, at #121) is now hip.

• *Regent Street arcs seductively into the ever-vibrant...*

❿ Piccadilly Circus

London's most touristy square got its name from the fancy ruffled shirts—*picadils*—made in the neighborhood long ago. In the late 20th century, the square veered toward the gimmicky and tacky—look no further than the gargantuan Ripley's Believe-It-or-Not Museum. But, it's trending back.

Until just a couple of years ago, this was a famously busy traffic circle, with cars and big red buses spinning around the tipsy-but-perfectly balanced Eros statue in the center. Now—though still busy with cars—it's also a packed people zone. At night, when neon pulses, the 20-foot-high video ads paint the classic Georgian facades in a rainbow of colors. Black cabs honk, tourists crowd the attractions, and Piccadilly shows off big-city London at its glitziest.

Piccadilly Circus is where common tastes steamroll the elegance of Regent Street. **Lillywhites** (at the bottom of the square, near the Eros fountain) is a sports store popular as a place to buy the jersey of your favorite football (soccer) team. Farther left (at the start of Coventry Street) is **Cool Britannia,** a tacky palace of English kitsch and a Union Jack fantasy for anyone needing to buy a Brit-themed gift.

• *For some more characteristic London shops—and a chance for a tea break—we'll do a little loop to the west. From Piccadilly Circus, turn right and wander down the busy...*

⓫ Piccadilly Street

After a block on your left (at #203), escape from the frenzy of Piccadilly into the quiet of **Waterstones,** Europe's largest bookshop and the flagship store of its widespread chain. Page through seven orderly floors. The fifth floor offers a hip bar with minimalist furniture and great views (see sidebar on page 86).

Next you'll pass Christopher Wren's **St. James's Church** (with free lunchtime concerts several days a week at 13:10—see page 461) and a tiny all-day flea market (antiques Tue 10:00-18:00, crafts Wed-Sat 11:00-18:00, closed Sun-Mon). One block farther (on the left, at #181) is the **Fortnum & Mason** department store, which eschews the glitz of bigger stores and revels in understated, old-school elegance. At the top of the hour the fancy clock on the facade is the scene of a low-key spectacle, as the venerable store's founders—Fortnum and Mason—come out and bow to each other (best viewed from across the street). This reminds shoppers of the store's humble beginnings 300 years ago, when it was started by these two footmen of Queen Anne. With rich displays and deep red carpet, Fortnum's feels classier and more relaxed than Harrods. The Queen, Camilla, and Kate—three generations of royalty—enjoyed tea here together in 2012.

Across the street from Fortnum & Mason is the delightful covered shopping street of **Burlington Arcade** (at #51, just beyond the entrance to Burlington House).

An elegant way to cap your shopping stroll (we'll finish just a block from here) is with a traditional **afternoon tea.** While pricey, many consider this ritual an essential part of any London visit. My two favorite places in town for a traditional afternoon tea are within a block of here: Fortnum & Mason (with several restaurants and price ranges), and a block farther down Piccadilly Street, **The Wolseley,** the grand 1920s former showroom of a now defunct car manufacturer (where couples are allowed to split a £22.50 tea in sumptuous sur-

roundings; on the left at #160); for details on F&M and The Wolseley, see "Taking Tea in London" on page 433. Beyond that is the original **Ritz Hotel,** where the tea is much fancier.

• *But before we part ways, we'll stroll a block south of big and busy Piccadilly Street. Opposite the Burlington Arcade, the Piccadilly Arcade leads to quiet...*

⑰ Jermyn Street

A statue of **Beau Brummell,** the ultimate dandy, meets you as if to say, "Within a block in either direction are numerous fine gentlemen's shirtmakers and many other delightful small shops."

Stand by the statue and survey your menswear shopping options (all to the right): **Bates Hats** (#73) still sells bowlers and top hats, as it has for a century. **Turnbull & Asser** (#71) has dressed Winston Churchill, Prince Charles, and James Bond with its "bespoke" (custom-made) shirts and suits. **John Lobb** (#88) has sold boots to Princes William and Harry. **Tricker's** (#67) has been making shoes for the gentleman since the days of Beau Brummell.

It was Brummell (1778-1840) who popularized the understated jacket-trousers-and-tie ensemble that men still wear today. As the quote on his statue reads, "To be truly elegant, one should not be noticed."

• *Our walk is finished. From here, you have several nearby options. If you're ready for **teatime**, cut back through the block to Piccadilly Street and the places I mentioned earlier.*

*Or, to head back to **Piccadilly Circus** (and its handy Tube stop), walk east down Jermyn Street, pausing at the classic perfume shop Floris (at #89) and at Paxton & Whitfields (#93), which has served exceptional cheese since 1797, with generous tastings. On the little Duke of York Street (behind St. James's Church) is an old-fashioned barbershop called Geo. F. Trumper (selling top-quality shaving gear) and the classic Red Lion Pub. If all of this is just too elegant, dip into Piccadilly Square's Cool Britannia and buy some Union Jack underwear.*

COURTAULD GALLERY TOUR

The Courtauld Gallery (part of the Courtauld Institute of Art) is just small enough that you can see it all in a single visit, which makes for a pleasant experience. The collection spans the history of Western painting, from medieval altarpieces through the Italian Renaissance to the 20th century. But its highlight is Impressionist and Post-Impressionist works, some of which you'll recognize. Besides the pieces I've featured, you'll likely see many other well-known Post-Impressionist, Fauvist, and early modern paintings, part of the museum's rotating collection of loaners. For some, the Van Gogh self-portrait alone is worth the price of admission.

The gallery is located at Somerset House, a grand 18th-century civic palace that offers a marvelous public space (housing temporary exhibits) and a riverside terrace with several eateries (between the Strand and the Thames). The palace once held the national registry that recorded Britain's births, marriages, and deaths: "...where they hatch 'em, match 'em, and dispatch 'em." Step into the courtyard to enjoy the fountain. Go ahead...walk through it. The 55 jets get playful twice an hour. In the winter, this becomes a popular ice-skating rink with a toasty café for viewing.

Orientation

Cost: £6 (£3 on Mon). Admission includes temporary exhibits.

Hours: Daily 10:00-18:00, last entry 30 minutes before closing, occasionally open late on Thu (until 21:00, usually the first and second Thu of the month—check their website) when there may be concerts or other events—check their website.

Getting There: The Courtauld is located in Somerset House, a major arts and cultural center on the Strand. It's a 10-minute walk from Trafalgar Square. Tube: Temple or Covent Garden, or catch bus #6, #9, #11, #13, #15, or #23 from Trafalgar Square. The gallery is right at the Strand entrance to the huge Somerset House.

Information: Lunchtime art talks are generally offered Mon and Fri at 13:15 (15 minutes, included in ticket). Recorded info tel. 020/7848-2526, gallery shop tel. 020/7848-2579, www.courtauld.ac.uk.

Length of This Tour: Allow one hour. With limited time, don't miss Manet's *A Bar at the Folies-Bergère* and Van Gogh's *Self-Portrait with Bandaged Ear.*

Services: The coin-op lockers are free (you get your £1 coin back). WCs are in the basement.

Photography: Permitted without flash.

Cuisine Art: The café (serving soups, salads, sandwiches, pastries, and drinks), with the same hours as the gallery, is in the basement. The recommended Sitar Indian Restaurant is next door (see page 425).

Starring: Van Gogh, Manet, Cézanne, Degas, and many other artists spanning the centuries.

OVERVIEW

The museum is arranged more or less chronologically, from the bottom up. Wealthy collectors created this museum by donating their personal collections. Sam-uel Courtauld (1876-1947)—a philanthropist, industrialist, and wealthy great-nephew of a textile magnate—gave his paintings (Van Gogh, Manet, Cézanne, and others on the first floor) and his name to the bud-ding museum.

Occasionally, the paintings described in this tour are loaned to other museums. If there's a piece you really want to see, check with a guard or at the front desk (the ticket seller has a notebook that lists pieces currently on loan).

This tour covers just enough to introduce you to the wide range of art in the collection. Take time to explore the gallery's many other masterpieces.

The Tour Begins

• *Start on the ground floor, in Room 1 (a.k.a. Gallery I, directly across from the ticket counter), filled with religious paintings.*

Robert Campin—*The Seilern Triptych—The Entombment* (c. 1425)

As the earliest known work of this pioneering artist, the altarpiece is a mix of medieval piety and proto-Renaissance techniques.

Christ's followers prepare to lower him into the tomb. In medieval fashion, it's set on a gold-leaf background with intricate vines and flowers hammered in. Christ's body is spindly, weightless, and presented at an unnatural angle. But the faces! With knit brows, they bear their sorrow solemnly. Even the angels are choked up. The man kneeling at left (who donated the money for the altarpiece) has a day's growth of beard—that's spot-on realism.

• *Climb the stairs two flights up to the "first" floor. Here you'll survey the rooms clockwise, in chronological order. Begin by turning left from the top of the stairs into Room 2 (with large painted chests), dedicated to the Renaissance.*

Lucas Cranach the Elder—*Adam and Eve* (1526)

Eve takes a bite of Knowledge, gazes into the distance, and passes the forbidden fruit to a puzzled Adam, standing in a lush garden amid peaceful animals. Strategic branches fuzz their genitals, but otherwise they're nude, with the pale, thin bodies of the aristocrats for whom Cranach painted. (Adam, beware of antlers.) Though the subject is biblical, it captures the worldly spirit of Germany's Renaissance. The northern version of humanism saw humans not as noble Greek gods (as the Italian Renaissance did), but as fallible, lusty, and even a bit cynical.

• *Continue into Room 3, devoted to Baroque.*

Peter Paul Rubens—*The Family of Jan Brueghel the Elder* (1613-1615)

Rubens paints his close friend and occasional collaborator, along with his wife and two kids. Rubens and Brueghel, Antwerp's two best painters, tag-teamed a couple of dozen works. Brueghel focused on his specialty—background, flowers, animals, and garlands—and Rubens did the people. Also in Room 3 is Rubens' dreamy *Landscape by Moonlight* (1635-1640).

• *Head through Room 4 (with stuffy canvases of 18th-century Europe) and proceed into Room 5 (a.k.a. the Harry Neal Room).*

Edgar Degas—*Two Dancers on the Stage* (1874)

Degas differs from his Impressionist peers in that he often painted interiors with people, especially dancers, rather than landscapes. These two ballerinas look at each other while we observe them from above, perhaps from balcony seating. The dancers are most likely performing the *Ballet des Roses* at the Paris Opera company's rendition of Mozart's *Don Giovanni*.

• *Continue into the long, elegant Room 6 (a.k.a. the Wolfson Room). The walls shimmer with Impressionist masterpieces, the most striking of which is...*

Edouard Manet—*A Bar at the Folies-Bergère* (1882)

While we look at the barmaid and her wares, Manet also shows us the barmaid's-eye view of the crowded nightclub, reflected in the

(slightly tilted) mirror behind her. We see the glittering chandeliers rendered in Impressionist smudges, the bottles of wine, the swirl of activity, and even a trapeze artist (upper left). From the barmaid's own reflection, we see that she's facing a mustachioed man in a top hat. This may be a self-portrait, but whoever he is, he's standing right where we are.

Manet, in his last major painting, places us in the center of the scene, surrounded with glitter. Reflected in the mirror, the gaiety all looks a bit fake, and, judging from her blank expression, that's the way the barmaid sees it.

• *To the left is...*

Edouard Manet—*Le Dejeuner sur l'Herbe* (c. 1863-1868)

This is a smaller, cruder version Manet did of his famous painting (now in Paris' Orsay Museum, pictured here) that launched the Impressionist revolution. The nude woman in a classical pose wasn't shocking. It was the presence of the fully clothed men in everyday dress that suddenly made the nude naked. Manet and the Impressionists rejected goddesses and romance for the landscapes, café scenes, and still lifes of the real world.

• *Sometimes this room also contains a famous sculpture.*

Edgar Degas—*Study in the Nude for Dressed Ballet Dancer* (1879-1917)

The naked 14-year-old girl splays her feet out (fourth position), bends her arms back, and turns her face up, exuding the sheer joy of dancing. Like a stripped Barbie doll, this is a smaller-scale, nude version of the famous statue Edgar Degas exhibited in Paris in 1881. The original was made of wax and plaster over a wire frame. (The Courtauld's version is a bronze cast of a wax statue, done after Degas' death.) Degas dressed his original wax statue in a cloth tutu and ballet slippers and attached real human hair to the wax head, creating a modern collage of materials that shocked and intrigued the Parisians. Critics of the day both praised its modernism and lambasted the angular, adolescent body and "ugly" face.

The model for the statue was an aspiring dancer who, like so many adolescent girls then and now, dreamed of finding a career on stage. Degas sketched and painted her many times. But this well-known painter was also a closet sculptor, fashioning dozens of small-scale statues in the privacy of his studio, especially in his later years as his eyesight failed and painting became more difficult. Only *The Little Fourteen-Year-Old Dancer* was exhibited.

• *Proceed from Impressionism to Post-Impressionism, and over by the window, find...*

Paul Gauguin—*Nevermore* (1897)

A nude Tahitian woman lies daydreaming. The curves of her body and of the headboard soften the horizontal lines of the bed and the verticals of the wall.

Gauguin—who quit his stockbroker job, abandoned his wife and family, and moved to Tahiti—paints in the "primitive" style he found there. With complete simplicity, he draws the girl with a thick outline (so different from Impressionists who "built" a figure with a mosaic of brushstrokes) and then fills it in with solid Crayola colors. Gauguin emphasizes only the two dimensions of height and width, so that the women and clouds in the "background" blend into the flowery wallpaper in the "foreground." Gauguin rejected the camera-eye literalness of Western art. His simple style requires the viewer's imagination to fill in the blanks, perhaps evoking the romance of a bygone world that is...nevermore.

COURTAULD GALLERY

By the way, Gauguin insisted that the title and the raven were not from Poe's poem, but "a bird of the devil who watches." Hmm.
• *Next, dominating Room 7 (a.k.a. the Sydney Butler Room) is...*

Vincent van Gogh—*Self-Portrait with Bandaged Ear* (1889)

On the night of December 23, 1888, Vincent van Gogh went ballistic. Drunk, self-doubting, clinically insane, and enraged at his

friend Gauguin's smug superiority, he waved a knife in Gauguin's face, and later that night cut off a piece of his own ear and gave it to a prostitute. Gauguin hightailed it back to Paris, and the locals in Arles persuaded the mad Dutchman to get help. A week later, just released from the hospital, Vincent stood in front of a blank canvas and looked at himself in the mirror.

What he saw looking back was a calm man with an unflinching gaze, dressed in a heavy coat (painted with thick, vertical strokes of blue and green) and fur-lined hat. The slightly stained bandage over his ear is neither hidden in shame nor worn as a badge of honor—it's just another accessory. The scene is evenly lit, with no melodramatic shadows.

Vincent must have been puzzled and unnerved by his "artist's fit," as he called it. Does this man suspect it would be only the first of many he'd suffer over the next year and a half before finally taking his own life?
• *If you're ready for an encore, head upstairs to the top floor to Room 8, where you'll find 10 Cézanne paintings, including...*

Paul Cézanne—*La Montagne Sainte-Victoire* (1882)

Cézanne could look out his studio window at this 3,300-foot-high mountain in Provence. Over a 20-year span, he painted the same mountain 60 different ways, each with its own color scheme and mood. This one—with a windblown branch framing the mountain from above—may reflect the turmoil of the fortysomething's life (father's death, stalled Impressionist career, shuttling between Paris and hometown Aix-en-Provence, the recent humiliation of having his childhood friend Emile Zola parody him in a novel).

The mountain is realistic, but the scene is carefully composed. The tree branch echoes the curving ridgeline, uniting foreground and background. A patch of paint forming a house (in the foreground) is the same size as a patch depicting a rock formation (in the background), further flattening this "distant" scene into a wall of brushstrokes. (Cézanne's "cube"-shaped brushstrokes inspired the Cubists, a decade later, to build figures using geometric shapes, to mix foreground and background, and to emphasize style over realism.) Cézanne juggles many technical balls of modern painting—a roughed-up surface texture done with thick brushwork, a self-imposed color scheme, abstract composition—and still manages to stay true to his Impressionist roots, painting the mountain he sees.

• *Move onward to see...*

The Rest of the Courtauld

Rooms 9-13 contain paintings by Seurat and 20th-century artists Derain, Dufy, Kandinsky, Jawlensky, Modigliani, Vlaminck, and more. Many have the bright, bold colors and thick brushstrokes of the Fauvist style, from the time when Impressionism was merging into abstract. The museum rotates its large collection, so you may see a different mix. Temporary exhibits also occupy the second floor.

In Room 11a, you'll also see works by members of Britain's own Bloomsbury Group—Roger Fry, Vanessa Bell, and Duncan Grant. This group of intellectual friends also included Virginia Woolf (Bell's sister), E. M. Forster, and the economist John Maynard Keynes. During the 1910s and 1920s, they met for cocktails, flirting, and high-minded discussions in their Bloomsbury neighborhood (east of the British Museum), and went on to fame in their respective fields.

Rounding out the collection (in Rooms 14 and 15) are temporary exhibits.

BRITISH MUSEUM TOUR

In the 19th century, the British flag flew over one-fourth of the world. London was the world's capital, where women in saris walked the streets with men in top hats. And England collected art as fast as it collected colonies.

The British Museum is *the* chronicle of Western civilization. History is a modern invention. Three hundred years ago, people didn't care about crumbling statues and dusty columns. Nowadays, we value a look at past civilizations, knowing that "those who don't learn from history are condemned to repeat it."

The British Museum is the only place I can think of where you can follow the rise and fall of three great civilizations—Egypt, Assyria, and Greece—in a few hours, with a coffee break in the middle. And, while the sun never set on the British Empire, it will on you, so on this tour we'll see just the most exciting two hours.

Orientation

Cost: Free, but a £5 donation is requested. (Take this opportunity to unload your spare change.) Interesting temporary exhibits usually require a separate admission (and a timed ticket).

Hours: The museum is open daily 10:00-17:30, Fri until 20:30 (not all galleries are open Fri night, but most of our tour is). The **Great Court**—the grand entrance with eateries, gift shops, and an exhibit gallery—is open daily 9:00-18:00, Fri until 20:30.

When to Go: Rainy days and Sundays are the most crowded times; the same goes for school holidays. The museum is least crowded late on weekday afternoons.

Getting There: The main entrance is on Great Russell Street. From the Tottenham Court Road Tube stop, take exit #3, then with

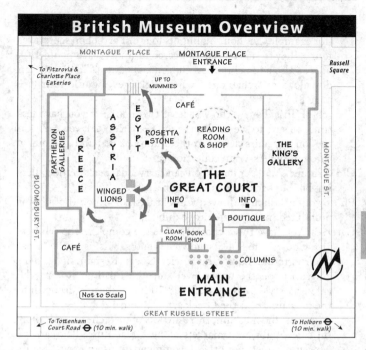

British Museum Overview

MONTAGUE PLACE

MONTAGUE PLACE ENTRANCE

Russell Square

← To Fitzrovia & Charlotte Place Eateries

UP TO MUMMIES

CAFÉ

E G Y P T

A S S Y R I A

ROSETTA STONE

READING ROOM & SHOP

THE KING'S GALLERY

PARTHENON GALLERIES

G R E E C E

THE GREAT COURT

MONTAGUE ST.

BLOOMSBURY ST.

WINGED LIONS

INFO

INFO

BOUTIQUE

CAFÉ

CLOAK-ROOM

BOOK-SHOP

COLUMNS

Not to Scale

MAIN ENTRANCE

GREAT RUSSELL STREET

← To Tottenham Court Road ⊖ (10 min. walk)

To Holborn ⊖ (10 min. walk) →

BRITISH MUSEUM

the tall Centrepoint building on your right, walk to Museum Street and hang a left. The Holborn and Russell Square Tube stops are also nearby. Buses #38, #168 and #24 are among the many that stop here (see page 30).

Information: Information desks are just inside the Great Court. You can pick up the basic map (£1 donation), but it's not essential for this tour. The *Visitor's Guide* (£3.50) offers 15 different tours and skimpy text. The main bookstore is inside the entrance on the left. General info tel. 020/7323-8299, ticket desk tel. 020/7323-8181, www.britishmuseum.org.

Tours: Free 30-minute **eyeOpener tours** are led by volunteers, who focus on select rooms (daily 11:00-15:45, generally every 15 minutes). Free 45-minute **gallery talks** on specific subjects are offered Tue-Sat at 13:15; a free 20-minute highlights tour is available on Friday evening.

The £5 **multimedia guide** offers dial-up audio commentary and video on 200 objects, as well as several theme tours (for example, 1.5-hour highlights tour or Parthenon sculptures tour). They're substantial and cerebral (must leave photo ID). There's also a fun children's multimedia guide (£3.50). You can download this chapter as a free Rick Steves **audio tour** (see page 8).

Length of This Tour: Allow at least two hours. If you have less time, be sure to see the Parthenon Galleries (㉖); you can skip the long upstairs detour to the mummies (❻) and go quickly through the Assyrian collection (⓬-⓱).

Cloakroom: £1.50 per item. You can carry a daypack in the galleries, but big backpacks must be checked.

Photography: Photos allowed without flash or tripod (but photos prohibited in the temporary exhibits).

Eateries: You have three choices inside the complex. The self-service Court Café (£4-5 sandwiches and salads) is in the Great Court ground floor. The pricier Court Restaurant (£15-18 entrées) is on the upper level atop the Reading Room. The cafeteria-style Gallery Café (£8-10 hot dishes) is deeper into the museum, near the Greek art in Room 12.

Near the museum, there are lots of fast, cheap, and colorful cafés, pubs, and markets along Great Russell Street and Museum Street. For other recommendations and some handy sit-down chains, see page 426. The sumptuous Princess Louise Pub is nearby (see page 414). No picnicking is allowed indoors, except on weekends and holidays, when the museum opens a family area in the basement under the Great Court. Karl Marx picnicked on the benches near the museum entrance and in nearby Russell Square.

Starring: Rosetta Stone, Egyptian mummies, Assyrian lions, and the Parthenon sculptures.

The Tour Begins

The main entrance on Great Russell Street spills you into the Great Court, a glass-domed space with the round Reading Room in the center. From the Great Court, doorways lead to all wings. To the left are the exhibits on Egypt, Assyria, and Greece—our tour. You'll notice that this tour does not follow the museum's numbered sequence of rooms. Instead, we'll try to hit the highlights as we work chronologically.

Enjoy the Great Court, Europe's largest covered square, which is bigger than a football field. This people-friendly court—delightfully

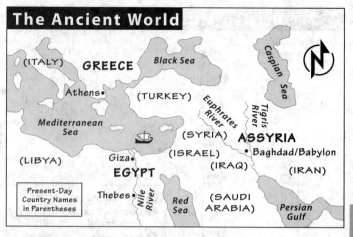

The Ancient World

(ITALY) GREECE Black Sea

Athens• (TURKEY)

Mediterranean Sea

(SYRIA) ASSYRIA

(LIBYA) Giza• (ISRAEL) •Baghdad/Babylon

EGYPT (IRAQ) (IRAN)

Thebes• Nile River Red Sea (SAUDI ARABIA) Persian Gulf

Caspian Sea

Euphrates River Tigris River

Present-Day Country Names in Parentheses

BRITISH MUSEUM

spared from the London rain—was for 150 years one of London's great lost spaces...closed off and gathering dust. Since the year 2000, it's been the 140-foot-wide hub of a two-acre cultural complex.

The stately Reading Room now hosts special exhibitions, but in years past, it was a study hall for Oscar Wilde, Arthur Conan Doyle, Rudyard Kipling, T. S. Eliot, Virginia Woolf, W. B. Yeats, Mark Twain, and V. I. Lenin. Karl Marx formulated his ideas on communism and wrote *Das Kapital* here.

• *The Egyptian Gallery is in the West Wing, to the left of the round Reading Room. Enter the Egyptian Gallery. The Rosetta Stone is directly in front of you.*

ANCIENT EGYPT

Egypt was one of the world's first "civilizations"—a group of people with a government, religion, art, free time, and a written language. The Egypt we think of—pyramids, mummies, pharaohs, and guys who walk funny—lasted from 3000 to 1000 B.c. with hardly any change in the government, religion, or arts. Imagine two millennia of Nixon.

❶ The Rosetta Stone

When this rock was unearthed in the Egyptian desert in 1799, it was a sensation in Europe. This black slab, dating from 196 B.C., caused a quantum leap in the study of ancient history. Finally, Egyptian writing could be decoded.

The hieroglyphic writing in the upper part of the stone was indecipherable for a thousand years. Did a picture of a bird mean "bird"? Or was it a sound, forming part of a larger word, like "burden"? As it turned out, hieroglyphics are a complex combination of

British Museum—Egypt

Not to Scale

GREAT
COURT &
READING
ROOM

ASSYRIA

WINGED
LIONS

CLOAKROOM

❶ Rosetta Stone
❷ Colossal Statue of Ramesses II
❸ Egyptian Gods as Animals
❹ Monumental Granite Scarab
❺ Up to Nebamun Hunting in the Marshes
❻ Up to Mummies & Coffins
❼ Head of Amenhotep III
❽ Four Figures of Sekhmet
❾ Fragment of Great Sphinx Beard
❿ False Door of Ptahshepses
⓫ Statue of Nenkheftka

BRITISH MUSEUM

the two, surprisingly more phonetic than symbolic. (For example, the hieroglyph that looks like a mouth or eye is the letter "R.")

The Rosetta Stone allowed scientists to break the code. It contains a single inscription repeated in three languages. The bottom third is plain old Greek (find your favorite frat or sorority), while the middle is medieval Egyptian. By comparing the two known languages with the one they didn't know, translators figured out the hieroglyphics.

The breakthrough came when they discovered that the large ovals (such as in the sixth line from the top) represented the name of the ruler, Ptolemy. Simple.

• *In the gallery to the right of the Stone, find the huge head of Ramesses.*

❷ Colossal Statue of Ramesses II

When Moses told the king of Egypt, "Let my people go!" this was the stony-faced look he got. Ramesses II ruled for 66 years (c.

1290-1223 B.C.) and may have been in power when Moses cursed Egypt with plagues, freed the Israeli slaves, and led them out of Egypt to their homeland in Israel (according to the Bible, but not exactly corroborated by Egyptian chronicles).

This seven-ton statue (c. 1250 B.C.), made from two different colors of granite, is a fragment from a temple in Thebes. It shows Ramesses with the traditional features of a pharaoh—goatee, cloth headdress, and cobra diadem on his forehead. Ramesses was a great builder of temples, palaces, tombs, and statues of himself. There are probably more statues of him in the world than there are cheesy fake *Davids*. He was so concerned about achieving immortality that he even chiseled his own name on other people's statues. Very cheeky.

Picture what the archaeologists saw when they came upon this: a colossal head and torso separated from the enormous legs and toppled into the sand—all that remained of the works of a once-great pharaoh. Kings, megalomaniacs, and workaholics, take note.

• Say, *"Ooh, heavy,"* and climb the ramp behind Ramesses, *looking for animals.*

❸ Egyptian Gods as Animals

Before technology made humans the alpha animal on earth, it was easier to appreciate our fellow creatures. Animals were stronger, swifter, and fiercer than puny *Homo sapiens.* The Egyptians worshipped animals as incarnations of the gods.

The powerful ram is the god Amun (king of the gods), protecting a puny pharaoh under his powerful chin. The falcon is Horus, the god of the living. The speckled, standing hippo (with lion head) is Tawaret, protectress of childbirth. Her stylized breasts and pregnant belly are supported by ankhs, symbols of life. (Is Tawaret grinning or grimacing in labor?) Finally, the cat (with ear- and nose-rings) served Bastet, the popular goddess of stress relief.

Scattered around the floor are huge stone boxes. The famous mummies of ancient Egypt were wrapped in linen and then encased in finely decorated wooden coffins, which were then placed in these massive stone outer coffins.

• *At the end of the Egyptian Gallery is a big stone beetle.*

❹ Monumental Granite Scarab

This species of beetle would burrow into the ground, then reappear—it's a symbol of resurrection, like the sun rising and setting, or dying and rebirth. Scarab amulets were placed on mummies' chests to protect the spirit's heart from acting impulsively. Pharaohs wore the symbol of the beetle, and tombs and temples were decorated with them (this one, from c. 332 B.C., probably once sat in a temple). The hieroglyph for scarab meant "to come into being."

Like the scarab, Egyptian culture was buried—first by Greece, then by Rome. Knowledge of the ancient writing died, condemning the culture to obscurity. But since the discovery of the Rosetta Stone, Egyptology has boomed, and Egypt has come back to life.

• *You can't call Egypt a wrap until you visit the mummies upstairs. Continue to the end of the gallery past the giant stone scarab and up the West Stairs (four flights or elevator) to Floor 3. At the top, turn left into Room 61, with objects and wall paintings from the tomb of Nebamun.*

❺ Painting of Nebamun Hunting in the Marshes

Nebamun stands in a reed boat, gliding through the marshes. He raises his arm, ready to bean a bird with a snakelike hunting

stick. On the right, his wife looks on, while his daughter crouches between his legs, a symbol of fatherly protection.

This nobleman walks like Egyptian statues look—stiff and flat, like he was just run over by a pyramid. We see the torso from the front and everything else—arms, legs, face—in profile, creating the funny walk that has become an Egyptian cliché. (Like an early version of Cubism, we see various perspectives at once.)

But the stiffness is softened by a human touch. It's a family snapshot of loved ones from a happy time. The birds, fish, and plants are painted realistically, like encyclopedia entries. (The first "paper" came from papyrus plants like the bush on the left.) The only unrealistic element is the house cat (thigh-high, in front of the man) acting as a retriever—possibly the only cat in history that ever did anything useful.

When Nebamun passed into the afterlife, his awakening soul could look at this painting (c. 1350 B.C.) on the tomb wall and think of his wife and daughter—doing what they loved for all eternity.

• *Browse through Rooms 61-64, filled with displays in glass cases.*

❻ The Egyptian Funeral

To mummify a body, you first disembowel it (but leave the heart inside), then pack the cavities with pitch, and dry it with natron, a

natural form of sodium carbonate (and, I believe, the active ingredient in Twinkies). Then carefully bandage it head to toe with hundreds of yards of linen strips. Let it sit 2,000 years, and...*voilà!* Or just dump the corpse in the desert and let the hot, dry, bacteria-killing Egyptian sand do the work—you'll get the same results.

The mummy was placed in a wooden coffin, which was put in a stone coffin, which was placed in a tomb. (The pyramids were super-sized tombs for the rich and famous.) The result is that we now have Egyptian bodies that are as well preserved as Joan Rivers.

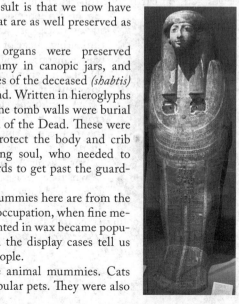

The internal organs were preserved alongside the mummy in canopic jars, and small-scale statuettes of the deceased *(shabtis)* were scattered around. Written in hieroglyphs on the coffins and the tomb walls were burial rites from the Book of the Dead. These were magical spells to protect the body and crib notes for the waking soul, who needed to know these passwords to get past the guardians of eternity.

Many of the mummies here are from the time of the Roman occupation, when fine memorial portraits painted in wax became popular. X-ray photos in the display cases tell us more about these people.

Don't miss the animal mummies. Cats (Room 62) were popular pets. They were also considered incarnations of the cat-headed goddess Bastet. Worshipped in life as the sun god's allies, preserved in death, and memorialized with statues, cats were given the adulation they've come to expect ever since.

• *Linger in Rooms 62 and 63, but remember that eternity is about the amount of time it takes to see this entire museum. In Room 64, in a glass case, you'll find what's left of a visitor who tried to see it all...*

Egyptian Grave Containing a Naturally Preserved Body

This man died 5,400 years ago, a thousand years before the pyramids. His people buried him in the fetal position, where he could "sleep" for eternity. The hot sand naturally dehydrated and protected the body. With him are a few of his possessions: bowls, beads, and the flint blade next to his arm. His grave was covered with stones. Named "Ginger" by scientists for his wisps of red hair, this man from a distant time seems very human.

• *Backtrack to Room 61 and head back down the stairs to the Egyptian Gallery and the Rosetta Stone. Just past the Rosetta Stone, find a huge head (facing away from you) with a hat like a bowling pin.*

❼ Colossal Head of Amenhotep III

Art served as propaganda for the pharaohs, kings who called themselves gods on earth. Put this red granite head (c. 1370 B.C.) on

top of an enormous body (which still stands in Egypt), and you have the intimidating image of an omnipotent ruler who demands servile obedience. Next to the head is, appropriately, the pharaoh's powerful fist—the long arm of the law.

Amenhotep's crown is actually two crowns in one. The pointed upper half is the royal cap of Upper Egypt. This rests on the flat, fez-like crown symbolizing Lower Egypt. A pharaoh wearing both crowns together is bragging that he rules a combined Egypt. As both "Lord of the Two Lands" and "High Priest of Every Temple," the pharaoh united church and state.

• *Along the wall to the left of the red granite head (as you're facing it) are four black lion-headed statues.*

❽ Four Figures of the Goddess Sekhmet

The lion-headed goddess Sekhmet looks pretty sedate here (in these sculptures dating c. 1360 B.C.), but she could spring into a

fierce crouch when crossed. She was the pharaoh's personal bodyguard, who could burn his enemies to a crisp with flaming arrows.

The gods ruled the Egyptian cosmos like dictators in a big banana republic (or the US Congress). Egyptians bribed their gods for favors, offering food, animals, or money, or erecting statues like these.

Sekhmet holds an ankh. This key-shaped cross was the hieroglyph meaning "life" and was a symbol of eternal life. Later, it was adopted as a Christian symbol because of its cross shape and religious overtones.

• *Continuing down the Egyptian Gallery, a few paces directly in front of you and to the left, find a glass case containing a...*

❾ Fragment of the Beard of the Great Sphinx

The Great Sphinx—a statue of a pharaoh-headed lion—crouches in the shadow of the Great Pyramids in Cairo. Time shaved off

the sphinx's soft limestone, goatee-like beard, and a piece is now preserved here in a glass case. This hunk of stone is only a whisker—about three percent of the massive beard—giving an idea of the scale of the six-story-tall, 250-foot-long statue.

The Sphinx is as old as the pyramids (c. 2500 B.C.), built during the time known to historians as the Old Kingdom (2686-2181 B.C.), but this beard may have been added later, during a restoration (c. 1420 B.C., or perhaps even later under Ramesses II).

• *Ten steps past the Sphinx's soul patch is a 10-foot-tall, red-tinted "building" covered in hieroglyphics.*

False Door of Ptahshepses

This limestone "false door" (c. 2400 B.C.) was a ceremonial entrance (never meant to open) for a sealed building, called a *mastaba*, that marked the grave of a man named Ptahshepses. The hieroglyphs of eyes, birds, and rabbits serve as his epitaph, telling his life story, how he went to school with the pharaoh's kids, became an honored vizier, and married the pharaoh's daughter.

The deceased was mummified, placed in a wooden coffin that was encased in a stone coffin, then in a stone sarcophagus (like the **red-granite sarcophagus** in front of Ptahshepses' door), and buried 50 feet beneath the *mastaba* in an underground chamber (see the diagram of "Old Kingdom Tombs," on a nearby wall).

Mastabas like Ptahshepses' were decorated inside and out with statues, steles, and frescoes like those displayed nearby. These pictured things that the soul would find useful in the next life—magical spells, lists of the deceased's accomplishments, snapshots of the deceased and his family while alive, and secret passwords from the Egyptian Book of the Dead. False doors like this allowed the soul (but not grave robbers) to come and go.

• *Just past Ptahshepses' false door is a glass case with a statue.*

⓫ Statue of Nenkheftka

Painted statues such as this one (c. 2400 B.C.) represented the soul of the deceased. Meant to keep alive the memory and personality

of the departed, this image would have greeted Nenkheftka's loved ones when they brought food offerings to place at his feet to nourish his soul. (In the mummification rites, the mouth was ritually opened, to prepare it to eat soul food.)

In ancient Egypt, you *could* take it with you. The Egyptians believed that after death, your soul lived on, enjoying its earthly possessions—sometimes including servants, who might be walled up alive with their dead master. (Remember that even the great pyramids were just big tombs for Egypt's most powerful.)

Statues functioned as a refuge for the soul on its journey after death. The rich scattered statues of themselves everywhere, just in case. Statues needed to be simple and easy to recognize, mug shots for eternity: stiff, arms down, chin up, nothing fancy. This one has all the essential features, like the simplified human figures on international traffic signs. To a soul caught in the fast lane of astral travel, this symbolic statue would be easier to spot than a detailed one.

With their fervent hope for life after death, Egyptians created calm, dignified art that seems built for eternity.

• *Relax. One civilization down, two to go. Near the end of the gallery are two huge, winged Assyrian lions (with bearded human heads) stand-ing guard over the Assyrian exhibit halls.*

ANCIENT ASSYRIA

Long before Saddam Hussein, Iraq was home to other palace-building, iron-fisted rulers—the Assyrians.

Assyria was the lion, the king of beasts of early Middle East-ern civilizations. These Semitic people from the agriculturally challenged hills of northern Iraq became traders and conquerors, not farmers. They conquered their southern neighbors and domi-nated the Middle East for 300 years (c. 900-600 B.C.).

Their strength came from a superb army (chariots, mounted cavalry, and siege engines), a policy of terrorism against enemies ("I tied their heads to tree trunks all around the city," reads a royal inscription), ethnic cleansing and mass deportations of the van-quished, and efficient administration (roads and express postal ser-vice). They have been called the "Romans of the East."

⑫ Two Human-Headed Winged Lions

These stone lions guarded an Assyrian palace (11th-8th century B.C.). With the strength of a lion, the wings of an eagle, the brain of a man, and the beard of ZZ Top, they protected the king from evil spirits and scared the heck out of foreign ambassadors and left-wing newspaper reporters. (What has five legs and flies? Take a close look. These quintupeds, which appear complete from both the front and the side, could guard both di-rections at once.)

Carved into the stone between the bearded lions' loins, you can see one of civilization's most impressive achievements—writ-

ing. This wedge-shaped **(cuneiform)** script is the world's first written lan-guage, invented 5,000 years ago by the Sumerians (of southern Iraq) and passed down to their less-civilized descendants, the Assyrians.

• *Walk between the lions, glance at the large reconstructed wooden gates from an Assyrian palace, and turn right into the long, narrow red gallery (Room 7) lined with stone relief panels.*

⑬ Ashurnasirpal II's Palace at Nimrud

This gallery is a mini version of the throne room and royal apart-ments of King Ashurnasirpal II's Northwest Palace at Nimrud (9th

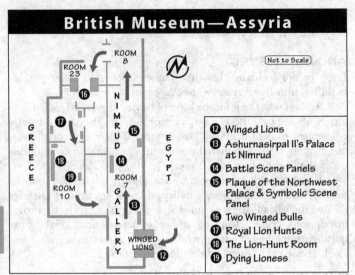

British Museum—Assyria

ROOM 8
ROOM 23

Not to Scale

NIMRUD GALLERY

GREECE

EGYPT

ROOM 7

ROOM 10

WINGED LIONS

⑫ Winged Lions
⑬ Ashurnasirpal II's Palace at Nimrud
⑭ Battle Scene Panels
⑮ Plaque of the Northwest Palace & Symbolic Scene Panel
⑯ Two Winged Bulls
⑰ Royal Lion Hunts
⑱ The Lion-Hunt Room
⑲ Dying Lioness

BRITISH MUSEUM

century B.C.). Entering, you'd see the king on his throne at the far end, surrounded by these pleasant, sand-colored, gypsum relief panels (which were, however, originally painted and varnished).

That's Ashurnasirpal himself in the **first panel on your right,** with braided beard, earring, and fez-like crown, flanked by his supernatural hawk-headed henchmen, who sprinkle incense on him with pinecones. The bulging forearms tell us that Ashurnasirpal II (r. 883-859 B.C.) was a conqueror's conqueror who enjoyed his reputation as a merciless warrior, using torture and humiliation as part of his distinct management style. The room's panels chronicle his bloody career.

Under Ashurnasirpal's reign, the Assyrians dominated the Mideast from their capital at Nineveh (near modern Mosul). Ashurnasirpal II proved his power by building a brand-new palace in nearby Nimrud (called "Calah" in the Bible).

The cuneiform inscription running through the center of the panel is Ashurnasirpal's résumé: "The king who has enslaved all mankind, the mighty warrior who steps on the necks of his enemies, tramples all foes and shatters the enemy; the weapon of the gods, the mighty king, the King of Assyria, the king of the world, B.A., M.B.A., Ph.D., etc...."

• A dozen paces farther down, on the left wall, you'll find...

⓮ Panels with Battle Scenes

Many "nations" conquered by the Assyrians consisted of little more than a single walled city. Look for the **upper panel,** in which the Assyrians lay siege with a crude "tank" that shields them as they advance to the city walls to smash down the gate with a battering ram. The king stands a safe distance away behind the juggernaut and bravely shoots arrows.

In the **next panel to the right,** enemy soldiers flee the slings and arrows of outrageous Assyrians by swimming across the Euphrates, using inflated animal bladders as life preservers. Their friends in the castle downstream applaud their ingenuity.

Just **to the left** (under the attack), prisoners are paraded before the Assyrian king, who is shaded by a parasol. Ashurnasirpal II sneers and tells the captured chief, "Drop and give me 50." Above the prisoners' heads, we see the rich spoils of war—elephant tusks, metal pots, and so on. The Assyrians, whose economy depended on booty, depopulated conquered lands by slavery and ethnic cleansing, then moved in Assyrian settlers.

• *On the opposite wall, a few steps farther along, is an artist's rendering of what the palace would have looked like.*

⓯ Plaque of the Northwest Palace and Symbolic Scene Panel

The plaque shows the king at the far end of the throne room, shaded by a parasol and flanked by winged lions. (In the diagram of the palace's floor plan, the throne room is Room B.) The 30,000-square-foot palace was built atop a 50-acre artificial mound. The new palace was inaugurated with a 10-day banquet (according to an inscription), where the king picked up the tab for 69,574 of his closest friends.

The relief panel (immediately to the right) labeled **Symbolic Scene** stood behind the throne. It shows the king (and his double) tending the tree of life while reaching up to receive the ring of kingship from the winged sun god.

• *Exit the gallery at the far end, then hang a U-turn left. Pause at the entrance of Room 10c to see the impressive...*

⓰ Two Winged Bulls from the Palace of Sargon

These marble bulls (c. 710-705 B.C.) guarded the entrance to the city of Dur-Sharrukin ("Sargonsburg"), a new capital (near Nineveh/

Mosul) with vast palaces built by Sargon II (r. 721-705 B.C.). The 30-ton bulls were cut from a single block, tipped on their sides, then dragged to their place by POWs. (In modern times, when the British transported them here, they had to cut them in half; you can see the horizontal cracks through the bulls' chests.)

Sargon II gained his reputation as a general by subduing the Israelites after a three-year siege of Jerusalem (2 Kings 17:1-6). He solidified his conquest by ethnically cleansing the area and deporting many Israelites (inspiring legends of the "Lost" Ten Tribes).

In 710 B.C., while these bulls were being carved for his palace, Sargon II marched victoriously through the streets of Babylon (near present-day Baghdad), having put down a revolt there against him. His descendants would also have to deal with the troublesome Babylonians.

• *Sneak between these bulls and veer right (into Room 10), where horses are being readied for the big hunt.*

⓱ Royal Lion Hunts from the North Palace of Ashurbanipal

Lion hunting was Assyria's sport of kings. On the right wall are horses; on the left are the hunting dogs. And next to them, lions, resting peacefully in a garden, unaware that they will shortly be rousted, stampeded, and slaughtered.

Lions lived in Mesopotamia up until modern times, and it was the king's duty to keep the lion population down to protect farmers and herdsmen. This duty soon became sport, with staged hunts and zoo-bred lions, as the kings of men proved their power by taking on the king of beasts.

• *Continue ahead into the larger lion-hunt room. Reading the panels like a comic strip, start on the right and gallop counterclockwise.*

⓲ The Lion-Hunt Room
In these panels (c. 650 B.C.), the king's men release lions from their cages, then riders on horseback herd them into an enclosed arena. The king has them cornered. Let the slaughter begin. The chariot carries King Ashurbanipal, the great-grandson of Sargon II (not to be confused with Ashurnasirpal II, who ruled 200 years earlier, mentioned previously).

The last of Assyria's great kings, Ashurbanipal has reigned now for 50 years. Having left a half-dozen corpses in his wake, he moves on, while spearmen hold off lions attacking from the rear.

• *At about the middle of the long wall...*

The fleeing lions, cornered by hounds, shot through with arrows, and weighed down by fatigue, begin to fall. The lead lion carries on even while vomiting blood.

This low point of Assyrian cruelty is, perhaps, the high point of their artistic achievement. It's a curious coincidence that civilizations often produce their greatest art in their declining years. Hmm.

• *On the wall opposite the vomiting lion is the...*

⓳ Dying Lioness
A lion roars in pain and frustration. She tries to run, but her body is too heavy. Her muscular hind legs, once a source of power, are now paralyzed.

Like these brave, fierce lions, Assyria's once-great warrior nation was slain. Shortly after Ashurbanipal's death, Assyria was conquered, and its capital at Nineveh was sacked and looted by an ascendant Babylon (612 B.C.). The mood of tragedy, dignity, and proud struggle in a hopeless cause makes this dying lioness one of the most beautiful of human creations.

• *Exit the lion-hunt room at the far end and make your way back to the huge, winged lions at the start of the Assyrian exhibit. To reach the Greek section, exit Assyria between the winged lions and make a U-turn to the right, into Room 11.*

*You'll walk past (**20**) early Greek Barbie and Ken dolls from the Cycladic period (2500 B.C.). Continue into Room 12 (the hungry can go straight to the Gallery Café), and turn right, into Room 13, filled with Greek vases in glass cases.*

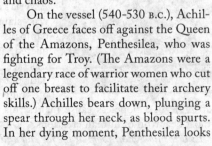

ANCIENT GREECE

The history of ancient Greece (600 B.C.-A.D. 1) could be subtitled "making order out of chaos." While Assyria was dominating the Middle East, "Greece"—a gaggle of warring tribes roaming the Greek peninsula—was floundering in darkness. But by about 700 B.C., these tribes began settling down, experimenting with democracy, forming self-governing city-states, and making ties with other city-states. Scarcely two centuries later, they would be a relatively united community and the center of the civilized world.

During its Golden Age (500-430 B.C.), Greece set the tone for all of Western civilization to follow. Democracy, theater, literature, mathematics, philosophy, science, gyros, art, and architecture, as we know them, were virtually all invented by a single generation of Greeks in a small town of maybe 80,000 citizens.

• *Roughly in the middle of Room 13 is a Z-shaped glass case marked #8. On the upper shelf, find a...*

21 Black-Figured Amphora with Achilles Killing Penthesilea

Greeks poured wine from jars like this one, which is painted with a legend from the Trojan War. The Trojan War (c. 1200 B.C.)— part fact but mostly legend—symbolized Greece's long struggle to rise above war and chaos.

On the vessel (540-530 B.C.), Achilles of Greece faces off against the Queen of the Amazons, Penthesilea, who was fighting for Troy. (The Amazons were a legendary race of warrior women who cut off one breast to facilitate their archery skills.) Achilles bears down, plunging a spear through her neck, as blood spurts. In her dying moment, Penthesilea looks

BRITISH MUSEUM

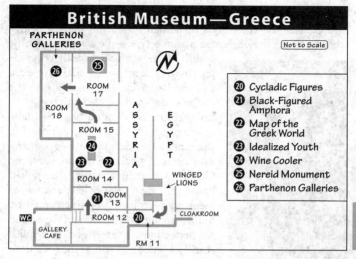

up, her gaze locking on Achilles. His eyes bulge wide, and he falls instantly in love with her. She dies, and Achilles is smitten.

Greek pottery was a popular export product for the sea-trading Greeks. Their earliest pots featured geometric patterns (8th century B.C.), then evolved into painted black silhouettes on the natural orange clay, before switching to red figures on black backgrounds. On this jar, see the names of the two enemies/lovers ("AXILEV" and "PENOESIIEA") as well as the signature of the craftsman, Exekias.

• *Continue to Room 15, then relax on a bench and read, surrounded by statues and vases in glass cases. On the entrance wall, find a...*

㉒ Map of the Greek World, 520-430 B.C.

After Greece drove out Persian invaders in 480 B.C., the city of Athens became the most powerful of the city-states and the center of the Greek world. Golden Age Greece was never really a full-fledged empire, but more a common feeling of unity among Greek-speaking people.

A century after the Golden Age, Greek culture was spread still farther by Alexander the Great, who conquered the Mediterranean world and beyond (including Persia). By 300 B.C., the "Greek" world stretched from Italy and Egypt to India (including most of what used to be the Assyrian Empire). Two hundred years later, this Greek-speaking Hellenistic Empire was conquered by the Romans.

• *There's a nude male statue on the left side of the room.*

㉓ Torso of an Idealized Youth

The Greeks saw their gods in human form...and human beings were godlike. They invented a statue type—the kouros (literally,

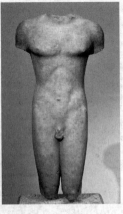

"youth")—to showcase idealized bodies. In this example (c. 520-510 B.C.), the youth would have exemplified the divine orderliness of the universe with his once perfectly round head (it's now missing), symmetrical pecs, and navel in the center. The ideal man was geometrically perfect, a balance of opposites, the Golden Mean. In a statue, that meant finding the right balance between movement and stillness, between realistic human anatomy (with human flaws) and the perfection of a Greek god. Our youth is still a bit uptight, stiff as the rock from which he's carved. But—as we'll see—in just a few short decades, the Greeks would cut loose and create realistic statues that seemed to move like real humans.

• *Two-thirds of the way down Room 15 (on the left) is a glass case containing a vase.*

㉔ Wine Cooler Signed by Douris as Painter

This clay vessel (490 B.C.), called a *psykter*, would have been topped off with wine and floated in a bowl of cooling water. Its red-figure drawings show satyrs at a *symposium*, or

drinking party. These half-man/half-animal creatures (notice their tails) had a reputation for lewd behavior, reminding the balanced and moderate Greeks of their rude roots.

    The reveling figures painted on this jar are realistic and three-dimensional; their movements are more naturalistic than the literally three-dimensional but quite stiff kouros. The Greeks are beginning to conquer the natural world in art. The art, like life, is more in balance. And speaking of "balance," if that's a Greek sobriety test, revel on.

• *Carry on into Room 17 and sit facing the Greek temple at the far end.*

㉕ Nereid Monument

Greek temples (like this reconstruction of a temple-shaped tomb from Xanthos, c. 390-380 B.C.) housed a statue of a god or goddess. Unlike Christian churches, which serve as meeting places, Greek temples were the gods' homes. Worshippers gathered outside, so the most impressive part of the temple was its exterior. Temples

were rectangular build-
ings surrounded by rows
of columns and topped by
slanted roofs.

The triangle-shaped
space above the col-
umns—the pediment—is
filled with sculpture. Supporting the pediment are
decorative relief panels,
called metopes. Now look
through the columns to the building itself. Above the doorway,
another set of relief panels—the frieze—runs around the building
(under the eaves).

The statues between the columns (and three more facing
the monument) are Nereids—friendly sea nymphs with dramatic
wave-like poses and wind-blown clothes; some appear to be borne
aloft by sea animals. Notice the sculptor's delight in capturing the
body in motion, and the way the wet clothes cling to the figures'
anatomy.

Next, we'll see pediment, frieze, and metope decorations from
Greece's greatest temple.

• *Enter through the glass doors labeled* Parthenon Galleries. *(The rooms
branching off the entryway usually have helpful exhibits that reconstruct
the Parthenon and its once-colorful sculptures.)*

❷❻ Parthenon Galleries

If you were to leave the British Museum, take the Tube to Heathrow, and fly to Athens, there, in the center of the old city, on top of

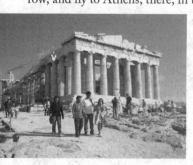

the high, flat hill known as the
Acropolis, you'd find the Parthenon—the temple dedicated
to Athena, goddess of wisdom
and the patroness of Athens. It
was the crowning glory of an
enormous urban-renewal plan
during Greece's Golden Age.
After Athens was ruined in a
war with Persia, the city—under
the bold leadership of Pericles—
constructed the greatest building of its day (447-432 b.c.). The
Parthenon was a model of balance, simplicity, and harmonious elegance, the symbol of the Golden Age. Phidias, the greatest Greek
sculptor, decorated the exterior with statues and relief panels.

While the building itself remains in Athens, many of the Parthenon's best sculptures are right here in the British Museum—the

so-called Elgin Marbles, named for the shrewd British ambassador who had his men hammer, chisel, and saw them off the Parthenon in the early 1800s. Though the Greek government complains about losing its marbles, the Brits feel they rescued and preserved the sculptures. The often-bitter controversy continues.

The marble panels you see lining the walls of this large hall are part of the frieze that originally ran around the exterior of the

Parthenon, under the eaves. The statues at either end of the hall once filled the Parthenon's triangular-shaped pediments. Near the pediment sculptures, we'll also find the relief panels known as metopes.

The Frieze: These 56 relief panels show Athens' "Fourth of July" parade, celebrating the birth of the city. On this day, citizens marched up the Acropolis to symbolically present a new robe to the 40-foot-tall gold-and-ivory statue of Athena housed in the Parthenon.

• *Start at the panels by the entrance (#136), and work counterclockwise.*

Men on horseback, chariots, musicians, children, animals for sacrifice, and young maidens with offerings are all part of the grand parade, all heading in the same direction—uphill. Prance on.

Notice the muscles and veins in the horses' legs and the intricate folds in the cloaks and dresses. Some panels have holes

drilled in them, where gleaming bronze reins were fitted to heighten the festive look. All of these panels were originally painted in realistic colors. As you move along, notice that, despite the bustle of figures posed every which way, the frieze has one unifying element—all the people's heads are at the same level, creating a single ribbon around the Parthenon.

• *Cross to the opposite wall.*

A three-horse chariot (#67), cut from only a few inches of

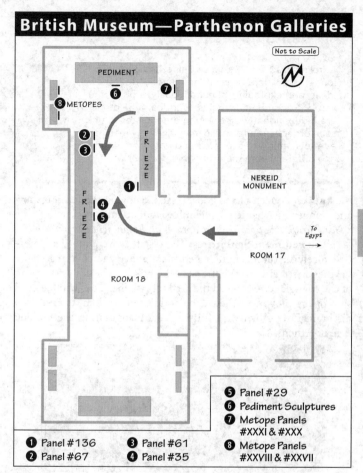

British Museum—Parthenon Galleries

Not to Scale

PEDIMENT

8 METOPES

❶ Panel #136
❷ Panel #67
❸ Panel #61
❹ Panel #35
❺ Panel #29
❻ Pediment Sculptures
❼ Metope Panels #XXXI & #XXX
❽ Metope Panels #XXVIII & #XXVII

FRIEZE

FRIEZE

NEREID MONUMENT

To Egypt →

ROOM 17

ROOM 18

BRITISH MUSEUM

marble, is more lifelike and three-dimensional than anything the Egyptians achieved in a freestanding statue.

Enter the girls (five yards to the left, #61), the heart of the procession. Dressed in pleated robes, they shuffle past the parade marshals, carrying incense burners and jugs of wine and bowls to pour out an offering to the thirsty gods.

The procession culminates (#35) in the presentation of the robe to Athena. A man and a child fold the robe for the goddess while the rest of the gods look on. There are Zeus and Hera (#29),

Centaurs Slain Around the World

Dateline 500 B.C.—Greece, China, India: Man no longer considers himself an animal. Bold new ideas are exploding simultaneously around the world. Socrates, Confucius, Buddha, and others are independently discovering a nonmaterial, unseen order in nature and in man. They say man has a rational mind or soul. He's separate from nature and different from the other animals.

the king and queen of the gods, seated, enjoying the fashion show and wondering what length hemlines will be this year.

• *Head for the set of pediment sculptures at the far right end of the hall.*

The Pediment Sculptures: These statues were originally nestled nicely in the triangular pediment above the columns at the Parthenon's main (east) entrance. The missing statues at the peak of the triangle once showed the birth of Athena. Zeus had his head split open, allowing Athena, the goddess of wisdom, to rise from his brain fully grown and fully armed, inaugurating the Golden Age of Athens.

The other gods at this Olympian banquet slowly become aware of the amazing event. The first to notice is the one closest to them, Hebe, the cupbearer of the gods (tallest surviving fragment). Frightened, she runs to tell the others, her dress whipping behind her. A startled Demeter (just left of Hebe) turns toward Hebe.

The only one who hasn't lost his head is laid-back Dionysus (the cool guy farther left). He just raises another glass of wine to his lips. Over on the right, Aphrodite, goddess of love, leans back into her mother's lap, too busy admiring her own bare shoulder to even notice the hubbub. A chess-set horse's head screams, "These people are nuts—let me out of here!"

The scene had a message. Just as wise Athena rose above the lesser gods, who were scared, drunk, or vain, so would her city, Athens, rise above her lesser rivals.

This is amazing workmanship. Compare Dionysus, with his natural, relaxed, reclining pose, to all those stiff Egyptian statues standing eternally at attention.

Appreciate the folds of the clothes on the female figures (on the right half), especially Aphrodite's clinging, rumpled robe.

Some sculptors would first build a nude model of their figure, put real clothes on it, and study how the cloth hung down before actually sculpting in marble. Others found inspiration at the *taverna* on wet T-shirt night.

Even without their heads, these statues, with their detailed anatomy and expressive poses, speak volumes.

Wander behind. The statues originally sat 40 feet above the ground. The backs of the statues, which were never intended to be seen, are almost as detailed as the fronts.

• *The metopes are the panels on the walls to either side. Start with the three South Metope panels on the right wall.*

The Metopes: In the central panel of the three (#XXXI), a centaur grabs a man by the throat while the man pulls his hair. The humans have invited some centaurs—wild half-man/half-horse creatures—to a wedding feast. All goes well until the brutish centaurs, the original party animals, get too drunk and try to carry off the women. A battle ensues. The centaur does the hair-pulling, and begins to drive the man to his knees (#XXX).

The Greeks prided themselves on creating order out of chaos. Within just a few generations, they went from nomadic barbarism to the pinnacle of early Western civilization.

These metopes tell the story of this struggle between the forces of human civilization and animal-like barbarism.

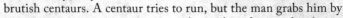

On the opposite wall (center, #XXVIII), the centaurs take control of the party, as one rears back and prepares to trample the helpless man. The leopard skin draped over the centaur's arm roars a taunt. The humans lose face.

To the left (#XXVII), the humans finally rally and drive off the brutish centaurs. A centaur tries to run, but the man grabs him by the neck and raises his (missing) right hand to run him through. The man's folded cloak sets off his smooth skin and graceful figure.

The centaurs have been defeated. Civilization has triumphed over barbarism, order over chaos, and rational man over his half-animal alter ego.

Why are the Parthenon sculptures so treasured? The British of the 19th century saw themselves as the new "civilized" race, subduing "barbarians" in their far-flung empire. Maybe these carved stones made them stop and wonder—will our great civilization also turn to rubble?

THE REST OF THE MUSEUM

You've toured only the foundations of Western civilization on the ground floor of the West Wing. Upstairs you'll find still more artifacts from these ancient lands, plus Rome and the medieval civilization that sprang from it. Pick up the free map, locate the rooms with themes you find interesting (Etruscan, Persian, Roman Britain, Dark Age Europe, and so on) and explore. Some highlights:

Lindow Man (a.k.a. the Bog Man): This victim of a Druid human-sacrifice ritual, with wounds still visible, was preserved for 2,000 years in a peat bog (Room 50, upper floor, via East Stairs).

Sutton Hoo Ship-Burial: Finds from a seventh-century Anglo-Saxon burial site (Room 41, upper floor, via East Stairs).

Treasures of the Persian Civilization: The collection here is far better than what remains to be seen in Iran (Room 52, upper floor).

Michelangelo's Drawings: The museum owns a complete cartoon (a full-scale preliminary drawing for another work of art) by Michelangelo—it's one of only two that survive (Room 90, level 4, accessed via the North Stairs or from the top of the Reading Room).

Enlightenment Gallery: Formerly known as the King's Library, this room held the British Library's treasures when it was founded in 1753. Today it displays objects that reveal the learning and wonder of the Age of Discovery (Room 1; the long hall to the right of the main entry).

And, of course, history doesn't begin and end in Europe. Look for remnants of the sophisticated, exotic cultures of Asia and the Americas (in North Wing, ground floor) and Africa (lower floor)—all part of the totem pole of the human family.

BRITISH LIBRARY TOUR

The British Empire built its greatest monuments out of paper. It's through literature that England has made her lasting contribution to history and the arts. These national archives of Britain include more than 150 million items. A copy of every publication in the UK and Ireland is sent here. It's all housed on 380 miles of shelving in the deepest basement in London.

But everything that matters for your visit is in the delightful Sir John Ritblat Gallery and an adjacent room containing the Magna Carta. We'll concentrate on a handful of documents—literary and historical—that changed the course of history. Start with these top stops, then stray according to your interests.

Orientation

Cost: Free (£5 suggested donation); admission charged for some special exhibits.

Hours: Mon-Fri 9:30-18:00, Tue until 20:00, Sat 9:30-17:00, Sun 11:00-17:00.

Getting There: From the King's Cross St. Pancras Tube station, exit to Euston Road, turn right, and walk a block west to 96 Euston Road, where you'll see a humble brick building dating from 1998. Euston Tube station is also nearby. Buses #10, #30, #59, #63, #73, and #91 (among others) also stop nearby.

Rotating Exhibits: Exhibits change often, and many of the museum's old, fragile manuscripts need to "rest" periodically in order to stay well-preserved. Even some of the major items I describe here could be napping out of view (likely candidates are the Lindisfarne Gospels, *Beowulf*, *The Canterbury Tales*, Handel's *Messiah*, and *Alice's Adventures in Wonderland*). Items usually on view include the Magna Carta, Shakespeare's First

Folio, Leonardo da Vinci's notebooks, and at least one book by Jane Austen. If your heart's set on seeing that one particular rare Dickens book or letter penned by Gandhi, call ahead to make sure it's on display.

Information: Tel. 019/3754-6060; general info tel. 020/7412-7676, www.bl.uk.

Tours: There are no guided tours or audioguides for the permanent collection. There are, however, **guided tours** of the building itself—the archives and reading rooms (for details, call 020/7412-7639 or see the website). **Touch-screen computers** in the permanent collection let you page virtually through some of the rare books.

You can download this chapter as a free Rick Steves **audio tour** (see page 8).

Length of This Tour: Allow one hour.

Cloakroom: Free. Lockers require £1 coin deposit (no large bags). For security, bags may be searched at the library entrance.

Services: There's free Wi-Fi throughout the library.

Photography: No photos allowed.

Eating: The upper-level restaurant has good hot meals. The ground-floor café (sandwiches and drinks) is next to the vast and fun pull-out stamp collection. From either café, you'll see the 50-foot-tall wall of 65,000 books, a present to the people from King George IV in 1823. The high-tech bookshelf is behind glass and has movable lifts.

Starring: Bibles, Shakespeare, English Lit 101, Magna Carta, and—ladies and gentlemen—the Beatles.

The Tour Begins

Entering the library courtyard, you'll see a big statue of a naked Isaac Newton bending forward with a compass to measure the universe. The statue symbolizes the library's purpose: to gather all knowledge and promote humanity's endless search for truth.

Stepping inside, you'll find the information desk and shop. The cloakroom and WC are down a short staircase to the right. The reading rooms upstairs are not open to the general public. The PACCAR Gallery, down a few steps to the left, houses temporary exhibits (sometimes requiring an admission charge).

Our tour is of the tiny but exciting area to the left. It's variously called "The Sir John Ritblat Gallery," "Treasures of the British Library," or just "The Treasures." This priceless literary and historical collection is held in one large, carefully designed, dimly lit room.

Enter and let your eyes adjust. The room has display cases grouped according to themes: maps, sacred texts, music, and so on.

Focus on the big picture, and don't be too worried about locating every specific exhibit in this tour.

❶ Maps

The historic maps show how humans' perspective of the world expanded over the centuries. These pieces of paper, encoded with information gleaned from travelers, could be passed along to future generations—each building upon the knowledge of the last.

The collection changes year to year, but you may see maps similar to these: A crude 13th-century map of Britain put medieval man in an unusual position—looking down on his homeland from 50 miles in the air. A few centuries later, maps of Britain were of such high quality they could still be used today to plan a trip. And only a few generations after Columbus' first journey, the entire globe was fairly well-mapped, except for the mysterious expanse of unknown land that lay beyond America's east coast—"Terra Incognita."

• *Move into the area dedicated to sacred texts from several cultures—the Hebrew Torah, Muslim Quran, Buddhist sutras, and Hindu Upanishads. Start by browsing the different versions of the sacred text of Christians, the Bible.*

❷ Early Bibles

My favorite excuse for not learning a foreign language is "If English was good enough for Jesus Christ, it's good enough for me!" I don't know what that has to do with anything, but obviously Jesus didn't speak English—nor did Moses or Isaiah or Paul or any other Bible author or character. As a result, our present-day English Bible came not directly from the mouths and pens of these religious figures, but is instead the fitful product of centuries of evolution and translation.

The Bible is not a single book; it's an anthology of books by many authors from different historical periods writing in various languages (usually Hebrew or Greek). So there are three things that editors must do in compiling the most accurate Bible: 1) decide which books actually belong, 2) find the oldest and most accurate version of each book, and 3) translate it accurately.

The **Codex Sinaiticus,** from A.D. 350, is one of the oldest complete Bibles in existence ("codex" means it's an ancient, bound manuscript). It's one of

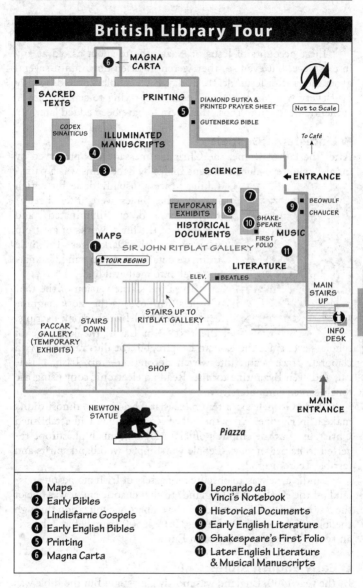

British Library Tour

MAGNA CARTA — **6**

SACRED TEXTS

PRINTING

DIAMOND SUTRA & PRINTED PRAYER SHEET

GUTENBERG BIBLE

Not to Scale

CODEX SINAITICUS — **2**

ILLUMINATED MANUSCRIPTS — **4**

3

5

To Café

SCIENCE

← ENTRANCE

TEMPORARY EXHIBITS

7

8

HISTORICAL DOCUMENTS

9

BEOWULF

CHAUCER

SHAKE-SPEARE

10

MAPS — **1**

SIR JOHN RITBLAT GALLERY

FIRST FOLIO

MUSIC

11

TOUR BEGINS

LITERATURE

ELEV. — ■ BEATLES

MAIN STAIRS UP

STAIRS UP TO RITBLAT GALLERY

STAIRS DOWN

INFO DESK

PACCAR GALLERY (TEMPORARY EXHIBITS)

SHOP

NEWTON STATUE

Piazza

MAIN ENTRANCE

BRITISH LIBRARY

1 Maps
2 Early Bibles
3 Lindisfarne Gospels
4 Early English Bibles
5 Printing
6 Magna Carta

7 Leonardo da Vinci's Notebook
8 Historical Documents
9 Early English Literature
10 Shakespeare's First Folio
11 Later English Literature & Musical Manuscripts

the first attempts to collect various books by different authors into one authoritative anthology. The parchment is made from animal skin. It's in Greek, the language in which most of the New Testament was written. The Old Testament portions are Greek translations from the original Hebrew. This particular Bible, and the nearby **Codex Alexandrinus** (A.D. 425), contain some books not included in most modern English Bibles. (Even today, Catholic Bibles contain books not found in Protestant Bibles.)

These accounts of Jesus of Nazareth are about as old as any in existence, but even so, they weren't written down until several generations after Jesus' death. Today, Bible scholars pore diligently over every word in the New Testament, trying to separate Jesus' authentic words from those that seem to have been added later.

❸ Lindisfarne Gospels

After the fall of Rome, the Christian message was preserved by monks, who reproduced ancient Bibles by hand. This was a painstaking process, usually done for a rich patron. The Bibles were often beautifully illustrated, or "illuminated," and are some of the finest works of art from what we call the Dark Ages. The little intimate details offer a rare and fascinating peek into medieval life.

The Lindisfarne version of the four Gospels (A.D. 698) is the most magnificent of medieval British monk-uscripts. The text is in Latin, the language of scholars ever since the Roman Empire, but the illustrations—with elaborate tracery and interwoven decoration—mix Irish, classical, and even Byzantine forms. (Read an electronic copy using the touch-screen computers.)

These Gospels are a reminder that Christianity almost didn't make it in Europe. After the fall of Rome (which had established Christianity as the empire's official religion), much of Europe reverted to its pagan ways. People worshipped woodland spirits and terrible Teutonic gods.

Lindisfarne was an obscure monastery of Irish monks on an island off the east coast of England. In that chaotic era, it was one of the few beacons of light, tending the embers of civilization through the long night of the Dark Ages. It took 500 years before Christianity was fully re-established in Europe.

❹ Early English Bibles

By the year 1400, England was mostly Christian. But the Bible was still written in Latin, even though only a small percentage of the population understood that language. A few brave reformers risked death to translate the sacred books into English and print them using Gutenberg's new invention, the printing press. Within two centuries, English translations were both legal and popular.

These Bibles are written in the same language you speak, but try reading them. The strange letters and archaic words clearly show how quickly languages evolve. Jesus spoke Aramaic, a form of Hebrew. His words were written down in Greek. Greek manuscripts were translated into Latin, the language of medieval monks and scholars. In the 1400s, English scholars began translating the Greek and Latin into the King's English.

The King James version (made during his reign) has been the most widely used English translation. Fifty scholars worked for four years, borrowing heavily from previous translations, to produce the work. Its impact on the English language was enormous. It made Elizabethan English something of the standard, even after ordinary people had long since stopped saying "thee," "thou," and "verily, verily."

Recent translations are not only more readable but also more accurate, based on better scholarship and original manuscripts. But scholars still encounter problems when trying to translate old phrases to fit contemporary viewpoints (case in point: our generation's debate over whether the God of the Bible should be a he or a she).

❺ Printing

Printing was invented by the Chinese (what wasn't?). The **Diamond Sutra** (c. 868) is the world's earliest, complete printed book bearing a date. It's written in Chinese even though the Buddhist faith originated in India. Considered one of Buddhism's most important sacred works, it addresses the nature of perception, reality, enlightenment, and impermanence. The **Printed Prayer Sheet** (c. 618-907) was made seven centuries before the printing press was "invented" in Europe. A bodhisattva (an incarnation of Buddha) rides a lion, surrounded by a prayer in Chinese characters. The faithful gained a blessing by saying the prayer, and so did the printer by reproducing it. Texts such as this were printed using wooden blocks carved with Chinese characters, then dipped into paint or ink.

The Gutenberg Bible

It looks like just another monk-made Latin manuscript, but it was the first book printed in Europe using movable type (c. 1455). Printing is one of the most revolutionary inventions in history.

Johann Gutenberg (c. 1397-1468), a German silversmith, devised a convenient way to reproduce written materials quickly, neatly, and cheaply—by printing with movable type. You scratch each letter onto a separate metal block, then arrange them into words, ink them up, and press them onto paper. When one job was done you could reuse the same letters for a new one.

This simple idea had immediate and revolutionary consequences. Suddenly, the Bible was available for anyone to read, fueling the Protestant Reformation. Knowledge became cheap and accessible to a wide audience, not just the rich. Books became the mass medium of Europe, linking people by a common set of ideas.

❻ Magna Carta

Duck into the Magna Carta Room to answer this question: How did Britain, a tiny island with a few million people, come to rule a quarter of the world? Not by force, but by law. The 1215 Magna Carta was the basis for England's constitutional system of government. Though historians talk about *the* Magna Carta, several different versions of the document exist, some of which are kept in this room.

The Articles of the Barons (labeled *King John*): In 1215, England's barons rose in revolt against the slimy King John. (The same King John appears as a villain in the legends of Robin Hood.) After losing London, John was forced to negotiate. The barons presented him with this list of demands. John, whose rule was worthless without the barons' support, had no choice but to affix his seal to it.

Magna Carta: A few days after John agreed to this original document, it was rewritten in legal form, and some 35 copies of the

final version of the "Great Charter" were distributed around the kingdom.

This was a turning point in the history of government. Before, kings had ruled by God-given authority, above the laws of men. Now, for the first time, there were limits—in writing—on how a king could treat his subjects. More generally, it established the idea of "due process"— the notion that a government can't infringe on citizens' freedom without a legitimate legal reason. This small step became the basis for all constitutional governments, including yours.

So what did this radical piece of paper actually say? Not much, by today's standards. The specific demands had to do with things such as inheritance taxes, the king's duties to widows and orphans, and so on. It wasn't the specific articles that were important, but the simple fact that the king had to abide by them as law.

• *Now return to the main room to find...*

❼ Leonardo da Vinci's Notebook

Books also spread secular knowledge. During the Renaissance, men turned their attention away from heaven and toward the nuts and bolts of the material world around them.

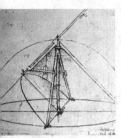

These pages from Leonardo's notebook show his powerful curiosity, his genius for invention, and his famous backward and inside-out handwriting, which makes sense only if you know Italian and have a mirror. Leonardo's restless mind pondered diverse subjects, from how birds fly, to the flow of the Arno River, to military fortifications, to an early helicopter, to the "earthshine" reflecting onto the moon.

One person's research inspired another's, and books allowed knowledge to accumulate. Galileo championed the counter-commonsense notion that the earth spun around the sun, and Isaac Newton later explained the mathematics of those moving celestial bodies.

❽ Historical Documents

Nearby are many more historical documents. The displays change frequently, but you may see letters by Henry VIII, Queen Elizabeth I, Darwin, Freud, Gandhi, and others. But for now, let's trace the evolution of...

❾ Early English Literature

Four out of every five English words have been borrowed from other languages. The English language, like English culture (and London today), is a mix derived from foreign invaders. Some of the historic ingredients that make this cultural stew:

- The original Celtic tribesmen
- Latin-speaking Romans (A.D. 1-500)
- Germanic tribes called Angles and Saxons (English is a Germanic language, and the name England comes from "Angle-land"—island of the Angles)
- Vikings from Denmark (A.D. 800)
- French-speaking Normans under William the Conqueror (1066-1250)

Beowulf

Ponder this first English literary masterpiece. The Anglo-Saxon epic poem, written in Old English (the earliest version

William Shakespeare (1564-1616)

William Shakespeare is the greatest author in any language, period. He expanded and helped define modern English. In one fell swoop, he made the language of everyday people as important as Latin. In the process, he gave us phrases like "one fell swoop," which we quote without knowing they're Shakespeare. (Without him, no one would ever "vanish into thin air," "play fast and loose," "have seen better days," do anything "without rhyme or reason," become a "laughingstock," or wish anything "good riddance.")

Shakespeare was born in Stratford-upon-Avon in 1564 to John Shakespeare and Mary Arden. Though his parents were probably illiterate, Shakespeare is thought to have attended Stratford's grammar school, finishing his education at age 14. When he was 18, he married a 26-year-old local girl, Anne Hathaway, who was three months pregnant at the time with their daughter Susanna.

The next few years are a blank—following his marriage, Shakespeare disappeared from any historical record, not turning up again until seven years later. By this point, he was a budding poet and playwright in London. He soon hit the big time, writing and performing for royalty, founding (along with his troupe) the Globe Theatre (a replica of which now sits along the Thames' South Bank—see page 88), and raking in enough dough to buy New Place, a swanky mansion back in his hometown. Around 1611, the rich-and-famous playwright retired from the theater, moving back to Stratford, where he died at the age of 52.

With plots that entertained both the highest and the lowest minds, Shakespeare taught the play-going public about human nature. His tool was an unrivaled mastery of the English language. Using borrowed plots, outrageous puns, and poetic language,

of our language), almost makes the hieroglyphics on the Rosetta Stone look easy. The manuscript is from A.D. 1000, although the story itself dates to about 750. In this epic story, the young hero Beowulf defeats two half-human monsters threatening the kingdom. Beowulf symbolizes England's emergence from the chaos and barbarism of the Dark Ages.

The Canterbury Tales

Six hundred years later, England was Christian, but it was hardly the pious, predictable, Sunday-school world we might imagine. Geoffrey Chaucer's bawdy collection of stories (c. 1410), told by pilgrims on their way to Canterbury, gives us the full range of life's experiences—happy, sad, silly, sexy, and devout. (Late in life,

Shakespeare wrote comedies (c. 1590—*Taming of the Shrew*, *As You Like It*), tragedies (c. 1600—*Hamlet*, *Othello*, *Macbeth*, *King Lear*), and fanciful combinations (c. 1610—*The Tempest*), exploring the full range of human emotions and reinventing the English language.

Perhaps as important was his insight into humanity. His father was a glove maker and wool merchant, and his mother was the daughter of a landowner from a Catholic family. Some scholars speculate that Shakespeare's parents were closet Catholics, practicing their faith during the rise of Protestantism. It is this tug-of-war between two worlds, some think, that helped enlighten Shakespeare's humanism. Think of his stock of great characters and great lines: Hamlet ("To be or not to be, that is the question"), Othello and his jealousy ("It is the green-eyed monster"), ambitious Mark Antony ("Friends, Romans, countrymen, lend me your ears"), rowdy Falstaff ("The better part of valor is discretion"), and the star-crossed lovers Romeo and Juliet ("But soft, what light through yonder window breaks"). Shakespeare probed the psychology of human beings 300 years before Freud. Even today, his characters strike a familiar chord.

The scope of his brilliant work, his humble beginnings, and the fact that no original Shakespeare manuscripts survive raise a few scholarly eyebrows. Some have wondered if maybe Shakespeare had help on several of his plays. After all, they reasoned, how could a journeyman actor with little education have written so many masterpieces? And he was surrounded by other great writers, such as his friend and fellow poet, Ben Jonson. Most modern scholars, though, agree that Shakespeare did indeed write the plays and sonnets attributed to him.

His contemporaries had no doubts about Shakespeare—or his legacy. As Jonson wrote in the preface to the First Folio, "He was not of an age, but for all time!"

Chaucer wrote an apology for those works of his "that tend toward sin.")

While most serious literature of the time was written in scholarly Latin, the stories in *The Canterbury Tales* were written in Middle English, the language that developed after the French invasion of 1066 added a Norman twist to Old English.

⓾ Shakespeare's First Folio

Shakespeare wrote his plays to be performed, not read. He published a few, but as his reputation grew, unauthorized "bootleg" versions began to circulate. Some of these were written by actors who were trying (with faulty memories) to re-create plays they had appeared in years before. Publishers also put out different versions of his plays.

It wasn't until seven years after his death, in 1623, that a complete collection of Shakespeare's plays was published, commonly known as the First Folio. Of the 700 printed, about 150 survive (most are in the US). Western literature owes much to this folio, which collects 36 of the 37 known Shakespeare plays (*Pericles* missed out). If the First Folio is not out for viewing, the library should have other Shakespeare items on display.

The engraving of Shakespeare on the title page is reportedly one of only two portraits done during his lifetime. Is this what he really looked like? No one knows. The best answer probably comes from Ben Jonson, in the introduction on the facing page. Jonson concludes, "Reader, look not on his picture, but his book."

⓫ Later English Literature and Musical Manuscripts

Look for the wall with a greatest-hits sampling of literature in English, featuring works that have enlightened and brightened our lives for centuries. The displays rotate frequently, but there's always a tasty selection of famous works, from Brontë to Kipling to Woolf to Joyce to Dickens, whose novels were as popular in his time as blockbuster movies are today. Jane Austen's novels of upper-class young women seeking suitable husbands, though set in the 19th century, have become enormously popular in the 21st. The original *Alice's Adventures in Wonderland* by Lewis Carroll created a fantasy world, where grown-up rules and logic were turned upside down. Also on display are superb works by contemporary writers, making it clear that Britain continues to be a powerful force in the world of ideas and imagination.

The Beatles

Bach, Beethoven, Brahms, Bizet...Beatles. Future generations will have to judge whether this musical quartet ranks with such artists, but no one can deny their historical significance. The Beatles burst onto the scene in the early 1960s to unheard-of popularity. With their long hair and loud music, they brought counterculture and revolutionary ideas to the middle class, affecting the values of a whole generation. Touring the globe, they served as a link between young people everywhere. Look for photos of John Lennon, Paul

McCartney, George Harrison, and Ringo Starr before and after their fame.

Most interesting are the manuscripts of song lyrics written by Lennon and McCartney, the two guiding lights of the group. "I Want to Hold Your Hand" was the song that launched them to superstardom in America. "A Hard Day's Night" and "Help" were title songs of two films capturing the excitement and chaos of their hectic touring schedule. Some call "Ticket to Ride" the first heavy-metal song. "Michelle," with a line in French, seemed oh-so-sophisticated. "Yesterday," by Paul, was recorded with guitar and voice backed by a string quartet—a touch of class from producer George Martin. Also, glance at the rambling, depressed, and cynical but humorous "untitled verse" by a young John Lennon. Is that a self-portrait at the bottom?

Handel's *Messiah* and Other Music Manuscripts

Kind of an anticlimax after the Fab Four, I know, but there

are manuscripts by Mozart, Beethoven, Schubert, and others. George Frideric Handel's famous oratorio, the *Messiah* (1741), was written in a flash of inspiration—three hours of music in 24 days. Here are the final bars of its most famous tune. Hallelujah.

THE CITY WALK

From Trafalgar Square to London Bridge

In Shakespeare's day, London consisted of a one-square-mile area surrounding St. Paul's. Today, that square mile, the neighborhood known as "The City," is still the financial heart of London, densely packed with history and bustling with business.

This two-mile walk from Trafalgar Square to London Bridge parallels the Thames, on the same main road that's been used for centuries. Along the way, you'll see sights from The City's storied past, such as St. Paul's Cathedral, the steeples of other Wren churches, historic taverns, a Crusader church, and narrow alleyways with faint remnants of the London of Shakespeare and Dickens.

But you'll also catch The City in action today, especially if you visit on a weekday at lunchtime, when workers spill out onto the streets and The City is at its liveliest. See lawyers and judges in robes and wigs taking cigarette breaks, brokers in pin-striped power suits buying newspapers from Cockneys, and the last of a dying breed—elderly gentlemen with bowler hats and brollies (umbrellas) browsing for tailored shirts and Cuban cigars. Sip a pint in the same pub where Dickens did, and eavesdrop on a power lunch. Use this walk to help resurrect the London that was, then let The City of today surprise you with what is.

Orientation

Length of This Walk: Allow three or more hours, depending on what you visit. If you have less time, you could skip a mile's worth of the Strand by taking the Tube directly to Temple, picking up the walk at St. Clement Danes, then ending at St. Paul's. Less-important stops along the way include the Temple Church, Inns of Court, and Dr. Johnson's House.

Getting There: Start at Trafalgar Square (Tube: Charing Cross or Embankment). You'll head east on the Strand and end at London Bridge (where the Bankside Walk begins). Handy buses #15 and #11 (see page 30) travel along the Strand and Fleet Street from Trafalgar Square.

Tourist Information: The City of London TI is located next to St. Paul's (Mon-Sat 9:30-17:30, Sun 10:00-16:00).

Courtauld Gallery: £6 (£3 on Mon), daily 10:00-18:00, last entry at 17:30. ✪ See the Courtauld Gallery Tour chapter.

St. Clement Danes: Free, daily 9:00-16:00, closed to sightseers during worship (generally Sun at 11:00, Wed and Fri at 12:30).

Royal Courts of Justice: Free, Mon-Fri 10:00-16:30, closed Sat-Sun, no photos, on the Strand, www.hmcourts-service.gov.uk.

Twinings Tea Shop: Mon-Fri 9:30-17:00, Sat 10:00-16:00, closed Sun.

St. Dunstan-in-the-West: Mon-Fri 9:30-17:00, free 45-minute recital on Wed at 13:15; you're welcome to bring a bag lunch; confirm schedule at www.stdunstaninthewest.org.

Dr. Johnson's House: £4.50, Mon-Sat 11:00-17:30, closed Sun, closes at 17:00 Oct-April, audioguide-£2, tel. 020/7353-3745, www.drjohnsonshouse.org.

St. Bride's Church: Free, Mon-Fri 8:00-18:00, Sat hours generally 11:00-15:00, Sun 10:00-18:30; free lunch concerts usually Tue and Fri at 13:15; Sun choral Eucharist at 11:00 and evensong at 17:30, www.stbrides.com.

Old Bailey: Free, public galleries only; opening hours depend on court schedule, but generally Mon-Fri 9:45-13:00 & 14:00-16:00, last entry at 15:40 but often closes an hour or so earlier, closed Sat-Sun, reduced hours in Aug, no kids under 14, on Old Bailey Street. No bags, mobile phones, cameras, iPods, or food, but small purses OK; you can check bags at the Capable Travel agency just down the street at Old Bailey 4—£5/bag, £1 per phone or camera.

St. Paul's Cathedral: £16, includes church entry, dome climb, crypt, tour, and audioguide; Mon-Sat 8:30-16:30, last entry for sightseeing at 16:00; dome opens at 9:30, last entry at 16:15; closed Sun except for worship. ✪ See the St. Paul's Cathedral Tour chapter.

St. Mary-le-Bow: Free, Mon-Wed 7:30-18:00, Thu 7:30-18:30, Fri 7:30-16:00, closed Sat-Sun.

Bank Museum: Free, Mon-Fri 10:00-17:00, closed Sat-Sun.

The Monument: £3 to climb the steps for the view, daily 9:30-18:00, until 17:30 Oct-March, last entry 30 minutes before closing.

Tours: You can download this chapter as a free Rick Steves audio tour (see page 8).

Services: You'll find WCs toward the back of the terrace café at Somerset House, in front of the Royal Courts of Justice (50p, in a traffic island), and in the basement of St. Paul's (free entry, around the left side).

OVERVIEW

The City stretches from Temple Church (near Blackfriars Bridge) to the Tower of London. This was the London of the ancient Romans, William the Conqueror, Henry VIII, Shakespeare, and Elizabeth I.

But The City has been stripped of its history by the Great Fire (1666), the WWII Blitz (1940-1941), and modern economic realities. Today, it's a neighborhood of modern bank buildings and retail stores. Only about 7,000 people actually live here, but The City is a hive of business activity on workdays—packed with hundreds of thousands of commuting bankers, legal assistants, and coffee-shop baristas. At night and on weekends, it's a ghost town.

The route is simple—a two-mile walk east along a single street that changes names as you go. The Strand becomes Fleet Street, which becomes Cannon Street.

The Walk Begins

• *From Trafalgar Square (Tube: Charing Cross or Embankment), head east on the Strand. (Or you can skip a mile's worth of the Strand by taking the Tube directly to Temple and starting the walk at St. Clement Danes.)*

The Strand

This busy boulevard, home to theaters and retail stores, was formerly a high-class riverside promenade, back before the Thames was tamed with retaining walls in the 19th century.

The venerable **Charing Cross Station** still has a terminus hotel (a standard part of station design in the early days of rail travel) and remains a busy transportation hub.

The station is named for the **Charing Cross monument,** which stands quietly out of place amid all the commotion in front of the station. This monument is a Victorian Age replacement of the original, medieval "Eleanor Cross." When Queen Eleanor died in 1290, her body was carried from Nottingham to Westminster Abbey. King Edward I had a memorial "Eleanor Cross" built at each of the 12 places his wife's funeral procession spent the night during that long, sad trek. Charing Cross marks the final overnight stop.

A few blocks up the Strand on the left is Southampton Street, which leads to **Covent Garden** (described on page 58).

Ahead on the right is the drive-up entrance to the **Savoy Hotel** and **Savoy Theatre.** The hotel sparkles after a recent £100 million renovation. Its shiny gold knight represents the Earl of Savoy, who built the original riverside palace here in 1245. This is one of London's ritziest locales, with Rolls-Royces, fancy shops, Simpson's Restaurant, Donald Trump luxury, and the doorman in top hat and tails. Everyone has stayed here. Monet painted the Thames at the Savoy; Oscar Wilde romanced Lord Douglas; Chaplin, Sinatra, and Burton-and-Taylor made the scene; as did the Beatles, The Who, and Bob Dylan, who filmed his cue-card-flipping film for *Subterranean Homesick Blues* in an alley around back—one of the earliest examples of a music video. Step inside to see the spiffy foyer under the pretext of asking about their (overpriced) afternoon tea under the glass cupola.

At the next major intersection, a side-trip out onto **Waterloo Bridge** affords one of the best London views, overlooking the city in both directions.

A half-block farther is **Gibraltar House** (at 150 Strand), a quasi-embassy and visitors center for one of Britain's last little "colonies," located on the southern tip of Spain.

Next up is **Somerset House,** the last of the many great riverside mansions that once lined the Strand. Today, it has a people-friendly courtyard with playful fountains, a riverside terrace, a café (with WCs), an exhibition hall, and the **Courtauld Gallery**—a fine art collection including Impressionist and Post-Impressionist gems (✪ see the Courtauld Gallery Tour chapter).

You'll encounter two different churches left Strand-ed in the middle of traffic when the road was widened around them. **St. Mary-le-Strand,** with its clean, white interior lit by blue-and-green stained glass, is an oasis of quiet (see photo). Charles Dickens' parents were married here. To the right of the church (in the ugly concrete building) is **King's College,** one of the world's top universities, with 20,000 current stu-

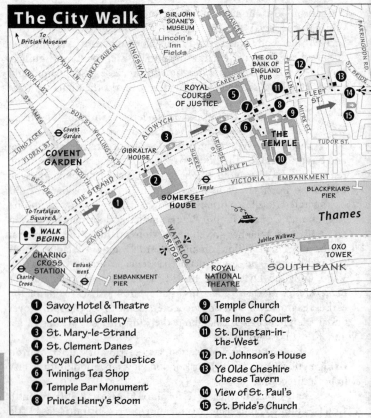

The City Walk

SIR JOHN SOANE'S MUSEUM
Lincoln's Inn Fields
THE OLD BANK OF ENGLAND PUB
ROYAL COURTS OF JUSTICE
THE TEMPLE
COVENT GARDEN
GIBRALTAR HOUSE
SOMERSET HOUSE
WALK BEGINS
CHARING CROSS STATION
EMBANKMENT PIER
WATERLOO BRIDGE
ROYAL NATIONAL THEATRE
Thames
OXO TOWER
SOUTH BANK
BLACKFRIARS PIER
Jubilee Walkway
TUDOR ST.
FLEET ST.
To British Museum
To Trafalgar Square &

1 Savoy Hotel & Theatre
2 Courtauld Gallery
3 St. Mary-le-Strand
4 St. Clement Danes
5 Royal Courts of Justice
6 Twinings Tea Shop
7 Temple Bar Monument
8 Prince Henry's Room
9 Temple Church
10 The Inns of Court
11 St. Dunstan-in-the-West
12 Dr. Johnson's House
13 Ye Olde Cheshire Cheese Tavern
14 View of St. Paul's
15 St. Bride's Church

dents and a distinguished list of former students that includes John Keats, Florence Nightingale, and Desmond Tutu.

Across the street is **Bush House,** former home of the BBC's World Service. And just beyond is **Australia House,** a kind of embassy for that member of the British Commonwealth. It's most famous for its role as the goblin-run Gringotts Wizarding Bank in the *Harry Potter* movies. (Though it's not open to visiting Muggles, you can peek into the chandeliered lobby from the door.) The building sits on a multibranched intersection where the flow of traffic is a marvel to watch.

• *Also in the intersection is the church of* **St. Clement Danes.** *(To reach St. Clement Danes from the Temple Tube stop, walk uphill on Arundel Street until it intersects with the Strand.)*

St. Clement Danes

Built by Christopher Wren (1682), the church was blitzed heavily in World War II. Today, it's a busy Royal Air Force chapel and a

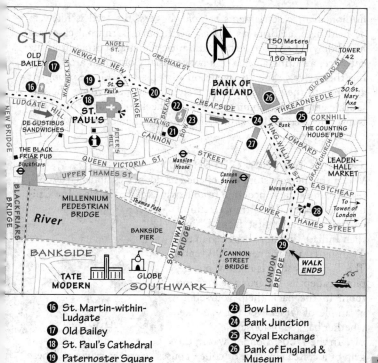

⑯ St. Martin-within-Ludgate	㉓ Bow Lane
⑰ Old Bailey	㉔ Bank Junction
⑱ St. Paul's Cathedral	㉕ Royal Exchange
⑲ Paternoster Square	㉖ Bank of England & Museum
⑳ Cheapside	㉗ Mansion House
㉑ Mermaid Tavern Site	㉘ The Monument
㉒ St. Mary-le-Bow	㉙ London Bridge

memorial to the 125,000 RAF servicemen who gave their lives in both world wars. Outside stand statues of brave airmen. Inside, hundreds of gray medallions in the stone floor are dedicated to various squadrons. Lining the walls are Books of Remembrance—10 thick volumes (with a page respectfully turned each day). This is the first of several Wren-built churches (steeple added later) we'll see on the walk. Of the 50-some he originally built, 23 Wren churches still dot London.

• *Past St. Clement Danes, on the left side of street are the...*

Royal Courts of Justice

When former Spice Girls sue tabloids for libel, when media mogul Rupert Murdoch is called to testify in a corruption inquiry, or when ex-Beatles pay $50

million divorce settlements to gold diggers, the trial is likely to be held here, at Britain's highest civil court. (Criminal cases are heard down the street at the Old Bailey.) Paparazzi often litter the entrance, awaiting a celeb or a lawyer (many of whom are celebrities themselves). The 76 courtrooms in this Neo-Gothic complex are open to the public. At least step into the lobby to see the vast Gothic entry hall (submit to a security check to go farther in). This is just one of several legal buildings in the neighborhood.

• *Across the street is...*

Twinings Tea Shop (216 Strand)

When this narrow store first opened its doors ("established 1706"), tea was an exotic concoction from newly explored lands. (The Chinese statues at the entrance remind us that tea came first from China, then India.) This store has been in the Twining family for nearly 300 years. The Twinings shop is narrow, but explore its depths—there's a tea-tasting room in the back (help yourself to a sample of whichever tea you like, whether bagged or loose).

In the 1700s, London was in the grip of a coffee craze, and "coffee houses" were everywhere. These were rather seedy places, where "gentlemen" went for coffee, tobacco, and female companionship. Tea offered a refreshing change of pace, and the late-in-the-day "cuppa" (as well as "afternoon tea") soon became a national institution. These days—as you'll see on this walk—coffee has made a comeback in London in the form of modern Starbucks-style coffee shops.

• *Pass a Thai restaurant at #229, which used to be a pub called The Wig and Pen. There's a small plaque on the front of the wood and stained-glass facade that commemorates the old pub—the only building on the Strand to survive the Great Fire of 1666. Up ahead, in the middle of the street, is a small statue of a winged creature.*

Temple Bar Monument

A statue of a griffin, a mythological beast with an eagle's wings and a lion's body, marks the official border between the City of Westminster and The City of London. The Queen, who presides over Westminster, does not pass this point without ceremonial permission of The

City's Lord Mayor. The relief at its base shows Queen Victoria submitting to this ritual in 1837.

• *Cross the border, leaving Westminster and entering The City. Ahead on the left (194 Fleet Street) is The Old Bank of England pub—a former bank with a lavish late-Victorian interior that serves lunches to the 9-to-5 crowd. (To imagine a fancy 19th-century bank, pop inside.) Up a few storefronts, on the right side of the street, look above a beauty shop to find an old building with black-framed, stained-glass bay windows.*

Prince Henry's Room (17 Fleet Street)

This half-timbered, three-story, Tudor-style building (1610) on Fleet Street is one of the few to survive the Great Fire. In Shakespeare's day, the entire City was packed, rooftop to rooftop, with wood and plaster buildings like this. Many were five and six stories high, with narrow frontage. Little wonder that a small fire could spread so quickly and become the Great Fire of 1666.

The building flies the red-and-yellow flag of Spain's Catalan region, as it now houses the Catalan tourist board.

The upper floor of the building is "Prince Henry's Room," once an office for King Charles I's son. It's likely closed—seemingly indefinitely—for restoration, but if it's open, admire the elaborate plaster ceiling and stained glass, and check out any temporary exhibitions (free, Mon-Fri 11:00-14:00, closed Sat-Sun, tel. 020/7332-1097, www.cityoflondon.gov.uk).

• *Pass underneath the house, through the passageway called Inner Temple Lane that leads a half-block to the exotic...*

Temple Church

Exterior: The round, crenellated, castle-turret roof and tiny statue of a knight on horseback (on a pillar in the courtyard) mark this as a

Crusader church (1185) from the days of King Richard the Lionhearted. The church was the headquarters of the Knights Templar, a band of heavily armed, highly trained monks who dressed in long white robes (decorated with red crosses) beneath heavy armor. In their secret rituals, the knights were sworn to chastity and to the protection of pilgrims on their way to the Muslim-held Holy Land.

Interior: Inside, some honored knights lie face-up on the floor under the rotunda of the circular "nave," patterned after the Church of the Holy Sepulchre in Jerusalem. A knight's crossed legs indicate that he probably died peacefully at home. Surrounding the serene knights are grotesque faces, perhaps the twisted expressions seen in distant wars (£4, visiting hours are irregular, often 11:00-16:00, but not every day, www.templechurch.com).

Fans of *The Da Vinci Code* will recognize the Temple Church as a place the protagonist comes to find clues leading to a special

tomb. For the film version, some footage was shot here.

By 1300, the Knights Templar's mission of protecting pilgrims had become a corrupt "protection" racket, and they'd grown rich loaning money to kings and popes. Those same kings and popes condemned the monks as heretics and sodomites, and confiscated their lands (1312). The Temple Church was rented to lawyers, who built the Inns of Court around it.

• *Abutting, surrounding, and extending from the Temple Church is a vast complex of buildings covering a full city block between the Strand/Fleet Street and the Thames, known collectively as...*

THE CITY

The Inns of Court

Wander through the peaceful maze of buildings, courtyards, narrow lanes, nooks, gardens, fountains, and century-old gas lamps, where lawyers take a break from the Royal Courts. The complex is a self-contained city of lawyers, with offices, lodgings, courtrooms, chapels, and dining halls. Law students must live here (and are even required to eat a number of meals on the premises) to complete their legal internship.

You'll see barristers in modern business suits and ties, plus a few in traditional wigs and robes, as they prepare to do legal battle. The wigs are a remnant of French manners of the 1700s, when every self-respecting European gentleman wore one.

• *Get lost. Don't worry—you'll eventually spill back out onto the busy street. Return to the building that houses Prince Henry's Room, which marks the spot where the Strand becomes...*

Fleet Street

"The Street" was the notorious haunt of a powerful combination—lawyers and the media. In 1500, Wynkyn de Worde moved here with a newfangled invention, a printing press, making this area the center of an early Information Age. In 1702, the first daily newspaper appeared. Soon you had the *Tatler*, the *Spectator*, and many others pumping out both hard news and paparazzi gossip for the hungry masses. Just past St. Dunstan church (described next), you'll see a building decorated with mosaic signs with the names of some bygone newspapers: the *Dundee Evening Telegraph*, the *People's Journal*, and so on.

London became the nerve center of a global, colonial empire, and Fleet Street was where every twitch found expression. Hard-drinking, ink-stained reporters gathered in taverns and coffeehouses, pumping lawyers for juicy pretrial information, scrambling for that choice bit of must-read gossip that would make their paper number one. They built an industry that still endures. Even in this digital age, Britain supports about a dozen national newspapers, selling more than 9 million papers a day.

Today, busy Fleet Street bustles with almost every business *except* newspapers. The industry made a mass exodus in the 1980s for offices elsewhere, replaced by financial institutions. As you walk along, you'll see the former offices of the *Daily Telegraph* (135 Fleet Street) and the *Daily Express* (#121-128—peek into the lobby to see its classic 1930s Art Deco interior). The last major institution to leave (in the summer of 2005) was the Reuters news agency (#85, opposite the *Daily Express*).

• *Heading 50 yards east past Prince Henry's Room along Fleet Street, you'll find...*

St. Dunstan-in-the-West

This church stands where the Great Fire of September 1666 finally ended. The fire started near London Bridge. For three days it swept westward, fanned by hot and blustery weather, leveling everything in its path. As it approached St. Dunstan, 40 theology students battled the blaze, holding it off until the wind shifted, and the fire slowly burned itself out.

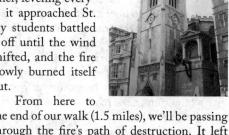

From here to the end of our walk (1.5 miles), we'll be passing through the fire's path of destruction. It left London a Sodom-and-Gomorrah wasteland so hot it couldn't be walked on for weeks. (For more on the fire, ✪ see the end of the Bankside Walk chapter.)

Today, St. Dunstan is one of the few

The Great Fire

The stones of St. Paul's flew from the building, the lead melting down the streets in a stream.... God grant mine eyes may never behold the like.... Above 10,000 homes all in one flame, the noise and crackling and thunder of the impetuous flames, the shrieking of women and children, the hurry of the people, the fall of the towers, houses, and churches was like a hideous storm.

—John Evelyn, eyewitness

churches with a thriving congregation (of Orthodox Romanians) in this now depopulated and secularized district. An unbroken line of vicars dating back to 1237 is listed in the vestibule. The clock on the bell tower outside (1670) features London's first minute hand and has two slaves gonging two bells four times an hour.

The church usually hosts Wednesday lunch-time concerts from 13:15-14:00; you can bring a bag lunch.

Alongside the church is a rare contemporary statue of Queen Elizabeth I. Surviving from her reign, this 1586 depiction of Elizabeth is as accurate as anything we have. The scepter and orb symbolize her religious and secular authority.

• *Continue east on Fleet Street. A half-block past Fetter Lane, turn left through a covered alleyway (at #167, immediately across from #54). Follow signs through the narrow lanes directing you to* Dr. Johnson's House.

Narrow Lanes—1700s London

"Sir, if you wish to have a just notion of the magnitude of this city, you must...survey the innumerable little lanes and courts," said the writer Samuel Johnson in 1763 to his young friend and biographer, James Boswell. These twisting alleyways and cramped buildings that house urban hobbits give a faint glimpse of rebuilt 1700s London, a crowded city of half a million people. After the Great Fire, London was resurrected in brick and stone instead of wood, but they stuck to the same medieval street plan, resulting in narrow lanes of brick buildings like these.

• *The narrow lanes eventually spill out onto Gough Square, about a block north of Fleet Street, where you'll find...*

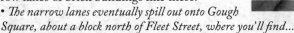

Dr. Johnson's House (17 Gough Square)

"When a man is tired of London, he is tired of life," wrote Samuel Johnson, "for there is in London all that life can afford." Johnson (1709-1784) loved to wander these twisting lanes, looking for pungent slices of London street life that he could pass along in his weekly columns called "The Rambler" and "The Idler."

At age 28, Johnson arrived in London with one of his former students, David Garrick, who went on to revolutionize Lon-

don theater. Dr. Johnson prowled the pubs, brothels, coffeehouses, and illicit gaming pits where terriers battled cornered rats while men bet on the outcome. Johnson—described as "tall, stout," and "slovenly in his dress"—became a well-known eccentric and man-about-town, though he always seemed to live on the fringes of poverty. At the far end of Gough Square is a statue of Johnson's beloved cat Hodge, who dined on oysters.

Johnson inhabited this house from 1748 to 1759. He prayed at St. Clement Danes, drank in Fleet Street pubs, and, in the attic of the house, produced his most famous work, *A Dictionary of the English Language*. Published in 1755, it was the first great English-language dictionary, starring Johnson's 42,773 favorite words culled from all the books he'd read. It took Johnson and six assistants more than six years to sift through all the alternate spellings and Cockney dialects of the world's most complex language. He standardized spelling and pronunciation, explained each word's etymology, and occasionally put his own droll spin on words. ("Oats: a grain, which is generally given to horses, but in Scotland supports the people.")

Today, the house is a museum. While the exhibits are fascinating for hard-core Johnson fans (I met one once), the old house is interesting in itself, even for the casual visitor. See a video and climb four stories through period furniture, passing a first edition of Johnson's dictionary and pictures of Johnson, Garrick, and Boswell. Nothing is roped off or behind glass, and you can browse at will. See objects Johnson once owned: his walking stick, a chair, a letter carrier, and a brick from something that fascinated him—the Great Wall of China. Portraits bring to life his urbane circle of friends, which, in addition to Boswell and Garrick (pictured in the role of Richard III), included actress Sarah Siddons, painter Sir Joshua Reynolds, and writer Oliver Goldsmith, many of whom socialized at the home of the sophisticated Elizabeth Montagu. Finally you arrive in the top-floor garret where literary history was

London's Great Plague of 1665

The Grim Reaper—in the form of the bacteria *Yersinia pestis* (bubonic plague)—rode through London on fleas atop a black rat. It killed one in six people, while leaving the buildings standing. (The next year, the Great Fire consumed the buildings.) It started in the spring as "the Poore's Plague," neglected until it spread to richer neighborhoods. During the especially hot summer, 5,000 died each week. By December, St. Bride's congregation was 2,111 souls fewer.

Victims passed through several days of agony: headaches, vomiting, fever, shivering, swollen tongue, and swollen buboes (lumps) on the groin glands. After their skin turned blotchy black (the "Black Death"), they died. "Searchers of the Dead" carted bodies off to mass graves, including one near St. Bride's (see page 254). Both the victims and their families were quarantined under house arrest, with a red cross painted on the door and a guard posted nearby, and denied access to food, water, or medical attention for 40 days—a virtual death sentence even for the uninfected.

The disease was blamed on dogs and cats, and paid dog-killers destroyed tens of thousands of pets—which brought even more rats. People who didn't die tried to leave. The Lord Mayor quarantined the whole city within the walls, so the only way out was to produce (or purchase) a "certificate of health."

By fall, London was a ghost town, and throughout England, people avoided Londoners like the Plague. It took the Great Fire of 1666 to fully cleanse the city of the disease. Some scholars have suggested that a popular nursery rhyme refers to the dreaded disease (while others brush this off as bunk):

Ring around the rosie (flower garlands
   to keep the Plague away)
A pocket full of posies (buboes on the groin)
Ashes, ashes (your skin turns black)
We all fall down (dead).

made—the birthplace of the dictionary that standardized our English language.

• *At the other end of Gough Square, turn right at the statue of Hodge and head back toward Fleet Street, noticing the lists of barristers (trial lawyers) on the doorways (e.g., next to the door at 9 Gough Square). They work not as part of a firm, but as freelancers sharing offices and clerks. Stay to the left as you wind downhill through the alleys, and look near Fleet Street for the entrance of...*

Ye Olde Cheshire Cheese Tavern

Johnson often—and I do mean often—popped 'round here for a quick one, sometimes with David Garrick and his sleazy actor friends.

"The Cheese" dates from 1667, when it was rebuilt after the Great Fire, but it's been a tavern since 1538. It's a four-story warren of small, smoky, wood-lined rooms, each offering different menus, from pub grub to white-tablecloth meals. A traditional "chop house," it serves hearty portions of meats to power-lunching businessmen.

Sit in Charles Dickens' favorite seat, next to a coal fireplace (in the "Chop Room," main floor) and order a steak-and-kidney

pie and some spotted dick (sponge pudding with currants). Sip a pint of Samuel Smith (the house beer of the current owners) and think of Samuel Johnson, who drank here pondering various spellings: "pint" or "pynte," "color" or "colour," "theater" or "theatre." Immerse yourself in a world largely unchanged for centuries, a world of reporters scribbling the news over lunch, of Alfred Lord Tennyson inventing rhymes and Arthur Conan Doyle solving crimes, of W. B. Yeats, Teddy Roosevelt, and Mark Twain.

• *Back out on Fleet Street, you're met with a cracking...*

View of St. Paul's

If you were standing here on December 30, 1940, the morning after a German Luftwaffe firebomb raid, you'd see nothing but a flat, smoldering landscape of rubble, with St. Paul's rising above it almost miraculously intact. (For more on the Blitz, see the sidebar on page 274.)

Standing here in September of 1666, you'd see nothing but smoke and ruins. The Great Fire razed everything, including the original St. Paul's Cathedral. And standing here a year earlier, in September of 1665, you'd hear "Bring out yer dead!" as they carted away 70,000 victims of the bubonic plague. After the double-

Christopher Wren (1632-1723)

After London burned, King Charles II turned to his childhood friend, Christopher Wren, to rebuild it. The 33-year-old Wren was not an architect, but he'd proven his ability in every field he'd touched: astronomy (mapping the moon and building a model of Saturn), medicine (using opium as a general anesthetic, making successful blood transfusions between animals), mathematics (a treatise on spherical trigonometry), and physics (his study of the laws of motion influenced Newton's "discovery" of gravity). Wren also invented a language for the deaf, studied refraction and optics, and built weather-watching instruments.

Though domed St. Paul's is Wren's most famous church, the smaller churches around it better illustrate his distinctive style: a steeple over the west entrance; an uncluttered, well-lit interior; Neoclassical (Greek-style) columns; a curved or domed plaster ceiling; geometrical shapes (e.g., round rosettes inside square frames); and fine carved woodwork, often by his favorite whittler, Grinling Gibbons.

whammy of plague and fire, the architect Christopher Wren was hired to rebuild St. Paul's and The City.

Even today, we see the view that Wren intended—a majestic dome hovering above the hazy rooftops, surrounded by the thin spires of his lesser churches. In the foreground below St. Paul's is the slender, lead-covered steeple of St. Martin-within-Ludgate, perfectly offsetting the more massive dome. Wren's 23 surviving churches are more than plenty for today's secular ghost town of a city.

• *A block east of Ye Olde Cheshire Cheese, and a half-block down St. Bride's Avenue, is the stacked-tier steeple of...*

St. Bride's Church

The 226-foot steeple, Wren's tallest, is stacked in layers as it tapers to a point. It's said to have inspired the wedding cake. Supposedly, a Fleet Street baker named Mr. Rich gazed out his shop window at St. Bride's as he made the first multitiered cake. (By the way, the word "Bride" in St. Bride's is only coincidental. The church was dedicated to St. Bridgit—or Bride—of Kildare long before the steeple or any wedding cakes.)

St. Bride's, built between 1671 and 1675, was one of the first of Wren's churches to open its doors after the Fire. St. Bride's is nicknamed both "The Cathedral of Fleet Street" and "The Printer's Church." Notice that the pews bear the names of departed journalists. It has been home to newspaper reporters, scholars, and literati ever since 1500, when Wynkyn de Worde set up his printing press here on church property. De Worde's press first served the literate clergy of St. Bride's, but was soon adopted by secular scholars, bookmakers, and newspapers, as Fleet Street became a global center for printed information.

During World War II, St. Bride's suffered terribly in the Blitz. (Today's structure was largely rebuilt after the war.) But thanks to Hitler's bombs, St. Bride's was instantly excavated down to its sixth-century Saxon foundations. Layers of previously unknown history were revealed from six previous churches that stood on this spot, including items such as Roman coins, medieval stained glass, and 17th-century tobacco pipes.

Also in the crypt is a wedding dress—worn by the wife of the Fleet Street baker whose wedding cake was inspired by St. Bride's steeple.

• *A block past St. Bride's Church on Fleet Street is* **The Punch Tavern,** *draped with memories of the venerable London political magazine famous for its satirical cartoons. Peek in to see Punch and his twin wife Judy looking down on a perfectly Victorian scene. These characters from a popular puppet show came onto the London scene 350 years ago. The characters gave the magazine its name, and the pub became the magazine staff's hangout. In the back room hang huge, colorful Victorian-era pastels of Punch and Judy (good £6-15 lunches, Mon-Fri 8:00-24:00, Sat–Sun 11:00-24:00, 99 Fleet Street, tel. 020/7353-6658). The valley between St. Bride's and St. Paul's is the...*

THE CITY

Fleet River and Ludgate

The Fleet River—now covered over by Farringdon Road—still flows southward, crossing underneath Fleet Street on its way to the Thames at Blackfriars Bridge. In medieval times, the river formed the western boundary of the walled city. Between you and the towering dome of St. Paul's stands Wren's

steeple-topped church of **St. Martin-within-Ludgate.** It incorporates the old city wall into its west wall, at the old city entrance known as Ludgate.

• *After crossing Farringdon Road, look left down Old Bailey Street to see a dome crowned by a golden statue of justice, which marks the...*

Old Bailey—Central Criminal Court

England's most infamous criminals—from the king-killers of the Civil War to the radically religious William Penn, from the

"criminally homosexual" Oscar Wilde to the Yorkshire Ripper—were tried here, in Britain's highest criminal court. On top of the copper dome stands the famous golden Lady who weighs and executes Justice with scale and sword. The Old Bailey is built on the former site of Newgate Prison, with its notorious execution-by-hanging site. Inside, you can visit courtrooms and watch justice doled out the old-fashioned way (see page 73). Bewigged barristers argue before stern judges while the accused sit in the dock.

• *Continue up Ludgate Hill to...*

St. Paul's Cathedral

The greatest of Wren's creations is the rebuilt St. Paul's, England's national church and the heart of The City. Wren labored for over

40 years on the church, both designing and overseeing construction of what was then the second-largest dome in the world. Unlike many church architects, Wren lived long enough to see his masterpiece completed. (✪ See the St. Paul's Cathedral Tour chapter.)

If you're not paying to enter the great church, you can pop into the basement (entry to left of front) for a café, fine WCs, a shop, and a peek at the memorials in the crypt. Belly up to the iron Churchill Gates. Standing on a plaque honoring Churchill, you can see the tomb of Admiral Lord Nelson directly below the dome.

• *A right turn at St. Paul's would take you to the Millennium Bridge, leading across the Thames to the Tate Modern and Bankside area. Instead, look for the Temple Bar gate—a white stone archway—directly to the left of the church. The gate was once the west entrance to the City of London. Relocated here, it now welcomes you to...*

Paternoster Square

This gate originally stood a half-mile west of here. It marked "Temple Bar," the boundary between the City of London and Westminster, where the griffin monument now stands (see page 246). The original Temple Bar gate was built of stone by St. Paul's architect, Christopher Wren, in 1672. But given the increase in traffic and new construction around it, the gate didn't "fit" at Temple Bar anymore. It was disassembled in 1878 and carted off to ornament the rural estate of a brewery owner. Finally, in 2004, the 2,700 stones were brought back to The City and painstakingly rebuilt here in Paternoster Square.

Enjoy a view of the dome from behind the church's red-brick Chapter House (a good example of Wren's Neoclassicism). This square was designed in the early 21st century to save views of the church, while allowing maximum modern development here in the city center.

• *Stride right past the* Shepherd and Sheep *statue and head up the pedestrian street, then bear right onto the busy, noisy street called...*

Cheapside—Shakespeare's London

This was the main east-west street of Shakespeare's London, which had a population of about 200,000. The wide street hosted The

City's marketplace ("cheap" meant market), seen today in the names of the streets that branch off from it: Bread, Milk, Honey. Rebuilt cheaply after the war, more recently it has been upgraded with brand-new glassy facades—leaving Cheapside anything but. Between New Change and Bread Streets is a shopping mall with a glass elevator; ride it to the rooftop terrace for a free view of St. Paul's Cathedral. On the street there are also some fancy offices, mobile-phone shops, clothing stores, and Ye Olde Starbucks.

If you were to detour two blocks south on Bread Street (to the corner of Bread and Cannon streets), you would not see even a trace of the **Mermaid Tavern,** Shakespeare's favorite haunt—but that's where it stood. In the early 1600s, "Sweet Will" would meet Ben Jonson, Sir Walter Raleigh, and John Donne at the Mermaid for food, ale, and literary conversation. Francis Beaumont, one of the group, wrote: "What things have we seen / Done at the

Cockney Rhyming Slang

The East End (specifically, the area around the Church of St. Mary-le-Bow) is known as the traditional home of the Cockneys. This colorful, working-class group spoke in a quirky pastiche that was the opposite of the Queen's English...think Audrey Hepburn as Eliza Doolittle in *My Fair Lady*, Dick van Dyke as the chimneysweep in *Mary Poppins*, or Don Cheadle in *Ocean's Eleven*.

One colorful Cockney invention that survives from the mid-19th century is the neighborhood's unique rhyming slang. According to urban legend, the Cockneys devised this secret way of talking to confuse policemen who might be listening. Another theory suggests that it was used between market vendors in order to rip off customers. Either way, Cockney rhyming slang helped create a sort of neighborhood pride for this downtrodden community.

Here's how it works: Simply replace an everyday word with a nonsensical phrase that rhymes with it. Instead of stairs, it's "apples and pears"—often shortened to simply "apples," as in, "I'm walking up the apples." For teeth, it's "Hampstead Heath" (or just "hampstead": "The dentist took a bloody good whack at me hampsteads").

Some Cockney rhyming slang words have become integrated into everyday American speech. For example, "blow a raspberry" comes from the slang "raspberry tart" for fart. And did you ever notice that "getting down to brass tacks" rhymes with "facts"? Many others—including several on the list on the next page—remain widely used as slang throughout the UK (if not in the US).

The tradition has continued into the 21st century—though these days it's done as a fun bit of irony, rather than as an actual secret language. For curry, they might say "Ruby Murray"—also the name of an Irish pop singer from the 1950s. Someone might

Mermaid! heard words that have been / So nimble, and so full of subtle flame..."

• *Head straight ahead for the pointy steeple that is past the shopping mall on the right. This marks...*

St. Mary-le-Bow

From London's earliest Christian times, a church has stood here. The steeple of St. Mary-le-Bow, rebuilt after the Fire, is one of Wren's most impressive. He incorporated the ribbed-arch design of the former church (a "bow" is an arch) in the steeple's midsection. In the courtyard is a statue of a smiling Captain John Smith, who in 1607 established an English colony in Jamestown, Virginia, USA, before retiring here near the church. Inside the church, see suggest, "After work, let's head to the pub for some Britneys" (Britney Spears = beers), or "Go wash yer Chevy" (Chevy Chase = face).

Cockney Rhyming Slang	Translation
a la mode	code
Adam and Eve	believe
Barnet Fair (barnet)	hair (hairstyle)
bubble and squeak (bubble)	Greek
butcher's hook (butcher's)	look
china plate (china)	mate (friend)
deep sea diver	fiver (£5 note)
loaf of bread (loaf)	head
Mutt and Jeff (mutton)	deaf
plates of meat (plates)	feet
porkpies (porkies)	lies
rabbit and pork (rabbit)	talk
Scapa Flow (scarper)	go
septic tank (septic, seppo)	Yank (American)
tea leaf	thief
trouble and strife	wife
whistle and flute	suit

So the next time you find yourself 'avin' a rabbit with a Cockney, slip the bartender a deep sea diver to buy him a Britney and ask him about his trouble and strife's new barnet. Or take a butcher's at his fancy whistle and flute, and try out the local a la mode. Maybe he'll tap his loaf and say, "Not bad fer a septic."

not one but two pulpits, used today for point-counterpoint debates of moral issues.

This is the very center of old London, where, in medieval times, the church's bells rang each evening, calling Londoners safely back in to the walled town before the gates were locked. To be born "within the sound of Bow bells" long defined a true local, or "Cockney."

This is also the "Cockney" neighborhood of plucky streetwise urchins, where a distinctive Eliza Doolittle dialect is sometimes still spoken. Today's Cockney is the hard accent of rough-and-tumble, working-class Londoners—and the Geico gecko on American TV ads. There are no Hs. "Are you 'appy, 'arry?" "Where's your 'orse? ...'urry up now." (Another fun element of the Cockney dialect—its creative rhyming slang—is described in the sidebar.)

Nineteenth-century social climbers added extra H's in order not to sound Cockney. "I hunderstand you are hinterested in renting my hattic."

These days, few people actually live within the sound of Bow bells. The City's population, while 300,000 during working hours, falls to about 7,000 at night.

• *Just past St. Mary-le-Bow is...*

Bow Lane

Today, pedestrian-only Bow Lane features smart clothing shops, sandwich bars, and pubs. The entire City once had narrow lanes like Bow, Watling, and Bread Streets. Explore this area between Cheapside and Cannon Street.

When Shakespeare bought his tights and pointy shoes in Bow Lane, the shops were wooden, the streets were dirt, and the bathroom was a ditch down the middle of the road. (The garbage brought rats, and rats brought plagues, like the one in 1665.) You bought your water in buckets carted up from the Thames. And at night, the bellman walked the streets, ringing the hour.

(For more Shakespearean ambience, it's a three-block walk south from St. Paul's to the river, where the Millennium Bridge crosses the Thames to Shakespeare's Globe, a reconstruction of the theater where many of Shakespeare's plays premiered. See page 88.)

• *Continue east on Cheapside a few blocks to the long, wide intersection where nine streets meet, called Bank Junction (Tube: Bank). Looking east, survey the buildings before you. There may be a historical plaque at the street corner with a helpful diagram of Bank Junction's buildings. A good place to view it all is from the front of Mansion House, the building with the six-columned (not eight-columned) entrance, standing where Victoria Street empties onto Bank Junction.*

Bank Junction

You're at the center of financial London. The Square Mile hosts 500 foreign and British banks. London, centrally located amid the globe's time zones, can find someone around the world to trade with 24 hours a day. In 2009, thousands of protesters packed this square, smashing bank windows in anger over Britain's severe financial downturn.

• *Look across the square at the eight-columned entrance to the...*

Royal Exchange: When London's original stock exchange opened, "stock" meant whatever could be loaded and unloaded onto a boat in the Thames. Remember, London got its start as a river-trading town. Soon, Londoners were gathering here, trading slips of paper and "futures" in place of live goats and chickens. Traders needed money changers, who needed bankers...and London's financial district boomed. Today, you can step inside under the *Trading Since 1571* sign to a skylight-covered courtyard lined with traders of retail goods and cappuccinos.

• *To the left of the Royal Exchange is the city-block-sized Bank of England (main entrance just across Threadneedle Street from the Royal Exchange entrance).*

Bank of England: This 3.5-acre, two-story complex houses the country's national bank. In 1694, it loaned £1.2 million to King William III at 8 percent interest to finance a war with France; it's managed the national debt ever since. It's an investment bank (a banker's bank), loaning money to other financial institutions. Working in tandem with the government (nationalized 1946, independent 1997), "The Old Lady of Threadneedle Street" sets interest rates, prints pound notes, and serves as the country's Fort Knox, housing stacks of gold bars.

The complex has a good **Bank Museum** inside (enter from far side, on St. Bartholomew Lane). See banknotes from 1699, an old safe, account books, and mannequins of CPAs in powdered wigs. Also see current pound notes—with a foil hologram and numbers visible under UV light (to stay one step ahead of counterfeiters). The museum's highlight is under the rotunda, displaying a real gold bar that's worth more than $500,000 (check today's rates at the entrance) and weighs 28 pounds. Try lifting it.

• *Rising up behind the Bank of England is...*

Tower 42: The black-capped skyscraper at 600 feet is The City's tallest (but not London's tallest—that's the shiny new Shard, on the opposite bank of the Thames).

• *Rising to the right is the tip of the bullet-shaped, spiral-ribbed, glass building called...*

30 St. Mary Axe: Built in 2003, the 40-story building houses the London office of a Swiss re-insurance company (an insurer's insurer). The building, nicknamed "The Gherkin" (pickle), is ventilated by natural air entering the balconies spiraling around the perimeter.

London keeps adding even more new skyscrapers to the scene (rendering the Bank Junction plaque obsolete). Look to the right of St. Mary Axe to see the Leadenhall Building (a.k.a. "The Cheesegrater"), and still farther right is the Fenchurch Building (a.k.a. "The Walkie-Talkie"). Who says there was a financial crisis in 2008?

• *You're standing in front of...*

Mansion House: This is the official residence of The City's Lord Mayor. The Lord Mayor governs not all of London but just this neighborhood. In the year 2000, a new post was created—"Mayor of London"—overseeing all of London. But the "Lord Mayor of the City" still carries out the old traditions, presiding from this palatial building. Once a year, he rides the streets in the Lord Mayor's Coach, a gilded carriage pulled by six white horses that looks like something out of *Cinderella* (the rest of the year, you can see the coach in the Museum of London).

• *Another classic bank-turned-pub, The Counting House, is two blocks up Cornhill Street (to the right of the Royal Exchange)—see page 432. From Bank Junction, turn right on Lombard Street, which turns into King William Street, and curves right (southeast) toward London Bridge. Near the northeast corner of the bridge, look to your left and find a lone column poking its bristly bronze head above the modern rooftops.*

The Monument

The 202-foot hollow column is Wren's tribute to the Great Fire that gave him a blank canvas on which to create modern London. At 2:00 in the morning of September 2, 1666, a small fire broke out in a baker's oven in nearby Pudding Lane. Supposedly, if you tipped the Monument over (to the east), its top would fall on the exact spot. Fanned by hot, blustery weather, the fire swept westward, leaping from house to house until The City was a square mile of flame.

You can climb the Monument's 311 steps for a view that's still pretty good, despite modern buildings.

• *From here, hike out over the river on...*

London Bridge

End our walk at The City's beginning. (For the history of London Bridge, see page 293.)

The City was born as a river-trading town. The Thames flows west to east, from the interior of England to the open sea. It's a tidal river from here to the sea, so ancient boats hitched rides on the tide in both directions. London Bridge, first built by the ancient Romans, established a north-south axis. Soon, goods from every corner of the world were pouring into this, one of the modern world's first great urban centers. Surviving plagues, fires, blitzes, economic changes, and even the Great Recession, with its worldwide financial network and cultural heritage, The City thrives.

• *From here, the **Tower of London** (❂ see the Tower of London Tour chapter) is a seven-minute walk east, down either Eastcheap*

THE CITY

or *Lower Thames Street. The **Bankside Walk** (✪ see the Bankside Walk chapter) begins across London Bridge. The **East End Walk** (see page 79 in the Sights in London chapter) begins a 20-minute walk (up Gracechurch/Bishopsgate) or one Tube stop to the north, at Liverpool Street Station. Or you can return to **Trafalgar Square** on the Tube (Monument stop nearby) or bus #15 (from Cannon Street).*

ST. PAUL'S CATHEDRAL TOUR

No sooner was Sir Christopher Wren selected to refurbish Old St. Paul's Cathedral than the Great Fire of 1666 incinerated it. Within a week, Wren had a plan for a whole new building...and for the city around it, complete with some 50 new churches. For the next four decades he worked to achieve his vision—a spacious church, topped by a dome, surrounded by a flock of Wrens.

St. Paul's is England's national church. There's been a church on this spot since 604. It was the symbol of London's rise from the Great Fire of 1666 and of the city's survival of the Blitz of 1940. It's been the site of important weddings (Prince Charles and Lady Diana) and state funerals (Prime Ministers Churchill and Thatcher). Architecturally, it's the masterpiece of England's greatest Neoclassical architect. Today, it's the center of the Anglican faith. Military buffs will find memorials to many great wars and their war heroes. Dome climbers will be rewarded with expansive views over London's skyline.

Orientation

Cost: £16 (includes church entry, dome climb, crypt, tour, and audioguide). Free on Sun but officially open only to worshippers.

Hours: Mon-Sat 8:30-16:30, last entry for sightseeing at 16:00 (dome opens at 9:30, last entry at 16:15), closed Sun except for worship. Sometimes closed for special events—check online. The church is also open Mon-Sat 16:15-18:00 for evening worship. It's always free to enter the church to worship, but your visit is restricted to the back of the nave.

Avoiding Lines: To miss the summer and weekend crowds, arrive first thing in the morning or late in the afternoon.

Getting There: Located in The City; Tube: St. Paul's (other nearby Tube stops include Mansion House, Cannon Street, and Blackfriars). You can take handy buses #15 and #11 (see page 30), as well as #4, #23, or #26. Careful: Don't head for tiny St. Paul's Church near Covent Garden;

your destination is St. Paul's Cathedral, in The City.

Information: Pick up the free visitor's map. Recorded info tel. 020/7236-4128, reception tel. 020/7246-8350, www.stpauls. co.uk.

Music and Church Services: If interested, check the website for worship times the day of your visit. Communion is generally Mon-Sat at 8:00 and 12:30. On Sunday, services are held at 8:00, 10:15 (Matins), 11:30 (sung Eucharist), 15:15 (evensong), and 18:00. The rest of the week, evensong is at 17:00 Tue-Sat (not Mon). If you come 20 minutes early for evensong worship (under the dome), you may be able to grab a big wooden stall in the choir, next to the singers. On some Sundays, there's a free organ recital at 16:45.

Tours: Guided 1.5-hour **tours** are offered Mon-Sat at 10:00, 11:00, 13:00, and 14:00 (confirm schedule at church or call 020/7246-8357). Free 20-minute **introductory talks** are offered throughout the day. The **audioguide** (included in admission) contains video clips that show the church in action. You can also download this chapter as a free Rick Steves **audio tour** (see page 8).

Climbing the Dome: It's 528 steps to the top and a mere 257 to the first viewing level. (While there's an elevator for people with disabilities, it does not go up into the dome's galleries—only down to the crypt.) Allow an hour to go up and down. The tower has three levels, called galleries. The climb gets steeper, narrower, and more claustrophobic as you go higher. It's a one-way system, so you can't come back down until you reach the next level.

Length of This Tour: Allow one hour, two if you climb the dome. If you're in a rush, skip the crypt and the dome.

Photography: No photography allowed.

Eating: There's a good café (£5 soups and sandwiches, £8 main dishes) and a pricier restaurant (£15 "express lunch," £22-26 meals, afternoon tea) in the crypt; free access from north side of church. There are several places to get a quick bite in Paternoster Square; for another choice, see page 432.

ST. PAUL'S CATHEDRAL

Nearby: A helpful TI is located to the right of the church. Just behind the church, to the east, is a modern shopping mall topped by a terrace with great views of the church—not a bad substitute for the dome climb for those disinclined to pay the entry fee and/or climb so many steps (free elevator to top floor). Millennium Bridge is a five-minute walk south, leading to the South Bank (Tate Modern and Shakespeare's Globe).

Starring: Sir Christopher Wren, his dome, and World War II.

The Tour Begins

Even now, as skyscrapers encroach, the 365-foot-high dome of St. Paul's rises majestically above the rooftops of the neighborhood. The tall dome is set on classical columns, capped with a lantern, topped by a six-foot ball, and iced with a cross. As the first Anglican cathedral built in London after the Reformation, it is Baroque: St. Peter's in Rome filtered through clear-eyed English reason.

Viewing St. Paul's facade from in front of the church, you can see the story of Paul's conversion told in the stone pediment. A blinding flash leaves Saul sightless on the road to Damascus (see cityscape, lower left). When his sight was restored he became Paul, the Christian. This was the pivotal moment in the life of the man who established Christianity

as a world religion through his travels, writing, and evangelizing.

While Paul stands on the top, Peter (with the annoying cock that crowed three times, symbolizing his betrayal of Jesus) is to the left and James is on the right. The four evangelists at the towers' bases each carry the gospel they wrote. As Queen Anne was on the throne when the church was finished in 1710, the statue in front portrays her.

• *Enter, buy your ticket, pick up the free visitor's map, and stand at the far back of the nave, near the font.*

❶ Nave

Look down the nave through the choir stalls to the stained glass at the far end. This big church feels big. At 515 feet long and 250 feet wide, it's Europe's fourth largest, after Rome (St. Peter's), Se-

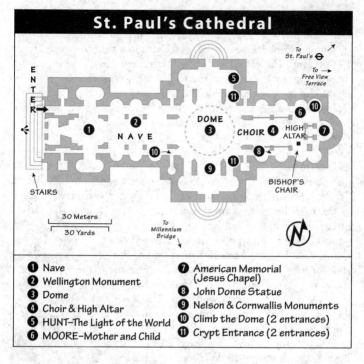

St. Paul's Cathedral

To
St. Paul's ⊖

To
Free View
Terrace

ENTER

NAVE

DOME

CHOIR

HIGH ALTAR

BISHOP'S CHAIR

STAIRS

30 Meters

30 Yards

To
Millennium
Bridge

N

❶ Nave
❷ Wellington Monument
❸ Dome
❹ Choir & High Altar
❺ HUNT–The Light of the World
❻ MOORE–Mother and Child

❼ American Memorial
(Jesus Chapel)
❽ John Donne Statue
❾ Nelson & Cornwallis Monuments
❿ Climb the Dome (2 entrances)
⓫ Crypt Entrance (2 entrances)

villa, and Milan. The spaciousness is accentuated by the relative lack of decoration. The simple, cream-colored ceiling and the clear glass in the windows light everything evenly. Wren wanted this: a simple, open church with nothing to hide. Unfortunately, only this entrance area keeps his original vision—the rest was encrusted with 19th-century Victorian ornamentation.

A diamond-shaped plaque on the floor honors the guards ("St. Paul's Watch") who worked so valiantly from 1939 until 1945 to save the church from WWII destruction. On the wall next to the door a dirty panel of stone remains, reminding visitors how dark the entire church was before undergoing a recent huge cleaning in preparation for the 300th anniversary of the first service held in the church. Remarkably, this is the first great church completed in the lifetime of its architect (built 1675-1710).

• *Glance up and behind. The organ trumpets say, "Come to the evensong and hear us play." Ahead and on the left is the towering, black-and-white...*

❷ Wellington Monument

It's so tall that even Wellington's horse has to duck to avoid bumping its head. Wren would have been appalled, but his church has become so central to England's soul that many national heroes are buried here (in the basement crypt). General Wellington, Napoleon's conqueror at Waterloo (1815) and the embodiment of British stiff-upper-lippedness, was honored here in a funeral packed with 13,000 fans. The church is littered with memorials. While all the monuments are upstairs, all the tombs are downstairs.

• *Stroll up the same nave Prince Charles and Lady Diana walked on their 1981 wedding day. Imagine how they felt making the hike to the altar with the world watching. Grab a chair underneath the impressive...*

❸ Dome

The dome you see from here, painted with scenes from the life of St. Paul, is only the innermost of three. From the painted interior of the first dome, look up through the opening to see the light-filled lantern of the second dome. Finally, the whole thing is covered on the outside by the third and final dome, the shell of lead-covered wood that you see from the street. Wren's ingenious three-in-one design was psychological as well as functional—he wanted a low, shallow inner dome so worshippers wouldn't feel diminished.

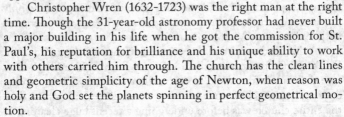

You'll see tourists walking around the base of the dome in the Whispering Gallery. The dome is constructed with such acoustic precision that secrets whispered from one side of it are heard on the opposite side, 170 feet away.

Christopher Wren (1632-1723) was the right man at the right time. Though the 31-year-old astronomy professor had never built a major building in his life when he got the commission for St. Paul's, his reputation for brilliance and his unique ability to work with others carried him through. The church has the clean lines and geometric simplicity of the age of Newton, when reason was holy and God set the planets spinning in perfect geometrical motion.

For more than 40 years, Wren worked on this site, overseeing every detail of St. Paul's and the 65,000-ton dome. It's estimated that the dome cost $850 million (in today's dollars). At age 75, Wren got to look up and see his son place the cross on top of the dome, completing the masterpiece.

On the floor directly beneath the dome is a brass grate—part of a 19th-century attempt to heat the church. Encircling it is Christopher Wren's name and epitaph, written in Latin: *Lector, si monumentum requiris circumspice (Reader, if you seek his monument, look around you).*

Now review the ceiling: Behind is Wren simplicity and ahead is Victorian ornateness.

• *The choir area blocks your way, but you can see the altar at the far end under a golden canopy.*

❹ Choir and High Altar

English churches, unlike most in Europe, often have a central choir area (a.k.a. a "quire" or "chancel"), where church officials and the

singers sit. (You can see St. Paul's well-known choir of 30 boys and 12 men in action, singing psalms, at the evensong service, held daily except Monday.) St. Paul's—a cathedral since 604—is home to the local Anglican bishop, who presides in the chair nearest the altar on the south, or right, side (the carved bishop's hat hangs over the chair).

The ceiling above the choir is a riot of glass mosaics, representing God (above the altar) and his creation. The mosaics are very Victorian. In fact, Queen Victoria complained that the earlier ceiling was "dreary and undevotional." The Dean and chapter wisely took note and had it spiffed up with this brilliant mosaic work... textbook late Victorian. In separate spheres, eight "Angels of the Morning" hold up creatures of the earth, sea, and sky.

The high altar (the marble slab with crucifix and candlesticks— you'll get a close look later) sits under a huge canopy with corkscrew columns. The canopy looks ancient, but it only dates from 1958, when it was rebuilt after being heavily damaged in October of 1940 by the bombs of Hitler's Luftwaffe. For regular services, the priest stands beneath the dome on the low wooden platform.

• *In the north transept (to your left as you face the altar), find the big painting of Christ, in a golden wood altarpiece. Glare? Try walking side-to-side to find the best viewing angle.*

❺ *The Light of the World* (1904)

In the dark of night, Jesus—with a lantern, halo, jeweled cape, and crown of thorns—approaches an out-of-the-way home in the woods, knocks on the door, and listens for an invitation to come in. A Bible passage on the picture frame says: "Behold, I stand at the door and knock..." (Revelation 3:20).

In his early twenties, William Holman Hunt (1827-1910) was in the dark night of a spiritual crisis when he heard this verse knocking in his head. He opened his soul to Christ, his life changed forever, and he tried to capture the experience in paint.

ST. PAUL'S CATHEDRAL

The Anglican Communion

St. Paul's Cathedral is the symbolic (but not official) nucleus of earth's 70 million Anglicans. The Anglican Communion is a loose association of churches—including the Church of England and the Episcopal Church in the US—with common beliefs. The rallying point is *The Book of Common Prayer*, their handbook for worship services.

Forged in the fires of Europe's Reformation, Anglicans see themselves as a "middle way" between Catholics and Protestants. They retain much of the pomp and ceremony of traditional Catholic worship but with Protestant elements such as married priests (and, recently, female priests); attention to Scripture; and a less hierarchical, more consensus-oriented approach to decision making. Among Anglicans there are divisions, from Low Church congregations (more evangelical and "Protestant") to High Church (more traditional and "Catholic").

The Church of England, the largest single body, is still the official religion of the state, headed by the Archbishop of Canterbury (who presides in Canterbury but lives in London). In 1982, Pope John Paul II and the then Archbishop of Canterbury met face-to-face. In 2010, Pope Benedict XVI visited London and joined the Archbishop in prayer. Pope Francis has indicated that he wants to continue bridging the gap that has existed since the Reformation. These symbolic gestures signal a new ecumenical spirit.

As one of the Pre-Raphaelites who adored medieval art (see page 342), he used symbolism, but only images the average Brit-on-the-street could understand. The door is the closed mind, the weeds the neglected soul, the darkness is malaise, while Christ carries the lantern of spiritual enlightenment.

In 1854, Hunt debuted *The Light of the World* (not this version, but a smaller one now at Oxford). The critics savaged it—"syrupy," "too Catholic," "simple"—but the masses lapped it up. It became the most famous painting in Victorian England—in fact, in the whole world. It was taken on tour through the vast British Empire, and was reproduced in countless engravings. It became a pop icon that inspired sermons, poems, hymns, and countless Christ-at-the-door paintings in churches and homes. Hunt's humble-hippie image of Christ was stamped forever on the minds of generations of schoolkids. It was so popular that late in life Hunt was asked to do this larger version specifically for St. Paul's. Nearly blind, he needed an assistant. (*The Guardian* newspaper once published a list of "Britain's Ten Worst Paintings." They honored *The Light of the World* as number seven, comparing it to a plastic crucifix.)

• *Return to the area underneath the dome and walk toward the altar, along the left side of the choir, pausing at a modern statue.*

❻ Mother and Child (1983)

Britain's (and perhaps the world's?) greatest modern sculptor, Henry Moore, rendered a traditional subject in marble in an abstract, minimalist way. This Mary and Baby Jesus was inspired by the sight of British moms nursing babies in WWII bomb shelters. Moore intended the viewer to touch and interact with the art. It's OK.

• *Continue to the altar at the far end of the church. The area behind it has three bright and modern stained-glass windows.*

❼ American Memorial Chapel (Jesus Chapel)

This special spot in St. Paul's honors the Americans who sacrificed their lives to save Britain in World War II. An inscription on the floor reads: "To the American Dead of the Second World War, From the People of Britain."

Each of the three windows has a central core of religious scenes, but the brightly colored panes that arch around them have some unusual iconography: American. Spot the American eagle (center window, to the left of Christ), George Washington (right window, upper-right corner), and symbols of all 50 states (find your state seal). In the carved wood beneath the windows, you'll see birds and foliage native to the US. And at the very far right of the paneling, check out the tiny tree "trunk" (amid foliage, below the bird)—it's a US rocket ship circa 1958, shooting up to the stars.

Britain is very grateful to its WWII saviors, the Yanks, and remembers them religiously with the Roll of Honor (immediately behind the altar). This 500-page book under glass lists the names of 28,000 US servicemen and women based in Britain who gave their lives during the war.

• *Take a close look at the high altar and the view back to the entrance from here. Look up and enjoy the Victorian mosaic ceiling above the choir. Then continue around the altar and head back toward the entrance. On the left wall of the aisle, standing white in a black niche, is a statue of...*

❽ John Donne

John Donne (1573-1631), shown here wrapped in a burial shroud,

was not only a great poet, but also a passionate preacher. He spent the last decade of his
life working in old St. Paul's. Donne personally chose to be portrayed here in a shroud to
capture the melancholy he felt after his wife's
death. The statue is one of the few treasures to
survive the Great Fire of 1666. You can still
see the dark scorch marks on the urn beneath
Donne's feet.

Imagine hearing Donne deliver a funeral
sermon here, with the huge church bell toll-
ing in the background: "No man is an island....
Any man's death diminishes me, because I am involved in Mankind. Therefore, never wonder for whom the bell tolls—it tolls for
thee."

• *And also for dozens of people who lie buried beneath your feet, in the
crypt where you'll end your tour. But first, in the south transept, find
the...*

❾ Horatio Nelson Monument and Charles Cornwallis Monument

Admiral Horatio Nelson (1758-1805) leans on
an anchor, his coat draped discreetly over the
arm he lost in battle.

In October of 1805, England trembled in
fear as Napoleon—bent on world conquest—
prepared to invade from across the Channel.
Meanwhile, hundreds of miles away, off the
coast of Spain, the daring Lord Nelson sailed
the HMS *Victory* into battle against the French
and Spanish navies. His motto: England expects that every man shall do his duty.

Nelson's fleet smashed the enemy at Trafalgar, and Napoleon's
hopes for a naval invasion of Britain sank. Unfortunately, Nelson
took a sniper's bullet in the spine and died. The lion at Nelson's feet
groans sadly, and two little boys gaze up—one at Nelson, one at
Wren's dome. You'll find Nelson's tomb directly beneath the dome,
downstairs in the crypt.

Opposite Nelson is a monument to another great military
man, Charles Cornwallis (1738-1805), honored here for his service
as Governor General of Bengal (India). Yanks know him better as
the general who lost the American Revolutionary War (or "American War," as it's known here) when George Washington—aided by
French ships—forced his surrender at Yorktown in 1780.

• *There are several entrances to the dome and its galleries, but only one is
open to the public at any given time, so check the free visitor's map.*

ST. PAUL'S CATHEDRAL

❿ Climb the Dome

The 528-step climb is worthwhile, and each level (or gallery) offers something different.

First you get to the Whispering Gallery (257 steps, with views of the church interior). Whisper sweet nothings into the wall, and your partner (and anyone else) standing far away can hear you. Exactly how it works is debated (some even question *if* it works). Most likely, the sound does not travel up and over the dome to the dia-metrically opposite side (as it would in a perfect sphere). Rather, it goes around the curved wall horizontally, so you don't have to stand in any particular spot. For best effects, try whispering (not talking) with your mouth close to the wall, while your partner stands a few dozen yards away with his or her ear to the wall.

After another set of stairs, you're at the Stone Gallery, with views of London. If you're exhausted, claustrophobic, or wary of heights, this middle level might be high enough. (The top level has very little standing room for tourists.)

Finally a long, tight, metal staircase takes you to the very top of the cupola, the Golden Gallery. (Just before the final dozen

stairs to the top, there's a tiny window at your feet that allows you to peek directly down—350 feet—to the church floor.) Once at the top, you emerge to stun-ning unobstructed views of the city. Looking west, you'll see the London Eye and Big Ben. To the south, across the Thames, is the rectangular smokestack of the Tate Modern, with Shakespeare's Globe nestled nearby. To the east sprouts a glassy garden of new skyscrapers, including the 600-foot-tall, black-topped Tower 42 and the bullet-shaped 30 St. Mary Axe building (nicknamed "The Gherkin"). Looking farther into the distance, you'll see London's future—the teeming, fast-growing expanse of the East End and the Docklands. The cluster of skyscrapers marks Canary Wharf. Just north of that was the site of the 2012 Olympic Games.

• *Descend the dome to church level, then follow signs directing you down-stairs to the...*

⓫ Crypt

Many famous people are buried here. Start by locating the central

ST. PAUL'S CATHEDRAL

St. Paul's, the Blitz, and the Battle of Britain

Nazi planes mercilessly firebombed London in 1940. Even though The City around it burned to the ground, St. Paul's survived, giving hope to the citizens. The church took two direct hits, crumbling the altar and collapsing the north transept. On December 29, 1940, some 28 bombs fell on the church. The surrounding neighborhood was absolutely flattened, while the church rose above it, nearly intact. Some swear that many bombs bounced miraculously off Wren's dome, while others credit the heroic work of local firefighters. (There's a memorial chapel to the firefighters who kept watch over St. Paul's with hoses cocked.) Still, it's clear from the damage that St. Paul's was not fully Blitz-proof.

Often used synonymously, the Blitz and the Battle of Britain are actually two different phases of the Nazi air raids of 1940-1941. The Battle of Britain (June-Sept 1940) pitted Britain's Royal Air Force against German planes trying to soften up Britain for a land-and-sea invasion. The Blitz (Sept 1940-May 1941) was Hitler's punitive terror campaign against civilian London.

In the early days of World War II, the powerful, technologically superior Nazi army quickly overran Poland, Belgium, and France. The British army hightailed it out of France, crossing the English Channel from Dunkirk, and Britain hunkered down, waiting to be invaded. Hitler bombed R.A.F. airfields while his

tomb of **Horatio Nelson,** who wore down Napoleon. It's a big coffin-on-a-pedestal in a round alcove at the center of the crypt, directly beneath the dome. Nearby is the granite tomb of the Duke of Wellington (who finished Napoleon off). The flags near the tomb were carried at his funeral procession.

Continuing up the central axis of the crypt, you enter a chapel. At the chapel's altar, turn right to reach **Christopher Wren's** tomb—a simple black slab with no statue. Next to it is a hunk of rough Portland stone quarried but unused by Wren while building St. Paul's; see his triangle brand on the left end. These few stones are not much of an honor ground troops massed along the Channel. Britain was hopelessly outmatched, but Prime Minister Winston Churchill vowed, "We shall fight on the beaches...We shall fight in the fields and in the streets...We shall never surrender."

Britain fought back. Though greatly outgunned, they had a new and secret weapon—radar—that allowed them to get the jump on puzzled Nazi pilots. Speedy Spitfires flown by a new breed of young pilots shot down 1,700 German planes. By September of 1940, the German land invasion was called off, Britain counterattacked with a daring raid on Berlin...and the Battle of Britain was won.

A frustrated Hitler retaliated with a series of punishing air raids on London itself, known as the Blitz. All through the fall, winter, and spring of 1940-1941, including 57 consecutive nights, Hermann Göring's Luftwaffe pummeled a defenseless London, killing 20,000 and leveling half the city (mostly from St. Paul's eastward). Residents took refuge deep in the Tube stations. From his Whitehall bunker, Churchill made radio broadcasts exhorting his people to give their all, their "blood, toil, sweat, and tears."

Late in the war (1944-1945), Hitler ordered another round of terror-inducing attacks on London (sometimes called the "second Blitz") using car-sized V-1 and V-2 bombs, an early type of cruise missile. But Britain's resolve had returned, the United States had entered the fight, and the pendulum shifted. Churchill could say that even if the empire lasted a thousand years, Britons would look back and say, "This was their finest hour."

Churchill's state funeral was held in 1965 at St. Paul's in a bittersweet remembrance of Britain's victory.

for the man who built this great church. "If you seek his monument..." you'll be disappointed.

Use your visitor's map to find other **tombs and memorials:** of painters Turner and Reynolds (located near Wren); of Florence Nightingale (near Wellington); and a memorial to George Washington, who lies buried back in old Virginny.

Back near Nelson's tomb is a stand-up, wrap-around film program titled *Oculus: An Eye into St. Paul's.* Relaxing movies show the view from atop the dome (helping you decide whether it's worth the huff to see in person). Clips illustrate a day in the life of this great church. A timeline of church history provides context.

Temporary exhibits (they change frequently) often chronicle important events that have been held at the cathedral. There are also models of previous churches that stood on this spot.

The crypt contains a fine gift shop, a WC, a restaurant, and the grim-sounding **Crypt Café,** which nevertheless serves tasty food.

TOWER OF LONDON TOUR

William I, still getting used to his new title of "the Conqueror," built the stone "White Tower" (1077-1097) to keep the Londoners in line. The Tower also served as an effective lookout for seeing invaders coming up the Thames. His successors enlarged it to its present 18-acre size. Because of the security it provided, the Tower served over the centuries as a royal residence, the Royal Mint, the Royal Jewel House, and, most famously, as the prison and execution site of those who dared oppose the Crown.

The Tower's hard stone and glittering jewels represent the ultimate power of the monarch. So does the executioner's block. You'll find more bloody history per square inch in this original tower of power than anywhere else in Britain. Today, though its military purpose is history, it's still home to the Yeoman Warders, a.k.a. the "Beefeaters," who host three million visitors a year.

Your visit has four parts: the lively Beefeater tour (included in admission price, 1 hour), the White Tower (a serious museum and armory, which many rush through and underappreciate), the crown jewels (best in Europe, generally with a bit of a wait), and the grounds and walls (a simple and enjoyable stroll).

Orientation

Cost: £22, family-£57 (prices include a 10 percent optional donation).

Hours: March-Oct Tue-Sat 9:00-17:30, Sun-Mon 10:00-17:30; Nov-Feb Tue-Sat 9:00-16:30, Sun-Mon 10:00-16:30; last entry 30 minutes before closing.

Advance Tickets: To avoid the long ticket-buying lines at the Tower, the easiest option is to buy your ticket at the Trader's Gate gift shop, located down the steps from the Tower Hill

Tube stop (tickets here are generally slightly cheaper than at the gate—they don't include the voluntary donation). Tickets are also sold at various locations (such as travel agencies) throughout London. You can also buy tickets, with credit card only, at the Tower Welcome Centre to the left of the normal ticket lines—though on busy days, it can be crowded here as well. It's easy to book online (www.hrp.org.uk, £1 discount, no fee) or by phone (tel. 0844-482-7799 within UK or tel. 011-44-20-3166-6000 from the US; £2 fee), then pick up your tickets at the Tower.

More Crowd-Beating Tips: It's most crowded in summer, on weekends (especially Sundays), and during school holidays. Any time of year, the line for the crown jewels—the best on earth—can be just as long as the line for tickets. For fewer crowds, arrive before 10:00 and go straight for the jewels. Alternatively, arrive in the afternoon, tour the rest of the Tower first, and see the jewels an hour before closing time, when crowds die down.

Getting There: The Tower is located in East London (Tube: Tower Hill). For speed, take the Tube there (about 10-12 minutes from central London); for romance, take the boat. Thames Clippers boats make the trip between the Tower of London and Westminster Pier near Big Ben in 30 minutes; the boat continues on to Greenwich from the Tower Pier. For details about these cruises, see page 42. Buses #15 and #RV1 make the trip from Trafalgar Square (see map on page 30).

Information: Upon arrival, pick up the free map/guide, and check the schedule of the day's events and special demonstrations (such as knights in armor explaining medieval fighting techniques; these are most common on particularly busy days such as school holidays). Everything inside is well described, so skip the £5 Tower guidebook. Switchboard tel. 0844-482-7777, www.hrp.org.uk.

Sunday Worship: On Sunday morning, visitors are welcome on the grounds for free to worship in the Chapel Royal of St. Peter ad Vincula. You get in without the lines, but you can only see the chapel—no sightseeing (9:15 Communion or 11:00 service with fine choral music, meet at west gate 30 minutes early, dress for church, may be closed for ceremonies—call ahead; phone number listed above).

Yeoman Warder (Beefeater) Tours: Free, worthwhile, one-hour Beefeater tours leave every 30 minutes from inside the gate (first tour Tue-Sat at 10:00, Sun-Mon at 10:30, last one at 15:30—or 14:30 in Nov-Feb). The boisterous Beefeaters are great entertainers, whose historical talks include lots of bloody anecdotes and corny jokes. Check the clock inside the gate. If you just miss the start of a tour, you can join it in progress (just catch up to the group a bit ahead). You won't need the £4 audioguide.

Length of This Tour: Allow two hours. If you have less time, see the crown jewels, and try to squeeze in a Beefeater tour to get an overview. If time allows, also tour the White Tower Museum.

Photography: Photos allowed, except of the jewels and in chapels.

Eating: The New Armouries Café, inside the Tower, is a big, efficient, inviting cafeteria (large, splittable meals for £8-10). Outside the Tower, there's an Apostrophe food shop along the river; the big, modern Eat, uphill from the ticket lines; a row of familiar fast-food joints just behind the Welcome Centre; and various take-out stands all around. Picnicking is allowed on Tower grounds but not inside the buildings.

Nearby: Adjacent to the Tower is **Tower Hill,** with two memorials (WWI and WWII). Looming above this area, with a gigantic decorative tower, is the building called Ten Trinity Square, which was designed to house the London Port Authority.

The Tower is also close to three of my self-guided walks: You could walk from Trafalgar Square to the Tower following ✪ The City Walk. Across the river is the start of the ✪ Bankside Walk (begins at London Bridge, upstream). And just to the north, near Liverpool Street Station, is the start of the ✪ East End Walk (see page 79).

Starring: The crown jewels, Beefeaters, William the Conqueror, and Henry VIII.

The Tour Begins

❶ Entrance Gate

Even an army the size of the ticket line couldn't storm this castle. After the drawbridge was pulled up and the iron portcullis slammed down, you'd have to swim a 120-foot moat; cross an island prowled by wild animals; then toss a grappling hook onto a wall and climb up while the enemy poured boiling oil on you. If you made it this far, you'd only

be halfway there. You'd still have to swim a second moat (eventually drained to make the grassy parade ground we see today), then, finally, scale a second, higher wall. In all, the central keep (tower) was surrounded by two concentric rings of complete defenses. Yes,

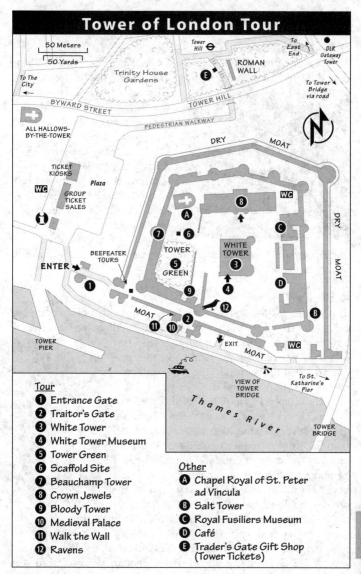

Tower of London Tour

Tour
1. Entrance Gate
2. Traitor's Gate
3. White Tower
4. White Tower Museum
5. Tower Green
6. Scaffold Site
7. Beauchamp Tower
8. Crown Jewels
9. Bloody Tower
10. Medieval Palace
11. Walk the Wall
12. Ravens

Other
A. Chapel Royal of St. Peter ad Vincula
B. Salt Tower
C. Royal Fusiliers Museum
D. Café
E. Trader's Gate Gift Shop (Tower Tickets)

TOWER OF LONDON

it was difficult to get into the Tower (if you were a foreign enemy)... but it was almost as impossible to get out (if you were an enemy of the state).

• Show your ticket, enter, check the posted daily event schedule, and consider catching a one-hour Beefeater tour. The information booth is nearby. If you didn't get a free map on the way in, pick one up at the bookstore up ahead (you may have to ask for it). WCs are 100 yards ahead.

When you're all set, go 50 yards straight ahead to the...

❷ Traitor's Gate

This was the boat entrance to the Tower from the Thames. Princess Elizabeth, who was a prisoner here before she became Queen

Elizabeth I, was carried down the Thames and through this gate on a barge, thinking about her mom, Anne Boleyn, who had been decapitated inside just a few years earlier. Many English leaders who fell from grace entered through here—Elizabeth was one of the lucky few to walk out.

• *Pass underneath the "Bloody Tower" into the inner courtyard. The big, white tower in the middle is the...*

❸ White Tower

This square, 90-foot-tall tower was the original structure that gave this castle complex of 20 towers its name. William the Conqueror built it more than 900 years ago to put 15 feet of stone between himself and those he conquered. Over the centuries, the other walls and towers were built around it.

The keep was a last line of defense. The original entry (on the south side) is above ground level so that the wooden approach (you'll climb its modern successor to get in, and lots more stairs once you're inside) could be removed, turning the tower into a safe refuge. Originally, there were even fewer windows—the lower windows were added during a Christopher Wren-ovation in 1660. In the 13th century, the tower was painted white (hence the name).

Standing high above the rest of old London, the White Tower provided a gleaming reminder of the monarch's absolute power over subjects. If you made the wrong move here, you could be feasting on roast boar in the Banqueting Hall one night and chained to the walls of the prison the next. Torture ranged from stretching on the rack to the full monty: hanging by the neck until nearly dead, then "drawing" (cut open to be gutted), and finally quartering, with your giblets displayed on the walls as a warning. (Guy Fawkes, who tried to blow up Parliament with 36 barrels of gunpowder, received this treatment after being tortured here.) Any cries for help were muffled by the thick stone walls—15 feet at the base, a mere 11 feet at the top.

• *Either now or later, find time to go inside the White Tower for its excellent museum.*

❹ White Tower Museum

Inside the White Tower, a one-way route winds through exhibits re-creating medieval life and the Tower's bloody history of torture and executions.

In the **Royal Armory,** you'll see some suits of armor of Henry VIII—on a horse, slender in his youth (c. 1515), then more heavy-set by 1540 (with his bigger-is-better codpiece). Next to Henry is the child-size armor once thought to be for his long-awaited male heir, Edward VI, who died young. But the armor actually belonged to Henry, Prince of Wales (1594-1612), the popular son of James I. Get up close to see the incredibly detailed battle scenes. Continuing along, other suits of armor, including those of a 6'8" giant and a 3'1" midget (more likely a child), and swords are identified by king. End this section by finding some memorabilia of Princes William and Harry.

The **Line of Kings,** spread throughout this level, is a colorful row of painted wooden horses (some carved in the 17th century by revered sculptor Grinling Gibbons, the "King's Carver"), which once held the suits-of-armor of the monarchs who rode them.

Upstairs, pass through the long hall to reach the rare and lovely **St. John's Chapel** (1080). This is where Lady Jane Grey (described later) offered up a last unanswered prayer. The oldest surviving part of the original Tower—and the oldest church in London—the chapel's round Norman (Romanesque) arches and column capitals decorated with the T-shaped Tau cross evoke the age of William the Conqueror.

Moving on, the **Arsenal** displays the heaviest suit of armor in the world (130 pounds!), as well as various weapons used through the ages, including machine guns and the jeweled "Tiffany Revolver."

On the top floor, ogle the giant dragon made out of old weapons. In the case at the end of this hall, see the Tower's actual **execution ax** and chopping block. In 1747, this seven-pound ax sliced through the neck of Lord Lovat, a Scottish supporter of

The Beefeaters

The original duty of the Yeoman Warders (called "Beefeaters") was to guard the Tower, its prisoners, and the jewels. Their nickname may come from an original perk of the job—large rations of the king's beef. The Beefeaters dress in blue knee-length coats with red trim and a top hat. The "ER" on the chest stands for the monarch they serve—Queen Elizabeth II (Elizabetha Regina in Latin). On special occasions, they wear red. All are retired non-commissioned officers from the armed forces with distinguished service records.

These days, the Yeoman Warders are no longer expected to protect the Tower. Instead, they've evolved into great entertainers, leading groups of tourists through the Tower. At night, they ritually lock up the Tower in the Ceremony of the Keys. There are 35 Yeoman Warders, including one woman. They and their families make for a Beefeating community of 120 that live inside the Tower.

Bonnie Prince Charlie's claim to the throne. With his death, the ax was retired.

In the next room, kid-oriented, hands-on exhibits bring the history engagingly to life. I learned how hard it is to nock an arrow (to properly align the arrow on the bow prior to release).

• *Back outside, find the courtyard to the left of the White Tower, called...*

❺ Tower Green

In medieval times, this spacious courtyard within the walls was the "town square" for those who lived in the castle. Knights exercised and jousted here, and it was the last place of refuge in troubled times. The Tower is still officially a royal residence, and the Queen's lodgings are on the south side of the green, in the white half-timbered buildings where a bearskin-hatted soldier stands guard.

The north side of the Green is bordered by the stone **Chapel Royal of St. Peter ad Vincula** ("in Chains"). The current structure was built by Henry VIII, and his most famous victims are buried here (among them his wives Anne Boleyn and Catherine Howard). The chapel's interior is open only on the Beefeater tour, except during the last hour of the day, when anyone can go inside to see it. If you aren't on a tour, wait for one to come around, discreetly squeeze into the group while the Beefeater is talking outside the chapel, and go in with the group.

• *Near the middle of Tower Green is a granite-paved square marked* Site of Scaffold.

❻ Scaffold Site

The actual execution site looks pleasant enough today; the chopping block has been moved to inside the White Tower, and a modern sculpture encourages visitors to ponder those who died.

It was here that enemies of the Crown would kneel before the king for the final time. With their hands tied behind their backs, they would say a final prayer, then lay their heads on a block, and—*shlit*—the blade would slice through their necks, their heads tumbling to the ground. The headless corpses were buried in unmarked graves in Tower Green or under the floor of the Chapel Royal of St. Peter ad Vincula. The heads were stuck on a stick and displayed at London Bridge. Passersby did not really see the heads—they saw spheres of insects and parasites.

Tower Green was the most prestigious execution site at the Tower. Common criminals were hanged outside the Tower. More prominent evil-doers were decapitated before jeering crowds atop Tower Hill (near today's Tube station). Inside the Tower walls was reserved for the most heinous traitors.

Henry VIII axed a couple of his ex-wives here (divorced readers can insert their own cynical joke). Anne Boleyn was the appealing young woman Henry had fallen so hard for that he broke with the Catholic Church in order to divorce his first wife and marry her. But when Anne failed to produce a male heir, the court turned against her. She was locked up in the Tower, tried in a kangaroo court, branded an adulteress and traitor, and decapitated.

Henry's fifth wife, teenage Catherine Howard, was beheaded and her body laid near Anne's in the church. Jane Boleyn (Anne's sister-in-law) was also executed here for arranging Catherine's adulterous affair behind Henry's back. Next.

Henry even beheaded his friend Thomas More (a Catholic) because he refused to recognize (Protestant) Henry as head of the Church of England. (Thomas died at the less-prestigious Tower Hill site near the Tube stop.)

The most tragic victim was 17-year-old Lady Jane Grey, who

was manipulated into claiming the Crown for nine days during the scramble for power after Henry's death and the six-year reign and death of his sickly young son, Edward VI. When Bloody Mary (Mary I, Henry's daughter) took control, she forced her Protestant cousin Jane to kneel before the executioner. Young Jane bravely blindfolded herself, but then couldn't find the block. She crawled around the scaffolding pleading, "Where is it?!" (The scene is depicted, beautifully if not entirely accurately, in sharp Pre-Raphaelite detail in one of the National Gallery's most popular paintings; see page 162.)

Years ago, a Beefeater, tired of what he called "Hollywood coverage" of the Tower, grabbed my manuscript, read it, and told me that in more than 900 years as a fortress, palace, and prison, the place held 8,500 prisoners. But only 120 were executed, and, of those, only six were executed inside it. Stressing the hospitality of the Tower, he added, "Torture was actually quite rare here."

• *Overlooking the scaffold site is the...*

❼ Beauchamp Tower—Prisoners

The Beauchamp Tower (pronounced "BEECH-um") was one of several places in the complex that housed Very Important Prisoners. Climb upstairs to a room where the walls are covered with dozens of final messages—graffiti carved into the stone by bored and despondent inmates.

Picture Philip Howard, the Earl of Arundel (c. 1555-1595), warming himself by this fireplace and glancing out at the execution site during his 10-year incarceration. Having lived a devil-may-care life of pleasure in the court of Queen Elizabeth, the pro-Catholic Arundel was charged with treason by the Protestant government. He pleaded with the queen—his former friend—  to at least let him see his wife and young children. She refused, unless he would renounce his faith. On June 22, 1587, he carved his family name "Arundell" into the chimney (graffiti #13) and wrote in Latin: *"Quanto plus afflictionis..."* ("The more we suffer for Christ in this world, the more glory with Christ in the next.") Arundel suffered faithfully another eight years here before he wasted away and died at age 40.

Graffiti #85 belongs to Lady Jane Grey's young husband, Lord Guilford Dudley. Locked in the Beauchamp Tower and executed the same day as his wife, Dudley vented his despair by scratching "IANE" into the stone. Cynics claim he was actually whining for his mommy, who was also named Jane.

Read other pitiful graffiti, like the musings of James Typping (#18). Imprisoned for three years "in great disgrace," he wonders what will happen to him: "I cannot tell but be death." Consider the stoic cry of Thomas Miagh (#29), an Irish rebel, who writes: "By torture straynge my truth was tried," having suffered some form of the rack. Thomas Clarke (#28), a Catholic priest who later converted to Protestantism, wrote pathetic poetry: "Unhappy is that man whose acts doth procure/the misery of this house in prison to endure." Many held onto their sense of identity by carving their family's coats of arms.

The last enemy of the state imprisoned in the Tower complex was one of its most infamous: the renegade Nazi Rudolf Hess. In 1941, Hitler's henchman secretly flew to Britain with a peace proposal (Hitler denied any such plan). He parachuted into a field, was arrested and held for four days in the Tower, and was later given a life sentence.

• *Join the looooong line leading to the crown jewels. Pass time in line reading ahead—it's too dark inside to read.*

❽ Crown Jewels

When you finally enter the building, you'll pass through a series of rooms with instructive warm-up videos. Don't let the crowd rush you—just step aside if you want to keep watching. The videos touch on the many kings and queens who have worn the crown jewels, from William I the Conqueror (1066), to Henry VIII, to his daughter Elizabeth I, to the current Queen Elizabeth II. Film clips show you close-up highlights of coronation regalia, as well as the most recent coronation—Elizabeth II's, in 1953.

After the videos, you enter the exhibits, seeing each of the actual coronation items in the order that they're used whenever a new king or queen is crowned. First, you walk down a hallway displaying the ceremonial maces, swords, and trumpets that lead the actual coronation procession into Westminster Abbey.

Next comes a room with the royal regalia. The monarch-to-be is anointed with holy oil poured from the eagle-beak flask; handed the jeweled Sword of Offering; and dressed in the 20-pound gold robe and other gear. (Other items in the first case are simply standing by. The 12th-century coronation spoon, last used in 1953 to anoint the head of Queen Elizabeth, is the most ancient object here.) Most of the original crown jewels from medieval times were lost during Cromwell's 1648 revolution.

After being dressed and anointed, the new monarch prepares for the "crowning" moment.

• *Five glass cases display the various crowns, orbs, and scepters used in various royal ceremonies. Ride the moving sidewalk that takes you past them. You're welcome to circle back and glide by again (I did, several times). Or, to get away from the crowds, hang out on the elevated view-ing area with the guard. Chat with the guards—they're actually here to provide information (and to keep you from taking photos, which aren't allowed). As you glide by on the walkway, you'll see the following items. (The collection rotates, so you may not see all of the crowns described here.)*

Scepter and Orb: After being crowned, the new monarch is handed these items. The **Sovereign's Scepter** is encrusted with the world's largest cut diamond—the 530-carat Star of Africa, beefy as a quarter-pounder. This was one of nine stones cut from the origi-nal 3,106-carat (1.37-pound) Cullinan diamond. The **orb** symbol-izes how Christianity rules over the earth, a reminder that even a "divine monarch" is not above God's law. The coronation is a kind of marriage between the church and the state in Britain, since the king or queen is head of both, and the ceremony celebrates the monarch's power to do good for the whole of the nation.

St. Edward's Crown: This coronation crown is the one placed by the archbishop upon the head of each new monarch on coro-nation day in Westminster Abbey. It's worn for 20 minutes, then locked away until the next coronation. The original crown, de-stroyed by Cromwell, was older than the Tower itself and dated back to 1061, the time of King Edward the Confessor, "the last English king" before William the Conqueror invaded from France (1066). This 1661 remake is said to contain some of the original's gold amid its 443 precious and semiprecious stones. Because the crown weighs nearly five pounds, weak or frail monarchs have opted not to wear it.

Other Crowns: Various other crowns illustrate a bit of regalia symbolism. Kings and queens get four arches on their crowns, em-perors get eight arches (e.g., the Imperial Crown of India you'll see in the case at the exit), and princes get only two (for example, see the crowns of Prince George—before he became King George V—and Prince Frederick; today's Prince Charles keeps his two-arch crown in Wales).

The Crown of the Queen Mother: This crown, last worn by Elizabeth II's famous mum (who died in 2002), has the 106-carat Koh-I-Noor diamond glittering on the front. The Koh-I-Noor dia-mond is considered unlucky for male rulers and, therefore, only adorns the crown of the king's wife. If Charles becomes king, Ca-milla might wear this. This crown was remade in 1937 and given an innovative platinum frame.

Queen Victoria Small Diamond Crown: It's tiny. Victoria had a normal-sized head, but this was designed to sit atop the wid-ow's veil she insisted on wearing for decades after the death of her husband, Prince Albert. This four-ounce job was made in 1870 for £50,000—personally paid for by the queen.

• *Continuing on from the moving walkway, you'll enter a room with walls lined by the gilded platters and bowls used in the post-coronation banquet. Continuing on, you reach one final room, with one last crown.*

The **Imperial State Crown** is what the Queen wears for official functions such as the State Opening of Parliament. When

Victoria was queen, she insisted on wearing her small crown, but by law, this State Crown had to be carried next to her on a pillow, as it represents the sovereign. Among its 3,733 jewels are Queen Elizabeth I's former earrings (the hanging pearls, top center), a stunning 13th-century ruby look-alike in the center, and Edward the Confessor's ring (the blue sapphire on top, in the center of the Maltese cross of diamonds). When Edward's tomb was exhumed—a hundred years after he was buried—his body was "incorrupted." The ring on his saintly finger featured this sapphire and ended up on the crown of all future monarchs. This is the stylized crown you see representing the royalty on Britain's coins and stamps. It's depicted on the Beefeater uniforms and on the pavement at the end of the sliding walk.

• *The final room is the epilogue of the jewels collection, with videos showing attendants putting all of these precious items back into their cases after the last coronation—emphasizing that these aren't just pretty museum pieces, but a vital part of an ongoing tradition.*

Leave the jewels by exiting through the thick vault doors. Back near the Traitor's Gate you'll find the next two sights. The entrance to the Bloody Tower is at the far end of Tower Green.

❾ Bloody Tower

Not all prisoners died at the block. The 13-year-old King Edward V and his kid brother were kidnapped in 1483 during the Wars of the Roses by their uncle Richard III ("Now is the winter of our discontent...") and locked in the Bloody Tower, never to be seen again. End of story? Two centuries later, the skeletons of two unidentified children were found here; the 2013 discovery of the remains of Richard III (in Leicester, in central England) may allow modern forensics to solve this centuries-old mystery.

Sir Walter Raleigh—poet, explorer, and political radical—was imprisoned here for 13 years. In 1603, the English writer and adventurer was accused of plotting against King James and sentenced to death. The king commuted the sentence to life imprisonment in the Bloody Tower. While in prison, Raleigh wrote the first volume of his *History of the World.* Check out his rather cushy bedroom, study, and walkway (courtesy of the powerful tobacco lobby?). Raleigh promised the king a wealth of gold if he would release him to search for El Dorado. The expedition was a failure. Upon Raleigh's return, the displeased king had him beheaded in 1618.

• *Next door to the Bloody Tower, inside the base of the Lower Wakefield Tower, is a cellar filled with some replica torture equipment*

To reach the next sight, walk under the Bloody Tower, cross the cobbled road, and bear right a few steps to find the stairs up onto the wall.

❿ Medieval Palace

The Tower was a royal residence as well as a fortress. These rooms were built around 1240 by Henry III, the king most responsible for the expansive Tower of London complex we see today. The well-described rooms are furnished as they might have been during the reign of his son, Edward I ("Longshanks"). You'll see his re-created bedroom, then—up a flight of stairs—his throne room, both with massive fireplaces to keep this cold stone palace cozy. After Cromwell temporarily deposed the monarchy (in the 17th century), the Tower ceased to be a royal residence except in name.

• *From the throne room, continue up the stairs to...*

⓫ Walk the Wall

The Tower was defended by state-of-the-art walls and fortifications in the 13th century. This walk offers a good look. From the walls, you also get a fine view of the famous bridge straddling the Thames, with the twin towers and blue spans. It's not London Bridge (which is the nondescript bridge just upstream), but **Tower Bridge.**

Although it looks somewhat medieval, this drawbridge was built in 1894, of steel and concrete. Sophisticated steam engines raise and lower the bridge, allowing tall-masted ships to squeeze through.

Gaze out at the bridge, the river, City Hall (the egg-shaped glass building across the river—see page 93), The Shard (London's bold new exclamation point—see page 92), and life-filled London.

• *Between the White Tower and the Bloody Tower are cages housing the...*

⓬ Ravens

According to goofy tradition, the Tower and the British throne are only safe as long as ravens are present here. Their wings are clipped so they'll stay, and eight (the traditional six, plus two spares) are kept in the cage. World War II bombing raids reduced the population to one. Some years ago, with their clipped wings, the birds had trouble mating, so a slide was built to help them get a bit of lift to mate. Happily, that worked, and a baby raven was born.

A children's TV show sponsored a nationwide contest to come up with a name. The winner: "Ronald Raven." As you leave through the riverside exit, look into the moat on the right for the tiny raven graveyard. There lie Cedric (2003), Gundolf (2005), and Hardey (2006). RIP.

Other Sights

Get out your Tower-issued map to check out other areas you can visit. The **Salt Tower** has graffiti by Henry Walpole, a staunch Catholic who was imprisoned here by Queen Elizabeth I, tortured on the rack, and had a finger torn off. At the **Royal Fusiliers Regimental Museum** you can see the uniforms, swords, and fusils (flintlock rifles) of the army of Redcoats who've fought Napoleon, the American War of Independence, two World Wars ("Monty"—Field Marshal Bernard Montgomery of D-Day fame—was a Fusilier), and wars in the Persian Gulf.

Take one final look at the stern stone walls of the Tower. Be glad you can leave.

BANKSIDE WALK

Along the South Bank of the Thames

Bankside—the neighborhood between London Bridge and Blackfriars Bridge—is the historic heart of the revamped southern bank of the Thames. In ancient times "greater London" consisted of two Roman settlements straddling the easiest place to ford the river: One settlement was here, and the other was across the river—in the financial district known today as "The City."

From the Roman era until recently, the south side of the river was the wrong side of the tracks. For centuries, it was London's red light district. In the 20th century, it became an industrial wasteland of empty warehouses and street crime. Today, the prostitutes and pickpockets are gone, replaced by a riverside promenade dotted with pubs, cutesy shops, and historic tourist sights.

This half-mile Bankside Walk gives you plenty of history and sights to choose from—you can see it all, design your own plan, or just enjoy the view of London's skyline across the river.

Orientation

Length of This Walk: One hour (or up to an entire day if you tour Vinopolis, Shakespeare's Globe, and the Tate Modern).

Getting There: Take the Tube to the London Bridge stop to begin the walk. (The Monument stop, on the Circle Line, is nearby.) The walk ends near Blackfriars Bridge (closest Tube stop: Blackfriars; the Southwark stop is several blocks south of the bridge on the South Bank). Bus #RV1 stops along Southwark Street behind the Tate Modern, and runs east to Tower Bridge or west to Covent Garden.

Old Operating Theatre Museum and Herb Garret: £6.50, cash only, daily 10:30-16:45, closed Dec 15-Jan 5.

Southwark Cathedral: Free, but £4 donation requested (be prepared with at least £1 or a simple "No"); Mon-Fri 8:00-18:00, Sat-Sun 8:30-18:00 (but partially closed during frequent services—schedule posted out front), last entry 30 minutes before closing.

Borough Market: Wed-Thu 10:00-17:00, Fri 10:00-18:00, Sat 8:00-17:00, closed Sun-Tue.

Golden Hinde **Replica:** £6, daily 10:00-17:00, last entry at 16:15, sometimes closed for private events.

The Clink Prison Museum: Overpriced at £7.50; July-Sept daily 10:00-21:00; Oct-June Mon-Fri 10:00-18:00, Sat-Sun until 21:00, last entry 30 minutes before closing.

Vinopolis: £27-38 self-guided tour packages, more expensive packages include a meal; Wed 18:00-21:30, Thu-Fri 14:00-22:00, Sat 12:00-21:30, Sun 12:00-18:00, closed Mon-Tue; last entry 2 hours before closing (4 hours on Sun).

Shakespeare's Globe: The complex is open daily 9:00-17:00. To see the theater interior, you must either take a 40-minute guided tour (£13.50, includes Globe Exhibition museum and audioguide; £10 when only the Exhibition is open; see page 88) or buy a ticket to a performance (see the Entertainment in London chapter).

Tate Modern: Free, but £4 donation appreciated (fee for special exhibits), daily 10:00-18:00, Fri-Sat until 22:00, last entry to temporary exhibits 45 minutes before closing, view restaurant on top floor. ✪ See the Tate Modern Tour chapter.

Starring: Shakespeare's world, London Bridge, historic pubs, and views of the London skyline.

The Walk Begins

• *Start at the south end of London Bridge. From the London Bridge Tube stop, take the "Borough High Street east" exit and turn right (north), pass the One London Bridge complex, and walk out on the bridge about 100 yards.*

❶ London Bridge

The City (across the river) is to the north, Tower Bridge is east, and the Thames flows from west to east (left to right). Looking to the east (downstream) and turning counterclockwise, you'll see the following:

Downstream

• Tower Bridge (the Neo-Gothic-towered drawbridge that many Americans mistakenly call London Bridge).

• The HMS *Belfast* (in the foreground, docked on the southern bank), a WWII cruiser that's open to tourists.

• Canary Wharf Tower (the distant 800-foot skyscraper with pyramid top and blinking light), built in 1990 on the Isle of Dogs. It recently lost its standing as the UK's tallest building to The Shard.

• The "Pool of London." This is the stretch of river between Tower Bridge (a drawbridge) and London Bridge, which marks the farthest point seagoing vessels can sail inland. In the 18th century this was the busiest port in the world.

North Bank

• The Tower of London (four domed spires and a flag rising above the trees).

• The Monument (north end of London Bridge but almost completely buried among modern buildings), a column topped with a shiny bronze knob, marking the start of the 1666 Great Fire.

• St. Paul's Cathedral (to the northwest, with a dome like a state capitol and twin spires).

• St. Bride's Church, the pointed, stacked steeple (nestled among office buildings) that supposedly inspired the wedding cake.

• BT Tower (a communications tower).

• Southwark Bridge (the next bridge upstream).

South Bank

• The Tate Modern art museum (square brick smokestack tower, barely visible).

• Southwark Cathedral (100 yards away, may not be visible from where you're standing).

• Borough High Street, the busy street that London Bridge spills onto.

• The small griffin statues (winged lions holding shields) at the south end of London Bridge guard the entrance to The City. They marked the jurisdiction of The City to include both sides of the all-important river. For centuries, they said, "Neener neener" to late-night partiers who got locked out of town when the gates shut tight at curfew.

• The Shard, one of London's newer skyscrapers. At 1,020 feet, it's the tallest building in Western Europe. It looks unfinished, but that's art. (For details on the building—including the observation deck at its tip, see page 92.)

• *The best view of London Bridge is not from the bridge itself, but from the riverbank. Retrace your steps back to the south end of the bridge and hang a right at the ice-cream stand. Find the staircase next to the southwest*

BANKSIDE

griffin, by the building marked Two London Bridge. *These stairs will impress fans of Charles Dickens'* Oliver Twist—*they're the setting of the infamous "Meeting on the Bridge."*

❷ View of London Bridge

The bridge of today—three spans of boring, traffic-clogged concrete, built in 1972—is (at least) the fourth incarnation of this

2,000-year-old river crossing. The Romans (A.D. 50) built the first wooden footbridge to Londinium (rebuilt many times), which was pulled down by boatmen in 1014 to retake London from Danish invaders. (They celebrated with a song passed down to us as "London Bridge is falling down, my fair lady.")

The most famous version—crossed by everyone from Richard the Lionhearted, to Henry VIII, to Shakespeare, to Newton, to Darwin—was built around 1200 and stood for more than six centuries, the only crossing point into this major city. Built of stone on many thick pilings, stacked with houses and shops that arched over the roadway and bulged out over the river, with its own chapel and a fortified gate at each end, it was a neighborhood unto itself (pop. 300). Picture Mel Gibson's head boiled in tar and stuck on a spike along the bridge (like the Scots rebel William Wallace in 1305, depicted in Gibson's movie *Braveheart*), and you'll capture the local color of that time.

In 1823, the famous bridge was replaced with a more modern (but less impressive) brick one. In 1967, that brick bridge was sold to an American, dismantled, shipped to Arizona, and reassembled (all 10,000 bricks) in Lake Havasu City. (Humor today's Brits, who'd like to believe the Yank thought he was buying Tower Bridge.)

• *Circle around the cathedral and find the entrance on the opposite side.*

❸ Southwark Cathedral

This neighborhood parish church is where Shakespeare prayed while brother Edmund rang the bells. The Southwark (SUTH-uck) church dates back to 1207, though the site has had a church for at least a thousand years, and inhabitants for 2,000.

❹ **View down the Nave:** Clean and sparse, with warm golden stone, the church is a symbol of the urban renewal

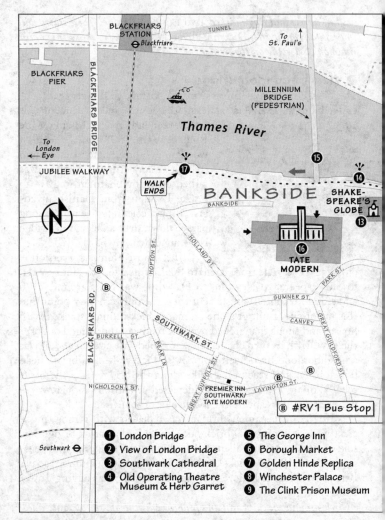

❶ London Bridge	❺ The George Inn
❷ View of London Bridge	❻ Borough Market
❸ Southwark Cathedral	❼ Golden Hinde Replica
❹ Old Operating Theatre Museum & Herb Garret	❽ Winchester Palace
	❾ The Clink Prison Museum

of the whole Bankside/Southwark area. Its WWII damage has been repaired, with replacement windows of unstained glass on the right side. The nave bends slightly to the left (the chandelier, ceiling arches, and altar don't line up until you take two baby steps left) as a medieval tribute to Christ's bent body on the cross.

• *Work your way counterclockwise around the church.*

   ❸ **Shakespeare Monument:** William reclines in front of a backdrop of the 16th-century Bankside skyline (view looking north). Find (left to right) the original Globe Theatre, Winchester Palace, Southwark Cathedral, and the old London Bridge with its arched gate. Shakespeare seems to be dreaming about the many

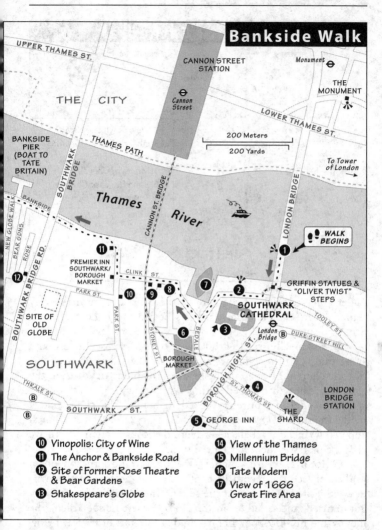

Bankside Walk

UPPER THAMES ST.

CANNON STREET STATION

Monument ⊖

THE MONUMENT

THE CITY

Cannon Street ⊖

LOWER THAMES ST.

BANKSIDE PIER (BOAT TO TATE BRITAIN)

THAMES PATH

200 Meters

200 Yards

To Tower of London

SOUTHWARK BRIDGE

BANKSIDE

NEW GLOBE WALK

BEAR GDNS.

ROSE

Thames River

LONDON BRIDGE

🚶 WALK BEGINS

❶

⓬

PREMIER INN SOUTHWARK/ BOROUGH MARKET

CLINK ST.

❷

GRIFFIN STATUES & "OLIVER TWIST" STEPS

PARK ST.

⓫

⑩

❾ ❽

❼

SOUTHWARK CATHEDRAL

SITE OF OLD GLOBE

PARK ST.

STONEY ST.

BEDALE

❻

❸

London Bridge ⊖ Ⓑ

DUKE STREET HILL

TOOLEY ST.

SOUTHWARK

BOROUGH MARKET

BOROUGH HIGH ST.

ST. THOMAS ST.

LONDON BRIDGE STATION

THRALE ST.

Ⓑ

Ⓑ

SOUTHWARK ST.

❹

❺ GEORGE INN

THE SHARD

⑩ Vinopolis: City of Wine
⑪ The Anchor & Bankside Road
⑫ Site of Former Rose Theatre & Bear Gardens
⑬ Shakespeare's Globe

⑭ View of the Thames
⑮ Millennium Bridge
⑯ Tate Modern
⑰ View of 1666 Great Fire Area

characters of his plays, depicted in the stained-glass window above (see Hamlet addressing a skull, right window). To the right is a plaque to the American actor Sam Wanamaker, who spearheaded the building of a replica of Shakespeare's Globe Theatre (explained later in this chapter). Shakespeare's brother Edmund is buried in the church, possibly

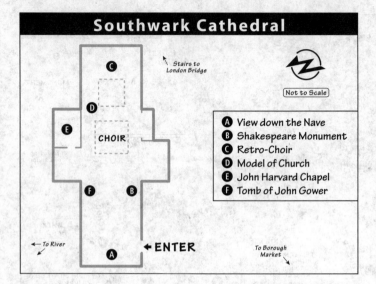

Southwark Cathedral

Stairs to
London Bridge

Not to Scale

CHOIR

Ⓐ View down the Nave
Ⓑ Shakespeare Monument
Ⓒ Retro-Choir
Ⓓ Model of Church
Ⓔ John Harvard Chapel
Ⓕ Tomb of John Gower

← To River

← ENTER

To Borough
Market

under a marked slab on the floor of the choir area, near the very center of the church. (The Bard lies buried in his hometown of Stratford-upon-Avon.)

Ⓒ **Retro-Choir:** The 800-year-old crisscross arches and stone tracery in the windows are some of the oldest parts of this historic church. Located in the heart of the industrial district, the church was heavily bombed during World War II.

Ⓓ **Model of Church:** Tucked in behind the choir, find a model (marked *Church and Priory of St. Mary Overy*) of the church and old Winchester Palace—a helpful reconstruction before we visit the paltry Winchester Palace ruins.

Ⓔ **John Harvard Chapel:** The Southwark-born son of an innkeeper (see the record of baptism at the bottom of the window) inherited money from the sale of The Queen's Head tavern, got married, and sailed to Boston (1637), where he soon died. The money and his 400-book library funded the start of Harvard University.

Ⓕ **Tomb of John Gower:** The poet and friend of Chaucer (c. 1400) rests his head on his three books, one written in Middle English, one in French, and one in Latin—the three languages from which modern English soon emerged

• *This walk is a pick-and-choose collection of sights. If you're interested in visiting the Old Operating Theatre Museum and Borough High Street inns, described next, see those sights first before heading west: Exiting Southwark Cathedral, turn left to the end of the churchyard and go up the stairs to the busy Borough High Street (the one that crosses the bridge). Turn right and hike 100 yards south (along the left-hand side of this busy thoroughfare) to the Old Operating Theatre Museum (turn left on St. Thomas Street) and The George Inn.*

❹ Old Operating Theatre Museum and Herb Garret

Back when the common cold was treated with a refreshing blood-letting, the Old Operating Theatre—a surgical operating room from the 1800s—was a shining example of "modern" medicine. Today a museum, this is a quirky, sometimes gross, look at that painful transition from folk remedy to clinical health care. Originally part of a larger hospital complex, the Old Operating Theatre was boarded up when the hospital relocated, lying untouched for 100 years until its chance discovery in 1956. The location alone—in a long-forgotten attic above a church, reached by a steep spiral staircase—makes this odd place worth a visit.

After buying your ticket, climb a few more stairs into a big room under heavy timbers—the Herb Garret, which was used to dry herbs for the former hospital. Today, it displays healing plants used for millennia—different ones for each of the traditional four ailments (melancholic, choleric, sanguine, phlegmatic), supposedly caused by an imbalance in the body's traditional four substances, or "humours" (black bile, yellow bile, blood, and phlegm), corresponding to the earth's traditional four elements (earth, wind, fire, and Ringo). Florence Nightingale, the nurse famed for saving so many Crimean War soldiers wounded in Russia, worked here to improve sanitation and to turn nurses from low-paid domestics into trained doctors' assistants.

The small hallway leading to the theater displays crude anesthetics (ether, chloroform, three pints of ale), surgical instruments by Black & Decker (knives, saws, drills), and a glaring lack of antiseptics—that is, until young Dr. Joseph Lister discovered carbolic acid, which reduced the high rates of mortality (and halitosis).

Up the stairs, the Old Operating Theatre is the highlight—a semicircular room surrounded by railings for 150 spectators (truly a "theater"), where doctors operated on patients while med students observed.

The patients were often poor women, blindfolded for their own modesty. The doctors donated their time to help, practice, and teach (see the motto *Miseratione non Mercede:* "Out of compassion, not for profit"). The surgeries, usually amputations, were performed under very crude working conditions—under the skylight or by gaslight, with no sink, and only sawdust to sop up blood. (A false floor held another layer of sawdust to stop the blood before it dripped through to the ceiling of the church below.) The wood still bears bloodstains. Nearly one in three patients died. There was a fine line between Victorian-era surgeons and Jack the Ripper.

• *Farther down Borough High Street (on the left-hand side), you'll find...*

❺ The George Inn and (Faint Echoes of) Other Historic Taverns

The George is the last of many "coaching inns" that lined the main highway from London to all points south. Like Greyhound bus stations, each inn was a terminal for far-flung journeys, since coaches were forbidden inside The City. They offered food, drink, beds, and entertainment for travelers—Shakespeare, as a young actor, likely performed in The George's courtyard. On a sunny day, the courtyard is a fine place for a break from the Borough High Street bustle (food served all day long, five ales on tap including their own brew).

Along Borough High Street are plaques locating the alleyway ("yard") of long-gone taverns known to book lovers. **The White Hart** (north of The George) was where Shakespeare and Dickens drank and set scenes. **The Queen's Head** (south of The George) was owned by the mother of John Harvard, of university fame. At **The Tabard** (now called "Talbot," also south of The George), Chaucer's band began its fictional trip south in *The Canterbury Tales*—"Befell that in that season on a day/In Southwark at The Tabard as I lay/Ready to wander on my pilgrimage/To Canterbury with full courage."

• *Walk back to Southwark Cathedral. Next to the church, you'll find the...*

❻ Borough Market

The first trading starts at 2:00 in the morning at this open-air wholesale produce market. Workers can knock off by sunrise for a pint at the specially licensed Market Porter tavern (on Park Street). On Thursday, Friday, and Saturday, the colorful market opens for retail sales to Londoners seeking trendy specialty and organic foods. It's great for gathering a picnic on a sunny day. Of the many market stalls, the Ginger Pig is *the* place for serious English sausage and  bacon (west end of market, across from Park Street), while Maria's Market Café is a colorful eatery popular with market workers (the red stall in the middle of the market).

First started a thousand years ago on London Bridge, where country farmers brought fresh goods to the city gates, the market

now sits here under a Victorian arcade. The railroad rumbling overhead, knifing right through dingy apartment houses (and the Globe Tavern), only adds to the color of London's oldest vegetable market and public gathering spot.

A detour westward through the market leads to Park Street, with an old 19th-century ambience that makes it popular as a filming location. Check out the colorful pub and the fragrant cheese shop at Neal's Yard Dairy.

• Walk to the river along Cathedral Street, veering left at the Y. (Alternatively, from the far end of the market, turn right down Stoney Street, then right again on Clink Street.)

❼ Golden Hinde Replica

As we all learned in school, "Sir Francis Drake circumcised the globe with a hundred-foot clipper." Or something like that...

Imagine a hundred men on a boat this size (yes, this replica is full-size) circling the globe on a three-year voyage, sleeping on the wave-swept decks, suffering bad food, floggings, doldrums, B.O., and attacks from foreigners. They explored unknown waters and were paid only from whatever riches they could find or steal along the way. (I took a bus tour like that once.)

The *Golden Hinde* (see the female deer, or hind, on the prow and stern) was Sir Francis Drake's flagship as he circumnavigated the globe (1577-1580). Drake, a farmer's son who

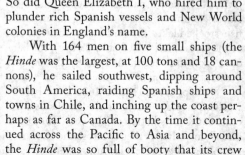

followed the lure of the sea, hated Spaniards. So did Queen Elizabeth I, who hired him to plunder rich Spanish vessels and New World colonies in England's name.

With 164 men on five small ships (the *Hinde* was the largest, at 100 tons and 18 cannons), he sailed southwest, dipping around South America, raiding Spanish ships and towns in Chile, and inching up the coast perhaps as far as Canada. By the time it continued across the Pacific to Asia and beyond, the *Hinde* was so full of booty that its crew replaced the rock ballast with gold ingots and silver coins. Three years later, Drake—with only one remaining ship and 56 men—sailed the *Hinde* up the Thames, unloading a fabulously valuable hoard of gold, silver, emeralds, diamonds, pearls, silks, cloves, and spices before the queen. A grateful Elizabeth knighted Drake on the main deck and kissed him on his *Golden Hinde*.

The *Hinde* was retired gloriously, but rotted away from neglect. Drake received a large share of the wealth, became enormously famous, and later gained more glory defeating the Spanish Armada (aided by "the winds of God") in the decisive battle in the English Channel, off Plymouth (1588), making England ruler of the waves.

The galleon replica, a working ship that has itself circled the globe, is berthed at St. Mary Overie Dock ("St. Mary's over the river"), a public dock available for free to all Southwark residents. A victim of WWII bombing and container ships that require big berths and deep water, the Thames river trade that used to thrive even this far upstream is now concentrated east of Tower Bridge. Only a few brick warehouses remain (just west of here), waiting to be leveled or yuppified. Although you can pay to enter the ship, it's not worth the cost of admission.

• *There's a fine view (with a handy chart to identify things) from the riverside. The beach below is fun for beachcombing—old red roof tiles and little chunks of disposable clay tobacco pipes litter the rocks at low tide. From here, the Monument is visible across London Bridge, poking its bristly bronze head above the ugly postwar buildings. Beyond that is the bullet-shaped tip of the modern 30 St. Mary Axe Tower (also known as the "Swiss Re Tower" as well as "The Gherkin" and "Towering Innuendo" for its unusual design). Now go up the street across from the* Golden Hinde's *gangplank (Pickfords Wharf) and head west. About 25 yards ahead on the left are the excavated ruins of...*

❽ Winchester Palace

All that remains today is a wall with a medi-eval rose window, but this was once a lavish 80-acre estate stretching along 200 feet of wa-terfront. It had a palace, gardens, fountains, stables, tennis courts, a working farm, and a fish-stocked lake. The wall marks the west end of the Great Hall (134 feet by 29 feet), the ban-quet room for receptions held by the palace's owner, the Bishop of Winchester.

Bishops from 1106 to 1626 lived here as wealthy, worldly rulers of the Bankside area, outside the jurisdiction of The City. They prof-ited from activities illegal across the river, such as prostitution and gambling. They were a law unto themselves, with their own courts and prisons. One famous prison—the Clink—built by the bishops remained, even after its creators were ousted by a Puritan Parliament.

• *Fifty yards farther west (along what is now called Clink Street) is...*

❾ The Clink Prison Museum

The prison—now an overpriced and disappointing museum—gave us our expression "thrown in the Clink" from the sound of prison-

ers' chains. It burned down in 1780, but the underground cells remain, featuring historical information on wall plaques, many torture devices, and a generally creepy, claustrophobic atmosphere.

Originally part of Winchester Palace, it housed troublemakers who upset the smooth running of the bishop's 22 licensed brothels (called "the stews"), gambling dens, and taverns. Bouncers delivered drunks who were out of control, johns who couldn't pay, and prostitutes ("women living by their bodies") who tried to go freelance or cheated loyal customers. Offending prostitutes had their heads shaved and breasts bared, and were carted through the streets and whipped while people jeered. They might share cells side by side with "heretics"—namely, priests who'd crossed their bishops.

In 1352, debtors (who'd maxed out their Visa cards) became criminals, housed here among harder criminals in harsh conditions. Prisoners were not fed. They had to bribe guards to get food, to avoid torture, or even to gain their release. (The idea was that you'd brought this on yourself.) Prisoners relied on their families for money, prostituted themselves to guards and other inmates, or reached through the bars at street level, begging from passersby. Murderers, debtors, Protestants, priests, and many innocent people experienced this strange brand of justice...all part of the rough crowd that gave Bankside such a seedy reputation.

• *Continuing west and crossing under the Cannon Street Bridge, you could detour a half-block to the left to find...*

❿ Vinopolis: City of Wine

This warehouse of wine—with a splash of France, a dash of ancient Rome, and a taste of Italian *vino*—seems out of place in

London, but no one's complaining. For more on this wine-tasters' Disneyland, see page 90.

• *Switching from wine to beer, across the street is...*

⓫ The Anchor and Bankside Road

The Anchor is the last of the original 22 licensed "inns" (tavern/brothel/restaurant/nightclub/casino) of Bankside's red light district

ANCHOR TAP

heyday in the 1600s. A tavern has stood here for 800 years. The big brick buildings behind the inn were once part of the mass-producing Anchor brewery, with the inn as its brew pub. (Even back in the 1300s, Chaucer wrote, "If the words get muddled in my tale/Just put it down to too much Southwark ale.")

In the cozy, maze-like interior are memories of greats who've drunk here (I have) or indulged in a new drug that hit London in the 1560s—tobacco. Shakespeare, who may have lived along Clink Street, may have tippled here, especially because the original Globe Theatre was right behind The Anchor (see map on page 295). Dr. Samuel Johnson also worked here while writing the famous dictionary that helped codify the English language and spelling (for more on Dr. Johnson, see page 251).

The Anchor marks the start of once-notorious Bankside Road that runs along a river retaining wall. In Elizabethan times (16th century), the street was lined with "inns" offering one-stop shopping for addictive personalities. The streets were jammed with sword-carrying punks in tights looking for a fight, prostitutes, gaping tourists from the Borough High Street coaching inns, pickpockets, river pirates, highwaymen, navy recruiters kidnapping drunks, and many proper ladies and gentlemen who ferried across from The City for an evening's entertainment. And then there were the really seedy people—yes, actors.

• *Crossing under the green-and-yellow Southwark Bridge, notice the metal reliefs depicting London's "Frost Fair" of 1564. Because the old London Bridge was such a wall of stone, the swift-flowing Thames would back up and even freeze over during cold winters.*

Emerging from under the bridge, head farther west on Bankside to ⓭ *Shakespeare's Globe.*

Possible detour: Die-hard theater fans may wish to detour inland to the site of the Rose Theatre. I don't recommend it, since the Rose is rarely open (free, Sat only 10:00–17:00, www.rosetheatre.org.uk), and there's not much to see. But if I can't talk you out of it, here's how to get there: Emerging from under the bridge, turn at the first left (Bear Gardens

Lane), then go left on Park Street. Go one block to the gray-granite modern building located on the site of the former Rose Theatre. Even if you don't go to the site, you might enjoy knowing some background:

⑫ Site of the Former Rose Theatre and Bear Gardens

When the 2,200-seat Rose first raised its curtain in 1587, it signaled four decades of phenomenal popularity (centered in Bankside) for a rapidly evolving form of entertainment—theater. Soon there were four great theaters in the area: the Rose, the Hope, the Swan, and the Globe. (Theatrical types can find the unimpressive plaque marking the site of the original Globe Theatre—a half-block east of the Rose—and be as disappointed as Sam Wanamaker, who was inspired to build the replica of Shakespeare's Globe. More on the Globe when we arrive at the replica.)

It's thought that the young Will Shakespeare, recently arrived from the country, got his start at the Rose tending theatergoers' horses ("What?" he said, "and give up show business?!"). Soon, though, the struggling actor saw his first play *(Henry VI, Part I)* come to life on the Rose stage.

Closer to the river was a theatrical venue called the Bear Gardens (only a plaque marks the spot today). Bankside theaters presented everything from serious drama, to light comedy, to vaudeville, to circus acts, to...animal fights. Bearbaiting was the most popular. A bear was chained to a stake while a pack of dogs (mastiffs) attacked, and spectators bet on the winner. The bears, often with teeth filed down or jaws wired shut, fought back with their paws, sweeping dogs into the crowd. Now, that's entertainment.

⑬ Shakespeare's Globe

All the world's a stage,
And all the men and women merely players.
They have their exits and their entrances,
And one man, in his time, plays many parts.
—As You Like It

By 1599, 35-year-old William Shakespeare was a well-known actor, playwright, and businessman in the booming theater trade (see sidebar on page 236). His acting company, the Lord Chamberlain's Men, built the 3,000-seat Globe Theatre,

by far the largest of its day (200 yards from today's replica, where only a plaque stands now). The Globe premiered Shakespeare's

BANKSIDE

greatest works—*Hamlet, Othello, King Lear, Macbeth*—in open-air summer afternoon performances, though occasionally at night by the light of torches and buckets of tar-soaked ropes.

In 1612, it featured Shakespeare's *All Is True (Henry VIII)*. During Scene 4, a stage cannon boomed, announcing the arrival of King Henry, who started flirting with Anne Boleyn. As the two actors generated sparks onstage, play-watchers smelled fire. Some stray cannon wadding had sparked a real fire offstage. Within an hour, the wood-and-thatch building had burned completely to the ground, but with only one injury: A man's pants caught fire and were quickly doused with a tankard of ale.

Built in 1997, the new Globe—round, half-timbered, thatched, with wooden pegs for nails—is a quite realistic replica, though slightly smaller (seating 1,500 spectators), located a block away from the original site, and constructed with fire-repellent materials. Performances are staged almost nightly in summer—check at the box office (at the east end of the complex). A recent addition is the indoor Sam Wanamaker Playhouse, behind the Globe complex, around the left side. For more on touring the Globe, see page 88.

Bankside's theater scene vanished in the 1640s, closed by a Parliament dominated by hard-line Puritans. Drama seemed to portray and promote immoral behavior, and actors—men who also played women's roles—parodied and besmirched fair womanhood. Bearbaiting was also outlawed by the outraged moralists (to paraphrase the historian Thomas Macaulay)—not because it caused bears pain, but because it gave people pleasure.

⑭ View of the Thames

From the Cotswolds to the North Sea, the river winds eastward a total of 210 miles. London is close enough to the estuary to be affected by the North Sea's tides, so the river level does indeed rise and fall twice a day. In fact, one of the reasons Romans found this a practical location—even though it was about 40 miles inland—was that their boats could hitch a free ride with the tides between the sea and the town twice a day. But tides also mean floods. After centuries of periodic flooding (spring rains plus high tides), barriers to regulate the tides were built in 1982, east of Tower Bridge. The barriers also slow down the once fast-moving river.

The Thames is still a major commercial artery (east of Tower Bridge). In the previous two centuries, it ran brown with Industrial Revolution pollution. Today it's brown because of es-

tuary silt—the Thames is now one of the cleanest rivers in the industrialized world.

• *Fifty yards west of the Globe, spanning the river, is the...*

⓯ Millennium Bridge

This pedestrian bridge was built in 2000 to connect the Tate Modern with St. Paul's Cathedral and The City. For its first two glorious days, Londoners made the pleasant seven-minute walk across...before the $25 million "bridge to the next millennium" started wobbling dangerously (insert your own ironic joke here) and was closed for rethinking. After much work, 20 months, and $8 million in retrofits, the bridge reopened. Nicknamed the "blade of light," it was designed (partly by Lord Norman Foster, who also did the 30 St. Mary Axe Tower and City Hall downstream) to allow a wide-open view of St. Paul's. Now stabilized, it links two revitalized sections of London.

⓰ Tate Modern

London's large, impressive modern art collection is housed in a former power station—typical of the move to renovate empty, ugly Industrial Age hulks on the South Bank. Even if you don't tour the collection, pop inside the north entrance (free) to view the spacious interior, decorated each year with a new industrial-sized installation by one of the world's top contemporary artists. As the Tate is in the process of adding a new annex (behind the building), it's interesting to see what new spaces they've opened up to the public.

✪ See the Tate Modern Tour chapter.

• *Bankside—maybe at The Founder's Arms pub along the river—is a great place to contemplate the...*

⓱ Great Fire of 1666

On Sunday, September 2, 1666, stunned Londoners quietly sipped beers in Bankside pubs and watched The City across the river go up in flames. ("When we could endure no more upon the water," wrote Samuel Pepys in his diary, "we went to a little alehouse on the Bankside.") Started in a bakery shop near the Monument (north end of London Bridge) and fanned by strong winds, the fire swept westward, engulfing the mostly wooden city, devouring Old St. Paul's, and moving past what is now Blackfriars Bridge and St. Bride's to Temple Church (near the pointy, black, gold-tipped steeple of the Royal Courts of Justice).

In four days, 80 percent of The City was incinerated, including 13,000 houses and 89 churches. The good news? Incredibly, only nine people died, the fire cleansed a plague-infested city, and Christopher Wren was around to rebuild London's skyline.

The fire also marked the end of Bankside's era as London's naughty playground. Having recently been cleaned up by the Puritans, it now served as a temporary refugee camp for those displaced by the fire. And, with the coming Industrial Age, businessmen demolished the inns and replaced them with brick warehouses, docks, and factories to fuel the economy of a world power.

• From here, the closest **Tube** stops are Southwark (a several-block walk to the south) and Blackfriars (just over Blackfriars Bridge, to the north).

Handy **bus #RV1** has two stops about a five-minute walk away: From The Founder's Arms, the nearest stop is called "Southwark Street/Blackfriars Road": Go around behind the tavern and along the river. At Blackfriars Rail Station, turn left and go up Hopton Street, then turn right on busy Southwark Street under the bridge to find the stop. From the Tate or the Globe, the other stop—"Lavington Street"—is a bit closer (also along Southwark Street, but directly behind the Tate). From either of these stops, the westbound bus goes to the London Eye, Waterloo Station (Tube stop), then across Waterloo Bridge to Covent Garden. Eastbound buses go to London Bridge Station (Tube stop), City Hall, and over Tower Bridge to the Tower of London (and Tower Hill Tube stop).

To continue on **foot**, follow the Jubilee Walkway along the South Bank of the Thames to the London Eye and Big Ben. (The 20-minute stroll is particularly enjoyable in the evening.) Or you can cross the Thames on the Millennium Bridge, where a pedestrian mall leads past the glassy Salvation Army headquarters (good café and small, free Salvation Army history display in daylight basement) to St. Paul's Cathedral and Tube station.

TATE MODERN TOUR

Remember the 20th century? Accelerated by technology and frag-mented by war, it was an exciting and chaotic time, with art as turbulent as the world that created it. The Tate Modern lets you walk through the explosive last century with a glimpse at its brave new art.

The Tate Modern is (controversially) displayed by concept—"Poetry and Dream," for example—rather than by artist and chro-nology. But unlike the museum, this chapter is neatly chronologi-cal. It's not intended as a painting-by-painting tour. Read through this chapter for a general introduction, use it as a reference, then take advantage of the Tate's excellent videoguide to focus on spe-cific works. With this background in 20th-century art, you'll ap-preciate the Tate's even greater strength: art of the 21st century.

Future Expansion: The Tate Modern opened in 2000 antici-pating two million visitors a year. More than twice that number visit, mostly on Saturdays. To meet the growing demand, the Tate is constructing a new wing to the south, which will double the museum's exhibition space. Although the new building's exterior facade matches the Tate's industrial brick look, its shape and in-terior are slick, modern, and custom-built to display great art, in-cluding large-scale installations. In addition to showing off more of the Tate's impressive collection (much of which, sadly, is often in storage or on loan), the museum plans to go beyond its current European and North American focus by adding exhibits of Latin American, African, and Asian art. A new 11th-floor restaurant promises some of the grandest views over London.

The new wing is opening bit by bit. Once finished, the perma-nent collection will likely be rearranged, with some pieces moving to the new building.

TATE MODERN

Orientation

Cost: Free (but £4 donations appreciated); fee for special exhibits.

Hours: Daily 10:00-18:00, Fri-Sat until 22:00, last entry to special exhibits 45 minutes before closing.

When to Go: This popular place is especially crowded on weekend days (crowds thin out on Fri and Sat evenings).

Getting There: Located on the South Bank of the Thames, across from St. Paul's and near the Globe Theatre. You can get here by Tube, ferry, or foot:

    By Tube: Take the Tube to Southwark, London Bridge, St. Paul's, or Mansion House; then walk 10-15 minutes. ✪ See the Bankside Walk chapter.

    By Ferry: Catch Thames Clippers' Tate Boat ferry from the Tate Britain (£6.50 one-way, £15 day ticket, discount with Travelcard or Oyster card, buy ticket at gallery desk or on board, departs every 40 minutes from 9:55 to 17:00, about 15 minutes, www.tate.org.uk/visit/tate-boat).

    On Foot: Walk across the Millennium Bridge from St. Paul's Cathedral.

Information: The two lowest floors (levels 0 and 1) have the basic services: info desks, baggage check, bookstores, videoguide rentals, and tickets for temporary exhibits. The helpful staff at the info desk (level 1) can tell you the location of specific works. The floor plan (suggested £1 donation) is also useful. In addition, several **touch-screen computers** are scattered throughout the museum. Tel. 020/7887-8888, www.tate.org.uk.

Tours: The £4 interactive **videoguide** covers the entire permanent collection, and includes a tour geared for kids ages 8-12. Free 45-minute **guided tours** are offered at 11:00, 12:00, 14:00, and 15:00 (see info desk for details).

Length of This Tour: Allow at least an hour. Read this chapter ahead of time, then browse according to your tastes.

Cloakroom: Level 0 (free, £2 suggested donation).

Photography: Photos are only permitted in the entrance hall.

Cuisine Art: View coffee shops with food are on levels 1 and 3. On level 6, there's a table-service restaurant (£24 for two courses, £29 for three courses, £15 afternoon tea served 15:00-17:30, until 17:00 Fri-Sun); even better, you can sit at one of the many stools at the casual bar, with the best views of all and lower prices (£3-5 drinks, limited

£9-12 main courses). This perch provides stunning panoramas of St. Paul's (see photo on previous page). Some trendy restaurants are several blocks southwest of the Tate, along the street named "the Cut" (near Southwark Tube stop).

Starring: Picasso, Matisse, Dalí, and all the "classic" modern artists, plus the Tate Modern's specialty—British and American artists of the last half of the 20th century.

Know Your Tates: Don't confuse the Tate Modern with the Tate Britain (south of Big Ben), which features British art (✪ see the Tate Britain Tour chapter).

OVERVIEW

Even though the layout of the Tate Modern changes constantly, the collection's focus is the same: the postwar period. Don't just come

to see the Old Masters of modernism (Matisse, Picasso, Kandinsky, and so on). Push your mental envelope with works by Pollock, Miró, Bacon, Picabia, Beuys, Twombly, and others.

More modern art from British artists is on display at the Tate Britain museum (✪ see the Tate Britain Tour chapter).

Reminder: The following is not a painting-by-painting tour but rather a chronological overview of modern art.

The Tour Begins

• *Start at the main entrance (on the west side of the building). To reach it from the river: With the Thames at your back, walk to the right around the corner of the building, down the slope and into the massive empty space of the former industrial powerhouse.*

This huge, grand entrance usually dwarfs the art it houses (a metaphor for the triumph of 20th-century technology, perhaps?). The Turbine Hall displays major art installations by contemporary artists—always one of the highlights of the art world.

You're on underground level 0 (the riverfront entrance leads to level 1). To see the core of the permanent collection—and the artwork described in this chapter—head upstairs (via the escalator near the ground-floor cloakroom) to visit levels 2, 3, and 4, where you're most likely to find the permanent collection.

Paintings are arranged according to theme, not artist. Paintings by Picasso, for example, are scattered all over the building. Special exhibits are on levels 2 and 3.

Overview of Modern Art

1900—VICTORIA'S LEGACY

Anno Domini 1900, a new century dawns. Europe is at peace, Britannia rules the world. Technology is about to usher in a golden age.

Claude Monet (1840-1926)

Monet captures the relaxed, civilized spirit of belle époque France and Victorian England with Impressionist snapshots of peaceful landscapes and middle-class family picnics. But the true subject is the shimmering effect of reflected light, rendered with rough brushstrokes and bright paints that look messy up close but blend at a distance. The newfangled camera made camera-eye realism obsolete. Artists began placing more importance on *how* something was painted rather than on *what* was painted.

1905—COLONIAL EUROPE

Europe ruled a global empire, tapping its dark-skinned colonials for raw materials, cheap labor, and bold new ways to look at the world. The cozy Victorian world was shattering. Nietzsche murdered God. Darwin stripped off Man's robe of culture and found a naked ape. Primitivism was modern. Ooga-booga.

Henri Matisse (1869-1954)

Matisse was one of the Fauves, or "wild beasts," who tried to inject a bit of the jungle into civilized European society. Inspired by "primitive" African and Oceanic masks and voodoo dolls, the Fauves made modern art that looked primitive: long, mask-like faces with almond eyes; bright, clashing colors; simple figures; and "flat," two-dimensional scenes.

Matisse simplifies. A man is a few black lines and blocks of paint. A snail is a spiral of colored paper. A woman's back is an outline. Matisse's colors are unnaturally bright. The "distant" landscape is as crisp and clear as close objects, and the slanted lines meant to suggest depth are crudely done.

Traditionally, the canvas was like a window that you looked "through" to see a slice of the real world stretching off into the horizon. With Matisse, you look "at" the canvas, like wallpaper, to appreciate the decorative pattern of colors and shapes.

Though his style is modern, Matisse builds on 19th-century art—the bright colors of Van Gogh, the primitive figures of Gauguin, the colorful designs of Japanese wood-block prints, and the Impressionist patches of paint that blend together only at a distance.

Paul Cézanne (1839-1906)

Cézanne brings Impressionism into the 20th century. Whereas Monet uses separate dabs of different-colored paint to "build" a figure, Cézanne "builds" a man with somewhat larger slabs of paint, giving him a kind of 3-D chunkiness. It's not hard to see the progression from Monet's dabs to Cézanne's slabs to Picasso's cubes—Cubism.

1910—THE MODERNS

The modern world was moving fast, with automobiles, factories, and mass communication. Motion pictures captured the fast-moving world, while Einstein explored the fourth dimension: time.

Cubism: Pablo Picasso (1881-1973)

Born in Spain, Picasso moved to Paris as a young man. He worked with painter and sculptor Georges Braque in poverty so dire they often didn't know where their next bottle of wine was coming from.

Picasso's Cubist works show the old European world shattering to bits. He pieces the fragments back together in a whole new way, showing several perspectives at once (for example, looking up the left side of a woman's body and, at the same time, down at her right).

Whereas newfangled motion pictures capture several perspectives in succession, Picasso achieves it on a canvas with overlapping images. A single "cube" might contain an arm (in the foreground) and the window behind (in the background), both painted the same color. The foreground and background are woven together so that the subject dissolves into a pattern.

Picasso, the most famous and—OK, I'll say it—the greatest artist of the 20th century, constantly explored and adapted his style to new trends. He made collages, tried his hand at "statues" out of wood, wire, or whatever, and even made art out of everyday household objects. These multimedia works, so revolutionary at the time, have become stock-in-trade today. Scattered throughout the museum are works from the many periods of Picasso's life.

Futurism

The Machine Age is approaching, and the whole world gleams with promise in cylinder shapes ("Tubism"), like an internal-combustion engine. Or is it the gleaming barrel of a cannon?

1914—WORLD WAR I

A soldier—shivering in a trench, ankle-deep in mud, waiting to be ordered "over the top," to run through barbed wire, over fallen comrades, and into a hail of machine-gun fire, only to capture a few hundred yards of meaningless territory that would be lost the next day. This soldier was not thinking about art.

World War I left nine million dead. (At times, England lost more men per month than America lost during the entire Vietnam War.) The war also killed the optimism and faith in humankind that had guided Europe since the Renaissance.

Expressionism

Cynicism and decadence settled over postwar Europe. Artists such as Grosz, Beckmann, and Kokoschka "expressed" their disgust by showing a distorted reality that emphasized the ugly. Using the lurid colors and simplified figures of the Fauves, they slapped paint on in thick brushstrokes, depicting a hypocritical, hard-edged, dog-eat-dog world—a civilization watching its Victorian moral foundations collapse.

Dada

When they could grieve no longer, artists turned to grief's giddy twin, laughter. The war made all old values a joke, including artistic ones. The Dada movement, choosing a purposely childish name, made art that was intentionally outrageous: a moustache on the *Mona Lisa*, a shovel hung on the wall, or a modern version of a Renaissance "fountain"—a urinal (by Marcel Duchamp...or was it I. P. Freeley?).

It was a dig at all the pompous prewar artistic theories based on the noble intellect of Rational Women and Men. While the experts ranted on, Dadaists sat in the back of the class and made cultural fart noises.

Hey, I love this stuff. My mind says it's sophomoric, but my heart belongs to Dada.

1920s—ANYTHING GOES

In the Jazz Age, the world turned upside down. Genteel ladies smoked cigarettes. Gangsters laid down the law. You could make a fortune in the stock market one day and lose it the next. You could dance the Charleston with the opposite sex, and even say the word "sex" while talking about Freud over cocktails. It was almost...surreal.

Surrealism

Artists caught the jumble of images on a canvas. A telephone made from a lobster, an elephant with a heating-duct trunk, Venus sleep-

Abstract Art

Abstract art simplifies. A man becomes a stick figure. A squiggle is a wave. A streak of red expresses anger. Arches make you want a cheeseburger. These are universal symbols that everyone from a caveman to a banker understands. Abstract artists capture the essence of reality in a few lines and colors, boldly capturing objects and ideas that even a camera can't—emotions, abstract concepts, musical rhythms, and spiritual states of mind.

With abstract art, you don't look "through" the canvas to see the visual world, but "at" it to read the symbolism of lines, shapes, and colors. Most 20th-century paintings are a mix of the real world (representation) and colorful patterns (abstraction).

walking among skeletons. Take one mixed bag of reality, jumble it in a blender, and serve on a canvas—Surrealism.

The artist scatters seemingly unrelated things on the canvas, leaving us to trace the connections in a kind of connect-the-dots without numbers.

Further complicating the modern world was Freud's discovery of the "unconscious" mind, which thinks dirty thoughts while we sleep. Surrealists let the id speak. The canvas is an uncensored, stream-of-consciousness "landscape" of these deep urges, revealed in the bizarre images of dreams. Salvador Dalí, the most famous Surrealist, combined an extraordinarily realistic technique with an extraordinarily twisted mind. He painted "unreal" scenes with photographic realism, making us believe they could really happen. Dalí's images—crucifixes, political and religious figures, and naked bodies—pack an emotional punch.

1930s—DEPRESSION

As capitalism failed around the world, governments propped up their economies with vast building projects. The architecture style was modern, stripped-down (i.e., cheap), and functional. Propagandist campaigns championed noble workers in the heroic Social Realist style.

Piet Mondrian (1872-1944)

Like blueprints for modernism, Mondrian's T-square style boils painting down to its basic building blocks: a white canvas, black lines, and the three primary colors—red, yellow, and blue—arranged in orderly patterns. (When you come right down to it, that's all painting ever has been. A schematic drawing of, say, the *Mona*

Lisa shows that it's less about a woman than about the triangles and rectangles she's composed of.)

Mondrian started out painting realistic landscapes of the orderly fields in his native homeland of Holland. Increasingly, he simplified his style into horizontal and vertical patterns. For Mondrian, who was heavily into Eastern mysticism, "up versus down" and "left versus right" were the perfect metaphors for life's dualities: good versus evil, body versus spirit, fascism versus communism, man versus woman. The canvas is a bird's-eye view of Mondrian's personal landscape.

1940s—WORLD WAR II

World War II was a global war (involving Europe, the Americas, Australia, Africa, and Asia) and a total war (saturation bombing of civilians and ethnic cleansing). It left Europe in ruins.

Alberto Giacometti's skinny statues have the emaciated, haunted, and faceless look of concentration-camp survivors. In the sweep of world war and overpowering technology, man is frail and fragile. All he can do is stand at attention and take it like a man.

Meanwhile, Francis Bacon's caged creatures speak for all of war-torn Europe when they scream, "Enough!" (For more on Bacon, see page 348.)

1950s—AMERICA, THE GLOBAL SUPERPOWER

As converted war factories turned swords into kitchen appliances, America helped rebuild Europe while pumping out consumer goods for its own booming population. Prosperity, a stable government, national television broadcasts, and a common fear of Soviet communism threatened to turn America into a completely homogeneous society.

Some artists, centered in New York, rebelled against conformity and superficial consumerism. (They'd served under Eisenhower in war and now had to in peace, as well.) They created art that was the very opposite of the functional, mass-produced goods of the American marketplace.

Art was a way of asserting your individuality by creating a completely original and personal vision. The trend was toward bigger canvases, abstract designs, and experimentation with new materials and techniques. It was called "Abstract Expressionism"— expressing emotions and ideas using color and form alone.

Jackson Pollock (1912-1956)

"Jack the Dripper" attacks convention with a can of paint, dripping and splashing a dense web onto the canvas. Picture Pollock in his studio, jiving to the hi-fi, bouncing off the walls, throwing paint in a moment of enlightenment. Of course, the artist loses some control this way—over the paint flying in midair and over himself in an ecstatic trance. Painting becomes a whole-body activity, a "dance" between the artist and his materials.

The intuitive act of creating is what's important, not the final product. The canvas is only a record of that moment of ecstasy.

Big, Empty Canvases

With all the postwar prosperity, artists could afford bigger canvases. But what reality are they trying to show?

In the modern world, we find ourselves insignificant specks in a vast and indifferent universe. Every morning, each of us must confront that big, blank, existential canvas, and decide how we're going to make our mark on it.

Another influence was the simplicity of Japanese landscape painting. A Zen master studies and meditates for years to achieve the state of mind in which he can draw one pure line. These canvases, again, are only a record of that state of enlightenment. (What is the sound of one brush painting?)

On more familiar ground, postwar painters were following in the footsteps of artists such as Mondrian. The geometrical forms here reflect the same search for order, but these artists painted to the musical 5/4 asymmetry of the Dave Brubeck Quartet's jazzy *Take Five*.

Patterns and Textures

Enjoy the lines and colors, but also a new element: texture. Some works have very thick paint piled on, where you can see the brushstrokes clearly. Some have substances besides paint applied to the canvas, or the canvas is punctured so the fabric itself (and the hole) becomes the subject. Artists show their skill by mastering new materials. The canvas is a tray, serving up a delightful buffet of different substances with interesting colors, patterns, shapes, and textures.

Mark Rothko (1903-1970)

Rothko makes two-toned rectangles, laid on their sides, that seem to float in a big, vertical canvas. The edges are blurred, so if you get close enough to let the canvas fill your field of vision (as Rothko intended), the rectangles appear to rise and sink from the cloudy depths like answers in a Magic 8 Ball.

Serious students appreciate the subtle differences in color between the rectangles. Rothko experimented with different bases for the same color and used a single undercoat (a "wash") to unify them. His early works are warmer, with brighter reds, yellows, and oranges; his later works are maroon and brown, approaching black.

Still, these are not intended to be formal studies in color and form. Rothko was trying to express the most basic human emo-

20th-Century British Artists

Since 1960, London has rivaled New York as a center for the visual arts. You'll find British artists displayed in both the Tate Modern and the Tate Britain. Check out the Tate Britain Tour chapter for more on the following artists: David Hockney, Stanley Spencer, Jacob Epstein, Gilbert and George, Henry Moore, Francis Bacon, and Barbara Hepworth.

tions in a pure language. (A "realistic" painting of a person is inherently fake because it's only an illusion of the person.) Staring into these windows onto the soul, you can laugh, cry, or ponder, just as Rothko did when he painted them.

Rothko, the previous century's "last serious artist," believed in the power of art to express the human spirit. When he found out that his nine large Seagram canvases were to be hung in a corporate restaurant, he refused to sell them, and they ended up in the Tate. (A 2010 Tony Award-winning play called *Red* dealt with Rothko's anguished decision.)

In his last years, Rothko's canvases—always rectangles—got bigger, simpler, and darker. When Rothko finally slashed his wrists in his studio, one nasty critic joked that what killed him was the repetition. Minimalism was painting itself into a blank corner.

1960s—POP AND POLITICS

The decade began united in idealism—young John F. Kennedy pledged to put a man on the moon, newly launched satellites signaled a united world, the Beatles sang exuberantly, peaceful race demonstrations championed equality, and the Vatican II Council preached liberation. By decade's end, there were race riots, assassinations, student protests, and America's floundering war in distant Vietnam. In households around the world, parents screamed, "Turn that down...and get a haircut!"

Culturally, every postwar value was questioned by a rising wealthy and populous baby-boom generation. London—producer of rock-and-roll music, film actors, mod fashions, and Austin Powers joie de vivre—once again became a world cultural center.

Though government-sponsored public art was dominated by big, abstract canvases and sculptures, other artists pooh-poohed the highbrow seriousness of abstract art. Instead, they mocked lowbrow, popular culture by embracing it in a tongue-in-cheek way (Pop Art), or they attacked authority with absurd performances to make a political statement (conceptual art).

Pop Art

America's postwar wealth made the consumer king. Pop Art is created from the popular objects of that throwaway society—soup cans, car fenders, tacky plastic statues, movie icons. Take a Sears product, hang it in a museum, and you have to ask: Is this art? Are mass-produced objects beautiful? Or crap? Why do we work so hard to acquire them? Pop Art, like Dadaism before it, questions our society's values.

Andy Warhol (who coined "15 minutes of fame") concentrated on another mass-produced phenomenon: celebrities. He took publicity photos of famous people and reproduced them. The repetition—like the constant bombardment we get from recurring images on TV—cheapens even the most beautiful things.

Roy Lichtenstein took a comic strip, blew it up, hung it on a wall, and charged a million bucks—whaam, Pop Art. Lichtenstein supposedly was inspired by his young son, who challenged him to do something as good as Mickey Mouse. The huge newsprint dots never let us forget that the painting—like all commercial art—is an illusionistic fake. The work's humor comes from portraying a lowbrow subject (comics and ads) on the epic scale of a masterpiece.

Op Art

Optical illusions play tricks with your eyes, the way a spiral starts to spin when you stare at it. These obscure scientific experiments in color, line, and optics suddenly became trendy in the psychedelic '60s.

1970s—THE "ME DECADE"

All forms of authority—"The Establishment"—seemed bankrupt. America's president resigned in the Watergate scandal, corporations were polluting the earth, and capitalism nearly ground to a halt when Arabs withheld oil.

Artists attacked authority and institutions, trying to free individuals to discover their full human potential. Even the concept of "modernism"—that art wasn't good unless it was totally original and progressive—was questioned. No single style could dictate in this postmodern period.

Earth Art

Fearing for the health of the earth's ecology, artists rediscovered the beauty of rocks, dirt, trees, even the sound of the wind, using them to create natural art. A rock placed in a museum or urban square is certainly a strange sight.

Performance Art

The Tate Modern's collection of "sculptures" by Joseph Beuys—assemblages of steel, junk, wood, and, especially, felt and animal fat—only hint at his greatest artwork: Beuys himself.

Imagine Beuys ("boyss") walking through the museum, carrying a dead rabbit, while he explains the paintings to it. Or taking off his clothes, shaving his head, and smearing his body with fat.

This charismatic, ex-Luftwaffe art shaman did ridiculous things to inspire others to break with convention and be free. He choreographed "Happenings"—spectacles where people did absurd things while others watched—and pioneered performance art, in which the artist presents himself as the work of art. Beuys inspired a whole generation of artists to walk on stage, cluck like a chicken, and stick a yam up themselves. Beuys will be Beuys.

New Media

Minimalist painting and abstract sculpture were old hat, and there was an explosion of new art forms. Performance art was the most controversial, combining music, theater, dance, poetry, and the visual arts. New technologies brought video, assemblages, installations, artists' books (paintings in book form), and even (gasp!) realistic painting.

Conceptual Art

Increasingly, artists are not creating an original work (painting a canvas or sculpting a stone) but assembling one from premade objects. The *concept* of which object to pair with another to produce maximum effect ("Let's stick a crucifix in a jar of urine," to cite one notorious example) is the key.

1980s—MATERIAL GIRL

Ronald Reagan in America, Margaret Thatcher in Britain, and corporate executives around the world ruled over a conservative and materialistic society. On the other side were starving Ethiopians, gay men with the new disease AIDS, people of color, and women—all demanding power. Intelligent, peaceful, straight white males assumed a low profile.

The art world became big business, with a Van Gogh fetching $54 million. Corporations paid big bucks for large, colorful, semi-abstract canvases. Marketing became an art form. Gender and sexual orientation were popular themes. Many women picked up paintbrushes, creating bright-colored abstract forms hinting at vulva and penis shapes. Visual art fused with popular music, bringing us installations in dance clubs and fast-edit music videos. The crude style of graffiti art demanded to be included in corporate society.

1990s—MULTICULTURAL DIVERSITY

The communist-built Berlin Wall was torn down, ending four decades of a global Cold War between capitalism and communism. The new battleground was the "Culture Wars," the struggle to include all races, genders, and lifestyles within an increasingly corporate-dominated, global society.

Artists looked to Third World countries for inspiration and championed society's outsiders against government censorship and economic exclusion. A new medium, the Internet, arose, allowing instantaneous multimedia communication around the world through electronic signals carried by satellites and telephone lines.

2000—?

A new millennium dawned, with Europe and America at a peak of prosperity unmatched in human history....

VICTORIA AND ALBERT MUSEUM TOUR

With one of the biggest, most eclectic collections of objects any-where, the Victoria and Albert (V&A) has something for every-one. It bills itself as a museum for the decorative arts, and Martha Stewart types will be in hog heaven. You'll see furniture, glass-ware, clothing, jewelry, and carpets from every corner of the world. Throw in historical artifacts, a few fine-arts masterpieces (painting and sculpture), and a bed that sleeps seven, and you have a museum built for browsing.

The V&A grew out of the Great Exhibition of 1851, that ul-timate celebration of the Industrial Revolution. Now "art" could be brought to the masses through modern technology and mass production. The museum was founded on the idealistic Victorian notion that anyone can be continually improved by education and example. After much support from Queen Victoria and Prince Al-bert, the museum was renamed for the royal couple, and its present building was opened in 1909.

You could spend days in this place. The museum is large and gangly, with 150 rooms and more than 12 miles of corridors. My quick tour gives you a sample of the V&A's range, covering fine art, historical objects, interior design, fashion, and beautiful objects from around the globe. Use this tour to get your bearings, then use the museum's map to wander at will.

The V&A is in the midst of a 10-year update and expansion. Changes so far include a new café, sculpture gallery, Islamic Art room, refurbished Medieval and Renaissance galleries, and new galleries covering Europe from 1600-1800. Future plans include a spiffed-up entrance from Exhibition Road and new state-of-the-art permanent exhibition spaces. During this chaotic time, exhibits may be rearranged, so check with the information desk for current room closures, carry a copy of the museum's detailed map, and ask a nearby guard if you can't find one of the objects in this tour.

Orientation

Cost: Free (£3 donation requested), sometimes pricey fees for (optional) special exhibits.

Hours: Daily 10:00-17:45. Some galleries—including most on this tour—stay open Fri until 22:00 (though Tube tunnel may be closed at this time).

Getting There: The Grand Entrance—where our tour begins—is on Cromwell Road in the South Kensington neighborhood (Tube: South Kensington). You can also reach the Grand Entrance via a tunnel that leads directly from the Tube station: Once inside the museum (on level 1), continue straight down the long sculpture gallery. After about 100 yards, turn right through the gift shop, which takes you to the Grand Entrance lobby.

Information: Pick up the much-needed museum map (£1 suggested donation). The V&A's helpful website lists its current exhibitions. Once at the museum, strategically located computer terminals tell you more about the collection. Tel. 020/7942-2000, www.vam.ac.uk.

Tours: Free one-hour tours (general orientation and other, more specific topics) leave from the Grand Entrance lobby daily on the half-hour from 10:30 to 15:30. Additional tours and lectures are offered sporadically; check the website for details.

Length of This Tour: Allow 1.5 hours (not counting the British Galleries). With limited time, don't miss the Cast Courts (❽, ❾, and ❿), the Fashion Galleries (❻), and the Raphael Cartoons (❻).

Cloakroom: Free, mandatory for large bags.

Photography: Permitted in most of the galleries without flash or tripod, but not allowed for the Raphael Cartoons, the Jewelry gallery, special exhibits, and works loaned by other museums.

Cuisine Art: The V&A Café offers self-service lunch and tea in the elegant Morris, Gamble, and Poynter rooms. These three rooms formed the world's first museum restaurant (£10-13 meals, £5 sandwiches and salads). In summer, a self-service café (£4-6 sandwiches) sets up in the Madejski Garden—grab a bite

there or bring a picnic. For a list of recommended eateries in the neighborhood, see page 429.

Starring: A little of everything—and all of it beautiful.

The Tour Begins

• *Start at the Grand Entrance lobby, on level 1. Look up into the rotunda.*

❶ Dale Chihuly Chandelier

This modern chandelier/sculpture by the American glass artist epitomizes the spirit of the V&A's collection—beautiful manufac-

tured objects that demonstrate technical skill and innovation, wedding the old with the new, and blurring the line between arts and crafts.

Each blue-and-yellow strand of the chandelier is tied with a wire to a central spine. When the chandelier first went up in 2001, Chihuly said, "Too small," had it disassembled, and fired up still more glass bubbles.

Dale Chihuly (b. 1941)—face-famous for the eye-patch he's worn since a car accident—studied glassmaking in Venice, then set up his own studio/factory in Seattle, making art as the director of a creative team. He makes an old medium seem fresh and modern...and the V&A keeps his chandelier looking fresh with a long feather duster.

• *From the lobby, look up to the balcony and see the pointed arches of the...*

❷ Hereford Screen (1862)

In the 1800s, just as Britain was steaming into the future on the cutting edge of the Industrial Revolution, the public's taste went

retro. This 35-by-35-foot, eightton rood screen (built for the Hereford Cathedral's sacred altar area) looks medieval, but it was created with the most modern materials the Industrial Revolution could produce. The metal parts were not hammered

and hand-worked as in olden days, but are made of electroformed copper. The parts were first cast in plaster, then bathed in molten copper with an electric current running through it, leaving a metal skin around the plaster. The entire project—which might have taken years in medieval times—was completed in five months.

George Gilbert Scott (1811-1878), who built the screen, re-designed all of London in the Neo-Gothic style, restoring old churches such as Westminster Abbey, renovating the Houses of Parliament, and building new structures like St. Pancras Station and the Albert Memorial—some 700 buildings in all.

The world turns, and a century later (1960s), the Gothic style was "out" again, modernism was in, and this screen was neglected and ridiculed. Considering that the V&A was originally called the Museum of Manufactures (1857), it's appropriate that the screen was brought here, where it shows off the technical advances of the Industrial Revolution.

• *To the right of the Grand Entrance lobby, look into a large hall of statues (Room 50a), including a spiraling statue of two battling men.*

❸ *Samson Slaying a Philistine*, by Giambologna (c. 1562)

Carved from a single block of marble, the statue shows the testy Israelite warrior rearing back, brandishing the jawbone of an ass, preparing to decapitate a man who'd insulted

him. Samson pauses to make sure the Philistine looks him in the eye so he can see what's coming. Circle the statue and watch it spiral around its axis. Giambologna was clearly influenced by Michelangelo, who pioneered both the theme of the fallen enemy and the spiral-shaped pose that many artists imitated. The V&A has (arguably) the best collection of Italian Renaissance sculpture outside Italy.

• *From the Grand Entrance lobby (near the main doorway), find the entrance to the rooms labeled* Medieval & Renaissance, 300-1500. *It's down a few steps, on level 0 (Rooms 8-10).*

❹ Medieval and Renaissance Galleries, A.D. 300-1500

Walk through 1,200 years of decorative arts, seeing how the mix of pagan-Roman and medieval-Christian elements created modern Europe.

It's A.D. 300, and Rome's Europe-wide empire is beginning to unravel. Within two centuries, its political dominance would be over, but Rome's culture lived on in the Christian faith. Rooms 8-10 show how traditional Roman media (mosaics, carved ivory, column-and-arch building techniques) were adapted to make Christian-themed art and churches.

• *About three-fourths of the way down the long Room 8 is a glass case displaying the shoebox-sized...*

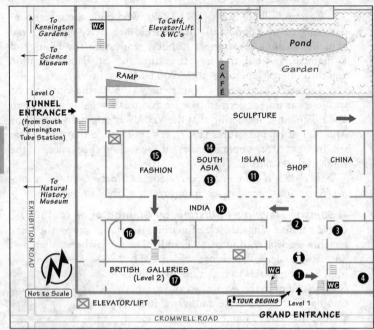

❺ Becket Casket (c. 1180)

The blue-and-gold box contains the mortal remains (or relics) of St. Thomas Becket, who was brutally murdered. Look at the scene depicted along the side—the Archbishop of Canterbury is about to grab a chalice from the altar, when knights tiptoe up, draw their swords, and slice off his head. Two shocked priests throw up their hands.

Becket's soul (upper right) is borne aloft on a sling by two angels. His body is laid to rest (upper left) and blessed by the new bishop. Mourners kneel at the tomb, just as the man behind Becket's murder—King Henry II—is said to have done, out of remorse.

Henry II had handpicked his good friend Thomas Becket (1118-1170) for the job of archbishop, assuming he'd follow the king's orders. In two days, Thomas was made a priest, a bishop, then archbishop—the head of all England's Christians. But when Becket proved loyal to the Church and opposed Henry's policies, the king, in a rash fit of anger, said he wanted Becket dead. Remorseful after his knights murdered the archbishop, Henry had

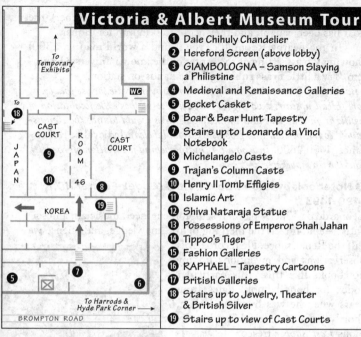

Victoria & Albert Museum Tour

1. Dale Chihuly Chandelier
2. Hereford Screen (above lobby)
3. GIAMBOLOGNA – Samson Slaying a Philistine
4. Medieval and Renaissance Galleries
5. Becket Casket
6. Boar & Bear Hunt Tapestry
7. Stairs up to Leonardo da Vinci Notebook
8. Michelangelo Casts
9. Trajan's Column Casts
10. Henry II Tomb Effigies
11. Islamic Art
12. Shiva Nataraja Statue
13. Possessions of Emperor Shah Jahan
14. Tippoo's Tiger
15. Fashion Galleries
16. RAPHAEL – Tapestry Cartoons
17. British Galleries
18. Stairs up to Jewelry, Theater & British Silver
19. Stairs up to view of Cast Courts

To Temporary Exhibits

To 18

WC

CAST COURT

CAST COURT

ROOM 46

JAPAN

9

10

8

19

KOREA

5

7

6

To Harrods & Hyde Park Corner →

BROMPTON ROAD

V&A MUSEUM

80 monks whip him, and then he spent all night at the foot of the tomb.

Just three years after his death, Becket was made a saint. Pieces of Becket's DNA—valuable relics—were conserved in this enamel-and-metal work box, a specialty of Limoges, France.

• *Continue straight to the far end of this long set of rooms. In Room 10a, you'll run right into...*

❻ Boar and Bear Hunt Tapestry (c. 1425-1430)

Though most medieval art depicted the Madonna and saints, this colorful wool tapestry—woven in Belgium—provides a secular slice of life.

"Read" it from right to left: The nobles want to go hunting, so they hire some professional guides. One pro (in red) enters with his dogs and hunting horn, leading two nobles. His colleague (above) rousts bear cubs from their den, so the mama and papa bears can be flushed out into the open. Men and dogs (in the center) surround a bear, while another is lanced by a nobleman on horseback. Below, well-dressed ladies look on.

Continuing to the left, the hunt turns to wild boar, as two

dogs flush one out of hiding. Finally (far left, bottom corner), the boar has been caught, and they begin to skin him for dinner.

In the nearby Room 10c, you'll find a **world map** (c. 1300) showing Christ sitting at the center of the known universe: Jerusalem. Try a little **brass rubbing** at the hands-on station.

• *Backtrack 20 more paces and find the nearby staircase (or use the elevator). Head upstairs two flights to level 2 to see how the foundation of civilization that was laid in medieval times would launch the Renaissance. You'll spill out into Rooms 62-64b, labeled* Medieval & Renaissance, 1400-1600. *In Room 64 (hiding behind a partition on the left), find the tiny, pocket-size...*

❼ Notebook by Leonardo da Vinci *(Codex Forster III)*, 1490-1493

Leonardo da Vinci—painter, sculptor, engineer, musician, and scientist—epitomized the merging of art, knowledge, and science we call the Renaissance. He recorded his observations and inventions in tiny notebooks like this. This particular codex (or bound book) dates from years when he was living in Milan, shortly before undertaking his famous *Last Supper* fresco. He was always busy, but completed little from this time.

The book's contents are all over the map: meticulous sketches of the human head, diagrams illustrating nature's geometrical perfection, a horse's leg for a huge equestrian statue, and even drawings of the latest ballroom fashions. The adjacent computer lets you flip his backwards handwriting to make the secret code legible.

In Room 64a (off to the left), an exhibit shows works by the sculptor Donatello, who blazed the artistic path followed by his fellow Florentine, Michelangelo. This all leads (in Room 63, at the opposite end of Room 64) to works showing the new wealth of Europe as it enters the modern age.

• *Get out your V&A map to help you find our next destination, in Rooms 46a and 46b. To get there, go back down the stairs one flight to the ground floor (level 1). Cross the big sculpture hall and find Rooms 46a and 46b, labeled* The Cast Courts—*filled with replicas of famous statues.*

These two rooms are taking turns being renovated. Room 46b (❽, below) will likely reopen sometime in 2015; after that, Room 46a (❾, below) will close. Because these plaster casts are gigantic and hard to move, they're being rehabbed right here where they stand. If you'd like to see the conservation work in action, go up the stairs at the Cast Courts entryway to a gallery overlooking both rooms.

But first, visit whichever of the next two rooms you find open.

❽ Michelangelo Casts and Other Replica Statues

These plaster-cast versions of famous Renaissance statues by Michelangelo and others allowed 19th-century art students who couldn't afford a rail pass to go study the classics.

The statues were made by coating the original with a non-stick substance, then laying wet plaster strips over it that dried to form a mold, from which a plaster cast was made. They look solid but are very fragile. In a single glance, you can follow Michelangelo's career, from youthful optimism *(David)*, to his never-finished masterpiece (statues from the tomb of Julius II, including *Moses* and two *Slaves*), to

full-blown midlife crisis (while sculpting the brooding Medici Tomb statues of Lorenzo and Giuliano). Compare Michelangelo's monumental *David* with Donatello's girlish *David* (at the other end of the room), and see Ghiberti's bronze Baptistery doors, which inspired the Florentine Renaissance.

David was a gift from Tuscany to Queen Victoria, who immediately donated it to the museum. Circle behind *David* to see the clip-on fig leaf that was hung on him when modest aristocrats visited (this was "the Victorian Age," after all).

• *Across the hall, in Room 46a, you can't miss the two halves of...*

❾ Trajan's Column Casts

Rising 140 feet and decorated with a spiral relief of 2,500 figures trumpeting the exploits of the Roman Emperor Trajan (c. A.D. 100), this is a copy of the world's grandest column from antiquity. The original column still stands in Rome, but the V&A's version was cast from a copy in Paris. In fact, they had to cut it in half to fit it here.

The column's relief unfolds like a scroll, telling the story of Trajan's conquest of Dacia (modern-day Romania). It starts at the bottom (the half with the pedestal) with a trickle of water that becomes a river and soon picks up boats full of supplies. Then come the soldiers themselves, who spill out from the gates of the city. A river god surfaces to bless the journey. Along the way (second band), they build roads and forts to sustain the vast enterprise. Trajan himself (fourth band, in military skirt with toga over his arm) mounts a podium to fire up the troops. They hop into a Roman galley (fifth band) and head off to fight the valiant Dacians in the middle of a forest (eighth band). Finally, at the very top, the Romans hold a sacrifice to give thanks for the victory, while the captured armor is displayed on the pedestal.

Originally, the entire story was painted in bright colors. If you unwound the scroll, it would stretch the length of two football fields—it's far longer than the frieze around Athens' Parthenon.

• *Near Trajan's column, find several casts of knights and ladies on their backs, staring at the ceiling (in faded hues of red, gold, and blue). Some of these (near where you entered, top row, far end) are the...*

❿ Plaster Casts of Tomb Effigies of Henry II and Family

This was a remarkable and dysfunctional royal family. England's King Henry II (1133-1189)—Becket's murderer—lies alongside his wife and their children.

Henry's wife, Eleanor of Aquitaine (the one reading a book while dead), was the ex-wife of the King of France and was renowned as Europe's most sophisticated lady. The wedding of Henry and Eleanor united their two families' large land holdings, creating an "England" that stretched as far down as southern France. It would eventually take the Hundred Years' War (1336-1453) to sort out the current border between England and France.

As king, Henry placed church courts under secular control, causing the rift that led to Becket's bloody murder. In Henry's old age, his children rebelled, taking arms against him for their slice of the royal pie. Henry's heir, Richard the Lionhearted, famous as the good guy in the Robin Hood legend, was actually an absentee monarch—a French-speaking dandy allied with the King of France. Younger son John, the "evil" King John of the Robin Hood legend, became a tyrant, prompting English nobles to make him sign the document called the Magna Carta, which established the principle that even kings must follow the law. (The British Library has a copy of the Magna Carta—❂ see the British Library Tour chapter.)

• *From the Cast Court entryway, head down the long hallway, past*

Asian art in Rooms 47g, 47f, 47e, etc. Pass the shop, then turn right into Room 42, which contains art of the Islamic Middle East.

⓫ Islamic Art

While owing much to Islam as a religion, Islamic art also reflected a sophisticated secular culture. Many Islamic artists expressed themselves with beautiful but functional objects.

In the center of the room is the 630-square-foot Ardabil Carpet (1539-1540). Its silk-thread underpinnings are topped by a dense wool pile made of 304 knots per square inch. (Carpet connoisseurs will nod approvingly at this impressively high KPI number.) Woven on a huge standing loom, it likely took a dozen workers years to make. In the center of the design is a yellow medallion ringed with ovals, supporting two hanging lamps. If you sat on the carpet near the smaller of the two lamps, you'd have the illusion of a symmetrical pattern. The carpet is illuminated on the hour and half-hour.

Also in the room are more carpets, ceramics (mostly blue-and-white or red-and-white), and glazed tile—all covered top to bottom in similarly complex patterns. The intricate interweaving, repetition, and unending lines suggest the complex, infinite nature of God (Allah).

You'll likely see only a few pictures of humans or animals—the Islamic religion is wary of any "graven images," or idols forbidden by God. However, secular art for homes and palaces was not bound by this, and you may see realistic depictions of men and women enjoying a garden paradise, a symbol of the Muslim heaven.

Notice floral patterns (twining vines, flowers, arabesques) and geometric designs (stars, diamonds). But the most common pattern is calligraphy—elaborate lettering of an inscription in Arabic, the language of the Quran (and the lettering used even in non-Arabic languages). A quote from the Quran on a vase or lamp combines the power of the message with the beauty of the calligraphy.

• *Return to the hall and continue on. In the hallway (technically "Room" 47b) is a glass case with a statue of...*

⓬ Shiva Nataraja (12th Century)

The Hindu god Shiva (SHEE-vah)—one of the hundreds, if not thousands, of godlike incarnations of Hinduism's eternal being, Brahma—steps lively and creates the world by dancing. His four arms are busy creating, and he treads on the sleepy dwarf of ignorance.

This bronze statue, one of Hinduism's most popular, is loaded with symbolism, summing up where humans came from and where we're going. Surrounded by a ring of fire, Shiva crosses a leg in time to the music. Smiling serenely, he blesses with one hand, while another beats out the rhythm of life with a hand drum. The cobra draped over his arm symbolizes the *Kundalini Sakti*, the cosmic energy inside each of us that can, with the right training, uncoil and bring us to enlightenment.

As long as Shiva keeps dancing, the universe will continue. But Shiva also holds a flame, a reminder that, at the end of time, he will transform into his female alter ego, Kali, and destroy the world by fire, clearing the slate for another round of existence.

• *Head through the doorway into the adjoining Room 41 (labeled South Asia). You'll run right into a glass case in the center of the room containing small items that were the...*

⓭ Possessions of Emperor Shah Jahan (r. 1628-1658)

Look at the cameo portrait, thumb ring, and wine cup (made of white nephrite jade, 1657) that belonged to one of the world's most powerful men.

Shah Jahan—or "King of the World"—ruled the largest empire of the day, covering northern India, Pakistan, and Afghanistan. His Mughal Empire was descended from Genghis Khan and the Mongol horde, who conquered and then settled in central Asia and converted to Islam.

Shah Jahan was known for his building projects, especially the Taj Mahal (see a picture of it nearby), built as a mausoleum for his favorite wife, Mumtaz, who bore him 14 children before dying in childbirth.

His unsuccessful attempts to expand the empire drained the treasury. In his old age, his sons quarreled over the inheritance. Imprisoned by his sons in the Agra fort, Shah Jahan died gazing across the river at the Taj Mahal, where he, too, would be buried. India's glory days were ending.

Then came the British.

• *At the far end of Room 41 (facing the door) is the huge wood-carved...*

The British in India

December 31, 1600—The British East India Company—a multinational trading company owned by stockholders—is founded with a charter from Queen Elizabeth I. They're given a virtual monopoly on trade with India.

1600s—The British trade peacefully with Indian locals on the coast, competing with France, Holland, and Portugal for access to spices, cotton, tea, indigo, and jute (for rope-making).

1700s—As the Mughal (Islamic) Empire breaks down, Britain and France vie for trade ports and inland territory. By the 1750s, Britain is winning. Britain establishes itself in Bombay, Madras, and Calcutta. First they rule through puppet Mughal leaders, then dump local leaders altogether.

1800s—By midcentury, two-thirds of the subcontinent is under British rule, exporting opium and tea (transplanted from its native China) and importing British-made cloth. Britain tries to reform Indian social customs (such as outlawing widow suicides) with little long-lasting effect. They build railways, roads, and irrigation systems.

1857-1858—The "Indian Mutiny"—sparked by high taxes, British monopoly of trade, and a chafing against foreign rule—is the first of many uprisings that slowly erode British rule.

1900s—Two world wars drain and distract Britain while Indians lobby for self-rule.

August 15, 1947—After a decade of peaceful protests led by Mahatma Gandhi, India gains its independence.

⓮ Tippoo's Tiger (1790s)

This life-size robotic toy, once owned by an oppressed Indian sultan (see Tipu's portrait and belongings nearby), is perhaps better called "India's revenge." The Bengal tiger has a British redcoat down, sinking its teeth into his neck. When you turned the crank, the Brit's left arm would flail, and both he and the tiger would roar through organ pipes. (The mechanism still works.)

Tipu, the Sultan of Mysore (1750-1799), called himself "The Tiger of Mysore." He was well educated in several languages and collected a library of 2,000 books. An enlightened ruler, he built roads and dams and promoted new technology. Tipu could see that India was being swallowed up by the all-powerful British East India Company. He allied himself with France and fought several successful wars against the British, but he was eventually defeated and forced to give up half his kingdom to them. Tipu was later killed by the Brits in battle (1799), his palace ransacked, and his possessions—including this toy—were taken, like much of India, by the British East India Company.

• *Backtrack out of Room 41 and turn right, then right again into Room 40. Here you'll find the...*

⓯ Fashion Galleries

Centuries of English fashion are corseted into 40 display cases. The cases around the perimeter show the evolution of a particular article of clothing. You'll see ladies' underwear through the ages, formal wear, men's suits, and so on. Temporary exhibits here usually enliven the displays. For more on old English fashion, visit the British Galleries (described below).

• *Directly across the hall from Room 40 is the cavernous Room 48a, filled with...*

⓰ Raphael's Tapestry Cartoons

For Christmas in 1519, Pope Leo X unveiled 10 new tapestries in the Sistine Chapel, designed by the famous artist Raphael. The project was one of the largest ever undertaken by a painter—it cost far more than Michelangelo's Sistine ceiling—and when it was done, the tapestries were a hit, inspiring princes across Europe to decorate their palaces in masterpieces of cloth.

The V&A owns seven of the full-size designs by Raphael that were used to produce the tapestries (approximately 13 feet by 17 feet, done in tempera on paper, now mounted on canvas). The cartoons were sent to factories in Brussels, cut into strips (see the lines), and placed on the looms. The scenes are the reverse of the final product—lots of left-handed saints.

Raphael (1483-1520) chose scenes from the Acts of the Apostles—particularly of Peter and Paul, the two early saints most as-

sociated with Rome, the seat of the popes. Knowing where the tapestries were to be hung, Raphael was determined to top Michelangelo's famous Sistine ceiling, with its huge, dramatic figures and subtle color effects. He matched Michelangelo's body-builder muscles (for example, the fishermen in *The Miraculous Draught of Fishes*), dramatic gestures, and reaction shots (as in the busy crowd scenes in *St. Paul Preaching in Athens*), and he exceeded Michelangelo in the subtleties of color.

Unfortunately, it was difficult to reproduce Raphael's painted nuances in the tapestry workshop. Traditional tapestries were simple, depicting either set patterns or block figures on a neutral background. Raphael challenged the Flemish weavers. Each brushstroke had to be reproduced by a colored thread woven horizontally. The finished tapestries (which are still in the Vatican) were glorious, but these cartoons capture Raphael's original vision.

• *From the Raphael room (48a), go up the staircase. At the top of the stairs (on level 2), turn left into Room 57. This is the heart of the British Galleries, featuring the Great Bed of Ware and Elizabethan miniatures.*

⑰ British Galleries

Room 57 covers the era of Queen Elizabeth I. Find rare miniature portraits—a popular item of the day—including Hilliard's oft-reproduced *Young Man Among Roses* miniature, capturing the romance of a Shakespeare sonnet. Also in the room are musical instruments and suits of armor—a love-and-war combination appropriate to the Elizabethan Age. Finally, there's the Great Bed of Ware. Built as a tourist-attracting gimmick by an English inn around 1600, this four-poster bed still wows. You and six of your favorite friends could bed down here, taking a well-earned rest after this eclectic tour.

Continue into the next room (Room 58), dedicated to *Birth, Marriage and Death,* and displaying swaddling clothes, a wedding

portrait, and a casket pall. Continuing on, you'll pass through a couple of alcoves with Tudor-era tapestries. The far end of Room 58, devoted to Henry VIII, has a portrait of him; his writing box (with quill pens, ink, and sealing wax); and a whole roomful of the fancy furniture, tapestries, jewelry, and dinnerware that may have decorated his palaces.

If you're interested, there's much more to the British Galleries, which sweep chronologically through 400 years of British high-class living (1500-1900)—all laid out over two floors and beautifully described.

• *For now, pop out the doorway of Room 58. You'll notice we've come full circle: You're overlooking the Grand Entrance lobby. This tour is officially over. But if you'd like more suggestions, there's great stuff upstairs.*

⓲ Jewelry, Theater, Silver, and More

• *From the Grand Entrance lobby, pass through the shop, turn right into Room 24, and climb the staircase to level 3.*

Jewelry (Rooms 90-93): This collection is understandably popular. In one long glittering gallery, you can trace the evolution of jewelry from ancient Egyptian, Greek, and Roman to the 20th century. The Art Nouveau style of Parisian jeweler Rene Lalique is hard not to love.

• *Exit the jewelry rooms at the far end and turn right to find...*

Theater and Performance (Rooms 103-106): With artifacts from Hamlet skulls to rock-and-roll tour posters, this exhibit re-

cords the history of live performance in the UK. Kids will enjoy the costumes from *The Lion King* and the dress-up costume box. Nearby, aging boomers will see Mick Jagger's jumpsuit...and marvel that he used to fit into it.

• *Exit the collection where you entered, turn right (into "Prints & Drawings"), then left to find...*

British Silver (Rooms 65-68): The displays in these galleries are bursting with flamboyant silver treasures dating from the 1600s to modern times, including teething rattles, gambling counters, punch bowls, and pitchers.

• *I'll leave you here (find exit stairs at the far-right end of Room 74), but there's plenty left to see. If you have stamina, use your V&A map to plot the rest of your Grand Tour of this museum.*

TATE BRITAIN TOUR

The National Gallery of British Art, otherwise known as the Tate Britain, features the world's best collection of British art—sweeping you from 1500 until today. This is people's art, with realistic paintings rooted in the people, landscape, and stories of the British Isles. The recently renovated Tate shows off Hogarth's stage sets, Gainsborough's ladies, Blake's angels, Constable's clouds, Turner's tempests, the naturalistic realism of the Pre-Raphaelites, and the camera-eye portraits of Hockney and Freud. Even if these names are new to you, don't worry. You'll likely see a few "famous" works you didn't know were British and exit the Tate Britain with at least one new favorite artist.

Orientation

Cost: Free (£4 donation requested); special exhibits require separate admission.

Hours: Daily 10:00-18:00, last entry 45 minutes before closing.

Getting There: It's on the Thames River, south of Big Ben and north of Vauxhall Bridge. The museum has two entrances: the main entrance on Millbank, facing the Thames, and the Manton entrance on Atterbury Street (wheelchair-accessible). You can reach the museum by Tube, ferry, bus, or on foot:

By Tube: Tube: Pimlico plus seven-minute walk, or Tube: Westminster plus 15-minute walk.

By Ferry: Hop on Thames Clippers' Tate Boat ferry from the Tate Modern (£6.50 one-way, £15 day ticket, discount with Travelcard or Oyster card, buy ticket at gallery desk or on board, departs every 40 minutes from 10:15 to 16:30, about 15 minutes, www.tate.org.uk/visit/tate-boat).

By Bus: Bus #87 leaves from the National Gallery, and

drops off in front of the Tate. Bus #88 leaves from Oxford Circus, and drops off behind museum. Both connect the museum to Westminster.

On Foot: Walk 15 minutes south along the Thames from Big Ben.

Information: Pick up a map (£1 suggested donation) at the information desk. The spacious reading room downstairs is designed as a creative thinking space for the public. The museum's shops are great for books, magazines, and trinkets. Tel. 020/7887-8888, www.tate.org.uk.

Tours: Free **guided tours** are generally offered daily at 11:00, 12:00, 14:00, and 15:00, but call to confirm schedule. Use the Tate's Wi-Fi and download their handy room-by-room **audio tour.** The museum also hosts games, activities, and art projects for children (Sat-Sun 11:00-15:00 plus other times as scheduled).

Length of This Tour: Allow one hour. If you have less time, focus on the Pre-Raphaelites and Turner.

Cloakroom: Bag and coat check are free (£2 suggested donation).

Photography: Photos are allowed without a flash or tripod.

Cuisine Art: Your options are a café with an affordable gourmet buffet line (£4-7 sandwiches or salads, £7-11 hot meals) or a pricey-but-delightful restaurant (one course for £17, two courses for £24, three courses for £29, daily 12:00-15:00; £14 afternoon tea served Mon-Sat 15:30-17:00, Sun 16:00-17:00).

Starring: Hogarth, Gainsborough, Reynolds, Blake, Constable, Pre-Raphaelites, and Turner.

Know Your Tates: Don't confuse the Tate Britain (British art) with the Tate Modern (at Bankside, on the South Bank of the Thames across from St. Paul's Cathedral), which features modern art (♥ see the Tate Modern Tour chapter).

ORIEN-TATE: GALLERY IN MOTION

This tour covers, in roughly chronological order, British paintings from 1500 to today. Works from the early centuries are located in the west half of the building, 20th-century art is in the east half, and the works of J. M. W. Turner are in an adjacent wing (the Clore Gallery). Temporary exhibits (some free, some requiring an entrance fee) are in the east wing and in the basement.

Though the Tate's layout is roughly chronological, the emphasis here is on *rough*. Certain artists' work (such as Blake's and Henry Moore's) are placed in special rooms outside the chronological flow. Other rooms focus on a particular aspect of British art. In addition, the Tate rotates its vast collection of paintings, so it's difficult to predict exactly which works will be on display. Pick up the latest map as you enter, or download the handy audio tour. Consider reading this chapter ahead of time as an overview of British art, then let the Tate surprise you with its current array of masterpieces.

The Tour Begins

British artists painted people, countrysides, and scenes from daily life, realistically and without the artist passing judgment (substance over style). What you won't see here are the fleshy goddesses, naked baby angels, and Madonna-and-child altarpieces so popular elsewhere in Europe. The largely Protestant English abhorred the "graven images" of the wealthy Catholic world; many such images were destroyed during the 16th-century Reformation. They preferred portraits of flesh-and-blood English folk.

• *From the main Millbank entrance, walk through the bright, white rotunda and down the long central hall, usually adorned with sculpture or temporary installations. Near the far end, enter the rooms on the left, where you'll find the beginnings of British painting (as you enter each room, you'll find the year etched into the floor).*

1500-1700—Portraits of Lord and Lady Whoevertheyare

Stuffy portraits of a beef-fed society try to turn crude country nobles into refined men and delicate women. Men in ruffled collars clutch symbols of power. Women in ruffled collars, puffy sleeves, and elaborately patterned dresses display their lily-white complexions, turning their pinkies out.

English country houses often had a long hall built specially to hang family portraits. You could stroll along and see your noble

forebears looking down their noses at you. Britain's upper crust had little interest in art other than as a record of themselves along with their possessions—their wives, children, jewels, furs, ruffled collars, swords, and guns.

You'll see plenty more portraits in the Tate Britain, right up to modern times. Each era had its own style. Portraits from the 1500s are stern and dignified. The 1600s brought a more relaxed and elegant style and more décolletage.

1700s—ART BLOSSOMS

With peace at home (under three King Georges), a strong overseas economy, and a growing urban center in London, England's artistic life began to bloom. As the English grew more sophisticated, so did their portraits. Painters branched out into other subjects, cap-

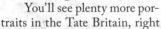

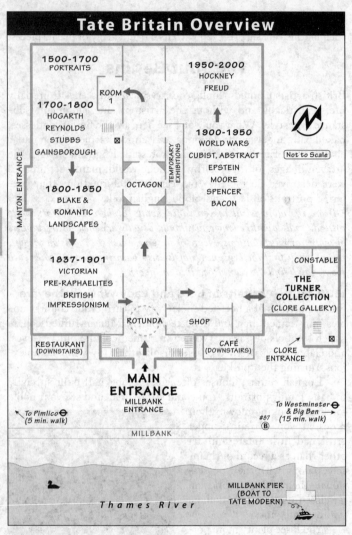

Tate Britain Overview

1500-1700 PORTRAITS

ROOM 1

1700-1800
HOGARTH
REYNOLDS
STUBBS
GAINSBOROUGH

1800-1850
BLAKE &
ROMANTIC
LANDSCAPES

OCTAGON

TEMPORARY EXHIBITIONS

MANTON ENTRANCE

1837-1901
VICTORIAN
PRE-RAPHAELITES
BRITISH
IMPRESSIONISM

1950-2000
HOCKNEY
FREUD

1900-1950
WORLD WARS
CUBIST, ABSTRACT
EPSTEIN
MOORE
SPENCER
BACON

Not to Scale

CONSTABLE

THE TURNER COLLECTION (CLORE GALLERY)

ROTUNDA

SHOP

RESTAURANT (DOWNSTAIRS)

CAFÉ (DOWNSTAIRS)

CLORE ENTRANCE

MAIN ENTRANCE
MILLBANK ENTRANCE

To Pimlico ⊖ (5 min. walk)

To Westminster ⊖ & Big Ben (15 min. walk)
#87 Ⓑ

MILLBANK

Thames River

MILLBANK PIER (BOAT TO TATE MODERN)

TATE BRITAIN

turing slices of everyday life. The Royal Academy added a veneer of classical Greece to even the simplest subjects.

William Hogarth (1697-1764)

Hogarth loved the theater. "My picture is my stage," he said, "and my men and women my players." The curtain goes up, and we see one scene that tells a whole story, often satirizing English high society. The London theater scene came into its own (after post-Shakespeare censorship) during Hogarth's generation. He often painted series based on popular plays of the time.

A born Londoner, Hogarth loved every gritty aspect of the big city. You'd find him in seedy pubs and brothels, at the half-price ticket booth in Leicester Square, at prize-fights, cockfights, duels, and public executions—all with sketchbook in hand. An 18th-century Charles Dickens, he exposed the hypocrisy of fat-bellied squires, vain ladies, and gluttonous priests. He also gave the upper classes a glimpse into the hidden poverty of "merry olde England"—poor soldiers with holes in their stockings, overworked servants, and unwed mothers.

Hogarth's portraits (and self-portraits) are unflinchingly honest, quite different from the powdered-wig fantasies of his contemporaries. Hogarth was an accomplished engraver; his works were mass-produced, giving Londoners a sense of their city and themselves.

Sir Joshua Reynolds (1723-1792) and the "Grand Manner"

Real life wasn't worthy of a painting. So said Sir Joshua Reynolds, the pillar of Britain's Royal Academy. Instead, people, places, and

things had to be gussied up with Greek columns, symbolism, and great historic moments, ideally from classical Greece.

In his portraits, he'd pose Lady Bagbody like the Medici Venus, or Lord Milquetoast like Apollo Belvedere. In landscapes you get Versailles-type settings of classical monuments amid perfectly manicured greenery. Inspired by Rembrandt, Reynolds sometimes used dense, clotted paint to capture the look of the Old Masters.

This art was meant to elevate the viewer, to appeal to his rational nature and fill him with noble sentiment. Sir Joshua Reynolds, the pillar of England's art establishment, stood for all that was upright, tasteful, rational, brave, clean, reverent, and...zzzzzzz....

George Stubbs (1724-1806)

Stubbs was the Michelangelo of horse painters. He understood these creatures from the inside out, having dissected them in his studio. He even used machinery to prop the corpses up into lifelike poses. He painted the horses first on a blank canvas, then filled in the background landscape around them (notice the heavy outlines that make them stand out clearly from the countryside). The result is both incredibly natural—from the veins in their noses to their freshly brushed coats—and geometrically posed.

Thomas Gainsborough (1727-1788)

Gainsborough showcased the elegant, educated women of his generation. He portrayed them as they wished to see themselves: a

feminine ideal, patterned after fashion magazines. The cheeks are rosy, the poses relaxed and S-shaped, the colors brighter and more pastel, showing the influence of the refined French culture of the court at Versailles. His ladies tiptoe gracefully toward us, with clear, Ivory-soap complexions that stand out from the swirling greenery of English gardens. (Though he painted portraits, he longed to do landscapes.) Gainsborough worked hard to prettify his subjects, but the results were always natural and never stuffy.

1800-1850—THE INDUSTRIAL REVOLUTION

Newfangled inventions were everywhere. Railroads laced the land. You could fall asleep in Edinburgh and wake up in London, a trip that used to take days or weeks. But along with technology came factories coating towns with soot, urban poverty, regimentation, and clock-punching. Machines replaced honest laborers, and once-noble Man was viewed as a naked ape.

Strangely, you'll see little of the modern world in paintings of the time—except in reaction to it. Many artists rebelled against "progress" and the modern world. They escaped the dirty cities to commune with nature (Constable and the Romantics). Or they found a new spirituality in intense human emotions (dramatic scenes from history or literature). Or they left the modern world altogether.

• *The work of William Blake may be displayed in a dedicated room on the other side of the central sculpture hall.*

William Blake (1757-1827)

At the age of four, Blake saw the face of God. A few years later, he ran across a flock of angels swinging in a tree. Twenty years later, he was living in a run-down London flat with an illiterate wife, scratching out a thin existence as an engraver. But even in this squalor, ignored by all but a few fellow artists, he still had his heavenly visions, and he described them in poems, paintings, drawings, and prints.

One of the original space cowboys, Blake also was a unique

artist, often classed with
the Romantics because he
painted in a fit of ecstatic
inspiration rather than by
studied technique. He painted angels, not the dull material world. While Britain
was conquering the world
with guns and nature with
machines, and while his fel-

low Londoners were growing rich, fat, and self-important, Blake
turned his gaze inward, illustrating the glorious visions of the soul.

Blake's work hangs in a darkened room to protect his watercolors from deterioration. Enter his mysterious world and let your
pupils dilate opium-wide.

His pen and watercolor sketches glow with an unearthly aura.
In visions of the Christian heaven or Dante's hell, his figures have
superhero musculature. The colors are almost translucent.

Blake saw the material world as bad, trapping the divine spark
inside each of our bodies and keeping us from true communion
with God. Blake's prints illustrate his views on the ultimate weak-
ness of material, scientific man. Despite their Greek-god anatomy,
his men look noble but tragically lost.

A famous poet as well as painter, Blake summed up his dis-
trust of the material world in a poem addressed to "The God of this
World"—that is, Satan:

> *Tho' thou art Worship'd by the Names Divine*
> *Of Jesus and Jehovah, thou art still*
> *The Son of Morn in weary Night's decline,*
> *The lost Traveller's Dream under the Hill.*

"Romantic" Landscapes—Art and the Sublime

Artists in the Romantic style saw the most intense human emotions
reflected in the drama and mystery of nature. Some of them mixed

landscapes with intense human emotion to produce huge, colorful canvases depicting storms, burning sun-
sets, towering clouds, and crashing
waves, all dwarfing puny humans.

History paintings reflected great
moments from the past, from ancient
Greece to medieval knights, Napoleon to Britain's battles abroad. These
were seen as the classiest form of art, combining the high drama of
heroic acts with refined technique.

Other artists made supernatural, religious fantasy-scapes.

God is found within nature, and nature is charged with the grandeur and power of God.

1837-1901—THE VICTORIAN ERA

In the world's wealthiest nation, the prosperous middle class dictated taste in art. They admired paintings that were realistic (showcasing the artist's talent and work ethic), depicting Norman Rockwell-style slices of everyday life.

We see families and ordinary people eating, working, and relaxing. Some paintings tug at the heartstrings, with scenes of parting couples, the grief of death, or the joy of families reuniting. Dramatic scenes from classical (Chaucer and Shakespeare) and popular literature get the heart beating. There's the occasional touching look at the plight of the honest poor, reminiscent of Dickens. Many paintings warn us to be good little boys and girls by showing the consequences of a life of sin. And then there are the puppy dogs with sad eyes.

The Pre-Raphaelites

You'll see medieval damsels in dresses and knights in tights, legendary lovers from poetry, and even a very human Virgin Mary as a delicate young woman. The women wear flowing dresses and have long, wavy hair and delicate, elongated, curving bodies. Beautiful.

Overdosed with the gushy sentimentality of their day, a band of 20-year-old artists—including Sir John Everett Millais, Dante Gabriel Rossetti, and William Holman Hunt—said "Enough!" and dedicated themselves to creating less saccharine art. Their "Pre-Raphaelite Brotherhood" (you may see the initials P. R. B. by the artist's signature) returned to a style "pre-Raphael"—that is, "medieval" in its simple style, in its melancholy mood, and often in its subject matter.

"Truth to Nature" was their slogan. Like the Impressionists who followed them, they donned their scarves, barged out of the stuffy studio, and set up outdoors, painting trees, streams, and people, like scientists on a field trip. Still, they often captured nature with such a close-up clarity that it's downright unnatural. And despite the Pre-Raphaelite claim to paint life just as it is, this is so beautiful it hurts.

This is art from the cult of femininity, worshipping Woman's haunting beauty, compassion, and depth of soul (proto-feminism or nouveau-chauvinism?). The artists' wives and lovers were their models and muses, and the art echoed their love lives. The people are surrounded by nature at its most beautiful, with every detail

painted crystal clear. Even
without the people, there
is a mood of melancholy.

The Pre-Raphaelites
hated overacting. Their
subjects—even in the face
of great tragedy, high pas-
sions, and moral dilem-
mas—barely raise an eye-
brow. Outwardly, they're
reflective, accepting their
fate. But sinuous postures—with lovers swooning into each other,
and parting lovers swooning apart—speak volumes. These volumes
are footnoted by the small objects with symbolic importance placed
around them: red flowers denoting passion, lilies for purity, pets for
fidelity, and so on.

The colors—greens, blues, and reds—are bright and clear,
with everything evenly lit, so that we see every detail. To get the

luminous color, some painted a
thin layer of bright paint over a
pure white, still-wet undercoat,
which subtly "shines" through.
These canvases radiate a pure
spirituality, like stained-glass
windows.

Stand for a while and enjoy
the exquisite realism and human emotions of these Victorian-era
works...flesh-and-blood people painted realistically. Get your fill,
because beloved Queen Victoria is about to check out, the modern
world is coming, and, with it, new art to express modern attitudes.

BRITISH IMPRESSIONISM

Realistic British art stood apart from the modernist trends in
France, but some influences drifted across the Channel. John
Singer Sargent (American-born) stud-
ied with Parisian Impressionists, learning the thick, messy brushwork and play
of light at twilight. James Tissot used
Degas' snapshot technique to capture a
crowded scene from an odd angle. And
James McNeill Whistler (born in America, trained in Paris, lived in London)
composed his paintings like music—see
some of his paintings' titles. These col-

lages of shapes and colors please the eye like a song tickles the
ear. Whistler signed his paintings with his initials in the shape

of a butterfly. You may also see sophisticated works by London's own "Bloomsbury Group," who put a British spin on French Post-Impressionism.

• *Before moving on to 20th-century art, first visit the Turner Collection. You'll find it in a wing adjacent to the main building: Pass through the rotunda to the east side of the gallery and just keep going through a few rooms till you enter The Turner Collection, housed in the Clore Gallery.*

THE TURNER COLLECTION

The Tate Britain has the world's best collection of works by J. M. W. Turner (1775-1851). Walking through his life's work, you can trace his progression from a painter of realistic historical scenes, through his wandering years, to Impressionist paintings of color-and-light patterns.

• *As you explore the collection, you'll watch Turner's style evolve from clear-eyed realism to hazy proto-Impressionism. You'll also see how Turner dabbled in different subjects: landscapes, seascapes, Roman ruins, snapshots of Venice, and so on.*

Self-Portrait as a Young Man

At 24, Turner has just been elected the youngest Associate of the Royal Academy. The son of a Covent Garden barber now dresses like a gentleman. His clear, realistic painting style caught the public's fancy. The full-frontal pose and intense gaze of this portrait show a young man ready to take on the world.

The Royal Academy Years

Trained in the Reynolds school of grandiose epics, Turner painted the obligatory big canvases of great moments in history—*The Destruction of Sodom, Hannibal and His Army Crossing the Alps, The Lost ATM Card, Jason and the Argonauts,* and various shipwrecks. Not content to crank them out in the traditional staid manner, he sets them in expansive landscapes. Nature's stormy mood mirrors the human events, but is so grandiose it dwarfs them.

This is a theme we'll see throughout his works: The forces of nature—the burning sun, swirling clouds, churning waves, gathering storms, and the weathering of time—overwhelm men and wear down the civilizations they build.

Travels with Turner

Turner's true love was nature—he was a born hobo. Oblivious to the wealth and fame that his early paintings gave him, he set out traveling—mostly on foot—throughout England and the Continent, with a rucksack full of sketch pads and painting gear. He sketched the English countryside—not green, leafy, and placid as so many others had done, but churning in motion, hazed over by a burning sunset.

He found the "sublime" not in the studio or in church, but in the overwhelming power of nature. The landscapes throb with life and motion. He sets Constable's clouds on fire.

Italy's Landscape and Ruins

With a Rick Steves guidebook in hand, Turner visited the great museums of Italy, drawing inspiration from the Renaissance masters. He painted the classical monuments and Renaissance architecture. He copied masterpieces, admired the works of the French classicist Claude Lorrain, and fused a great variety of styles—a true pan-European vision. Turner's Roman ruins are not grand; they're dwarfed by the landscape around them and eroded by swirling, misty, luminous clouds.

Stand close to a big canvas of Roman ruins, close enough so that it fills your whole field of vision. Notice how the buildings seem to wrap around you. Turner was a master of using multiple perspectives to draw the viewer in. On the one hand, you're right in the thick of things, looking "up" at the tall buildings. Then again, you're looking "down" on the distant horizon, as though standing on a mountaintop.

Venice

I know what color the palazzo is. But what color is it at sunset? Or through the filter of the watery haze that hangs over Venice? Can I paint the glowing haze itself? Maybe if I combine two different colors and smudge the paint on....

Venice stoked Turner's lust for reflected, golden sunlight. You'll see both finished works and unfinished sketches...uh, which is which?

Seascapes

The ever-changing sea was his specialty, with waves, clouds, mist, and sky churning and mixing together, all driven by the same forces.

Turner used oils like many painters use watercolors. First, he'd lay down a background (a "wash") of large patches of color, then he'd add a few dabs of paint to suggest a figure. (Some artists might use pencil lines to sketch out their figures, but Turner avoided that.) The final product lacked photographic clarity but showed the power and constant change in the forces of nature. He was perhaps the most prolific painter ever, with some 2,000 finished paintings and 20,000 sketches and watercolors.

Late Works

The older Turner got, the messier both he and his paintings became. He was wealthy, but he died in a run-down dive, where he'd set up house with a prostitute.
Yet the colors are brighter and the subjects less pessimistic than in the dark and brooding early canvases. His last works—whether landscape, religious, or classical scenes—are a blur and swirl of colors in motion, lit by the sun or a lamp burning through the mist. Even Turner's own cre-
ations were finally dissolved by the swirling forces of nature.

These paintings are "modern" in that the subject is less important than the style. You'll have to read the title to "get" it. You could argue that an Englishman helped invent Impressionism a generation before Monet and his ilk boxed the artistic ears of Paris in the 1880s. Turner's messy use of paint to portray reflected light "Chunneled" its way to France to inspire the Impressionists.
• *Now, head for the corner room of the Clore Gallery that's dedicated to Turner's great rival and contemporary...*

John Constable (1776-1837)

Constable brought painting back into the real world. Although the Royal Academy thought Nature needed makeup, Constable

thought she was just fine. He painted the English landscape as it was—realistically, without idealizing it. With simple earth tones he caught leafy green trees, gathering gray skies, brown country lanes, and rivers the color of the clouds reflected in them. Many details came from actual landscapes and villages from his childhood roots in Suffolk.

Clouds are Constable's trademark. Appreciate the effort involved in sketching ever-changing cloud patterns for hours on end—the mix of dark clouds and white clouds, cumulus and stratus, the colors of sunset. A generation before the Impressionists, he actually set up his easel outdoors and painted on the spot, a painstaking process before the invention of ready-made paints-in-a-tube (about 1850).

It's rare to find a Constable (or any British) landscape that doesn't have the mark of man in it—a cottage, hay cart, field hand, or a country road running through the scene. For him, the English countryside and its people were one.

In his later years, Constable's canvases became bigger, the style more "Impressionistic" (messier brushwork), and he worked more from memory than observation.

Constable's commitment to unvarnished nature wasn't fully recognized in his lifetime, and he was forced to paint portraits for his keep. The neglect caused him to ask a friend, "Can it therefore be wondered at that I paint continual storms?"

• *Now, back to where we left off: the beginning of the 20th century. Retrace your steps to the main building, where you'll find 20th-century art in the east half of the building.*

1900-1950—WORLD WARS

As two world wars whittled down the powerful British Empire, it still remained a major cultural force.

British art mirrored many of the trends and "-isms" pioneered in Paris. You'll see Cubism like Picasso's, abstract art like Mondrian's, and so on. But British artists also continued the British tradition of realistic paintings of people and landscapes. (Note: You'll find 20th-century artists' work both here in the Tate Britain and in the Tate Modern—✪ see also the Tate Modern Tour chapter.)

World War I, in which Britain lost a million men, cast a long shadow over the land. Artists expressed the horror of war, particularly of dehumanizing battles pitting powerful machines against puny human pawns. Jacob Epstein's (1880-1959) gleaming, abstract statues suggest mangled half-human/half-machine forms.

Henry Moore (1898-1986)

Twice a week, young Henry Moore went to the British Museum to sketch ancient statues, especially reclining ones (as in the Parthenon pediment or the Mayan god, Chac Mool, which he saw in a photo). His statues—mostly female, mostly reclining—catch the primitive power of carved stone. Moore almost always carved with his own hands (unlike, say, Rodin, who modeled a small clay figure and let assistants chisel the real thing), capturing the human body in a few simple curves, with minimal changes to the rock itself.

The statues do look vaguely like what their titles say, but it's the stones themselves that are really interesting. Notice the texture and graininess of these mini-Stonehenges; feel the weight, the space they take up, and how the rock forms intermingle.

During World War II, Moore passed time in the bomb shelters sketching mothers with babes in arms, a theme found in later works.

Moore carves the human body with the epic scale and restless poses of Michelangelo but with the crude rocks and simple lines of the primitives.

Stanley Spencer (1891-1959)

Spencer paints unromanticized landscapes, portraits, and hometown scenes. Even the miraculous *Resurrection of the Dead* is portrayed absolutely literally, with the dead climbing out of their Glasgow graves. In fully modern times, Spencer carried on the British tradition of sober realism.

Francis Bacon (1909-1992)

With a stiff upper lip, Britain survived the Blitz, World War II, and the loss of hundreds of thousands of men—but at war's end, the bottled-up horror came rushing out. Bacon's 1945 exhibition, opening just after Holocaust details began surfacing, stunned London with its unmitigated ugliness.

His deformed half-humans/half-animals—caged in a claustrophobic room, with twisted hunk-of-meat bodies and quadriplegic, smudged-mouth helplessness—can do nothing but scream in anguish and frustration. The scream becomes a blur, as though it goes on forever.

Bacon, largely self-taught, uses "traditional" figurativism, painting somewhat recognizable people and things. His subjects express the existential human predicament of being caught in a world not of your making, isolated and helpless to change it.

1950-2000—MODERN WORLD

No longer a world power, Britain in the Swinging '60s became a major exporter of pop culture. British art's traditional strengths—realism, portraits, landscapes, and slice-of-life scenes—were redone in the modern style.

David Hockney (b. 1937)

The "British Andy Warhol"—who is bleach-blonde, horn-rimmed, gay, and famous—paints "pop"-ular

culture with photographic realism. Large, airy canvases of L.A. swimming pools, double portraits of his friends in their stylish homes, or mundane scenes from the artist's own life capture the superficial materialism of the 1970s and 1980s. (Is he satirizing or glorifying it by painting it on a monumental scale with painstaking detail?)

Hockney saturates the canvas with bright (acrylic) paint, eliminating any haze, making distant objects as clear and bright as close ones. This technique, combined with his slightly simplified "cutout" figures, gives the painting the flat look of a billboard.

Lucian Freud (1922-2011)

Sigmund's grandson (who emigrated from Nazi Germany as a boy) puts every detail on the couch for analysis, then reassembles them

into works that are still surprisingly realistic. His subjects look you right in the eye, slightly on edge. Even the plants create an ominous mood. Everything is in sharp focus (unlike in real life, where you concentrate on one thing while your peripheral vision is blurred). Thick brushwork is especially good at capturing the pallor of British flesh.

In the great tradition of British portrait painting, Freud recently did an unflinching (and controversial) portrait of Queen Elizabeth.

Bridget Riley (b. 1931)

The pioneer of Op Art paints patterns of lines and alternating colors that make the eye vibrate (the way a spiral will "spin") when you stare at them. These obscure, scientific experiments in human optics suddenly became trendy in the psychedelic, cannabis-fueled 1960s. Like, wow.

Barbara Hepworth (1903-1975)

Hepworth's small-scale carvings in stone and wood—like "mini-Moores"—make even holes look interesting. Though they're not exactly realistic, it isn't hard to imagine them being inspired by, say, a man embracing a woman (she called it "sex harmony"), or the shoreline encircling a bay near her Cornwall-coast home, or a cliff penetrated by a cave—that is, two forms intermingling.

Gilbert (b. 1943) and George (b. 1942)

The Siegfried and Roy of art satirize the "Me Generation" and its shameless self-marketing by portraying their nerdy, three-piece-suited selves on the monumental scale normally dedicated to kings, popes, and saints.

THE REST OF THE MUSEUM

We've covered 500 years, with social satire from Hogarth to Hockney, from Constable's placid landscapes to Turner's churning scenes, from Blake's inner visions to Pre-Raphaelite fantasies, from realistic portraits to...realistic portraits.

But the Tate's great strength is championing contemporary British art in special exhibitions. There are generally two exhibition spaces: one in the east half of the main floor (often free), and another downstairs (usually requiring separate admission). Explore the cutting-edge art from one of the world's thriving cultural capitals: London.

Enough Tate? Great. It's late.

GREENWICH TOUR

Still well within the city limits of London, the Royal Borough of Greenwich (GREN-ich)—England's maritime capital—feels like a small town all its own. Visitors come here for all things salty, including the *Cutty Sark* clipper, the area's premier attraction. Greenwich is synonymous with timekeeping and astronomy, and at the Royal Observatory Greenwich, you can learn how those pursuits relate to seafaring. Greenwich also has stately Baroque architecture, appealing markets, a fleet of nautical shops, plenty of parks, kid-friendly museums, and hordes of tourists. Since many of the major sights here are free to enter, and you can travel between central London and Greenwich on a cheap Tube ticket, it's a wonderfully inexpensive day out. And where else can you set your watch with such accuracy?

Note that Greenwich pairs perfectly with a quick visit to the Docklands, London's glittering skyscraper zone (just across the river from Greenwich, and covered in the next chapter).

GETTING TO GREENWICH

It's a joy by boat or a snap by DLR. I enjoy a mix-and-match approach: Ride the boat to Greenwich for the scenery and commentary, and take the Docklands Light Railway (DLR) back—especially if you want to stop at the Docklands on the way home. On pleasant weekends, the early evening London-bound boats fill up quickly as everyone leaves around the same time (17:00-18:00)—another reason to boat here and take the DLR back to central London.

By Boat: From central London, you can cruise scenically down the Thames to Greenwich. Various tour boats—with commentary and open-deck seating up top—leave from the piers at Westminster, Waterloo, and the Tower of London (2/hour, 30 minutes-1.25 hours). Most boats have commentary only on the way to Greenwich, but if you really want it on the way back, you can ask the boat staff to provide it.

Thames Clippers offers faster trips, with no commentary and only a small deck at the stern (departs every 20-30 minutes from several piers in central London, 20-45 minutes). Thames Clippers also connects Greenwich to the Docklands' Canary Wharf Pier (2-3/hour, 10 minutes).

For cruising details, see page 40.

By Docklands Light Railway (DLR): From Bank Station in central London (also accessible from the Monument Tube station), take the DLR to Cutty Sark Station in central Greenwich; it's one stop before the main—but less central—Greenwich Station (departs at least every 10 minutes, 20 minutes, all in Zone 2, covered by any Tube pass). The DLR works like the Tube; be sure to touch your card to the reader on the platform before and after your journey, or risk being fined.

Many DLR trains terminate at Canary Wharf, so make sure you get on one that continues to Lewisham or Greenwich. Some DLR trains terminate at Island Gardens, from where you can generally catch another train to Greenwich's Cutty Sark Station within a few minutes. Or, disembark at Island Gardens for the unique experience of walking under the Thames into Greenwich: To reach the pedestrian tunnel, exit the station, cross the street, and follow signs to *Island Gardens* for a good photo op. Then enter the red-brick Greenwich Foot Tunnel (opened in 1902), descend 86 spiral stairs (or ride the lift), hold your breath, and re-emerge on dry land at the bow of the *Cutty Sark*.

By Train: Mainline trains also go from London (Cannon Street and London Bridge stations) several times an hour to Greenwich Station (10-minute walk from the sights). Although the train is fast and cheap, the DLR is preferable because it drops you right in the heart of Greenwich.

By Bus: Catch bus #188 from Russell Square near the British Museum (about 45 minutes to Greenwich).

Orientation to Greenwich

When to Go: To allow enough time to see everything—and to fit in a Docklands visit on your way back—head to Greenwich in the morning. Some of the sights can get crowded with families and school groups, especially in summer and on weekends. You can reserve your *Cutty Sark* visit in advance (explained on page 355).

Opening Times: Greenwich's main sights are open daily from 10:00 to 17:00; some stay open later (complete hours are listed later for each individual sight). On Mondays, the town's popular market is closed.

Information: The TI is within the Discover Greenwich visitors center, right next to the Cutty Sark entrance (daily 10:00-17:00, Pepys House, 2 Cutty Sark Gardens, tel. 0870-608-2000, www.visitgreenwich.org.uk). For more on Discover Greenwich, see the listing later in this chapter.

Tours: Guided city walks, which depart from the TI within Discover Greenwich, offer an overview and go past most of the big sights (£8, daily at 12:15 and 14:15, 1.5 hours; the only sights you enter are the Painted Hall and Chapel of Sts. Peter and Paul, and only on the 14:15 tour; the 12:15 tour leaves you at the door of the Naval Observatory).

Picnicking: Greenwich's parks are picnic-perfect. Gather picnic supplies before heading up the hill to the National Maritime Museum and observatory. The colorful **Greenwich Market,** just down the street from the DLR station, hosts food stalls (described later, under "Markets"). **Marks & Spencer Simply Food** sells ready-made lunches (between the DLR station and the *Cutty Sark* at 55 Greenwich Church Street).

Pub Grub: Greenwich has almost 100 pubs, with some boasting that they're mere milliseconds from the prime meridian. **Meantime The Old Brewery,** in the Discover Greenwich center, is a gastropub decorated with all things beer. An adjacent café serves cheap lunches. A brewery on this site once provided the daily ration of four pints of beer for pensioners at the hospital. Today it's a microbrewery offering 50 different beers, while a beer sommelier suggests the right pairings with food on the menu (£4 bar snacks, £12 lunches, at night part of the pub becomes a fancier restaurant with £5-10 starters and £10-

17 main courses; daily 10:00-23:00, lunch 12:00-17:00, dinner from 18:00, tel. 020/3327-1280).

The **Trafalgar Tavern,** with a casual pub and elegant ground-floor dining room, is a historical place for an over-priced meal (£15-22 main courses in restaurant, food served Mon-Sat 12:00-22:00, Sun 12:00-16:00, Park Row, tel. 020/8858-2909).

Markets: Thanks to its markets, Greenwich throbs with brows-ing Londoners on weekends. The **Greenwich Market** is an entertaining mini-Covent Garden, located in the middle of the block between the Cutty Sark DLR station and the Old Royal Naval College—right on your way to the sights (farmers market, arts and crafts, and food stands; open Tue-Sun 10:00-17:30, closed Mon; antiques-only on Thu, www.greenwichmarketlondon.com).

The **Clocktower Market** sells old odds and ends at high prices on Greenwich High Road, near the post office (Sat-Sun and bank holidays only 10:00-17:00, www.clocktowermarket.co.uk).

Exploring Back Streets: Allow time to browse the town. Wander beyond the touristy Church Street and Greenwich High Road to where flower stands spill onto the side streets and antique shops sell brass nautical knickknacks. King William Walk, College Approach, Nelson Road, and Turnpin Lane (all in the vicinity of Greenwich Market) are all worth a look.

Length of This Tour: Allow about two hours simply to stroll the area and enjoy the parks, but add several hours more to enter the sights (figure about an hour for the *Cutty Sark,* 30 minutes for the Royal Naval College, and an hour or two apiece for the National Maritime Museum and the Royal Observatory).

Starring: Glorious parks and stately buildings, maritime history, and the prime meridian.

BACKGROUND

Tudor kings favored the palace at Greenwich. Henry VIII was born here. Later kings commissioned architects Inigo Jones and Christopher Wren to beautify the town and palace, and William and Mary built a grand hospital to care for retired seamen (which later became a college for training naval officers). Today, Green-wich is a pincushion of royal, maritime, and scientific sights from Britain's illustrious past.

The Tour Begins

I've linked Greenwich's major sights with handy walking directions. Each attraction is described in full and rated; you can pick and choose which ones you enter. If you're in a rush, make a beeline to only the sights that interest you.

• *Our first stop is the* Cutty Sark. *If you're arriving by boat, it's right in front of you. If you're coming by DLR, you'll get off at the Cutty Sark stop, exit the station to the left, pass under the brick archway, cross the street, and continue straight ahead one block to the monumental gateway for the Old Royal Naval College complex. The* Cutty Sark *is just inside the gate on the left.*

▲▲Cutty Sark

The Scottish-built *Cutty Sark* was the last of the great China tea clippers and the queen of the seas when first launched in 1869.

She was among the fastest clippers ever built, the culmination of centuries of ship design. With 32,000 square feet of sail—and favorable winds—she could travel 300 miles in a day. But as a new century dawned, steamers began to outmatch sailing ships for speed, and by the mid-1920s the *Cutty Sark* was the world's last operating clipper ship. After a stint as a training ship, she was retired and turned into a museum in the 1950s.

Following a five-year-long restoration, interrupted by a devastating fire, the ship reopened to the public in the spring of 2012. The spectacular new display space has one major drawback: The glass building obscures the elegant lines of the hull that gave the *Cutty Sark* her record-breaking speed (one critic groused that the ship now "looks like it has run aground in a giant greenhouse"). On the plus side, the building allows visitors to walk directly below the ship, which has been raised 11 feet above her dry dock. Above deck, the ship's rigging has been restored to original specifications, while below deck, displays explore the *Cutty Sark*'s 140-year history and the cargo she carried—everything from tea to wool to gunpowder—as she raced between London and ports all around the world.

Cost and Hours: £13.50, includes voluntary 10 percent donation, kids aged 5-15-£7, free for kids under age 5, family tickets available; daily 10:00-17:00, may stay open until 18:00 during school holidays; last entry one hour before closing; £5 guidebook available but hardly necessary, reservation tel. 020/8312-6608, www.rmg.co.uk/cuttysark.

GREENWICH

GREENWICH

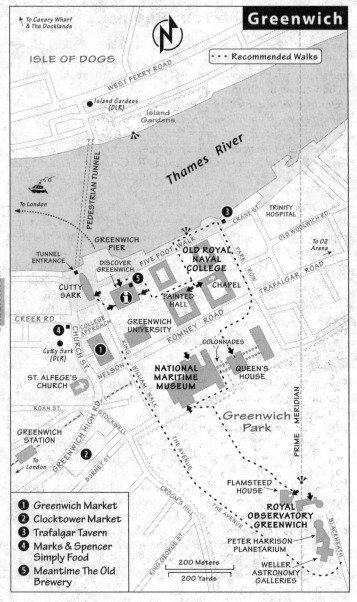

Greenwich

To Canary Wharf
& The Docklands

ISLE OF DOGS

WEST FERRY ROAD

- - - Recommended Walks

Island Gardens
(DLR)

Island
Gardens

Thames River

To London

PEDESTRIAN TUNNEL

TRINITY
HOSPITAL

OLD WOOLWICH RD

To O2
Arena

GREENWICH
PIER

CRANE ST

❸

FIVE FOOT WALK

PARK ROW

TRAFALGAR ROAD

TUNNEL
ENTRANCE

DISCOVER
GREENWICH

OLD ROYAL
NAVAL
COLLEGE

CUTTY
SARK

❺

CHAPEL

PAINTED
HALL

CREEK RD.

❹

COLLEGE APPROACH

CHURCH ST.

GREENWICH
UNIVERSITY

ROMNEY ROAD

Cutty Sark
(DLR)

❶

KING WILLIAM WALK

NELSON

COLONNADES

ST. ALFEGE'S
CHURCH

NATIONAL
MARITIME
MUSEUM

QUEEN'S
HOUSE

ROAN ST.

GREENWICH
STATION

GREENWICH HIGH RD

STOCKWELL

Greenwich
Park

PRIME MERIDIAN

To
London

❷

BURNEY ST.

THE AVENUE

FLAMSTEED
HOUSE

❶ Greenwich Market
❷ Clocktower Market
❸ Trafalgar Tavern
❹ Marks & Spencer
   Simply Food
❺ Meantime The Old
   Brewery

CROOM'S HILL

THE AVENUE

ROYAL
OBSERVATORY
GREENWICH

BLACKHEATH

PETER HARRISON
PLANETARIUM

KING GEORGE ST.

200 Meters

200 Yards

WELLER
ASTRONOMY
GALLERIES

Crowd-Beating Tips: The ship can get busy on school holidays and on weekends. To skip the line, you can reserve ahead online or by phone, or just try showing up around 13:00, when there's often a lull in visitors.

Visiting the *Cutty Sark:* The first deck you'll visit harkens back to the ship's days in the Chinese tea trade...which didn't last long, as the Suez Canal soon opened, allowing steam-powered ships to reach China much faster than sailboats. The *Cutty Sark* turned to trading wool with Australia, as explored on the next deck up. This "Tween Deck" is full of not-quite-gimmicky displays that mostly succeed in making the ship's history come alive, even for adults. Find the fun video game that lets you attempt to beat Captain Woodget's record voyage sailing a wool-laden *Sark* from Sydney to London. Sit on the tilting benches of tea crates for a seaborne feel, try your hand at some knots, enjoy the oddly mesmerizing video at the stern, and get the figurehead's take on *Sark* history in the bow.

Sailing fans will like the gorgeously restored top deck best. Notice how pathetic the crew's mattresses were, and don't miss the video showing the rigger's-eye-view as he climbs high above the deck. Your visit ends down below, where you can take a coffee break directly under the shiny stern (it may gleam like gold, but the hull's covering is actually an alloy of copper and zinc). Near the bow is a colorful collection of figureheads from other ships, and a great photo op from the top of the stairs. On the floor directly under the front of the hull, note the compass rose that shows how many days at sea it'd take to reach major ports from here.

• *Leaving the museum, head straight across the path through a gate in the fence to the visitors center called...*

Discover Greenwich

While it's hardly a museum, this center offers a decent introduction to Greenwich and some fun exhibits for kids. In the middle, a model of the town lights up to tell its history. Surrounding the model are displays and artifacts from various people who have left their mark on the town, along with exhibits about the architecture and construction of Greenwich's fine buildings. Tours of the Royal Naval College leave from the reception desk. Adjoining Discover Greenwich are the TI and a recommended pub, Meantime The Old Brewery.

Cost and Hours: Free, daily 10:00-17:00, tel. 020/8269-4799, www.ornc.org.

• *Leave through the front or side exits, and walk away from the* Cutty Sark, *continuing through the manicured park to the dramatic identical-twin buildings that make up the heart of the...*

GREENWICH

▲Old Royal Naval College

The college was originally a hospital founded by Queen Mary II and King William III in 1692 as a charity to care for retired or injured naval officers (called pensioners). William and Mary spared no expense, hiring the great Christopher Wren to design the complex (though other architects completed it). Its days as a hospital ended in 1869, and it served as a college for training naval officers from 1873 to 1998. Now that the Royal Navy has moved out, the public is invited to view the college's elaborate Painted Hall and Chapel of Sts. Peter and Paul, which are in symmetrical buildings that face each other overlooking a broad riverfront park.

Cost and Hours: Free, daily 10:00-17:00, sometimes closed for private events, service Sun at 11:00 in chapel—all are welcome, www.ornc.org.

Tours: Guides give one-hour tours covering the hall and chapel, along with other areas not open to the general public (£6, daily at 12:00, departs from Discover Greenwich, call ahead to check availability, tel. 020/8269-4799).

◑ Self-Guided Tour: Each building sells a descriptive guide (50p-£1), or you can buy the fun *Nasty Naval College* brochure (made for children, but with entertaining offbeat facts about the place; £1). Volunteers are often standing by to answer questions. Visit the highlight—the Painted Hall—first, before touring the chapel.

GREENWICH

Painted Hall

Originally intended as a dining hall for pensioners, this sumptuously painted room was deemed too glorious (and, in the winter, too cold) for that purpose. So almost as soon as it was completed, it became simply a place to impress visitors.

Enter the hall, climb the stairs, and gape up at one of the largest painted ceilings in Europe—112 feet long. It's a big propaganda scene, glorifying the building's founders, Queen Mary II and King William III (who, as a Protestant monarch, had recently trounced the Catholic French King Louis XIV in a pivotal battle). Crane your neck—

or use the clever wheeled mirrors—to examine the scene. In the center are William and Mary. Under his foot, William is crushing a dark figure with a broken sword...Louis XIV. William is handing a red cap (representing liberty) to the woman on the right, who holds the reins of a white horse (symbolizing Europe). On the left, a white-robed woman hands him an olive branch, a sign of peace. The message: William has granted Europe liberty by saving it from the tyranny of Louis XIV. Below the royal couple, the Spirit of Architecture shows them the plans for this very building (commemorating the sad fact that Mary died before its completion). Ringing the central image are the four seasons (represented by Zodiac signs), the four virtues, and—at the top and bottom—a captured Spanish galleon and a British man-of-war battleship.

Up the steps at the end of the room, along the wall of the upper hall, is a portrait of the family of King George I. On the right is the artist who spent 19 years of his life painting this hall, James Thornhill (he finally finished it in 1727). He's holding out his hand—reportedly, he didn't feel he was paid enough for this Sistine-sized undertaking.

• *Exit the hall, and cross the field to enter the...*

Chapel of Sts. Peter and St. Paul

Not surprisingly, you'll sense a nautical air in this fine chapel. Notice the rope motif in the floor tiles down the aisle. The painting above the altar, by American Benjamin West, depicts the shipwreck of St. Paul on the island of Malta. According to the Bible, Paul disturbed a poisonous viper but managed to throw it in

a fire, miraculously without being harmed. Soon after the chapel was completed, it was gutted by a fire and had to be redecorated all over again. The plans were too ambitious, so the designers cut corners. Some of the columns and capitals are fake, and the "sculptures" lining the nave high above are actually trompe l'oeil—3-D paintings meant to look real. But some items, such as the marble frame around the main door, are finely crafted from expensive materials.

• *Leave the chapel, and walk straight down to the water—enjoying the sweeping views across to the Docklands. When you hit the river, turn right for a quick...*

Riverside Stroll

Looking back toward the Old Royal Naval College, notice how it's split into two parts; reportedly, Queen Mary didn't want the view from the Queen's House blocked. The college's twin-domed towers (one giving the time, the other the direction of the wind) frame the Queen's House, and the Royal Observatory Greenwich crowns the hill beyond.

Wander east along the Thames on Five Foot Walk (named for the width of the path). From here you can see the big, white, spiky

O2 dome a mile downstream. This stadium languished for nearly a decade after its controversial construction and brief life as the Millennium Dome. Intended to be a world's fair-type site and the center of London's year 2000 celebration, it ended up as the topic of heated debates about cost overruns and its controversial looks. The site was finally bought by a developer a few years ago and rechristened "The O2" (a telecommunications company paid for the naming rights). Today it hosts sporting events and concerts. Next to the O2 are the towers of the Emirates Air Line aerial gondola, which ferries passengers from the O2 and across the Thames to, essentially, nowhere.

Continuing downstream, just outside the fenced college grounds, you'll find the recommended **Trafalgar Tavern.** Dickens

knew the pub well, and he used it as the setting for the wedding breakfast in *Our Mutual Friend.* Built in 1837 in the Regency style to attract Londoners downriver, the upstairs Nelson Room is still used for weddings. Its formal moldings and elegant windows with balconies over the Thames are a step back in time and worth a peek.

• *From the Trafalgar Tavern, walk two long blocks up Park Row. After crossing busy Romney Road, turn right (through the gate near the corner) into the park. The palatial buildings in the middle of the park are the Queen's House and the National Maritime Museum; the Royal Observatory Greenwich is on the hilltop beyond. Together, this trio is known as the Royal Museums of Greenwich.*

Queen's House

This building, the first Palladian-style villa in Britain, was designed in 1616 by Inigo Jones for James I's wife, Anne of Denmark. All traces of the queen are long gone, and the Great Hall and Royal

Apartments now serve as an art gallery for the National Maritime Museum. Predictably, most of the art is nautical-themed, with plenty of paintings of ships and sea battles, and portraits of admirals and captains. Among these is the great J. M. W. Turner painting *The Battle of Trafalgar* (1824), the artist's only royal commission. The painting is often out on loan, so ask at the entry before you look for it. If you're short on time or energy, skip this sight.

Cost and Hours: Free, daily 10:00-17:00, tel. 020/8858-4422, www.rmg.co.uk.

Tours: Skip the free (and outdated) audioguide and instead ask about the daily tour (free, 2-3/day).

• *Exiting the Queen's House, walk toward the hill, pass through a colon-nade, and turn right. About 300 yards farther on, you'll see a giant ship in a bottle and the...*

▲National Maritime Museum

Great for anyone interested in the sea, this museum holds everything from a giant working paddlewheel to the uniform Admiral

Horatio Nelson wore when he was killed at Trafalgar (look for the bullet hole, in the left shoulder). A big glass roof tops three levels of slick, modern, kid-friendly exhibits about all things seafaring.

The Explorers exhibit covers early expeditions and an ill-fated Arctic trip, complete with a soundtrack of creaking wooden ships and crashing waves. One room displays stained-glass windows honoring members of London's Baltic Exchange (an important shipping consortium) killed in World War I, while the somber Atlantic Worlds hall thoughtfully describes how the movements of goods, ideas, and enslaved people shaped the 17th to 19th centuries. Kids like the All Hands and Bridge galleries, where they can send secret messages by Morse code and operate a miniature dockside crane. Along with displays of lighthouse technology and a whaling cannon, you'll see model ships, nautical paintings, and various salty odds and ends.

Cost and Hours: Free, daily 10:00-17:00, last entry 30 minutes before closing, tel. 020/8858-4422, www.rmg.co.uk. The museum hosts frequent family-oriented events—singing, treasure hunts, and storytelling—particularly on weekends; ask at the desk. Inside, listen for announcements alerting visitors to free tours on various topics.

• *The final sight in town—the Royal Observatory Greenwich—is at the top of the hill just behind the National Maritime Museum. To reach it,*

The Longitude Problem

Around 1700, as the ships of seafaring nations began to venture farther from their home bases, the alarming increase in the number of shipwrecks made it clear that navigational tools had to be improved. Determining latitude—the relative position between the equator and the North or South Pole—was straightforward; sailors needed only to measure the angle of the sun at noon. But figuring out longitude, or their east-west position, was not as easy without a fixed point (such as the equator) from which to measure.

In 1714, the British government offered the £20,000 Longitude Prize. Two successful solutions emerged, and both are tied to Greenwich.

The first approach was to observe the position of the moon, which moves in relation to the stars. Sailors would compare the night sky they saw with the sky over Greenwich by consulting a book of tables prepared by Greenwich astronomers. This told them how far they were from Greenwich—their longitude. Visitors to the Royal Observatory can still see the giant telescopes—under retractable roofs—that were used to carefully chart the heavens to create these meticulous tables.

The second approach was to create a clock that would remain completely accurate on voyages—no easy feat back then, when turbulence and changes in weather and humidity made timepieces notoriously unreliable at sea. John Harrison spent 45 years working on this problem, finally succeeding in 1760 with his fourth effort, the H4 (which won him the Longitude Prize). All four of his attempts are on display at the Royal Observatory.

So, how can a clock determine longitude? Every 15° of longitude equals an hour when comparing the difference in sunrise or sunset times between two places. For example, the time gap between Greenwich and New York City is five hours, which translates into a longitudinal difference of 75°. Equipped with an accurate timepiece set to Greenwich Mean Time, sailors could figure out their longitude by comparing sunset time at their current position with sunset time back in Greenwich.

Notice that both approaches use Greenwich as a baseline—either on an astral map or on a clock. That's why, to this day, the prime meridian and official world time are both centered in this unassuming London suburb.

exit the Maritime Museum and follow signs leading you to a tree-lined uphill path, then follow the crowds as they huff up the steep hill (allow 10–15 minutes).

As you hike up, look along the observatory's roof for the red **Time Ball** *(also visible from the Thames), which drops daily at 13:00.*

▲▲Royal Observatory Greenwich

Located on the prime meridian (0° longitude), the observatory is famous as the point from which all time is measured. The observatory's early work, however, had nothing to do with coordinating the world's clocks to Greenwich Mean Time (GMT). The observatory was founded in 1675 by King Charles II for the purpose of improving navigation by more accurately charting the night sky. Today, the Greenwich time signal is linked with the BBC (which broadcasts the famous "pips" worldwide at the top of the hour). A visit here gives you a taste of the sciences of astronomy, timekeeping, and seafaring—and how they all meld together—along with great views over Greenwich and the distant London skyline. The Royal Observatory grounds are made up of the observatory (with the prime meridian and three worthy exhibits), the Weller Astronomy Galleries, and the Peter Harrison Planetarium.

If your only interest in the Royal Observatory is the famous prime meridian line, you can go through the iron gate near the entrance for a free, more simplistic (and significantly less crowded) display of the prime meridian. Under the analog clock just outside the courtyard, see how your foot measures up to the foot where the public standards of length are cast in bronze.

Observatory: £7, £11.50 combo-ticket with planetarium saves money if you visit both; daily 10:00-17:00, later in summer, last entry 30 minutes before closing; audioguide-£3.50, 1 hour.

Weller Astronomy Galleries: Free, daily 10:00-17:00, last entry 30 minutes before closing.

Peter Harrison Planetarium: £6.50, £11.50 combo-ticket with observatory; 30-minute shows generally run every hour (usually Mon-Fri 13:00-16:00, Sat-Sun 11:00-16:00, fewer in winter). Confirm times in advance by phone or online, or by picking up a flier at the observatory. As these shows can sell out, consider calling ahead to order tickets. Most shows are family-oriented, with early shows intended for young children.

Information: Tel. 020/8858-4422, www.rmg.co.uk.

➜ **Self-Guided Tour:** Entering the complex, you're directed either to the observatory entrance or the Weller Astronomy Galleries. Since the ob-

GREENWICH

servatory is more interesting, do that first (but note that the Weller Galleries won't let you in after 16:30).

• *After purchasing your ticket, enter the courtyard.*

Running through the middle of this space is The Line—the **prime meridian.** Visitors wait patiently to have their photographs

taken as they straddle the line in front of the monument, with one foot in each hemisphere. While watching all this fuss over a little line, consider that— unlike the equator—the placement of the prime meridian is totally arbitrary. It could well have been at my house, in Timbuktu, or just a few feet over—as, for a time, it was (the trough along the building's roofline shows where one as- tronomer had placed it).

Three different attractions are scat- tered around this courtyard. First, hiding in a corner is a **camera obscura.** This thrillingly low-tech device projects a live image from Greenwich onto a flat disc in a darkened room simply by manipu- lating light, without electricity or machinery (although the image can be pretty dim on cloudy days). Imagine how astonishing it was in the days before television.

The smaller building is the **Flamsteed House,** named for John Flamsteed, the first king-appointed Astronomer Royal (in 1675). It contains the apartments that he lived in and the Wren-designed Octagon Room, where he carried out some of his work. Down- stairs is a fascinating exhibit on the "Longitude Problem" and how it was solved (see sidebar). Also on display are all four of John Har- rison's sea clocks. Compared to his other contraptions, the fourth and final attempt looks like an oversized pocket watch. But, in terms of its impact, this little timepiece is right up there with the printing press, the cotton gin, the telegraph, and the money belt on the scale of human achievement.

The **Meridian Building,** in the larger house, has a wide as- sortment of historical telescopes, including a room-sized one de- signed by George Airy that was used to define the prime meridian. Watch the video (in the back corner of this room) of the telescope

in action. If the meridian was too crowded outside, you can straddle it when you walk around this tele- scope. Upstairs from the gift shop, a skippable exhibit explores the role of timekeeping in our society.

• *Now head out back.*

Walk past the giant rusted-copper cone top of the planetarium. The building beyond houses the **Weller Astronomy Galleries,** where interactive, kid-pleasing displays allow you to guide a space mission and touch a 4.5-billion-year-old meteorite. You can also buy tickets for and enter the state-of-the-art, 120-seat **Peter Harrison Planetarium** from here.

Before you leave the observatory grounds, enjoy the **view** from the overlook—the symmetrical royal buildings, the Thames, and the Docklands and its busy cranes (including the prominent Canary Wharf Tower, with its pyramid cap). You may be able to see—poking up between buildings—the white stadium and red Orbit tower in Queen Elizabeth Olympic Park. To the right is the

huge O2 dome and the towers of the Emirates Air Line gondola. To the left lies the square-mile City of London, with skyscrapers and the dome of St. Paul's Cathedral. The Shard is to the far left. At night (17:00-24:00), look for the green laser beam the observatory projects into the sky (best viewed in winter), which extends along the prime meridian for 15 miles.

• *Our tour through Greenwich is finished. Enjoy the views from this hilltop perch, then wander back down through the parklands and town to the river, where you can catch a boat or DLR train back to downtown London. If you have time, on your way back, remember that it's easy to hop off the DLR for a quick visit to the Docklands; for details, just turn the page.*

THE DOCKLANDS WALK

Survey London's skyline (or a Tube map), and it becomes clear that London is shifting east. The thundering heart of this new London is the Docklands. Nestled around a hairpin bend in the Thames, this area was London's harbor and warehouse district back in the 19th century, when Britannia ruled the waves. Today it's been gentrified into a futuristic, skyscraper-filled landscape rising from the canals and docks.

The heart of the Docklands is the Isle of Dogs, a marshy peninsula in the river's curve. From the Isle rises the 800-foot-tall Canary Wharf Tower (officially the "One Canada Square" building), which is surrounded by a cluster of other office buildings.

Don't expect Jolly Olde England here. The Docklands is more about businessmen in suits, creatively planned parks, art-filled plazas, and trendy cafés. But there are also traces of its rugged dock-worker past. You'll see canals, former docks, brick warehouses, and a fine history museum. Most impressive of all, there's not a tourist in sight.

If your London visit is brief and focused on the big, famous sights, the Docklands is not worth a special trip. But if you're visiting nearby Greenwich, it's very easy to add on a quick peek at the Docklands (which you'll pass by—or under—as you travel to Greenwich anyway). You can also combine the Docklands with a quick look at London's newest park, Queen Elizabeth Olympic Park, to the north.

If you want to say you've seen today's London, visit the Docklands.

Orientation

Length of This Walk: 1.5 hours, including museum tour.

When to Go: As it's now a financial district, the Docklands bustles only on weekdays. (On weekends, it can either be laid-back and festive if it's sunny, or empty and dead if rainy.)

Ideally time your visit here for late afternoon on a week-day, when the area is enlivened by business workers headed for happy hour. But don't wait too long—the fine museum at the end of this walk closes at 18:00. To catch the *après*-work bustle, and still make it to the museum before last-entry time at 17:30, I'd aim to begin this walk by 16:00. (If the museum interests you most, you could either start the walk earlier or make a beeline to the museum.)

Getting There: This walk starts at the Canary Wharf Tube sta-tion. You can get there via the Tube, Docklands Light Railway (DLR), or boat.

By Tube: Take the Jubilee Line to the Canary Wharf sta-tion (15 minutes from Westminster, frequent departures).

By Docklands Light Railway (DLR): If you're returning from Greenwich, the DLR's the way to go (described later). If you're coming from central London, though, it's usually easier to take the Tube, unless you're already near a DLR stop (the Bank/Monument stops are the most central).

By Boat: Catch the Thames Clippers boat from central London (£6.50 one-way, £15 all-day pass, discounts with Travelcard or Oyster Card; boats leave every 20-30 minutes from major London docks; 10-30-minute trip). You arrive at Canary Wharf Pier, a 10-minute walk straight ahead on West India Avenue to the heart of the Docklands.

Combining the Docklands with Greenwich or Queen Eliza-beth Olympic Park: All three places lie along the north-south DLR train line, a few minutes apart. You could sightsee Greenwich in the morning and early afternoon, then make a brief stop at the Docklands on your way back to central Lon-don. Or, to reach Greenwich from the Docklands, hop a DLR train bound for Greenwich or Lewisham, then get off at the Cutty Sark station (for Greenwich coverage, see the previous chapter).

To reach Queen Elizabeth Olympic Park (described on page 103), catch a DLR train heading north toward Stratford and get off at the Pudding Mill Lane DLR stop (about 10 minutes).

Shopping and Eating: Three different subterranean shopping malls all flow into each other via underground corridors. There's Cabot Place shopping mall (enter at Cabot Square), the

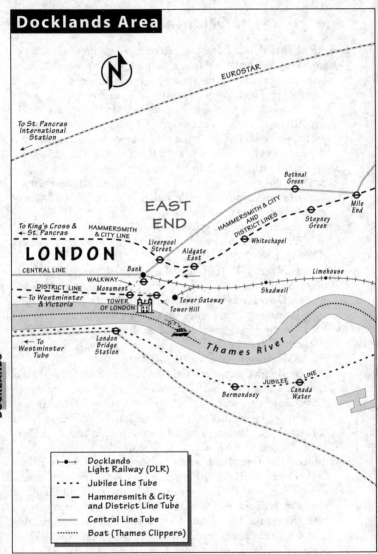

Docklands Area

EUROSTAR

To St. Pancras
International
Station

Bethnal
Green

EAST
END

HAMMERSMITH & CITY
AND
DISTRICT LINES

Mile
End

To King's Cross &
← St. Pancras

HAMMERSMITH
& CITY LINE

Stepney
Green

LONDON

Liverpool
Street

Whitechapel

CENTRAL LINE

Aldgate
East

Bank

Limehouse

WALKWAY

DISTRICT LINE

Monument

Shadwell

← To Westminster
& Victoria

TOWER
OF LONDON

Tower Gateway
Tower Hill

To
Westminster
Tube

London
Bridge
Station

Thames River

JUBILEE LINE

Bermondsey

Canada
Water

Legend:

|—•—| Docklands
Light Railway (DLR)

- - - Jubilee Line Tube

– – – Hammersmith & City
and District Line Tube

——— Central Line Tube

.... Boat (Thames Clippers)

DOCKLANDS

mall beneath Canary Wharf Tower, and Jubilee Place (enter from Jubilee Place Park).

Waterside restaurants abound—at the West India Dock, along Mackenzie Walk, and elsewhere. Or enjoy a picnic in Jubilee Place Park (delis and sandwich shops abound).

Safety and Services: Despite its rough past, the area we'll visit is now very safe and clean (almost sterile). Public WCs are plentiful in the malls.

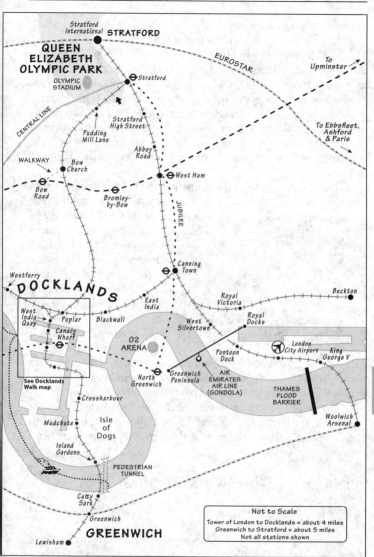

OVERVIEW

Centuries ago, this end of town was notorious for its smelly industries (bone boiling, glue making, chemical works). It was conveniently downwind from the rest of London. By the late 1700s, 13,000 ships a year were loaded and unloaded in central London, congesting the Thames. So in 1802, the world's largest-of-its-kind harbor was built in the Docklands, organizing shipping for the capital of the empire upon which the sun never set. When Britannia ruled the waves, the Isle of Dogs hosted the world's leading harbor, with direct connections to the North Sea.

After being destroyed by Nazi bombers during World War II, the Docklands struggled for several decades and never regained its status as a port. With the advent of container shipping in the 1960s, London's shipping industry moved farther east, to deep-water docks. The old Docklands became a derelict and dangerous wasteland. Until a generation ago, local surveys ranked it as one of the least desirable places to call home. It's said that for every Tube stop you lived east of central London, your life expectancy dropped one year.

But all of this misfortune paid off in the 1980s, when investors realized that the Docklands was ripe for redevelopment...the per-

fect place to host a new and vibrant economic center. Over the past few decades, Britain's new Information Age industries—banking, finance, publishing, and media—have vacated downtown London and set up shop here. You'll still see remnants of the past—those 1802 West India warehouses survive, but rather than trading sugar and rum, today they house the excellent Museum of London Docklands and a row of happening restaurants.

Our walk takes us from the heart of the modern Docklands (the plaza by the Canary Wharf Tower and Tube stop), through some pleasant squares, and ends at the Museum of London Docklands.

The Walk Begins

• *Start at the Canary Wharf Tube station. If arriving by Tube, ride up the escalators to the west exit.*

If arriving on the DLR: From any of the six platforms, go down the escalator one level towards Cabot Place East, walk straight through this shopping mall, then walk through the One Canada Square office building, veering right as you exit the revolving doors.

Either way, you'll wind up in...

❶ Canada Square

Stand in the square and take it all in. You're surrounded by towering skyscrapers, three glitzy shopping malls, lively cafés, and hurried businesspeople.

Standing in this busy square, it can seem like continual rush hour—with the young high-tech workforce coursing through the battery of turnstiles. Flash back 200 years, to this area's heyday as a shipping harbor. "Canary Wharf"—the name for the whole neighborhood—is a reminder of the trading connection London had with distant ports such as the Canary Islands, off the western coast of Africa. Where sailors once drank grog while stevedores unloaded cargo, today thousands of office workers (the stevedores of the Information Age) populate a forest of skyscrapers, towering high above the remnants of the Industrial Age.

• *Of the many skyscrapers, the tallest one, in the center, is...*

❷ One Canada Square (a.k.a. Canary Wharf Tower)

The 800-foot, 50-story building is known throughout London for its distinctive pyramid cap. (You can't see the top from this angle—we'll get views later.) Once the tallest building in the UK, and, for a time, in Europe, it was topped by The Shard in 2012.

Canary Wharf Tower is filled with big banks and financial and media companies. The plaza just under it has a playful display of clocks on lampposts. If you like modern art, enter the lobby from street level and poke around to see what's on display. Flanking skyscrapers are owned by HSBC (Hong Kong Shanghai Banking Corporation) and Citigroup.

• *Behind the Tube station is a grassy park. You can reach it by a path to the right of the Tube entrance.*

❸ Jubilee Place Park

Opened in 2002 on the 50th anniversary ("Golden Jubilee") of Queen Elizabeth's rule, this delightful little park is an example of how the new Canary Wharf was designed with a futuristic people-friendliness. Workers and residents enjoy plenty of green spaces, waterways, public art, and good public-transit service. The entire ensemble sits upon an underground shopping mall. (The entrance to the mall is in the middle of the park.) Stroll through the park past meandering fountains and outdoor art.

• *Return to Canada Square. Head south (directly away from Canary Wharf Tower),*

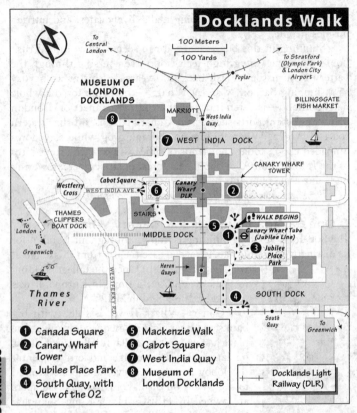

Docklands Walk

MUSEUM OF LONDON DOCKLANDS

To Central London

100 Meters
100 Yards

To Stratford (Olympic Park) & London City Airport

Poplar

MARRIOTT

West India Quay

7 WEST INDIA DOCK

BILLINGSGATE FISH MARKET

8

CANARY WHARF TOWER

Westferry Cross

Cabot Square

WEST INDIA AVE.

6

Canary Wharf DLR

2

THAMES CLIPPERS BOAT DOCK

STAIRS

MIDDLE DOCK

5

1

● WALK BEGINS

To London

To Greenwich

Canary Wharf Tube (Jubilee Line)

3 Jubilee Place Park

Heron Quays

WESTFERRY RD.

4

SOUTH DOCK

Thames River

South Quay

To Greenwich

1	Canada Square	**5**	Mackenzie Walk
2	Canary Wharf Tower	**6**	Cabot Square
3	Jubilee Place Park	**7**	West India Quay
4	South Quay, with View of the O2	**8**	Museum of London Docklands

Docklands Light Railway (DLR)

DOCKLANDS

pass through the glassy building, and exit at the far end. Cross the canal over the curvy, modernistic footbridge, reaching the...

❹ South Quay, with View of the O2

Gazing across the water, in the distance, you see Greenwich. The prickly white dome pierced with crane-like projections is the O2 (a.k.a. "the Dome," described on page 359), a costly and long-unpopular edifice that's now primarily the locus of sports matches, arena concerts, and Londoners' habitual disdain.

• *Return to Canada Square. Once there, face the water (so that Canary Wharf Tower is to your right). Start walking along the right side of the canal, along the promenade called...*

❺ Mackenzie Walk

Stroll along the canal, called Middle Dock, past All Bar One and

other inviting eateries, and under the train bridge. The canal is a surviving remnant of the many artificial harbors and canals from the Docklands' 19th-century shipping heyday. The land here on the Isle of Dogs was marshy, flooded by the Thames, and unsuitable for farming or habitation. But it was perfect for accommodating large seagoing vessels. Beginning around 1800, industrious Londoners channeled the water into canals and lined them with docks. Picture the lively scene: burly men off-loading goods from ships at anchor, while an army of poor laborers bustled between storage warehouses, dry docks for ship repair, and various ship-building enterprises. Each dock specialized in a particular product to ship—spices, coal, whatever. By the mid-1800s, the Docklands had siphoned away shipping from London's traditional port (near London Bridge) and was the world's busiest port.

• *Cross under the DLR bridge and keep going. When you reach the arched footbridge, turn right, passing a sculpture of two figures sitting on a bench, and hike up Cubitt Steps, into...*

❻ Cabot Square

Enjoy the square's big fountain and views of domineering skyscrapers. From the west (left) end of the square, you have the iconic photo-op of Canary Wharf Tower with the fountain in the foreground. Many newlyweds come here for their wedding photos.

• *Exit the square at the north side (near another sculpture couple), where steps lead down to a footbridge that crosses another canal to the...*

❼ West India Quay

This row of 19th-century brown-brick warehouses typifies today's Docklands. Standing side by side are elements of the old Docklands (the warehouses, canal, a few barges) and the new (the esplanade of umbrella-shaded restaurants, the futuristic Marriott skyscraper). Back in the 19th century, the water originally lapped up right against those buildings. You can still see the rustic gates to the lofts. Imagine heavily laden cargo boats off-loading there.

The Docklands thrived as a shipping port until the mid-20th century; two big gray cranes-on-tracks are reminders of the two events that eventually doomed the area. First, the Blitz of World War II obliterated the Docklands—it was hit by more than 2,000 bombs. Of course, Hitler's aim was to wipe out this vital industrial area.

Though it survived the Blitz, the Docklands couldn't survive the next hit—when the shipping industry converted to containers. The large container ships couldn't make it this far up the shallow Thames, and almost overnight, the industry rapidly shifted to seaports. In the 1970s, the Docklands became London's poorest area.
• *In the left part of the row of warehouses you'll find the...*

❽ Museum of London Docklands

This modern and interesting museum, which fills an old sugar warehouse, gives the Docklands historic context. In telling the story of the world's leading 19th-century port, it also conveys the story of London. It has a nice café, a hip bar, and a great kids' play area. Ride the elevator up to the third floor, then work your way down, going on a 2,000-year walk through the story of commerce on the Thames.

Cost and Hours: Free, daily 10:00-18:00, last entry 30 minutes before closing

Visiting the Museum: Start on the **third floor,** in old London, back when London's port was at London Bridge, and the Docklands was a barely inhabited swamp far to the east. You'll see fascinating models of Old London Bridge, crammed with little houses and shops—not unlike how Florence's Ponte Vecchio still looks.

Continuing on, exhibits show how the Docklands rapidly developed in the 1800s. A reconstruction of a "Legal Quay," where cargo was processed, has a life-size mannequin in a hamster-wheel contraption used for lifting cargo from ships. Displays show the brutality of punishment in those days: Executed pirates were displayed publicly, suspended in metal cages called "gibbets." The next, thought-provoking section analyzes the connection between sugar and slavery—a frank and sober look at the terrible human toll taken by several centuries of transatlantic trade.

The **second floor** explores London's growth after 1800—its population was more than one million by 1810. Stroll through a gritty reconstruction of "Sailortown," listening to the salty voices of those who lived and worked in quarters like this. A painted *Stevedores* banner from the 1889 Dock Strike is a reminder that while the Industrial Revolution first exploited workers, it later provoked them to rise up. During World War II, the Docklands was a prime target for Nazi bombers bent on crippling British shipping. Find the claustrophobic, dome-shaped "consul shelter," where dock-workers could take cover in case of attack. There's also a re-creation of the fuel pipeline that was laid under the English Channel to supply the Allies on the Continent.

The final section, "New Port, New City," traces the Dock-lands' post-WWII rebuilding. In the 1980s, a combination of government and private investors remade the area into an office zone. The area has prospered, but not without controversy—there's still tension between the yuppie newcomers and the blue-collar old-timers.

When you're finished, step out into today's Docklands and take in this combination of old and new.

• *Our walk is over. You have several options from here:*

Return to Central London: *The Tube is your fastest way back into the city—to take it, you can retrace your steps to the Canary Wharf Tube*

station and catch the Jubilee line. Depending on where you're going in London, it may be more convenient to head to the other end of the West India Quay to catch the DLR there (stop: West India Quay), and get off at Bank, where you can transfer to the Tube's Central line.

To catch a boat (slower but very scenic), return to Cabot Square, turn right, and walk five minutes along West India Avenue to the round Westferry Circus park; the Thames Clippers dock is just beyond (see "Orientation" at the top of this chapter).

Visiting Greenwich or Queen Elizabeth Olympic Park: *Catch a DLR train south to Greenwich or north to the Olympic Park.*

Riding the Emirates Air Line Gondola: *The much-hyped aerial gondola makes a pointless trip across the Thames between the O2 dome and what has to be London's least-interesting district. There's not much to see from here, but the ride itself is a thrill, reasonably priced, and easily tacked on to a day of Docklands sightseeing.*

To reach the gondola, take the Jubilee Line from Canary Wharf one stop to North Greenwich Pier. Above ground, follow signs to Air Emirates (about 5 minutes away). The ride costs £3.20 with an Oyster card (otherwise £4.40); you can head right to the turnstiles if you have enough credit on your Oyster card. The gondola ride itself is a 10-minute dangle 300 feet above the Thames that lands you at the Royal Docks station.

From there it's a two-minute walk to the Royal Victoria DLR station; ride one stop (on either line) to Canning Town. From Canning Town, you can hop a Bank-bound train back to central London.

DOCKLANDS

SLEEPING IN LONDON

Contents

I favor hotels and restaurants that are handy to your sightseeing activities. I've chosen several favorite neighborhoods (Victoria Station, South Kensington, Bayswater, Notting Hill, and Paddington Station, among others) and recommend the best accommodations values for each, from dorm beds to fancy doubles with all of the comforts. I've also listed big, good-value, modern hotels scattered throughout London, along with hostels, dorms, and apartment rentals.

    London is an expensive city for lodging. Cheaper rooms are relatively dumpy. Don't expect £130 cheeriness in a £70 room. For £70, you'll get a double with breakfast in a safe, cramped, and dreary place with minimal service and the bathroom down the hall. For £90, you'll get a basic, clean, reasonably cheery double with a private bath in a usually cramped, cracked-plaster building, or a soulless but comfortable room without breakfast in a huge Motel 6-type place. My London splurges, at £160-290, are spacious, thoughtfully appointed places good for entertaining or romancing.

    A major feature of this book is its extensive and opinionated

Sleep Code

£1 = about $1.60, country code: 44, area code: 020

Price Rankings

To help you easily sort through my listings, I've divided the accommodations into three categories based on the highest price for a double room with bath during high season:

$$$ **Higher Priced**—Most rooms £125 or more.

$$ **Moderately Priced**—Most rooms between £75-125.

$ **Lower Priced**—Most rooms £75 or less.

I always rate hostels as $, whether or not they have double rooms, because they have the cheapest beds in town.

Prices can change without notice; verify the hotel's current rates online or by email. For the best prices, always book directly with the hotel.

Abbreviations

To pack maximum information into minimum space, I use the following code to describe accommodations in this book. Prices are listed per room, not per person. When a price range is given for a type of room (such as double rooms listing for £80-120), it means the price fluctuates with the season, size of room, or length of stay; expect to pay the upper end for peak-season stays.

S = Single room (or price for one person in a double).

D = Double or twin room. "Double beds" can be two twins sheeted together and are usually big enough for non-romantic couples.

T = Triple (generally a double bed with a single).

Q = Quad (usually two double beds; adding an extra child's bed to a T is usually cheaper).

b = Private bathroom with toilet and shower or tub.

s = Private shower or tub only (the toilet is down the hall).

According to this code, a couple staying at a "Db-£90" hotel would pay a total of £90 (about $144) per night for a double room with a private bathroom. Unless otherwise noted, breakfast is included and credit cards are accepted. For most places, the rates I list include the 20 percent VAT tax—but it's smart to ask when you book your room.

There's almost always Wi-Fi and/or a guest computer available, either free or for a fee.

SLEEPING

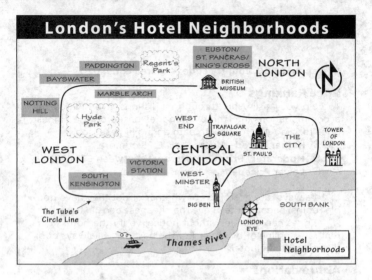

listing of good-value rooms. I like places that are clean, central, relatively quiet at night, reasonably priced, friendly, small enough to have a hands-on owner and stable staff, run with a respect for British traditions, and not listed in other guidebooks. (In London, for me, meeting six out of these eight criteria means it's a keeper.) I'm more impressed by a convenient location and a fun-loving philosophy than flat-screen TVs and a pricey laundry service.

Book your accommodations well in advance, especially if you'll be traveling during busy times. See page 584 for a list of major holidays and festivals in London; for tips on making reservations, see page 382.

RATES AND DEALS

I've described my recommended accommodations using a Sleep Code (see sidebar). Prices listed are for one-night stays in peak season, include a hearty breakfast unless otherwise noted, and assume you're booking directly with the hotel (not through a TI or online hotel-booking engine). Booking services extract a commission from the hotel, which logically closes the door on special deals. Book direct.

Staying in B&Bs and small hotels can sometimes be a great way to save money over sleeping in big hotels, but lately the big, impersonal chain hotels are offering rooms even cheaper than the mom-and-pop places (but without breakfast); see "Big, Good-Value, Modern Hotels" on page 400. When comparing prices between these chain hotels and B&Bs, remember you're getting two breakfasts (about a £25 value) for each double room at a B&B. Some fancy hotels rent for a third off if you arrive late on a slow day and ask for a deal. Official "rack rates" (the highest rates a hotel charges) can be misleading, because they often omit cheaper oddball rooms and special promo deals.

All of my recommended hotels have a website (which often has a built-in booking form) and an email address; you can expect a response within a day (and often sooner).

If you're on a budget, it's smart to email several hotels to ask for their best price. Comparison-shop and make your choice. This is especially helpful when dealing with the larger hotels that use "dynamic pricing," a computer-generated system that predicts the demand for particular days and sets prices accordingly: High-demand days will often be more than double the price of low-demand days. This makes it impossible for a guidebook to list anything more accurate than a wide range of prices. I regret this trend. While you can assume that hotels listed in this book are good, it's very difficult to say which ones are the better value unless you email to confirm the price.

As you look over the listings, you'll notice that some accommodations promise special prices to Rick Steves readers who book directly with the hotel. To get these rates, you must book direct (that is, not through a booking site like TripAdvisor or Booking.com), mention this book when you reserve, and then show the book upon arrival. Rick Steves discounts apply to readers with ebooks as well as printed books. Because we trust hotels to honor this, please let me know if you don't receive a listed discount. Note, though, that discounts understandably may not be applied to promotional rates.

In general, prices can soften if you do any of the following: offer to pay cash, stay at least three nights, or mention this book. You can also try asking for a cheaper room or a discount, or offer to skip breakfast.

Looking for Hotel Deals Online

Given London's high hotel prices, using the Internet can help you score a deal. Various websites list rooms in high-rise, three- and four-star business hotels. You'll give up the charm and warmth of a family-run establishment, and breakfast probably won't be included, but you might find that the price is right.

Start by browsing the websites of several chains to get a sense of typical rates and online deals. For listings of no-frills, Motel 6-type places, see "Big, Good-Value, Modern Hotels," on page 400.

Pricier London hotel chains include Millennium/Copthorne, Thistle, InterContinental/Holiday Inn, Radisson, Hilton, and Red Carnation. Auction-type sites (such as Priceline and Hotwire) match flexible travelers with empty hotel rooms, often at prices well below the hotel's normal rates.

My readers report good experiences with these accommodation discount sites: www.londontown.com (an informative site with a discount booking service), athomeinlondon.co.uk and www.londonbb.com (both list central B&Bs), www.lastminute.com, www.visitlondon.com, roomsnet.com, and www.eurocheapo.com.

Types of Accommodations

HOTELS

Many of my recommended hotels have three floors of rooms and steep stairs. Elevators are rare except in the larger hotels. If you're concerned about stairs, call and ask about ground-floor rooms or pay for a hotel with a lift (elevator). Air-conditioning is rare (I've noted which of my listings have it), but most places have fans. On hot summer nights, you'll want your window open—and unfortunately, in this big city, street noise is a fact of life. If concerned, request a room on the back side or on an upper floor.

"Twin" means two single beds, and "double" means one double bed. If you'll take either one, let them know, or you might be needlessly turned away. Most hotels offer family deals, which means that parents with young children can easily get a room with an extra child's bed or a discount for larger rooms. Call to negotiate the price. Teenagers are generally charged as adults. Kids under five sleep almost free.

Be careful of the terminology: An "en suite" (pronounced "on sweet") room has a bathroom (toilet and shower/tub) actually inside the room; a room with a "private bathroom" can mean that the bathroom is all yours, but it's across the hall; and a "standard" room has access to a bathroom down the hall that's shared with other rooms. Figuring there's little difference between "en suite" and "private" rooms, some places charge the same for both. If you want your own bathroom inside the room, request "en suite."

If money's tight, ask for a standard room. You'll almost always have a sink in your room, and as more rooms go "en suite," the hallway bathroom is shared with fewer standard rooms.

Confusingly, pricey hotels might call an en suite room "standard" to differentiate it from a fancier "superior" or "deluxe" room—if you're not sure, ask for clarification.

Note that to be called a "hotel," a place technically must have certain amenities, including a 24-hour reception (though this rule is loosely applied). TVs are standard in rooms, but may come with limited channels (no cable). Note that all of Britain's accommodations are now non-smoking.

If you're arriving early in the morning, your room probably

won't be ready. You can drop your bag safely at the hotel and dive right into sightseeing.

Hoteliers can be a great help and source of advice. Most know their city well, and can assist you with everything from public transit and airport connections to finding a good restaurant, the nearest launderette, or Wi-Fi hotspots.

Even at the best places, mechanical breakdowns occur: Air-conditioning malfunctions, sinks leak, hot water turns cold, and toilets gurgle and smell. Report your concerns clearly and calmly at the front desk. For more complicated problems, don't expect instant results.

To guard against theft in your room, keep valuables out of sight. Some rooms come with a safe, and other hotels have safes at the front desk. I've never bothered using one.

Checkout can pose problems if surprise charges pop up on your bill. If you settle up your bill the afternoon before you leave, you'll have time to discuss and address any points of contention (before 19:00, when the night shift usually arrives).

Above all, keep a positive attitude. Remember, you're on vacation. If your hotel is a disappointment, spend more time out enjoying the city you came to see.

SMALL HOTELS AND B&BS

Places with "townhouse" or "house" in their name (such as "London House") are like big B&Bs or small family-run hotels—with fewer amenities but more character than a hotel. Places named "B&B"—rare in big and bustling London—typically have six rooms or fewer.

Small hotels and B&Bs come with their own etiquette and quirks. Keep in mind that owners are at the whim of their guests—if you're getting up early, so are they; and if you check in late, they'll wait up for you. Be considerate.

Small places usually serve a hearty fried breakfast of eggs and much more (for details on breakfast, see page 406 in the Eating in London chapter). Because your B&B or small-hotel owner is often also the cook, there's usually a quite limited time span when breakfast is served (typically about an hour—make sure you know when it is before you turn in for the night). It's an unwritten rule that guests shouldn't show up at the very end of the breakfast period and expect a full cooked breakfast. If you do arrive late (or if you need to leave before breakfast is served), most establishments are happy to let you help yourself to cereal, fruit or juice, and coffee; ask politely if it's possible.

Most places stock rooms with an electric kettle, along with cups, tea bags, and coffee packets (if you prefer decaf, buy a jar at a grocery and dump the contents into a baggie for easy packing).

Making Hotel Reservations

Reserve your rooms several weeks in advance—or as soon as you've pinned down your travel dates. Note that some national holidays merit your making reservations far in advance (see page 584).

Requesting a Reservation: It's easiest to book your room through the hotel's website. (For the best rates, always use the hotel's official site and not a booking agency's site.) If there's no reservation form, or for complicated requests, send an email (see below for a sample request).

The hotelier wants to know:
- the number and type of rooms you need
- the number of nights you'll stay
- your date of arrival
- your date of departure
- any special needs (such as bathroom in the room or down the hall, twin beds vs. double bed, etc.)

Mention any discounts—for Rick Steves readers or otherwise—when you make the reservation.

Confirming a Reservation: Most places will request a credit-card number to hold your room. If they don't have a secure on-line reservation form—look for the *https*—you can email your card number (I do), but it's safer to share that confidential info via a phone call or two emails (splitting your number between them).

Canceling a Reservation: If you must cancel your reservation, it's courteous—and smart—to do so with as much notice as possible, especially for smaller family-run places. Be warned that

Electrical outlets sometimes have switches that turn the current on or off; if your electrical appliance isn't working, flip the switch at the outlet. When you unplug your appliance, don't forget your adapter—most B&Bs have boxes of various adapters and converters that guests have left behind (which is handy if you left yours at the last place).

You're likely to encounter unusual bathroom fixtures. The "pump toilet" has a flushing handle or button that doesn't kick in unless you push it just right: too hard or too soft, and it won't go. (Be decisive but not ruthless.) There's also the "dial-a-shower," an electronic box under the shower head where you'll turn a dial to select the heat of the water and (sometimes with a separate dial or button) turn on or shut off the flow of water. If you can't find the switch to turn on the shower, it may be just outside the bathroom.

Many B&Bs and small hotels come with thin walls and doors that can make for a noisy night. If you're a light sleeper, bring earplugs. And please be quiet in the halls and in your rooms at night

From: rick@ricksteves.com
Sent: Today
To: info@hotelcentral.com
Subject: Reservation request for 19-22 July

Dear Hotel Central,

I would like to reserve a room for 2 people for 3 nights, arriving 19 July and departing 22 July. If possible, I would like a quiet room with a double bed and a bathroom inside the room.

Please let me know if you have a room available and the price.

Thank you!
Rick Steves

cancellation policies can be strict; read the fine print or ask about these before you book. Internet deals may require prepayment, with no refunds for cancellations.

Reconfirming a Reservation: Always call to reconfirm your room reservation a few days in advance. For smaller hotels and B&Bs, I call again on my day of arrival to tell my host what time I expect to get there (especially important if arriving late—after 17:00).

Phoning: For tips on how to call hotels overseas, see page 566.

(talk softly, and keep the TV volume low)...those of us getting up early will thank you for it.

HOSTELS AND DORMS

London hostels charge about £20-30 per bed. Travelers of any age are welcome if they don't mind sleeping in dorm-style accommodations and meeting other travelers. Cheap meals are sometimes available. Most hostels offer kitchen facilities, Wi-Fi, a guest computer, and a self-service laundry. Nowadays, concerned about bedbugs, hostels are likely to provide all bedding, including sheets. Family and private rooms may be available on request.

Hostelling International hostels (also known as **"official hostels"** and run by the YHA in Britain) charge a few extra pounds a night for nonmembers. If you'll be staying for several days in an official hostel, consider buying a membership card before you go (www.hihostels.com).

Independent hostels tend to be easygoing, colorful, and in-

SLEEPING

formal (no membership required). For London independent hostel listings, try www.hostellondon.com; www.hostelworld.com is the standard way backpackers search and book hostels, but also try www.hostels.com and www.hostelz.com.

Many London colleges rent out their dorms during school holidays, mainly during July, August, and early September. Types of accommodations vary, but are usually somewhat spartan (no phones or TVs in the rooms) and come with single or twin beds. For listings, see "Dorms" on page 403.

APARTMENTS

Renting an apartment, house, or villa can be a fun and cost-effective, though not necessarily cheap, way to delve into London. Websites such as HomeAway and its sister sites VRBO and Great-Rentals let you correspond directly with European property owners or managers. Consider this option if you're traveling with a family or staying a week or longer. For listings, see "Apartment Rentals" at the end of this chapter.

PRIVATE HOMES

Airbnb.com and Roomorama.com make it reasonably easy to find a place to sleep in someone's home. Beds range from air-mattress-in-living-room basic to plush-B&B-suites. One Fine Stay (www.onefinestay.com) offers a more upscale version, where you coordinate through an agency that sweeps in and turns traveling Londoners' apartments into an "unhotel" with fresh linens and a loaner iPhone.

If you want a place to sleep that's free, www.couchsurfing.org is a vagabond's alternative to Airbnb. It lists millions of outgoing members, who host fellow "surfers" in their homes.

Accommodations

VICTORIA STATION NEIGHBORHOOD

The streets behind Victoria Station teem with little, moderately-priced-for-London B&Bs. It's a safe, surprisingly tidy, and decent area without a hint of the trashy, touristy glitz of the streets in front of the station. I've divided these accommodations into two broad categories: Belgravia, west of the station, feels particularly posh, while Pimlico, to the east, is still upscale and dotted with colorful eateries. While I wouldn't go out of my way just to dine here, each area has plenty of good restaurants (see page 427). All of my recommended hotels

The Good and Bad of Online Reviews

User-generated travel review websites—such as TripAdvisor, Booking.com, and Yelp—have quickly become a huge player in the travel industry. These sites give you access to actual reports—good and bad—from travelers who have experienced the hotel, restaurant, tour, or attraction.

My hotelier friends in Europe are in awe of these sites' influence. Small hoteliers who want to stay in business have no choice but to work with review sites—which often charge fees for good placement or photos, and tack on commissions if users book through the site instead of directly with the hotel.

While these sites work hard to weed out bogus users, my hunch is that a significant percentage of reviews are posted by friends or enemies of the business reviewed. I've even seen hotels "bribe" guests (for example, offer a free breakfast) in exchange for a positive review. Also, review sites can become an echo chamber, with one or two flashy businesses camped out atop the ratings, while better, more affordable, and more authentic alternatives sit ignored farther down the list. (For example, I find review sites' restaurant recommendations skew to very touristy, obvious options.)

Remember that a user-generated review is based on the experience of one person. That person likely stayed at one hotel and ate at a few restaurants, and doesn't have much of a basis for comparison. A guidebook is the work of a trained researcher who has exhaustively visited many alternatives to assess their relative value. I recently checked out some top-rated TripAdvisor listings in various towns; when stacked up against their competitors, some are gems, while just as many are duds.

Both types of information have their place, and in many ways, they're complementary. If a hotel or restaurant is well-reviewed in a guidebook or two, and also gets good ratings on one of these sites, it's likely a winner.

are within a five-minute walk of the Victoria Tube, bus, and train stations. On hot summer nights, request a quiet back room; most of these B&Bs lack air-conditioning and may front busy streets.

The nearest laundry option is **Pimlico Launderette,** on the east—Pimlico—side about five blocks southwest of Warwick Square. Low prices and friendly George brighten your chore (£7.40 same-day full service, £5-6 self-service, daily 8:00-19:00; 3 Westmoreland Terrace—go down Clarendon Street, turn right on Sutherland, and look for the launderette on the left at the end of the street; tel. 020/7821-8692).

Drivers like the 400-space Semley Place NCP **parking garage,** near the hotels on the west—Belgravia—side (£40/day,

Victoria Station Neighborhood

1. Lime Tree Hotel
2. Morgan House
3. Luna Simone Hotel
4. Bakers Hotel
5. New England Hotel
6. Best Western Victoria Palace
7. Jubilee Hotel
8. Cherry Court Hotel
9. easyHotel Victoria
10. Ebury Wine Bar
11. La Bottega Deli
12. The Thomas Cubitt Pub
13. To The Duke of Wellington Pub
14. The Orange Pub
15. Daylesford Deli
16. Grumbles Restaurant
17. Pimlico Fresh
18. Seafresh Fish Restaurant
19. The Jugged Hare Pub
20. St. George's Tavern
21. Nando's
22. Grocery Stores (4)
23. To Launderette
24. Bus Tours – Day (2)
25. Bus Tours – Night
26. Tube, Taxis, City Buses
27. Green Line Coach Terminal
28. Buses to Luton & Stansted Airports

possible discounts with hotel voucher, just west of Victoria Coach Station at Buckingham Palace Road and Semley Place, tel. 0845-050-7080, www.ncp.co.uk).

West of Victoria Station (Belgravia)

Here in Belgravia, the prices are a bit higher and your neighbors include some of the world's wealthiest people. These two places sit nearly kitty-corner from each other on tranquil Ebury Street, two

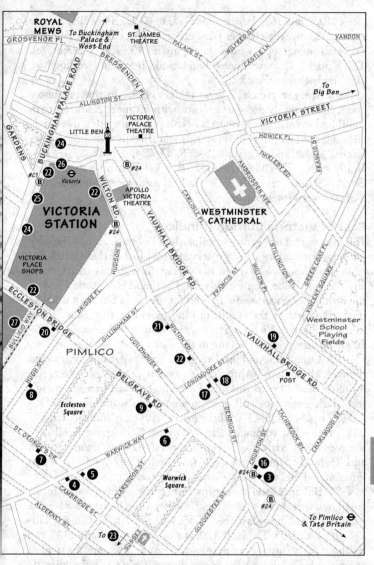

blocks over from Victoria Station (or a slightly shorter walk from the Sloane Square Tube stop). You can cut the walk from Victoria Station to nearly nothing by taking a short ride on frequent bus #C1 (leaves from Buckingham Palace Road side of Victoria Station and drops you off directly in front of Morgan House).

$$$ **Lime Tree Hotel,** enthusiastically run by Charlotte and Matt, is a gem, with 25 spacious, stylish, comfortable, thoughtfully decorated rooms, a helpful staff, and a fun-loving breakfast room

(Sb-£110, Db-£165, larger superior Db-£195, Tb-£205, family room-£225, usually cheaper Jan-Feb, free guest computer and Wi-Fi, small lounge opens onto quiet garden, 135 Ebury Street, tel. 020/7730-8191, www.limetreehotel.co.uk, info@limetreehotel.co.uk, Alex manages the office).

$$ Morgan House, a great budget choice in this neighborhood, has 11 nicely decorated rooms with far more character than you'll find in other nearby hotels in this price range. It's also entertainingly run, with lots of travel tips and friendly chat from owner Rachel Joplin and her staff (S-£58, D-£84, Db-£108, T-£108, family suites: Tb-£148, Qb-£158, free Wi-Fi can be spotty, 120 Ebury Street, tel. 020/7730-2384, www.morganhouse.co.uk, morganhouse@btclick.com).

East of Victoria Station (Pimlico)

This area is a bit less genteel-feeling than Belgravia, but still plenty inviting, with eateries and grocery stores. Most of these hotels are on or near Warwick Way, the main drag through this area. Generally the best Tube stop for this neighborhood is Victoria (though the Pimlico stop works equally well for the Luna Simone). Bus #24 runs right through the middle of Pimlico, connecting Tate Britain to the south with Victoria Station, the Houses of Parliament, Trafalgar Square, and much more to the north.

$$ Luna Simone Hotel rents 36 fresh, spacious, remodeled rooms with modern bathrooms. It's a smartly managed place, run for more than 40 years by twins Peter and Bernard—and Bernard's son Mark—and they still seem to enjoy their work (Sb-£80, Db-£115, Tb-£140, Qb-£170, these prices with cash and this book in 2015, free guest computer and Wi-Fi, at 47 Belgrave Road near the corner of Charlwood Street, handy bus #24 to Victoria Station and Trafalgar Square stops out front, tel. 020/7834-5897, www.lunasimonehotel.com, stay@lunasimonehotel.com).

$$ Bakers Hotel shoehorns 11 brightly painted rooms into a small building, but it's conveniently located and offers modest prices and a small breakfast (S-£45-55, Sb-£70-80, D-£70-85, Db-£85-95, T-£85-95, Tb-£110-120, family room with bath-£135, can be about £5-8 cheaper per person off-season, discounts for stays of at least a week, ask for Rick Steves discount when booking directly with hotel, free Wi-Fi, 126 Warwick Way, tel. 020/7834-0729, www.bakershotel.co.uk, reservations@bakershotel.co.uk, Amin Jamani).

$$ New England Hotel, run by Jay and the Patel family, has very worn public spaces but well-priced rooms in a tight old corner building. The family plans a major facelift for 2015 (small Sb-£69-79, Db-£79-109, Tb-£109-139, Qb-£119-149, prices soft during slow times, breakfast is very basic, pay Wi-Fi, 20 Saint George's

Drive, tel. 020/7834-8351, www.newenglandhotel.com, mystay@
newenglandhotel.com).

$$ **Best Western Victoria Palace** offers modern business-
class comfort compared to the other creaky old hotels listed here.
Choose between the 43 rooms in the main building (Db-£120,
Tb-£200, prices flex with demand—often around Db-£90/Tb-
£160 off-season, sometimes includes breakfast, elevator, 60-64
Warwick Way), or pay about 20 percent less by booking a nearly
identical room in one of the two annexes, each a half-block away—
an excellent value for this neighborhood if you skip breakfast. All
three buildings were recently renovated (annex Db-£85-90, break-
fast-£12.50, air-con, no elevator). Book in advance for the best rates
(free guest computer and Wi-Fi, 17 Belgrave Road and 1 War-
wick Way, reception at main building, tel. 020/7821-7113, www.
bestwesternvictoriapalace.co.uk, info@bestwesternvictoriapalace.
co.uk).

$$ **Jubilee Hotel** is a well-run but slightly shabby slumbermill
with 24 tiny, simple rooms and many tiny, neat beds. The cheap-
est rooms, which share bathrooms, are just below street level (S-
£39-45, Sb-£59-65, tiny twin D-£55-65, Db-£79-89, T-£65, Tb-
£89-95, Qb-£99-109, rates depend on season and length of stay,
5 percent discount for Rick Steves readers if you book direct and
pay cash, free guest computer, free Wi-Fi for Rick Steves readers,
31 Eccleston Square, tel. 020/7834-0845, www.jubileehotel.co.uk,
stay@jubileehotel.co.uk, Bob Patel).

$ **Cherry Court Hotel,** run by the friendly and industrious
Patel family, rents 12 very small but bright and well-designed
rooms in a central location. Considering London's sky-high prices,
this is a fine budget choice (Sb-£60, Db-£75, Tb-£110, Quint/b
family room-£135, these prices with this book in 2015, 5 percent
fee to pay with credit card, fruit-basket breakfast in room, air-con,
free guest computer and Wi-Fi, laundry, peaceful garden patio, 23
Hugh Street, tel. 020/7828-2840, www.cherrycourthotel.co.uk,
info@cherrycourthotel.co.uk, daughter Neha answers emails and
offers informed restaurant advice).

$ **easyHotel Victoria,** at 36 Belgrave Road, is part of the bud-
get chain described on page 401.

"SOUTH KENSINGTON," SHE SAID, LOOSENING HIS CUMMERBUND

To stay on a quiet street so classy it doesn't allow hotel signs, surrounded by trendy shops and colorful restaurants, call "South Ken"
your London home. Shoppers like being a short walk from Harrods and the designer shops of King's Road and Chelsea. When
I splurge, I splurge here. Sumner Place is just off Old Brompton
Road, 200 yards from the handy South Kensington Tube station

(on Circle Line, two stops from Victoria Station; and on Piccadilly Line, direct from Heathrow).

$$$ Aster House, well-run by friendly and accommodating Simon and Leonie Tan, has a cheerful lobby, lounge, and breakfast room. Its 13 rooms are comfy and quiet, with TV, phone, and air-conditioning. Enjoy breakfast or just lounging in the whisper-elegant Orangery, a glassy greenhouse. Simon and Leonie offer free loaner mobile phones to their guests (Sb-£135, Db-£200, bigger Db-£250 or £295, does not include 20 percent VAT; significant discount offered to readers of this book in 2015—up to 20 percent discount if you book three or more nights, up to 25 percent discount for five or more nights; additional 5 percent off when you pay cash, check website for specials, pay guest computer, free Wi-Fi, 3 Sumner Place, tel. 020/7581-5888, www.asterhouse.com, asterhouse@gmail.com).

$$$ Number Sixteen, for well-heeled travelers, packs over-the-top class into its 41 artfully imagined rooms, plush designer-chic lounges, and tranquil garden. It's in a labyrinthine building, with boldly modern decor—perfect for an urban honeymoon (Sb-from £180, "superior" Db-from £294—but soft, ask for discounted "seasonal rates," especially on weekends and in Aug—subject to availability, larger "luxury" Db-£330, breakfast buffet in the conservatory-£19 continental or £20 full English, elevator, free guest computer and Wi-Fi, 16 Sumner Place, tel. 020/7589-5232, US tel. 800-553-6674, www.numbersixteenhotel.co.uk, sixteen@firmdale.com).

$$$ The Pelham Hotel, a 51-room business-class hotel with crisp service and a pricey mix of pretense and style, is genteel, with low lighting and a pleasant drawing room among the many perks (Db-£190-290, rate depends on room size and season, breakfast-£15 continental or £19.50 full English, slightly lower prices on weekends and in Aug, Web specials can include free breakfast; air-con, elevator, free guest computer, pay Wi-Fi, fitness room, 15 Cromwell Place, tel. 020/7589-8288, US tel. 1-888-757-5587, www.pelhamhotel.co.uk, reservations@pelhamhotel.co.uk, Jamie will take good care of you).

$$$ Brompton Hotel has 26 plain rooms above a jumble of cafés and clubs. There's a noisy bar and some street noise, so ask for a room in the back if you want quiet. Since it has no public spaces, they serve breakfast in your room. Although the hotel is humble, its rates are reasonable for this upscale neighborhood (Sb-£100, Db-£110-140 but can fall to £75 when demand is down, Tb-£140-150, "deluxe" rooms are just like the others but with a tub, save a little by booking via their website, includes continental breakfast, free Wi-Fi, piles of stairs, across from the South Kensington Tube station at

SLEEPING

South Kensington Neighborhood

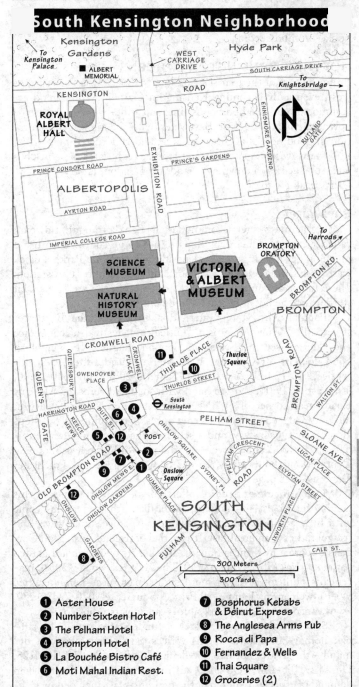

1 Aster House
2 Number Sixteen Hotel
3 The Pelham Hotel
4 Brompton Hotel
5 La Bouchée Bistro Café
6 Moti Mahal Indian Rest.
7 Bosphorus Kebabs & Beirut Express
8 The Anglesea Arms Pub
9 Rocca di Papa
10 Fernandez & Wells
11 Thai Square
12 Groceries (2)

SLEEPING

30 Old Brompton Road, tel. 020/7584-4517, www.bromhotel.com, book@bromhotel.com).

NORTH OF KENSINGTON GARDENS

From the core of the tourist's London, the vast Hyde Park spreads west, eventually becoming Kensington Gardens. Three good accommodations neighborhoods line up side-by-side along the northern edge of the park: Bayswater (with the highest concentration of good hotels) anchors the area, and is bordered by Notting Hill to the west and Paddington to the east. This area has quick bus and Tube access to downtown, and, for London, is very "homely" (Brit-speak for cozy).

Bayswater

Most of my Bayswater accommodations flank a tranquil, tidy park called Kensington Gardens Square (not to be confused with the much bigger Kensington Gardens adjacent to Hyde Park), a block west of bustling Queensway, north of Bayswater Tube station. These hotels are quiet for central London, but the area feels a bit sterile, and the hotels here tend to be impersonal.

Popular with young international travelers, the Bayswater street called **Queensway** is a multicultural festival of commerce and eateries (see the Eating in London chapter). The neighborhood does its dirty clothes at **Kornelia Launderette** (£6-8 self-service, £10-12 full-service, Mon-Sat 8:00-20:00, Sun 9:00-20:00, last wash at 19:00, staff on hand with soap and coins, 67 Moscow Road, near corner of St. Petersburgh Place and Moscow Road, tel. 020/3305-6310). For **Internet access,** you'll find several stops along busy Queensway, and a self-serve bank of computer terminals on the food-circus level—third floor—of Whiteleys Shopping Centre (long hours daily, corner of Queensway and Porchester Gardens—see page 432).

$$$ Vancouver Studios offers one of the best values in this neighborhood. Its 48 modern, tastefully furnished rooms come with fully equipped kitchenettes (utensils, stove, microwave, and fridge) rather than breakfast. It's nestled between Kensington Gardens Square and Princes Square, and has its own tranquil garden patio out back (Sb-£97, Db-£140, Tb-£179, extra bed-£20, 10 percent discount for seven or more nights, pay guest computer, free Wi-Fi, welcoming lounge, 30 Princes Square, tel. 020/7243-1270, www.vancouverstudios.co.uk, info@vancouverstudios.co.uk).

$$$ Garden Court Hotel is understated, with 40 simple, homey-but-tasteful rooms (prices vary seasonally with demand—these are normal/low-demand rates: Sb-£74, D-£125, Db-£129, Tb-£149, Qb-£179, all rooms can be £20 more when demand is especially high, continental breakfast included or English breakfast-£3.50, elevator, pay guest computer, free Wi-Fi, 30-31 Kensington Gardens Square, tel. 020/7229-2553, www. gardencourthotel.co.uk, info@gardencourthotel.co.uk).

$$$ **London House Hotel** has 103 spiffy, modern cookie-cutter rooms on Kensington Gardens Square. Its rates are great considering the quality and fine location (rates fluctuate, but generally Db-£105 weekdays and £130 on weekends, expect to pay more during busiest times and less in winter, smaller rooms not facing the square are about £10-20 cheaper, basement family rooms-£140, check online for specific rates and last-minute deals, continental breakfast-£7, elevator, free Wi-Fi, 81 Kensington Gardens Square, tel. 020/7243-1810, www.londonhousehotels.com, reservations@londonhousehotels.com).

$$$ **Phoenix Hotel,** a Best Western modernization of a 125-room hotel, offers spacious public spaces and modern-feeling rooms. Its prices—which range from fine-value to rip-off—are determined by a greedy computer program, with huge variations according to expected demand. Book online to save money (Sb-£80-110, Db-£110-140, Tb-£150-180, elevator, free guest computer and Wi-Fi, 1-8 Kensington Gardens Square, tel. 020/7229-2494, US tel. 800-528-1234, www.phoenixhotel.co.uk, info@phoenixhotel.co.uk).

$$ **Princes Square Guest Accommodation** is a crisp (if impersonal) place renting 50 businesslike rooms with pleasant, modern decor. It's well-located, practical, and a very good value, especially if you can score a good rate (prices fluctuate with demand, but generally Db-£100-110, £20 less for a single, £40 more for a triple; email to ask for best price, breakfast likely included if you book direct—ask, elevator, pay Wi-Fi, 23-25 Princes Square, tel. 020/7229-9876, www.princessquarehotel.co.uk, info@princessquarehotel.co.uk).

$$ **Kensington Gardens Hotel** laces 17 pleasant, slightly scuffed rooms together in a tall, skinny building (Ss-£59, Sb-£69, Db-£98, Tb-£120; continental breakfast served at Phoenix Hotel, free Wi-Fi, 9 Kensington Gardens Square, tel. 020/7243-7600, www.kensingtongardenshotel.co.uk, info@kensingtongardenshotel.co.uk, Rowshanak).

$$ **Bayswater Inn Hotel**'s 140 tidy, perfectly adequate rooms come with dated style, an impersonal feel, and outrageously high official rack rates. But rooms commonly go for much lower prices, making this a decent—sometimes great—budget option (if booked in advance roughly Sb-£60, Db-£90, Tb-£125, Qb-£150, stay for free on fifth consecutive night, elevator, pay guest computer and Wi-Fi, 8-16 Princes Square, tel. 020/7727-8621, www. bayswaterinnhotel.com, reservations@bayswaterinnhotel.com).

North of Kensington Gardens

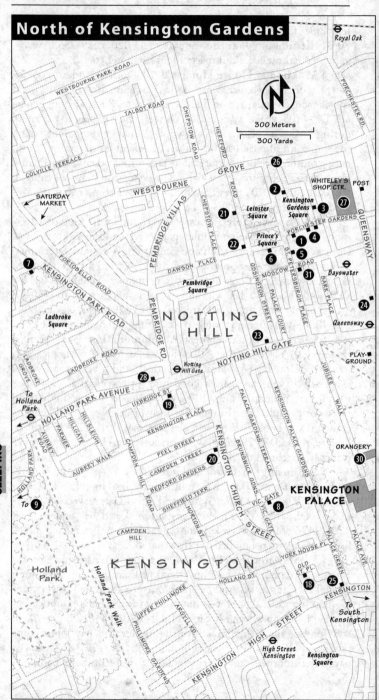

1 Vancouver Studios
2 Garden Court Hotel
3 London House Hotel
4 Phoenix & Kensington Gardens Hotels
5 Princes Square Guest Accommodation
6 Bayswater Inn Hotel
7 Portobello Hotel
8 London Vicarage Hotel
9 To Norwegian YWCA
10 Tudor Court Hotel
11 St. David's Hotels
12 Falcon Hotel
13 easyHotel
14 The Royal Park Hotel
15 Stylotel
16 Olympic House Hotel
17 Caring Hotel
18 Maggie Jones Restaurant
19 Geales Restaurant
20 The Churchill Arms Pub & Thai Kitchen
21 Hereford Road Restaurant
22 The Prince Edward Pub
23 Café Diana
24 Royal China Restaurant
25 Wagamama
26 More Chain Eateries
27 Whiteleys Shopping Centre (Eateries, Grocery, Internet)
28 Tesco Grocery
29 Spar Market
30 The Orangery (Afternoon Tea)
31 Launderette

SLEEPING

Notting Hill and Nearby

The Notting Hill neighborhood, just west of Bayswater (spreading out from the northwest tip of Kensington Gardens) is famous for two things: It's the site of the colorful Portobello Road Market (see page 448 of the Shopping in London chapter), and the setting of the 1999 Hugh Grant/Julia Roberts film of the same name. While the neighborhood is now a bit more upscale and less funky than the one seen in that film, it's still a pleasant place to stay.

$$$ Portobello Hotel is on a quiet, residential street in the heart of Notting Hill. Its 21 freshly refurbished rooms are funky yet elegant. Prices vary greatly with the season and size of the room (Sb-£140-175, "Good" Db-£175-240, "Better" Db-£195-245, "Great" Db-£225-315, elevator, free guest computer and Wi-Fi, 22 Stanley Gardens, tel. 020/7727-2777, www.portobellohotel.com, stay@portobellohotel.com, Hannah).

West of Kensington Gardens: **$$$ London Vicarage Hotel** is family-run, understandably popular, and located in a quiet, classy neighborhood just south of the core of Notting Hill. It has 17 quality rooms, a modest TV lounge, a grand staircase, and facilities on each floor. Mandy and Monika maintain a homey atmosphere (S-£67, Sb-£112, D-£112, Db-£140, T-£143, Tb-£184, Q-£155, Qb-£205, 20 percent less in winter—check website, free Wi-Fi; 8-minute walk from Notting Hill Gate and High Street Kensington Tube stations, near Kensington Palace at 10 Vicarage Gate; tel. 020/7229-4030, www.londonvicaragehotel.com, vicaragehotel@btconnect.com).

Near Holland Park: **$ Norwegian YWCA (Norsk K.F.U.K.)**—where English is definitely a second language—is open to any Norwegian woman, and to non-Norwegian women under 30. (Men must be under 30 with a Norwegian passport.) Located on a quiet, stately street, it offers a study, TV room, piano lounge, and an open-face Norwegian ambience (goat cheese on Sundays!). They have mostly quads, so those willing to share with strangers are most likely to get a bed (Ss-£54, shared double-£46/bed, shared triple-£43/bed, shared quad-£40/bed, includes sheets and towels, includes breakfast year-round plus sack lunch and dinner Sept-June, £20 key deposit and £3 membership fee required, pay Wi-Fi, 52 Holland Park, Tube: Holland Park, tel. 020/7727-9346 or 020/7727-9897, www.kfukhjemmet.org.uk, kontor@kfukhjemmet.org.uk). With each visit, I wonder which is easier to get—a sex change or a Norwegian passport?

Paddington Station Neighborhood

Just to the east of Bayswater, the neighborhood around Paddington Station—while much less charming than the other areas I've recommended—is pleasant enough, and very convenient to the

Heathrow Express airport train. The area is flanked by the Paddington and Lancaster Gate Tube stops. Most of my recommendations circle Norfolk Square, just two blocks in front of Paddington Station, yet are still quiet and comfortable. The main drag, London Street, is lined with handy eateries—pubs, Indian, Italian, Moroccan, Greek, Lebanese, and more—plus convenience stores and an Internet café. (Better restaurants are a short stroll to the west, near Queensway and Notting Hill—see page 430.) To reach this area, exit the station toward Praed Street (with your back to the tracks, it's to the left). Once outside, continue straight across Praed Street and down London Street; Norfolk Square is a block ahead on the left.

On Norfolk Square

These places (and many more on the same street) are similar; all offer small rooms at a reasonable price, in tall buildings with lots of stairs and no elevator. I've chosen the ones that offer the most reasonable prices and the warmest welcome.

$$ Tudor Court Hotel has 38 colorful rooms conscientiously run by Connan and the Gupta family. While the tiny rooms are tight (with prefab plastic bathrooms) and the rates are a bit high, this place distinguishes itself with its warm welcome and attention to detail. If you smell them cooking up a big batch of curry rice, the Guptas are getting ready to take it to the homeless shelter, where they volunteer each week (S-£54-63, Sb-£95-108, "compact" Db-£99-120, larger "standard" Db-£135-165, "compact" Tb-£144-180, larger "standard" Tb-£162-198, family room-£180-225, higher rates are for Fri-Sat and other busy times, free Wi-Fi, 10-12 Norfolk Square, tel. 020/7723-5157, www.tudorcourtpaddington.co.uk, reservations@tudorcourtpaddington.co.uk).

$$ St. David's Hotels, run by the Neokleous family, has 60 rooms in several adjacent buildings. The rooms are small—as is typical for less-expensive hotels in London with minimal amenities, but the staff is friendly, and their non-en-suite rooms are a workable budget option (S-£50-60, Sb-£70-85, D-£70-85, Db-£90-120, Tb-£100-130, pay Wi-Fi in rooms, free Wi-Fi in lobby, 14-20 Norfolk Square, tel. 020/7723-3856, www.stdavidshotels.com, info@stdavidshotels.com).

$$ Falcon Hotel, a lesser value, has less personality and 19 simple, old-school, slightly dingy rooms (S-£59, Sb-£69, D-£85, Db-£95, twin Db-£99, Tb-£139, Qb-£149, rates flex with demand, free guest computer, pay Wi-Fi, 11 Norfolk Square, tel. 020/7723-8603, www.falcon-hotel.com, info@falcon-hotel.com).

$ easyHotel, the budget chain described on page 401, has a branch at 10 Norfolk Place.

SLEEPING

Elsewhere near Paddington Station

To reach these hotels, follow the directions on the previous page, but continue away from the station past Norfolk Square to the big intersection with Sussex Gardens; the Royal Park is a couple of blocks to the right, and the others are immediately to the left.

$$$ The Royal Park is the neighborhood's classy splurge, with 48 plush rooms, polished service, a genteel lounge, and all the little extras, including a welcome drink upon arrival and cookie at bedtime ("classic" Db-official rates-£189-279, bigger "executive" Db for £20 more, prices vary with demand, does not include 20 percent VAT, breakfast-£14-18, elevator, free guest computer and Wi-Fi, 3 Westbourne Terrace, tel. 020/7479-6600, www.theroyalpark.com, info@theroyalpark.com).

$$ Stylotel feels like the stylish, super-modern, aluminum-clad big sister of the easyHotel chain. Their tidy 39 rooms come with hard surfaces—hardwood floors, prefab plastic bathrooms, and metallic walls. While rooms can be a little cramped, the beds have space for your luggage underneath. You may feel like an astronaut in a retro science-fiction film, but if you don't need ye olde doilies, this place offers a good value (Sb-£65, Db-£95, Tb-£115, Qb-£135, prices go up with demand—book early and direct to get these rates, elevator, pay Wi-Fi, 160-162 Sussex Gardens, tel. 020/7723-1026, www.stylotel.com, info@stylotel.com, well-run by Andreas). They also have eight fancier, pricier, air-conditioned suites across the street (£180-220 for 2-4 people, kitchenettes, no breakfast).

$$ Olympic House Hotel has stark public spaces and a stern welcome, but its 38 business-class rooms offer predictable comfort and fewer old-timey quirks than many hotels in this price range (Sb-£75, Db-£105, Tb-£135, rates vary with demand, air-con in most rooms costs extra, elevator, pay Wi-Fi, 138-140 Sussex Gardens, tel. 020/7723-5935, www.olympichousehotel.co.uk, olympichousehotel@btinternet.com).

Between Paddington and Bayswater: About halfway between these two hotel neighborhoods, **$$ Caring Hotel,** plain but affordable, has 25 tidy, nondescript-bordering-on-depressingly dull rooms in a nice, quiet location just off Hyde Park (basic D-£75, Ds-£80, small Db-£90, standard Db-£100, extra bed-£15, these rates are approximate—prices change with demand, free Wi-Fi, 24 Craven Hill Gardens—it's the second road with this name as you come from the park, Tube: Queensway, tel. 020/7262-8708, www.caringhotel.co.uk, enquiries@caringhotel.co.uk).

ELSEWHERE IN CENTRAL LONDON

$$$ The Sumner Hotel rents 19 rooms in a 19th-century Georgian townhouse sporting a lounge decorated with fancy modern Italian

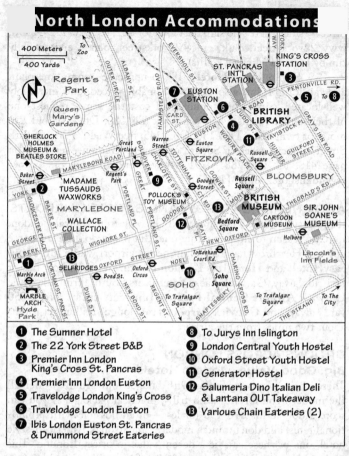

North London Accommodations

1. The Sumner Hotel
2. The 22 York Street B&B
3. Premier Inn London King's Cross St. Pancras
4. Premier Inn London Euston
5. Travelodge London King's Cross
6. Travelodge London Euston
7. Ibis London Euston St. Pancras & Drummond Street Eateries
8. To Jurys Inn Islington
9. London Central Youth Hostel
10. Oxford Street Youth Hostel
11. Generator Hostel
12. Salumeria Dino Italian Deli & Lantana OUT Takeaway
13. Various Chain Eateries (2)

SLEEPING

furniture and large contemporary rooms. This swanky place packs in all the amenities and is conveniently located north of Hyde Park and near Oxford Street, a busy shopping destination—with a convenient Marks & Spencer (see page 443) within walking distance (queen Db-£193, king Db-£213, "deluxe" Db-£229, mention this book to get these Rick Steves rates, can be cheaper off-season, extra bed-£60, air-con, elevator, free Wi-Fi, 54 Upper Berkeley Street, a block and a half off Edgware Road, Tube: Marble Arch, tel. 020/7723-2244, www.thesumner.com, reservations@thesumner. com).

$$$ **The 22 York Street B&B** offers a casual alternative in the city center, renting 10 traditional, hardwood, comfortable rooms, each named for a notable London landmark (Sb-£120, Db-£150, Tb-£180, free guest computer and Wi-Fi, inviting lounge; near Marylebone/Baker Street: from Baker Street Tube station,

walk 2 blocks down Baker Street and take a right to 22 York Street—since there's no sign, just look for #22; tel. 020/7224-2990, www.22yorkstreet.co.uk, mc@22yorkstreet.co.uk, energetically run by Liz and Michael Callis).

$$ Seven Dials Hotel's 18 no-nonsense rooms are plain and fairly tight, but also clean, reasonably priced, and incredibly well-located. Since their doubles all cost the same, request one of their larger rooms when you book (Sb-£80, Db-£105 but £10 more for twin beds, Tb-£130, Qb-£145, free Wi-Fi, 7 Monmouth Street, Tube: Leicester Square or Covent Garden—see map on page 418, tel. 020/7681-0791, www.sevendialshotel.com, info@sevendialshotel.co.uk, Hanna).

AT OR NEAR HEATHROW AND GATWICK AIRPORTS

It's so easy to get to Heathrow and Gatwick from central London, I see no reason to sleep at either one. But if you do, here are some options. Heathrow has a **Yotel** inside the airport, while **Jurys Inn, easyHotel,** and **Hotel Ibis London Heathrow** are a short bus or taxi ride away. Gatwick has a **Yotel** in its South Terminal, while **Gatwick Airport Central Premier Inn** rents cheap rooms 350 yards away, and **Gatwick Airport Travelodge** has budget rooms about two miles from the airport.

OPTIONS ACROSS LONDON
Big, Good-Value, Modern Hotels

These chain hotels—popular with budget tour groups—offer all the modern comforts in a no-frills, practical package. If you can score a double for £90-100 (or less—often possible with promotional rates) and don't mind a modern, impersonal, American-style hotel, one of these can be a decent value in pricey London. This option is especially worth considering for families, as kids often stay for free. While most of these hotels have 24-hour reception and elevators, extras such as breakfast and Wi-Fi cost extra, and the service lacks a personal touch (at some, you'll check in at an automated kiosk). When comparing your options, keep in mind that for about the same price, you can get a basic room at a budget hotel or B&B that has less predictable comfort, but more funkiness and friendliness in a more enjoyable neighborhood.

On each chain's website, you can see information about individual branches and book a stay. The rate you'll pay changes from day to day, and varies depending on how far ahead you book. Midweek prices are generally higher than weekend rates, and Sunday nights can be shockingly cheap. To comparison-shop, visit several sites and punch in the dates you're considering to see what the going rate is. The best deals generally must be prepaid a few weeks ahead and may not be refundable—read the fine print carefully.

I've listed and briefly described a few of the dominant chains below, along with a quick rundown on their more convenient London locations. Many of these hotels sit on busy streets in dreary train-station neighborhoods, so use common sense after dark and wear your money belt. For a sneak preview, try looking up the "Street View" for the address in Google Maps.

Premier Inn's locations include a branch inside **London County Hall** (next door to the London Eye), at **Southwark/Borough Market** (near Shakespeare's Globe on the South Bank, 34 Park Street, Tube: London Bridge), **Southwark/Tate Modern** (on Great Suffolk Street), **London King's Cross St. Pancras** (across the street from the east end of King's Cross Station and near the Eurostar terminus at St. Pancras), **London Euston** (handy but noisy location at corner of Euston Road and Dukes Road), **Kensington/Earl's Court** (11 Knaresborough Place, Tube: Earl's Court or Gloucester Road), **Victoria** (82-83 Eccleston Square, Tube: Victoria), and **Putney Bridge** (farther out, 3 Putney Bridge Approach). Avoid the **Tower Bridge** location, which is an inconvenient 15-minute walk from the nearest Tube stop. Book online at www.premierinn.com or call 0871-527-9222; from North America, dial 011-44-1582-567-890.

Travelodge has quite a few locations in London, including at **King's Cross** (200 yards in front of King's Cross Station, Grays Inn Road, Tube: King's Cross St. Pancras), **Kings Cross Royal Scot, Euston, Marylebone, Covent Garden, Liverpool Street,** and **Farringdon** (www.travelodge.co.uk).

Ibis has only two locations that are convenient to London's center: **Euston St. Pancras** (on a quiet street a block west of Euston Station, 3 Cardington Street, Tube: Euston) and **The City** (5 Commercial Street, Tube: Aldgate East); book at www.ibishotel.com.

Jurys Inn's locations include **Islington** (near King's Cross Station, 60 Pentonville Road, Tube: Angel), and **Chelsea** (Imperial Road, Tube: Imperial Wharf); book at www.jurysinns.com.

easyHotel: With several branches in good neighborhoods around London, easyHotel (www.easyhotel.com) has a unique business model inspired by its parent company, the easyJet budget airline. The generally tiny, super-efficient, no-frills rooms feel popped out of a plastic mold, down to the prefab ship's head-type "bathroom pod." Rates can be surprisingly low (with doubles as cheap as £30 if you book early enough)—but you'll be charged à la carte for add-ons that are included at most hotels, such as TV use, luggage storage, fresh towels, and daily cleaning (breakfast, if available, comes from a vending machine). If you go with the basic package, it's like hosteling with privacy—a hard-to-beat value. But you get what you pay for (walls can be thin, construction can be flimsy, fellow guests can be noisy, and so on). They're only a good

SLEEPING

deal if you book far enough ahead to get a good price, and skip the many extras...which add up fast. Locations include **Victoria** (34-40 Belgrave Road—see map on page 386, Tube: Victoria), **South Kensington** (14 Lexham Gardens, Tube: Earl's Court or Gloucester Road), **Earl's Court** (44-48 West Cromwell Road, Tube: Earl's Court), and **Paddington** (10 Norfolk Place, Tube: Paddington).

Hostels

Hostels can slash accommodation costs while meeting your basic needs. Prices listed here include sheets and lockers (bring your own lock), but you'll likely have to rent towels and pay a bit extra for breakfast. All of these places are open 24 hours, give members a £3 discount, and have guest computers and Wi-Fi (usually for a fee).

$ London Central Youth Hostel is the flagship of London's hostels, with 300 beds and all the latest in security and comfortable efficiency. Families and travelers of any age will feel welcome in this wonderful facility. You'll pay the same price for any bed in a four- to eight-bed single-sex dorm—with or without private bathroom—so try to grab one with a bathroom (£17-34/bunk depending on demand, twin D-£50-70, families welcome to book an entire room, members' kitchen, book long in advance, between Oxford Circus and Great Portland Street Tube stations at 104 Bolsover Street—see map on page 399, tel. 0845-371-9154, www.yha.org.uk, londoncentral@yha.org.uk).

$ Oxford Street Youth Hostel is right in the shopping and clubbing zone in Soho, with 90 beds (£20-30/bunk, twin D-£50-70, members' kitchen, 14 Noel Street, Tube: Oxford Street, tel. 0845-371-9133, www.yha.org.uk, oxfordst@yha.org.uk).

$ St. Paul's Youth Hostel, near St. Paul's Cathedral, is modern, friendly, well-run, and a bit scruffy. Most of the 210 beds are in shared, single-sex 3- to 11-bunk rooms (£20-30/bunk depending on demand, twin D-£50-70, cheap meals, 36 Carter Lane, Tube: St. Paul's, tel. 020/7236-4965 or 0845-371-9012, www.yha.org.uk, stpauls@yha.org.uk).

$ Generator Hostel is a brightly colored, hip hostel with a café, a DJ spinning the hits, and 870 beds in 220 rooms, including doubles. It's in a renovated building tucked behind a busy street halfway between Kings Cross and the British Museum (£18-30/bunk depending on demand, twin Db-£70-120, breakfast-£4.50, free Wi-Fi, 37 Tavistock Place: Tube: Russell Square, tel. 020/7388-7666, www.generatorhostels.com, london@generatorhostels.com).

$ A cluster of three **St. Christopher's Inn** hostels, south of the Thames near London Bridge, have cheap dorm beds; one branch (the Oasis) is for women only. All have loud and friendly bars attached (£22-36, higher price is for weekends, less in off-season, D-£60 or thereabouts, includes small breakfast, must be over 18 years old, free Wi-Fi, 161-165 Borough High Street, Tube: Borough or London Bridge, reservations tel. 020/8600-7500, www.st-christophers.co.uk, bookings@st-christophers.co.uk).

Dorms

$$ The **University of Westminster** opens its dorm rooms to travelers during summer break, from June through mid-September. Located in several high-rise buildings scattered around central London, the most convenient are Marylebone Hall and Wigram House—which have the higher rates. Some rooms have private bathrooms; others have shared bathrooms nearby. They all come with access to well-equipped kitchens and big lounges (S-£37-43, Sb-£61-73, D-£56-65, Db-£72-93, discounts for long stays, tel. 020/7911-5181, www.westminster.ac.uk/summeraccommodation, summeraccommodation@westminster.ac.uk).

$$ The **London School of Economics** has openings in its dorms from July through September (S-£42, Sb-£55-70, D-£50-65, Db-£75-100, prices vary according to location and length of stay, may include breakfast, pay guest computer, tel. 020/7955-7676, www.lsevacations.co.uk, vacations@lse.ac.uk).

$ **University College London** has rooms for travelers from late June until mid-September (S-£36-41, Sb-£53, 2-night minimum, linens and towels provided, cable Internet access in rooms, Wi-Fi available in some common areas, tel. 020/7387-4537, www.ucl.ac.uk/residences, accommodation@ucl.ac.uk@ucl.ac.uk).

Apartment Rentals

Consider the advantages that come with renting a furnished apartment—or "flat," as the British say. Complete with a small, equipped kitchen and living room, this option can also work for families or groups on shorter visits.

Be careful to avoid getting scammed: Follow all of the website's safety advice and use their internal payment procedures. Never wire money directly to an apartment owner, or you may find yourself with no place to stay—and no hope of getting your money back. It's also a good idea to buy trip cancellation/interruption insurance, as many weekly rentals are nonrefundable.

Be sure to read the rental conditions carefully and ask lots of questions. If a certain amenity is important to you (such as Wi-Fi or a washing machine in the unit), ask specifically about it and what to do if it stops working. Plot the location carefully (plug the address into maps.google.com), and remember to factor in travel time and costs from outlying neighborhoods to central London.

Cross-Pollinate is an online booking agency representing B&Bs and apartments in a handful of European cities, including London. Search their website for a listing you like, then submit your reservation online. If the place is available, you'll be charged a small deposit and emailed the location and check-in details. Policies vary from owner to owner, but in most cases you'll pay the balance on arrival in cash. London listings range from a Chelsea B&B room for two for £100 per night to a two-bedroom Marble Arch apartment sleeping four for £280 per night. Minimum stays vary from one to five nights (US tel. 800-270-1190, UK tel. 020/3514-0083, www.cross-pollinate.com, info@cross-pollinate.com).

Coach House Rentals offers a range of hand-selected apartments around the city, nearly all of them in real homes. As with any apartment rental, these can be an especially smart option if you're traveling as a group of four or more. Generally speaking, the more central the apartment, the more you pay (around £200/night for place in Pimlico, £425/night right by Westminster Abbey, £120-150/night farther afield). Each comes with a packet of neighborhood info, a "starter pack" of breakfast snacks, and usually either cable Internet access or Wi-Fi. A staff member meets you when you first arrive, and someone's always available over the phone (5-night minimum, £90 fee on top of quoted rental, tel. 020/8133-8332, rentals.chslondon.com, rentals@chslondon.com).

Many other organizations are ready to help; the following have been recommended by local guides and readers: www.perfectplaces.com, www.homefromhome.co.uk, www.londonhouse.com, www.gowithit.co.uk, www.aplacelikehome.co.uk, and www.regentsuites.com.

SLEEPING

EATING IN LONDON

Contents

England's reputation for miserable food, while once well-deserved, is now woefully dated. The British cuisine scene is lively, trendy, and pleasantly surprising. (Unfortunately, it's also expensive.) Even the basic, traditional pub grub has gone "upmarket," with gastropubs that serve fresh vegetables rather than soggy fries and mushy peas.

With "modern English" cuisine on the rise, you could try a different cuisine for each meal and never eat "local" English food, even on a lengthy stay in London. The sheer variety of foods—from every corner of its former empire and beyond—is astonishing. You'll be amazed at the number of hopping, happening new restaurants of all kinds.

If you want to dine (as opposed to eat), drop by a London newsstand to get a weekly entertainment guide or an annual restaurant guide (both have extensive restaurant listings). Visit www. london-eating.co.uk or www.squaremeal.co.uk for more options.

The thought of a £50 meal in Britain generally ruins my appetite, so my London dining is limited mostly to easygoing, fun, moderately priced alternatives. I've listed places by neighborhood—handy to your sightseeing or hotel. Considering how expensive London can be, if there's any good place to cut corners to stretch your budget, it's by eating cheaply (see "Lunch and Dinner on a Budget," later).

When restaurant-hunting, choose a spot filled with Londoners, not tourists. Venturing even a block or two off the main drag leads to higher-quality food for less than half the price of the tourist-oriented places. Londoners eat better at lower-rent locales.

London (and all of Britain) is smoke-free. Expect restaurants and pubs that sell food to be non-smoking indoors, with smokers occupying patios and doorways outside.

From Breakfast to Dessert

BREAKFAST FRY-UP

The traditional "fry-up" or "full English" breakfast is famous as a hearty way to start the day. Also known as a "heart attack on a plate," the breakfast is especially feast-like if you've just come from the land of the skimpy continental breakfast across the Channel. Your standard fry-up is a heated plate with a fried egg, Canadian-style bacon and/or sausage, a grilled tomato, sautéed mushrooms, baked beans, toast, and sometimes potatoes. The toast comes in a rack (to cool quickly and crisply) with butter and marmalade. The meal is typically topped off with tea or coffee. At a B&B or hotel, it may start with juice and cereal or porridge, and many progressive B&B owners offer vegetarian, organic, or other creative variations on the traditional breakfast.

This protein-stuffed meal is great for stamina, and tides many travelers over until dinner (or at least afternoon tea). You'll be asked which elements of the full fry-up you want; your B&B host appreciates it if you order only what you'll eat. There's nothing wrong with skipping some or all of the fry-up—few locals actually start their day with this heavy breakfast. They are more likely to eat Weetabix, a soggy British cousin of Shredded Wheat and perhaps the most absorbent material known to man.

LUNCH AND DINNER ON A BUDGET

You have plenty of inexpensive £8-12 choices: pub grub, daily lunch and early-bird dinner specials, ethnic restaurants, cafeterias, fast food, picnics, fish-and-chips, greasy-spoon cafés, or pizza.

I've found that portions are huge, and with locals feeling the pinch of their recession, **sharing plates** is generally just fine. Ordering two drinks, a soup or side salad, and splitting a £10 meat pie can make a good, filling meal. If you are on a limited budget, I'd recommend sharing a main course in a more expensive place for a nicer eating experience.

Tipping

Tipping is an issue only at restaurants and fancy pubs that have waiters and waitresses. If you order food at a counter (as is common at many pubs), don't tip.

If the menu states that service is included, there's no need to tip beyond that. If service isn't included, tip about 10 percent by rounding up. Leave the tip on the table, or hand it to your server with your payment for the meal and say, "Keep the rest, please." Most restaurants in London now add a 12.5 percent "optional" tip onto the bill—read your bill carefully, and tip only what you think the service warrants.

Pub grub is the most atmospheric budget option. Many of London's 7,000 pubs serve fresh, tasty buffets under ancient timbers, with hearty lunches and dinners priced reasonably at £6-10 (see "Pubs," later).

Classier restaurants have some affordable deals. Lunch is usually cheaper than dinner; many a top-end £25-for-dinner-type restaurant serves the same quality two-course lunch deals for £10. Look for early-bird dinner specials, allowing you to eat well and affordably (generally two courses-£15, three courses-£20), but early (about 17:30-19:00, last order by around 19:00).

Ethnic restaurants from all over the world add spice to London's cuisine scene. Eating Indian, Bangladeshi, Chinese, or Thai

is cheap (even cheaper if you do takeout). Middle Eastern stands sell gyros, falafel, and *shwarmas* (lamb in pita bread). An Indian samosa (greasy, flaky meat-and-vegetable pie) costs £2, can be microwaved, and makes a very cheap, if small, meal. You'll find all-you-can-eat Chinese and Thai places serving £6 meals and offering £3.50 takeaway boxes. While you can't "split" a buffet, you can split a takeaway box. Stuff the box full, and you and your partner can eat in a park for under £2 each—making this London's cheapest hot meal.

Most large **museums** (and many historic **churches**) have handy, moderately priced cafeterias.

Fast-food places, both American and British, are everywhere.

Cheap chain restaurants, such as steak houses and pizza places, serve no-nonsense food in a family-friendly setting (steak-house meals cost about £10, all-you-can-stomach pizza around £5). For

EATING

specific chains to keep an eye out for, see "Good Chain Restaurants," later.

Bakeries sell yogurt, cartons of "semi-skimmed" milk, pastries, and pasties (PASS-teez). Pasties are hearty, savory meat pies that originated in the Cornish mining country; they had big crimped edges so miners with filthy hands could eat them and toss the dirty crust. The most traditional filling is beef stew, but you'll also find them with chicken, vegetable, lamb and mint, and even Indian flavors inside.

Picnicking saves time and money. Fine park benches and polite pigeons abound in most neighborhoods. You can easily get prepared food to go. Munch a relaxed "meal on wheels" picnic during your open-top bus tour or river cruise to save 30 precious minutes for sightseeing.

Good **sandwich shops** and corner **grocery stores** are a hit with local workers eating on the run. Try boxes of orange juice (pure, by the liter), fresh bread, tasty English cheese, meat, a tube of Colman's English mustard, local eatin' apples, bananas, small tomatoes, a small tub of yogurt (drinkable), trail mix, nuts, plain or chocolate-covered digestive biscuits (cookies), and any local specialties. At **open-air markets** and **supermarkets,** you can get fruit and veggies in

small quantities. Supermarkets often have good deli sections, even offering Indian dishes, and sometimes salad bars. Decent packaged sandwiches are sold everywhere (£3-4).

DESSERTS (SWEETS)

To the British, the traditional word for dessert is "pudding," although it's also referred to as "sweets" these days. Sponge cake, cream, fruitcake, and meringue are key players.

Trifle is the best-known British concoction, consisting of sponge cake soaked in brandy or sherry (or orange juice for children), then covered with jam and/or fruit and custard cream. Whipped cream can sometimes put the final touch on this "light" treat.

Castle puddings are sponge puddings cooked in small molds and topped with Golden Syrup (a popular brand and a cross between honey and maple syrup). Bread-and-butter pudding consists of slices of French bread baked with milk, cream, eggs, and raisins (similar to the American preparation), served warm with cold cream. Hasty pudding, supposedly the invention of people in

British Chocolate

My chocoholic readers are enthusiastic about British chocolates. As with other dairy products, chocolate seems richer and creamier here than it does in the US, so even the basics like Mars, Kit Kat, and Twix have a different taste. Some favorites include Cadbury Gold bars (filled with liquid caramel), Cadbury Crunchie bars, Nestle's Lion bars (layered wafers covered in caramel and chocolate), Cadbury's Boost bars (a shortcake biscuit with caramel in milk chocolate), Cadbury Flake (crumbly folds of melt-in-your-mouth chocolate), Aero bars (with "aerated" chocolate filling), and Galaxy chocolate bars (especially the ones with hazelnuts). Thornton shops (in larger train stations) sell a box of sweets called the Continental Assortment, which comes with a tasting guide. (The highlight is the mocha white-chocolate truffle.) British M&Ms, called Smarties, are better than American ones. Many Brits feel that the ultimate treat is a box of either Nestlé Quality Street or Cadbury Roses—assortments of filled chocolates in colorful wrappers. At ice-cream vans, look for the beloved traditional "99p"—a vanilla soft-serve cone with a small Flake bar stuck right into the middle.

a hurry to avoid the bailiff, is made from stale bread with dried fruit and milk. Queen of puddings is a breadcrumb pudding topped with warm jam, meringue, and cream. Treacle pudding is a popular steamed pudding whose "sponge" mixture combines flour, suet (animal fat), butter, sugar, and milk. Christmas pudding (also called plum pudding) is a dense mixture with dried and candied fruit served with brandy butter or hard sauce. Sticky toffee pudding is a moist cake made with dates, heated and drizzled with toffee sauce, and served with ice cream or cream. Banoffee pie is the delicious (and better) British answer to banana cream pie.

The English version of custard is a smooth, yellow liquid. Cream tops most everything that custard does not. There's single cream for coffee. Double cream is really thick. Whipped cream is familiar, and clotted cream is the consistency of whipped butter.

Fool is a dessert with sweetened pureed fruit (such as rhubarb, gooseberries, or black currants) mixed with cream or custard and chilled. Elderflower is a popular flavoring for sorbet.

Flapjacks here aren't pancakes, but are dense, sweet oatmeal cakes (a little like a cross between a granola bar and a brownie). They come with toppings such as toffee and chocolate.

Scones are tops, and many inns and restaurants have their secret recipes. Whether made with fruit or topped with clotted cream, scones take the cake.

EATING

Types of Eateries

GOOD CHAIN RESTAURANTS

I know—you're going to London to enjoy characteristic little hole-in-the-wall pubs, so mass-produced food is the furthest thing from your mind. But several excellent chains with branches around London (and across the UK) can be a nice break from pub grub.

Sit-Down Chains

Like any restaurants in London, most branches of the chains listed here open daily no later than noon (several at 8:00 or 9:00), and close sometime between 22:00 and midnight. Occasionally a place may close on Sundays or in the afternoon between lunch and dinner, but these are rare exceptions.

Busaba Eathai is a hit with Londoners for its snappy (sometimes rushed) service, boisterous ambience, and good, inexpensive Thai cuisine. Wedge yourself at one of the 16-person hardwood tables or at a two-person table by the window—with everyone in the queue staring at your noodles (£7-12 meals, www.busaba.com). New locations pop up often, with outlets in Soho, Covent Garden, near the British Museum, and across from the Bond Street Tube stop.

Thai Square is another dependable Thai option with a much swankier atmosphere (£8-10 salads, noodle dishes, and curries; £9 daily lunch box specials; £13-18 meat dishes, www.thaisq.com). Handy locations include Soho, Trafalgar Square, Covent Garden, the Strand, South Kensington, near Oxford Circus, and The City (one on The Strand at Fleet Street and another near the Mansion House Tube stop).

Wagamama Noodle Bar, serving up pan-Asian cuisine (udon noodles, fried rice, and curry dishes), is a noisy, organic slurpathon. Portions are huge and splittable. There's one in almost every mid-size city in the UK, usually located in sprawling halls filled with long shared tables and busy servers who scrawl your order on the placemat. While the quality has gone downhill a bit as they've expanded, this remains a reliable choice with reasonable prices (£8-12 main dishes big enough for light eaters to share, good veggie options, www.wagamama.com). Branches are all over, including Soho, Piccadilly Circus, Leicester Square, Covent Garden, Kensington, near the British Museum, in the Harvey Nichols department store, near the Holborn Tube stop, in The City along Fleet Street and another near the Mansion House Tube stop, next to the Tower of London, and on the South Bank across from Vinopolis.

Masala Zone, serving accessible Indian food, makes a predictable, good alternative to the many one-off, hole-in-the-wall Indian joints around town. Try a curry-and-rice dish, a *thali* (platter with several small dishes), or their street food specials. Each branch has its own personality (£8-12 meals, www.masalazone. com). Locations include Soho, Covent Garden, Bayswater, and in the Selfridges department store on Oxford Street.

Côte Brasserie is a contemporary French chain serving good-value French cuisine in reliably pleasant settings, and at the right prices (£9-14 main dishes, early dinner specials, www.cote-restaurants.co.uk). Côte has locations in Soho, Covent Garden, Leicester Square, Oxford Circus, Fitzrovia, Kensington, Bayswater, and near St. Paul's on Ludgate Hill.

Byron, an upscale-hamburger chain with hip interiors, is worth seeking out if you need a burger fix. While British burgers aren't exactly like American ones—they tend to be a bit overcooked by our standards—Byron's burgers are your best bet (£7-10 burgers, www.byronhamburgers.com). Locations are in Soho, Covent Garden, Leicester Square, between Piccadilly Circus and Trafalgar Square, near St. Paul's, Fitzrovia, South Kensington, Kensington, and Greenwich. **Gourmet Burger Kitchen (GBK)** provides a cheaper alternative, serving burgers that are, if not quite gourmet, very good. Choices range from a simple cheeseburger to more elaborate options, such as Jamaican. Choose a table and order at the counter—they'll bring the food to you (£7-8 burgers, many outposts throughout London).

Loch Fyne Fish Restaurant is part of a Scottish chain that raises its own oysters and mussels. Its branches offer an inviting, lively atmosphere with a fine fishy energy and no pretense (£12-20 main dishes, two- and three-course specials often available before 19:00, www.lochfyne-restaurants.com). In London, there's one near Covent Garden, and another in The City (near Leadenhall Market).

Nando's is understandably popular as a casual, affordable place to get flame-broiled chicken with a range of Portuguese and South African flavors (£10 meals, www.nandos.co.uk). They're all over, including Soho, near Piccadilly Circus, between Covent Garden and Leicester Square, near Victoria Station, near the Baker Street Tube stop, Fitzrovia, two blocks behind St. Paul's, near Leadenhall Market, on Clink Street along the South Bank, and in South Kensington, Kensington, Notting Hill, and Bayswater.

At **Yo! Sushi,** sushi dishes trundle past on a conveyor belt. Color-coded plates tell you how much each dish costs (£1.80-5), and a picture-filled menu explains what you're eating. For £1.50, you get unlimited green tea (water for £1.05). Snag a bar stool and grab dishes as they rattle by (www.yosushi.com). Yo!s abound in London, with about 25 locations around town, including a handy branch a block from the London Eye on Belvedere Road, as well as outlets on Rupert Street, and on Haymarket—both a block from

EATING

Piccadilly Circus, within Selfridges and Harvey Nichols department stores, in the Whiteleys Shopping Centre on Queensway, and in several major train stations.

Ask and **Pizza Express** serve quality pasta and pizza in a pleasant, sit-down atmosphere that's family-friendly. **Jamie's Italian** (from celebrity chef Jamie Oliver) is hipper and pricier, and feels more upmarket.

Carry-Out Chains

While the following places might have some seating, they're best as an easy place to grab some prepackaged food on the run.

Major supermarket chains have smaller, offshoot branches that specialize in sandwiches, salads, and other prepared foods to go. These can be a picnicker's dream come true. Some shops are stand-alone, while others are located inside a larger store. The most prevalent—and best—is **M&S Simply Food** (an offshoot of the Marks & Spencer department-store chain; there's one in every major train station). **Sainsbury's Local** grocery stores also offer some decent prepared food; **Tesco Express** and **Tesco Metro** run a distant third.

Some "cheap and cheery" chains, such as **Pret à Manger, Eat, Apostrophe,** and **Pod** provide office workers with good, healthful sandwiches, salads, and pastries to go. Among these, Eat has a reputation for slightly higher quality...and higher prices.

West Cornwall Pasty Company and **Cornish Bakehouse** sell a variety of these traditional savory pies for around £3—as do many smaller, independent bakeries.

PUBS

Pubs are a basic part of the British social scene, and, whether you're a teetotaler or a beer-guzzler, they should be a part of your travel here. "Pub" is short for "public house." It's an extended living room where, if you don't mind the stickiness, you can feel the pulse of London. Smart travelers use the pubs to eat, drink, get out of the rain, watch sporting events, and make new friends.

Though hours vary, pubs generally serve beer Monday-Saturday 11:00-23:00 and Sunday 12:00-22:30, though many are open later, particularly on Friday and Saturday. As it nears closing time, you'll hear shouts of "Last orders." Then comes the 10-minute warning bell. Finally, they'll call "Time!" to pick up your glass, finished or not, when the pub closes.

A cup of darts is free for the asking. People go to a public house to be social. They want to talk. Get vocal with a local. This is easiest at the bar, where people assume you're in the mood to talk (rather than at a table, where you're allowed a bit of privacy). The pub is the next best thing to having relatives in town. Cheers!

Pub Grub

Pub grub gets better each year. It's London's best indoor eating value. For £6-10, you'll get a basic budget hot lunch or dinner in friendly surroundings. (For something more refined, try a gastropub, which serves higher-quality meals for £12-18.) The *Good Pub Guide* is an excellent resource (www.thegoodpubguide.co.uk). Pubs that are attached to restaurants, advertise their food, and are crowded with locals are more likely to have fresh food and a chef—and less likely to be the kind of pub that sells only lousy microwaved snacks.

Pubs generally serve traditional dishes, such as fish-and-chips, vegetables, "bangers and mash" (sausages and mashed potatoes), roast beef with Yorkshire pudding (batter-baked in the oven), and assorted meat pies, such as steak-and-kidney pie or shepherd's pie (stewed lamb topped with mashed potatoes). Sunday afternoons at most pubs are reserved for a traditional favorite, "Sunday Roast," usually roast beef, pork, or lamb served with vegetables. Side dishes include salads (sometimes even a nice self-serve salad bar), vegetables, and—invariably—"chips" (French fries). "Crisps" are potato chips. A "jacket potato" (baked potato stuffed with fillings of your choice) can almost be a meal in itself. A "ploughman's lunch" is a "traditional English meal" of bread, cheese, and sweet pickles that nearly every tourist tries...once. These days, you'll likely find more Italian pasta, curried dishes, and quiche on the menu than traditional fare.

Meals are usually served 12:00-14:00 and 18:00-20:00—generally not throughout the day. Since they make more money selling beer, many pubs stop serving meals early in the evening. There's often no table service. Order at the bar, then take a seat and they'll bring the food when it's ready (or sometimes you pick it up at the bar). Pay at the bar (sometimes when you order, sometimes after you eat). Don't tip unless it's a place with full table service. Servings are hearty, service is quick, and you'll rarely spend more than £10. (If you're on a tight budget, consider sharing a meal—note the size of portions around you before ordering.) A beer or cider adds another couple of pounds. (Free tap water is always available.)

Beer

The British take great pride in their beer. Many Brits think that drinking beer cold and carbonated, as Americans do, ruins the taste. Most pubs will have **lagers** (cold, refreshing, American-style beer), **ales**

EATING

Pub Appreciation

The pub is the heart of the people's England, where all manner of folks have, for generations, found their respite from work and a home-away-from-home. England's classic pubs are national treasures, with great cultural value and rich history, not to mention good beer and grub.

Their odd names can go back hundreds of years. Because so many medieval pub-goers were illiterate, pubs were simply named for the picture hung outside (e.g., The Crooked Stick, The Queen's Arms—meaning her coat of arms).

The Golden Age for pub-building was in the late Victorian era (c. 1880-1905), when pubs were independently owned and land prices were high enough to make it worthwhile to invest in fixing them up. The politics were pro-pub as well: Conservatives, backed by Big Beer, were in, and temperance-minded Liberals were out.

Especially in class-conscious Victorian times, traditional pubs were divided into sections by elaborate screens (now mostly gone), allowing the wealthy to drink in a more refined setting, while commoners congregated on the pub's rougher side. These were really "public houses," featuring nooks (snugs) for groups and clubs to meet, friends and lovers to rendezvous, and families to get out of the house at night.

Historic pubs still dot the London cityscape. The only place to see the very oldest-style tavern in the "domestic tradition" is at **Ye Olde Cheshire Cheese,** which was rebuilt in 1667 (after the Great Fire) from a 16th-century tavern (see description on page 252; £5-10 pub grub, £9-14 meals in the restaurant, open daily, 145 Fleet Street, Tube: Blackfriars, tel. 020/7353-6170). Imagine this mazelike place, with three separate bars, in the pre-Victorian era: With no bar, drinkers gathered around the fireplaces, while tap boys shuttled tankards up from the cellar. (This was long before barroom taps were connected to casks in the cellar. Oh, and don't say "keg"—that's a gassy modern thing.)

Late-Victorian pubs are more common, such as the lovingly restored 1897 **Princess Louise** (daily midday until 23:00, lunch and dinner served in less atmospheric upstairs lounge Mon-Fri, no food Sat-Sun, 208 High Holborn, see map on page 418, Tube: Holborn, tel. 020/7405-8816). These places are fancy, often with heavy embossed wallpaper ceilings, decorative tile work, fine-etched glass, ornate carved stillions (the big central hutch for storing bottles and glass), and even urinals equipped with a place to set your glass.

London's best Art Nouveau pub is **The Black Friar** (c. 1900-1915), with fine carved capitals, lamp holders, and quirky phrases worked into the decor (£9-15 meals, daily 10:00-23:00, outdoor seating, 174 Queen Victoria Street, Tube: Blackfriars, tel.

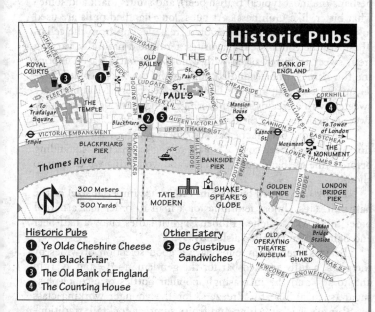

Historic Pubs

Historic Pubs
1. Ye Olde Cheshire Cheese
2. The Black Friar
3. The Old Bank of England
4. The Counting House

Other Eatery
5. De Gustibus Sandwiches

020/7236-5474).

The "former-bank pubs" represent a more modern trend in pub-building. As banks increasingly go electronic, they're moving out of lavish, high-rent old buildings. Many of these former banks are being refitted as pubs with elegant bars and freestanding stillions, which provide a fine centerpiece. Three such pubs are **The Old Bank of England** (£7-10 meals, Mon-Fri 11:00-23:00, food served 12:00-21:00, closed Sat-Sun, 194 Fleet Street, Tube: Temple, tel. 020/7430-2255), **The Jugged Hare** (open daily, 172 Vauxhall Bridge Road—see map on page 386, Tube: Victoria, tel. 020/7614-0134, also see listing on page 429), and **The Counting House** (Mon-Fri 11:00-23:00, closed Sat-Sun, 50 Cornhill, Tube: Bank, tel. 020/7283-7123, see listing on page 432).

Go pubbing in the evening for a lively time, or drop by during the quiet late morning (from 11:00), when the pub is empty and filled with memories.

(amber-colored, cellar-temperature beer), **bitters** (hop-flavored ale, perhaps the most typical British beer), and **stouts** (dark and somewhat bitter, like Guinness). At pubs, long-handled pulls are used to pull the traditional, rich-flavored "real ales" up from the cellar. These are the connoisseur's favorites: fermented naturally, varying from sweet to bitter, often with a hoppy or nutty flavor. Notice the fun names. Short-handled pulls at the bar mean colder, fizzier, mass-produced, and less interesting keg beers. Mild beers are sweeter, with a creamy malt flavoring. Irish cream ale is a smooth, sweet experience. Try the draft cider (sweet or dry)...carefully.

Order your beer at the bar and pay as you go, with no need to tip. An average beer costs £3. Part of the experience is standing before a line of "hand pulls," or taps, and wondering which beer to choose.

Drinks are served by the pint (20-ounce imperial size) or the half-pint. (It's almost feminine for a man to order just a half; I order mine with quiche.) Proper English ladies enjoy a half-beer and half-7-Up mix called a **shandy.**

Besides beer, many pubs have a good selection of wines by the glass, a fully stocked bar for the gentleman's "G and T" (gin and tonic), and the increasingly popular bottles of alcohol-plus-sugar (such as Bacardi Breezers) for the younger working-class set. **Pimm's** is a refreshing and fruity summer cocktail, traditionally popular during Wimbledon. It's an upper-class drink...a rough bloke might insult a pub by claiming it sells more Pimm's than beer. Teetotalers can order from a wide variety of soft drinks. Children are served food and soft drinks in pubs, but you must be 18 to order a beer.

INDIAN CUISINE

Eating Indian food is "going local" in cosmopolitan, multiethnic London. Take the opportunity to sample food from Britain's former colony. Indian cuisine is as varied as the country itself. In general, they use more exotic spices than British or American cuisine—some hot, some sweet. Indian food is very vegetarian-friendly, offering many meatless dishes to choose from on any given menu.

For a simple meal that costs about £10-12, order one dish with rice and naan (Indian flatbread that can be served plain, with garlic, or other ways). Many restaurants offer a fixed-price combination called a *thali* that offers more variety, and is simpler and cheaper than ordering à la carte. For about £20, you can make a mix-and-match platter out of several sharable dishes, including dal (lentil soup) as a starter, one or two meat or vegetable dishes with sauce (e.g., chicken curry, chicken *tikka masala* in a creamy tomato sauce, grilled fish tandoori, chickpea *chana masala*, or the spicy vindaloo dish), *raita* (a cooling yogurt that's added to spicy dishes), rice, naan, and an Indian beer (wine and Indian food don't really mix) or chai (a cardamom- and cinnamon-spiced tea, usually served with milk).

Restaurants

CENTRAL LONDON

I've arranged these options by neighborhood, but they're all within about a 15-minute walk of each other. Survey your options before settling on a place.

Near Soho and Chinatown

London has a trendy scene that most Beefeater-seekers miss entirely. Foodies who want to eat well skip the more staid and touristy zones near Piccadilly and Trafalgar Square, and head to Soho instead. Make it a point to dine in Soho at least once, to feel the pulse of London's eclectic urban melting pot of international flavors. These restaurants are scattered throughout a chic, creative, and borderline-seedy zone that teems with hipsters, theatergoers, and London's gay community. Even if you plan to have dinner elsewhere, it's a treat just to wander around Soho. (For a guided visit, see my West End Walk.)

Note: While gentrification has mostly stripped this area (no pun intended) of its former "red light district" vibe, a few pockets of sex for sale survive. Beware of the extremely welcoming women standing outside the strip clubs (especially on Great Windmill Street). Enjoy the sales pitch—but know that only fools fall for the "£5 drink and show" lure.

On and near Wardour Street, in the Heart of Soho

Running through the middle of Soho, rumbling past what's left of the strip-club zone, Wardour Street is ground zero for creative restaurateurs hoping to break into the big leagues. Strolling up this street—particularly from Brewer Street northward—you can take your pick from a world of options: Thai, Indonesian, Vietnamese, Italian, French and even...English. Not yet tarnished by the corporatization creeping in from areas to the south, this drag still seems to hit the right balance between trendy and accessible. While I've listed several choices below (including some that are a block or two off Wardour Street), simply strolling the length of the street and following your appetite to the place that looks best is a great plan.

Princi is a vast, bright, efficient, wildly popular Italian deli/bakery with Milanese flair. Along one wall is a long counter with display cases offering a tempting array of pizza *rustica*, *panini* sandwiches, focaccia, a few pasta dishes, and desserts (look in the win-

Central London Eateries

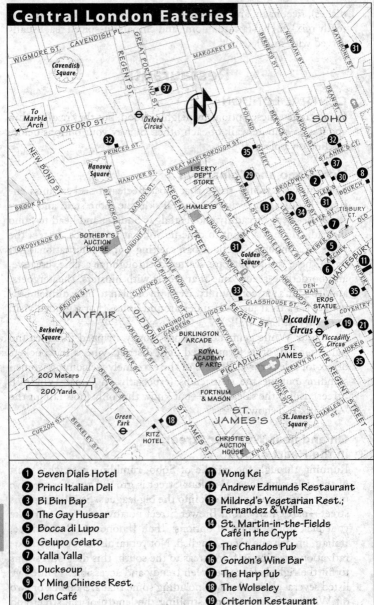

1 Seven Dials Hotel	**11** Wong Kei
2 Princi Italian Deli	**12** Andrew Edmunds Restaurant
3 Bi Bim Bap	**13** Mildred's Vegetarian Rest.; Fernandez & Wells
4 The Gay Hussar	**14** St. Martin-in-the-Fields Café in the Crypt
5 Bocca di Lupo	
6 Gelupo Gelato	**15** The Chandos Pub
7 Yalla Yalla	**16** Gordon's Wine Bar
8 Ducksoup	**17** The Harp Pub
9 Y Ming Chinese Rest.	**18** The Wolseley
10 Jen Café	**19** Criterion Restaurant

EATING

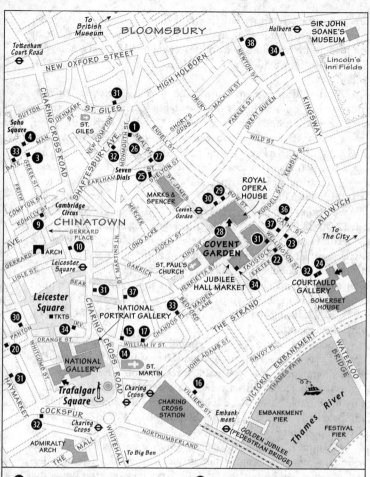

20 West End Kitchen
21 Woodlands South Indian Vegetarian Restaurant
22 Joe Allen
23 Sofra Turkish Restaurant
24 Sitar Indian Restaurant
25 Belgo Centraal
26 Neal's Yard Eateries
27 Food for Thought Café
28 Union Jacks

29 Masala Zone (2)
30 Busaba Eathai (3)
31 Byron (7)
32 Thai Square (5)
33 Nando's (3)
34 Wagamama Noodle Bar (4)
35 Yo! Sushi (3)
36 Loch Fyne Fish Restaurant
37 Côte Brasserie (4)
38 The Princess Louise Pub

EATING

dow from the street to see their wood-fired oven in action). Order your food at the counter, then find a space at a long shared table; or get it to go for an affordable and fast meal (£7-13 meals, Mon-Sat 8:00-24:00, Sun 8:30-22:00, 135 Wardour Street, tel. 020/7478-8888).

Bi Bim Bap is named for what it sells: *bibimbap* (literally "mixed rice"), a scalding stone bowl filled with rice and thinly sliced veggies, topped with a fried egg. Mix it up with your spoon, flavor it to taste with the two sauces, then dig in with your chopsticks. While purists go with the straightforward rice bowl, you can pay a few pounds extra to add other toppings—including chicken, *bulgogi* (marinated beef strips), and mushrooms. Though the food is traditional Korean, the stylish, colorful interior lets you know you're in Soho (£7-10 meals, Mon-Fri 12:00-15:00 & 18:00-23:00, Sat 12:00-23:00, closed Sun, 11 Greek Street, tel. 020/7287-3434).

The Gay Hussar squeezes several cozy tables into what the owners say is the only Hungarian restaurant in England. It's traditional fare: cabbage, sauerkraut, sausage, paprika, and pork, as well as duck and chicken. Wash down this Hungarian comfort food with a Hungarian wine (£15-18 meals, Mon-Sat 12:15-14:30 & 17:30-22:30, closed Sun, 2 Greek Street, tel. 020/7437-0973, gayhussar.co.uk).

Bocca di Lupo, a pricey and popular splurge, serves small portions of classic regional Italian food. Dressy and a bit snooty, it's a place where you're glad you made a reservation. The counter seating, on cushy stools with a view into the open kitchen, is particularly memorable (Mon-Sat 12:30-15:00 & 17:30-23:00, Sun 12:30-15:30 & 17:30-21:30, 12 Archer Street, tel. 020/7734-2223, www.boccadilupo.com).

Gelupo, Bocca di Lupo's sister *gelateria* across the street, has a wide array of ever-changing but always creative and delicious dessert favorites—ranging from popular standbys like the incredibly rich chocolate sorbet to fresh-mint *stracciatella* to hay (yes, hay). A £3 sampler cup or cone gets you two flavors (and little taster spoons are generously offered to help you choose). Everything is homemade, and the white subway-tile interior feels clean and bright. They also have espresso drinks and—at lunchtime—£5-6 deli sandwiches (daily 12:00 until late, 7 Archer Street, tel. 020/7287-5555).

Yalla Yalla is a hole-in-the-wall serving up high-quality Beirut street food—hummus, baba ghanoush, tabbouleh, and *shawarmas*. Stylish as you'd expect for Soho, it's tucked down a seedy alley across from a sex shop. Eat in the cramped and cozy interior or at one of the few outdoor tables, or get your food to go (£3-4 sandwiches, £4-6 *meze*, £8 *mezes* platter available until 17:00, £10-15 bigger dishes, Mon-Sat 10:00-23:00, Sun 10:00-22:00, 1 Green's Court—just north of Brewer Street, tel. 020/7287-7663).

Ducksoup, a short block over from Wardour Street, is an upscale-feeling yet cool and relaxed little bar, with a small but thoughtful menu of well-executed international and modern British dishes (£7 small plates, £14 big plates—sharing several items can add up). The menu is handwritten, the music is on vinyl, and the rough woodwork and cramped-but-convivial atmosphere give it the feeling of a well-loved wine bar. While a bit overpriced, the atmosphere is memorable (Mon-Sat 12:00-24:00, food served until 22:30, Sun 13:00-17:00, 41 Dean Street, tel. 020/7287-4599).

And for Dessert: In addition to the outstanding gelato at **Gelupo** and the treats at **Princi** (both described earlier), several other places along Wardour Street boast window displays that tickle the sweet tooth. In just a couple of blocks, you'll see pastry shops, a *crêperie,* and a Hummingbird cupcake shop.

Soho Chain Restaurants: Some of Britain's most popular chain restaurants started out here in Soho, but in this fast-evolving neighborhood, they're now a little like stale sushi. While I wouldn't waste a Soho meal on one of these places, they're a convenient fallback: **Byron** (particularly appealing industrial-mod branch at 97-99 Wardour Street), **Busaba Eathai** (106 Wardour Street), **Thai Square** (27-28 St. Anne's Court, plus one near Trafalgar Square at 21-24 Cockspur Street), **Wagamama** (10A Lexington Street), **Masala Zone** (9 Marshall Street), **Côte** (124-126 Wardour Street), and **Nando's** (10 Frith Street). For descriptions, see page 410.

Authentic Chinese Food in and near Chinatown

The main drag of Chinatown (Gerrard Street, with the ornamental archways) is lined with touristy, interchangeable Chinese joints—but these places seem to have an edge.

Y Ming Chinese Restaurant—across Shaftesbury Avenue from the ornate gates, clatter, and dim sum of Chinatown—has dressy European decor, serious but helpful service, and authentic Northern Chinese cooking. London's food critics consider this well worth the short walk from the heart of Chinatown for food that's a notch above (good £12 meal deal offered 12:00-18:00, £8-12 plates, open Mon-Sat 12:00-23:45, closed Sun, turquoise corner shop at 35-36 Greek Street, tel. 020/7734-2721).

Jen Café, across the little square called Newport Place, is a humble Chinese corner eatery much loved for its homemade dumplings. It's just stools and simple seating, with fast service, a fun, inexpensive menu, and a devoted following (£6-8 plates, daily 10:30-20:30, until 21:30 Thu-Sun, cash only, 4 Newport Place, tel. 020/7287-9708).

Wong Kei Chinese restaurant, at the Wardour Street (west) end of the Chinatown drag, offers a bewildering variety of dishes served by notoriously brusque waiters in a setting that feels like a hospital cafeteria. Londoners put up with the abuse to enjoy one of the satisfying BBQ rice dishes or hot pots. Individuals and couples are usually seated at communal tables, while larger parties are briskly shuffled up or down stairs (£7-12 main dishes, £10-15 fixed-price meals, cash only, Mon-Sat 11:30-23:30, Sun 11:30-22:30, 41-43 Wardour Street, tel. 020/7437-8408).

Sedate and Upscale Options on Lexington Street, in the Heart of Soho

Andrew Edmunds Restaurant is a tiny, candlelit space where you'll want to hide your camera and guidebook and not act like a tourist. This little place—with a jealous and loyal clientele—is the closest I've found to Parisian quality in a cozy restaurant in London. The extensive wine list, modern European cooking, and creative seasonal menu are worth the splurge (£5-8 starters, £12-20 main dishes, Mon-Sat 12:00-15:30 & 17:30-22:45, Sun 13:00-16:00 & 18:00-22:30, these are last-order times, come early or call ahead, request ground floor rather than basement, 46 Lexington Street, tel. 020/7437-5708, www.andrewedmunds.com).

Mildred's Vegetarian Restaurant, across from Andrew Edmunds, has an enjoyable menu and a pleasant interior filled with happy eaters (£8-11 meals, Mon-Sat 12:00-23:00, closed Sun, vegan options, 45 Lexington Street, tel. 020/7494-1634, www.mildreds.co.uk).

Fernandez & Wells is a cozy, convivial, delightfully simple little wine, cheese, and ham bar. Drop in and grab a stool as you belly up to the big wooden bar. Share a plate of top-quality cheeses and/or Spanish, Italian, or French hams with fine bread and oil, while sipping a nice glass of wine (daily 12:00-22:00, until 23:00 Thu-Sat, quality sandwiches at lunch, 43 Lexington Street, tel. 020/7734-1546).

Traditional Choices near Trafalgar Square

These places, all of which provide a more "jolly olde" experience than high cuisine, are within about 100 yards of Trafalgar Square.

St. Martin-in-the-Fields Café in the Crypt is just right for a tasty meal on a monk's budget—maybe even on a monk's tomb. You'll dine sitting on somebody's gravestone in an ancient crypt. Their enticing buffet line is kept stocked all day, serving breakfast, lunch, and dinner (£7-10 cafeteria plates, hearty traditional desserts, free jugs of water). They also serve a restful cream tea (£6, daily 14:00-18:00). You'll find the café directly under the St. Martin-in-the-Fields Church, facing Trafalgar Square—enter through the glass pavilion next to the church (Mon-Tue 8:00-20:00, Wed

8:00-22:30, Thu-Sat 8:00-21:00, Sun 11:00-18:00, profits go to the church, Tube: Charing Cross, tel. 020/7766-1158 or 020/7766-1100). Wednesday evenings at 20:00 come with a live jazz band (£5.50-12 tickets). While here, check out the concert schedule for the busy church upstairs (or visit www.smitf.org).

The Chandos Pub's Opera Room floats amazingly apart from the tacky crush of tourism around Trafalgar Square. Look for it opposite the National Portrait Gallery (corner of William IV Street and St. Martin's Lane) and climb the stairs (to the left or right of the pub entrance) to the Opera Room. This is a fine Trafalgar rendezvous point and wonderfully local pub. They serve £5 sandwiches and a better-than-average range of traditional pub meals for under £10—meat pies and fish-and-chips are their specialty. The ground-floor pub is stuffed with regulars and offers snugs (private booths) and more serious beer drinking. To eat on that level, you have to order upstairs and carry it down. Chandos proudly serves the local Samuel Smith beer at £3 a pint (kitchen open daily 11:00-19:00, Fri and Sun until 18:00, order and pay at the bar, 29 St. Martin's Lane, Tube: Leicester Square, tel. 020/7836-1401).

Gordon's Wine Bar is really a Back Door eatery—you have to enter through its leafy patio just past its locked street entrance. This candlelit 15th-century wine cellar is filled with dusty old bottles, faded British memorabilia, and nine-to-fivers. At the "English rustic" buffet, choose a hot meal or cold meat dish with a salad (figure around £7-8/dish); the £10 cheese plate comes with two cheeses, bread, and a pickle. Then step up to the wine bar and consider the many varieties of wine and port available by the glass (this place is passionate about port). The low, carbon-crusted vaulting deeper in the back seems to intensify the Hogarth-painting atmosphere. Although it's crowded, you can normally corral two chairs and grab the corner of a table. The crowd often spills out onto the patio, and on hot days a chef cooks at a barbecue for a long line of tables (arrive before 17:00 to get a seat, Mon-Sat 11:00-23:00, Sun 12:00-22:00, 2 blocks from Trafalgar Square, bottom of Villiers Street at #47, Tube: Embankment, tel. 020/7930-1408, manager Gerard Menan).

Ales: The Harp, clearly a local favorite, is a crowded and cluttered little pub just a block above Trafalgar Square. While they serve no food, this is a good, central spot to nurse a fine ale and befriend one of the Londoners crowded around the coaster-coated bar. This is a top choice for an après-work pint among nine-to-fivers, who stand in the dozens out front after the workday, sipping their beers (Mon-Sat 10:30-23:30, Sun 12:00-22:30, 47 Chandos Place, tel. 020/7836-0291).

Near Piccadilly

The first two places are upscale and snooty—but if you want something cheaper in this same area, you'll find plenty of other options.

Swanky Splurges

The Wolseley is the grand 1920s showroom of a long-defunct British car. The last Wolseley drove out with the Great Depression, but today this old-time bistro bustles with formal waiters serving traditional Austrian and French dishes in an elegant black-marble-and-chandeliers setting fit for its location next to the Ritz. Although the food can be unexceptional, prices are reasonable, and the presentation and setting are grand. Reservations are a must (£13-30 main courses; cheaper soup, salad, and sandwich "café menu" available; both menus available in all areas of restaurant, Mon-Fri 7:00-24:00, Sat 8:00-24:00, Sun 8:00-23:00, 160 Piccadilly—see map on page 418, tel. 020/7499-6996, www.thewolseley.com). They're popular for their fancy cream or afternoon tea (for details, see page 433).

The palatial **Criterion** offers grand-piano ambience beneath gilded tiles and chandeliers in a dreamy Byzantine church setting from 1880. It's right on Piccadilly Circus but a world away from the punk junk. It's a deal for the visual experience during lunch and if you order the £20-25 fixed-price meal (except on Sun, when you must order from the expensive à la carte menu). At any hour, the service couldn't care less. Anyone can drop in for coffee or a drink (Mon-Sat 12:00-14:30 & 17:30-23:30, Sun 12:00-15:30 & 17:30-22:30, 224 Piccadilly, tel. 020/7930-0488, www.criterionrestaurant.com).

Cheaper Options near Piccadilly

Hungry and broke in the theater district? Head for Panton Street (off Haymarket, two blocks southeast of Piccadilly Circus), where several hardworking little places compete, all seeming to offer a three-course meal for about £9. Peruse the entire block (vegetarian, Pizza Express, Moroccan, Chinese, and diners) before making your choice.

The **West End Kitchen** serves up Italian (£7-10 pizzas, £9-17 meals, daily 11:45-22:30, 5 Panton Street, tel. 020/7839-4241). The **Woodlands South Indian Vegetarian Restaurant** offers an impressive £19 *thali* combination plate (otherwise £7 main courses, daily 12:00-22:45, 37 Panton Street, tel. 020/7839-7258).

Good Chains near Piccadilly: **Busaba Eathai** (35 Panton Street), **Wagamama** (another in Leicester Square at 14 Irving Street), **Byron** (11 Haymarket, but enter around the corner on Whitcomb Street), and **Nando's** (46 Glasshouse Street). For descriptions, see page 410.

Near Covent Garden

Covent Garden bustles with people and touristy eateries. The area feels overrun, but if you must eat around here, you have some good choices.

Joe Allen, tucked in a brick cellar a block away from the market, serves modern international and American cuisine with both style and hubbub. Downstairs off a quiet street with candles and white tablecloths, it's comfortably spacious and popular with the theater crowd. It feels a bit old-fashioned and cluttered, but in a welcoming way (£7 starters, £10-30 main courses, £15 two-course specials and £20 three-course specials available at lunch and 17:00-18:45, open Mon-Fri 12:00-24:00, Sat-Sun 10:00-24:00, piano music after 19:00, 13 Exeter Street, tel. 020/7836-0651).

Sofra Turkish Restaurant is good for quality Turkish with a touch of class. They have several menus: *meze* (Turkish tapas, £4-7), vegetarian, and £11-13 fixed-price meals (also £10-15 main dishes, daily 9:00-23:00, 36 Tavistock Street, tel. 020/7240-3773).

Sitar Indian Restaurant is a well-respected Indian/Bangladeshi place serving dishes from many regions, fine fish, and a tasty £15 vegetarian *thali* (combo plate). It's small and dressy, with snappy service (£10-17 main dishes, Mon-Fri 12:00-24:00, Sat-Sun 15:00-23:00, next to Somerset House at 149 Strand, tel. 020/7836-3730).

Belgo Centraal serves hearty Belgian specialties in a vast 400-seat underground lair. It's a mussels, chips, and beer emporium dressed up as a mod-monastic refectory—with noisy acoustics and waiters garbed as Trappist monks. The classy restaurant section is more comfortable and less rowdy, but usually requires reservations. It's often more fun just to grab a spot in the boisterous beer hall, with its tight, communal benches (no reservations accepted). Both sides have the same menu and specials. Belgians claim they eat as well as the French and as heartily as the Germans. This place, which offers a stunning array of dark, blonde, and fruity Belgian beers, actually makes Belgian things trendy—a formidable feat (£10-14 main dishes, open daily 12:00-23:00; Mon-Fri £5-6.30 "beat the clock" meal specials 17:00-18:30—the time you order is the price you pay—including main dishes and fries; no meal-splitting after 18:30, and you must buy food with beer except Fri-Sat; daily £8 lunch special 12:00-17:00; 1 kid eats free for each parent ordering a regular entrée; 1 block north of Covent Garden Tube station at 50 Earlham Street, tel. 020/7813-2233, www.belgo-restaurants.co.uk).

Neal's Yard is a surprisingly colorful courtyard full of cheap, hip, and healthy eateries near Covent Garden. The neighborhood is a tabbouleh of fun, hippie-type cafés. One of the best—nearby—is the venerable and ferociously vegetarian **Food for Thought,** packed with local health nuts (good £8 vegetarian meals, Mon-Sat 12:00-20:30, Sun 12:00-17:30, 2 blocks north of Covent Garden Tube station at 31 Neal Street, tel. 020/7836-9072).

Union Jacks, a venture of British celebrity chef Jamie Oliver, fuses traditional British ingredients to make inventive modern dishes. Jamie's wood-fired pizzas are topped not with cheese and tomatoes, but roast pig shoulder or oxtail and brisket. While this sounds risky, he pulls it off with great flavors, plus fun "fizzy drinks." It sits right inside the Covent Garden market hall (£5-8 small plates are very small, £10-13 pizzas, £15 classic British dishes, daily 12:00-23:00, Covent Garden tel. 020/3640-7086).

Good Chains near Covent Garden: This area seems to have a branch of nearly every London chain, including **Masala Zone** (particularly fun branch at the top end of the market has giant, colorful marionettes suspended from the ceiling, 48 Floral Street), **Côte** (17-21 Tavistock Street and one closer to Leicester Square at 50-51 St. Martin's Lane), **Busaba Eathai** (44 Floral Street), **Thai Square** (166-170 Shaftesbury Avenue, plus one next to Sitar Indian Restaurant at 148 The Strand), **Wagamama** (1 Tavistock Street), **Byron** (behind the London Transport Museum at 33-35 Wellington Street), **Loch Fyne** (a couple of blocks behind the square at 2 Catherine Street), and **Nando's** (66-68 Chandos Place). For descriptions, see page 410.

Near the British Museum, in Fitzrovia

To avoid the touristy crush right around the museum (and just southwest, in Soho), Londoners head a few blocks west, to the Fitzrovia area. Here, tiny Charlotte Place is lined with small eateries (including the first two listed below); nearby, the much bigger Charlotte Street has several more good options. The higher street signs you'll notice on Charlotte Street are a holdover from a time when they needed to be visible to carriage drivers. This area is a short walk from the Goodge Street Tube station—convenient to the British Museum, and just two blocks from Pollock's Toy Museum.

Salumeria Dino serves up hearty sandwiches, pasta, and Italian coffee. Dino, a native of Naples, has run his little shop for more than 30 years and has managed to create a classic Italian deli that's so authentic, you'll walk out singing "O Sole Mio" (£3-5 sandwiches, £1 takeaway cappuccinos, Mon-Fri 9:00-18:00, closed Sat-Sun, 15 Charlotte Place, see map on page 399, tel. 020/7580-3938).

Lantana OUT, next door to Salumeria Dino, is an Australian coffee shop that sells modern soups, sandwiches, and salads at their takeaway window (£3-7 meals, pricier sit-down café—**Lantana IN** serving £8-10 meals—next door, Mon-Fri 7:30-15:00, café also open Sat-Sun 9:00-17:00, 13 Charlotte Place, see map on page 399, tel. 020/7637-3347).

Nearby Chains: Several recommended chain restaurants are a short walk from the museum, including **Busaba Eathai** (22 Store Street), **Wagamama** (4 Streatham Street and near Holborn Tube stop at 123 Kingsway), **Côte** (5 Charlotte Street), **Byron** (6 Store Street, with another at 6 Rathbone Place), and **Nando's** (9-10 Southampton Place). For descriptions, see page 410.

WEST LONDON
Near Victoria Station Accommodations

These restaurants are within a few blocks of Victoria Station—and all are places where I've enjoyed eating. As with the accommodations in this area, I've grouped them by location: east or west of the station (see the map on page 386).

Cheap Eats: For groceries, a handy **M&S Simply Food** is inside Victoria Station (Mon-Sat 7:00-24:00, Sun 8:00-23:00, near the front, by the bus terminus), along with a **Sainsbury's Local** (daily 6:00-23:00, at rear entrance, on Eccleston Street). A larger Sainsbury's is on Wilton Road near Warwick Way, a couple of blocks southeast of the station (Mon-Fri 7:00-23:00, Sat 7:00-22:00, Sun 11:00-17:00). A string of good ethnic restaurants lines Wilton Road, including this neighborhood's obligatory branch of **Nando's.** For affordable if forgettable meals, try the row of cheap little eateries on Elizabeth Street.

West of Victoria Station (Belgravia)

Ebury Wine Bar, filled with young professionals, provides a cut-above atmosphere (rumor has it that Prince William held his bachelor party here). In the delightful back room, the fancy menu features modern European cuisine with a French accent, including delicious £15-22 main dishes and a £21 two-course and £27 three-course special (available Mon-Fri at lunch and daily 18:00-20:00; three-course meal includes a glass of Prosecco that you're welcome to swap for house wine). At the wine bar, find a cheaper bar menu that's better than your average pub grub (£9-15 meals). This is emphatically a "traditional wine bar," with no beers on tap (restaurant open daily 12:00-15:00 & 18:00-22:30, wine bar open all day long, reservations smart, at intersection of Ebury and Elizabeth Streets, 139 Ebury Street, tel. 020/7730-5447, www.eburyrestaurant. co.uk).

La Bottega is an Italian delicatessen that fits its upscale Belgravia neighborhood. It offers tasty, freshly cooked pastas (£6), lasagnas, and salads (£9 lasagna-and-salad meal), along with great sandwiches (£3) and a good coffee bar with Italian pastries. It's fast (order at the counter), and the ingredients would please an Italian

EATING

grandmother. Grab your meal to go, or enjoy the Belgravia good life with locals, either sitting inside or on the sidewalk (Mon-Fri 8:00-19:00, Sat 9:00-18:00, Sun 9:00-17:00, on corner of Ebury and Eccleston Streets, tel. 020/7730-2730).

The Thomas Cubitt pub, named for the urban planner who designed much of Belgravia, is a trendy neighborhood gastropub packed with young professionals. It's pricey and a pinch pretentious, and prides itself on using sustainable ingredients in its modern English cooking. With a bright but slightly cramped interior and fine sidewalk seating, it's great for a drink or meal (£4-6 small plates, £14-17 main dishes, 44 Elizabeth Street). Upstairs is a more refined restaurant with the same kitchen, but an emphasis on finer technique and presentation (£8-12 starters, £19-29 main courses, reservations recommended, food served daily 12:00-22:00, tel. 020/7730-6060).

The Duke of Wellington pub is a classic neighborhood place with forgettable grub, sidewalk seating, and an inviting interior. A bit more lowbrow than my other Belgravia listings, this may be your best shot at meeting a local (£5 sandwiches, £7-10 meals, food served Mon-Sat 12:00-15:00 & 18:00-21:00, Sun lunch only, 63 Eaton Terrace, tel. 020/7730-1782).

South End of Ebury Street: A five-minute walk down Ebury Street, where it intersects with Pimlico Road, you'll find a pretty square with a few more eateries to consider—including **The Orange,** a high-priced gastropub with the same owners and a similar menu to The Thomas Cubitt (described earlier); and **Daylesford,** the deli and café of an organic farm (£3-5 light meals to go—a good picnic option).

East of Victoria Station (Pimlico)

Grumbles brags it's been serving "good food and wine at nonscary prices since 1964." Offering a delicious mix of "modern eclectic French and traditional English," this unpretentious little place with cozy booths inside (on two levels, including a cellar) and four nice sidewalk tables is the best spot to eat well in this otherwise workaday neighborhood. Their traditional dishes are their forte (£10-16 plates, £11 early-bird specials 18:00-19:00, open Mon-Sat 12:00-14:30 & 18:00-23:00, Sun 12:00-22:30, reservations wise, half a block north of Belgrave Road at 35 Churton Street, tel. 020/7834-0149, www.grumblesrestaurant.co.uk).

Pimlico Fresh's breakfasts and lunches feature fresh, organic ingredients, served up with good coffee and/or fresh-squeezed juices. Choose from the dishes listed on the wall-sized chalkboard that lines the small eating area, then order at the counter. This place is heaven if you've slept through your hotel's breakfast hour, or if you just need a break from the bacon-eggs-beans routine (£5-10 meals, take-out lunches, plenty of vegetarian options; Mon-Fri 7:30-19:30, breakfast served until 15:00; Sat-Sun 9:00-18:00, breakfast until 17:00; 86 Wilton Road, tel. 020/7932-0030).

Seafresh Fish Restaurant is the neighborhood place for plaice—and classic and creative fish-and-chips cuisine. You can either take out on the cheap or eat in, enjoying a white-fish ambience. Though Mario's father started this place in 1965, it feels like the chippie of the 21st century (meals-£5-8 to go, £12-17 to sit, Mon-Fri 12:00-15:00 & 17:00-22:30, Sat 12:00-22:30, closed Sun, 80-81 Wilton Road, tel. 020/7828-0747).

The Jugged Hare pub, a 10-minute walk from Victoria Station, sits in a lavish old bank building, with vaults replaced by tankards of beer and a fine kitchen. They have a fun, traditional menu with more fresh veggies than fries, and a plush, vivid pub scene good for a meal or just a drink (£6.50 sandwiches, £12 meals; Mon-Sat 11:00-23:00, food served 12:00-22:00; Sun 12:00-22:30, food served until 21:30; 172 Vauxhall Bridge Road, tel. 020/7828-1543).

St. George's Tavern is the neighborhood's best pub for a full meal. They serve dinner from the same menu in three zones: on the sidewalk to catch the sun and enjoy some people-watching, in the ground-floor pub, and in a classier downstairs dining room. They're proud of their sausages. The scene is inviting for just a beer, too (£8-14 meals, food served Mon-Sat 10:00-22:00, Sun until 21:30, corner of Hugh Street and Belgrave Road, tel. 020/7630-1116).

South Kensington

Popular eateries line Old Brompton Road and Thurloe Street (Tube: South Kensington), and a good selection of cheap eateries are clumped around the Tube station. For locations, see the map on page 391.

La Bouchée Bistro Café is a classy hole-in-the-wall touch of France. This candlelit and woody bistro, with very tight seating, serves a special fixed-price meal (£13.50 two courses, £14.50 three courses) on weekdays during lunch and 17:00-19:00 (also £16-20 à la carte main courses). Reservations are smart in the evening (daily 12:00-15:00 & 17:30-23:00, 56 Old Brompton Road, tel. 020/7589-1929).

Moti Mahal Indian Restaurant, with minimalist-yet-upscale ambience and attentive service, serves mostly Bangladeshi cuisine that's delicious. Consider chicken *jalfrezi* if you like spicy food, and buttery chicken if you don't (£9-15 main courses, daily 12:00-14:30 & 17:30-23:30, 3 Glendower Place, tel. 020/7584-8428).

Bosphorus Kebabs is the student favorite for a quick, fast, and hearty Turkish dinner. While mostly for takeaway, they have a few tight tables indoors and on the sidewalk (£5-7 meals, Turkish

EATING

kebabs, daily 10:30-24:00, 59 Old Brompton Road, tel. 020/7584-4048).

Beirut Express has fresh, well-prepared Lebanese cuisine. In the front, you'll find takeaway service as well as barstools for a quick bite (£4.50 sandwiches). In the back is a sit-down restaurant with £14-18 plates and £5-8 *mezes* (daily 12:00-24:00, 65 Old Brompton Road, tel. 020/7591-0123).

The Anglesea Arms, with a great terrace surrounded by classy South Kensington buildings, is a destination pub that feels like the classic neighborhood favorite. It's a thriving and happy place, with a woody ambience and a mellow step-down back dining room a world away from any tourism. While the food is the main draw, this is also a fine place to just have a beer (£6-8 starters, £12-17 main dishes, meals served daily 12:00-15:00 & 18:00-22:00; from Old Brompton Road, turn left at Onslow Gardens and go down a few blocks to 15 Selwood Terrace; tel. 020/7373-7960).

Rocca di Papa is a bright and dressy Italian place with a heated terrace (£6-8 pizza, pasta, and salads; daily 11:30-23:30, 73 Old Brompton Road, tel. 020/7225-3413).

Fernandez & Wells has a second outpost just north of the South Kensington Tube station (8 Exhibition Road; similar menu and hours as Soho location—see listing on page 422). Just up Exhibition Road (at #19) is a branch of **Thai Square** (described on page 410).

Supermarkets: **Tesco Express** (daily 6:00-24:00, 50-52 Old Brompton Road) and **Little Waitrose** (daily 7:00-22:00, 99-103 Old Brompton Road) are handy for picnics.

Near Bayswater and Notting Hill Accommodations

For locations, see the map on page 394.

Maggie Jones's has been feeding locals for 40 years in a neighborhood where eateries come and go. Its countryside antique decor, and candlelight make a visit a step back in time. It's a longer walk than most of my recommendations, but you'll get solid English cuisine. It's pricey, but the portions are huge (especially the meat-and-fish pies, their specialty). You're welcome to save lots by splitting your main course. The candlelit upstairs is the most romantic, while the basement is kept lively with the kitchen, tight seating, and lots of action. The staff is young and slightly aloof (lunch—£5 starters, £7 main dishes; dinner—£6-9 starters, £15-24 main dishes; daily 12:00-14:30 & 18:00-23:00, reservations recommended, 6 Old Court Place, just east of Kensington Church Street, near High Street Kensington Tube stop, tel. 020/7937-6462, www.maggie-jones.co.uk).

Geales, which opened its doors in 1939 as a fish-and-chips shop, has been serving Notting Hillbillies ever since. Today the menu is much more varied, but the emphasis is still on fish. The gingham-clad tables are casual, but the food is upscale. If you still want the crispy battered cod that put them on the map, it's the best around (lunch—£10 two-course express menu; dinner—£3-11 starters and salads, £10-22 main dishes; Mon 18:00-22:30, Tue-Fri 12:00-15:30 & 18:00-22:30, Sat 12:00-22:30, Sun 12:00-21:30, reservations smart, 2 Farmer Street, just south of Notting Hill Gate Tube stop, tel. 020/7727-7528, www.geales.com).

The Churchill Arms pub and **Thai Kitchen** (same location), are local hangouts, with good beer and a thriving old-English ambience in front, and hearty £8 Thai plates in an enclosed patio in the back. You can eat the Thai food in the tropical hideaway (table service) or in the atmospheric pub section (order at the counter and they'll bring it to you). The place is festooned with Churchill memorabilia and chamber pots (including one with Hitler's mug on it—hanging from the ceiling farthest from Thai Kitchen—sure to cure the constipation of any Brit during World War II). Arrive by 18:00 or after 21:00 to avoid a line. During busy times, diners are limited to an hour at the table (food served daily 12:00-22:00, 119 Kensington Church Street, tel. 020/7727-4242).

Hereford Road is a cozy, mod eatery tucked at the far end of Prince's Square. It's stylish but not pretentious, serving heavy, meaty English cuisine executed with modern panache. Cozy two-person booths face the open kitchen up top; the main dining room is down below. There are also a few sidewalk tables (£7-8 starters, £14-17 main courses, reservations smart, Mon-Sat 12:00-15:00 & 18:00-22:00, Sun 12:00-16:00 & 18:00-22:00, 3 Hereford Road, tel. 020/7727-1144, www.herefordroad.org).

The Prince Edward serves good grub in a comfy, upscale-pub setting and at its sidewalk tables (£10-15 meals, Mon-Sat 10:0-23:00, Sun 10:00-22:30, family-friendly, 2 blocks north of Bayswater Road at the corner of Dawson Place and Hereford Road, 73 Prince's Square, tel. 020/7727-2221).

Café Diana is a healthy little eatery serving sandwiches, salads, and Middle Eastern food. It's decorated—almost shrine-like—with photos of Princess Diana, who used to drop by for pita sandwiches. You can dine in the simple interior, or order some food from the counter to go (£3-5 sandwiches, £6-10 meat dishes, daily 8:00-23:00, cash only, 5 Wellington Terrace, on Bayswater Road, opposite Kensington Palace Garden Gates, where Di once lived, tel. 020/7792-9606, Abdul).

On Queensway: The road called Queensway is a multiethnic food circus, lined with lively and inexpensive eateries—browse the options along here and choose your favorite. For a cut above, head for **Royal China Restaurant**—filled with London's Chinese, who consider this one of the city's best eateries. It's dressed up in black,

EATING

white, and gold, with candles and brisk waiters. While it's pricier than most neighborhood Chinese restaurants, the food is noticeably better (£9-13 dim sum menu, served until 17:00, £10-40 main dishes, Mon-Sat 12:00-23:00, Sun 11:00-22:00, 13 Queensway, tel. 020/7221-2535). For a lowbrow alternative, **Whiteleys Shopping Centre Food Court**—at the top end of Queensway—offers fast-food chain eateries among Corinthian columns, and a multiscreen theater in a mall that dates back to 1912 (most restaurants daily 12:00-22:00, some eateries open shorter hours; options include Yo! Sushi, good salads at Café Rouge, pizza, gelato, Starbucks, and a coin-op Internet place; third floor, corner of Porchester Gardens and Queensway).

Supermarkets: Tesco is a half-block from the Notting Hill Gate Tube stop (Mon-Fri 7:00-24:00, Sat 7:00-23:00, Sun 12:00-18:00, near intersection with Pembridge Road, 114-120 Notting Hill Gate). Queensway is home to several supermarkets, including the smaller **Spar Market** at #18 (Mon-Sat 7:00-24:00, Sun 8:00-24:00). Nearby, **Marks & Spencer** can be found in Whiteleys Shopping Centre (Mon-Sat 8:30-22:00, Sun 12:00-18:00).

ELSEWHERE IN LONDON

Between St. Paul's and the Tower: The **Counting House,** formerly an elegant old bank, offers great £7-11 meals, nice homemade £10-11 meat pies, fish, and fresh vegetables. The fun "nibbles menu," with £4-6 snacks, is available starting in the early evening until 22:00 (or until 21:00 on Mon; open Mon-Fri 11:00-23:00, gets really busy with the buttoned-down 9-to-5 crowd after 12:15 especially Thu-Fri, closed Sat-Sun, near Mansion House in The City, 50 Cornhill—see map on page 415, tel. 020/7283-7123).

Near St. Paul's: **De Gustibus Sandwiches** is where an artisan bakery meets the public, offering fresh, you-design-it sandwiches, salads, and soups. Communication can be difficult, but it's worth the effort. Just one block below St. Paul's, it has simple seating or takeout picnic sacks for lugging to one of the great nearby parks (£4-8 sandwiches, £6 hot dishes, Mon-Fri 7:00-17:00, closed Sat-Sun, from church steps follow signs to youth hostel a block downhill—see map on page 415, 53-55 Carter Lane, tel. 020/7236-0056; another outlet is inside the Borough Market in Southwark).

Near the British Library: Drummond Street (running just west of Euston Station—see map on page 399) is famous for cheap and good Indian vegetarian food (£5-10 dishes, £7 lunch buffets). For a good *thali* (combo plate) consider **Chutneys** (124 Drummond, tel. 020/7388-0604) and **Ravi Shankar** (133-135 Drummond, tel. 020/7388-6458, both open long hours daily).

Near the Tower of London: In **The Medieval Banquet**'s underground, brick-arched room, costumed wenches bring you a tasty four-course medieval-themed meal (includes ale and red wine) as minstrels, knights, jesters, and contortionists perform. If you enjoy an act, pound on the table. Reserve in advance online or by phone (adult-£50, child-£30, family deal for 2 adults and 2 kids-£110—Sun-Thu only, 15 percent discount for Rick Steves readers—can't combine with family deal, Mon-Sat around 20:00, Sun around 18:00, veggie option possible, rentable medieval garb, The Medieval Banquet Ivory House, St. Katharine Docks, enter docks off East Smithfield Street, Tube: Tower Hill, tel. 020/7480-5353, www.medievalbanquet.com).

Near East End Street Markets: Brick Lane in "Banglatown" is where London's Bangladeshi community goes to dine at their favorite curry house. If you join them, be prepared for curbside hawkers pitching their eateries (Tube: Aldgate East, see page 79).

Taking Tea in London

Once the sole province of genteel ladies in fancy hats, afternoon tea has become more democratic in the 21st century. While some tearooms—such as the wallet-draining £50-a-head tea service at Claridges and the finicky Fortnum & Mason—still require a jacket and tie, most happily welcome tourists in jeans and sneakers.

Tea Terms
The cheapest "tea" on the menu is generally a "cream tea"; the most expensive is the "champagne tea." **Cream tea** is simply a pot of tea and a homemade scone or two with jam and thick clotted cream. (For maximum pinkie-waving taste per calorie, slice your scone thin like a miniature loaf of bread.) **Afternoon tea**—what many Americans would call "high tea"—generally is a cream tea plus a tier of three plates holding small finger foods (such as cucumber sandwiches) and an assortment of small pastries. **Champagne tea** includes all of the goodies, plus a glass of bubbly. **High tea** to the English generally means a more substantial late-afternoon or early-evening meal, often served with meat or eggs.

Tearooms, which often also serve appealing light meals, are usually open for lunch and close about 17:00, just before dinner. At all the places listed below, it's perfectly acceptable for two people to order one afternoon tea and one cream tea (at about £5) and share the afternoon tea's goodies.

Places to Sip Tea
The Wolseley serves a good afternoon tea between their meal service. Split one with your companion and enjoy two light meals at a great price in classic elegance (£11 cream tea, £24 afternoon tea,

served Mon-Fri 15:00-18:30, Sat 15:30-17:30, Sun 15:30-18:30, see full listing on page 424).

The Orangery at Kensington Palace serves a £24 "Orangery tea" and a £30-34 champagne tea in its bright white hall near Princess Di's former residence. You can also order treats à la carte. The portions aren't huge, but who can argue with eating at a princess' orangery or on the terrace? (Tea served 14:00-17:00, no reservations taken; a 10-minute walk through Kensington Gardens from either Queensway or High Street Kensington Tube stations to the orange brick building, about 100 yards from Kensington Palace—see map on page 394; tel. 020/3166-6113, www.hrp.org.uk.)

The Capital Hotel, a luxury hotel a half-block from Harrods, caters to weary shoppers with its intimate five-table, linen-tablecloth tearoom. It's where the ladies-who-lunch meet to decide whether to buy that Versace gown they've had their eye on. Even so, casual clothes, kids, and sharing plates are all OK (£30 afternoon tea, daily 14:00-17:30, call to book ahead—especially on weekends, 22 Basil Street—see color map on page v, Tube: Knightsbridge, tel. 020/7591-1202, www.capitalhotel.co.uk).

The **Fortnum & Mason** department store offers tea at several different restaurants within its walls. You can "Take Tea in the Parlour" for £18 (including ice-cream cakes; Mon-Sat 10:00-20:00, Sun 11:30-18:00), or try the all-out "Gallery Tea" for £26 (daily 15:00-18:00). But the pièce de resistance is their Diamond Jubilee Tea Salon, named in honor of the Queen's 60th year on the throne (and, no doubt, to remind visitors of Her Majesty's visit for tea here in 2012 with Camilla and Kate). At these royal prices, consider it dinner (£40-44, Mon-Sat 12:00-21:00, Sun 12:00-20:00, dress up a bit—no shorts, "children must be behaved," 181 Piccadilly—see map on page 418, smart to reserve online or by phone at least a week in advance, tel. 0845-602-5694, www.fortnumandmason.com).

Other Places Serving Good Tea: The **National Dining Rooms,** within the National Gallery on Trafalgar Square, offers a £7 cream tea and £17.50 afternoon tea with a great view (served 14:30-17:00, in Sainsbury Wing of National Gallery, Tube: Charing Cross or Leicester Square, tel. 020/7747-2525, www.peytonandbyrne.co.uk). The **National Café,** at the other end of the building, is a bit cheaper (£16.50 afternoon tea served 14:30-17:30). **The Café at Sotheby's,** on the ground floor of the auction giant's headquarters, gives shoppers a break from fashionable New Bond Street (£9-25, tea served Mon-Fri only 15:00-16:45, reservations smart, 34-35 New Bond Street—see map on page 418, Tube: Bond Street or Oxford Circus, tel. 020/7293-5077, www.sothebys.com/cafe).

Cheaper Options: Taking tea is not just for tourists and the wealthy—it's a true English tradition. If you want the teatime experience but are put off by the price, most department stores on Oxford Street (including those between Oxford Circus and Bond Street Tube stations) offer an afternoon tea. **John Lewis'** mod third-floor brasserie serves a nice afternoon tea from 15:30 (£10, on Oxford Street one block west of the Bond Street Tube station, tel. 020/7629-7711, www.johnlewis.com). Many museums and bookstores have cafés serving afternoon tea goodies à la carte, where you can put together a spread for less than £10—**Waterstones'** fifth-floor café and the **Victoria and Albert Museum** café are two of the best. **Teapod,** a modern place near the Tower Bridge, serves cream tea for £5.50 and afternoon tea for £13.50 (Mon-Fri 8:00-18:00, Sat-Sun 9:30-18:30, 31 Shad Thames, tel. 020/7407-0000).

LONDON WITH CHILDREN

The key to a successful family trip to London is making everyone happy, including the parents. My family-tested recommendations have this objective in mind. Consider these tips:

- Take advantage of Time Out London's frequently updated website, which includes handy kids' calendars listing activities, shows, and museum events, all searchable by date and location (www.timeout.com/london/kids). Their annually updated guidebook, *London for Children* (£12, available in bookstores and many newsstands), is chockablock with ideas for the serious parent tour guide in London.

- Give each of your kids business cards with your hotel's address just in case they make a wrong turn and get lost.

- London's big, budget chain hotels generally allow kids to sleep for free (see page 400).

- Eat dinner early (around 18:00) to miss the romantic crowd. Skip the famous places. Look instead for relaxed cafés, pubs (kids are welcome, though sometimes restricted to the restaurant section or courtyard area), or even fast-food restaurants where kids can move around. Picnic lunches and dinners work well.

- Public WCs can be hard to find. Try department stores, museums, and restaurants, particularly fast-food places.

- Follow this book's crowd-beating tips. Kids get antsy standing in line for a museum. At each sight, ask about a kids' guide or flier.

- Most of the big museums—such as the Tate Modern, Tate Britain, and National Gallery—schedule children's activities on weekends. Some museums also offer "backpacks" with activities to make the visit more interesting. Ask at museum information desks.

- Many museums—such as the Science Museum and Museum of London Docklands—have play areas for children under age seven. (The Army Museum will, too, when it reopens in the summer of 2016.)
- Hamleys is the biggest toy store in Britain, with seven floors of toys (daily, 188-196 Regent Street, Tube: Oxford Circus, www.hamleys.com). It's also included in the shopping-oriented second half of my West End Walk (see page 191). Hamleys has branches at Heathrow and Stansted airports, and at St. Pancras International Station.
- Harry Potter fans (and Muggle parents) enjoy visiting places in London where scenes from the movies were filmed (see page 108)—or, better yet, visit the actual sets at the studio where the movie magic was made (see "The Making of Harry Potter," later in this chapter).

Sights and Activities

EAST LONDON
Tower of London
The crown jewels are awesome, and the Beefeater tour plays off kids in a memorable and fun way. Avoid the long ticket lines by buying your ticket in advance (must use within seven days) at the gift shop just below the Tower Hill Tube station ticket office, London travel agencies, or online at a slight discount.

✪ See the Tower of London Tour chapter.

Museum of London
The museum has a very kid-friendly presentation that takes you from prehistoric times to the present. The events guide at the entrance details current kids' activities (see listing on page 74).

Unicorn Theatre
This modern complex presents professional theater for children on two stages (ask about family discounts, check play's recommended ages before booking, café, on the South Bank just behind City Hall, 147 Tooley Street, Tube: London Bridge; tel. 020/7645-0560, www.unicorntheatre.com).

CENTRAL LONDON
Covent Garden
This is a great area for people-watching and candy-licking. Kids like the **London Transport Museum,** with its interactive zone (see page 58).

Trafalgar Square

The grand square is fun for kids (Tube: Charing Cross). Climb the lions, munch a meal in a crypt (at St. Martin-in-the-Fields, see later), and tour the National Gallery.

National Gallery

Begin your visit in the ArtStart multimedia room. Your child can list his or her interests (cats, naval battles, and so on) and print out a tailor-made tour map for free. Ask about their children's printed guides, audioguide programs, and events—Sunday mornings are especially kid-friendly.

   ○ See the National Gallery Tour chapter.

St. Martin-in-the-Fields

Next to the church on Trafalgar Square is a glass pavilion with a brass-rubbing center below that's fun for kids who'd like a souvenir to show for their efforts (£4.50 and up, Mon-Wed 10:00-18:00, Thu-Sat 10:00-20:00, Sun 11:30-17:00, tel. 020/7766-1122; for details on the church, see page 55). The affordable Café in the Crypt has just the right spooky tables-on-gravestones ambience (see page 422).

London Eye

The grand observation wheel is a delight for the whole family (for specifics, including crowd-avoidance tips, see page 82).

Sealife Aquarium

Part of the London Eye complex and run by the same company as Madame Tussauds, this small, pricey, but entertaining aquarium resembles an overpriced theme park. Even though there are far better aquariums elsewhere, this place packs in school groups and families looking for a break from museums (daily, check for discounts online, Tube: Waterloo or Westminster, www.visitsealife.com).

Changing of the Guard

Kids enjoy the bands and pageantry of the Buckingham Palace Changing of the Guard, but little ones get a better view at the inspection; guards assemble daily May-July (every other day Aug-April) at 11:00 at Wellington Barracks, and march out at 11:30 for Buckingham Palace (see page 61). The Horse Guards change daily at 11:00 (10:00 on Sun) and have a colorful dismounting ceremony daily at 16:00 (on Whitehall, between Trafalgar Square and #10 Downing Street, Tube: Westminster, www.royal.gov.uk—search "Changing the Guard"—see page 53).

Piccadilly Circus

This titillating district has lots of schlocky amusements, such as the pricey Ripley's Believe It or Not. Be careful of fast-fingered riffraff.

Hamleys toy store is just two blocks up Regent Street at 188-196 (listed earlier).

Shopping

If your teenager wants to bring home a few chic and cheap London fashions, Oxford Street (at the intersection of Regent Street) is a good place to start. Take the Tube to the Oxford Circus stop, and you'll be surrounded by lots of shops selling inexpensive, trendy clothes for teens. Stores include Topshop, Miss Selfridge, Zara, two H&M shops, and music stores like HMV. Sandwich-to-go shops and coffeehouses (including a half-dozen Starbucks) offer easy rest stops for families. Also see Part 2 of my West End Walk ("Shopping Streets and Piccadilly Circus" on page 190), which goes down Regent Street. Harrods in Knightsbridge, with its over-the-top toy and food departments, can be fun for kids of all ages (see page 444). Markets, particularly the Camden Lock Market, will hit the spot for finicky teenagers in need of loud music, cool clothes, and plenty of food choices (see page 448).

Theater

Long-running shows are kid- and parent-pleasers (see Entertainment in London chapter).

WEST LONDON

Hyde Park

London's backyard is the perfect place for museumed-out kids to play and run free. For older kids, the park has a tennis court, a putting green, and trails for running or biking. Young children will enjoy the Diana, Princess of Wales Memorial Playground in adjacent Kensington Gardens, with its Peter Pan-themed climbing equipment, including a huge wooden pirate ship (Tube: Queensway). Events such as music, plays, and clown acts are scheduled throughout the summer. The Serpentine Lake offers paddleboat rentals and a swimming area with a playground and a shallow kiddie pool (Easter-Oct daily 10:00-dusk, closed off-season; Tube: Knightsbridge, South Kensington, and more). The park is open daily from 5:00 in the morning until midnight (www.royalparks.org.uk).

Natural History Museum

This wonderful world of dinosaurs, volcanoes, meteors, and creepy-crawlies offers creative interactive displays (see page 101).

Science Museum

Next door to the Natural History Museum, this museum offers lots of hands-on fun and IMAX movies (see page 102). The Garden play area on Floor B entertains younger children with water, textures, sounds, and climbing areas.

Both the Natural History and Science museums are kid-friendly and can be clogged with school groups during the school year. Check for special events and exhibits (noted at each museum's entry and on their websites).

NORTH LONDON
Madame Tussauds Waxworks
Despite the lines outside and the crowds inside, the waxworks are popular with kids for gory stuff, pop and movie stars, everyone's favorite royals, and more (see page 66).

London Zoo and Regent's Park
This venerable animal habitat features more than 8,000 creatures and a fine petting zoo. Call for feeding and event times (daily, in Regent's Park, Tube: Camden Town, then bus #274, tel. 020/7722-3333, www.zsl.org).

For a scenic treat that also happens to be a good value, take the London Waterbus down Regent's Canal to the zoo. They drop you off right at the entry (ticket includes one-way trip and admission to the zoo; board at Camden Lock Market, Tube: Camden Town, or at Little Venice, Tube: Warwick Avenue; www.londonwaterbus.com).

Regent's Park also has rental rowboats.

Pollock's Toy Museum
Kids will wonder how their grandparents ever survived without Xbox, as they wander through this rickety old house filled with toys that predate batteries and microchips. Be aware, though, that you must exit through a neat toy shop (see page 69).

SOUTH LONDON
The Bankside Walk (see page 290) links several sights children might enjoy: The *Golden Hinde* ship, Clink Prison, and Old Operating Theatre. Nearby is the...

HMS *Belfast*
Older kids might enjoy scrambling across the decks of this World War II warship (see page 93).

GREATER LONDON
The *Cutty Sark*
This beautifully restored sailing ship, now on dry land in Greenwich, is full of kid-friendly, hands-on displays (see page 355).

The Making of Harry Potter: Warner Bros. Studio Tour
A nirvana for Potterphiles, this attraction (in Leavesden, a 20-minute train ride from London) lets fans young and old see the actual sets and props that were used to create the Harry Potter films.

Shuttle buses run to the studio from the Leavesden train station; for details, see page 107.

Kew Gardens

These famous 300-acre gardens include the Rhizotron and Xstrata Treetop Walkway, which lets kids explore the canopy 60 feet above the ground on a 200-yard-long scenic steel walkway. Younger children will love the Climbers and Creepers indoor play area and kid-size zip line (see page 103).

London Museum of Water and Steam

This impressive collection of steam-powered pumping engines that once powered waterworks across the UK is mesmerizing for children. The engines operate only on weekends—search the website for "What's On" to make sure they're "in steam." An outdoor water-play area is fun in nice weather (£5 kids, £12 adults, check for discounts online; daily 11:00-16:00, Green Dragon Lane, tel. 020/8568-4757, www.waterandsteam.org.uk).

FUN TRANSPORTATION
Thames Cruise

Young sailors delight in boats. Westminster Pier (near Big Ben) offers a lot of action, with round-trip cruises and boats to the Tower of London, Greenwich, and Kew Gardens. For details, see page 40.

Hop-On, Hop-Off London Bus Tours

These two-hour double-decker bus tours, which drive by all the biggies, are fun for kids and stress-free for parents. You can stay on the bus the entire time, or hop on and hop off at any of the nearly 30 stops and catch a later bus (every 10-15 minutes in summer, every 10-20 minutes in winter, see page 34). The Original London Sightseeing Tour's "City Sightseeing Tour" bus (marked with a red triangle) has a kids' soundtrack on the earphones.

DAY TRIP TO WINDSOR
Legoland Windsor

If your kids are loopy over Legos, they'll love a day trip to Legoland Windsor. While older kids will probably enjoy it, the park is really aimed at the 11-and-under crowd (see page 500 for cost, hours, and other details).

WHAT TO AVOID

The **London Dungeon's** popularity with teenagers makes it one of London's most-visited sights. I enjoy gore and torture as much as the next boy, but this is lousy gore and torture, and I would not waste the time or money on it with my child. **The London Bridge Experience** (not to be confused with the Tower Bridge Exhibition) and **The London Tombs** are also to be avoided. They are copycat rip-offs of the London Dungeon.

SHOPPING IN LONDON

London is great for shoppers—and, thanks to the high prices, perhaps even better for window-shoppers. This chapter will tell you where to get essentials, where to get souvenirs, where to browse through colorful street markets, and where to gawk at some high-end stores in this major fashion capital.

Most stores are open Monday through Saturday from roughly 10:00 to 18:00, and many close Sundays. Large department stores stay open later during the week (until 20:00 or 21:00) and are open shorter hours on Sundays. If you're looking for bargains, you can visit one of the city's many street markets.

Consider these tips for shopping in London:

If all you need are souvenirs, a surgical strike at any souvenir shop will do.

- London's museums have extraordinarily good shops. The Transport Museum's is one of the best, and stays open a half-hour later than the museum itself (listed on page 58). Other sights with great shops include the British Museum (page 64), the Victoria and Albert Museum (page 101), the Museum of London (page 74), the National Portrait Gallery (page 54), the Tate Modern (page 88), and the wacky selections at Pollock's Toy Museum (page 69) and the Old Operating Theatre (page 91).

- Large department stores offer relatively painless one-stop shopping. Consider the down-to-earth Marks & Spencer (Mon-Fri 8:00-21:00, Sat 9:00-21:00, Sun 12:00-18:00, 173 Oxford Street, Tube: Oxford Circus; another at 458 Oxford Street, Tube: Bond Street or Marble Arch; see www.marksandspencer.com for more locations).

- Connect small shops with a pleasant walk (✪ see the West End Walk chapter, particularly "Part 2").

- For flea-market fun, try one of the many street markets.
- Gawkers as well as serious bidders can attend auctions.

Warning: Refuse any offers to charge your credit card in dollars. This is called dynamic currency conversion (DCC), and it's offered by some stores (including Harrods) as a "convenience." The very bad exchange rate they use is convenient only for increasing the store's profits.

For information on **VAT refunds** and **customs regulations,** see page 562.

SHOPPING STREETS

London is famous for its shopping. The best and most convenient

shopping streets are in the West End and West London (roughly between Soho and Hyde Park). You'll find midrange shops along **Oxford Street** (running east from Tube: Marble Arch), and fancier shops along **Regent Street** (stretching south from Tube: Oxford Circus to Piccadilly Circus) and **Knightsbridge** (where you'll find Harrods and Harvey Nichols, described later; Tube: Knightsbridge). Other streets are more specialized, such as **Jermyn Street** for old-fashioned men's clothing (just south of Piccadilly Street) and **Charing Cross Road** for books. **Floral Street,** connecting Leicester Square to Covent Garden, is lined with fashion boutiques.

The second half of my ✪ West End Walk chapter is designed to connect several shopping areas, including Regent Street and Jermyn Street; even if you're not taking the entire walk, consider riding the Tube to Oxford Circus, walking south two blocks to Liberty department store, and starting the walk with "Part 2" on page 190.

FANCY DEPARTMENT STORES IN WEST LONDON

Harrods: Harrods is London's most famous and touristy department store. With more than four acres of retail space covering seven floors, it's a place where some shoppers could spend all day. (To me, it's still just a department store.) Big yet classy, Harrods has everything from elephants to toothbrushes (Mon-Sat 10:00-20:00, Sun 11:30-18:00; to check bags enter from Basil Street or look for *left luggage* signs at back of the store, £3/bag; Brompton Road, Tube: Knightsbridge, tel. 020/7730-1234, www.harrods.com).

Sightseers should pick up the free *Store Guide* at any info post. Here's what I enjoy: On the ground floor, find the Food Halls, with their Edwardian tiled walls, creative and exuberant displays, and staff in period costumes—not quite like your local supermarket back home.

Descend to the lower ground floor and follow signs to the Egyptian Escalator (in the center of the store). Here you'll find a memorial to Princess Diana and her boyfriend, Dodi Fayed, who both died in a car crash in Paris in 1997 (Dodi's father, Mohamed Al Fayed, was the store's former owner). Photos and flowers honor the late princess and her lover. Inside a small, clear pyramid, you can see a wine glass still dirty from their last dinner and the engagement ring that Dodi purchased the day before they died. True Di-hards can go back up one level to the ground floor and follow signs to Door #3 in Menswear (near Men's Designer and Men's Tailoring, at the escalator). A huge (and more than a little creepy) bronze statue shows Di and Dodi releasing a symbolic albatross.

Back in the center of the store, ride the Egyptian Escalator—lined with pharaoh-headed sconces, papyrus-plant lamps, and hieroglyphic balconies—to the fourth floor. From the escalator, make a U-turn left and head to the far end to find the incredible Toy Land, which includes an impressive Harry Potter section (wands go for upwards of £100), and child-size luxury pedal cars (£7,000)—the perfect gift for the child who has everything.

More than two dozen eateries are scattered throughout the store, including a sushi bar, deli, pizzeria, Ladurée *macaron* parlor, and—for the truly homesick—an American diner.

Many of my readers report that Harrods is overpriced, snooty, and teeming with American, Japanese, and Middle Eastern tourists with zero concept of bargain shopping. It's the only shopping mall I've seen with its own gift store. Still, it's the palace of department stores. The nearby Beauchamp Place is lined with classy and fascinating shops.

Harvey Nichols: Once Princess Diana's favorite, "Harvey Nick's" remains the department store *du jour* (Mon-Sat 10:00-20:00, Sun 11:30-18:00, near Harrods, 109-125 Knightsbridge, Tube: Knightsbridge, tel. 020/7235-5000, www.harveynichols.com). Want to pick up a little £20 scarf for the wife? You won't do it here, where they're more like £200. The store's fifth floor is a veritable food fest, with a gourmet grocery store, a fancy restaurant, a Yo! Sushi bar, and a lively café. Consider a takeaway tray of sushi to eat on a bench in the Hyde Park rose garden two blocks away.

Fortnum & Mason: The official department store of the

SHOPPING

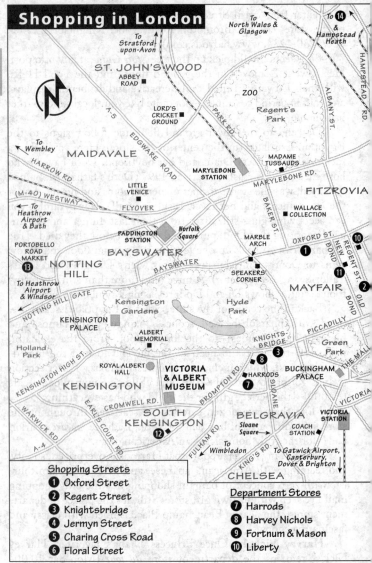

Shopping in London

To North Wales & Glasgow

To 14 & Hampstead Heath

To Stratford-upon-Avon

ST. JOHN'S WOOD

ABBEY ROAD

ZOO

Regent's Park

LORD'S CRICKET GROUND

MADAME TUSSAUDS

MARYLEBONE STATION

MARYLEBONE RD.

To Wembley

MAIDAVALE

EDGWARE ROAD

FITZROVIA

HARROW RD.

LITTLE VENICE

WALLACE COLLECTION

(M-40) WESTWAY

FLYOVER

OXFORD ST. ❶

To Heathrow Airport & Bath

PADDINGTON STATION

Norfolk Square

MARBLE ARCH

❿

PORTOBELLO ROAD MARKET ⓭

BAYSWATER

BAYSWATER

SPEAKERS CORNER

⓫

❷

NOTTING HILL

To Heathrow Airport & Windsor

NOTTING HILL GATE

Kensington Gardens

Hyde Park

MAYFAIR

KENSINGTON PALACE

ALBERT MEMORIAL

PICCADILLY

Holland Park

ROYAL ALBERT HALL

VICTORIA & ALBERT MUSEUM

KNIGHTS-BRIDGE ❸

❽

Green Park

KENSINGTON HIGH ST.

KENSINGTON

CROMWELL RD.

Harrods

❼

BUCKINGHAM PALACE

THE MALL

WARWICK RD.

EARLS COURT RD.

SOUTH KENSINGTON

⓬

A-4

FULHAM RD.

BROMPTON RD.

SLOANE

BELGRAVIA

Sloane Square

KING'S RD.

VICTORIA

VICTORIA STATION

COACH STATION

CHELSEA

To Wimbledon

To Gatwick Airport, Canterbury, Dover & Brighton

Shopping Streets
1. Oxford Street
2. Regent Street
3. Knightsbridge
4. Jermyn Street
5. Charing Cross Road
6. Floral Street

Department Stores
7. Harrods
8. Harvey Nichols
9. Fortnum & Mason
10. Liberty

Queen, Fortnum & Mason embodies old-fashioned, British upper-class taste. While some may find it too stuffy, you won't find another store with the same storybook atmosphere (Mon-Sat 10:00-21:00, Sun 12:00-18:00, elegant tea served in their Diamond Jubilee Tea Salon—see page 433, 181 Piccadilly, Tube: Green Park, tel. 020/7734-8040, www.fortnumandmason.com, also see ✪ West End Walk).

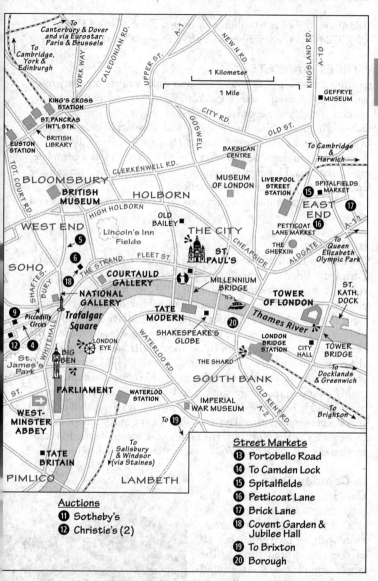

1 Kilometer

1 Mile

Street Markets

⓭ Portobello Road
⓮ To Camden Lock
⓯ Spitalfields
⓰ Petticoat Lane
⓱ Brick Lane
⓲ Covent Garden & Jubilee Hall
⓳ To Brixton
⓴ Borough

Auctions

⑪ Sotheby's
⑫ Christie's (2)

Liberty: Designed to make well-heeled shoppers feel at home, the half-timbered, mock-Tudor emporium is a 19th-century institution that thrives today. Known for its gorgeous floral fabrics and well-stocked crafts department, it's fun to stroll through just for a look at its hip, artful displays and castle-like interior, constructed of two decommissioned battleships (Mon-Sat 10:00-20:00, Sun

12:00-18:00, Great Marlborough Street, Tube: Oxford Circus, tel. 020/7734-1234, www.liberty.co.uk, also see ❂ West End Walk).

STREET MARKETS

Antiques buffs, people-watchers, and folks who brake for garage sales love London's street markets. There's good early-morning market activity somewhere any day of the week. The best markets—which combine lively stalls and a colorful neighborhood with cute and characteristic shops of their own—are Portobello Road and Camden Lock Market. Any London TI has a complete, up-to-date list. Hagglers will enjoy the no-holds-barred bargaining encouraged in London's street markets.

Warning: Markets attract two kinds of people—tourists and pickpockets.

In Notting Hill

Portobello Road Market: Arguably London's best street market, Portobello Road stretches for several blocks through the delightful, colorful, funky-yet-quaint Notting Hill neighborhood. Already charming streets lined with pastel-painted houses and offbeat antique shops are enlivened on Fridays and Saturdays with 2,000 additional stalls (9:00-19:00), plus food, live music, and more. (The best strategy is to come on Friday; most stalls are open, with half the crowds of Saturday.) If you start at Notting Hill Gate and work your way north, you'll find these general sections: antiques, new goods, produce, more new goods, and a flea market. While Portobello Road is best on Fridays and Saturdays, it's enjoyable to stroll this street on most other days as well, since the quirky shops are fun to explore (Tube: Notting Hill Gate, near recommended accommodations, tel. 020/7727-7684, www.portobelloroad.co.uk).

In Camden Town

Camden Lock Market: This huge, trendy arts-and-crafts festival is divided into three areas, each with its own vibe (but all of them fresh and funky). The whole complex sprawls around an old-fashioned, still-functioning lock (used mostly for leisure boats) and its retro-chic,  yellow-brick industrial buildings. The main market, set alongside the picturesque canal, features a mix of shops and stalls selling boutique crafts and artisanal foods. The market on the opposite side of Chalk Farm Road is edgier, with cheap ethnic food stalls, lots of canalside seating, and punk crafts. The Stables, a sprawling, incense-scented complex, is decorated with fun statues of horses and squeezed into tunnels under the old rail bridge just behind the main market. It's a little lowbrow and wildly creative, with cheap clothes, junk jewelry, and loud music (daily 10:00-18:00, busiest on weekends, Tube: Chalk Farm, bus #24 heads from Pimlico to Victoria Station to Trafalgar Square and then straight up to Camden—before continuing on to Hampstead Heath, tel. 020/7485-7963, www.camdenlockmarket.com).

Avoid the tacky, crowded area between the market and the Camden Town Tube station (which bills itself as "The Camden Market," but lacks the real one's canalside charm) by getting off at the Chalk Farm stop; better yet, consider arriving via a scenic waterbus ride from Little Venice (tel. 020/7482-2660, www. londonwaterbus.com).

To escape the crowds, stroll for a while in either direction along the tranquil canal; it's possible to walk east from here all the way to Queen Elizabeth Olympic Park in Stratford (about six miles away).

In the East End

All three of these East End markets are busiest and most interesting on Sundays. For a walk tying together these three markets—and a lot more in this neighborhood, which combines Cockney memories with London's biggest Bangladeshi community—see page 79.

Spitalfields Market: This huge, mod-feeling market hall (pronounced "spittle-fields") combines a shopping mall with old brick buildings and sleek modern ones, all covered by a giant glass roof. While the shops, stalls, and a rainbow of restaurant options are open every day, the scene is best on Sundays, when you'll find a lively organic food market, many ethnic eateries, crafts, trendy clothes, bags, and an antiques-and-junk market (Mon-Wed 10:00-17:00, Thu and Sun 9:00-17:00, Fri 10:00-16:00, Sat 11:00-17:00, Tube: Liverpool Street; from the Tube stop, take Bishopsgate East exit, turn left, walk to Brushfield Street, and turn right; www. visitspitalfields.com).

Petticoat Lane Market: Just a block from Spitalfields Market, this line of stalls sits on the otherwise dull, glass-skyscraper-filled Middlesex Street; adjoining Wentworth Street is grungier and more characteristic. Expect budget clothing, leather, shoes, watches, jewelry, and crowds (Sun 9:00-14:00, sometimes later; smaller market Mon-Fri 8:00-16:00 on Wentworth Street only; closed Sat; Middlesex Street and Wentworth Street, Tube: Liverpool Street). The Columbia Road flower market is nearby (Sun 8:00-15:00, http://columbiaroad.info).

Brick Lane Markets: Housed in the former Truman Brewery, this cluster of markets is in the heart of the "Banglatown" Bangladeshi community. Of the three East End market areas, Brick Lane's markets are the grittiest and most avant-garde, selling handmade clothes and home decor as well as ethnic street food. The markets are in full swing on Sundays (roughly 10:00-17:00), though you'll still see some action on Saturdays (11:00-18:00). The Boiler House Food Hall and the Backyard Market (hipster arts and crafts) go all weekend—and the Vintage Market (clothes) even operates on Fridays (11:00-17:30). Surrounding shops and eateries are open all week (Tube: Liverpool Street or Aldgate East, tel. 020/7770-6028, www.bricklanemarket.com).

In the West End
Covent Garden Market: Originally the convent garden for West-minster Abbey, the iron-and-glass market hall hosted a produce market until the 1970s (earning it the name "Apple Market"). Now it's a mix of fun shops, eateries, and markets. Mondays are for an-tiques, while arts and crafts dominate the rest of the week. Yester-year's produce stalls are open daily 10:30-18:00, and on Thursdays, a food market brightens up the square (Tube: Covent Garden— will be exit-only through summer of 2015, Leicester Square is 5 minutes away, tel. 020/7420-5856, www.coventgardenlondonuk. com, also see ✪ West End Walk).

Jubilee Hall Market: Located on the south side of Cov-ent Garden, this market features antiques on Mondays; a general market Tuesday through Friday; and arts and crafts on Saturdays and Sundays (Mon 5:00-16:00, Tue-Fri 9:30-18:00, Sat-Sun 9:00-18:00, tel. 020/7379-4242, www.jubileemarket.co.uk).

In South London
Borough Market: London's oldest fruit and vegetable market has been serving the Southwark community for over 800 years. These days there are as many people taking photos as buying the fruit, cheese, and beautiful breads, but it's still a fun carnival at-mosphere with fantastic stall food. For maximum market and minimum crowds, join the locals on Thursdays (Mon-Tue open for lunch only, no market; Wed-Thu 10:00-17:00, Fri 10:00-18:00, Sat 8:00-17:00, closed Sun; Tube: London Bridge, tel. 020/7407-1002, www.boroughmarket.org.uk, also see ✪ Bankside Walk).

Brixton Market: This seedy neighborhood south of the Thames features yet another thriving market. Here the food, cloth-ing, records, and hair-braiding throb with an Afro-Caribbean beat (stalls open Mon-Sat 8:00-17:00, Wed until 15:00, farmers market Sun 10:00-14:00 but otherwise dead on Sun; Tube: Brixton, www. brixtonmarket.net).

In Greenwich

With several sightseeing treats just a quick DLR ride from central London, Greenwich has its share of great markets, especially lively on weekends. For details, see page 353.

FAMOUS AUCTIONS

London's famous auctioneers welcome the curious public for viewing and bidding. You can preview estate catalogs or browse auction calendars online. To ask questions or set up an appointment, contact **Sotheby's** (opening times vary, tel. 020/7293-5000, www. sothebys.com; recommended café on site, 34-35 New Bond Street, Tube: Oxford Circus) or **Christie's** (Mon-Fri 9:30-16:30; 85 Old Brompton Road, Tube: South Kensington, tel. 020/7930-6074; second location at 8 King Street, Tube: Green Park, tel. 020/7839-9060; www.christies.com).

ENTERTAINMENT IN LONDON

London bubbles with top-notch entertainment seven days a week: plays, movies, concerts, exhibitions, walking tours, shopping, and children's activities.

For the best list of what's happening and a look at the latest London scene, check www.timeout.com/london. (Unfortunately, the once-dominant print version of *Time Out London*, though free, is paltry and hard to find.) The free monthly *London Planner* covers sights, events, and plays, though generally not as well as *Time Out* does.

Choose from classical, jazz, rock, and far-out music, Gilbert and Sullivan, tango lessons, comedy, Baha'i meetings, poetry readings, spectator sports, theater, and the cinema. In Leicester Square, you might be able to catch a film that has yet to be released in the States—if Colin Firth is attending an opening-night premiere in London, it will likely be at one of the big movie houses here.

There are plenty of free performances, such as lunch concerts at St. Martin-in-the-Fields (at Trafalgar Square) and summertime events at The Scoop amphitheater near City Hall (see "Summer Evenings Along the South Bank," later).

Theater (a.k.a. "Theatre")

London's theater scene rivals Broadway's in quality and sometimes beats it in price. Choose from 200 offerings—Shakespeare, musicals, comedies, thrillers, sex farces, cutting-edge fringe, revivals starring movie celebs, and more. London does it all well.

Seating Terminology: Just like at home, London's theaters sell seats in a range of levels—but the Brits use different terms: stalls (ground floor), dress circle (first balcony), upper circle (second balcony), balcony (sky-high third balcony), and slips (cheap seats

on the fringes). For floor plans of the various theaters, see www.
theatremonkey.com.

BIG WEST END SHOWS

Nearly all big-name shows are hosted in the commercial (nonsub-
sidized) theaters of the West End, clustering around Soho (especially along Shaftesbury Avenue) between Piccadilly and Covent
Garden. With a centuries-old tradition of pleasing the masses, they
present London theater at its grandest.

I prefer big, glitzy—even bombastic—musicals over serious
chamber dramas, simply because London can deliver the lights,
booming voices, dancers, and multimedia spectacle I rarely get
back home. If that's not to your taste—or you already have access
to similar spectacles at home—you might prefer some of London's
more low-key offerings.

Well-known musicals may draw the biggest crowds, but the
West End offers plenty of other crowd-pleasers, from revivals of
classics to cutting-edge works by the hottest young playwrights.
These productions tend to have shorter runs than famous musicals.
A few relatively recent cinematic hits (including *The King's Speech*
and *War Horse*) started out as London plays. Many productions star
huge-name celebrities—London is a magnet for movie stars who
want to stretch their acting chops.

You'll see the latest offerings advertised all over the Tube and
elsewhere. The free *Official London Theatre Guide*, updated weekly,
is a handy tool (find it at hotels, box offices, the City of London TI,
and online at www.officiallondontheatre.co.uk). If you're picky,
check the reviews at www.timeout.com/london.

Most performances are nightly except Sunday, usually with
two or three matinees a week. The few shows that run on Sundays
are mostly family fare (*Matilda, The Lion King*, and so on). Tickets
range from about £25 to £120 for the best seats at big shows. Matinees are generally cheaper and rarely sell out.

Buying Tickets for West End Shows

For most visitors, it makes the most sense to simply buy tickets
in London. But if your time in London is limited and you have
your heart set on a particular show that's likely to sell out (usually
the newest shows), you can buy peace of mind by prebooking your
tickets from home.

Before You Go

Once you know what show you want to see, buy your tickets directly from its theater's website (which may reroute you to a third-party
ticket vendor such as Ticketmaster). You can also call the theater
box office (which may ring through to a central ticketing office).

ENTERTAINMENT

London's Major Theaters

❶ Adelphi
❷ Aldwych
❸ Ambassadors & St. Martin's
❹ Apollo
❺ Cambridge
❻ Criterion
❼ Dominion
❽ Donmar Warehouse
❾ Drury Lane
❿ Duke of York's
⓫ Fortune
⓬ Garrick
⓭ Haymarket
⓮ Her Majesty's
⓯ Lyceum
⓰ Lyric
⓱ New London
⓲ Noël Coward
⓳ Novello
⓴ Palace
㉑ Phoenix
㉒ Playhouse
㉓ Prince Edward
㉔ Prince of Wales
㉕ Queen's & Gielgud
㉖ Savoy
㉗ Shaftesbury
㉘ Trafalgar Studios
㉙ Wyndham's

Whether you book online or over the phone, you'll pay with your credit card. A service charge of £3 per ticket is typical if you book directly with the theater. You may be offered the option of having your tickets emailed to you (you print them out); otherwise, arrive about 30 minutes before the show starts to pick up your tickets at Will Call.

Avoid buying tickets through third-party middleman agencies, which mark up their prices dramatically (explained in "Booking Through Other Agencies," later).

ENTERTAINMENT

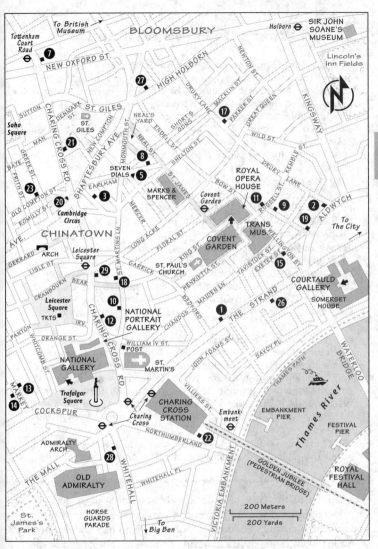

Buying Tickets in London

Most shows have tickets available on short notice—likely at a discount. While very recent and/or popular shows sell out early (especially for weekend performances), nearly-as-popular shows may offer discounted tickets to fill seats.

You have two good options for booking tickets—the official discount TKTS booth at Leicester Square and the theater's box office...and one bad option—a middleman ticket agency (only worthwhile if you're desperate). All three alternatives are described next.

ENTERTAINMENT

What's On in the West End

Here are some of the perennial favorites that you're likely to find among the West End's evening offerings. If spending the time and money for a London play, I like a full-fledged, high-energy musical (which all of these are). Generally ticket prices range from £25-120; you can book tickets for free at the box office or for a £2-3 fee by phone or online. Shows typically run Monday through Saturday at 19:30, with two or three matinees a week—confirm specifics on show websites. See the map on page 454 for locations.

Billy Elliot—This adaptation of the popular British film is part family drama, part story of a boy who just has to dance, set to a score by Elton John (Mon-Sat 19:30, matinees Thu and Sat 14:30, Victoria Palace Theatre, Victoria Street, Tube: Victoria, tel. 0844-248-5000, www.billyelliotthemusical.com).

Jersey Boys—This fast-moving, easy-to-follow show tracks the rough start and rise to stardom of Frankie Valli and the Four Seasons. It's light, but the music is so catchy that everyone leaves whistling the group's hits (Tue-Sat 19:30; matinees Tue and Sat 15:00, Sun 17:00; Piccadilly Theatre, 16 Denman Street, Tube: Piccadilly Circus, box office tel. 0844-871-7630, www.jerseyboyslondon.com).

Les Misérables—Claude-Michel Schönberg's musical adaptation of Victor Hugo's epic follows the life of Jean Valjean as he struggles with the social and political realities of 19th-century France. This inspiring mega-hit takes you back to the days of France's struggle for a just and modern society (Mon-Sat 19:30, matinees Wed and Sat 14:30, Queen's Theatre, Shaftesbury Avenue, Tube: Piccadilly Circus, box office tel. 0844-482-5160, www.lesmis.com).

The Lion King—In this Disney extravaganza, Simba the lion learns about the delicately balanced circle of life on the savanna (Tue-

Which of the two good options is best for you? It depends on how committed you are to seeing a particular show, how picky you are about seating, and how important it is to nab the cheapest possible ticket. If you have a handful of shows in mind, head to the TKTS booth—it's centrally located, its booking fee is small, and you stand a good chance of getting a discount on a good seat for one of your preferred shows (check the frequently updated www.tkts.co.uk before heading out). The box office may also sell same-day discounted tickets—but if TKTS has discounts on good seats, you might as well head there first. The TKTS booth doesn't, however, have seating plans for each theater, and it doesn't sell the absolutely cheapest seats, which are only available directly from the box office. For example, a top-notch seat to *Billy Elliot* costs £96 if you buy

Sat 19:30; matinees Wed, Sat, and Sun 14:30; Lyceum Theatre, Wellington Street, Tube: Charing Cross or Covent Garden, theater info tel. 020/7420-8100, box office tel. 0844-871-3000, www. thelionking.co.uk).

Mamma Mia!—This energetic, spandex-and-platform-boots musical weaves together a slew of ABBA hits to tell the story of a bride in search of her real dad as her promiscuous mom plans her Greek Isle wedding. The production has the audience dancing in their seats (Mon-Sat 19:30, matinees Thu and Sat 15:00, Novello Theatre, Aldwych, Tube: Covent Garden, box office tel. 0844-482-5115, www.mamma-mia.com).

Matilda—Based on the Roald Dahl children's book, this hit is a family favorite for its tale of a precocious young girl who's unappreciated by her parents (Tue 19:00, Wed-Sat 19:30, matinees Wed and Sat 14:30 and Sun 15:00, Cambridge Theatre, Seven Dials, Tube: Covent Garden or Leicester Square, box office tel. 0844-412-4652, www.matildathemusical.com).

Phantom of the Opera—A mysterious masked man falls in love with a singer in this haunting Andrew Lloyd Webber musical about life beneath the stage of the Paris Opera (Mon-Sat 19:30, matinees Thu and Sat 14:30, Her Majesty's Theatre, Haymarket, Tube: Piccadilly Circus or Leicester Square, US toll-free tel. 800-334-8457, box office tel. 0844-412-2707, www. thephantomoftheopera.com).

Wicked—This lively prequel to *The Wizard of Oz* examines how the Witch of the West met Glinda the Good Witch, and later became so, you know... (Mon-Sat 19:30, matinees Wed and Sat 14:30, Apollo Victoria Theatre, just east of Victoria Station, Tube: Victoria, AGT Tickets tel. 0844-871-3001, www.wickedthemusical. co.uk).

directly from the theater; the same seat costs £41 through TKTS. The cheapest (restricted view) seat is £23 through the theater. See www.londontheatretickets.org and www.timeout.com/london for plenty more cheap-ticket advice.

Discount TKTS Booth: This famous ticket booth at Leicester (LESS-ter) Square, run by the Society of London Theatre, sells discounted tickets for top-price seats to shows on the push list. Big-name shows frequently turn up on this list. Most tickets are around half-price; other shows are discounted 25 percent (in either case, you'll pay a £3 service charge per ticket). For some extremely popular shows, they sell full-price tickets without the service charge (so it costs the same as at the box office). For about half of the shows, discounted tickets are available only on the day of the performance, although theaters are beginning to offer discounted tickets through TKTS up to a week ahead. Their website (www.tkts.co.uk) lists ticket availability and prices, and is updated throughout the day—but you must buy in person at their kiosk. A similar list is posted next to the kiosk—survey your options before you queue (or, if the line is long, while you're in the queue). It's smart to have two or three options in mind, just in case your first choice is sold out when you reach the counter. While the line forms early, it tends to move fast. Unless you have your heart set on a particular show that has only same-day tickets, consider dropping by later in the day, when it's a bit less crowded—TKTS receives tickets throughout the day (open Mon-Sat 9:00-19:00, Sun 11:00-16:30). Note: If TKTS runs out of its ticket allotment for a certain show, it doesn't necessarily mean that the show is sold out—you can still try the theater's box office.

Warning: The real booth (with its prominent *TKTS* sign) is a freestanding kiosk at the south edge of the garden in Leicester Square. Several dishonest outfits nearby advertise "official half-price tickets"—avoid these, where you'll rarely pay anything close to half-price.

Booking Direct (at the Theater's Box Office): While TKTS generally has seats that are as cheap or cheaper than at the theater itself, the advantage of buying direct is that you may have access to deals that you can't get anywhere else. Most theaters offer cheap returned tickets, standing-room, matinee, senior or student standby deals, and more. (Discounted tickets, called "concessions," are indicated with a "conc" or "s" in the listings.) Picking up a late return can get you a great seat at a cheap-seat price. A good plan for same-day deals is to arrive at the box office right when it opens (most open at 10:00; a few open at 9:00). For example, the popular show *Wicked* saves its front-row tickets to sell at half-price at 10:00 on the day of the show, but you must buy them in person at the box office...and on busy days, people line up early. (Restrictions may apply—for example, you may be limited to two half-price tickets, and even if you can buy more, the seats may not be together.) To find deals, look at the show's website, call the box office, or simply drop by (the theaters are mostly in highly trafficked tourist areas, so you're likely to pass your chosen theater at some point during your visit). Even if a show is "sold out," there's usually a way to get a seat. Call the theater box office and ask how, or check www.timeout.com/london for show-by-show info on same-day tickets at West End theaters.

If you don't care where you sit, you can often buy the absolute cheapest seats at the box office; these tickets usually cost £20 or less. These seats tend to be either in the nosebleed rows and/or have a restricted view (behind a pillar or extremely far to one side), and are often available only as same-day tickets. (For smaller theaters where every seat's a decent one, TKTS may indeed beat the best box-office price: Compare online before heading out.) After the lights go down, scooting up is less than a capital offense. Shakespeare did it.

Booking Through Other Agencies: Although booking through a middleman (such as your hotel or a ticket agency) is quick and easy, prices are inflated by a standard 25 percent fee. Ticket agencies (whether in the US or in London) are just scalpers with an address. As a rule of thumb, if anyone other than the box office charges you more than £100 per ticket, you're almost certainly getting ripped off. If you're buying from an agency, look at the ticket carefully (your price should be no more than 30 percent over the printed face value; the 20 percent VAT is already included in the face value) and understand where you're sitting according to the floor plan (if your view is restricted, it will state this on the ticket).

Agencies are worthwhile only if a show you've just got to see is sold out at the box office. They scarf up hot tickets, planning to make a killing after the show is sold out. US booking agencies get their tickets from another agency, adding to your expense by involving yet another middleman. Many tickets sold on the street are forgeries. Although some theaters use booking agencies to handle their advance sales, you'll likely save money by avoiding the middleman.

THEATER BEYOND THE WEST END

Tickets for lesser-known shows tend to be cheaper (figure £15-30), in part because most of the smaller theaters are subsidized. Remember that plays don't need a familiar title or famous actor to be a worthwhile experience—read up on the latest offerings online; Time Out's site is a great place to start.

Major Noncommercial Theaters: One particularly good venue is the **National Theatre,** which has a range of impressive options, often starring recognizable names; while the building is ugly on the outside, the acts that play out upon its stage are beautiful—as are the deeply discounted tickets it commonly offers (looming on the South Bank by Waterloo Bridge, Tube: Waterloo, www. nationaltheatre.org.uk).

The **Barbican Centre** puts on high-quality, often experimental work (right by the Museum of London, just north of The City, Tube: Barbican, www.barbican.org.uk), as does the **Royal Court Theatre,** which has £10 tickets for its Monday shows (west of the West End in Sloane Square, Tube: Sloane Square, www. royalcourttheatre.com).

Royal Shakespeare Company: If you'll ever enjoy Shakespeare, it'll be in Britain. The RSC performs at various theaters around London and in Stratford-upon-Avon year-round. To get a schedule, contact the RSC (Royal Shakespeare Theatre, Stratford-upon-Avon, tel. 0844-800-1110, www.rsc.org.uk).

Shakespeare's Globe: To see Shakespeare in a replica of the theater for which he wrote his plays, attend a play at the Globe. In this round, thatch-roofed, open-air theater, the plays are performed much as Shakespeare intended—under the sky, with no amplification.

The play's the thing from late April through early October (usually Tue-Sat 14:00 and 19:30, Sun either 13:00 and/or 18:30, tickets can be sold out months in advance). You'll pay £5 to stand and £15-39 to sit, usually on a backless bench. Because only a few rows and the pricier Gentlemen's Rooms have seats with backs, £1 cushions and £3 add-on backrests are considered a good investment by many. Dress for the weather.

The £5 "groundling" tickets—which are open to rain—are most fun. Scurry in early to stake out a spot on the stage's edge, where the most interaction with the actors occurs. You're a crude peasant. You can lean your elbows on the stage, munch a picnic dinner (yes, you can bring in food), or walk around. I've never enjoyed Shakespeare as much as here, performed as it was meant to be in the "wooden O." If you can't get a ticket, consider waiting around. Plays can be long, and many groundlings leave before the end. Hang around outside and beg or buy a ticket from someone leaving early (groundlings are allowed to come and go). A few non-Shakespeare plays are also presented each year. If you can't attend a show, you can take a guided tour of the theater and museum by day (see page 88).

The new indoor Sam Wanamaker Playhouse allows Shakespearean-era plays and early-music concerts to be performed through the winter. Many of the productions in this intimate venue are one-offs and can be quite pricey.

To reserve tickets for plays at the Globe or Sam Wanamaker, call or drop by the box office (Mon-Sat 10:00-18:00, Sun 10:00-17:00, open one hour later on performance days, New Globe Walk entrance, no extra charge to book by phone, tel. 020/7401-9919).

You can also reserve online (www.shakespearesglobe.com, £2.50 booking fee). If the tickets are sold out, don't despair; a few often free up at the last minute. Try calling around noon the day of the performance to see if the box office expects any returned tickets. If so, they'll advise you to show up a little more than an hour before the show, when these tickets are sold (first-come, first-served).

The theater is on the South Bank, directly across the Thames over the Millennium Bridge from St. Paul's Cathedral (Tube: Mansion House or London Bridge). The Globe is inconvenient for public transport, but the courtesy phone in the lobby lets you get a minicab in minutes. (These minicabs have set fees—e.g., £8 to South Kensington—but generally cost less than a metered cab and provide fine and honest service.) During theater season, there's a regular supply of black cabs outside the main foyer on New Globe Walk.

Outdoor Theater in Summer: Enjoy Shakespearean drama and other plays under the stars at the Open Air Theatre, in leafy Regent's Park in north London. Food is allowed: You can bring your own picnic, order à la carte from the theater menu, or preorder a picnic supper from the theater at least 48 hours in advance (season runs late May-mid-Sept, tickets available beginning in mid-Jan; book at www.openairtheatre.org or—for an extra booking fee—by calling 0844-826-4242; grounds open 1.5 hours prior to evening performances, one hour prior to matinees; 10-minute walk north of Baker Street Tube, near Queen Mary's Gardens within Regent's Park; detailed directions and more info at www.openairtheatre. org).

Fringe Theater: London's rougher evening-entertainment scene is thriving. Choose from a wide range of fringe theater and comedy acts (generally £12).

Music, Opera, and Dance

CONCERTS AT CHURCHES

For easy, cheap, or free concerts in historic churches, attend a **lunch concert,** especially:
- St. Bride's Church, with free half-hour lunch concerts twice a week at 13:15 (usually Tue and Fri—confirm in advance, church tel. 020/7427-0133, www.stbrides.com).
- St. James's at Piccadilly, with 50-minute concerts on Mon, Wed, and Fri at 13:10 (suggested £3.50 donation, info tel. 020/7381-0441, www.sjp.org.uk).
- St. Martin-in-the-Fields, offering concerts on Mon, Tue, and Fri at 13:00 (suggested £3 donation, church tel. 020/7766-1100, www.smitf.org).

St. Martin-in-the-Fields also hosts fine **evening concerts** by

ENTERTAINMENT

Evensong

One of my favorite experiences in Britain is to attend evensong at a great church. Evensong is an evening worship service that is typically sung rather than said (though some parts—including scripture readings, a few prayers, and a homily—are spoken). It follows the traditional Anglican service in the Book of Common Prayer, including prayers, scripture readings, canticles (sung responses), and hymns that are appropriate for the early evening—traditionally the end of the working day and before the evening meal. In major churches with resident choirs, this service is filled with quality, professional musical elements. A singing or chanting priest leads the service, and a choir—usually made up of both men's and boys' voices (to sing the lower and higher parts, respectively)—sings the responses. The choir usually sings a cappella, or is accompanied by organ. While regular attendees follow the service from memory, visitors—who are welcome—are given an order of service or a prayer book to help them follow along. (If you're not familiar with the order of service, watch the congregation to know when to stand, sit, and kneel.)

You can attend services in many of England's grandest churches—but be aware that evensong typically takes place in the small choir area—which is far more intimate than the main nave. (To see the full church in action, a concert is a better choice.) Evensong generally occurs daily between 17:00 and 18:00 (often two hours earlier on Sun)—check with individual churches for specifics. At smaller churches, evensong is sometimes spoken, not sung.

Note that evensong is not a performance—it's a somewhat somber worship service. If you enjoy worshipping in different churches, attending evensong can be a trip-capping highlight. But if regimented church services aren't your thing, consider getting a different music fix. Most major churches also offer organ or choral concerts—look for posted schedules or ask at the information desk or gift shop.

candlelight (£8-28, several nights a week at 19:30) and live jazz in its underground Café in the Crypt (£5.50, £9, or £12, Wed at 20:00).

Evensong services are held at several churches, including St. Paul's Cathedral (see details on page 265), Westminster Abbey (see page 129), Southwark Cathedral (see page 91), and St. Bride's Church (Sun at 17:30, tel. 020/7427-0133, www.stbrides.com).

Free **organ recitals** are usually held on Sunday at 17:45 in Westminster Abbey (30 minutes, tel. 020/7222-5152). Many other churches have free concerts; ask for the *London Organ Concerts Guide* at the TI.

OTHER PERFORMANCES

Prom Concerts: For a fun classical event (mid-July–mid-Sept), attend a Prom Concert (shortened from "Promenade Concert") during the annual festival at the Royal Albert Hall. Nightly concerts are offered at give-a-peasant-some-culture prices (cheap standing-room "Promming" spots sold at the door, nearly-as-cheap restricted-view seats and pricier good ones sold in advance, Tube: South Kensington, www.bbc.co.uk/proms).

Opera: Some of the world's best opera is belted out at the prestigious Royal Opera House, near Covent Garden (www.roh. org.uk), and at the London Coliseum (English National Opera, St. Martin's Lane, Tube: Leicester Square, www.eno.org). Or consider taking in an unusual opera at the King's Head pub in Islington, home of London's Little Opera House (11 Upper Street, Tube: Angel, www.kingsheadtheatre.com).

Dance: The critically acclaimed Royal Ballet—where Margot Fonteyn and Rudolf Nureyev forged their famous partnership—is based at the Royal Opera House (www.roh.org.uk). Sadler's Wells Theatre features both international and UK-based dance troupes (Rosebery Avenue, Islington, Tube: Angel, www.sadlerswells. com).

Evening Sightseeing

Museum Visits: Many museums are open an evening or two during the week, offering fewer crowds. See the list on page 76.

Tours: Guided **walks** are offered several times a day and vary by theme: ancient London, museums, legal London, Dickens, Beatles, Jewish quarter, Christopher Wren, and so on. In the evening, expect a more limited choice: ghosts, Jack the Ripper, pubs, or literature. See a list of walking-tour companies on page 37.

To see the city illuminated at night, consider a **bus tour.** A two-hour London by Night Sightseeing Tour leaves several times an evening from Victoria Station and other points (see page 36).

Cruises: In summer, boats sail as late as 19:00 between Westminster Pier (near Big Ben) and the Tower of London. (For details, see page 40.)

A handful of outfits run expensive Thames River evening cruises with four-course meals and dancing. **London Showboat** offers the best value (nightly at 19:45, 3.5 hours, departs from Westminster Pier, reservations required, tel. 020/7740-0400, www.citycruises.com). Dinner cruises are also offered by **Bateaux London** (www.bateauxlondon.com).

Summer Evenings Along the South Bank

If you're visiting London in summer, consider hitting the South Bank neighborhood after hours.

Take a trip around the **London Eye** while the sun sets over the city (the wheel spins until late—last ascent at 21:00 April-Aug, 20:30 Sept-March, later on weekends). Then cap your night with an evening walk along the pedestrian-only **Jubilee Walkway,** which runs east-west along the river. It's where Londoners go to escape the heat. This pleasant stretch of the walkway—lined with pubs and casual eateries—goes from the London Eye past Shakespeare's Globe to Tower Bridge (you can walk in either direction).

If you're in the mood for a movie, take in a flick at the **BFI Southbank,** located just across the river, alongside Waterloo Bridge. Run by the British Film Institute, the state-of-the-art theater shows mostly classic films, as well as art cinema (Tube: Waterloo or Embankment, check www.bfi.org.uk for schedules and prices).

Farther east along the South Bank is **The Scoop**—an outdoor amphitheater next to City Hall. It's a good spot for movies, concerts, dance, and theater productions throughout the summer—with Tower Bridge as a scenic backdrop. These events are free, nearly nightly, and family-friendly. For the latest event schedule, see www.morelondon.com and click on "Events" (next to City Hall, Riverside, The Queen's Walkway, Tube: London Bridge).

Winter Diversions

London dazzles year-round, so consider visiting in winter, when airfares and hotel rates are generally cheaper and there are fewer tourists. Despite drearier weather and shorter days, London's museums, theaters, concert halls, and pubs offer a warm, cozy welcome.

London at Christmas is especially appealing, with its buildings dressed in their holiday best. Many holiday traditions have their roots in 19th-century Victorian Britain. Beginning in the 1840s, Queen Victoria's German husband, Prince Albert, popularized the decorating of Christmas trees and the sending of Christmas cards. And what could be more traditional than seeing the setting of

Charles Dickens' *A Christmas Carol* come to life? God bless us, every one.

NOVEMBER TO JANUARY

Pantomimes, or "pantos," are a British holiday tradition. Though they have nothing to do with silent mimes—and they don't mention Christmas—these campy fairy-tale plays entertain with outrageous costumes, sets, and dance numbers. Verbal participation is definitely encouraged, and it doesn't take long to learn the lines. Adults will laugh at the more risqué jokes; kids will giggle at the slapstick. Two London theaters that usually stage pantos are the Hackney Empire (291 Mare Street, northeast London, Tube: Bethnal Green, then 10 minutes on bus #106 or #254, tel. 020/8985-2424, www.hackneyempire.co.uk) or the Old Vic (corner of Waterloo Road and The Cut, southeast of Waterloo Station, Tube: Waterloo, tel. 0844-871-7628, www.oldvictheatre. com). For a rundown of all theater events, see www.timeout.com/london, www.theatremonkey.com, or www.officiallondontheatre. co.uk. For more about the panto tradition, see www.its-behind-you.com.

Get some exercise at the **outdoor ice rinks** at the London Eye, Somerset House, Tower of London, Natural History Museum, and Hampton Court Palace, among other locations (rental skates, generally mid-Nov-mid-Jan, reservations smart).

The **Hyde Park Winter Wonderland** offers kitschy carnival fun with a Ferris wheel, carousel, and other rides, as well as an ice rink and vendors selling silly hats and plenty of food and drink (late Nov-early Jan, southeast corner of park, Tube: Hyde Park Corner, www.hydeparkwinterwonderland.com).

Stroll around and enjoy the elaborate **light displays** and store windows on major shopping streets from mid-November to early January, especially on Oxford Street, Bond Street, Regent Street, and Brompton Road. Post-holiday sales start December 26 for many stores, including the famous Harrods January sale.

The Trafalgar Square **Christmas tree** is given to London every year from the people of Oslo, Norway, in appreciation for British help during World War II (lighting ceremony first Thu in Dec, stays up until Jan 6, www.london.gov.uk). Free carol concerts are held beneath the tree in December.

The **Geffrye Museum**'s 11 historic rooms are decorated for Christmas every year, highlighting holiday customs from the 17th century to today (free, see page 81).

The grand, red-velvet-draped **Royal Albert Hall** hosts seasonal concerts; ask about "carols by candlelight" events (Tube: South

Christmas Travel Strategies

- There is no public transit in London (Tube, train, or bus) at all on Christmas Day, and reduced services on Christmas Eve and Boxing Day (Dec 26). For specifics, see www.tfl. gov.uk. Taxis are scarce, so be prepared for a long wait (£4 holiday surcharge, tel. 0871-871-8710). Better yet, bundle up and walk.

- If arriving at Heathrow Airport on Christmas Day, research transport from the airport to your hotel in advance. There is no Tube or train service, but buses may run between Heathrow and Paddington Station, and between Gatwick Airport and Victoria Station (likely every 15-30 minutes; confirm in advance at www.heathrowexpress.com and www.nationalrail.co.uk/christmas, holiday schedules available in Nov). Or you could try a Hotel By Bus door-to-door shuttle van (about 2/hour, reservations tel. 0845-850-1900, www.hotelbybus.com).

- Pick a central location if staying over December 25, both to save money and avoid transportation difficulties. Stay somewhere with a kitchen (such as an apartment, hostel, or hotel room with kitchenette) so you can prepare some of your own meals. Don't forget to buy groceries before stores close on Christmas Eve. For tips on finding apartment rentals, see the Sleeping in London chapter.

- If you plan to eat out December 24-26 without reservations, go ethnic: Indian, Chinese, and Middle Eastern restaurants are usually open in Soho, Chinatown, along Edgware Road, or near the East End's Brick Lane.

- Expect closures. Museums are generally closed December 24-26, and smaller shops are usually closed December 26.

Kensington, box office tel. 0845-401-5034, www.royalalberthall. com).

Instead of visiting Santa Claus at the North Pole, British children see **Father Christmas** in his grotto. In London, the poshest Santa is at Harrods, and it may be worth reserving in advance to avoid long lines (early Nov-Christmas Eve, reservations available online as early as Sept, fees for reservations and photos; Tube: Knightsbridge, tel. 020/7730-1234). Father Christmas has also been known to visit the Hyde Park Winter Wonderland (described earlier), where you can see him for free.

Nibble your way through **Borough Market,** where you'll find lots of seasonal and gourmet treats (open daily the week before Christmas, closed Dec 25-26; otherwise open Mon-Tue 10:00-15:00, Wed-Thu 10:00-17:00, Fri-10:00-18:00, Sat 8:00-17:00, closed Sun; south of London Bridge, where Southwark

Street meets Borough High Street; Tube: London Bridge, tel. 020/7407-1002, www.boroughmarket.org.uk). While at the market, be sure to sample traditional favorites such as mulled wine, mince pie, Christmas cake, and Christmas pudding (see page 298).

Don't forget to pick up some **Christmas crackers** to give your holiday meals some extra bang. Not to be confused with something you eat, these fun party favors contain a paper crown, a teeny gift, and a corny joke. Buy them at grocery or department stores, find a friend, and pull hard.

Another popular holiday food event is the German **Christmas Market,** on the South Bank between the London Eye and the Royal Festival Hall (daily late Nov-Christmas Eve, Tube: Waterloo, www.xmas-markets.com).

CHRISTMAS DAY

Spending December 25 in London? While almost everything is closed, and there is no public transit (not even the Tube), you still have a few options for getting out.

Popular **church services** are held both Christmas Eve and Christmas Day at Westminster Abbey, Westminster Cathedral, St. Paul's, and St. Martin-in-the-Fields, among other places. Warning: These draw large crowds, so ask in advance about when to arrive. (For example, you may need to reserve free tickets in advance—available in Nov—and wait in line several hours for the Abbey's 16:00 service on Christmas Eve; 23:30 service is less crowded; tel. 020/7222-5152.)

The Peter Pan Cup **swim race,** held in Hyde Park every Christmas morning since 1864, is named in honor of *Peter Pan* playwright J. M. Barrie, who presented the first cup. Only members of the local swimming club may compete, but spectators are welcome (9:00, south side of The Serpentine—a lake in the center of the park). Break the ice by asking a local where to find the nearby Peter Pan statue.

London Walks offers two guided **walking tours** on December 25, with appropriate themes such as "Christmas Morning 1660" and "Charles Dickens' *A Christmas Carol*" (meet at Trafalgar Square Christmas tree, tel. 020/7624-3978 or recorded info tel. 020/7624-9255, www.walks.com).

Watch the Queen's annual **Christmas message** on the BBC at 15:00. If you miss it, you can watch it online on Her Majesty's Royal YouTube channel (www.youtube.com/TheRoyalChannel).

If your visit extends through the **New Year,** here are two events to be aware of: New Year's Eve **fireworks** from the London Eye attract at least 400,000 revelers to Trafalgar Square and the nearby riverbank, with good viewing spots staked out hours in advance. Public transport is free after the festivities (generally 23:45-04:30). The next day, a **parade** featuring 10,000 performers snakes two miles from the Ritz Hotel, past Piccadilly Circus and Trafalgar Square, to Big Ben (free to stand, or pay for grandstand seats, 11:45-15:00, tel. 020/3275-0190, www.londonparade.co.uk).

LONDON CONNECTIONS

By Plane

London has six airports; I've focused my coverage on the two most widely used—Heathrow and Gatwick—with a few tips for using the others (Stansted, Luton, London City, and Southend).

For accommodations at or near the major airports, see page 400.

HEATHROW AIRPORT

Heathrow Airport is one of the world's busiest airports. Think about it: 70 million passengers a year on 470,000 flights from

190 destinations riding 85 airlines, like some kind of global maypole dance. For Heathrow's airport, flight, and transfer information, call the switchboard at 0844-335-1801, or visit the helpful website at www.heathrowairport.com (airport code: LHR).

Heathrow has five terminals, numbered T-1 through T-5. Each terminal is served by different airlines and alliances; for example, T-5 is exclusively for British Air and Iberia Air flights, while T-1 serves mostly Star Alliance flights, such as United and Lufthansa. Screens posted throughout the airport identify which terminal each airline uses; this information should also be printed on your ticket or boarding pass.

To navigate, read signs and ask questions. You can walk between T-1, T-2, and T-3. From this central hub (called "Heathrow Central"), T-4 and T-5 split off in opposite directions (and are not

London's Airports

Luton
Luton
Stanstead

Reading
ST. PANCRAS
PADDINGTON
LIVERPOOL STREET
Southend
Southend

Windsor
#71 & #77
Rail Air Link
Tube
VICTORIA
D.L.R.
London City

To Bath
Heathrow
VICTORIA COACH STN.
London

Thames
Guildford

Gatwick
Ashford

To Paris

To Brighton
English Channel

EUROSTAR

Not to Scale

Rail
Eurostar Rail
Tube & D.L.R.
Bus

ALL BUSES ARE NATIONAL EXPRESS UNLESS NOTED

LONDON CONNECTIONS

walkable). To travel between the T-1/T-2/T-3 cluster and either T-4 or T-5, you can take a shuttle bus (free, serves all terminals), or the Tube (requires a ticket, serves all terminals). You can also connect T-1/T-2/T-3 and T-5 by Heathrow Express train (free, every 15-20 minutes); transfer by free spur train from Heathrow Central (T-1/T-2/T-3) to connect T-4.

If you're flying out of Heathrow, it's critical to confirm which terminal your flight will use (look carefully at your ticket/boarding pass, check online, or call your airline in advance)—because if it's T-4 or T-5, you'll need to allow extra time. Taxi drivers generally know which terminal you'll need based on the airline, but bus drivers may not.

Services: Each terminal has an airport information desk (generally daily 5:00-22:00), car-rental agencies, exchange bureaus, ATMs, a pharmacy, a VAT refund desk (tel. 0845-872-7627, you must present the VAT claim form from the retailer here to get your tax rebate on purchased items—see page 562 for details), room-booking services, and baggage storage (£5/item for up to 4 hours, £10/item for 24 hours, daily 6:00-23:00, opens 30-60 minutes earlier in some terminals, www.left-baggage.co.uk). Get online 24 hours a day at Heathrow's Internet access points (at each terminal—T-4's is up on the mezzanine level). Pay Wi-Fi is avail-

LONDON CONNECTIONS

able throughout the airport. A post office is on the first floor of T-3 (departures area). Each terminal has cheap eateries.

Heathrow's small **"TI"** (tourist info shop), even though it's a for-profit business, is worth a visit if you're nearby and want to pick up free information: a simple map, the *London Planner*, and brochures (daily 6:30-22:00, 5-minute walk from T-3 in Tube station, follow signs to Underground; bypass queue for transit info to reach window for London questions).

Getting to London from Heathrow Airport

You have five basic options for traveling the 14 miles between Heathrow Airport and downtown London: Tube (£5.50/person), bus (£6-9/person), direct shuttle bus (£18/person), express train with connecting Tube or taxi (including connecting Tube fare, about £12.50/person for slower train, £24/person for faster train), or taxi (about £70/group).

By Tube (Subway): The Tube takes you from any Heathrow terminal to downtown London in 50-60 minutes on the Piccadilly

Line (6/hour, buy ticket at Tube station ticket window or self-service machine). Depending on your destination in London, you may need to transfer (for example, if headed to the Victoria Station neighborhood, transfer at Hammersmith to the District line and ride six more stops). If you plan to use the Tube for

transport in London, it may make sense to buy a Travelcard or pay-as-you-go Oyster card at the airport's Tube station ticket window. (For details on these passes, see page 23.) If your Travelcard covers only Zones 1-2, it does not include Heathrow (Zone 6); however, you can pay a small supplement for the initial trip from Heathrow to downtown.

If you're taking the Tube from downtown London *to* the airport, note that Piccadilly Line trains don't stop at every terminal. Trains either stop at T-4, then T-1/T-2/T-3 (also called Heathrow Central), in that order; or T-1/T-2/T-3, then T-5. When leaving central London on the Tube, allow extra time if going to T-4 or T-5; to ensure you get on a train going to your terminal, carefully check the destination before you board.

By Bus: Most buses depart from the outdoor common area called the Central Bus Station, located a five-minute walk from the T-1/T-2/T-3 complex. To connect between T-4 or T-5 and the Central Bus Station, use Heathrow's free shuttle buses; if you just need to reach T-5, ride the free Heathrow Express train.

National Express has regular service from Heathrow's Central Bus Station to Victoria Coach Station in downtown London, near several of my recommended hotels. While slow, the bus is affordable and convenient for those staying near Victoria Station (£6-9, 1-2/hour, less frequent from Victoria Station to Heathrow, 45-75 minutes depending on time of day, tel. 0871-781-8178, www.nationalexpress.com). A less-frequent National Express bus goes from T-5 directly to Victoria Coach Station.

By Shuttle: Heathrow Shuttle is an economical shuttle-bus service that goes to/from your hotel and your terminal at Heathrow. You'll share a minivan with other travelers who are also being picked up or dropped off, so it's not much of a time-savings over taking the Tube (£18/person, progressive discounts for groups of two or more, 1 child under age 10 travels free with 2 adults, runs daily 4:00-18:00, book at least 24 hours in advance, office open daily 7:00-20:00, tel. 0845-257-8068, www.heathrowshuttle.com, info@heathrowshuttle.com). Another option is **Just Airports**, which offers a private car service between five London airports and the city center (from £32/car; see website for specific quote, tel. 020/8900-1666, www.justairports.com).

By Train: Two different trains run between Heathrow Airport and London's Paddington Station. At Paddington Station, you're in the thick of the Tube system, with easy access to any of my recommended neighborhoods—my Paddington hotels are just outside the front door, and Notting Hill Gate is just two Tube stops away. The **Heathrow Connect** train is the slightly slower, much cheaper option, serving T-1/T-2/T-3 at a single station called Heathrow Central; use free transfers to get from either T-4 or T-5 to Heathrow Central (£10 one-way, £20 round-trip, 2/hour Mon-Sat, 1-2/hour Sun, 40 minutes, tel. 0845-678-6975, www. heathrowconnect.com).

The **Heathrow Express** train is fast and runs more frequently, but it's pricey (£21 one-way, £34 round-trip, £5 more if you buy your ticket on board, 4/hour; 15 minutes to downtown from Heathrow Central station serving T-1/T-2/T-3, 21 minutes from T-5; transfer by free spur train from T-4 to Heathrow Central; covered by BritRail pass, daily 5:10-23:48, tel. 0845-600-1515, www. heathrowexpress.co.uk). At the airport, you can use the Heathrow Express as a free transfer between terminals.

By Taxi: Taxis from the airport cost £45-75 to west and central London (one hour). For four people traveling together, this can be a reasonable option. Hotels can often line up a cab back to the airport for about £40.

GATWICK AIRPORT

More and more flights land at Gatwick Airport, which is half-way between London and the south coast (airport code: LGW, tel. 0844-892-0322, www.gatwickairport.com). Gatwick has two terminals, North and South, which are easily connected by a free monorail (two-minute trip, runs 24 hours daily). Note that boarding passes say "Gatwick N" or "Gatwick S" to indicate your terminal. British Airways flights generally use Gatwick North. The Gatwick Express trains (described next) stop only at Gatwick South. Schedules in each terminal show only arrivals and departures from that terminal.

Getting to London: Gatwick Express trains are clearly the best way into London from this airport. They shuttle conveniently between Gatwick South and London's Victoria Station, with many of my recommended hotels close by (£20 one-way, £35 round-trip, at least 10 percent cheaper if purchased online, 4/hour, 30 minutes, runs 5:00-24:00 daily, a few trains as early as 3:30, tel. 0845-850-1530, www.gatwickexpress.com). If you buy your tickets at the station before boarding, ask about their deal where three or four adults travel for the price of two. (If you see others in the ticket line, suggest buying your tickets together—you'll save up to 50 percent.) When going *to* the airport, at Victoria Station note that Gatwick Express has its own ticket windows right by the platform (tracks 13 and 14).

A train also runs between Gatwick South and **St. Pancras International Station** (£10, 3-5/hour, 45-60 minutes, www.firstcapitalconnect.co.uk)—useful for travelers taking the Eurostar train (to Paris or Brussels) or staying in the St. Pancras/King's Cross neighborhood.

Even slower, but cheap and handy to the Victoria Station neighborhood, you can take the **bus** (1.5 hours). National Express runs a bus from Gatwick direct to Victoria Station (£8, at least hourly, tel. 0871-781-8178, www.nationalexpress.com); easyBus has one going to near the Earls Court Tube stop (£2-10 depending on how far ahead you book, 2-3/hour, www.easybus.co.uk).

LONDON'S OTHER AIRPORTS

Stansted Airport: From Stansted (airport code: STN, tel. 0844-335-1803, www.stanstedairport.com), you have several options for getting into or out of London. Two different **buses** connect the airport and London's Victoria Station neighborhood: National Express (£8-10, every 15 minutes, 1.75 hours, runs 24 hours a day, picks up and stops throughout London, ends at Victoria Coach Station or Liverpool Street Station, tel. 0871-781-8178, www.nationalexpress.com) and Terravision (£9, 2-3/hour, 1.25 hours, ends at Green Line Coach Station just south of Victoria Station).

Or you can take the faster, pricier Stansted Express **train** (£23.50, connects to London's Tube system at Tottenham Hale and Liverpool Street, 4/hour, 45 minutes, 4:30-23:00, www.stanstedexpress.com). Stansted is expensive by **cab**; figure £100-120 one-way from central London.

Luton Airport: For Luton (airport code: LTN, airport tel. 01582/405-100, www.london-luton.co.uk), there are two choices into or out of London. The fastest way to go is by **train** to London's St. Pancras International Station (£9.50-15.50 one-way, 1-5/hour, 25-45 minutes—check schedule to avoid slower trains, tel. 0845-712-5678, www.eastmidlandstrains.co.uk); catch the 10-minute shuttle bus (every 10 minutes, £1.50) from outside the terminal to the Luton Airport Parkway Station. The Green Line express **bus** #757 runs to Buckingham Palace Road, just south of Victoria Station, and stops en route near the Baker Street Tube station—best if you're staying near Paddington Station or in North London (£10 one-way, small discount for easyJet passengers who buy online, 2-4/hour, 1-1.5 hours, runs 24 hours, tel. 0844-801-7261, www.greenline.co.uk). If you're sleeping at Luton, consider easyHotel (see listing on page 401).

Other Airports: There's a slim chance you might use **London City Airport** (airport code: LCY, tel. 020/7646-0088, www.londoncityairport.com). To get into London, take the Docklands Light Railway (DLR) to the Bank Tube station, which is one stop east of St. Paul's on the Central Line (less than £5 one-way, covered by Travelcard, a bit cheaper with an Oyster card, 22 minutes, www.tfl.gov.uk/dlr). Some easyJet flights land even farther out, at **Southend Airport** (airport code: SEN, tel. 01702/538-500, www.southendairport.com). Trains connect this airport to London's Liverpool Street Station (£15 one-way, 3-8/hour, 55 minutes, www.abelliogreateranglia.co.uk).

CONNECTING LONDON'S AIRPORTS BY BUS

A handy **National Express bus** runs between Heathrow, Gatwick, Stansted, and Luton airports—easier than having to cut through the center of London—although traffic can be bad and can increase travel times (tel. 0871-781-8178, www.nationalexpress.com).

From Heathrow Airport to: Gatwick Airport (1-6/hour, about 1.25 hours—but allow at least three hours between flights, £25), **Stansted Airport** (1-2/hour, about 1.5 hours, £27), **Luton Airport** (roughly hourly, 1-1.5 hours, £23).

DISCOUNTED FLIGHTS FROM LONDON

London is the hub for many cheap, no-frills airlines, which affordably connect the city with other destinations in the British Isles and throughout Europe. A visit to www.kayak.com or similar search engines sorts the numerous options offered by the many discount airlines, enabling you to see the best schedules for your trip and find the best deal. Book in advance for the best deals. Although you can book right up until the flight departs, the cheap seats will have sold out long before, leaving the most expensive seats for late-comers.

Be aware of the potential drawbacks of flying on the cheap: nonrefundable and nonchangeable tickets, rigid baggage restrictions (and fees if you have more than what's officially allowed), use of airports far outside town, tight schedules that can mean more delays, little in the way of customer assistance if problems arise, and, of course, no frills. To avoid unpleasant surprises, read the small print—especially baggage policies—before you book.

EasyJet flies from Gatwick, Luton, Stansted, and Southend. Prices are based on demand, so the least popular routes make for the cheapest fares, especially if you book early (www.easyjet.com). **Ryanair** flies from London (mostly Stansted airport, though also Gatwick and Luton) to often-obscure airports near dozens of European cities (www.ryanair.com). While their fares can be shockingly low, Ryanair is notorious for charging additional fees for nearly everything.

Other airlines to consider include **CityJet** (based at London City Airport, www.cityjet.com), **Monarch** (specializes in connecting to Mediterranean resorts, www.monarch.co.uk), **Thomson** (similar to Monarch, www.thomsonfly.com), **Flybe** (www.flybe.com), and **Brussels Airlines** (with frequent connections from Heathrow to its Brussels hub, www.brusselsairlines.com).

By Train

Britain is covered by myriad rail systems (owned by different companies), which together are called National Rail. London, the country's major transportation hub, has a different train station for each region. There are nine main stations (see the map):

Euston—Serves northwest England, North Wales, and Scotland.

St. Pancras International—Serves north and south England, plus the Eurostar to Paris or Brussels (see "Crossing the Channel," later).

King's Cross—Serves northeast England and Scotland, including York and Edinburgh.

Liverpool Street—Serves east England, including Essex and Harwich.

London Bridge—Serves south England, including Brighton.

Waterloo—Serves south England, including Salisbury and Southampton.

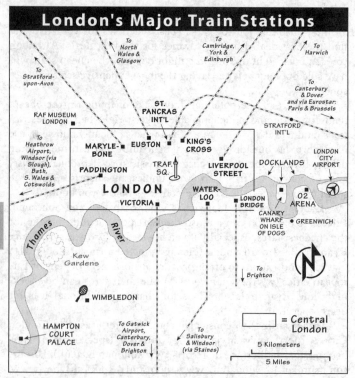

London's Major Train Stations

To North Wales & Glasgow

To Cambridge, York & Edinburgh

To Harwich

To Stratford-upon-Avon

To Canterbury & Dover and via Eurostar: Paris & Brussels

RAF MUSEUM LONDON

ST. PANCRAS INT'L

STRATFORD INT'L

To Heathrow Airport, Windsor (via Slough), Bath, S. Wales & Cotswolds

MARYLE-BONE   EUSTON   KING'S CROSS

LONDON CITY AIRPORT

PADDINGTON

TRAF. SQ.

LIVERPOOL STREET

DOCKLANDS

LONDON

WATER-LOO

LONDON BRIDGE

O2 ARENA

VICTORIA

CANARY WHARF ON ISLE OF DOGS

GREENWICH

Thames River

Kew Gardens

To Brighton

N

WIMBLEDON

= Central London

HAMPTON COURT PALACE

To Gatwick Airport, Canterbury, Dover & Brighton

To Salisbury & Windsor (via Staines)

5 Kilometers

5 Miles

Victoria—Serves Gatwick Airport, Canterbury, Dover, and Brighton.

Paddington—Serves south and southwest England, including Heathrow Airport, Windsor, Bath, South Wales, and the Cotswolds.

Marylebone—Serves southwest and central England, including Stratford-upon-Avon.

In addition, London has several smaller train stations that you're less likely to use, such as **Charing Cross** (serves southeast England, including Dover) and **Blackfriars.**

Any train station has schedule information, can make reservations, and can sell tickets for any destination. Most stations offer a baggage-storage service (£10/bag for 24 hours, look for *left luggage* signs); because of long security lines, it can take a while to check or pick up your bag (www.left-baggage.co.uk). For more details on the services available at each station, see www.nationalrail.co.uk/stations.

Buying Tickets: For general information, call 0845-748-4950 (or visit www.nationalrail.co.uk or www.eurostar.com). If you book far enough ahead, you might find discounted train tickets on

Public Transportation near London

To North England & Scotland

To York & Scotland

King's Lynn

Norwich

Coventry

ENGLAND

Stratford-upon-Avon

Warwick

Long Buckby

Bedford

Hunt.

Ely

To Hoek van Holland

Leam. Spa

Luton

Cambridge

Worcester

Moreton

Banbury

Stansted

Harwich

Chelten-ham

Stow

COTSWOLDS

Oxford

Didcot

London City

Southend

To Cardiff

Blenheim

Swindon

London

Greenwich

To Ostende

Avebury

Reading

Slough

Ramsgate

Bristol

Bath

Bedwyn

Windsor

Heathrow

EUROSTAR

Canterbury

Dover

Wells

Stonehenge

Gatwick

Glaston-bury

Salisbury

South-ampton

Ashford

Rye

(CHUNNEL)

Calais

To Cornwall

Brighton

East-bourne

Hastings

Calais-Fréthun

To Paris

Poole

Bourne-mouth

Portsmouth

Weymouth

Isle of Wight

English Channel

FRANCE

- - - - - Rail
- - - - Bus
.... Boat

Area covered by London Plus Pass

30 Kilometers

30 Miles (approx. scale)

Note: Bus Lines Follow Most Rail Lines

LONDON CONNECTIONS

certain routes at www.megabus.com (tel. 0871-266-3333; as they also sell bus tickets, be careful to specify that you want to take the train).

Rail Passes: For train travel outside London, consider getting a BritRail pass. Options include passes that cover England as well as Scotland and Wales, England-only passes, England/Ireland passes, "London Plus" passes (good for travel in most of southeast England but not in London itself), and BritRail & Drive passes (which include a car rental). For specifics, see www.ricksteves.com/rail.

TRAIN CONNECTIONS FROM LONDON
To Points West
From Paddington Station to: Bath (2/hour, 1.5 hours; also consider a guided Evan Evans tour by bus—see page 519), **Oxford** (2/hour direct, 1 hour, more possible with transfer in Reading), **Penzance** (every 1-2 hours, 5-5.5 hours, possible change in Plymouth), and **Cardiff** (2/hour, 2 hours).

To Points North
From King's Cross Station: Trains run at least hourly, stopping in **York** (2 hours), **Durham** (3 hours), and **Edinburgh** (4.5-4.75

hours). Trains to **Cambridge** also leave from here (2/hour, 45 minutes).

From Euston Station to: Conwy (nearly hourly, 3.25 hours, transfer in Chester), **Liverpool** (at least hourly, 2 hours, more with transfer), **Blackpool** (hourly, 3 hours, transfer at Preston), **Keswick** (hourly, 4-4.5 hours, transfer to bus at Penrith), and **Glasgow** (1-2/hour, 4.5-5.5 hours).

From London's Other Stations

Trains run between London and **Canterbury,** leaving from St. Pancras International Station and arriving in Canterbury West (1-2/hour, 1 hour), as well as from London's Victoria Station and arriving in Canterbury East or West (2/hour, 1.5-2 hours).

Direct trains leave for **Stratford-upon-Avon** from Marylebone Station, located near the southwest corner of Regent's Park (5/day direct, more with transfers, 2.25 hours).

To Other Destinations: Dover (hourly, 1.25 hours, from St. Pancras International Station; also hourly, 2 hours, direct from Victoria Station or Charing Cross Station), **Brighton** (4-5/hour, 1 hour, from Victoria Station and London Bridge Station), **Portsmouth** (3/hour, 1.5-2 hours, most from Waterloo Station, a few from Victoria Station), and **Salisbury** (2/hour, 1.5 hours, from Waterloo Station). For trains to **Windsor or Cambridge,** check the Day Trips section.

By Bus

Buses are slower but considerably cheaper than trains for reaching destinations around Britain, and beyond. Most depart from **Victoria Coach Station,** which is one long block south of Victoria Station (near many recommended accommodations and Tube: Victoria). Inside the station, you'll find basic eateries, kiosks, and a helpful information desk stocked with schedules and ready to point you to your bus or answer any questions. Watch your bags carefully—luggage thieves thrive at the station.

Most domestic buses are operated by **National Express** (tel. 0871-781-8178, www.nationalexpress.com); their international departures are called **Eurolines** (www.eurolines.co.uk).

A newer, smaller company called **Megabus** undersells National Express with deeply discounted promotional fares—the farther ahead you buy, the less you pay (some trips for just £1.50, toll tel. 0900-160-0900, www.megabus.com). While Megabus can be much cheaper than National Express—even half the price—they tend to be slower than their competitor and their routes mainly connect cities, not smaller towns. They also sell discounted train tickets on selected routes.

Public Transportation Routes in Britain

Legend:
- Rail
- Eurostar
- Bus
- (8H) Ferry with crossing time

Ferry Note:
Dover - Calais–1.5 H
Dover - Boul–1.5 H

Orkney Islands

Lewis

Burwick
Thurso
John o' Groats

Skye
Portree
Elgin
Inverness
Culloden
Kyle
Loch Ness
Aviemore
Aberdeen
Mallaig
Fort William
SCOTLAND
Pitlochry
Mull
Iona
Perth
Dundee
Leuchars
St. Andrews
Oban
Stirling
Edinburgh
Glasgow
Berwick

Holy Island

50 Kilometers
50 Miles

Larne (2H)
(2.5H)
Cairnryan
Stranraer
Hexham
Newcastle
Durham
To Amsterdam (15H)

North Sea

Belfast
NORTHERN IRELAND
(8H)
Carlisle
Keswick
Penrith
Whitby
Danby
North York Moors
Scarborough

Irish Sea
Windermere
Isle of Man
ENGLAND
York

Dublin
(7H)
Blackpool
Preston
Leeds
Hull
To Zeebrugge (10H)
Dun Laoghaire
(2-3H)
Holyhead
Conwy
Liverpool
Manchester
Grimsby

REPUBLIC OF IRELAND
Bangor
Caernarfon
Betws-y-Coed
Blaenau Ffest.
Pwllheli
Harlech
Chester
Stoke
Derby
Telford
Wolv.
Lincoln
Peter-borough
King's Lynn
Norwich

Aberystwyth
Ironbridge Gorge
Birmingham
Coventry
Warwick
Ely
Cambridge
To Esbjerg (18H)

(3.5H)
Rosslare
WALES
Cheltenham
Stratford
Stow
Moreton
Oxford
Harwich
To Hoek van Holland (6H)

Fishguard
Carmarthen
Newport
Reading
London
Ebbs-fleet
Canterbury
Dover (1.5H)

Swansea
Cardiff
Bath
STONE-HENGE
Woking
Ashford
Calais

Bristol
Wells
West-bury
Salisbury
Brighton

Glastonbury
Southampton
Newhaven
EUROSTAR (2.5H)

Exeter
Portsmouth
To Dieppe (4H)
To Paris & Brussels

Atlantic Ocean
Dartmoor
Truro
St. Ives
Plymouth
English Channel
To Ouistreham (6H)

Penzance
Falmouth
To Roscoff (6H)
To Cherbourg (3H)
FRANCE

Try to avoid bus travel on Friday and Sunday evenings, when weekend travelers are more likely to make buses sell out.

To ensure getting a ticket—and to save money with special promotions—you can book your ticket in advance online (National Express charges a £1 fee) or over the phone (£2 surcharge). The cheapest pre-purchased tickets can be changed (for a £5 fee), but they're usually nonrefundable within 72 hours of travel. If you have a British mobile phone, you can order online and have a "text ticket" sent right to your phone.

Ideally you'll buy your tickets online. But if you must buy one at the station, try to arrive an hour before the bus departs—or drop by the day before. Ticketing machines are scattered around the station (separate machines for National Express/Eurolines and Megabus; you can buy either for today or for tomorrow); there's also a ticket counter near gate 21.

National Express buses go to: **Oxford** (2/hour, about 2 hours), **Cambridge** (every 60-90 minutes, 2-2.5 hours), **Canterbury** (about hourly, 2-2.5 hours), **Dover** (about hourly, 2.5-3.25 hours), **Brighton** (hourly, 2 hours), **Penzance** (5/day, 8.5-10 hours, overnight available), **Cardiff** (hourly, 3.25-3.5 hours), **Stratford-upon-Avon** (3/day, 3.5 hours), **Liverpool** (8/day direct, 4.75-6 hours, overnight available), **Blackpool** (4/day direct, 6.25-7 hours, overnight available), **York** (4/day direct, 5.25-6.25 hours), **Durham** (3/day direct, 6-8 hours, train is better), **Glasgow** (2-4/day direct, 8-9 hours, train is a much better option), **Edinburgh** (2/day direct, 8.75-9.75 hours, go by train instead).

To Dublin, Ireland: This bus/boat journey, operated by National Express, takes 10-12 hours (£35-40, 1/day, departs Victoria Coach Station at 18:00, check in with passport one hour before). Consider a cheap 1.25-hour Ryanair flight instead (www.ryanair. com).

To the Continent: Especially in summer, buses run to destinations all over Europe, including Paris, Amsterdam, Brussels, and Germany (sometimes crossing the Channel by ferry, other times through the Chunnel). For any international connection, you need to check in with your passport one hour before departure. For details, call 0871-781-8178 or visit www.eurolines.co.uk. For information on crossing the Channel by bus, see page 483.

Crossing the Channel

BY EUROSTAR TRAIN

The fastest and most convenient way to get from Big Ben to the Eiffel Tower is by rail. The Eurostar is the speedy passenger train that zips you (and up to 800 others in 18 sleek cars) from downtown London to downtown Paris or Brussels (1-2/hour, 2.5 hours) faster and more easily than flying. The train goes 190 mph both before and after the English Channel crossing. The actual tunnel crossing is a 20-minute, silent, 100-mile-per-hour nonevent. Your ears won't even pop.

Get ready for more high-speed connections: Eurostar's monopoly expired at the beginning of 2010, and Germany's national railroad is negotiating to run bullet trains between Frankfurt, Amsterdam, and London by 2016.

Eurostar Fares

Unlike most trains in Western Europe, the Eurostar is not covered by rail passes and always requires a separate, reserved train ticket. Eurostar fares (essentially the same between London and Paris or Brussels) vary depending on how far ahead you reserve, whether you can live with restrictions (refundable vs. non-refundable tickets), and whether you're eligible for any discounts.

A **one-way, full-fare ticket** runs about $200-240 ("Standard"), $240-310 ("Standard Premier"), and $390 ("Business"). **Discounts** can lower fares substantially for children under age 12, youths under age 26, seniors age 60 or older, adults booking months ahead or traveling round-trip, and rail pass holders. The early bird gets the best price in each category. If you're ready to commit, you can book tickets as early as 4-9 months in advance.

A tour company called BritainShrinkers sells one- or two-day tours to Paris, Brussels, or Bruges, enabling you to side-trip to these cities from London for less than most train tickets alone. For example, you'll pay £129 for a one-day Paris "tour" (unescorted Mon-Sat day trip with Métro pass; tel. 020/7404-5100, www.britainshrinkers.com). This can be a particularly good option if you need to get to Paris from London on short notice, when only the costliest Eurostar fares are available.

Buying Eurostar Tickets

Because only the most expensive (full-fare, non-discounted) tickets are fully refundable, don't reserve until you're sure of your plans. But if you wait too long, the cheapest tickets will get bought up.

Once you're confident about the time and date of your crossing, you can check and book fares by phone or online. Ordering online offers a print-at-home eticket option (see www.ricksteves.com/eurostar or www.eurostar.com). You can also order by phone through Rail Europe at US tel. 800-387-6782, or through Eurostar (tel. 0843-218-6186, priced in euros). In Britain, tickets can be issued only at the Eurostar office in St. Pancras International Station. In continental Europe, you can buy your Eurostar ticket at any major train station in any country or at any travel agency that handles train tickets (expect a booking fee). You can purchase passholder discount tickets at Eurostar departure stations,

through US agents, or by phone with Eurostar, but they may be harder to get at other train stations and travel agencies, and are a discount category that can sell out.

Remember that Britain's time zone is one hour earlier than France and Belgium's. Times listed on tickets are local times (departure from London is British time, arrival in Paris is French time).

Taking the Eurostar

Eurostar trains depart from and arrive at London's St. Pancras International Station. Check in at least 30 minutes in advance for your Eurostar trip. It's very similar to an airport check-in: You pass through airport-like security, show your passport to customs officials, and find a TV monitor to locate your departure gate. There are a few airport-like shops, newsstands, horrible snack bars, and cafés (bring food for the trip from elsewhere), pay-Internet terminals, and a currency-exchange booth with rates about the same as you'll find on the other end.

CROSSING THE CHANNEL WITHOUT EUROSTAR

For speed and affordability, look into cheap flights. The old-fashioned ways of crossing the Channel are cheaper than Eurostar (taking the bus is cheapest). They're also twice as romantic, complicated, and time-consuming.

By Plane

Check with budget airlines for cheap round-trip fares to Paris or Brussels (see "Discounted Flights from London," earlier).

By Train and Boat

For additional European ferry info, visit www.aferry.to. For UK train and bus info, go to www.traveline.org.uk.

Building the Chunnel

The toughest obstacle to building a tunnel under the English Channel was overcome in 1986, when longtime rivals Britain and France reached an agreement to build it together. Britain began in Folkestone, France in Calais, planning a rendezvous in the middle.

By 1988, specially made machines three football fields long were boring 26-foot-wide holes under the ground. The dirt they hauled out became landfill in Britain and a hill in France. Crews crept forward 100 feet a day until June of 1991, when French and English workers broke through and shook hands midway across the Channel—the tunnel was complete. Rail service began in 1994.

The Chunnel is 31 miles long (24 miles of it underwater) and 26 feet wide. It sits 130 feet below the seabed in a chalky layer of sediment. It's segmented into three separate tunnels—two for trains (one in each direction) and one for service and ventilation. The walls are concrete panels and rebar fixed to the rock around it. Sixteen-thousand-horsepower engines pull 850 tons of railcars and passengers at speeds up to 100 mph through the tunnel.

The ambitious project—the world's longest undersea tunnel—helped to show the European community that cooperation between nations could benefit everyone.

To Paris: You'll take a train from London to the port of Dover (trains depart hourly from London's St. Pancras International Station to Dover's Priory Station, 1.25 hours), then catch a ferry to Calais, France, before boarding another train for Paris. P&O Ferries sail from Dover to Calais (up to 2/hour, 1.5 hours, www.poferries.com); TGV trains run from Calais to Paris.

To Amsterdam: Stena Line's Dutchflyer service combines train and ferry tickets between London and Amsterdam via the ports of Harwich and Hoek van Holland. Trains go from London's Liverpool Street Station to **Harwich** (hourly, 1.75 hours, most transfer in Manningtree). From Harwich, Stena Line ferries sail to Hoek van Holland (8 hours), where you can catch a train to Amsterdam (book ahead for best price, 13 hours total travel time, www.stenaline.co.uk, Dutch train info at www.ns.nl).

By Bus and Boat

You can take the bus from London direct to **Paris** (4/day, 8.25-9.75 hours), **Brussels** (4/day, 9 hours), or **Amsterdam** (4/day, 12 hours) from Victoria Coach Station (via ferry or Chunnel, day or overnight). Prices are the same to Paris, Brussels, or Amsterdam (around £60-70 one-way, cheaper in advance, tel. 0870-514-3219, www.eurolines.co.uk).

London's Cruise Ports

Many cruises begin, end, or call at one of several English ports offering easy access to London. Cruise lines favor two ports in particular: **Southampton**, 80 miles southwest of London; and **Dover**, 80 miles southeast of London (each one within about a 1.5-hour drive or train ride into the city).

While London offers plenty of public-transportation connections for getting you from your ship into town (explained below), most cruise lines offer an **"On Your Own" excursion** that includes an unguided bus trip from your ship to downtown London (usually Piccadilly Circus), then back again at an appointed time. While a bit pricey (usually around £65, compared to about £40 round-trip by train from Southampton, or about £36 from Dover), this can be efficient and avoids the potential stress of doing it on your own. Ask your cruise line for details.

SOUTHAMPTON CRUISE PORT

An important English port city for centuries, Southampton is best known for three ships that set sail from here and gained fame for very different reasons: the *Mayflower* in 1620, the *Titanic* in 1912, and the *Queen Mary* in 1936. Like many port cities, Southampton was badly damaged by WWII bombs, obliterating whatever cobbled charm it once had. These days, if Southampton is known for anything, it's for cruising. About 1.5 million cruise passengers pass through here every year.

Services: With 240,000 people, Southampton is a sprawling port town with a relatively compact downtown core. Everything is, to a point, walkable—though most of the cruise terminals (described later) are a long walk from the train station. The main drag stretching up from the waterfront, High Street (which becomes Above Bar higher up), is the easiest place to find ATMs, Wi-Fi hotspots, and a Boots pharmacy.

Transit Within Town: To reach the train station from your cruise ship, the easiest solution is to take a **taxi** (figure £5-8; around £125 one-way into central London). To save a bit of money, you can walk partway or all the way to the station; to shave some time off the walk, consider the free **Citylink bus**, which goes from the public ferry dock at Town Quay (between the two dock areas, where High Street meets the water, in front of the Red Funnel ticket office) up to the train station about every 15 minutes. As this bus doesn't stop at the cruise terminals themselves, you must walk to meet it: Figure 10 minutes from the Ocean Cruise Terminal, 15 minutes from the City Cruise Terminal, and even longer from the other terminals (from those, I'd take a taxi instead).

Cruise Terminals: Within Southampton's sprawling port (www.cruisesouthampton.com), cruises use two separate dock areas, each with two different terminals. All four terminal buildings have WCs, a rack of tourist brochures and maps, a basic café, a taxi stand out front, and possibly Wi-Fi (ask for the password). Most don't have ATMs or TIs.

Eastern Docks: The long piers jabbing straight out from Southampton have two cruise terminals (accessed through Dock Gate 4): **Ocean Cruise Terminal** at the near end (Berth 46, about a 5-minute walk to the mainland), and **QEII Cruise Terminal** at the tip (Berth 38/39, about a 15-minute walk to the mainland). From the QEII Terminal, I'd take a taxi; from Ocean Cruise Terminal, the walk-plus-bus combo is worth considering, though it takes longer: Walk down the pier and through Dock Gate 4, turn left, and follow the busy road (with the port on your left) about five more minutes to the Citylink bus stop at Town Quay.

Western Docks: This gloomy industrial zone, accessed through Dock Gate 8 (closer to town) or 10 (closer to the train station), hugs Southampton's coastline west of downtown. Shuffled between the endless parking lots and container shipping berths are two cruise terminals: **City Cruise Terminal,** close to the town center (Berth 101); and **Mayflower Cruise Terminal,** farther out (Berth 106). As Mayflower is a distant and dreary walk from the port gate, I'd spring for a taxi. From City Cruise Terminal, the walk-plus-bus combo may be worth considering: Exit the terminal to the right, then continue straight about 10 minutes through Dock Gate 8 and along the port to Town Quay and the free Citylink bus.

Trains to London: From Southampton Central Station, trains depart every 30 minutes to London's **Waterloo Station** (1.25 hours; additional departures require a change in Basingstoke and take 1.5 hours; slower trains go to London's Victoria Station in 2.5 hours). A same-day return (round-trip) ticket to London costs £39; a one-way ticket costs £34.10.

When returning to Southampton, be sure to get off at **Southampton Central Station;** the stop called Southampton Airport Parkway is much farther from the cruise port.

Sights in Southampton: While most people will make a beeline for London, the port city does have one sight worth considering: its excellent **SeaCity Museum,** with a beautifully presented exhibit about the *Titanic*. "Southampton's *Titanic* Story" explores every facet of the ill-fated ocean liner that set sail from here on April 10, 1912, and sank in the North Atlantic a few days later. Three-quarters of the *Titanic*'s 897 crew members lived in Southampton (£8.50, daily 10:00-17:00, last entry at 15:00, next to the

Civic Centre along Havelock Road, tel. 023/8083-3007, www.seacitymuseum.co.uk).

DOVER CRUISE PORT

For generations, Dover—with its easy ferry connections across the English Channel to the Continent—was the place where many travelers first set foot in Britain. But since the advent of cheap flights and the high-speed Eurostar train beneath the Channel, Dover is most useful these days for its cruise port.

Services: Like much of southern England, Dover sits on a foundation of chalk; its famous white cliffs are visible from your cruise ship. The workaday city center is anchored by Market Square, with a handy **TI** (inside the Dover Museum). Across the square begins the mostly pedestrianized (but not particularly charming) main shopping drag, Cannon Street/Biggin Street, with ATMs, Wi-Fi hotspots, and a Boots pharmacy.

Cruise Terminals: Little Dover has a huge port, and cruises put in at its far western edge—at the **Western Docks,** along the extremely long Admiralty Pier (www.whitecliffscountry.org.uk). Near the port gate at the base of the pier, Terminal 1 is a converted old railway station; farther out at the tip, Terminal 2 is a modern facility.

Getting into Town: From either terminal, the best way into town (or to the train station) is by shuttle bus or taxi. The bright-blue **shuttle bus** makes a loop connecting the cruise terminals, Market Square, and Dover Castle (bus costs £3 one-way into town; add £1 to continue up to the castle; www.opentopbus.co.uk). From Market Square, it's a 15-minute walk to the train station: Head up Cannon Street (directly across the square from the TI) for three blocks, turn left onto Priory Street, continue straight through the big roundabout, and head slightly uphill on Folkestone Road; a half-block after the gas station, watch for *Dover Priory* signs on the right marking the station.

For more than two people, it's cheaper to take a **taxi,** which will run you about £7-8 whether you're going downtown, to the train station, or up to Dover Castle (figure around £150 one-way to central London).

I'd avoid the long, dreary, 30-minute **walk** from the cruise terminals into town (you'll have to go down the entire length of the pier to the mainland, turn right along the busy road, and trudge the rest of the way into town; to reach the train station, turn left up York Street, then left again on Folkestone Road).

Trains to London: From Dover Priory Station, you can choose between the faster "Javelin" train (hourly, 1.25 hours to London's **St. Pancras International Station;** £38.10 one-way, £40.60 same-day return, £71.20 anytime return) and the slower train (hourly

LONDON CONNECTIONS

to **Victoria Station** or hourly to **Charing Cross Station,** each 2 hours; £31.20 one-way, £31.40 same-day return). When choosing a train, consider this: St. Pancras International and Victoria Stations are both well-connected to any point in the city by Tube or bus (and St. Pancras International is right next to the British Library), but Charing Cross Station is within easy walking distance of the sights many first-timers want to see (Trafalgar Square, National Gallery, West End, Whitehall, Houses of Parliament)—so the extra time spent on that train could save you time commuting to your sight-seeing in London.

Returning to Dover, you'll get off at the **Dover Priory** train station.

Sights in Dover: Most arriving cruisers will want to head straight into London. But if you're lingering in town, **Dover Castle** is well worth a look. Perched upon chalk cliffs, peering across the English Channel to France, it has sprawling grounds, a historic keep with a fine museum, and—its highlight—a chance to tour the WWII-era Secret Wartime Tunnels, where you'll hear the story of Operation Dynamo, a harrowing rescue operation across the English Channel (£16.50; April-Sept daily 10:00-18:00, from 9:30 in Aug; Oct daily 10:00-17:00; Nov-March Sat-Sun 10:00-16:00, closed Mon-Fri; tel. 01304/211-067, www.english-heritage.org.uk/dovercastle).

DAY TRIPS FROM LONDON

Windsor • Cambridge • Stonehenge

Windsor, Cambridge, and Stonehenge are three of the best day-trip possibilities near London. Any one of these very different but equally enjoyable destinations makes for an entertaining day out from London.

The primary residence of Her Majesty the Queen, **Windsor** hosts a castle that's regally lived-in, yet open to the public. This is simply a charming town to relax in—and its proximity to Heathrow Airport (45-60 minutes by train west of London) makes Windsor easy to combine with a flight into or out of London. Nearby is an oddball collection of intriguing sights, including Legoland Windsor, Eton College (Britain's most elite high school), Ascot

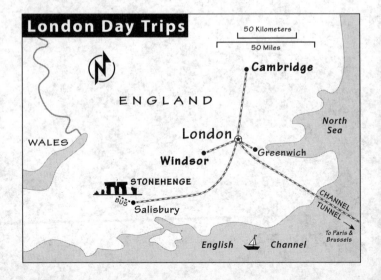

Racecourse (for horse racing), and Highclere Castle, where the TV series *Downton Abbey* is filmed.

Of Britain's many university towns, **Cambridge** (an hour north of London by train) is one of the best known—and, for travelers, simply the best. Combining a mellow, fun-to-explore townscape with a big-league university that churns out famous grads (from Charles Darwin to Isaac Newton), Cambridge delights.

Stonehenge, the world's most famous rock group, sits lonesome yet adored in a mysterious field 90 miles southwest of London. Though some consider it overrated, for others, this intricately arranged ring of boulders is a must-see.

Although these three destinations are my top picks, London's convenient public transit can easily whisk you to a wealth of daytrip destinations not covered in this book: Bath (Roman ruins and Georgian townhouses), Canterbury (cathedral), Dover (castle-crowned chalk cliffs), Portsmouth (treasure trove of maritime history), Stratford-upon-Avon (all things Shakespeare), Warwick (fine medieval castle), Oxford (another classic university town), and Brighton (beach and pier). For details, see *Rick Steves England*.

GETTING AROUND

By Train: Take advantage of British Rail's discounts for day-trippers from London. The "off-peak day return" ticket is a round-trip fare that costs virtually the same as one-way, provided you depart London outside rush hour (usually after 9:30 on weekdays and anytime Sat-Sun). Be sure to specifically ask for the "day return" ticket (round-trip within a single day) rather than the more expensive standard "return." You can also save a little money if you purchase tickets before 18:00 the day before your trip.

By Train Tour: London Walks offers a variety of "Daytrips from London" tours year-round by train, including a Salisbury and Stonehenge tour (see page 519), as well as a Cambridge itinerary (see page 37 for more on London Walks).

Windsor

Windsor, a compact and easy walking town of about 30,000 people, originally grew up around the royal residence. In 1070, William the Conqueror continued his habit of kicking Saxons out of their various settlements, taking over what the locals called "Windlesora" (meaning "riverbank with a hoisting winch")—which eventually became "Windsor." William built the first fortified castle on a chalk hill above the Thames; later kings added on to his early designs, rebuilding and expanding the castle and surrounding gardens.

By setting up their primary residence here, modern monarchs increased Windsor's popularity and prosperity—most notably, Queen Victoria, whose stern statue glares at you as you approach the castle. After her death, Victoria rejoined her beloved husband, Albert, in the Royal Mausoleum at Frogmore House, a mile south of the castle in a private section of the Home Park (house and mausoleum rarely open). The current Queen considers Windsor her primary residence, and the one where she feels most at home. She generally hangs her crown here on weekends, using it as an escape from her workaday grind at Buckingham Palace in the city. You can tell if Her Majesty is in residence by checking to see which flag is flying above the round tower: If it's the royal standard (a red, yellow, and blue flag) instead of the Union Jack, the Queen is at home.

While 99 percent of visitors just come to tour the castle and go, some enjoy spending the night. Daytime crowds trample Windsor's charm, which is most evident when the tourists are gone. Consider overnighting here—parking and access to Heathrow Airport are easy, and an evening at the horse races (on Mondays) is hoof-pounding, heart-thumping fun.

GETTING TO WINDSOR

By Train: Windsor has two train stations—Windsor & Eton Central (5-minute walk to palace; TI in adjacent shopping center) and Windsor & Eton Riverside (5-minute walk to palace and TI). First Great Western trains run between London's Paddington Station and Windsor & Eton Central (2-3/hour, 35 minutes, easy change at Slough; £9.50 one-way standard class, £10-13 same-day return, www.firstgreatwestern.co.uk). South West Trains run between London's Waterloo Station and Windsor & Eton Riverside (2/hour, 50 minutes; £9.50 one-way standard class, £10-17.50 same-day return, info tel. 0845-748-4950, www.nationalrail.co.uk). If deciding between these, notice that while Waterloo is more central within London and has a direct connection, it takes nearly twice as long as the alternative from Paddington.

If you're day-tripping into London *from* Windsor, ask at the train station about combining a same-day return train ticket with a One-Day Travelcard—you'll end up with one ticket that covers rail transportation to and from London and doubles as an all-day

Visiting Highclere Castle

If you're a fan of *Downton Abbey,* consider a day trip from London to Highclere Castle, the stately house where much of the show is filmed. Though the hugely popular TV series is set in Yorkshire, the actual house is located in Hampshire, about an hour's train ride west of London. Highclere has been home to the Earls of Carnarvon since 1679 (and the current residents enjoy watching the TV show), but the present, Jacobean-style house was rebuilt in the 1840s by Sir Charles Berry, who also designed London's Houses of Parliament. Noted landscape architect Capability Brown laid out the traditional gardens in the mid-18th century. The castle's Egyptian exhibit features artifacts collected by Highclere's fifth Earl, George Herbert, a keen amateur archaeologist. When Howard Carter discovered King Tut's tomb in 1922, he waited three weeks for his friend and patron Herbert to join him before looking inside. The Earl died unexpectedly a few months later, giving birth to the legend of a "mummy's curse."

Cost and Hours: Entrance is by timed-entry ticket for slots at 10:30 or 13:00, best bought well in advance online (although last-minute afternoon-entry tickets sometimes available—call ahead); £20 for castle, garden, and Egyptian exhibit; £13 for castle and garden only, or Egyptian exhibit and garden only; garden only—£5; open days sporadic but generally mid-April-Sept daily 10:30-17:00, last entry at 15:30; tickets available online several months ahead—sales begin as early as Feb for following summer; no photos inside, 24-hour info tel. 01635/253-204, www.highclerecastle.co.uk.

Getting There: Highclere is six miles south of Newbury, about 70 miles west of London, off A-34.

By Train and Taxi: First Great Western trains run from London's Paddington Station to Newbury (1-2/hour, 50-70 minutes, £22-40 same-day return, tel. 0845-748-4950, from the US or Canada call 011-44-20-7278-5240). From Newbury train station, you can take a taxi (£15-22 one-way, higher price is for Sun, taxis wait outside station or call 01635/33333) or reserve a car and driver (must arrange in advance, £12.50/person round-trip; £25 minimum, WebAir, tel. 07818/430-095, mapeng@msn.com).

By Tour: Brit Movie Tours offers an all-day bus tour of *Downton Abbey* filming locations, including Highclere Castle and the fictional village of Downton (sells out early, £99, includes transport and castle/garden entry, £5 extra for Egyptian exhibit, 9 hours, depart London from outside Gloucester Road Tube Station, reservations required, tel. 0844-247-1007, from the US or Canada call 011-44-20-7118-1007, http://britmovietours.com).

DAY TRIPS

Tube and bus pass in town (£13-22, lower price for travel after 9:30, rail ticket also qualifies you for some half-price London sightseeing discounts—ask or look for brochure at station, or go to www. daysoutguide.co.uk).

By Bus: Green Line buses #701 and #702 run from London's Victoria Colonnades (between the Victoria train and coach stations) to the Parish Church stop on Windsor's High Street, before continuing on to Legoland (1-2/hour, 1.5 hours to Windsor, £5.50-9.50 one-way, £9-16 round-trip, prices vary depending on time of day, tel. 0844-801-7261, www.rainbowfares.com).

By Car: Windsor is about 20 miles from London and just off Heathrow Airport's landing path. The town (and then the castle and Legoland) is well-signposted from the M-4 motorway. It's a convenient first stop if you're arriving at and renting a car from Heathrow, and saving London until the end of your trip.

From Heathrow Airport: First Bus Company's buses #71 and #77 run between Terminal 5 and Windsor, dropping you in the center of town on Peascod Street (about £8.50, 1-3/hour, 50 minutes, tel. 01753/524-144). London black cabs can (and do) charge whatever they like from Heathrow to Windsor; avoid them by calling a local cab company, such as Windsor Radio Cars (£26, includes 40 minutes waiting time—handy if you checked your luggage, tel. 01753/677-677, www.windsorcars.com).

Orientation to Windsor

Windsor's pleasant pedestrian shopping zone litters the approach to its famous palace with fun temptations. You'll find most shops and restaurants around the castle on High and Thames Streets, and down the pedestrian Peascod Street (PESS-cot), which runs perpendicular to High Street.

TOURIST INFORMATION
The TI is immediately adjacent to Windsor & Eton Central Station, in the Windsor Royal Shopping Centre's Old Booking Hall (May-Sept Mon-Sat 9:30-17:00, Sun 10:00-16:00; Oct-April Sun-Fri 10:00-16:00, Sat 10:00-17:00; tel. 01753/743-900, www.windsor.gov.uk). The TI sells discount tickets to Legoland.

ARRIVAL IN WINDSOR
By Train: The train to Windsor & Eton Central Station from Paddington (via Slough) spits you out into the Windsor Royal shop-

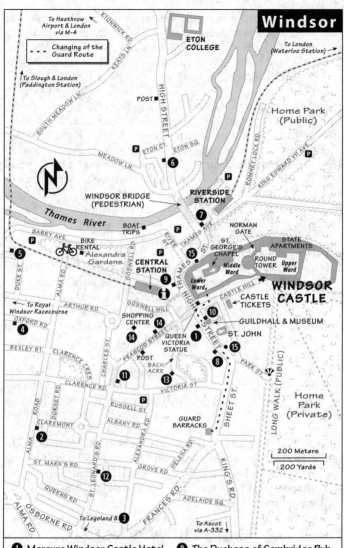

Windsor

Changing of the Guard Route

To Heathrow Airport & London via M-4

ETONWICK RD.

KEATS LN.

ETON COLLEGE

HIGH STREET

To London (Waterloo Station)

To Slough & London (Paddington Station)

SOUTH MEADOW LN.

POST

Home Park (Public)

MEADOW LN.

ETON CT.

ETON SQ.

ROMNEY LOCK RD.

KING EDWARD VII AVE.

P

WINDSOR BRIDGE (PEDESTRIAN)

RIVERSIDE STATION

P

Thames River

BOAT TRIPS

BARRY AVE.

BIKE RENTAL

Alexandra Gardens

RIVER ST.

THAMES AVE.

NORMAN GATE

ST. GEORGE'S CHAPEL

STATE APARTMENTS

ROUND TOWER

Upper Ward

P

P

DUKE ST.

ALMA RD.

CENTRAL STATION

GOSWELL RD.

Middle Ward

Lower Ward

CASTLE HILL

WINDSOR CASTLE

To Royal Windsor Racecourse

ARTHUR RD.

GOSWELL HILL

CASTLE TICKETS

OXFORD RD.

SHOPPING CENTER

GUILDHALL & MUSEUM

ST. JOHN

BEXLEY ST.

CLARENCE CRES.

CHARLES ST.

PEASCOD STREET

POST

QUEEN VICTORIA STATUE

BACH.ACRE

PARK ST.

LONG WALK (PUBLIC)

CLARENCE RD.

VICTORIA ST.

Home Park (Private)

ALMA ROAD

DORSET RD.

RUSSELL ST.

ALBANY RD.

ALEXANDRA RD.

SHEET ST.

GUARD BARRACKS

200 Meters

200 Yards

CLAREMONT

ST. MARK'S RD.

ST. LEONARD'S RD.

GROVE RD.

HELENA RD.

KING'S RD.

QUEENS RD.

OSBORNE RD.

ALMA RD.

To Legoland &

FRANCES RD.

ADELAIDE SQ.

To Ascot via A-332

DAY TRIPS

① Mercure Windsor Castle Hotel
② Langton House B&B
③ To Park Farm B&B
④ Dee & Steve's B&B
⑤ 76 Duke Street B&B
⑥ Crown & Cushion Rooms
⑦ Bel & The Dragon
⑧ Cornucopia Bistro
⑨ The Duchess of Cambridge Pub
⑩ The Crooked House Teahouse
⑪ Meimo Restaurant
⑫ Saffron Restaurant
⑬ Library (Internet Access)
⑭ Grocery Stores (2)
⑮ Legoland Bus Stops (2)

ping pavilion (which houses the TI), only a few minutes' walk from the castle. If you arrive instead at Windsor & Eton Riverside Station (from Waterloo Station), you'll see the castle as you exit—just follow the wall to the castle entrance.

By Car: Follow signs from the M-4 motorway for pay-and-display parking in the center. River Street Car Park is closest to the castle, but pricey and often full. The cheaper, bigger Alexandra Car Park (near the riverside Alexandra Gardens) is farther west. To walk to the town center from the Alexandra Car Park, head east through the tour-bus parking lot toward the castle. At the souvenir shop, walk up the stairs (or take the elevator) and cross the overpass to Windsor & Eton Central Station. Just beyond the station, you'll find the TI in the Windsor Royal Shopping Centre. The cheapest option is the King Edward VII Avenue car-park-and-ride, east of the castle on B-470, which includes a shuttle bus into town.

HELPFUL HINTS

Internet Access: Get online at the **library,** located on Bachelors' Acre, between Peascod and Victoria Streets (£1.50/30 minutes, free Wi-Fi, Mon-Sat 9:30-17:00, Tue and Fri until 19:00, Sun 11:00-14:00, tel. 01753/743-940, www.rbwm.gov.uk).

Supermarkets: Pick up picnic supplies at **Marks & Spencer** (Mon-Sat 8:00-19:00, Sun 11:00-17:00, 130 Peascod Street, tel. 01753/852-266) or at **Waitrose** (Mon-Fri 8:00-21:00, Sat 8:00-20:00, Sun 11:00-17:00, King Edward Court Shopping Centre, just south of Windsor & Eton Central Station, tel. 01753/860-565). Just outside the castle, you'll find long benches near the statue of Queen Victoria—great for people-watching while you munch.

Bike Rental: Extreme Motion, near the river in Alexandra Gardens, rents 21-speed mountain bikes (£12.50/4 hours, £18/day, includes helmet, £150 credit-card deposit required, bring passport as ID, summer daily 10:00-18:00, Sat-Sun only off-season, tel. 01753/830-220).

Sights in Windsor

▲▲WINDSOR CASTLE

Windsor Castle, the official home of England's royal family for 900 years, claims to be the largest and oldest occupied castle in the world. Thankfully, touring it is simple. You'll see sprawling grounds, lavish state-rooms, a crowd-pleasing dollhouse, a

gallery of Michelangelo and Leonardo da Vinci drawings, and an exquisite Perpendicular Gothic chapel.

Cost: If everything is open, a ticket costs £18.50 (family-£48); on (relatively rare) days that the Queen is hosting special events in her state rooms, the price is reduced to £10 (family-£26). Either ticket is valid for one year of re-entry if you get it stamped at the exit.

Crowd Control: Ticket lines can be long in summer; avoid the wait by purchasing tickets in advance online at www.royalcollection. org.uk or in person at the Buckingham Palace ticket office in London. Tickets in hand, you'll go in through a fast-entry door. There's nowhere in Windsor to buy advance tickets, so if you're already here and ticketless, you have to stand in line.

Hours: Grounds and most interiors open daily March-Oct 9:30-17:15, Nov-Feb 9:45-16:15, except St. George's Chapel, which is closed Sun to tourists (but open to worshippers). Last entry to grounds and St. George's Chapel 75 minutes before closing. Last entry to State Apartments and Queen Mary's Dolls' House 45 minutes before closing.

Possible Closures: If the queen is entertaining guests, the State Apartments may be closed—a big disappointment if you're not expecting it, but at least the ticket is cheaper (explained earlier). The entire palace occasionally closes for special events (such as the Garter Service in mid-June). It's smart to call ahead or check the website to make sure everything is open when you want to go. While you're at it, confirm the Changing of the Guard schedule.

Tours: As you enter, you'll pick up the dry, reverent, but informative audioguide, which covers both the grounds and interiors. For a good overview—and an opportunity to ask questions—consider the free 30-minute guided walks around the grounds (usually 2/hour, schedule posted next to audioguide desk). The official £5 guidebook is full of gorgeous images and makes a fine souvenir, but the information within is already covered by the audioguide and tour.

Information: Tel. 08453-302-898, www.royalcollection.org. uk.

Changing of the Guard:  The Changing of the Guard takes place Monday through Saturday at 11:00 (April-July) and on alternating days the rest of the year (check website to confirm schedule; get there by 10:30, or earlier if you expect a line for tickets). There is no Changing of the Guard on Sundays or in very wet weather. The

The Order of the Garter

In addition to being the royal residence, Windsor is the home of the Most Noble Order of the Garter—Britain's most prestigious chivalrous order. The castle's history is inexorably tied to this order.

Founded in 1348 by King Edward III and his son (the "Black Prince"), the Order of the Garter was designed to honor returning Crusaders. This was a time when the legends of King Arthur and the Knights of the Round Table were sweeping England, and Edward III fantasized that Windsor could be a real-life Camelot. (He even built the Round Tower as an homage to the Round Table.)

The order's seal illustrates the story of the order's founding and unusual name: a cross of St. George encircled with a belt and a French motto loosely translated as "Shame be upon he who thinks evil of it." Supposedly while the king was dancing with a fair maiden, her garter slipped off onto the floor; in an act of great chivalry, he rescued her from embarrassment by picking it up and uttering those words.

The Order of the Garter continues to the present day as the single most prestigious honor in the United Kingdom. There can be only 24 knights at one time (perfect numbers for splitting into two 12-man jousting teams), plus the sitting monarch and the Prince of Wales. Aside from royals and the nobility, past Knights of the Garter have included Winston Churchill, Bernard "Monty" Montgomery, and Ethiopian Emperor Haile Selassie. In 2008, Prince William became only the 1,000th knight in the order's 660-year history.

The patron of the order is St. George—the namesake of the State Apartments' most sumptuous hall and of the castle's own chapel. Both of these spaces—the grandest in all of Windsor—are designed to celebrate and to honor the Order of the Garter.

fresh guards, led by a marching band, leave their barracks on Sheet Street and march up High Street, hanging a right at Victoria, then a left into the castle's Lower Ward, arriving at about 11:00. After about a half-hour, the tired guards march back the way they came. To watch the actual ceremony inside the castle, you'll need to have already bought your ticket, entered the grounds, and staked out a spot. Alternatively, you could wait for them to march by on High Street or on the lower half of Castle Hill.

Evensong: An evensong takes place in the chapel nightly at 17:15 (free for worshippers, line up at exit gate to be admitted).

Best View: While you can get great views of the castle from any direction, the classic views are from the long, wooded walkway called the Long Walk, which stretches south of the palace and is open to the public.

Eating: There are a few shops scattered around the premises, but none sell real food (unless you count gifty boxes of chocolates)—though bottles of water are available. If you'll want a snack during your long castle visit, plan ahead and pack one in from outside.

⊙ Self-Guided Tour: After buying your ticket and going through the tight security checkpoint, head into the castle grounds to pick up your audioguide.

The Grounds: Turn right and head up the hill, enjoying the first of many fine castle views you'll see today. The tower-topped, conical hill on your left represents the historical core of the castle. William the Conqueror built this motte (artificial mound) and bailey (fortified stockade around it) in 1080—his first castle in England. Among the later monarchs who spiffed up Windsor were Edward III (flush with French war booty, he made it a palace fit for a 14th-century king), Charles II (determined to restore the monarchy properly in the 1660s), and George IV (Britain's "Bling King," who financed many such vanity projects in the 1820s). On your right, the circular bandstand platform has a seal of the Order of the Garter, which has important ties to Windsor (see sidebar).

Passing through the small gate, you approach the stately St. George's Gate. Peek through here to the Upper Ward's **Quadrangle,** surrounded by the State Apartments (across the field) and the Queen's private apartments (to the right).

Turn left and follow the wall. On your right-hand side, you enjoy great views of the **Round Tower** atop that original motte;

running around the base of this artificial hill is the delightful, peaceful garden of the castle governor. The unusual design of this castle has not one "bailey" (castle yard), but three, which today make up Windsor's Upper Ward (where the Queen lives, which we just saw), Middle Ward (the ecclesiastical heart of the complex, with St. George's Chapel, which you'll soon pass on the left), and Lower Ward (residences for castle workers).

Continue all the way around this mini-moat to the **Norman Gate,** which once held a prison. Walking under the gate, look up to see the bottom of the portcullis that could be dropped to seal off the inner courtyard. Three big holes are strategically situated to dump boiling goo or worse on whoever was outside the gate. Past the gate are even finer views of the Quadrangle we just saw from the other side.

Do a 180 and head back toward the Norman Gate, but before you reach it, go down the staircase on the right. You'll emerge onto a fine **terrace** overlooking the flat lands all around. It's easy to understand why this was a strategic place to build a castle. That's Eton College across the Thames. Imagine how handy it's been for royals to be able to ship off their teenagers to an elite prep school so close that they could easily keep an eye on them...literally. The power-plant cooling towers in the distance mark the workaday burg of Slough (rhymes with "plow," immortalized as the setting for Britain's original version of *The Office*).

Turn right and wander along the terrace. You'll likely see two lines: one long and one short. The long line leads to Queen Mary's Dolls' House, then to the State Apartments. The short line skips the dollhouse and lets you proceed directly to the apartments. While the State Apartments are certainly worth seeing, the Dolls' House may not be worth a long wait; read the following descriptions and decide (or return at the end of your castle visit; the dollhouse line tends to ease up at the end of the day). You can see the Drawings Gallery and the China Museum either way.

Queen Mary's Dolls' House: This palace in miniature (1:12 scale, from 1924) is "the most famous dollhouse in the world." It was a gift for Queen Mary (the wife of King George V, and the current Queen's grandmother), who greatly enjoyed miniatures, when she was already a fully grown adult. It's basically one big, dimly lit room with the large dollhouse in the middle, executed with an astonishing level of detail. Each fork, knife, and spoon on the expertly set banquet table is perfect and made of real silver—and the tiny pipes of its plumbing system actually have running water. But you're kept a few feet away by a glass wall, and are constantly jostled by fellow sightseers in this crowded space, making it difficult to fully appreciate. Unless you're a dollhouse devotee, it's probably not worth waiting a half hour for a five-minute peek at this, but if the line is short it's definitely worth a look.

Drawings Gallery and China Museum: Positioned at the exit of the Dolls' House, this collects a changing array of pieces from the Queen's collection—usually including some big names, such as Michelangelo and Leonardo. The China Museum features items from the Queen's many exquisite settings for royal shindigs.

State Apartments: Dripping with chandeliers, finely furnished, and strewn with history and the art of a long line of kings and queens, they're the best I've seen in Britain. This is where the Queen wows visiting dignitaries. The apartments are even more remarkable considering that many of these grand halls were badly damaged in a fire on November 20,

1992. They've been immaculately restored since. Take advantage of the talkative docents in each room, who are happy to answer your questions.

You'll climb the Grand Staircase up to the **Grand Vestibule,** decorated with exotic items seized by British troops during their missions to colonize various corners of the world. The **Waterloo Chamber** memorializes Wellington and others (from military officers to heads of state to Pope Pius VII) who worked together to defeat Napoleon. You'll pass through various bedchambers, dressing rooms, and drawing rooms of the king and queen (who traditionally maintained separate quarters). Many rooms are decorated with fine canvases by some of Europe's top artists, including Rubens, Van Dyck, and Holbein. Finally you emerge into **St. George's Hall,** decorated with emblems representing the knights of the prestigious Order of the Garter (see sidebar). This is the site of some of the most elaborate royal banquets—imagine one long table stretching from one end of the hall to the other, seating 160 VIPs. From here, you'll proceed into the rooms that were the most damaged by the 1992 fire, including the "Semi-State Apartments." The **Garter Throne Room** is where new members of the Order of the Garter are invested (ceremonially granted their titles).

Now head down to the opposite end of the terrace, and hook left back into the Middle Ward. From here, you're just above the chapel, with its buttresses; the entrance is about two-thirds of the way down.

St. George's Chapel: Housing numerous royal tombs, this chapel is an exquisite example of Perpendicular Gothic (dating from about 1500), with classic fan-vaulting spreading out from each pillar and with nearly every joint capped with an elaborate and colorful roof boss. Most of these emblems are associated with the Knights of the Garter, who consider St. George's  their "mother church." Under the upper stained-glass windows, notice the continuous frieze of 250 angels, lovingly carved with great detail, ringing the church.

In the corner, take in the melodramatic monument to the popular Princess Charlotte, the only child of King George IV. Heir to the throne, her death (at 21, in childbirth) devastated the nation. Farther along, find the simple chapel containing the tombs of the current Queen's parents, King George VI and "Queen Mum" Elizabeth; the ashes of her younger sister, Princess Margaret, are also kept here (see the marble slab against the wall).

Stepping into the choir area, you're immediately aware that you are in the inner sanctum of the Order of the Garter. The banners lining the nave represent the knights, as do the fancy helmets and half-drawn swords at the top of each wood-carved seat. These symbols honor only living knights; on the seats are some 800 golden panels memorializing departed knights. As you walk up the aisle, notice the marker in the floor: You're walking over the burial site of King Henry VIII and Jane Seymour, Henry's favorite wife (perhaps because she was the only one who died before he could behead her). The body of King Charles I, who was beheaded by Oliver Cromwell's forces at the Banqueting House (see page 121), was also discovered here...with its head sewn back on.

On your way out, you can pause at the door of the sumptuous 13th-century **Albert Memorial Chapel,** redecorated in 1861 after the death of Queen Victoria's husband, Prince Albert, and dedicated to his memory.

Lower Ward: You'll exit the chapel into the castle's Lower Ward. This area is a living town where some 160 people who work for the Queen reside; they include clergy, military, and castle administrators. Just below the chapel, you may be able to enter a tranquil little horseshoe-shaped courtyard ringed with residential doorways—all of them with a spectacular view of the chapel's grand entrance.

Back out in the yard, look for the guard posted at his pillbox. Like those at Buckingham Palace, he's been trained to be a ruthless killing machine...just so he can wind up as somebody's photo op. Click!

MORE SIGHTS IN WINDSOR
Legoland Windsor
Paradise for Legomaniacs under 12, this huge, kid-pleasing park has dozens of tame but fun rides (often with very long lines) scattered throughout its 150 acres.
The impressive Miniland has 40 million Lego pieces glued together to create 800 tiny buildings and a minitour of Europe; the Creation Centre boasts an 80 percent scale-model Boeing 747 cockpit, made of two million bricks. Several of the more exciting rides involve getting wet, so dress accordingly or  buy a cheap disposable poncho in the gift shop. While you may be tempted to hop on the Hill Train at the entrance, it's faster and

more convenient to walk down into the park. Food is available in the park, but you can save money by bringing a picnic.

Cost: Adults-£46.80, children-£41.40, about 25 percent cheaper if you book online at least seven days in advance, 10 percent discount if you buy tickets at Windsor TI, free for ages 3 and under; optional Q-Bot ride-reservation gadget allows you to bypass lines (£15-70 depending on when you go and how much time you want to save); coin lockers-£1.

Hours: Convoluted schedule, but generally late July-Aug daily 10:00-19:00; mid-March-late July and Sept-Oct Mon-Fri 10:00-17:00, Sat-Sun 10:00-18:00, often closed Tue-Wed; closed Nov-mid-March. Call or check website for exact schedule, tel. 0871-222-2001, www.legoland.co.uk.

Getting There: A £4.80 round-trip shuttle bus runs from opposite Windsor's Theatre Royal on Thames Street, and from the Parish Church stop on High Street (2/hour). If day-tripping from London, ask about rail/shuttle/park admission deals from Paddington or Waterloo train stations. For drivers, the park is on B-3022 Windsor/Ascot road, two miles southwest of Windsor and 25 miles west of London. Legoland is clearly signposted from the M-3, M-4, and M-25 motorways. Parking is easy (£4).

DAY TRIPS

Eton College

Across the bridge from Windsor Castle is the most famous "public" (the equivalent of our "private") high school in Britain. Eton was founded in 1440 by King Henry VI; today it educates about 1,300 boys (ages 13-18), who live on campus. Eton has molded the characters of 19 prime ministers as well as members of the royal family, most recently princes William and Harry. Already sparse on sights, the college is closed to the public during a building project until late 2015. When open, the public is typically allowed (via guided tour), into the schoolyard, chapel, cloisters, and the Museum of Eton Life.

Cost and Hours: Closed to visitors through late 2015. For updates, visit www.etoncollege.com or call 01753/671-000.

Eton High Street

Even if you're not touring the college, it's worth the few minutes it takes to cross the pedestrian bridge and wander straight up Eton's High Street. A bit more cutesy and authentic-feeling than Windsor (which is given over to shopping malls and chain stores), Eton has a charm that's fun to sample.

Windsor and Royal Borough Museum

Tucked into a small space beneath the Guildhall (where Prince Charles remarried), this little museum does its best to give some insight into the history of Windsor and the surrounding area. They also have lots of special activities for kids. Ask at the desk if tours are running to the Guildhall itself (visits are only possible with a guide); if not, it's probably not worth the admission.

Cost and Hours: £2, includes audioguide, Tue-Sat 10:00-16:00, Sun 12:00-16:00, closed Mon, located in the Guildhall on High Street, tel. 01628/685-686, www.rbwm.gov.uk.

Boat Trips

Cruise up and down the Thames River for classic views of the castle, the village of Eton, Eton College, and the Royal Windsor Racecourse. Choose from a 40-minute or two-hour tour, then relax onboard and nibble a picnic. Boats leave from the riverside promenade adjacent to Barry Avenue.

Cost and Hours: 40-minute tour—£6.70, family pass from £17.90, mid-Feb-Oct 1-2/hour daily 10:00-17:00, Nov hourly Sat-Sun 10:00-16:00; 2-hour tour—£10.50, family pass from £28.20, late March-Oct only, 1-2/day; closed Dec-mid-Feb; online discounts, tel. 01753/851-900, www.frenchbrothers.co.uk.

Horse Racing

The horses race near Windsor every Monday at the Royal Windsor Racecourse (£21-25 entry, online discounts, those under 18 free with an adult, April-Aug and Oct, no races in Sept, sporadic in Aug, off A-308 between Windsor and Maidenhead, tel. 01753/498-400, www.windsor-racecourse.co.uk). The romantic way to get there from Windsor is by a 10-minute shuttle boat (£6.50 round-trip, www.frenchbrothers.co.uk). The famous Ascot Racecourse (described next) is also nearby.

NEAR WINDSOR
Ascot Racecourse

Located seven miles southwest of Windsor and just north of the town of Ascot, this royally owned track is one of the most famous horse-racing venues in the world. The horses first ran here in 1711, and the course is best known for June's five-day Royal Ascot race meeting, attended by the Queen and 299,999 of her loyal subjects. For many, the outlandish hats worn on Ladies Day (Thu) are more interesting than the horses. Royal Ascot is usually the third week in June (June 16-20 in 2015). The pricey tickets go on sale the preceding November; while the Friday and Saturday races tend to sell out far ahead, tickets for the other days are often available close to the date (see website). In addition to Royal Ascot, the racecourse runs the ponies year-round—funny hats strictly optional.

Cost: Regular tickets generally £18-40—some may be available at a discount from the TI, Royal Ascot £25-75, online discounts, kids ages 17 and under free; parking from free to £20, de-

---

Sleep Code

Abbreviations
S = Single, **D** = Double/Twin, **T** = Triple, **Q** = Quad, **b** = bathroom, **s** = shower only.

Price Rankings
$$$ **Higher Priced**—Most rooms £105 or more.
$$ **Moderately Priced**—Most rooms between £60-105.
$ **Lower Priced**—Most rooms £60 or less.

---

pending on the event; dress code enforced in some areas and on certain days, tel. 0844-346-3000, www.ascot.co.uk.

Sleeping in Windsor

(£1 = about $1.60, country code: 44, area code: 01753)
Most visitors stay in London and do Windsor as a day trip. But here are a few suggestions for those staying the night.

Unless otherwise noted, credit cards are accepted and breakfast is included. All of these listings offer free Wi-Fi. Prices can change without notice; verify the hotel's current rates online or by email. For the best prices, always book directly with the hotel.

$$$ Mercure Windsor Castle Hotel, with 108 business-class rooms and elegant public spaces, is as central as can be, just down the street from Her Majesty's weekend retreat (official rates: Db-£149-189, breakfast-£17; but you'll likely pay around Db-£160 on weekdays and £150 on weekends including breakfast; £30-40 extra for fancy four-poster beds, nonrefundable online deals, air-con, parking-£10/day, 18 High Street, tel. 01753/851-577, www.mercure.com, h6618@accor.com).

$$ Langton House B&B is a stately Victorian home with five spacious, well-appointed rooms lovingly maintained by Paul and Sonja Fogg (S-£73, Sb-£85, D/Db-£105, huge four-poster Db-£115, Tb-£140, Qb-£155, 5 percent extra if paying by credit card, prices can be soft—especially off-season, family-friendly, guest kitchen, 46 Alma Road, tel. 01753/858-299, www.langtonhouse.co.uk, paul@langtonhouse.co.uk).

$$ Park Farm B&B, bright and cheery, is most convenient for drivers. But even if you're not driving, this beautiful place is such a good value, and the welcome is so warm, that you're unlikely to mind the bus ride into town (Sb-£65, Db-£89, Tb-£110, Qb-£125, family room with bunk beds, cash only—credit card solely for reservations, shared fridge and microwave, free off-street parking, 1 mile from Legoland on St. Leonards Road near Imperial

Road, 5-minute bus ride or 1-mile walk to castle, £5 taxi ride from station, tel. 01753/866-823, www.parkfarm.com, stay@parkfarm. com, Caroline and Drew Youds).

$$ 76 Duke Street has two nice rooms, but only hosts one set of guests at a time. While the bathroom is (just) outside your bedroom, you have it to yourself (Db-£80-100, rent both rooms for £160-200, 15-minute walk from station at—you guessed it—76 Duke Street, tel. 01753/620-636, www.76dukestreet.co.uk, bandb@76dukestreet.co.uk, Julia).

$$ Dee and Steve's B&B is a friendly four-room place above a window shop on a quiet residential street about a 10-minute walk from the castle and station. The rooms are cozy, Dee and Steve are pleasant hosts, and breakfast is served in the contemporary kitchen/lounge (S-£45, Sb-£55-60, Db-£75, 169 Oxford Road, tel. 01753/854-489, www.deeandsteve.com, dee@deeandsteve.com).

$$ Crown and Cushion is a good option on Eton's High Street, just across the pedestrian bridge from Windsor's waterfront (a short uphill walk to the castle). While the pub it's situated over is worn and drab, you're right in the heart of charming Eton, and the eight creaky rooms—with uneven floors and old-beam ceilings— are nicely furnished (Sb-£70, Db-£80, free parking, 84 High Street in Eton, tel. 01753/861-531, www.thecrownandcushioneton.co.uk, info@thecrownandcushioneton.com).

Eating in Windsor

ELEGANT SPOTS WITH RIVER VIEWS

Several places flank Windsor Bridge, offering romantic dining after dark. The riverside promenade, with cheap take-away stands scattered about, is a delightful place for a picnic lunch or dinner with the swans. If you don't see anything that appeals, continue up Eton's High Street, which is also lined with characteristic eateries.

IN THE TOURIST ZONE AROUND THE PALACE

Strolling the streets and lanes around the palace entrance—especially in the shopping zone near Windsor & Eton Station—you'll find countless trendy and inviting eateries. The central area also has a sampling of dependable British chains (including a Wagamama, Gourmet Burger Kitchen, Thai Square, and Nando's). Residents enjoy a wide selection of unpretentious little eateries (including a fire station turned pub-and-cultural center) just past the end of pedestrian Peascod Street.

Bel & The Dragon is the place to splurge on high-quality, classic British food in a charming half-timbered building with an upscale-rustic dining space (£6-9 starters, £14-26 main courses, food served daily 12:00-15:00 & 18:00-22:00, afternoon tea served between lunch and dinner, bar open longer hours, on Thames Street near the bridge to Eton, tel. 01753/866-056).

Cornucopia Bistro, with a cozy, woody atmosphere, serves tasty international dishes (£12 two-course meals and £16 three-course meals available Mon-Thu after 18:00 and Fri-Sat 18:00-19:00; £12-15 main courses, open daily 12:00-14:30 & 18:00-21:30, Fri-Sat until 22:00, closed Sun night, 6 High Street, tel. 01753/833-009).

The Duchess of Cambridge's friendly staff serves up the normal grub in a pub that's right across from the castle walls, and with an open fireplace to boot (£10-14 meals, daily 9:30-22:30 or later, 3-4 Thames Street, tel. 01753/864-405). While the pub pre-dates Kate, it was named in her honor following a recent remodel, and has the photos to prove her endorsement.

The Crooked House is a touristy 17th-century timber-framed teahouse, serving fresh, hearty £8-12 lunches and £10 cream teas in a tipsy interior or outdoors on its cobbled lane (Mon-Fri 10:00-17:30, Sat-Sun 9:30-18:30, 51 High Street, tel. 01753/857-534).

Meimo offers "Moroccan/Mediterranean" cuisine in a nicely subdued dining room (£9-14 main dishes, several fixed-price meal options, daily 10:00-22:00, 69-70 Peascod Street, tel. 01753/862-222).

Saffron Restaurant, while a fairly long walk from the castle, is the local choice for South Indian cuisine, with a modern interior and attentive waiters who struggle with English but are fluent at bringing out tasty dishes. Their vegetarian *thali* is a treat (£8-12 dishes, daily 12:00-14:30 & 17:30-23:30, 99 St. Leonards Road, tel. 01753/855-467).

Cambridge

Cambridge, 60 miles north of London, is world-famous for its prestigious university. Wordsworth, Isaac Newton, Tennyson, Darwin, and Prince Charles are a few of its illustrious alumni. The university dominates—and owns—most of Cambridge, a historic town of 100,000 people. Cambridge is the epitome of a university town, with busy bikers, stately residence halls, plenty of bookshops, and proud locals who can point out where DNA was originally modeled, the atom first split, and electrons discovered.

In medieval Europe, higher education was the domain of the Church and was limited to ecclesiastical schools. Scholars lived in "halls" on campus. This academic community of residential halls, chapels, and lecture halls connected by peaceful garden courtyards survives today in the colleges that make up the universities of Cambridge and Oxford. By 1350 (Oxford is roughly 100 years older), Cambridge had eight colleges, each with a monastic-type courtyard, chapel, library, and lodgings. Today, Cambridge has 31 colleges, each with its own facilities. In the town center, these grand old halls date back centuries, with ornately decorated facades that try to one-up each other. While students' lives revolve around their independent colleges, the university organizes lectures, presents degrees, and promotes research.

The university schedule has three terms: Lent term from mid-January to mid-March, Easter term from mid-April to mid-June, and Michaelmas term from early October to early December. During exam time (roughly the month of May), the colleges are closed to visitors, which can impede access to all the picturesque little corners of the town. But the main sights—King's College Chapel and Trinity Library—stay open, and Cambridge is never sleepy.

PLANNING YOUR TIME

Cambridge is worth most of a day. Start by taking the TI's walking tour, which includes a visit to the town's only must-see sight, the King's College Chapel (first tour at 11:00, later on Sun, call ahead to confirm and reserve—see "Tours in Cambridge," later). Spend the afternoon touring the Fitzwilliam Museum (closed Mon), or simply enjoying the ambience of this stately old college town.

GETTING TO CAMBRIDGE

By Train: It's an easy trip from London and less than an hour away. Catch the train from London's King's Cross Station (2/hour, trains leave King's Cross at :15 and :44 past the hour, 45 minutes, £22.60 one-way standard class, £23.70 same-day return after 9:30, operated by First Capital Connect, tel. 0845-748-4950, www.firstcapitalconnect.co.uk or www.nationalrail.co.uk). Direct trains also run from London's Liverpool Street Station, but take longer (2/hour, 1.25 hours).

By Bus: National Express coaches run from London's Victoria Coach Station to the Parkside stop in Cambridge (every 60-90 minutes, 2-2.5 hours, £11.90, £6 advance fares sometimes available online, tel. 0871-781-8178, www.nationalexpress.co.uk).

Orientation to Cambridge

Cambridge is congested but small. Everything is within a pleasant walk. There are two main streets, separated from the Cam River by the most interesting colleges. The town center, brimming with tearooms, has a TI and a colorful open-air market square. The train station is about a mile to the southeast.

TOURIST INFORMATION

Cambridge's TI is well run and well signposted, just off Market Square in the town center. They book rooms for £5, offer walking tours (see "Tours in Cambridge," later), and sell bus tickets and a £1.50 map/guide (Mon-Sat 10:00-17:00, Easter-Sept also Sun 11:00-15:00—otherwise closed Sun, phones answered from 9:00, Peas Hill, tel. 0871-226-8006, room-booking tel. 01223/457-581, www.visitcambridge.org). In the same building as the TI, you can duck into a former courtroom to catch a free video overview of the town and its history.

ARRIVAL IN CAMBRIDGE

By Train: Unfortunately, Cambridge's train station doesn't have baggage storage. The station also lacks a TI, but it does offer free maps and other brochures on an interior wall just before the turnstiles.

To get from the station to downtown Cambridge, you can **walk** for about 25 minutes (exit straight ahead on Station Road, bear right at the war memorial onto Hills Road, and follow it into town); take public **bus** #1, #3, #7, or #8 (buses are referred to as "Citi 1," "Citi 3," and so on in schedules, but only the number is marked on the bus; £1.60, pay driver, runs every 5-10 minutes, turn left when exiting station to find bus stop #7, get off when you see the Grand Arcade shopping mall on the left); pay about £6 for a **taxi;** or take a City Sightseeing **bus tour** (described later).

By Car: To park in the middle of town, follow signs from the M-11 motorway to any of the central short-stay parking lots. Or you can leave the car at one of five park-and-ride lots outside the city, then take the shuttle into town (free parking, shuttle costs £2.60 round-trip at machine, or £2.90 from driver).

HELPFUL HINTS

Festival: The **Cambridge Folk Festival** gets things humming and strumming in late July (tickets go on sale several months ahead and often sell out quickly; www.cambridgefolkfestival.co.uk).

Bike Rental: Station Cycles, inside the Grand Arcade shopping mall, rents bikes (£7/4 hours, £10/day, helmets-£1, £60 deposit, cash or credit card); Mon-Fri 8:00-18:00, Wed until

Cambridge

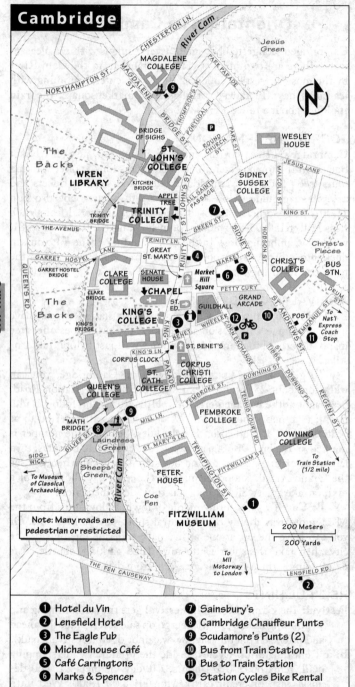

1. Hotel du Vin
2. Lensfield Hotel
3. The Eagle Pub
4. Michaelhouse Café
5. Café Carringtons
6. Marks & Spencer
7. Sainsbury's
8. Cambridge Chauffeur Punts
9. Scudamore's Punts (2)
10. Bus from Train Station
11. Bus to Train Station
12. Station Cycles Bike Rental

Note: Many roads are pedestrian or restricted

200 Meters
200 Yards

19:00, Sat 9:00-18:00, Sun 10:00-17:00, shorter Sun hours
Oct-March; tel. 01223/307-655, www.stationcycles.co.uk.
Their other location at the train station is closed through 2015
for renovation.

Tours in Cambridge

▲▲Walking Tour of the Colleges

A walking tour is the best way to understand Cambridge's mix of
"town and gown." The walks can be more educational (read: dry)
than entertaining. But they do provide a good rundown of the historic and scenic highlights of the university, some fun local gossip,
and plenty of university trivia. For example, why are entering students called "undergraduates"? Because long ago, new students at
Cambridge were assigned to a mentor who already had a degree...
so they were "under" the supervision of a "graduate."

The TI offers **daily walking tours** that include the King's
College Chapel, as well as another college—usually Queen's College (£18, 2 hours, includes entry fees; July-Aug daily at 11:00,
12:00, 13:00, and 14:00, no 11:00 tour on Sun; Sept-June Mon-
Sat at 11:00, 13:00, Sun at 13:00 only; tel. 01223/457-574, www.
visitcambridge.org). It's smart to call ahead to reserve a spot (they'll
take your credit-card number), or you can drop by in person (try
to arrive 30 minutes before the tour). Notice that the 12:00 tour
overlaps with the limited opening times of the Wren Library—so
you'll miss out on the library if you take the noon tour.

Private guides are available through the TI and affordable
if you can assemble a group to share the cost (basic 1-hour tour-
£4.75/person, £71.25 minimum; 1.5-hour tour-£5.25/person,
£78.75 minimum; 2-hour tour-£5.75/person, £86.25 minimum;
does not include individual college entrance fees, tel. 01223/457-
574, tours@cambridge.gov.uk).

Walking Ghost Tour

If you're in Cambridge on the weekend, consider a £6 ghost walk to
where spooky sightings have been reported (Fri at 18:00, organized
by the TI, tel. 01223/457-574).

Bus Tours

City Sightseeing hop-on, hop-off bus tours are informative and
cover the outskirts, including the American WWII Cemetery. But
keep in mind that buses can't go where walking tours can—right
into the center (£14, 80 minutes for full 19-stop circuit, buy ticket
with credit card at the bus-stop kiosk—or pay cash to driver when
you board, departs every 20 minutes in summer, every 40 minutes in
winter, first bus leaves train station at 10:06, last bus around 17:30,
recorded commentary, tel. 01223/423-250, www.city-sightseeing.

com). If arriving by train, you can buy your ticket from the kiosk directly in front of the station, then ride the bus into town.

Sights in Cambridge

Cambridge has many impressive old college buildings to explore, with fancy facades and tranquil grassy courtyards. I've featured the two most interesting (King's and Trinity), but feel free to wander beyond these. You might notice several bricked-up windows on the old buildings around town. This practice dates from a time when taxes were calculated per window...so filling them in saved money.

▲King's Parade and Nearby

The lively street in front of King's College, called King's Parade, seems to be where everyone in Cambridge gathers. Looming across the street from the college is **Great St. Mary's Church,** with a climbable bell tower (£3.50, Mon-Sat 9:30-16:30, Sun 12:30-16:00, 123 stairs). On the street out front, students hawk punting tours on the Cam River (see "Punting on the Cam," later).

Behind the church is the thriving **Market Hill Square.** The big market is on Sunday (9:30-16:30) and features produce, arts, and crafts. On other days, you'll find mostly clothes and food (Mon-Sat roughly 9:30-16:00).

The imposing Neoclassical building at the top (north) end of King's Parade is the **Senate House,** the meeting place of the university's governing body. In June, you might notice green boxes lining the front of this house. Traditionally, at the end of the term students would come to these boxes to see whether or not they'd earned their degree; if a name was not on the list, the student had flunked. Amazingly, until 2010 this was the only notification students received about their status. (Now they also get an email.)

In the opposite direction (south), at Benet Street, look for the strikingly modern **Corpus Clock.** Designed and commissioned by alum John Taylor, the clock was ceremonially unveiled by Stephen Hawking in 2008. It uses concentric golden dials with blue LED lights to tell the time, but it's precise only every five minutes; its otherwise-irregular timekeeping mimics the unpredictability of life. Perched on top is Chronophage, the "eater of time"—a grotesque giant grasshopper that keeps the clock moving and periodically winks at passersby. Creepy and disturbing? Exactly, says Taylor...so is the passage of time.

Just down Benet Street on the left is the recommended **Eagle Pub**—Cambridge's oldest pub and a sight in itself; it's worth poking into the courtyard to learn about its dynamic history, even if you don't eat or drink here. Across the street from the pub stands the oldest surviving building in Cambridgeshire, **St. Benet's Church.** The Saxons who built the church included circular holes in its bell tower, to encourage owls to roost there and keep the mouse population under control.

▲▲King's College Chapel

Built from 1446 to 1515 by Henrys VI through VIII, England's best example of Perpendicular Gothic architecture is the single most impressive building in town.

Cost and Hours: £7.50, erratic hours depending on school schedule and events; during academic term usually Mon-Fri 9:30-15:30, Sat 9:30-15:15, Sun 13:15-14:30; during breaks (see page 505) usually daily 9:30-16:30; recorded info tel. 01223/331-1212, www.kings.cam.ac.uk/chapel.

Evensong: When school's in session, you're welcome to enjoy an evensong service in this glorious space, with a famous choir made up of men and boys (free, Mon-Sat at 17:30, Sun at 15:30; for more on evensong, see page 462).

Getting There: You'll see the regal front facade of King's College along King's Parade. To enter the chapel, curl around the back: Facing the college on King's Parade, head right and take the first left possible (just after the Senate House, on Senate House passage); at the end, bear left on Trinity Lane to reach the gate where you can pay to enter the chapel.

● Self-Guided Tour: Stand inside, look up, and marvel, as Christopher Wren did, at what was then the largest single span of **vaulted roof** anywhere—2,000 tons of incredible fan vaulting, held in place by the force of gravity (a careful balancing act resting delicately on the buttresses visible outside the building).

While Henry VI—who began work on the chapel—wanted it to be austere, his descendants decided it should glorify the House of Tudor (of which his son, Henry VII, was the first king). Lining the walls are giant **Tudor**

coats-of-arms. The shield includes a fleur-de-lis because an earlier ancestor, Edward III, woke up one day and—citing his convoluted lineage—somewhat arbitrarily declared himself king of France. The symbols on the left (a rose and the red dragon of Wales, holding the shield) represent the Tudors, the family of Henry VII's father. On the right, the greyhound holding the shield and the portcullis (the iron grate) symbolize the family of Henry VII's mother, Lady Margaret Beaufort, who prodded her son for years to complete this chapel.

The 26 **stained-glass windows** date from the 16th century. It's the most Renaissance stained glass anywhere in one spot. (Most of the stained glass in English churches dates from Victorian times, but this glass is much older.) The lower panes show scenes from the New Testament, while the upper panes feature corresponding stories from the Old Testament. Considering England's turbulent history, it's miraculous that these windows

have survived for nearly half a millennium in such a pristine state. After Henry VIII separated from the Catholic Church in 1534, many such windows and other Catholic features around England were destroyed. (Think of all those ruined abbeys dotting the English countryside.) However, since Henry had just paid for these windows, he couldn't bear to get rid of them. A century later, in the days of Oliver Cromwell, another wave of iconoclasm destroyed more windows around England. Though these windows were slated for removal, they stayed put. (Historians speculate that Cromwell's troops, who were garrisoned in this building, didn't want the windows removed in the chilly wintertime.) Finally, during World War II, the windows were taken out and hidden away to keep them safe, and then painstakingly replaced after the war ended.

The **choir screen** that bisects the church was commissioned by King Henry VIII to commemorate his marriage to Anne Boleyn. By the time it was finished, so was she (beheaded). But it was too late to remove her initials, which were carved into the screen (look on the far left for *R.A.*, for *Regina Anna*—"Queen Anne").

Behind the screen is the **choir** area, where the King's College Choir performs a daily evensong. On Christmas Eve, a special service is held here and broadcast around the world on the BBC—a tradition near and dear to British hearts.

Walk to the altar and admire Rubens' masterful *Adoration of the Magi* (1634). It's actually a family portrait: The admirer in the front (wearing red) is a self-portrait of Rubens, Mary looks an awful lot like his much-younger wife, and the Baby Jesus resembles their own newborn at the time.

Finally, pop through the door to the left of the altar to find an exhibit with a basic history of the chapel, a nice model showing how the fan vaults were constructed, and an explanation of how the chapel has managed to hang together after all these years.

▲▲Trinity College and Wren Library

More than a third of Cambridge's 83 Nobel Prize winners have come from this richest and biggest of the town's colleges, founded in 1546 by Henry VIII. The college has three sights to see: the entrance gate, the grounds, and the magnificent Wren Library.

Cost and Hours: Grounds—£1, often free off-season, daily 10:00-16:30, last entry 45 minutes before closing; library—free, Mon-Fri 12:00-14:00, Nov-mid-June also Sat 10:30-12:30, closed Sun year-round; only small groups allowed in at a time, tel. 01223/338-400, www.trin.cam.ac.uk.

To see the Wren Library without paying for the grounds, access it from the riverside entrance: Head toward the Garret Hostel Bridge, and, if the gate's open, pass through the parking lot to your right immediately before the bridge. If the gate is not open, it's a long walk across the bridge and around the field to the path that leads back to the college.

Trinity Gate: You'll notice gates like these adorning facades of colleges around town. Above the door is a statue of **King Henry**

VIII, who founded Trinity because he feared that Cambridge's existing colleges were too cozy with the Church. Notice Henry's right hand holding a chair leg instead of the traditional crown jewels scepter. This is courtesy of Cambridge's Night Climbers, who first replaced the scepter a century ago, and continue to periodically switch it out for other items. According to campus legend, decades ago some of the world's most talented mountaineers enrolled at Cambridge...in one of the flattest parts of England. (Cambridge was actually a seaport until Dutch engineers drained the surrounding swamps.) Lacking opportunities to practice their skill, they began scaling the frilly facades of Cambridge's college buildings under cover of darkness (if caught, they'd have been expelled). In the 1960s, climbers actually managed to haul an entire automobile onto the roof of the Senate House. The university had to bring in the army to cut it into pieces and remove it. Only 50 years later, at a class reunion, did the guilty parties finally fess up.

In the little park to the right, notice the lone **apple tree.** Supposedly, this tree is a descendant of the very one that once stood in the garden of Sir Isaac Newton (who spent 30 years at Trinity). According to legend, Newton was inspired to investigate gravity when an apple fell from the tree onto his head. This tree stopped bearing fruit long ago; if you do see apples, they've been tied on by mischievous students.

• *If you like, head through the gate into the...*

Trinity Grounds: The grounds are enjoyable to explore. Inside the **Great Court,** the clock (on the tower on the right) double-

rings at the top of each hour. It's a college tradition to take off running from the clock when the high noon bells begin (it takes 43 seconds to clang 24 times), race around the courtyard, touching each of the four corners without setting foot on the cobbles, and try to return to the same spot before the ringing ends. Supposedly only one student (a young lord) ever managed the feat—a scene featured in *Chariots of Fire* (but filmed elsewhere).

The **chapel** (entrance to the right of the clock tower)—which pales in comparison to the stunning King's College Chapel—feels like a shrine to thinking, with statues honoring great Trinity minds both familiar (Isaac Newton, Alfred Lord Tennyson, Francis Bacon) and unfamiliar. Who's missing? The poet Lord Byron, who was such a hell-raiser during his time at Trinity that a statue of him was deemed unfit for Church property; his statue stands in the library instead.

Wren Library: Don't miss the 1695 Christopher Wren-designed library, with its wonderful carving and fascinating original manuscripts. Just outside the library entrance, Sir Isaac Newton clapped his hands and timed the echo to measure the speed of sound as it raced down the side of the cloister and back. In the library's 12 display cases (covered with cloth that you flip back), you'll see handwritten works by Sir Isaac Newton and John Milton, alongside A. A. Milne's original *Winnie the Pooh* (the real Christopher Robin attended Trinity College).

▲▲Fitzwilliam Museum

Britain's best museum of antiquities and art outside of London is the Fitzwilliam, housed in a grand Neoclassical building a 10-minute walk south of Market Square. The Fitzwilliam's broad collection is like a mini-British Museum/National Gallery rolled into one;

you're bound to find something you like. Helpful docents—many with degrees or doctorates in art history—are more than willing to answer questions about the collection. The ground floor features an extensive range of antiquities and applied arts—everything from Greek vases, Mesopotamian artifacts, and Egyptian sarcophagi to Roman statues, fine porcelain, and suits of armor.

Upstairs is the painting gallery, with works that span art history: Italian Venetian masters (such as Titian and Canaletto), a worthy English section (featuring Gainsborough, Reynolds, Hogarth, and others), and a notable array of French Impressionist art (including Monet, Renoir, Pissarro, Degas, and Sisley). Rounding out the collection are old manuscripts, including some musical compositions from Handel. Watch your step—in 2006, a visitor tripped and accidentally smashed three 17th-century Chinese vases. The vases were restored (with donations from the community) and are now on display in Gallery 17...in a protective case.

Cost and Hours: Free but £5 donation suggested, Tue-Sat 10:00-17:00, Sun 12:00-17:00, closed Mon except bank holidays, no photos, daypack-size lockers-£1 deposit, Trumpington Street, tel. 01223/332-900, www.fitzmuseum.cam.ac.uk.

Museum of Classical Archaeology

Although this museum contains no originals, it offers a unique chance to study accurate copies (19th-century casts) of virtually every famous ancient Greek and Roman statue. More than 450 statues are on display. If you've seen the real things in Greece, Istanbul, Rome, and elsewhere, touring this collection is like a high school reunion..."Hey, I know you!" But since it takes some time to get here, this museum is best left to devotees of classical sculpture.

Cost and Hours: Free, Mon-Fri 10:00-17:00, Sat 10:00-13:00 during term, closed Sun year-round, Sidgwick Avenue, tel. 01223/330-402, www.classics.cam.ac.uk/museum.

Getting There: The museum is a five-minute walk west of Silver Street Bridge; after crossing the bridge, continue straight until you reach a sign reading *Sidgwick Site*. The museum is in the long building on the corner to your right; the entrance is on the opposite side, and the museum is upstairs.

▲Punting on the Cam

For a little levity and probably more exercise than you really want, try hiring one of the traditional flat-bottom punts at the river and pole yourself up and down (or around and around, more likely) the lazy Cam. Once you get the hang of it, it's a fine way to enjoy the scenic side of

Cambridge. It's less crowded in late afternoon (and less embarrassing).

Several companies rent punts and offer tours. Hawkers try to snare passengers in the thriving people zone in front of King's College. Prices are soft in slow times—try talking them down a bit before committing.

Scudamore's has two locations: on Mill Lane, just south of the central Silver Street Bridge, and at the less convenient Quayside at Magdalene Bridge, at the north end of town (£25/hour, credit-card deposit required; 45-minute tours-£17.50/person, discount if you book at TI or online; open daily 9:00-dusk, tel. 01223/359-750, www.scudamores.com).

Cambridge Chauffeur Punts, just under the Silver Street Bridge, also rents punts. Take yourself and up to five friends for a spin, or they will chauffeur (£20/hour; passport, credit card, or £60 cash deposit required; 45-minute shared tours-£14/person, £12 if pre-booked online; open daily March-Nov 9:30-dusk, tel. 01223/354-164, www.punting-in-cambridge.co.uk).

NEAR CAMBRIDGE
Imperial War Museum Duxford
This former airfield, nine miles south of Cambridge, is nirvana for aviation fans and WWII buffs. Wander through seven exhibition halls housing 200 vintage aircraft (including Spitfires, B-17 Flying Fortresses, a Concorde, and a Blackbird) as well as military land vehicles and special displays on Normandy and the Battle of Britain. On many weekends, the museum holds special events, such as air shows (extra fee)—check the website for details.

Cost and Hours: £17.50 (includes small donation), show local bus ticket for discount, daily mid-March-late Oct 10:00-18:00, late Oct-mid-March 10:00-16:00, last entry one hour before closing; tel. 01223/835-000, http://duxford.iwm.org.uk.

Getting There: The museum is located off A-505 in Duxford. On Sundays, direct Myalls bus #132 runs to the museum from the train station (4/day, 30 minutes, www.travelineeastanglia.org.uk). On other days of the week, it's best to take a taxi from Cambridge. (Other buses do stop in Duxford, but too far from the museum to walk.)

Sleeping in Cambridge

(area code: 01223)
While Cambridge is an easy side-trip from London, its subtle charms might convince you to spend the night. Cambridge has very few accommodations in the city center, and none in the tight maze of colleges and shops where you'll spend most of your time. These

recommendations are about a 10- to 15-minute walk south of the town center, toward the train station. Both offer free Wi-Fi.

$$$ Hotel du Vin blends France, England, and wine. This worthwhile splurge has 41 comfortable, spacious rooms with all the amenities above a characteristic bistro that offers good deals for guests and nonguests alike. This mod place manages to be classy yet unpretentious (Db-£150-225, fancier suites available, check online for special offers, breakfast-£15-17, air-con, elevator, just down the street from the Fitzwilliam Museum at Trumpington Street 15-18, tel. 01223/227-330 or 0844-736-4253, www.hotelduvin.com, reception.cambridge@hotelduvin.com).

$$$ Lensfield Hotel, popular with visiting professors, has 30 old-fashioned rooms (Sb-£72, Db-£110, Tb-£136, newer "deluxe" Db-£150, pricier suites available, spa and fitness room, 53 Lensfield Road, tel. 01223/355-017, www.lensfieldhotel.co.uk, enquiries@lensfieldhotel.co.uk).

Eating in Cambridge

While picnicking is scenic and saves money, the weather may not always cooperate. Here are a few ideas for fortifying yourself with a lunch in central Cambridge.

The Eagle, near the TI, is the oldest pub in town, and a Cambridge institution with a history so rich that a visit here practically

qualifies as sightseeing. Find your way into the delightful courtyard, with outdoor seating and a good look at the place's past. The second-floor windows once lit guest rooms, back when this was a coachmen's inn as well as a pub. Notice that the window on the right end is open; any local will love to tell you why. Follow the signs into the misnamed "RAF Bar," where US Army Air Corps pilots signed the ceiling while stationed here during World War II. Science fans can celebrate the discovery of DNA—Francis Crick and James Watson first announced their findings here in 1953 (£8-15 lunches, £10-18 dinners, food served daily 9:00-22:00, drinks until 23:00, 8 Benet Street, tel. 01223/505-020).

The **Michaelhouse Café** is a heavenly respite from the crowds, tucked into the repurposed St. Michael's Church, just north of Great St. Mary's Church. At lunch, choose from salads, soups, and sandwiches, as well as a few hot dishes and a variety of tasty baked goods (£6-10 lunches, Mon-Sat 8:00-17:00, breakfast served 8:00-11:00, lunch served 12:00-15:30, hot drinks and baked goods always available, closed Sun, Trinity Street, tel. 01223/309-147).

Between 14:30 and 15:30 you can pay £4.45 to fill your plate with whatever they have left.

Café Carringtons is a cozy cafeteria that serves traditional British food at reasonable prices, including a Sunday roast lunch (£6-8 meals, £6 sandwiches, Mon-Sat 8:00-16:30, Sun 10:00-16:00, down the stairs at 23 Market Street, tel. 01223/361-792).

Supermarkets: There's a **Marks & Spencer Simply Food** at the train station (Mon-Fri 7:00-23:00, Sat 7:00-22:00, Sun 9:00-21:00) and a larger Marks & Spencer department store on Market Hill Square (Mon-Thu 8:00-18:00, Wed until 20:00, Fri-Sat 8:00-19:00, Sun 11:00-17:00, tel. 01223/355-219). **Sainsbury's** supermarket has longer hours (Mon-Sat 8:00-23:30, Sun 11:00-17:00, 44 Sidney Street, at the corner of Green Street).

A good picnic spot is Laundress Green, a grassy park on the river, at the end of Mill Lane near the Silver Street Bridge punts. There are no benches, so bring something to sit on. Remember, the college lawns are private property, so walking or picnicking on the grass is generally not allowed. When in doubt, ask at the college's entrance.

Cambridge Connections

From Cambridge by Train to: York (hourly, 2.5 hours, transfer in Peterborough), **Oxford** (2-3/hour, 2.5-3 hours, change in London involves Tube transfer between train stations), **London** (King's Cross Station: 2/hour, 45 minutes; Liverpool Street Station: 2/hour, 1.25 hours). Train info: Tel. 0845-748-4950, www.nationalrail.co.uk.

By Bus to: London (every 60-90 minutes, 2-2.5 hours), **Heathrow Airport** (hourly, 2-3 hours). Bus info: Tel. 0871-781-8178, www.nationalexpress.com.

Stonehenge

As old as the pyramids, and older than the Acropolis and the Colosseum, this iconic stone circle amazed medieval Europeans, who figured it was built by a race of giants. And it still impresses visitors today. As one of Europe's most famous sights, Stonehenge, worth ▲▲, does a valiant job of retaining an air of mystery and majesty (partly because cordons, which keep hordes of tourists from trampling all over

it, foster the illusion that it stands alone in a field). Although some people are underwhelmed by Stonehenge, most of its almost one million annual visitors find that it's worth the trip. And the ancient site continues to reveal its mysteries: In 2010, within sight of Stonehenge, archaeologists discovered another 5,000-year-old henge, which they believe once encircled a wooden "twin" of the famous circle. Recent excavations revealed that people had been living on the site since around 3,000 B.C.—about five centuries earlier than anyone had realized.

GETTING TO STONEHENGE

Stonehenge is about 90 miles southwest of central London. To reach it from London, you can take a bus tour; go on a guided tour that uses public transportation; or do it on your own using public transport, connecting via Salisbury. It's not worth the hassle or expense to rent a car just for a Stonehenge day trip.

By Bus Tour from London: Several companies offer big-bus day trips to Stonehenge from London, often with stops in Bath, Windsor, Salisbury, and/or Avebury. These generally cost about £45-85 (including admission to Stonehenge), last 8-12 hours, and pack a 45-seat bus. Some include hotel pickup, admission fees, and meals; understand what's included before you book. The more destinations listed for a tour, the less time you'll have at any one stop. Well-known companies are **Evan Evans** (their bare-bones Stonehenge Express gets you there and back for £44, tel. 020/7950-1777 or US tel. 866-382-6868, www.evanevanstours.co.uk) and **Golden Tours** (£44, tel. 020/7630-2028 or US toll-free tel. 800-509-2507, www.goldentours.com). **International Friends** runs pricier but smaller 16-person tours that include Windsor and Bath (£119, tel. 01223/244-555, www.internationalfriends.co.uk).

By Guided Tour on Public Transport: London Walks offers a guided "Stonehenge and Salisbury Tour" by train and bus on Tuesdays from April through October (£60, includes all transportation, Salisbury walking tour, entry fees and guided tours of Stonehenge and Salisbury Cathedral; buy all tickets from guide; cash only, Tue at 9:15, meet at Waterloo Station's main ticket office, opposite Platform 16, call or check website to verify price and schedule, advance booking not required, tel. 020/7624-3978, recorded info tel. 020/7624-9255, www.walks.com).

On Your Own on Public Transport: Catch a train to Salisbury, then go by bus or taxi to Stonehenge. Trains to Salisbury run from London's Waterloo Station (around £37 for same-day return leaving weekdays after 9:30, 2/hour, 1.5 hours, tel. 0871-200-4950 or 0845-748-4950, www.southwesttrains.co.uk or www.nationalrail.co.uk).

Once in Salisbury, you can take **The Stonehenge Tour** bus to

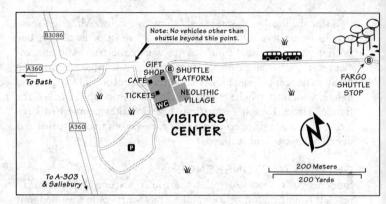

Note: No vehicles other than shuttle beyond this point.

B3086

A360
To Bath

GIFT SHOP   (B) SHUTTLE PLATFORM

CAFÉ

TICKETS   NEOLITHIC VILLAGE

WC

A360

VISITORS CENTER

P

To A-303 & Salisbury

(B) FARGO SHUTTLE STOP

N

200 Meters
200 Yards

DAY TRIPS

the site. Their distinctive red-and-black double-decker buses leave from the Salisbury train station (also stops at bus station) and make a circuit to Stonehenge and Old Sarum, with lovely scenery and a decent light commentary along the way (£14, £26 with Stonehenge and Old Sarum admission; tickets good all day; buy ticket from driver; daily June-Aug 10:00-18:00, 2/hour; may not run June 21 because of solstice crowds, shorter hours and hourly departures off-season; 30 minutes from station to Stonehenge, tel. 0845-072-7093, timetable at www.thestonehengetour.info).

By Taxi: A local cabbie named Brian will take you between Salisbury and Stonehenge, including an hour at the site (£40-50, 4 people max, best to reserve, contact for exact price, entry fee not included). He also offers a three-hour Stonehenge visit, which includes Old Sarum, Woodhenge, Durrington Walls, and Woodford's thatched cottages (£80, entry fee not included), and an Avebury and Stonehenge tour (£120-130, entry not included; tel. 07954/382-792, briantwort@ntlworld.com).

By Car: Stonehenge is well-signed just off the A-303, about 15 minutes north of Salisbury, an hour south of Bath, an hour east of Glastonbury, and an hour south of Avebury.

Stonehenge is about 70 miles and 1.5 hours west of **London Heathrow** (barring traffic). From the M-25 ring road, connect with the M-3 toward Southampton. Past Basingstoke, exit to the A-303. Continue west past Andover to Amesbury. In 3.5 miles, turn onto northbound A-360 at the roundabout, and follow "From Salisbury" directions from that point (see below).

From **Salisbury,** head north on A-360 (at the St. Paul's roundabout, take the second exit, direction: Devizes). Continue for eight miles, crossing the A-303 roundabout. In one more mile you'll encounter another roundabout; follow it around to the exit for the visitors center.

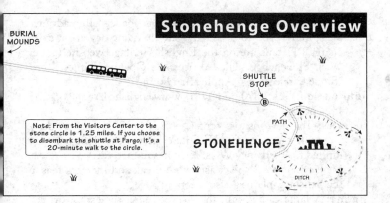

Orientation to Stonehenge

Cost: £14.90, save £1 and guarantee entry by pre-booking online, covered by English Heritage Pass (see page 565), includes shuttle-bus ride to the stone circle. In summer, there's a £5 refundable parking fee for drivers.

Advance Tickets: Pre-booking a timed-entry ticket online at least 24 hours in advance is strongly recommended, and the only way to assure you'll actually get in to the site, which caps the number of visitors per day at 7,000. (Some same-day tickets may be available at the ticket window, but in high season, it's risky to count on this.) Purchase your ticket online at www.english-heritage.org.uk/stonehenge. After booking a 30-minute arrival window, you'll receive a confirmation email with your e-ticket. Either print your ticket to present at the site, or bring your confirmation number.

If tickets are sold out for the day you planned to visit, you could consider a guided tour that includes entry (see various options under "Getting to Stonehenge," earlier).

Hours: Daily June-Aug 9:00-20:00, mid-March-May and Sept-mid-Oct 9:30-19:00, mid-Oct-mid-March 9:30-17:00. Note that last entry is two hours before closing. Expect shorter hours and possible closures June 20-22 due to huge, raucous solstice crowds.

Tours: Admission includes a worthwhile 45-minute audioguide; the same audio content can be downloaded for free to your mobile device from the English Heritage website.

Visiting the Inner Stones: For the true Stonehenge fan, special one-hour access to the stones' inner circle is available early in the morning (times vary depending on sunrise, but the earliest is 5:00 in June and July) or after closing to the general public. Touching the stones is not allowed. Only 26 people are allowed at a time, so reservations must be made well in advance (£22, allows you to revisit the site the same day at no extra charge). Details are on the English Heritage website (under "Visit Stonehenge," click "Prices and Opening Times," then "Stone Circle Access Application Form."

Information: Tel. 0870-333-1181, www.english-heritage.org.uk/stonehenge.

Services: The new visitors center, opened in 2013, has WCs, a large gift shop, and free Wi-Fi. Services at the circle itself are limited to emergency WCs. Even in summer, carry a jacket, as there are no trees to act as a wind-break and there's a reason the Salisbury plains are so green.

Eating: A large café within the visitors center serves hot drinks, soup, sandwiches, and salads along with hot light bites (£4-7).

Length of this Tour: Allow at least two hours to see everything.

Self-Guided Tour

DAY TRIPS

Whether you're using the audioguide or downloading the audio tour to your mobile device, this commentary will help make your visit even more meaningful. Start by touring the visitors center, then take a shuttle (or walk) to the stone circle.

• *Collect your ticket (or skip the line if you already have yours) and go straight to the excellent exhibit space.*

Visitors Center

The new visitors center, located 1.25 miles west of the circle, is a minimalist steel structure with a wavy roofline, intended to replicate the Salisbury plains.

The **permanent exhibit** uses an artful combination of high-tech multimedia displays and prehistoric bones, tools, and pottery shards to explore the history of the people who built Stonehenge, how they lived, and why they might have built the stone circle.

Stand in the virtual center of Stonehenge, as 5,000 years pass by around you. Be sure to find the forensic reconstruction of a Neolithic man, based on a skeleton unearthed in 1863. Then step outside and visit his ancient neighborhood—a village of **Neolithic huts** modeled after the traces of a village discovered just northeast of Stonehenge.

Pick up the handy audioguide as you make your way to the shuttle platform. (If nature calls, be sure to use the WCs within the Visitors Center, as there are only emergency WCs at the circle itself.)

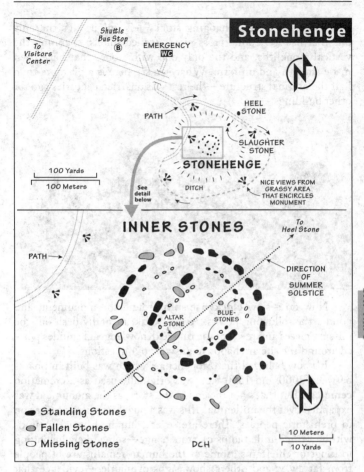

Stonehenge

Shuttle Bus Stop **B**

To Visitors Center

EMERGENCY **WC**

PATH

HEEL STONE

SLAUGHTER STONE

STONEHENGE

DITCH

NICE VIEWS FROM GRASSY AREA THAT ENCIRCLES MONUMENT

100 Yards
100 Meters

See detail below

INNER STONES

To Heel Stone

PATH →

DIRECTION OF SUMMER SOLSTICE

ALTAR STONE

BLUE-STONES

- **Standing Stones**
- **Fallen Stones**
- **Missing Stones**

DCH

10 Meters
10 Yards

• *Shuttle buses (green land-trains) depart about every 10 minutes from the platform behind the gift shop to the stone circle. The trip takes six minutes. If you'd prefer, you can walk the 1.25 miles to the site along a level, paved path.*

Along the way, you have the option of stopping at **Fargo Plantation,** *where you can see several burial mounds (tell the shuttle attendant if you want to disembark here). After wandering through the burial mounds, you'll need to walk the rest of the way to the stone circle (about 15 minutes).*

Stone Circle

As you approach the massive structure, walk right up to the knee-high cordon and let your fellow 21st-century tourists melt away. It's just you and the druids...

England has hundreds of stone circles, but Stonehenge—

which literally means "hanging stones"—is unique. It's the only one that has horizontal cross-pieces (called lintels) spanning the vertical monoliths, and the only one with stones that have been made smooth and uniform. What you see here is a bit more than half the original structure—the rest was quarried centuries ago for other buildings.

Now do a slow **clockwise spin** around the monument, and ponder the following points. As you walk, mentally flesh out the missing pieces and re-erect the rubble. Knowledgeable guides posted around the site are happy to answer your questions.

It's now believed that Stonehenge, which was built in phases between 3000 and 1500 B.C., was originally used as a cremation **cemetery.** But that's not the end of the story, as the monument was expanded over the millennia. This was a hugely significant location to prehistoric peoples. There are several hundred burial mounds within a three-mile radius of Stonehenge—some likely belonging to kings or chieftains. Some of the human remains are of people from far away, and others show signs of injuries—evidence that Stonehenge may have been used as a place of **medicine** or healing.

Whatever its original purpose, Stonehenge still functions as a celestial **calendar.** As the sun rises on the summer solstice (June 21), the "heel stone"—the one set apart from the rest, near the road—lines up with the sun and the altar at the center of the stone circle. A study of more than 300 similar circles in Britain found that each was designed to calculate the movement of the sun, moon, and stars, and to predict eclipses in order to help early societies know when to plant, harvest, and party. Even in modern times, as the summer solstice sun sets in just the right slot at Stonehenge, pagans boogie.

Some believe that Stonehenge is built at the precise point where six **"ley lines"** intersect. Ley lines are theoretical lines of magnetic or spiritual power that crisscross the globe. Belief in the power of these lines has gone in and out of fashion over time. They are believed to have been very important to prehistoric peoples, but then were largely ignored until the early 20th century, when the English writer Alfred Watkins popularized them (to the scorn of serious scientists). More recently, the concept has been embraced by the New Age movement. Without realizing it, you follow these ley lines all the time: Many of England's modern highways, following prehistoric paths, and churches, built over prehistoric monuments, are located where ley lines intersect. If you're a skeptic, ask one of the guides at Stonehenge to explain the mystique of this paranormal tradition that continued for centuries; it's creepy and convincing.

Notice that two of the stones (facing the entry passageway) are blemished. At the base of one monolith, it looks like someone has pulled back the stone to reveal a concrete skeleton. This is a clumsy **repair job** to fix damage done long ago by souvenir seekers, who actually rented hammers and chisels to take home a piece of Stonehenge. Look to the right of the repaired stone: The back of another stone is missing the same thin layer of protective lichen that covers the others. The lichen—and some of the stone itself—was sandblasted off to remove graffiti. (No wonder they've got Stonehenge roped off now.) The repairs were intentionally done in a different color, so as not to appear like the original stone.

Stonehenge's builders used two different types of stone. The tall, stout monoliths and lintels are sandstone blocks called **sarsen stones.** Most of the monoliths weigh about 25 tons (the largest is 45 tons), and the lintels are about 7 tons apiece. These sarsen stones were brought from "only" 20 miles away. The shorter stones in the middle, called **bluestones,** came from the south coast of Wales—240 miles away (close if you're taking a train, but far if you're packing a megalith). Imagine the logistical puzzle of floating six-ton stones across Wales' Severn Estuary and up the River Avon, then rolling them on logs about 20 miles to this position...an impressive feat, even in our era of skyscrapers. We know the stones came from Wales because geologists have chemically matched the bluestones to specific outcrops there.

Why didn't the builders of Stonehenge use what seem like perfectly adequate stones nearby? This, like many other questions about Stonehenge, remains shrouded in mystery. Think again about the ley lines. Ponder the fact that many experts accept none of the explanations of how these giant stones were transported. Then imagine congregations gathering here 5,000 years ago, raising thought levels, creating a powerful life force transmitted along the ley lines. Maybe a particular kind of stone was essential for maximum energy transmission. Maybe the stones were levitated here. Maybe psychics really do create powerful vibes. Maybe not. It's as unbelievable as electricity used to be.

BRITAIN: PAST AND PRESENT

Britain was created by force and held together by force. It's really a nation of the 19th century, when this rich Victorian-era empire reached its financial peak. Its traditional industry, buildings, and the popularity of the notion of "Great" Britain are a product of its past wealth.

To best understand the many fascinating sights you'll encounter in your travels, have a basic handle on the sweeping story of this land and its capital, London. (Generally speaking, the good and bad stories that tour guides tell are not true...and the boring ones are.)

London's History

I've divided London's story into major historical periods. For the full context of British history, see later in this chapter. In addition to the specific sights mentioned for each era, you'll find portraits of many of the big names in London's history in the National Portrait Gallery.

INVASIONS (2000 B.C.-A.D. 1100)

The mysterious Stonehenge-builders are replaced by the Celts, whose druid priests make human sacrifices and worship trees. The Romans bring 500 years of peace and stability, establishing London (Londinium) as a major city. Then civilization falls for 500 years, to German pirates (Angles and Saxons),

Danish Vikings, and, finally, William the Conqueror (A.D. 1066). During these Dark Ages, Christianity battles pagan gods for supremacy of the island.

Timeline

c. 1700 B.C. Stone slabs erected to create the ceremonial site now known as Stonehenge (90 miles west of London).

A.D. 43 Romans defeat the Celtic locals and establish Londinium as a seaport. They build the original London Bridge and a city wall, encompassing one square mile, which sets the city boundaries for 1,500 years.

c. 60 A queen of the Isle's indigenous people, Boadicea defies the Romans and burns Londinium before the revolt is squelched.

c. 200 London is the thriving, river-trading, walled, Latin-speaking capital of Roman-dominated England.

410 The city of Rome is looted by invaders, and the Europe-wide Roman infrastructure crumbles. England is soon overrun by "barbarian" Anglo-Saxon invaders from Germany. This begins 500 years of Viking invasions, poverty, ignorance, superstition, and hand-me-down leotards—the Dark Ages.

c. 600 The legend of "King Arthur" emerges—perhaps based on a real Roman Christian general battling barbarians after the Fall of Rome.

886 King Alfred the Great liberates London from Danish Vikings; he helps reunite England, re-establish Christianity, and encourage learning.

c. 1000 *Beowulf,* an epic tale written in Old English verse, is the first great work of Anglo-Saxon literature.

1052 King Edward the Confessor builds his palace and abbey at Westminster, a mile and a half from London.

1066 After Edward's death, England is conquered by Norman invaders (from northern France) under William the Conqueror. William builds the Tower of London and initiates two centuries of rule by French-speaking kings. London reasserts itself as a trade center.

1080 William builds his first castle on English soil: Windsor, which will become the residence of many monarchs to come.

Related Sights
- Boadicea statue near Westminster Bridge
- Roman Wall
- Lindisfarne Gospels, *Beowulf* manuscript (British Library)
- Westminster Abbey
- Tower of London
- Windsor Castle

WARS WITH FRANCE, WARS OF THE ROSES (1100-1500)

French-speaking kings rule England, and English-speaking kings invade France as the two budding nations define their modern borders. In the 1400s, feuding English nobles duke it out for control of the country.

PAST & PRESENT

Timeline

1100s   Robin Hood, a legendary (and possibly real) bandit, steals from the rich and gives to a poor populace that feels neglected and ignored by its francophone rulers.

1189-1199   England is ruled by Richard the Lionheart, a not-so-great king who prefers speaking French and spends his energy on distant Crusades. His influential mother, the French-born Eleanor of Aquitaine, outlives Richard and is considered one of the most powerful women of the Middle Ages.

1209   London Bridge—the famous stone version, topped with houses—is built. It stands until 1832.

1215   King John, under pressure from barons and London's powerful trade guilds, signs the Magna Carta, establishing that even kings must follow the rule of law.

1280   Old St. Paul's Cathedral is finished.

1337   Start of the Hundred Years' War with France.

1348   The Black Death (bubonic plague) kills half of London.

c. 1400   Poet Geoffrey Chaucer's (often bawdy) collection of stories, *The Canterbury Tales*, helps popularize common English.

1415   British victory over the French at Battle of Agincourt.

1431   In France, Joan of Arc—who has led French armies

to victory against invading English troops—is burned at the stake by English forces and local French supporters.

1455-1485 Prosperous London plays kingmaker in the Wars of the Roses, helping determine which noble becomes king.

Related Sights
• Magna Carta, *The Canterbury Tales* (British Library)
• Temple Church

THE TUDOR RENAISSANCE (1500s)

Powerful, charismatic Henry VIII thrusts England onto the world stage by defying the pope and sparking a century of Protestant/Catholic warfare. His daughter, Elizabeth I, reigns over a cultural renaissance of sea exploration, scientific discovery, and literature known as the "Elizabethan Age."

Timeline

1500 London's population swells to 50,000.

1534 Enraged by the pope's refusal to validate his second marriage (to Anne Boleyn), King Henry VIII breaks with Rome. He "dissolves" (destroys) the monasteries and forms his own Protestant Church of England (Anglican). This leads to centuries of religious division between Catholics and Protestants; generally speaking, London leans to the Protestant side.

1536 Henry VIII grows tired of Anne Boleyn and executes her; within days he marries Jane Seymour (the third of his six marriages).

1555 Attempting to convert England back to Catholicism, Queen Mary I—a.k.a. "Bloody Mary"—burns hundreds of Protestants at the stake.

1558 Elizabeth I—daughter of Henry VIII and Anne Boleyn, and half-sister of Mary I—is crowned queen, with London's backing. Her reign (the "Elizabethan Age") brings a renaissance of theater, literature, science, discovery, and manners to the city.

1577-1580	Explorer Sir Francis Drake circumnavigates the globe.
1585	Playwright William Shakespeare moves from Stratford-upon-Avon to London, beginning a remarkable career as the earth's greatest playwright.
1588	England's navy defeats the powerful Spanish Armada and starts to rule the waves. Overseas trade brings the world's wealth directly to London's wharves.
1594	Explorer Sir Walter Raleigh searches, unsuccessfully, for the legendary El Dorado ("City of Gold") in South America.

Related Sights

• Shakespeare's Globe
• Shakespeare folios (British Library)
• Tower of London execution site
• Chapel of Henry VII and Elizabeth I's tomb in Westminster Abbey
• Kings College Chapel in Cambridge

KINGS VS. PARLIAMENT (1600s)

The "Virgin Queen" Elizabeth dies without heirs, and the Crown passes to the Stuart family. Their arrogant, divine-right management style sparks a civil war, led by the commoner Oliver Cromwell, who beheads the king and briefly establishes a republic called the Commonwealth of England. The monarchy returns, along with back-to-back disasters—first the Great Plague (1665) and then the Great Fire (1666), which levels London.

Timeline

1600	London, population 200,000, is Europe's largest city, expanding beyond the medieval walls, stretching westward along the river to Charing Cross.
1642-1648	A civil war wracks England, pitting a Catholic aristocracy against a Protestant Parliament led by Oliver Cromwell.
1649	King Charles I is beheaded outside Whitehall as London backs the Protestant Parliament in England's Civil War.

PAST & PRESENT

1649-1653 Cromwell heads a democratic, Parliament-run commonwealth.

1653-1658 Cromwell—formerly an outspoken critic of royalty—becomes Lord Protector, a virtually "royal" lifelong title that compels others to refer to him as "Your Highness."

1658 Cromwell dies, passing the title of Lord Protector to his son; within a few years, the Protectorate is history, the king is back in power (see next), and Cromwell's corpse has been exhumed and posthumously beheaded.

1660 Charles II, son of Charles I, is invited to restore the monarchy under supervision by the Parliament.

1660-1669 Samuel Pepys (pronounced "peeps") keeps a diary, chronicling everyday London life, the Great Plague, and the Great Fire. Not a famous man himself, Pepys' diary, even today, makes his times come alive.

1665 The Great Plague kills 100,000.

1666 The Great Fire rages for four days, destroying the wooden city. The city is rebuilt in stone, largely by architect Christopher Wren—who designs more than 20 churches, including his masterpiece, St. Paul's Cathedral.

1666 Scientist Isaac Newton watches an apple fall from a tree to the ground, leading him to ponder the mysterious force of gravity.

1688 In the "Glorious Revolution," Parliament deposes the Catholic King James II and imports the Protestant William and Mary from the Netherlands to rule Britain.

1701 The Act of Settlement guarantees a line of succession for Protestant monarchs, assuaging noble nerves set on edge after William, Mary, and Mary's sister Queen Anne all die without heirs.

PAST & PRESENT

Related Sights
• Banqueting House (site of Charles I's beheading)
• Crown jewels (Tower of London)
• City of London
• Fire Monument
• St. Paul's and other Wren churches
• Isaac Newton's apple tree (outside Trinity College Gate, Cambridge)
• Kensington Palace (residence of William, Mary, and Anne)

COLONIAL EXPANSION (1700-EARLY 1800s)

Britannia rules the waves and becomes a world power, exploiting the wealth of India, Africa, Australia, and America...at least until the Yanks revolt in the "American War."

Timeline

1700s The London art scene blossoms, thanks to William Hogarth (paints realistic slices of English life), Sir Joshua Reynolds (embraces a "Grand Manner" of juxtaposing Londoners with classical settings), Thomas Gainsborough (depicts women as the feminine ideal), and others.

1700 London's population is 500,000 and growing fast. One in seven Brits lives in London.

1702 London's first daily newspapers hit the streets.

1714 The German Hanover family takes over the throne. While the first five Hanovers—Georges I-IV and William IV—are less than stellar monarchs, the sixth (Queen Victoria) redeems the clan.

1741 David Garrick takes the London stage. This actor and theater manager's naturalism on the stage—and business sense off it—greatly enhances the blossoming theater scene.

1741 George Frideric Handel (a German-born resident of London) composes one of the world's best-known choral works, *The Messiah*.

1755 Dr. Samuel Johnson publishes the first great English dictionary. The writer of a magazine column on everyday London life, Johnson is known to us today for witty remarks captured by his friend and biographer, James Boswell.

1763-1775 Scientist James Watt makes advances in engineering steam engines, laying the groundwork for a coming Industrial Revolution.

1776 Britain fights 13 of its colonies in the American War of Independence (1775-1783).

1779 On his final of three naval voyages to explore the South Pacific, Captain James Cook is killed by Hawaiian natives.

1789 The French Revolution sparks decades of war with France.

1800s-1830s John Constable paints the English countryside with an almost Impressionistic flair, specializing in cloudy skies.

1805 Admiral Nelson defeats the French navy at Trafalgar (Spain), ending the threat of invasion by Napoleon.

1815 The Duke of Wellington defeats Napoleon for good at Waterloo (Belgium); he later serves as a domineering prime minister. Britain becomes Europe's No. 1 power.

Related Sights

• Nelson's Column at Trafalgar Square
• Apsley House (Wellington Museum) and adjacent Wellington Arch
• Portraits by Reynolds and Gainsborough, slices of life by Hogarth, and cloudy skies by Constable in the Tate Britain
• Royal Observatory and National Maritime Museum, Greenwich
• Dr. Johnson's House in The City
• Georgian architecture in Bath

VICTORIAN GENTILITY AND THE INDUSTRIAL REVOLUTION (EARLY-LATE 1800s)

Britain under Queen Victoria reigns supreme, steaming into the modern age with railroads, factories, electricity, telephones, and the first Underground. Meanwhile, Romantic poets long for the innocence of nature, Charles Dickens questions the social order, and Rudyard Kipling criticizes the colonial system.

Timeline

Early 1800s A generation of Romantic poets (John Keats, Percy Shelley, Lord Byron, and William Wordsworth) return to nature and ponder mortality before dying young. Meanwhile, Jane Austen and the Brontë sisters write romantic tales about the landed gentry.

1800s-1850s J. M. W. Turner immerses himself in nature and paints moody landscapes.

c. 1830 Railroads lace the country together. The Industrial Revolution kicks into high gear.

1837 Eighteen-year-old Victoria becomes queen and presides over an era of peace and middle-class values. Britain's longest-reigning monarch (and great-great-grandmother of both Elizabeth II and

Queen Victoria (1819-1901)

Plump, pleasant, and barely five feet tall, Queen Victoria, with her regal demeanor and 64-year reign, came to symbolize the global dominance of the British Empire during its greatest era.

Born in Kensington Palace, Victoria was the granddaughter of "Mad" King George III, the tyrant who sparked the American Revolution. Her domineering mother raised her in sheltered seclusion, drilling into her the strict morality that would come to be known as "Victorian." At 18, she was crowned queen. Victoria soon fell madly, deeply in love with Prince Albert, a handsome German nobleman with mutton-chop sideburns. They married and set up house in Buckingham Palace (the first monarchs to do so) and at Windsor Castle. Over the next 17 years, she and Albert had nine children, whom they eventually married off to Europe's crowned heads. Victoria's royal descendants include Kaiser Wilhelm II of Germany (who started World War I); the current monarchs of Spain, Norway, Sweden, and Denmark; and England's Queen Elizabeth II, who is Victoria's great-great-granddaughter.

Victoria and Albert promoted the arts and sciences, organizing a world's fair in Hyde Park (1851) that showed off London as *the* global capital. Just as important, they were role models for an entire nation; this loving couple influenced several generations with their wholesome middle-class values and devoted parenting. Though Victoria is often depicted as dour and stuffy—she supposedly coined the phrase "We are not amused"—in private she was warm, easy to laugh, plainspoken, thrifty, and modest, with a talent for sketching and journal writing.

In 1861, Victoria's happy domestic life ended. Her mother's death was soon followed by the sudden loss of her beloved Albert to typhoid fever. A devastated Victoria dressed in black for the funeral—and for her remaining 40 years never again wore any other color. She hunkered down at Windsor with her family. Critics complained she was an absentee monarch. Rumors swirled that her kilt-wearing servant, John Brown, was not only her close friend but also her lover. For two decades, she rarely appeared in public.

Over time, Victoria emerged from mourning to assume her role as one of history's first constitutional monarchs. She had

her husband) reigns for 64 years. "Victorian" comes to describe the prim middle-class morality of the time.

1840 Victoria marries her German-born first cousin Prince Albert, whose support of the arts and sciences enriches London.

1840s-1860s Popular novelist Charles Dickens brings literature to the masses, educating them about Britain's harsh social and economic realities.

inherited a crown with little real power. But beyond her ribbon-cutting ceremonial duties, Victoria influenced events behind the scenes. She studiously learned politics from powerful mentors (especially Prince Albert and two influential prime ministers) and kept well-informed on what Parliament was doing. Thanks to Victoria's personal modesty and honesty, the British public never came to disdain the monarchy, as happened in other countries.

Victoria gracefully oversaw the peaceful transfer of power from the nobles to the people. The secret ballot was introduced during her reign, and ordinary workers acquired voting rights (though this applied only to men—Victoria opposed women's suffrage). The traditional Whigs and Tories morphed into today's Liberal and Conservative parties. Victoria personally promoted progressive charities, and even paid for her own crown.

Most of all, Victoria became the symbol of the British Empire, which she saw as a way to protect and civilize poorer peoples. Britain enjoyed peace at home, while its colonial possessions doubled to include India, Australia, Canada, and much of Africa. Because it was always daytime someplace under Victoria's rule, it was often said that "the sun never sets on the British Empire."

The Victorian era saw great changes. The Industrial Revolution was in full swing. When Victoria was born, there were no trains. By 1842, when she took her first train trip (with much fanfare), railroads crisscrossed Europe. The telegraph, telephone, and newspapers further laced the world together. The popular arts flourished—it was the era of Dickens novels, Tennyson poems, Sherlock Holmes stories, Gilbert and Sullivan operettas, and Pre-Raphaelite paintings. Economically, Britain saw the rise of the middle class. Middle-class morality dominated—family, hard work, honor, duty, and sexual modesty.

By the end of her reign, Victoria was wildly popular, both for her personality and as a focus for British patriotism. At her Golden Jubilee (1887), she paraded past adoring throngs to Westminster Abbey. For her Diamond Jubilee (1897), she did the same at St. Paul's Cathedral. Cities, lakes, and military medals were named for her. When she passed away in 1901, it was literally the end of an era.

PAST & PRESENT

1850   Alfred, Lord Tennyson is appointed poet laureate.

1851   With Britain at the peak of prosperity from its worldwide colonial empire, London—population one million—hosts a Great Exhibition in Hyde Park, trumpeting the latest triumphs of science and technology.

1859   Charles Darwin publishes *On the Origin of the Species*, articulating the principles of natural selection and evolution.

1863	First Underground (Tube) line is built.
1880-1914	Sherlock Holmes—a fictional detective living at 221b Baker Street—solves fictional crimes that the real Scotland Yard can't.
1888	Jack the Ripper, a serial killer of prostitutes, terrorizes east London; his (or her) identity remains unknown.

Related Sights

- Big Ben and Halls of Parliament
- Buckingham Palace, the Mall, and Hyde Park
- The Tube
- J. M. W. Turner paintings, Tate Britain
- Writers' manuscripts in the British Library
- Poets' Corner in Westminster Abbey
- Kensington Palace (Victoria Revealed exhibit)
- Sherlock Holmes Museum
- London's East End tenements (reminiscent of the Jack the Ripper days)

WORLD WARS AND RECOVERY (20TH CENTURY)

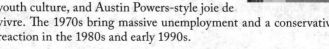

Two world wars whittle Britain down from a world empire to an island chain struggling to compete in a global economy. The German Blitz in World War II levels eastern London. Colonies rebel and gain their independence, then flood London with immigrants. Long-time residents flee to London's suburbs, and commute in on the Tube.

In the 1960s, "Swinging London" becomes a center for rock music, film, theater, youth culture, and Austin Powers-style joie de vivre. The 1970s bring massive unemployment and a conservative reaction in the 1980s and early 1990s.

Timeline

1914-1918	World War I. Britain, France, and other allies battle Germany from trenches dug in the open fields of France and Belgium. A million British men die.
1920s-1930s	A flourishing of literary talent hits London, including T. S. Eliot (American-turned-British), Virginia Woolf, and Dylan Thomas.
1936	King Edward VIII abdicates to marry an American commoner, Wallis Simpson. He is succeeded by his

PAST & PRESENT

brother, George VI ("Bertie" of *The King's Speech* fame).

1939-1945 World War II.

1940 Having failed to avert war with Nazi Germany, Neville Chamberlain resigns as prime minister. He is replaced by Sir Winston Churchill, whose resolve and charismatic speeches rally Britain during its darkest hour.

1940-1941 The Blitz. Preparing to invade the Isle, Nazi Germany air-bombs Britain, particularly London. Despite enormous devastation, Britain holds firm.

1945 Postwar recovery begins, aided by the United States. Many cheap, concrete (ugly) buildings rise from the rubble. Britain begins granting independence to many foreign colonies.

1950s Oxford professors and friends C. S. Lewis and J. R. R. Tolkien each publish fantasy stories (*The Chronicles of Narnia* and *The Lord of the Rings*, respectively).

1964 The Beatles bring counterculture ideas to the middle class, tour America, and spread "Swinging London" hipness to the world.

1970s Labor strikes, unemployment, and recession. Meanwhile, British musicians—Led Zeppelin, The Rolling Stones, The Who, Elton John, David Bowie, and so on—dominate American airwaves, and James Bond rules the box office.

1973 Britain joins what is now called the European Union, but maintains her distance.

1980s The Conservative administration of Margaret Thatcher—the "Iron Lady"—rules.

1981 Prince Charles marries Lady Diana Spencer in St. Paul's Cathedral.

1982 Britain battles Argentina over the Falkland Islands. Britain claims victory.

1994 The Channel Tunnel ("Chunnel") opens, linking London with Paris and Brussels.

1997 Tony Blair of the Labour Party becomes prime minister, signaling a shift toward moderate liberalism. Princess Diana dies in a car crash in Paris. The nation—and the world—mourn.

PAST & PRESENT

Related Sights
• Cabinet War Rooms
• Cenotaph
• Imperial War Museum

- Blitz photos at St. Paul's
- Beatles memorabilia in British Library

LONDON TODAY

London is one of the world's major cultural capitals, an exporter of art, science, and technology. In 2012, the city hosted the Olympics for the third time.

Timeline

2000 London puts on a big millennium celebration, building a Ferris wheel (the London Eye), the Millennium Bridge, and the Millennium Dome exhibition (now "The O2").

2002 Many EU nations adopt the euro currency, but Britain sticks with the pound sterling. Queen Elizabeth II celebrates her 50-year Jubilee.

2003 A wary and politically divided Britain joins America's "Coalition of the Willing," and invades Iraq.

2005 Four terrorist bombs rock London on "7/7."

2007 Tony Blair steps down as prime minister, and Gordon Brown takes over. A bank run on Northern Rock, the country's fifth-biggest mortgage lender, marks the beginning of an economic downturn.

2009 Construction starts on the Crossrail, an underground train line that will dramatically speed up east-west connections across town.

2010 After an extremely close election, embattled PM Gordon Brown of the Labour Party loses his job to Conservative David Cameron.

2011 Prince William marries Kate Middleton—the first royal wedding in a generation, watched by two billion people around the world.

2012 In a one-two punch of a giant year, London hosts the Summer Olympics, and Queen Elizabeth II celebrates her 60-year Diamond Jubilee.

2013 Will and Kate announce the birth of Prince George, third in line to the English throne.

2015 You visit Britain to make your own history.

Related Sights

- The London Eye
- Tate Modern contemporary art exhibits
- West End theaters
- The Docklands skyscraper zone

PAST & PRESENT

Basic British History for the Traveler

When Julius Caesar landed on the misty and mysterious isle of Britain in 55 B.C., England entered the history books. The primitive Celtic tribes Caesar fought were themselves invaders (who had earlier conquered the even more mysterious people who built Stonehenge). About 90 years later, the Romans came back, building towns and roads and establishing their capital at Londinium. The Celtic natives in Scotland and Wales—consisting of Gaels, Picts, and Scots—were not easily subdued. The Romans built Hadrian's Wall near the Scottish border as protection against their troublesome northern neighbors. Even today, the Celtic language and influence are strongest in these far reaches of Britain.

As Rome fell, so fell Roman Britain—a victim of invaders and internal troubles. Barbarian tribes from Germany and Denmark, called Angles and Saxons, swept through the southern part of the island, establishing Angle-land. These were the days of the real King Arthur, possibly a Christianized Roman general who fought valiantly—but in vain—against invading barbarians. In 793, England was hit with the first of two centuries of savage invasions by barbarians from Norway, called the Vikings or Norsemen. The island was plunged into 500 years of Dark Ages—wars, plagues, and poverty—lit only by the dim candle of a few learned Christian monks and missionaries trying to convert the barbarians. The sightseer sees little from this Anglo-Saxon period.

Modern England began with yet another invasion. William the Conqueror and his Norman troops crossed the English Channel from France in 1066. William crowned himself king in Westminster Abbey (where all subsequent coronations would take place) and began building the Tower of London. French-speaking Norman kings ruled the country for two centuries. Then followed two centuries of civil wars, with various noble families vying for the crown. In the bitterest feud, the York and Lancaster families fought the Wars of the Roses, so-called because of the white and red flowers the combatants chose as their symbols. Rife with battles, intrigues, and kings, nobles, and ladies imprisoned and executed in the Tower, it's a wonder the country survived its rulers.

England was finally united by the "third-party" Tudor family. Henry VIII, a Tudor, was England's Renaissance king. He was handsome, athletic, highly sexed, a poet, a scholar, and a musician. He was also arrogant, cruel, gluttonous, and paranoid. He went through six wives in 40 years, divorcing, imprisoning, or executing them when they no longer suited his needs. (To keep track of each one's fate, British kids learn this rhyme: "Divorced, beheaded, died; divorced, beheaded, survived.")

Henry "divorced" England from the Catholic Church, estab-

Get It Right

Americans tend to use "England," "Britain," and the "United Kingdom" (or "UK") interchangeably, but they're not quite the same.

- **England** is the country occupying the center and southeast part of the island.
- **Britain** is the name of the island.
- **Great Britain** is the political union of the island's three countries: England, Scotland, and Wales.
- The **United Kingdom** (UK) adds a fourth country, Northern Ireland.
- The **British Isles** (not a political entity) also includes the independent Republic of Ireland.
- The **British Commonwealth** is a loose association of possessions and former colonies (including Canada, Australia, and India) that profess at least symbolic loyalty to the Crown.

You can call the modern nation either the United Kingdom ("the UK"), "Great Britain," or simply "Britain."

lishing the Protestant Church of England (the Anglican Church) and setting in motion years of religious squabbles. He also "dissolved" the monasteries (c. 1540), left just the shells of many formerly glorious abbeys dotting the countryside, and pocketed their land and wealth for the Crown (for more on Henry, see the sidebar on page 170).

Henry's daughter, Queen Elizabeth I, who reigned for 45 years, made England a great trading and naval power (defeating the Spanish Armada) and presided over the Elizabethan era of great writers (such as William Shakespeare) and scientists (such as Sir Francis Bacon). But Elizabeth never married, so the English Parliament asked the Protestant ruler to the north, Scotland's King James (Elizabeth's first cousin twice removed), if he'd like to inherit the English throne. The two nations have been tied together, however fitfully, ever since (though recent stirrings toward Scottish independence may indeed shake up this long-standing union).

The enduring quarrel between England's divine-right kings and Parliament's nobles finally erupted into a civil war (1643). Parliament forces under the Protestant Puritan farmer Oliver Cromwell defeated—and beheaded—King Charles I. This civil war left its mark on much of what you'll see in Britain. Eventually, Parliament invited Charles' son to take the throne. This "restoration of the monarchy" was accompanied by a great colonial expansion and the rebuilding of London (including Christopher Wren's St. Paul's Cathedral), which had been devastated by the Great Fire of

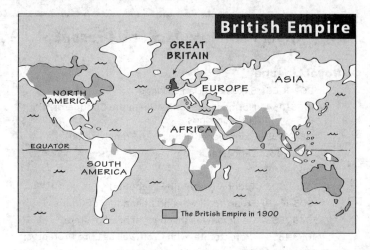

British Empire

GREAT
BRITAIN

NORTH
AMERICA

EUROPE

ASIA

AFRICA

EQUATOR

SOUTH
AMERICA

The British Empire in 1900

1666. Parliament gained ultimate authority over the throne when it deposed Catholic James II and imported the Dutch monarchs William and Mary in 1688, guaranteeing a Protestant succession.

Britain grew as a naval superpower, colonizing and trading with all parts of the globe (although it lost its most important colony to those ungrateful Americans in 1776). Admiral Horatio Nelson's victory over Napoleon's fleet at the Battle of Trafalgar secured her naval superiority ("Britannia rules the waves"), and 10 years later, the Duke of Wellington stomped Napoleon on land at Waterloo. Nelson and Wellington—both buried in London's St. Paul's Cathedral—are memorialized by many arches, columns, and squares throughout England.

Economically, Britain led the world into the Industrial Age with her mills, factories, coal mines, and trains. By the time of Queen Victoria's reign (1837-1901), Britain was at its zenith of power, with a colonial empire that covered one-fifth of the world (for more on Victoria, see sidebar).

The 20th century was not kind to Britain. After decades of rebellion, Ireland finally gained its independence—except for the more Protestant north. Two world wars devastated Britain's population. The Nazi Blitz of World War II reduced much of London to rubble, although the freedom-loving world was inspired by Britain's determination to stand up to Hitler. Britain was rallied through difficult times by two leaders: Prime Minister Winston Churchill, a remarkable orator, and King George VI, who overcame a persistent stutter. After the war, the colonial empire dwindled to almost nothing, and Britain lost its superpower economic status.

One post-Empire hot spot—Northern Ireland, plagued by the "Troubles" between Catholics and Protestants—heated up, and then finally started cooling off. In the spring of 2007, the unthink-

Royal Families: Past and Present

Royal Lineage

802-1066	Saxon and Danish kings
1066-1154	Norman invasion (William the Conqueror), Norman kings
1154-1399	Plantagenet (kings with French roots)
1399-1461	Lancaster
1462-1485	York
1485-1603	Tudor (Henry VIII, Elizabeth I)
1603-1649	Stuart (civil war and beheading of Charles I)
1649-1653	Commonwealth, no royal head of state
1653-1659	Protectorate, with Cromwell as Lord Protector
1660-1714	Restoration of Stuart dynasty
1714-1901	Hanover (four Georges, William IV, Victoria)
1901-1910	Saxe-Coburg (Edward VII)
1910-present	Windsor (George V, Edward VIII, George VI, Elizabeth II)

The Royal Family Today

It seems you can't pick up a British newspaper without some mention of the latest event, scandal, or oddity involving the royal family. Here is the cast of characters:

Queen Elizabeth II wears the traditional crown of her great-great grandmother Victoria. Elizabeth's husband is Prince Philip, who's not considered king.

Their son, Prince Charles (the Prince of Wales), is next in line to become king. But it's Prince Charles' sons who generate the tabloid buzz. The older son, Prince William (b. 1982), is a graduate of Scotland's St. Andrews University and served as a search-and-rescue helicopter pilot with the Royal Air Force. In 2011, when William married Catherine "Kate" Middleton, the TV audience was estimated at one-quarter of the world's population—more than two billion people. Kate—a commoner he met at university—is now the Duchess of Cambridge and will eventually become Britain's queen. Their son, Prince George Alexander Louis, born in 2013, will ultimately succeed William as sovereign. (A conve-

able happened when leaders of the ultra-nationalist party sat down with those of the ultra-unionist party. London returned control of Northern Ireland to the popularly elected Northern Ireland Assembly. Perhaps most important of all, after almost 40 years, the British Army withdrew from Northern Ireland that summer.

The tradition (if not the substance) of greatness continues, niently timed change in the law ensured that William and Kate's firstborn would inherit the throne, regardless of gender.)

William's brother, redheaded Prince Harry (b. 1984), has mostly shaken his reputation as a bad boy: He's proved his mettle as a career soldier, completing a tour in Afghanistan, doing charity work in Africa, and serving as an Apache aircraft commander pilot with the Army Air Corps. Nonetheless, Harry's romances and high-wire party antics are popular tabloid topics.

For years, their parents' love life was also fodder for the British press: Charles' 1981 marriage to Princess Di, their bitter divorce, Diana's dramatic death in 1997, and the ongoing drama with Charles' longtime girlfriend—and now wife—Camilla Parker Bowles. Camilla, trying to gain the respect of the Queen and the public, doesn't call herself a princess—she uses the title Duchess of Cornwall. (And even when Charles becomes king, she will not be Queen Camilla—instead she plans to call herself the "Princess Consort.")

Charles' siblings are occasionally in the news: Princess Anne, Prince Andrew (who married and divorced Sarah "Fergie" Ferguson), and Prince Edward (who married Di look-alike Sophie Rhys-Jones).

Royal Sightseeing

You can see the trappings of royalty at Buckingham Palace (the Queen's London residence) with its Changing of the Guard; Kensington Palace—with a wing that's home to Will, Kate, and baby George, and a cottage that serves as Harry's bachelor pad—plus good exhibits on Victoria, William and Mary, and the Hanovers; Clarence House, the London home of Prince Charles and Camilla; Althorp Estate (80 miles from London), the childhood home and burial place of Princess Diana; Windsor Castle, a royal country home near London; and the crown jewels in the Tower of London.

Your best chances to actually see the Queen are on three public occasions: State Opening of Parliament (mid-May, next in 2015), Remembrance Sunday (early November, at the Cenotaph), or Trooping the Colour (one Saturday in mid-June, parading down Whitehall and at Buckingham Palace).

Otherwise, check the "Latest news and diary" section of www.royal.gov.uk, where you can search for future royal events.

presided over by Queen Elizabeth II, her husband, Prince Philip, and their son Prince Charles. With economic problems, the marital turmoil of Charles and Diana, Princess Di's untimely death, and a relentless popular press, the royal family has had a tough time over the past few decades. But the Queen has stayed above it all, and most British people still jump at an opportunity to see royalty.

With the worldwide hubbub surrounding the 2011 wedding of the Queen's grandson, Prince William, to commoner Kate Middleton, it was clear that the concept of royalty is still alive and well in the third millennium.(And, according to pollsters, just one-fifth of the Queen's subjects are in favor of abolishing the monarchy.)

In 2012, Queen Elizabeth marked her 60th year on the throne—her Diamond Jubilee. Only her great-great-grandmother, Queen Victoria (see sidebar on page 534), had a longer reign—but Elizabeth is on pace to overtake her in September of 2015. While many wonder who will succeed her—and when—the situation is straightforward: The Queen sees her job as a lifelong position, and legally, Charles (who wants to be king) cannot be skipped over for his son William. Given the longevity in the family (the Queen's mum, born in August of 1900, made it to the ripe old age of 101), Charles may be in for a long wait.

Architecture in Britain

From Stonehenge to Big Ben, travelers are storming castle walls, climbing spiral staircases, and snapping the pictures of 5,000 years of architecture. Let's sort it out.

The oldest ruins—mysterious and prehistoric—date from before Roman times back to 3000 B.C. The earliest sites, such as Stonehenge and Avebury, were built during the Stone and Bronze ages. The remains from these periods are made of huge stones or mounds of earth, even man-made hills, and were created as celestial calendars and for worship or burial. Britain is crisscrossed with imaginary lines said to connect these mysterious sights (ley lines). Iron Age people (600 B.C.-A.D. 50) left desolate stone forts. The Romans thrived in Britain from A.D. 50 to 400, building cities, walls, and roads. Evidence of Roman greatness can be seen in lavish villas with ornate mosaic floors, temples uncovered beneath great English churches, and Roman stones in medieval city walls. Roman roads sliced across the island in straight lines. Today, unusually straight rural roads are very likely laid directly on these ancient roads.

As Rome crumbled in the fifth century, so did Roman Britain. Little architecture survives from Dark Ages England, the Saxon period from 500 to 1000. Architecturally, the light was switched on with the Norman Conquest in 1066. As William earned his title "the Conqueror," his French architects built churches and castles in the European Romanesque style.

English Romanesque is called Norman (1066-1200). Norman churches had round arches, thick walls, and small windows; Durham Cathedral and the Chapel of St. John in the Tower of London are prime examples. The Tower of London, with its square

Mysterious Ruins

Inverness

CLAVA CAIRNS

SCOTLAND

= Prehistoric Sites
Major

Keswick • **CASTLERIGG**

W
A
L
E
S

ENGLAND

AVEBURY

London

Bath •

CERNE ABBAS GIANT

STONEHENGE

GLASTONBURY

SCORHILL

keep, small windows, and spiral stone stairways, is a typical Norman castle. You can see plenty of Norman castles around England—all built to secure the conquest of these invaders from Normandy.

Gothic architecture (1200-1600) replaced the heavy Norman style with light, vertical buildings, pointed arches, soaring spires, and bigger windows. English Gothic is divided into three stages. Early English Gothic (1200-1300) features tall, simple spires; beautifully carved capitals; and elaborate chapter houses (such as the Wells Cathedral). Decorated Gothic (1300-1400) gets fancier, with more elaborate tracery, bigger windows, and ornately carved pinnacles, as you see at Westminster Abbey. Finally, the Perpendicular Gothic style (1400-1600, also called "rectilinear") returns to square towers and emphasizes straight, uninterrupted vertical lines from ceiling to floor, with vast windows and exuberant decoration, including fan-vaulted ceilings (King's College Chapel at Cambridge). Through this evolution, the structural ribs (arches meeting at the top of the ceilings) became more and more decorative and fanciful (the most fancy being the star vaulting and fan vaulting of the Perpendicular style).

As you tour the great medieval churches of Britain, remember that almost everything is symbolic. For instance, on the tombs of knights, if the figure has crossed legs, he was a Crusader. If his feet rest on a dog, he died at home; but if his legs rest on a lion, he died in battle. Local guides and books help us modern pilgrims understand at least a little of what we see.

Wales is particularly rich in English castles, which were needed to subdue the stubborn Welsh. Edward I built a ring of powerful castles in North Wales, including Conwy and Caernarfon.

Gothic houses were a simple mix of woven strips of thin wood, rubble, and plaster called wattle and daub. The famous black-and-white Tudor (or "half-timbered") look came simply from filling in heavy oak frames with wattle and daub.

PAST & PRESENT

Typical Church Architecture

History comes to life when you visit a centuries-old church. Even if you wouldn't know your apse from a hole in the ground, learning a few simple terms will enrich your experience. Note that not every church has every feature, and that a "cathedral" isn't a type of church architecture, but rather a designation for a church that's a governing center for a local bishop.

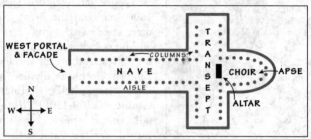

Aisles: The long, generally low-ceilinged arcades that flank the nave.

Altar: The raised area with a ceremonial table (often adorned with candles or a crucifix), where the priest prepares and serves the bread and wine for Communion.

Apse: The space beyond the altar, often bordered with small chapels.

Barrel Vault: A continuous round-arched ceiling that resembles an extended upside-down U.

Choir ("quire" in British English): A cozy area, often screened off, located within the church nave and near the high altar where services are sung in a more intimate setting.

Cloister: Covered hallways bordering a square or rectangular open-air courtyard, traditionally where monks and nuns got fresh air.

Facade: The exterior surface of the church's main (west) entrance, viewable from outside and usually highly decorated.

Groin Vault: An arched ceiling formed where two equal barrel vaults meet at right angles. Less common usage: term for a medieval jock strap.

Narthex: The area (portico or foyer) between the main entry and the nave.

Nave: The long, central section of the church (running west to east, from the entrance to the altar) where the congregation sits or stands through the service.

Transept: In a traditional cross-shaped floor plan, the transept is one of the two parts forming the "arms" of the cross. The transepts run north-south, perpendicularly crossing the east-west nave.

West Portal: The main entry to the church (on the west end, opposite the main altar).

The Tudor period (1485-1560) was a time of relative peace (the Wars of the Roses were finally over), prosperity, and renaissance. But when Henry VIII broke with the Catholic Church and disbanded its monasteries, scores of Britain's greatest churches were left as gutted shells. These hauntingly beautiful abbey ruins (Glastonbury, Tintern, Whitby, Rievaulx, Battle, St. Augustine's in Canterbury, St. Mary's in York, and lots more), surrounded by lush lawns, are now pleasant city parks.

Although few churches were built during the Tudor period, this was a time of house and mansion construction. Heating a home was becoming popular and affordable, and Tudor buildings featured small square windows and many chimneys. In towns, where land was scarce, many Tudor houses grew up and out, getting wider with each overhanging floor.

The Elizabethan and Jacobean periods (1560-1620) were followed by the English Renaissance style (1620-1720). English architects mixed Gothic and classical styles, then Baroque and classical styles. Although the ornate Baroque never really grabbed Britain, the classical style of the Italian architect Andrea Palladio did. Inigo Jones (1573-1652), Christopher Wren (1632-1723), and those they inspired plastered Britain with enough columns, domes, and symmetry to please a Caesar. The Great Fire of London (1666) cleared the way for an ambitious young Wren to put his mark on London forever with a grand rebuilding scheme, including the great St. Paul's Cathedral and more than 50 other churches.

The celebrants of the Boston Tea Party remember Britain's Georgian period (1720-1840) for its lousy German kings. But in architectural terms, "Georgian" is English for "Neoclassical." Its architecture was rich and showed off by being very classical. Grand ornamental doorways, fine cast-ironwork on balconies and railings, Chippendale furniture, and white-on-blue Wedgwood ceramics graced rich homes everywhere. John Wood Sr. and Jr. led the way, giving the trendsetting city of Bath its crescents and circles of aristocratic Georgian row houses.

The Industrial Revolution shaped the Victorian period (1840-1890) with glass, steel, and iron. Britain had a huge new erector set (so did France's Mr. Eiffel). This was also a Romantic period, reviving the "more Christian" Gothic style. London's Houses of Parliament are Neo-Gothic—they're just 140 years old but look 700, except for the telltale modern precision and craftsmanship. Whereas Gothic was stone or concrete, Neo-Gothic was often red brick. These were Britain's glory days, and there was more building in this period than in all previous ages combined.

The architecture of the mid-20th century obeyed the formula "form follows function"—it worried more about your needs than your eyes. But more recently, the dull "international style" has been

PAST & PRESENT

Typical Castle Architecture

Castles were fortified residences for medieval nobles. Castles come in all shapes and sizes, but knowing a few general terms will help you understand them.

The Keep (or Donjon): A high, strong stone tower in the center of the castle complex that was the lord's home and refuge of last resort.

Great Hall: The largest room in the castle, serving as throne room, conference center, and dining hall.

The Yard (or Bailey or Ward): An open courtyard inside the castle walls.

Loopholes: Narrow slits in the walls (also called embrasures, arrow slits, or arrow loops) through which soldiers could shoot arrows at the enemy.

Towers: Tall structures serving as lookouts, chapels, living quarters, or dungeons. Towers could be square or round, with either crenellated tops or conical roofs.

Turret: A small lookout tower projecting up from the top of the wall.

Moat: A ditch encircling the wall, often filled with water.

Motte-and-Bailey: A traditional form for early English castles, with a small fort on top of a hill (motte) next to an enclosed and fortified yard (bailey).

Wall Walk (or Allure): A pathway atop the wall where guards could patrol and where soldiers stood to fire at the enemy.

Parapet: Outer railing of the wall walk.

Crenellation: A gap-toothed pattern of stones atop the parapet.

Hoardings (or Gallery or Brattice): Wooden huts built onto the upper parts of the stone walls. They served as watch towers, living quarters, and fighting platforms.

nudged aside by a more playful style, thanks to cutting-edge architects such as Lord Norman Foster and Renzo Piano. In the last several years, London has added several creative buildings to its skyline: the City Hall (nicknamed "the Armadillo"), 30 St. Mary Axe ("the Gherkin"), and the tallest building in the European Union, the pointy Shard London Bridge (called...um, "the Shard").

Even as it sets trends for the 21st century, Britain treasures its heritage and takes great pains to build tastefully in historic districts and to preserve its many "listed" (government-protected) buildings. With a booming tourist trade, these quaint reminders of its past—and ours—are becoming a valuable part of the British economy.

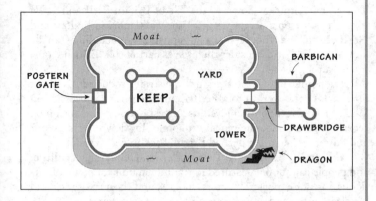

Machicolation: A stone ledge jutting out from the wall, fitted with holes in the bottom. If the enemy was scaling the walls, soldiers could drop rocks or boiling oil down through the holes and onto the enemy below.
Barbican: A fortified gatehouse, sometimes a stand-alone building located outside the main walls.
Drawbridge: A bridge that could be raised or lowered, using counterweights or a chain-and-winch.
Portcullis: A heavy iron grille that could be lowered across the entrance.
Postern Gate: A small, unfortified side or rear entrance used during peacetime. In wartime, it could become a "sally-port" used to launch surprise attacks, or as an escape route.

Britain Today

Regardless of the revolution we had 230-some years ago, many American travelers feel that they "go home" to Britain. This most popular tourist destination has a strange influence and power over us. The more you know of Britain's roots, the better you'll get in touch with your own.

WHAT'S SO GREAT ABOUT BRITAIN?

Geographically, the Isle of Britain is small (about the size of Uganda or Idaho)—600 miles long and 300 miles at its widest point (and just 75 miles at its narrowest). Similar in size to Louisiana, England occupies the southeastern part of Britain (with about 60 percent of its land and 80 percent of its population). England's highest mountain (Scafell Pike in the Lake District) is 3,206 feet, a foothill by our standards. The population is a fifth that of the United States. At its peak in the mid-1800s, Britain owned one-fifth of the world and accounted for more than half the planet's industrial output. Today, the Empire is down to the Isle of Britain itself and a few token, troublesome scraps, such as the Falklands, Gibraltar, and Northern Ireland (though many larger nations—including Canada and Australia—still consider themselves part of the "British Commonwealth").

Economically, Great Britain's industrial production is about 5 percent of the world's total. After emerging from a recession in 1992, Britain's economy enjoyed its longest period of expansion on record. But in 2008, the global economic slowdown, tight credit, and falling home prices pushed Britain back into a recession.

Culturally, Britain is still a world leader. Her heritage, culture, and people cannot be measured in traditional units of power. London is a major exporter of actors, movies, and theater; of rock and classical music; and of writers, painters, and sculptors.

Ethnically, the British Isles are a mix of the descendants of the early Celtic natives (in Scotland, Ireland, Wales, and Cornwall), the invading Anglo-Saxon "barbarians" who took southeast England in the Dark Ages, and the conquering Normans of the 11th century...not to mention more recent immigrants from around the world. Cynics call the United Kingdom an English Empire ruled by London, whose dominant Anglo-Saxon English (50 million) far outnumber their Celtic brothers and sisters (10 million).

Politically, Britain is ruled by the House of Commons, with some guidance from the mostly figurehead Queen and House of Lords. Just as the United States Congress is dominated by Democrats and Republicans, Britain's Parliament has traditionally been dominated by two parties: left-leaning Labour and right-leaning Conservative ("Tories"). But recently the center-left Liberal Democrats ("Lib Dems") have made inroads, and the current administration is a coalition between the Lib Dems and Tories.

Strangely, Britain's "constitution" is not one single document; the government's structures and policies are based on centuries of tradition, statutes, and doctrine, and much of it is not actually in writing. While this might seem potentially troublesome—if not dangerous—the British body politic takes pride in its ethos of civility and mutual respect, which has long made this arrangement work.

The prime minister is the chief executive. He or she is not elected directly by voters; rather, he or she assumes power as the head of the party that wins a majority in Parliamentary elections. In the interest of protocol, the Queen symbolically invites the winner to form a "government" (administration). Instead of imposing term limits, the Brits allow their prime ministers to choose when to leave office. The ruling party also gets to choose when to hold elections, as long as it's within five years of the previous one—so prime ministers carefully schedule elections for times that (they hope) their party will win. (Breaking with tradition, David Cameron's government announced their election date as soon as they took office: May 7, 2015.) When an election is announced, the Queen dissolves the Parliament so the parties can focus on a short-and-sweet, one-month campaign.

In the 1980s, Conservatives were in charge under Prime Minister Margaret Thatcher and Prime Minister John Major. As proponents of traditional, Victorian values—community, family, hard work, thrift, and trickle-down economics—they took a Reagan-esque approach to Britain's serious social and economic problems. In ending costly government subsidies to old-fashioned heavy industries, they caused many dated factories to close (earning working-class ire), but also nudged Britain toward a more 21st-century economy.

In 1997, a huge Labour victory brought Tony Blair to the prime ministership. Labour began shoring up a social-service system (health care, education, minimum wage) undercut by years of Conservative rule. Blair started out as a respected and well-liked PM, but his legacy became tarnished after he followed US President George W. Bush into war with Iraq. In 2007, Blair's Chancellor of the Exchequer and longtime colleague, Gordon Brown, succeeded him as prime minister. Elections in May of 2010 pitted a floundering Brown (who never achieved Blair's level of popularity) against a Conservative opponent, David Cameron, and a third-party Liberal Democrat challenger, Nick Clegg. No party won the number of seats needed for a majority, but the Conservatives and the Lib Dems formed a coalition government (the first since World War II)—vaulting David Cameron into the prime ministership. While Cameron's push for "austerity" (government-spending cutbacks) was initially met with approval, the promised results have not materialized; the election scheduled for May of 2015 will be a referendum on his approach.

In 2012, the Brits hosted two huge events: the Olympics and the Queen's Diamond Jubilee. The flurry of investment that swept Britain in the lead-up to that summer have left this already spruced-up country looking better than ever. This is the icing on top of a decades-long effort to rejuvenate some of Britain's former urban wastelands; cities like Liverpool and Cardiff have reclaimed their deserted, industrial waterfronts and converted them into hip, thriving people zones.

CURRENT CHALLENGES

From early 2008 to late 2009, the British economy shrank more than 6 percent—the largest decline since the Great Depression. Facing a huge—and growing—budget deficit, soon after his election Prime Minister Cameron announced an austerity program that dramatically cut back spending and increased the VAT (Value-Added Tax—the national sales tax) to 20 percent. The prime minister's budget eliminated more than 500,000 public-sector jobs, shortened long-term unemployment benefits to 12 months, imposed higher rents on public housing, slashed funding for the arts and the BBC, cut police services, and raised the retirement age to 66 by 2020. (Visitors might notice reduced bus schedules and unexpected closures of TIs or minor sights.) The initial result of these efforts was a double-dip recession (in 2012). The economy showed signs of recovery in 2014—but skeptics remain concerned that the growth isn't sustainable.

Other hot-button topics in Britain include terrorism, immigration, Scottish nationalism, and binge-drinking.

Like the US, Britain has been coping with its own string of terrorist threats and attacks. On the morning of July 7, 2005, London's commuters were rocked by four different bombs that killed dozens across the city. In the summer of 2006, authorities foiled a plot to carry liquid bombs onto a plane (resulting in the liquid ban air travelers are still experiencing today). On June 29, 2007, two car bombs were discovered (and defused) near London's Piccadilly Circus, and the next day, a flaming car drove into the baggage-claim level at Glasgow Airport. Most Brits have accepted that they now live with the possibility of terrorism at home—and that life must go on.

Britain has taken aggressive measures to prevent future attacks, such as installing CCTV (closed-circuit television) surveillance cameras everywhere, in both public and private places. (You'll frequently see signs warning you that you're being recorded.) As Brits trade their privacy for security, many wonder if they've given up too much.

The terrorist threats have also highlighted issues relating to Britain's large immigrant population (nearly 4 million). Three of the four suicide bombers responsible for the July 2005 attacks were second-generation Muslims, born in Britain. Some Brits reacted to the event known as "7/7" as if all the country's Muslims were to blame. At the same time, a handful of radical Islamic clerics attempted to justify the bombers' violent actions.

The large Muslim population is just one thread in the tapestry of today's Britain. While nine out of ten Brits are white, the country has large minority groups, mainly from Britain's former colonies: India, Pakistan, Bangladesh, Africa, the Caribbean, and many other places. Despite the tensions between some groups, for the most part Britain is relatively integrated, with minorities represented in most (if not all) walks of life.

But unemployment, the economic downturn, and cuts to programs for the working class have strained relations between communities within Britain. In August of 2011, London police shot and killed a young black man named Mark Duggan, inflaming tensions between the police and the black community. A peaceful protest against the police was followed by violent riots and looting. British society as a whole was left to grapple with its causes and social implications: Were the riots a sign of rising racial and economic tensions, or simply a chance for poor young people to grab a shiny new smartphone?

Throughout the British Isles, you'll also see many Eastern Europeans (mostly Poles, Slovaks, and Lithuanians) working in restaurants, cafés, and B&Bs. These transplants—who started arriving after their home countries joined the EU in 2004—can make a lot more money working here than back home. British small-business owners have found these new arrivals to be polite, responsible, and affordable. While a few Brits complain that the new arrivals are taking jobs away from the natives, and others are frustrated that their English can be far from perfect, for the most part Britain has absorbed this new set of immigrants gracefully.

Meanwhile Scottish nationalists have called for a vote on leaving the UK and becoming independent (but—like Canada and Australia—the Queen would remain Scotland's official head of state). Nationalists complain about the "shackles" of a London-based UK parliament and say that oil reserves would make Scotland rich. Opponents say the UK is one of the world's most successful political unions—and if the Scots leave, they would have to abandon the British pound and pay their "fair share" of the national debt.

In 2003, Tony Blair's Licensing Act deregulated alcohol sales and did away with the government-mandated 23:00 closing time for pubs. The goal was to encourage a lively, late-night café culture in Britain, but an unintended consequence has been an epidemic of binge-drinking among young people. A 2007 study revealed that one out of every three British men, and one out of every five British women, routinely drinks to excess. It's become commonplace for young adults (typically from their mid-teens to mid-20s) to spend weekend nights drinking at pubs and carousing in the streets. (And they ratchet up the debauchery even more when celebrating a "stag night" or "hen night"—bachelor and bachelorette parties.) While sociologists and politicians scratch their heads about this phenomenon, tourists are complaining about weekend noise and obnoxious (though generally harmless) young drunks on the streets.

PAST & PRESENT

BRITISH TV

Although it has its share of lowbrow reality programming, much British television is still so good—and so British—that it deserves a mention as a sightseeing treat. After a hard day of castle climbing, watch the telly over tea in the living room of your village B&B.

For many years there were only five free channels, but now nearly every British television can receive a couple dozen. BBC television is government-regulated and commercial-free. Broadcasting of its eight channels (and of the five BBC radio stations) is funded by a mandatory £145.50-per-year-per-household television and radio license (hmmm, 60 cents per day to escape commercials and public-broadcasting pledge drives...not bad). Channels 3, 4, and 5 are privately owned, are a little more lowbrow, and have commercials—but those "adverts" are often clever and sophisticated, providing a fun look at British life. About 60 percent of households pay for cable or satellite television.

Whereas California "accents" fill our airwaves 24 hours a day, homogenizing the way our country speaks, Britain protects and promotes its regional accents by its choice of TV and radio announcers. See if you can tell where each is from (or ask a local for help).

Commercial-free British TV, while looser than it used to be, is still careful about what it airs and when. But after the 21:00 "watershed" hour, when children are expected to be in bed, some nudity and profanity are allowed, and may cause you to spill your tea.

American programs (such as *Game of Thrones, CSI, Friends, Frasier, How I Met Your Mother, The Simpsons, Family Guy,* and trash-talk shows) are very popular. But the visiting viewer should be sure to tune the TV to more typically British shows, including a dose of British situation- and political-comedy fun, and the top-notch BBC evening news. British comedies have tickled the American funny bone for years, from sketch comedy *(Monty Python's Flying Circus)* to sitcoms *(Are You Being Served?, Fawlty Towers, Absolutely Fabulous,* and *The Office).* Quiz shows and reality shows are taken very seriously here *(American Idol, America's Got Talent, Dancing with the Stars, Who Wants to Be a Millionaire?,* and *The X Factor* are all based on British shows). Jonathan Ross is the David Letterman of Britain for sometimes edgy late-night talk. Other popular late-night "chat show" hosts include Graham Norton and Alan Carr. For a tear-filled, slice-of-life taste of British soaps dealing in all the controversial issues, see the popular and remarkably long-running *Emmerdale, Coronation Street,* or *EastEnders.* The costume drama *Downton Abbey,* the long-running sci-fi serial *Doctor Who,* and the small-town dramedy *Doc Martin* have all become hits on both sides of the Atlantic.

NOTABLE BRITS OF TODAY AND TOMORROW

Only history can judge which British names will stand the test of time, but these days big names in the UK include politicians (David Cameron, Nick Clegg, Ed Miliband), actors (Helen Mirren, Emma Thompson, Helena Bonham Carter, Jude Law, Stephen Fry, Ricky Gervais, Robert Pattinson, Daniel Radcliffe, Kate Winslet), musicians (Adele, Chris Martin of Coldplay, James Arthur, Emeli Sandé), writers (J. K. Rowling, Hilary Mantel, Tom Stoppard, Nick Hornby, Ian McEwan, Zadie Smith), artists (Damien Hirst, Rachel Whiteread, Tracey Emin, Anish Kapoor), athletes (David Beckham, Bradley Wiggins), entrepreneurs (Sir Richard Branson, Lord Alan Sugar)...and, of course, William, Kate, and their boy George.

For more about British history, consider Europe 101: History and Art for the Traveler *by Rick Steves and Gene Openshaw, available at* www.ricksteves.com.

PRACTICALITIES

Contents

This chapter covers the practical skills of European travel: how to get tourist information, pay for purchases, sightsee efficiently, use technology wisely, and get between destinations smoothly. To study ahead and round out your knowledge, check out "Resources" for a summary of recommended books and films.

Tourist Information

London has a fine tourist information office, called the **City of London Information Centre,** near St. Paul's Cathedral (see page 18). Note that tourist information offices are abbreviated "TI" in this book. TIs are good places to get a city map, advice on public transportation (including bus and train schedules), walking-tour information, tips on special events, and recommendations for nightlife. For all the help TIs offer, steer clear of their room-finding services (bloated prices, booking fee up to £4, no opinions, and they take a 10 percent cut from your B&B host).

Websites: Start with the TI's official website, www. visitlondon.com. Other helpful sites are www.timeout.com/london

and www.londontown.com. For information on London and beyond, try www.visitbritain.com.

Travel Tips

Emergency and Medical Help: In Britain, dial 999 for police help or a medical emergency. If you get sick, do as the Brits do and go to a pharmacist for advice. Or ask at your hotel for help—they know of the nearest medical and emergency services. St. Thomas' Hospital, across the river from Big Ben, has a fine reputation.

Theft or Loss: To replace a passport, you'll need to go in person to a US embassy (see page 583). If your credit and debit cards disappear, cancel and replace them (see "Damage Control for Lost Cards" on page 561). File a police report, either on the spot or within a day or two; you'll need it to submit an insurance claim for lost or stolen rail passes or travel gear, and it can help with replacing your passport or credit and debit cards. For more information, see www.ricksteves.com/help. Precautionary measures can minimize the effects of loss—back up your digital photos and other files frequently.

Time Zones: Britain, which is one hour earlier than most of continental Europe, is five/eight hours ahead of the East/West Coasts of the US. The exceptions are the beginning and end of Daylight Saving Time: Britain and Europe "spring forward" the last Sunday in March (two weeks after most of North America), and "fall back" the last Sunday in October (one week before North America). For a handy online time converter, see www.timeanddate.com/worldclock.

Business Hours: Most stores are open Monday through Saturday (roughly 10:00-17:00), with a late night on Wednesday or Thursday (until 19:00 or 20:00), depending on the neighborhood. On Sunday, when some stores are closed, many street markets are lively with shoppers.

Watt's Up? Britain's electrical system is 220 volts, instead of North America's 110 volts. Most newer electronics (such as laptops, battery chargers, and hair dryers) convert automatically, so you won't need a converter, but you will need an adapter plug with three square prongs, sold inexpensively at travel stores in the US. Avoid bringing older appliances that don't automatically convert voltage; instead, buy a cheap replacement in Britain. Low-cost hairdryers and other small appliances are sold at Superdrug and Boots (ask your hotelier for the closest branch). Or pop into a London department store (see the London shopping chapter).

Discounts: Discounts (called "concessions" or "concs" in Britain) are not listed in this book. However, many sights, buses, and trains offer discounts to youths (up to age 18), students (with

PRACTICALITIES

Exchange Rate

1 British pound (£1) = about $1.60

While the euro (€) is now the currency of most of Europe, Britain is sticking with its pound sterling. The British pound (£), also called a "quid," is broken into 100 pence (p). Pence means "cents." You'll find coins ranging from 1p to £2 and bills from £5 to £50. Fake pound coins are easy to spot (real coins have an inscription on their outside rims; the fakes look like tree bark).

To convert prices from pounds to dollars, add about 60 percent: £20 = about $32, £50 = about $80. (Check www.oanda.com for the latest exchange rates.) London is so expensive that some travelers try to kid themselves that pounds are dollars. But when they get home, that £1,000-pound Visa bill isn't asking for $1,000...it wants around $1,600.

proper identification cards, www.isic.org), families, seniors (loosely defined as retirees or those willing to call themselves seniors), and groups of 10 or more. Always ask. Some discounts are available only for citizens of the European Union (EU).

Money

This section offers advice on how to pay for purchases on your trip (including getting cash from ATMs and paying with plastic), dealing with lost or stolen cards, VAT (sales tax) refunds, and tipping.

WHAT TO BRING

Bring both a credit card and a debit card. You'll use the debit card at cash machines (ATMs) to withdraw local cash for most purchases, and the credit card to pay for larger items. Some travelers carry a third card, in case one gets demagnetized or eaten by a temperamental machine.

For an emergency stash, bring several hundred dollars in hard cash in $20 bills. If you need to exchange the bills, go to a bank; avoid using currency-exchange booths because of their lousy rates and/or outrageous fees.

CASH

Cash is just as desirable in Britain as it is at home. Small businesses (B&Bs, mom-and-pop cafés, shops, etc.) prefer that you pay your bills with cash. Some vendors will charge you extra for using a credit card, and some won't take credit cards at all. Cash is the best—and sometimes only—way to pay for cheap food, bus fare, taxis, and local guides.

Throughout Britain, ATMs are the standard way for travelers to get cash. To withdraw money from an ATM (known as a "cash-point"), you'll need a debit card (ideally with a Visa or MasterCard logo for maximum usability), plus a PIN code. Know your PIN code in numbers; there are only numbers—no letters—on European keypads. For increased security, shield the keypad when entering your PIN code, and don't use an ATM if anything on the front of the machine looks loose or damaged (a sign that someone may have attached a "skimming" device to capture account information). Try to withdraw large sums of money to reduce the number of per-transaction bank fees you'll pay.

Stay away from "independent" ATMs such as Travelex, Euronet, Moneybox, Cardpoint, and Cashzone, which charge huge commissions, have terrible exchange rates, and may try to trick users with "dynamic currency conversion" (described at the end of "Credit and Debit Cards," next). Instead, when possible, use ATMs located outside banks—a thief is less likely to target a cash machine near surveillance cameras, and if your card is munched by a machine, you can go inside for help.

Although you can use a credit card for an ATM transaction, it only makes sense in an emergency, because it's considered a cash advance (borrowed at a high interest rate) rather than a withdrawal.

While traveling, if you want to monitor your accounts online to detect any unauthorized transactions, be sure to use a secure connection (see page 576).

Even in jolly olde England, pickpockets target tourists. To safeguard your cash, wear a money belt—a pouch with a strap that you buckle around your waist like a belt and tuck under your clothes. Keep your cash, credit cards, and passport secure in your money belt, and carry only a day's spending money in your front pocket.

CREDIT AND DEBIT CARDS

For purchases, Visa and MasterCard are more commonly accepted than American Express. Just like at home, credit or debit cards work easily at larger hotels, restaurants, and shops. I typically use my debit card to withdraw cash to pay for most purchases. I use my credit card only in a few specific situations: to book hotel reservations by phone, to cover major expenses (such as car rentals, plane tickets, and long hotel stays), and to pay for things near the end of my trip (to avoid another visit to the ATM). While you could use a debit card to make most large purchases, using a credit card offers a greater degree of fraud protection (because debit cards draw funds directly from your account).

Ask Your Credit- or Debit-Card Company: Before your trip, contact the company that issued your debit or credit cards.

• Confirm that your **card will work overseas,** and alert them that you'll be using it in Europe; otherwise, they may deny transactions if they perceive unusual spending patterns.

• Ask for the specifics on transaction **fees.** When you use your credit or debit card—either for purchases or ATM withdrawals—you'll typically be charged additional "international transaction" fees of up to 3 percent (1 percent is normal) plus $5 per transaction. If your card's fees seem high, consider getting a different card just for your trip: Capital One (www.capitalone.com) and most credit unions have low-to-no international fees.

• If you plan to withdraw cash from ATMs, confirm your daily **withdrawal limit,** and if necessary, ask your bank to adjust it. Some travelers prefer a high limit that allows them to take out more cash at each ATM stop (saving on bank fees), while others prefer to set a lower limit in case their card is stolen. Note that foreign banks also set withdrawal limits for their ATMs (£300 is usually the maximum).

• Get your bank's emergency **phone number** in the US (but not its 800 number, which isn't accessible from overseas) to call collect if you have a problem.

• Ask for your credit card's **PIN** in case you need to make an emergency cash withdrawal or encounter Europe's "chip-and-PIN" system; the bank won't tell you your PIN over the phone, so allow time for it to be mailed to you.

Chip and PIN: Europeans are increasingly using chip-and-PIN cards, which are embedded with an electronic security chip (in addition to the magnetic stripe found on American-style cards). To make a purchase with a chip-and-PIN card, the cardholder inserts the card into a slot in the payment machine, then enters a PIN (like using a debit card in the US) while the card stays in the slot. The chip inside the card authorizes the transaction; the cardholder doesn't sign a receipt. Your American-style card might not work at payment machines using this system, such as those at train and subway stations, toll roads, parking garages, luggage lockers, bike-rental kiosks, and self-serve gas pumps.

If you have problems using your American card in a chip-and-PIN machine, here are some suggestions: For either a debit card or a credit card, try entering that card's PIN when prompted. (Note that your credit-card PIN may not be the same as your debit-card PIN; you'll need to ask your bank for your credit-card PIN.) If your cards still don't work, look for a machine that takes cash, seek out a clerk who might be able to process the transaction manually, or ask a local if you can pay them cash to run the transaction on their card.

And don't panic. Many travelers who use only magnetic-stripe cards don't run into problems. Still, it pays to carry plenty of pounds sterling; remember, you can always use an ATM to withdraw cash with your magnetic-stripe debit card.

If you're still concerned, you can apply for a chip card in the US (though I think it's overkill). One option is the no-annual-fee GlobeTrek Visa, offered by Andrews Federal Credit Union in Maryland (open to all US residents; see www.andrewsfcu.org). In the future, chip cards should become standard issue in the US: Visa and MasterCard have asked US banks and merchants to use chip-based cards by late 2015.

Dynamic Currency Conversion: If merchants offer to convert your purchase price into dollars (called dynamic currency conversion, or DCC), refuse this "service." You'll pay even more in fees for the expensive convenience of seeing your charge in dollars. "Independent" ATMs (such as Travelex and Moneybox) may try to confuse customers by presenting DCC in misleading terms. If an ATM offers to "lock in" or "guarantee" your conversion rate, choose "proceed without conversion." Other prompts might state, "You can be charged in dollars: Press YES for dollars, NO for GBP." Always choose the local currency in these situations.

DAMAGE CONTROL FOR LOST CARDS

If you lose your credit, debit, or ATM card, you can stop people from using your card by reporting the loss immediately to the respective global customer-assistance centers. Call these 24-hour US numbers collect: Visa (tel. 303/967-1096), MasterCard (tel. 636/722-7111), and American Express (tel. 336/393-1111). In Britain, to make a collect call to the US, dial 0-800-89-0011. Press zero or stay on the line for an operator. European toll-free numbers (listed by country) can be found at the websites for Visa and MasterCard. Diner's Club has offices in Britain (tel. 0845-862-2937) and the US (tel. 514/877-1577, call collect).

Providing the following information will allow for a quicker cancellation of your missing card: full card number, whether you are the primary or secondary cardholder, the cardholder's name exactly as printed on the card, billing address, home phone number, circumstances of the loss or theft, and identification verification (your birth date, your mother's maiden name, or your Social Security number—memorize this, don't carry a copy). If you are the secondary cardholder, you'll also need to provide the primary cardholder's identification-verification details. You can generally receive a temporary card within two or three business days in Europe (see www.ricksteves.com/help for more).

If you report your loss within two days, you typically won't be responsible for any unauthorized transactions on your account, although many banks charge a liability fee of $50.

TIPPING

Tipping in Britain isn't as automatic and generous as it is in the US. For special service, tips are appreciated, but not expected. As in the US, the proper amount depends on your resources, tipping philosophy, and the circumstances, but some general guidelines apply.

Restaurants: At pubs where you order at the counter, you don't have to tip. (Regular customers ordering a round sometimes say, "Add one for yourself" as a tip for drinks ordered at the bar—but this isn't expected.) At a pub or restaurant with waitstaff, check the menu or your bill to see if the service is included (generally 10-12.5 percent); if not, tip about 10 percent. (For more information, see page 407 in the Eating in London chapter.)

Taxis: To tip the cabbie, round up. For a typical ride, round up your fare a bit (for instance, if the fare is £4.50, pay £5). If the cabbie hauls your bags and zips you to the airport to help you catch your flight, you might want to toss in a little more. But if you feel like you're being driven in circles or otherwise ripped off, skip the tip.

Services: In general, if someone in the service industry does a super job for you, a tip of a pound or so is appropriate...but not required. If you're not sure whether (or how much) to tip for a service, ask your hotelier or the TI.

GETTING A VAT REFUND

Wrapped into the purchase price of your British souvenirs is a Value-Added Tax (VAT) of about 20 percent. You're entitled to get most of that tax back if you purchase more than £30 (about $48) worth of goods at a store that participates in the VAT-refund scheme (although individual stores can require that you spend more—Harrods, for example, won't process a refund unless you spend £50). Typically, you must ring up the minimum at a single retailer—you can't add up your purchases from various shops to reach the required amount.

Getting your refund is usually straightforward and, if you buy a substantial amount of souvenirs, well worth the hassle. If you're lucky, the merchant will subtract the tax when you make your purchase. (This is more likely to occur if the store ships the goods to your home.) Otherwise, you'll need to:

Get the paperwork. Have the merchant completely fill out the necessary refund document (either an official VAT customs form, or the shop or refund company's own version of it). The newest ones look like a long receipt. You'll have to present your passport at the store. Get the paperwork done before you leave the shop to ensure you'll have everything you need (including your original sales receipt).

Get your stamp at the border or airport. Process your VAT document at your last stop in the European Union (such as at the airport) with the customs agent who deals with VAT refunds. Arrive an additional hour early before you need to check in for your flight to allow time to find the local customs office—and to stand in line. It's best to keep your purchases in your carry-on. If they're too large or dangerous to carry on (such as knives), pack them in your checked bags and alert the check-in agent. You'll be sent (with your tagged bag) to a customs desk outside security, which will examine your bag, stamp your paperwork, and put your bag on the belt. You're not supposed to use your purchased goods before you leave. If you show up at customs wearing your new Wellingtons, officials might look the other way—or deny you a refund.

Collect your refund. You'll need to return your stamped document to the retailer or its representative. Many merchants work with a service that has offices at major airports, ports, or border crossings (at Heathrow, Travelex counters and customs desks are located before and after security in terminals 1-5). These services, which extract a 4 percent fee, can refund your money immediately in cash or credit your card (within two billing cycles). If the retailer handles VAT refunds directly, it's up to you to contact the merchant for your refund. You can mail the documents from home, or more quickly, from your point of departure (using an envelope you've prepared in advance or one that's been provided by the merchant). You'll then have to wait—it can take months.

CUSTOMS FOR AMERICAN SHOPPERS

You are allowed to take home $800 worth of items per person duty-free, once every 30 days. You can also bring in duty-free a liter of alcohol. As for food, you can take home many processed and packaged foods: vacuum-packed cheeses, dried herbs, jams, baked goods, candy, chocolate, oil, vinegar, mustard, and honey. Fresh fruits and vegetables and most meats are not allowed. However, canned meat is allowed if it doesn't contain any beef, veal, lamb, or mutton. Any liquid-containing foods must be packed in checked luggage, a potential recipe for disaster. To check customs rules and duty rates, visit www.cbp.gov.

Sightseeing

Sightseeing can be hard work. Use these tips to make your visits to London's finest sights meaningful, fun, efficient, and painless.

PLAN AHEAD

Set up an itinerary that allows you to fit in all your must-see sights. For a one-stop look at opening hours, see "London at a Glance" on page 48; also see the "Daily Reminder" on page 20. Most sights keep stable hours, but you can easily confirm the latest by checking with the TI or visiting museum websites.

Don't put off visiting a must-see sight—you never know when a place will close unexpectedly for a holiday, strike, or royal audience. Many museums are closed or have reduced hours at least a few days a year, especially on holidays such as Christmas, New Year's, and Bank Holiday Mondays in May and August. A list of holidays is on page 584; check museum websites for possible closures during your trip. Off-season, many museums have shorter hours.

Going at the right time helps avoid crowds. This book offers tips on the best times to see specific sights. Try visiting popular sights very early or very late. Evening visits are usually peaceful, with fewer crowds. In addition to the London Eye, at least one major London sight is open late every night (see the sidebar on page 76).

Study up. To get the most out of the self-guided tours and sight descriptions in this book, read them before you visit. The British Museum rocks if you understand the significance of the Rosetta Stone.

AT SIGHTS
Here's what you can typically expect:

Entering: Be warned that you may not be allowed to enter if you arrive 30 to 60 minutes before closing time. And guards start ushering people out well before the actual closing time, so don't save the best for last.

Some important sights have a security check, where you must open your bag or send it through a metal detector. Some sights require you to check daypacks and coats. (If you'd rather not check your daypack, try carrying it tucked under your arm like a purse as you enter.)

Admission Charges: Several major London museums are free, but they ask for a donation (which is completely optional). I see it as a good way to get rid of loose change while helping the arts. Admission at a half-dozen or so museums (identified in their sight listings in this book) includes a "voluntary donation" of about 10 percent, which is automatically tacked on. At these sights, the price you see posted includes the donation—and it is perfectly OK to ask to pay the price without the donation. At ticket desks, you'll see references to "Gift Aid"—a tax-deduction scheme that benefits museums—but this only concerns British taxpayers.

Photography: If the museum's photo policy isn't clearly posted, ask a guard. Generally, taking photos without a flash or tripod is allowed. Some sights ban photos altogether.

Special Exhibits: Museums may show special exhibits in addition to their permanent collection. An extra fee, which may not be optional, might be assessed for these shows.

Expect Changes: Artwork can be on tour, on loan, out sick, or shifted at the whim of the curator. To adapt, pick up a floor plan as you enter, and ask museum staff if you can't find a particular item.

Audioguides, Tours, and Videos: Many sights rent audioguides, which generally offer excellent recorded descriptions (about £4). If you bring your own earbuds, you can enjoy better sound and avoid holding the device to your ear. To save money, bring a Y-jack and share one audioguide with your travel partner. Increasingly, museums are offering apps (often free) that you can download to your mobile device. And I've produced free downloadable audio tours of the major sights in London; see page 8.

Guided tours are most likely to occur during peak season (usually £3-8 and widely ranging in quality). Some sights also run short introductory videos featuring their highlights and history. These are generally well worth your time and a great place to start your visit.

Services: Important sights and cathedrals may have an on-site café or cafeteria. These are an efficient way to rejuvenate during a long visit—try a cheap "cream tea" to pick up your energy in midafternoon, like Brits do. The WCs at sights are free and generally nearly always clean.

Before Leaving: At the gift shop, scan the postcard rack or thumb through a guidebook to be sure that you haven't overlooked something that you'd like to see.

Every sight or museum offers more than what is covered in this book. Use the information in this book as an introduction—not the final word.

SIGHTSEEING PASSES

The following sightseeing passes are sold online and at the City of London Information Centre, just south of St. Paul's Cathedral; see page 18.

The **London Pass,** which covers many big sights and lets you skip some lines, is expensive but potentially worth the investment for extremely busy sightseers (£47/1 day, £65/2 days, £78/3 days, £104/6 days; days are calendar days rather than 24-hour periods; comes with 160-page guidebook, also sold at major train stations and airports, tel. 0870-242-9988, www.londonpass.com). Among the many sights it includes are the Tower of London, Westminster Abbey, Churchill War Rooms, and Windsor Castle, as well as many temporary exhibits and audioguides at otherwise "free" biggies. Think through your sightseeing plans, study their website to see what's covered, and do the math before you buy.

The **English Heritage** society sells passes and memberships that include free entry to its 400 sights (which are exclusive to England); they're worth it only if you'll be thoroughly exploring England, not just London. You can buy passes or memberships at any participating sight. For most travelers, the Overseas Visitor Pass is a better choice than the pricier one-year membership (Visitor Pass: £25/9 days, £30/16 days, discounts for couples and families, www.english-heritage.org.uk/ovp; membership: £48 for one person, £84 for two, discounts for seniors and students, children under 19 free, www.english-heritage.org.uk/membership; tel. 0870-333-1181).

Communicating

"How can I stay connected in Europe?"—by phone and Internet—may be the most common question I hear from travelers. You have three basic options:

1. "Roam" with your US smartphone. This is the easiest option, but likely the most expensive. It works best for people who won't be making very many calls or using the Internet much, and who value the convenience of sticking with what's familiar (and their own phone number). In recent years, as data roaming fees have dropped and free Wi-Fi has become easier to find, the majority of travelers are finding this to be the best all-around option.

2. Use an unlocked mobile phone with European SIM cards. This is a much more affordable option if you'll be making lots of calls, since it gives you 24/7 access to cheap European rates. Although remarkably cheap, this option does require a willingness to grapple with the technology and do a bit of shopping around for the right phone and card. Savvy travelers who routinely use SIM cards swear by them.

3. Use public phones and get online at your hotel or at Internet cafés. These options can work in a pinch, particularly for travelers who simply don't want to hassle with the technology, or want to be (mostly) untethered from their home life while on the road.

Each of these options is explained in greater detail in the following pages. Mixing and matching works well. For example, I routinely bring along my smartphone for Internet chores and Skyping on Wi-Fi, but also carry an unlocked phone and buy cheap SIM cards for affordable calls on the go.

For an even more in-depth explanation of this complicated topic, see www.ricksteves.com/phoning.

HOW TO DIAL
Many Americans are intimidated by dialing European phone numbers. You needn't be. It's simple, once you break the code.

The English Accent

In the olden days, an English person's accent indicated his or her social standing. Eliza Doolittle had the right idea—elocution could make or break you. Wealthier families would send their kids to fancy private schools to learn proper pronunciation. But these days, in a sort of reverse snobbery that has gripped the nation, accents are back. Politicians, newscasters, and movie stars are favoring deep accents over the Queen's English. While it's hard for American ears to pick out all of the variations, most English people can determine where a person is from based on their accent...not just the region, but often the village, and even the part of a town.

Dialing Within Britain

The following instructions apply whether you're dialing from a British mobile phone or a landline (such as a pay phone or your hotel-room phone). If you're roaming with a US phone number, follow the "Dialing Internationally" directions described later.

Britain, like the US, uses an area-code dialing system. To make domestic calls anywhere within Britain, punch in just the phone number if you're dialing locally, and add the area code (which starts with a 0) if calling long distance.

Area codes are listed (with phone numbers) in this book, displayed by city on phone-booth walls, and available from directory assistance (dial 118-500, (£0.59/minute). It's most expensive to call within Britain between 8:00 and 13:00, and cheapest between 17:00 and 8:00. Still, a short call across the country is inexpensive, so don't hesitate to call long distance.

Certain phone numbers don't have area codes. For example, numbers beginning with 074, 075, 076, 077, 078, and 079 are mobile numbers, which are more expensive to call than a landline. Numbers starting with 080 are toll-free, but those beginning with 084, 087, or 03 are inexpensive toll numbers (£0.10/minute maximum from a landline, £0.20-40/minute from a mobile). Numbers beginning with 09 are pricey toll lines. If you have questions about a prefix, call 100 for free help.

Dialing Internationally

Always start with the **international access code**—011 if you're calling from the US or Canada, 00 from anywhere in Europe. If you're dialing from a mobile phone, simply insert a + instead (by holding the 0 key).

• Dial the **country code** of the country you're calling (44 for Britain, or 1 for the US or Canada).

• Then dial the area code (London's area code is 020—drop the initial zero if you're calling from outside Britain) and the local number. The European calling chart lists specifics per country.

Calling from the US to Britain: To call a recommended London hotel from the US, dial 011 (US access code), 44 (Britain's country code), then 7730-8191 (the hotel's number).

Calling from any European country to the US: To call my office in Edmonds, Washington, from anywhere in Europe, I dial 00 (Europe's access code), 1 (US country code), 425 (Edmonds' area code), and 771-8303.

More Dialing Tips

The chart on the next page shows how to dial per country. For online instructions, see www.countrycallingcodes.com or www.howtocallabroad.com.

If you're using a mobile phone, dial as if you're in that phone's country of origin. So, when roaming with your US phone number in Britain, dial as if you're calling from the US. But if you're using a British SIM card, dial as you would from Britain.

Note that calls to a European mobile phone are substantially more expensive than calls to a fixed line. Off-hour calls are generally cheaper.

USING YOUR AMERICAN SMARTPHONE IN EUROPE

Even in this age of email, texting, and near-universal Internet access, smart travelers still use the telephone. I call TIs to smooth out sightseeing plans, hotels to get driving directions, museums to confirm tour schedules, restaurants to check open hours or to book a table, and so on.

Most people enjoy the convenience of bringing their own smartphone. Horror stories about sky-high roaming fees are dated and exaggerated, and major service providers work hard to avoid surprising you with an exorbitant bill. With a little planning, you can use your phone—for voice calls, messaging, and Internet access—without breaking the bank.

Start by figuring out whether your phone works in Europe. Most phones purchased through AT&T and T-Mobile (which use the same technology as Europe) work abroad, while only some phones from Verizon or Sprint do—check your operating manual (look for "tri-band," "quad-band," or "GSM"). If you're not sure, ask your service provider.

Types of Roaming

"Roaming" with your phone—that is, using it outside of its home region, such as in Europe—generally comes with extra charges, whether you are making voice calls, sending texts, or reading your email. The fees listed here are for the three major American providers—Verizon, AT&T, and T-Mobile; Sprint's roaming rates tend to be much higher. But policies change fast, so get the latest details before your trip. For example, as of mid-2014, T-Mobile waived voice and data roaming fees for some plans.

Voice calls are the most expensive. Most providers charge from $1.29 to $1.99 per minute to make or receive calls in Europe. (As you cross each border, you'll typically get a text message explaining the rates in the new country.) If you plan to make multiple calls, look into a global calling plan to lower the per-minute cost, or buy a package of minutes at a discounted price (such as 30 minutes for $30). Note that you'll be charged for incoming calls whether or not you answer them; to save money ask your friends to stay in contact by texting, and to call you only in case of an emergency.

Text messaging costs 20 to 50 cents per text. To cut that cost, you could sign up for an international messaging plan (for example, $10 for 100 texts). Or consider apps that let you text for free (iMessage for Apple, Google Talk for Android, or WhatsApp for any device); however, these require you to use Wi-Fi or data roaming. Be aware that Europeans use the term "SMS" ("short message service") to describe text messaging.

Data roaming means accessing an Internet signal that's carried over the cellular telephone network. Prices have dropped dramatically in recent years, making this an affordable way to bridge gaps between Wi-Fi hotspots. You'll pay far less if you set up an international data roaming plan. Most providers charge $25-30 for 100-120 megabytes of data. That's plenty for basic Internet tasks—100 megabytes lets you view 100 websites or send/receive 1,000 text-based emails, but you'll burn through that amount quickly by streaming videos or music. If your data use exceeds your plan amount, most providers will automatically kick in an additional 100- or 120-megabyte block for the same price. (For more on Wi-Fi versus data roaming—including strategies for conserving your data—see "Using Wi-Fi and Data Roaming," later.)

Setting Up (or Disabling) International Service

With most service providers, international roaming (voice, text, and data) is disabled on your account unless you call to activate it. Before your trip, call your provider (or navigate their website), and cover the following topics:

• Confirm that your phone will work in Europe.

• Verify global roaming rates for voice calls, text messaging, and data.

• Tell them which of those services you'd like to activate.

• Consider any add-on plans to bring down the cost of international calls, texts, or data roaming.

PRACTICALITIES

European Calling Chart

Just smile and dial, using this key:
AC = Area Code, LN = Local Number.

European Country	Calling long distance within ...	Calling from the US or Canada to ...	Calling from a European country to ...
Austria	AC + LN	011 + 43 + AC (without initial zero) + LN	00 + 43 + AC (without initial zero) + LN
Belgium	LN	011 + 32 + LN (without initial zero)	00 + 32 + LN (without initial zero)
Bosnia-Herzegovina	AC + LN	011 + 387 + AC (without initial zero) + LN	00 + 387 + AC (without initial zero) + LN
Britain	AC + LN	011 + 44 + AC (without initial zero) + LN	00 + 44 + AC (without initial zero) + LN
Croatia	AC + LN	011 + 385 + AC (without initial zero) + LN	00 + 385 + AC (without initial zero) + LN
Czech Republic	LN	011 + 420 + LN	00 + 420 + LN
Denmark	LN	011 + 45 + LN	00 + 45 + LN
Estonia	LN	011 + 372 + LN	00 + 372 + LN
Finland	AC + LN	011 + 358 + AC (without initial zero) + LN	999 (or other 900 number) + 358 + AC (without initial zero) + LN
France	LN	011 + 33 + LN (without initial zero)	00 + 33 + LN (without initial zero)
Germany	AC + LN	011 + 49 + AC (without initial zero) + LN	00 + 49 + AC (without initial zero) + LN
Gibraltar	LN	011 + 350 + LN	00 + 350 + LN
Greece	LN	011 + 30 + LN	00 + 30 + LN
Hungary	06 + AC + LN	011 + 36 + AC + LN	00 + 36 + AC + LN
Ireland	AC + LN	011 + 353 + AC (without initial zero) + LN	00 + 353 + AC (without initial zero) + LN
Italy	LN	011 + 39 + LN	00 + 39 + LN

European Country	Calling long distance within ...	Calling from the US or Canada to ...	Calling from a European country to ...
Latvia	LN	011 + 371 + LN	00 + 371 + LN
Montenegro	AC + LN	011 + 382 + AC (without initial zero) + LN	00 + 382 + AC (without initial zero) + LN
Morocco	LN	011 + 212 + LN (without initial zero)	00 + 212 + LN (without initial zero)
Netherlands	AC + LN	011 + 31 + AC (without initial zero) + LN	00 + 31 + AC (without initial zero) + LN
Norway	LN	011 + 47 + LN	00 + 47 + LN
Poland	LN	011 + 48 + LN	00 + 48 + LN
Portugal	LN	011 + 351 + LN	00 + 351 + LN
Russia	8 + AC + LN	011 + 7 + AC + LN	00 + 7 + AC + LN
Slovakia	AC + LN	011 + 421 + AC (without initial zero) + LN	00 + 421 + AC (without initial zero) + LN
Slovenia	AC + LN	011 + 386 + AC (without initial zero) + LN	00 + 386 + AC (without initial zero) + LN
Spain	LN	011 + 34 + LN	00 + 34 + LN
Sweden	AC + LN	011 + 46 + AC (without initial zero) + LN	00 + 46 + AC (without initial zero) + LN
Switzerland	LN	011 + 41 + LN (without initial zero)	00 + 41 + LN (without initial zero)
Turkey	AC (if there's no initial zero, add one) + LN	011 + 90 + AC (without initial zero) + LN	00 + 90 + AC (without initial zero) + LN

PRACTICALITIES

- The instructions above apply whether you're calling to or from a European landline or mobile phone.

- If calling from any mobile phone, you can replace the international access code with "+" (press and hold 0 to insert it).

- The international access code is 011 if you're calling from the US or Canada.

- To call the US or Canada from Europe, dial 00, then 1 (country code for US and Canada), then the area code and number. In short, 00 + 1 + AC + LN = Hi, Mom!

When you get home from Europe, be sure to cancel any add-on plans that you activated for your trip.

Some people would rather use their smartphone exclusively on Wi-Fi, and not worry about either voice or data charges. If that's you, call your provider to be sure that international roaming options are deactivated on your account. To be double-sure, put your phone in "airplane mode," then turn your Wi-Fi back on.

Using Wi-Fi and Data Roaming

A good approach is to use free Wi-Fi wherever possible, and fill in the gaps with data roaming.

Wi-Fi (sometimes called "WLAN")—Internet access through a wireless router—is readily available throughout Europe. But just like at home, the quality of the signal may vary. Be patient, and don't get your hopes up. At accommodations, access is often free, but you may have to pay a fee, especially at expensive hotels. At hotels with thick stone walls, the Wi-Fi router in the lobby may not reach every room. If Wi-Fi is important to you, ask about it when you book—and be specific ("in the rooms?"). Get the password and network name at the front desk when you check in.

When you're out and about, your best bet for finding free Wi-Fi is often at a café. They'll usually tell you the password if you buy something. Or you can stroll down a café-lined street, smartphone in hand, checking for unsecured networks every few steps until you find one that works. Some towns have free public Wi-Fi in highly trafficked parks or piazzas. You may have to register before using it, or get a password at the TI.

Data roaming—that is, accessing the Internet through the cellular network—is handy when you can't find useable Wi-Fi. Because you'll pay by the megabyte (explained earlier), it's best to limit how much data you use. Save bandwidth-gobbling tasks like Skyping, watching videos, or downloading apps or emails with large attachments until you're on Wi-Fi. Switch your phone's email settings from "push" to "fetch." This means that you can choose to "fetch" (download) your messages when you're on Wi-Fi rather than having them continuously "pushed" to your device. And be aware of apps—such as news, weather, and sports tickers—that automatically update. Check your phone's settings to be sure that none of your apps are set to "use cellular data."

I like the safeguard of manually turning off data roaming on my phone whenever I'm not actively using it. To turn off data and voice roaming, look in your phone's menu—try checking under "cellular" or "network," or ask your service provider how to do it. If you need to get online but can't find Wi-Fi, simply turn on data roaming long enough for the task at hand, then turn it off again.

Figure out how to keep track of how much data you've used

Internet Calling

To make totally free voice and video calls over the Internet, all you need are a smartphone, tablet, or laptop; a strong Wi-Fi signal; and an account with one of the major Internet calling providers: Skype (www.skype.com), FaceTime (preloaded on most Apple devices), or Google+ Hangouts (www.google.com/hangouts). If the Wi-Fi signal isn't strong enough for video, try sticking with an audio-only call. Or...wait for your next hotel. Many Internet calling programs also work for making calls from your computer to telephones worldwide for a very reasonable fee—generally just a few cents per minute (you'll have to buy some credit before you make your first call).

(in your phone's menu, look for "cellular data usage"; you may have to reset the counter at the start of your trip). Some companies automatically send you a text message warning if you approach or exceed your limit.

There's yet another option: If you're traveling with an unlocked smartphone (explained later), you can buy a SIM card that also includes data; this can be far, far cheaper than data roaming through your home provider.

USING EUROPEAN SIM CARDS

Using your American phone in Europe is easy, but it's not always cheap. And unreliable Wi-Fi can make keeping in touch frustrating. If you're reasonably technology-savvy, and would like to have the option of making lots of affordable calls, it's worth getting comfortable with European SIM cards.

Here's the basic idea: First you need an unlocked phone that works in Europe. Then, in Europe, shop around for a SIM card—the little data chip that inserts into your phone—to equip it with a European number. Turn on the phone, and bingo! You've got service (and access to cheaper European rates).

Getting an Unlocked Phone

Your basic options are getting your existing phone unlocked, or buying a phone (either at home or in Europe).

Some phones are electronically "locked" so that you can't switch SIM cards (keeping you tied to your original service provider). But it's possible to "unlock" your phone—allowing you to replace the original SIM card. An unlocked phone is versatile; not only does it work with any European provider, but many US providers now offer no-contract, prepaid (or "pay-as-you-go") alternatives that work with SIM technology.

You may already have an old, unused mobile phone in a drawer somewhere. Call your service provider and ask if they'll send you the unlock code. Otherwise, you can buy one: Search an online shopping site for an "unlocked quad-band phone," or buy one at a mobile-phone shop in Europe. Either way, a basic model typically costs $40 or less.

Buying and Using SIM Cards

Once you have an unlocked phone, you'll need to buy a SIM card—a small, fingernail-size chip that stores your phone number and other information. (A smaller variation called "micro-SIM" or "nano-SIM" cards—used in most iPhones—are less widely available.)

SIM cards are sold at mobile-phone shops, department-store electronics counters, and newsstands for $5-10, and usually include about that much prepaid calling credit (making the card itself virtually free). Because SIM cards are prepaid, there's no contract and no commitment; I routinely buy one even if I'm in a country for only a few days.

In Great Britain, buying a SIM card is as easy as buying a pack of gum (though some European countries require you to register the SIM card with your passport as an antiterrorism measure).

When using a SIM card in its home country, it's free to receive calls and texts, and it's cheap to make calls—domestic calls average 20 cents per minute. You can also use SIM cards to call the US—sometimes very affordably (Lebara and Lycamobile, which operate in multiple European countries, let you call a US number for less than 10 cents a minute). Rates are higher if you're roaming in another country. But if you bought the SIM card within the European Union, roaming fees are capped no matter where you travel throughout the EU (about 25 cents/minute to make calls, 7 cents/minute to receive calls, and 8 cents for a text message).

While you can buy SIM cards just about anywhere, I like to seek out a mobile-phone shop, where a clerk can help explain my options, get my SIM card inserted and set up, and show me how to use it. When you buy your SIM card, ask about rates for domestic and international calls and texting, and about roaming fees. Also find out how to check your credit balance (usually you'll key in a few digits and hit "Send"). You can top up your credit at any newsstand, tobacco shop, mobile-phone shop, or many other businesses (look for the SIM card's logo in the window).

To insert your SIM card into the phone, locate the slot, which is usually on the side of the phone or behind the battery. Turning on the phone, you'll be prompted to enter the "SIM PIN" (a code number that came with your card).

If you have an unlocked smartphone, look for a European SIM card that covers both voice and data. This is often much cheaper than paying for data roaming through your home provider.

LANDLINE TELEPHONES AND INTERNET CAFÉS

If you prefer to travel without a smartphone or tablet, you can still stay in touch using landline telephones, hotel guest computers, and Internet cafés.

Landline Telephones

Phones in your **hotel room** can be great for local calls and for calls using cheap international phone cards (described in the sidebar). Many hotels charge a fee for local and "toll-free" as well as long-distance or international calls—always ask for the rates before you dial. Since you'll never be charged for receiving calls, it can be more affordable to have someone from the US call you in your room.

Phones are rare in **B&Bs,** but if your room has one, the advice above applies. If there's no phone in your B&B room, and you have an important, brief call to make, politely ask your hosts if you can use their personal phone. Keep in mind that most British people pay for each local call (whether from a fixed line or a mobile phone), and rates can be expensive. To be polite, ask to use someone's phone only in an emergency—and offer to pay for the call.

While **public pay phones** are relatively easy to find in Britain, they're expensive. Unlike most of Europe, British pay phones don't use dedicated, insertable phone cards; instead, you'll pay with a major credit card (which you insert into the phone—minimum charge for a credit-card call is £1.20) or coins (have a bunch handy; minimum fee is £0.60). The phone clearly shows how your money supply's doing. Only unused coins will be returned, so put in biggies with caution. Avoid using an international phone card at a pay phone.

Internet Cafés and Public Internet Terminals

Finding public Internet terminals in Europe is no problem. Many hotels have a computer in the lobby for guests to use. Otherwise, head for an Internet café, or ask the TI or your hotelier for the nearest place to access the Internet.

British computers typically use non-American keyboards. While familiar, a few letters are switched around. For example, the @ symbol appears to the right of the letter L, and the ⊠ symbol takes the place of the #. If you can't locate a special character (such as the @ symbol), simply copy it (Ctrl-C) from a Web page and paste it (Ctrl-V) into your email message.

PRACTICALITIES

International Phone Cards

In Britain, international phone cards are sold at newsstands, street kiosks, and train stations. These prepaid cards can be used to make inexpensive calls—within Europe, or to the US, for pennies a minute—from nearly any phone, including the one in your hotel room. The cards come with a toll-free number and a scratch-to-reveal PIN code. Be warned that the national telecom companies in Britain levy a hefty surcharge for using one of these cards from a pay phone—which effectively eliminates any savings. But you can still use them cheaply from a hotel-room phone.

SECURITY OVER THE INTERNET

Whether you're accessing the Internet with your own device or at a public terminal, using a shared network or computer comes with the potential for increased security risks. Ask the hotel or café for the specific name of their Wi-Fi network, and make sure you log on to that exact one; hackers sometimes create a bogus hotspot with a similar or vague name (such as "Hotel Europa Free Wi-Fi"). It's better if a network uses a password (especially a hard-to-guess one) rather than being open to the world.

While traveling, you may want to check your online banking or credit-card statements, or to take care of other personal-finance chores, but Internet security experts advise against accessing these sites entirely while traveling. Even if you're using your own computer at a password-protected hotspot, any hacker who's logged on to the same network can see what you're up to. If you need to log on to a banking website, try to do so on a hard-wired connection (i.e., using an Ethernet cable in your hotel room), or if that's not possible, use a secure banking app on a cellular Internet connection.

If using a credit card online, make sure that the site is secure. Most browsers display a little padlock icon, and the URL begins with *https* instead of *http*. Never send a credit-card number over a website that doesn't begin with *https*.

If you're not convinced a connection is secure, avoid accessing any sites (such as your bank's) that could be vulnerable to fraud.

MAIL

You can mail one package per day to yourself worth up to $200 duty-free from Europe to the US (mark it "personal purchases"). If you're sending a gift to someone, mark it "unsolicited gift." For details, visit www.cbp.gov and search for "Know Before You Go."

The British postal service works fine, but for quick transatlantic delivery (in either direction), consider services such as DHL (www.dhl.com). For postcards, get stamps at the neighborhood post office, newsstands within fancy hotels, and some mini-marts and card shops.

Resources

RESOURCES FROM RICK STEVES

Rick Steves London 2015 is one of many books in my series on European travel, which includes country guidebooks (including Great Britain), city and regional guidebooks (including England), Snapshot guides (excerpted chapters from my country guides), Pocket Guides (full-color little books on big cities, including London), and my budget-travel skills handbook, *Rick Steves Europe Through the Back Door*. Most of my titles are available as ebooks. My phrase books—for Italian, French, German, Spanish, and Portuguese—are practical and budget-oriented. My other books include *Europe 101* (a crash course on art and history designed for travelers); *Mediterranean Cruise Ports* and *Northern European Cruise Ports* (how to make the most of your time in port); and *Travel as a Political Act* (a travelogue sprinkled with tips for bringing home a global perspective). A more complete list of my titles appears near the end of this book.

Video: My public television series, *Rick Steves' Europe*, covers European destinations in 100 shows, with 10 episodes on Great Britain. To watch full episodes online for free, see www.ricksteves.com/tv. Or to raise your travel I.Q. with video versions of our popular classes, see www.ricksteves.com/travel-talks.

Audio: My weekly public radio show, *Travel with Rick Steves*, features interviews with travel experts from around the world. I've also produced free, self-guided **audio tours** of the top sights in London, based on tours in this book: Westminster Walk, British Museum, British Library, St. Paul's Cathedral, and The City Walk. All of this audio content is available for free at Rick Steves Audio Europe, an extensive online library organized by destination. Choose whatever interests you, and download it for free via the Rick Steves Audio Europe smartphone app, www.ricksteves.com/audioeurope, iTunes, or Google Play.

Begin Your Trip at
www.RickSteves.com

My **website** is *the* place to explore Europe. You'll find thousands of fun articles, videos, photos, and radio interviews on European destinations; money-saving tips for planning your dream trip; monthly travel news; my travel talks and travel blog; my latest guidebook updates (www.ricksteves.com/update); and my free Rick Steves Audio Europe app. You can also follow me on Facebook and Twitter.

Our **Travel Forum** is an immense, yet well-groomed collection of message boards, where our travel-savvy community answers questions and shares their personal travel experiences (www.ricksteves.com/forums).

Our **online Travel Store** offers travel bags and accessories that I've designed specifically to help you travel smarter and lighter. These include my popular bags (rolling carry-on and backpack versions), money belts, totes, toiletries kits, adapters, other accessories, and a wide selection of guidebooks, planning maps, and DVDs.

Choosing the right **rail pass** for your trip—amid hundreds of options—can drive you nutty. Our website will help you find the perfect fit for your itinerary and your budget: We offer easy, one-stop shopping for rail passes, seat reservations, and point-to-point tickets.

Want to travel with greater efficiency and less stress? We organize **tours** with more than three dozen itineraries and more than 700 departures reaching the best destinations in this book...and beyond. Three of our tours include London: our seven-day in-depth London city tour, our 14-day England tour, and our Family Best of Europe tour, which kicks off in London. You'll enjoy great guides, a fun bunch of travel partners (with small groups of 24 to 28 travelers), and plenty of room to spread out in a big, comfy bus when touring between towns. You'll find European adventures to fit every vacation length. For all the details, and to get our Tour Catalog and a free Rick Steves Tour Experience DVD (filmed on location during an actual tour), visit www.ricksteves.com or call us at 425/608-4217.

PRACTICALITIES

MAPS

The black-and-white maps in this book are concise and simple, designed to help you locate recommended places and get to local TIs, where you can pick up more in-depth maps of cities and regions (usually free). Better maps are sold at newsstands and bookstores. Before you buy a map, look at it to be sure it has the level of detail you want. The color city maps and Tube map at the front of this book are also useful.

For more detail, buy a city map at a London newsstand—the red *Bensons Map & Guide* (£3.50) is excellent. Even the vending-machine maps sold in Tube stations are good. The *Rough Guide* map to London is well-designed (£5, sold at London bookstores). The *Rick Steves Britain, Ireland & London City Map* has a good map of London ($8.99, www.ricksteves.com). Many Londoners, along with obsessive-compulsive tourists, rely on the highly detailed *London A-Z* map book (generally £5-7, called "A to Zed" by locals, available at newsstands). Before you buy a map, look at it to be sure it has the level of detail you want.

RECOMMENDED BOOKS AND MOVIES

To learn more about London past and present, check out a few of these books or films.

Nonfiction

A History of London (Inwood), topping out at 1,000 pages, covers 2,000 years. *London* (Ackroyd) takes the form of a biography rather than a conventional history. *Elizabeth's London* (Picard) re-creates 16th-century life in the era of England's first great queen.

Originally published in the *New Yorker* magazine, *Letters from London* (Barnes) captures life in the city in the early 1990s. The book *84, Charing Cross Road* is a collection of letters between a stiff-upper-lip London bookseller and a witty writer, Helene Hanff, in the post-WWII years. (Also worth reading is the sequel, *The Duchess of Bloomsbury Street*.) Although not specific to London, consider *Notes from a Small Island*, which is chock-full of Bill Bryson's witty observations about Great Britain. Dava Sobel's *Longitude*—a must-read if you plan to visit Greenwich—tells the story of the clockmaker who solved a problem that had thwarted previous geniuses. Kids of all ages enjoy the whimsical and colorful impressions of the city in Miroslav Sasek's classic picture-book *This Is London*.

Fiction

Describing the classics of British literature is a book in itself. But some favorites that feature London include *Pygmalion* (Shaw), the story of a young Cockney girl groomed for high society; *Persuasion*, a beloved Jane Austen book partially set in Bath; and Charles Dickens' tale of a workhouse urchin, *Oliver Twist*.

Dating from the turn of the century, P. G. Wodehouse's Jeeves series, with a problem-solving valet as the lead character, has endured. *A Study in Scarlet* (Doyle) introduced the world to detective Sherlock Holmes.

Edward Rutherfurd's *London*, which begins in ancient times and continues through to the 20th century, is as big and sprawling as its namesake. *The Jupiter Myth* (Davis) takes place in the days

PRACTICALITIES

when the city was called Londinium. In *The Great Stink* (Clark), the sewer system is also a metaphor for the blight that plagued the city.

Lucia in London (Benson) sends the protagonist of this 1920s series to the big city. Helen Fielding created another well-loved heroine in her *Bridget Jones* books, which began in the late 1990s as a newspaper column (and inspired two fun films). *Confessions of a Shopaholic* (Kinsella) continues the Bridget Jones formula. Nick Hornby explores a young male perspective of life and love in *Fever Pitch, High Fidelity,* and *About a Boy*.

London's movers and shakers commit bad deeds in the detective story *In the Presence of the Enemy* (George). *Murder in Mayfair* (Barnard) is based on a true crime from the 1980s. *Rumpole of the Bailey*, created by Sir John Mortimer, is a popular detective series, spawning both books and television shows.

Ian McEwan's highly praised post-9/11 novel, *Saturday*, takes place over the course of a day all over the sprawling city. Many recent works feature the city's thriving immigrant communities, including *The Buddha of Suburbia* (Kureishi), *White Teeth* (Smith), and *Brick Lane* (Ali, also a 2007 film).

Film and Television

In terms of world influence, Britain's filmmaking output rivals its substantial literary contributions. Britain gave birth to the two top-grossing film series of all time: Harry Potter and James Bond. Add to that the fact that much of the Star Wars series (ranked third) was filmed in England, and that the casts of the Lord of the Rings (fourth) and Pirates of the Caribbean (sixth) series were both dominated by British actors—and it's impossible to deny Britain's cinematic clout. But it's not all super-blockbusters. Here are some films that will flesh out your understanding of this small island, past and present.

For a taste of Tudor-era London, try *Shakespeare in Love* (1999), which is set in the original Globe Theatre. In *A Man for All Seasons* (1966), Sir Thomas More faces down Henry VIII. Showtime's racy, lavish series *The Tudors* (2007-2010) is an entertaining, loosely accurate chronicle of the marriages of Henry VIII.

For equally good portraits of Elizabeth I, try *Elizabeth* (1998) and its sequel *Elizabeth: The Golden Age* (2007), or the BBC/HBO miniseries *Elizabeth I* (2005). In *The Duchess* (2008), the 18th-century Duchess of Devonshire glides languidly through life in big skirts and even bigger wigs.

Written and set in the early 19th century, the works of Jane Austen have fared well in film. Among the many versions of *Pride and Prejudice,* the 1995 BBC miniseries starring Colin Firth is the winner. *Persuasion* (1995) was partially filmed in Bath. Other Austen adaptations include *Sense and Sensibility* (1995, with Emma

Thompson, Hugh Grant, and Kate Winslet) and *Emma* (1996, with Gwyneth Paltrow). Charlotte Brontë's *Jane Eyre* was filmed in 2011 with Mia Wasikowska and Michael Fassbinder.

In *The Elephant Man* (1980), the cruelty of Victorian London is starkly portrayed in a black-and-white film. *Sweeney Todd* (2007) captures the gritty Victorian milieu, as does the highly stylized *Sherlock Holmes* (2009). Sherlock shows up again in the excellent BBC update of the detective's story, set in present-day London (2010-present). On a lighter note, *Goodbye, Mr. Chips* (1939) is set in a boys' boarding school during Victorian England.

The Edwardian era of the early 20th century has provided a setting for many films. Producer Ismail Merchant and director James Ivory teamed up to create many well-regarded films about this era, including *Howard's End* (1992, which captures the stifling societal pressure underneath the gracious manners), *A Room with a View* (1985), and *The Remains of the Day* (1993). The critically acclaimed TV series *Downton Abbey* (2011-present), filmed at Highclere Castle about 70 miles west of London, so far has taken viewers from 1912 to the mid-1920s.

The all-star *Gosford Park* (2001) is part comedy, part murder mystery, and part critique of England's class stratification in the 1930s. *Chariots of Fire* (1981) ran away with the Academy Award for Best Picture. *Shadowlands* (1993), set largely in Oxford, tells a fictionalized account of author C. S. Lewis' relationship with his future wife.

Wartime London has been captured in many fine movies. *The King's Speech* (2010) won the Oscar for Best Picture, with Colin Firth named Best Actor for his portrayal of King George VI on the cusp of World War II. *Hope and Glory* (1987) is a semi-autobiographical story of a boy growing up during WWII's Blitz. *Waterloo Bridge* (1940) recalls the lost love between a woman and a WWI officer. In *Passport to Pimlico* (1949), an explosion in a Tube station is the source of riches and comedy in a time of post-WWII rationing.

In the 1960s, British acts were all the rage in the States, thanks to a little band called the Beatles, whose *A Hard Day's Night* (1964) is filled with wit and charm. During this time, "swinging London" also exploded on the international scene, with films such as *Alfie* (1966), *Blowup* (1966), and *Georgy Girl* (1966). (For a swinging spoof of this time, try the Austin Powers comedies.) In *To Sir, with Love* (1967), Sidney Poitier brings order to his undisciplined students.

You can watch Hugh Grant charming the ladies in *Four Weddings and a Funeral* (1994) and *Notting Hill* (1999); Gwyneth Paltrow living two lives in *Sliding Doors* (1998); and John Cleese,

PRACTICALITIES

Jamie Lee Curtis, and Kevin Kline hilariously double-crossing one other in *A Fish Called Wanda* (1988).

For a departure from the typical Hollywood fare, see *My Beautiful Laundrette* (1985), a gritty story of two gay men (with Daniel Day-Lewis). For another portrayal of urban London—and the racial tensions found in its multiethnic center—look for *Sammy and Rosie Get Laid* (1987). *Lock, Stock and Two Smoking Barrels* (1998) is a violent crime caper set in the city.

Billy Elliot (2000), about a young boy ballet dancer, and *Bend It Like Beckham* (2003), about a young girl of Punjabi descent who plays soccer, were both huge crowd-pleasers. *An Education* (2009), about a bright schoolgirl who falls for an older man, takes place in 1960s London. *V for Vendetta* (2006), based on a British graphic novel, shows a sci-fi future of a London ruled with an iron fist.

In *The Queen* (2006), Helen Mirren expertly channels Elizabeth II during the days after Princess Diana's death. If you enjoy *The Queen*, consider two other reality-based films with the same screenwriter and many of the same cast members (most notably Michael Sheen as Tony Blair): *The Special Relationship* (2010, about the friendship between Tony Blair and Bill Clinton) and *The Deal* (2003, about Tony Blair's early relationship with Gordon Brown).

Britain has offered up plenty of comedy choices over the years. If you're in the mood for something completely different, try *Monty Python and the Holy Grail* (1975), a surreal take on the Arthurian legend. The BBC's deeply irreverent "mockumentary" series *The Office* (by Ricky Gervais and Stephen Merchant) inspired the gentler US television show. In *The Full Monty* (1997), some working-class Yorkshire lads take it all off to pay the bills. *Calendar Girls* (2003) has a similar setting and premise, if a slightly more noble cause. *Shaun of the Dead* (2004) combines comedy and horror, when the city's residents turn into zombies.

Anglophiles of all ages are likely to enjoy *Mary Poppins* (1964), *My Fair Lady* (1964), *A Little Princess* (1995), the *Wallace & Gromit* movies, Rowan Atkinson's *Mr. Bean* television series and movies, and the *Harry Potter* films.

APPENDIX

Contents

Useful Contacts

Emergency Needs
Police and Ambulance: Tel. 999

Embassies and Consulates
US Consulate and Embassy: Tel. 020/7499-9000 (all services), no walk-in passport services; for emergency 36-hour passport service, email LondonEmergencyPPT@state.gov or call all-services number (24 Grosvenor Square, Tube: Bond Street, http://london.usembassy.gov)

Canadian High Commission: Tel. 020/7258-6600, passport services available Mon-Fri 9:30-12:30 (38 Grosvenor Street, Tube: Bond Street, www.unitedkingdom.gc.ca)

Directory Assistance
Operator Assistance: Tel. 100 (free)

Directory Assistance: Toll tel. 118-500 (£0.59/minute, plus £0.23/minute connection charge from fixed lines)

International Directory Assistance: Toll tel. 118-505 (£1.99/minute, plus £0.69 connection charge)

2015

JANUARY
S	M	T	W	T	F	S
				1	2	3
4	5	6	7	8	9	10
11	12	13	14	15	16	17
18	19	20	21	22	23	24
25	26	27	28	29	30	31

FEBRUARY
S	M	T	W	T	F	S
1	2	3	4	5	6	7
8	9	10	11	12	13	14
15	16	17	18	19	20	21
22	23	24	25	26	27	28

MARCH
S	M	T	W	T	F	S
1	2	3	4	5	6	7
8	9	10	11	12	13	14
15	16	17	18	19	20	21
22	23	24	25	26	27	28
29	30	31				

APRIL
S	M	T	W	T	F	S
			1	2	3	4
5	6	7	8	9	10	11
12	13	14	15	16	17	18
19	20	21	22	23	24	25
26	27	28	29	30		

MAY
S	M	T	W	T	F	S
					1	2
3	4	5	6	7	8	9
10	11	12	13	14	15	16
17	18	19	20	21	22	23
$^{24}/_{31}$	25	26	27	28	29	30

JUNE
S	M	T	W	T	F	S
	1	2	3	4	5	6
7	8	9	10	11	12	13
14	15	16	17	18	19	20
21	22	23	24	25	26	27
28	29	30				

JULY
S	M	T	W	T	F	S
			1	2	3	4
5	6	7	8	9	10	11
12	13	14	15	16	17	18
19	20	21	22	23	24	25
26	27	28	29	30	31	

AUGUST
S	M	T	W	T	F	S
						1
2	3	4	5	6	7	8
9	10	11	12	13	14	15
16	17	18	19	20	21	22
$^{23}/_{30}$	$^{24}/_{31}$	25	26	27	28	29

SEPTEMBER
S	M	T	W	T	F	S
		1	2	3	4	5
6	7	8	9	10	11	12
13	14	15	16	17	18	19
20	21	22	23	24	25	26
27	28	29	30			

OCTOBER
S	M	T	W	T	F	S
				1	2	3
4	5	6	7	8	9	10
11	12	13	14	15	16	17
18	19	20	21	22	23	24
25	26	27	28	29	30	31

NOVEMBER
S	M	T	W	T	F	S
1	2	3	4	5	6	7
8	9	10	11	12	13	14
15	16	17	18	19	20	21
22	23	24	25	26	27	28
29	30					

DECEMBER
S	M	T	W	T	F	S
		1	2	3	4	5
6	7	8	9	10	11	12
13	14	15	16	17	18	19
20	21	22	23	24	25	26
27	28	29	30	31		

Holidays and Festivals

This list includes selected festivals in London, plus national holidays observed throughout Great Britain. Many sights and banks close on national holidays—keep this in mind when planning your itinerary. Before planning a trip around a festival, make sure to verify its dates by checking the festival's website or TI sites (www.visitlondon.com and www.visitbritain.com).

In London, hotels get booked up on major holidays—New Year's Day, Easter weekend, Christmas, and Boxing Day—and on Fridays and Saturdays year-round. Some hotels require you to book the full three-day weekend around Bank Holiday Mondays.

Included in this list are major events in the nearby towns of Windsor and Cambridge.

Jan 1	New Year's Day
Feb 14-18	London Fashion Week (www.londonfashionweek.co.uk)
April 3	Good Friday
April 5-6	Easter Sunday and Monday
May 4	Early May Bank Holiday (first Monday in May)
May 25	Spring Bank Holiday (last Monday in May)
Late May	Chelsea Flower Show, London (book tickets ahead for this popular event at www.rhs.org.uk/chelsea)
June 14	Trooping the Colour, London (military bands and pageantry, Queen's birthday parade; www.trooping-the-colour.co.uk)
Late June	Royal Ascot Horse Race (www.ascot.co.uk), Ascot (near Windsor)
Late June-early July	Wimbledon Tennis Championship, London (www.wimbledon.com)
Late July-early Aug	Cambridge Folk Festival, Cambridge (buy tickets early at www.cambridgefolkfestival.co.uk)
Late Aug	Notting Hill Carnival, London (costumes, Caribbean music, www.thenottinghillcarnival.com)
Aug 31	Late Summer Bank Holiday (last Monday in August)
Sept (one week)	London Fashion Week (www.londonfashionweek.co.uk)
Nov 5	Bonfire Night (bonfires, fireworks, effigy burning of 1605 traitor Guy Fawkes)
Nov 8	Remembrance Sunday (second Sunday in November, royals lay wreaths at Cenotaph for WWI dead)
Mid-Nov	Lord Mayor's Show, London (second Saturday in November; huge parade in The City with fireworks, www.lordmayorsshow.org)
Dec 24-26	Christmas holidays (many sights close; limited or no public transport)

Conversions and Climate

NUMBERS AND STUMBLERS

- Some British people write a few of their numbers differently than we do: 1 = 1, 4 = 4, 7 = 7.
- In Europe, dates appear as day/month/year, so Christmas 2015 is 25/12/15.
- What Americans call the second floor of a building is the first floor in Britain.
- On escalators and moving sidewalks, Brits keep the left "lane" open for passing. Keep to the right.
- To avoid the British version of giving someone "the finger," don't hold up the first two fingers of your hand with your palm facing you. (It looks like a reversed victory sign.)
- And please...don't call your waist pack a "fanny pack" (see the British-Yankee Vocabulary list at the end of this appendix).

UNITS OF MEASUREMENT

Britain is becoming more metric, but imperial units are still used in a few official measurements.

Metric Conversions

Weight and volume are typically calculated in metric: A kilogram is 2.2 pounds, and a liter is about a quart (almost four to a gallon). Temperatures are generally given in Celsius, although some newspapers also list them in Fahrenheit.

1 foot = 0.3 meter	1 square yard = 0.8 square meter
1 yard = 0.9 meter	1 square mile = 2.6 square kilometers
1 mile = 1.6 kilometers	1 ounce = 28 grams
1 centimeter = 0.4 inch	1 quart = 0.95 liter
1 meter = 39.4 inches	1 kilogram = 2.2 pounds
1 kilometer = 0.62 mile	32°F = 0°C

Imperial Weights and Measures

Driving distances and speed limits are measured in miles. Beer is sold as pints (though milk can be measured in pints or liters), and a person's weight is measured in stone (a 168-pound person weighs 12 stone).

1 stone = 14 pounds	1 British pint = 1.2 US pints
1 imperial gallon = 1.2 US gallons or about 4.5 liters	

CLOTHING SIZES

When shopping for clothing, use these US-to-UK comparisons as general guidelines (but note that no conversion is perfect).

- Women's dresses and blouses:
  Add 4 (US women's size 10 = UK size 14)

- Men's suits, jackets, and shirts: US and UK use the same sizing
- Women's shoes: Subtract 2½ (US size 8 = UK size 5½)
- Men's shoes: Subtract about ½ (US size 9 = UK size 8½)

LONDON'S CLIMATE

First line, average daily high; second line, average daily low; third line, average days without rain. For more detailed weather statistics for destinations throughout Britain (as well as the rest of the world), check www.wunderground.com.

J	F	M	A	M	J	J	A	S	O	N	D
43°	44°	50°	56°	62°	69°	71°	71°	65°	58°	50°	45°
36°	36°	38°	42°	47°	53°	56°	56°	52°	46°	42°	38°
16	15	20	18	19	19	19	20	17	18	15	16

FAHRENHEIT AND CELSIUS CONVERSION

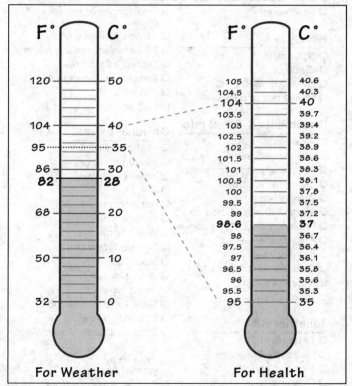

For Weather   For Health

Britain uses both Celsius and Fahrenheit to take its temperature. For a rough conversion from Celsius to Fahrenheit, double the number and add 30. For weather, remember that 28°C is 82°F—perfect. For health, 37°C is just right. At a launderette, 30°C is cold, 40°C is warm (usually the default setting), 60°C is hot, and 95°C is boiling.

Packing Checklist

Whether you're traveling for five days or five weeks, you won't need more than this. Pack light to enjoy the sweet freedom of true mobility.

Clothing

- ❑ 5 shirts: long- & short-sleeve
- ❑ 2 pairs pants or skirt
- ❑ 1 pair shorts or capris
- ❑ 5 pairs underwear & socks
- ❑ 1 pair walking shoes
- ❑ Sweater or fleece top
- ❑ Rainproof jacket with hood
- ❑ Tie or scarf
- ❑ Swimsuit
- ❑ Sleepwear

Money

- ❑ Debit card
- ❑ Credit card(s)
- ❑ Hard cash ($20 bills)
- ❑ Money belt or neck wallet

Documents & Travel Info

- ❑ Passport
- ❑ Airline reservations
- ❑ Rail pass/train reservations
- ❑ Car-rental voucher
- ❑ Driver's license
- ❑ Student ID, hostel card, etc.
- ❑ Photocopies of all the above
- ❑ Hotel confirmations
- ❑ Insurance details
- ❑ Guidebooks & maps
- ❑ Notepad & pen
- ❑ Journal

Toiletries Kit

- ❑ Toiletries
- ❑ Medicines & vitamins
- ❑ First-aid kit
- ❑ Glasses/contacts/sunglasses (with prescriptions)
- ❑ Earplugs
- ❑ Packet of tissues (for WC)

Miscellaneous

- ❑ Daypack
- ❑ Sealable plastic baggies
- ❑ Laundry soap
- ❑ Spot remover
- ❑ Clothesline
- ❑ Sewing kit
- ❑ Travel alarm/watch

Electronics

- ❑ Smartphone or mobile phone
- ❑ Camera & related gear
- ❑ Tablet/ereader/media player
- ❑ Laptop & flash drive
- ❑ Earbuds or headphones
- ❑ Chargers
- ❑ Plug adapters

Optional Extras

- ❑ Flipflops or slippers
- ❑ Mini-umbrella or poncho
- ❑ Travel hairdryer
- ❑ Belt
- ❑ Hat (for sun or cold)
- ❑ Picnic supplies
- ❑ Water bottle
- ❑ Fold-up tote bag
- ❑ Small flashlight
- ❑ Small binoculars
- ❑ Insect repellent
- ❑ Small towel or washcloth
- ❑ Inflatable pillow
- ❑ Some duct tape (for repairs)
- ❑ Tiny lock
- ❑ Address list (to mail postcards)
- ❑ Postcards/photos from home
- ❑ Extra passport photos
- ❑ Good book

BRITISH-YANKEE VOCABULARY

For a longer list, plus a dry-witted primer on British culture, see *The Septic's Companion* (Chris Rae). Note that instead of asking, "Can I help you?" many Brits offer a more casual, "You alright?" or "You OK there?"

advert: advertisement

afters: dessert

anticlockwise: counterclockwise

Antipodean: An Australian or New Zealander

aubergine: eggplant

banger: sausage

bangers and mash: sausage and mashed potatoes

bank holiday: legal holiday

bap: small roll

bespoke: custom-made

billion: a thousand of our billions (a million million)

biro: ballpoint pen

biscuit: cookie

black pudding: sausage made from dried blood

bloody: damn

blow off: fart

bobby: policeman ("the Bill" is more common)

Bob's your uncle: there you go (with a shrug), naturally

boffin: nerd, geek

bollocks: testicles (used in many colorful expressions)

bolshy: argumentative

bomb: success or failure

bonnet: car hood

booking: reservation

boot: car trunk

braces: suspenders

bridle way: path for walkers, bikers, and horse riders

brilliant: cool

brolly: umbrella

bubble and squeak: cabbage and potatoes fried together

builder: construction worker

bum: butt

candy floss: cotton candy

caravan: trailer

car boot sale: temporary flea market, often for charity

car park: parking lot

cashpoint: ATM

casualty: emergency room

cat's eyes: road reflectors

ceilidh (KAY-lee): informal evening of song and folk fun (Scottish and Irish)

cheap and cheerful: budget but adequate

cheap and nasty: cheap and bad quality

cheers: good-bye or thanks; also a toast

chemist: pharmacist

chicory: endive

chippie: fish-and-chip shop; carpenter (see also "joiner")

chips: French fries

chock-a-block: jam-packed

chuffed: pleased

cider: alcoholic apple cider

clearway: road where you can't stop

coach: long-distance bus

concession: discounted admission

concs (pronounced "conks"): short for "concession"

cos: romaine lettuce

cot: baby crib

cotton buds: Q-tips

council estate: public housing

courgette: zucchini

craic (pronounced "crack"): fun, good conversation

(Irish and spreading to England)

crisps: potato chips

cuppa: cup of tea

curry: any Indian meal flavored with curry, popular with all Brits

dear: expensive

dicey: iffy, risky

digestives: round graham cookies

dinner: lunch or dinner

diversion: detour

donkey's years: ages, a long time

draughts: checkers

draw: marijuana

dual carriageway: divided highway (four lanes)

dummy: pacifier

elevenses: coffee-and-biscuits break before lunch

elvers: baby eels

engaged tone: busy signal

estate car: station wagon

face flannel: washcloth

faff: bumble (about)

fag: cigarette

fagged: exhausted

faggot: meatball

fairy cake: cupcake

fancy: to like, to be attracted to (a person)

fanny: vagina

fell: hill or high plain (Lake District)

first floor: second floor

fixture: sports schedule

fizzy drink: pop or soda

flat: apartment

flutter: a bet

football: soccer

force: waterfall (Lake District)

fortnight: two weeks

fringe: hair bangs

Frogs: French people

fruit machine: slot machine

full Monty: whole shebang; everything

gallery: balcony

gammon: ham

gangway: aisle

gaol: jail (same pronunciation)

gateau (or gateaux): cake

gear lever: stick shift

geezer: dude (slang for young man)

ginger-haired: redhead

give way: yield

glen: narrow valley (Scotland)

goods wagon: freight truck

green fingers: green thumbs

grizzle: grumble, fuss (especially by a baby)

gutted: deeply disappointed

half eight: 8:30 (not 7:30)

hash sign: pound sign, as on a phone

heath: open treeless land

hen night: bachelorette party

High Street: Main Street (in a generic sense)

hire: rent, as in a car or bike

hire car: rental car

hob: stove burner

holiday: vacation

homely: homey or cozy

hoover: vacuum cleaner

ice lolly: Popsicle

interval: intermission

ironmonger: hardware store

ish: more or less

jacket potato: baked potato

jelly: Jell-O

Joe Bloggs: John Q. Public

joiner: carpenter (see also "chippie")

jumble sale: rummage sale

jumper: sweater

just a tick: just a second

kipper: smoked herring

knackered: exhausted (Cockney: cream crackered)

knickers: ladies' panties

knocking shop: brothel

knock up: wake up or visit (old-fashioned)

ladybird: ladybug

lady fingers: flat, spongy cookie

lady's finger: okra

lager: light, fizzy beer

left luggage: baggage check

lemon squash: lemonade, not fizzy

lemonade: lemon-lime pop, fizzy

let: rent, as in property

licenced: restaurant authorized to sell alcohol

lie-in, having a: sleeping in late

lift: elevator

listed: protected historic building

loo: toilet or bathroom

lorry: truck

mac: mackintosh raincoat

main: entrée

mains: electrical outlet

mangetout: snow peas

Marmite: yeast paste, spread on sandwiches

marrow: summer squash

mate: buddy (boy or girl)

mean: stingy

mental: wild, memorable

mews: former stables converted to two-story rowhouses (London)

mince: hamburger meat

mobile (MOH-bile): cell phone

moggie: cat

M.O.T.: mandatory annual car safety certificate

motorway: freeway

naff: dorky

nappy: diaper

natter: talk on and on

neep: Scottish for turnip

newsagent: corner store

nought: zero

noughts & crosses: tic-tac-toe

O.A.P.: old-age pensioner, retiree

off-licence: liquor store

on offer: for sale

one-off: unique; one-time event

panto, pantomime: fairy-tale play performed at Christmas (silly but fun)

pants: (noun) underwear, briefs; (adj.) terrible, ridiculous

paracetamol: acetaminophen, Tylenol

pasty (PASS-tee): crusted savory (usually meat) pie from Cornwall

pavement: sidewalk

people mover: minivan

pear-shaped: messed up, gone wrong

pensioner: senior citizen, retiree

petrol: gas

pillar box: mailbox

pissed (rude), **paralytic, bevvied, wellied, popped up, merry, trollied, ratted, rat-arsed, pissed as a newt:** drunk

pitch: playing field

plaster: Band-Aid

pram: baby carriage

publican: pub manager (old-fashioned)

public school: private "prep" school (e.g., Eton)

pudding: dessert in general

pull, to be on the: looking for love

punter: customer, especially in gambling

pushchair: stroller

put a sock in it: shut up

queue: line

queue up: line up

quid: a pound (money)

randy: horny

rasher: slice of bacon

redundant, made: laid off

Remembrance Day: Veterans' Day

return ticket: round-trip

revising; doing revisions: studying for exams

ring up: call (telephone)

rocket: arugula

roundabout: traffic circle

rubber: eraser

rubbish: bad

salad cream: mayo, mustard, and vinegar dressing

Sat Nav: GPS device

sausage roll: sausage wrapped in a flaky pastry

Scotch egg: hard-boiled egg wrapped in sausage meat

scrumpy: type of hard cider

self-catering: accommodation with kitchen

Sellotape: Scotch tape

services: freeway rest area

serviette: napkin

settee: couch

shag: intercourse (cruder than in the US)

shandy: lager and 7-Up

silencer: car muffler

single ticket: one-way ticket

skip: Dumpster

sleeping policeman: speed bumps

smalls: underwear

snogging: kissing, making out

sod: mildly offensive insult

sod it, sod off: screw it, screw off

soda: soda water (not pop)

solicitor: lawyer (a.k.a. barrister)

spanner: wrench

sparkie: electrician

spend a penny: urinate

stag night: bachelor party

starkers: buck naked

starters: appetizers

state school: public school

sticking plaster: Band-Aid

sticky tape: Scotch tape

stone: 14 pounds (measurement of weight)

stroppy: bad-tempered

subway: underground walkway

suet: fat from animal rendering (sometimes used in cooking)

sultanas: golden raisins

surgical spirit: rubbing alcohol

suspenders: garters

suss out: figure out

swede: rutabaga

ta: thank you

take the mickey: tease

tatty: worn out or tacky

taxi rank: taxi stand

telly: TV

tenement: stone apartment house (not necessarily a slum)

tenner: £10 bill

theatre: live stage

tick: a check mark

tight as a fish's bum: cheapskate (watertight)

tights: panty hose

tin: can

tip: public dump

tipper lorry: dump truck

top hole: first rate

top up: refill a drink

torch: flashlight
towel, press-on: panty liner
towpath: path along a river
trainers: sneakers
Tube: subway
twee: quaint, cute
twitcher: bird watcher
Underground: subway
verge: grassy edge of road
verger: church official
way out: exit
wee (adj.): small (Scottish)

wee (verb): urinate
Wellingtons, wellies: rubber boots
whacked: exhausted
whinge (rhymes with hinge): whine
wind up: tease, irritate
witter on: gab and gab
yob: hooligan
zebra crossing: crosswalk
zed: the letter Z

INDEX

MAP INDEX

Our website enhances this book and turns

Explore Europe

At ricksteves.com you can browse through thousands of articles, videos, photos and radio interviews, plus find a wealth of money-saving travel tips for planning your dream trip. And with our mobile-friendly website, you can easily access all this great travel information anywhere you go.

TV Shows

Preview the places you'll visit by watching entire half-hour episodes of Rick Steves' Europe (choose from all 100 shows) on-demand, for free.

ricksteves.com

your travel dreams into affordable reality

Radio Interviews

Enjoy ready access to Rick's vast library of radio interviews covering travel

tips and cultural insights that relate specifically to your Europe travel plans.

Travel Forums

Learn, ask, share! Our online community of savvy travelers is a great resource

for first-time travelers to Europe, as well as seasoned pros. You'll find forums on each country, plus travel tips and restaurant/hotel reviews. You can even ask one of our well-traveled staff to chime in with an opinion.

Travel News

Subscribe to our free Travel News e-newsletter, and get monthly updates from Rick on what's happening in Europe.

Audio Europe™

Experience maximum Europe

Save time and energy

This guidebook is your independent-travel toolkit. But for all it delivers, it's still up to you to devote the time and energy it takes to manage the preparation and logistics that are essential for a happy trip. If that's a hassle, there's a solution.

Rick Steves Tours

A Rick Steves tour takes you to Europe's most interesting places with great

great tours, too!

with minimum stress

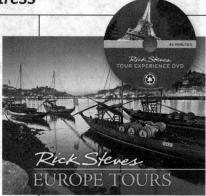

guides and small groups of 28 or less. We follow Rick's favorite itineraries, ride in comfy buses, stay in family-run hotels, and bring you intimately close to the Europe you've traveled so far to see. Most importantly, we take away the logistical headaches so you can focus on the fun.

customers—along with us on 40 different itineraries, from Ireland to Italy to Istanbul. Is a Rick Steves tour the right fit for your travel dreams? Find out at ricksteves.com, where you can also get Rick's latest tour catalog and free Tour Experience DVD.

Join the fun

This year we'll take 18,000 free-spirited travelers— nearly half of them repeat

Europe is best experienced with happy travel partners. We hope you can join us.

See our itineraries at ricksteves.com

Rick Steves

EUROPE GUIDES

Best of Europe
Eastern Europe
Europe Through the Back Door
Mediterranean Cruise Ports
Northern European Cruise Ports

COUNTRY GUIDES

Croatia & Slovenia
England
France
Germany
Great Britain
Ireland
Italy
Portugal
Scandinavia
Spain
Switzerland

CITY & REGIONAL GUIDES

Amsterdam, Bruges & Brussels
Barcelona
Budapest
Florence & Tuscany
Greece: Athens & the Peloponnese
Istanbul
London
Paris
Prague & the Czech Republic
Provence & the French Riviera
Rome
Venice
Vienna, Salzburg & Tirol

SNAPSHOT GUIDES

Berlin
Bruges & Brussels
Copenhagen & the Best of
   Denmark
Dublin
Dubrovnik
Hill Towns of Central Italy
Italy's Cinque Terre
Krakow, Warsaw & Gdansk
Lisbon
Madrid & Toledo
Milan & the Italian Lakes District
Munich, Bavaria & Salzburg
Naples & the Amalfi Coast
Northern Ireland
Norway
Scotland
Sevilla, Granada & Southern Spain
Stockholm

POCKET GUIDES

Amsterdam
Athens
Barcelona
Florence
London
Paris
Rome
Venice

Rick Steves guidebooks are published by Avalon Travel,
a member of the Perseus Books Group.

NOW AVAILABLE:
eBOOKS, DVD & BLU-RAY

Credits

Researchers
To help update this book, Rick and Gene relied on...

Amanda Buttinger

Amanda is a Rick Steves' Europe guide and guidebook researcher. While her adopted home-town is Madrid, where she has lived since 1998, she was lucky enough to have spent two years in London. She returned to Spain with a darling baby, an older boy with a lovely British accent, and a certain taste for flat whites and good ales with her mates.

Lynne McAlister

Lynne, from a small town in Tennessee, popped out of the Westminster Tube on a drizzly London evening to spy the glow of Big Ben and the Houses of Parliament. It was love at first sight. The history, art, architecture, parks, and people kept her coming back. Now she writes about travel from her flat in Notting Hill, where she lives with husband, Tony, and dog, Coco.